MONEY,
FINANCIAL INSTITUTIONS,
AND ECONOMIC ACTIVITY

MONEY, FINANCIAL INSTITUTIONS, AND ECONOMIC ACTIVITY

Bruce R. Dalgaard
University of Minnesota

SCOTT, FORESMAN AND COMPANY
Glenview, Illinois   London, England

To Kathy

Library of Congress Cataloging-in-Publication Data

Dalgaard, Bruce R.
   Money, financial institutions, and economic
activity.

   Includes bibliographies.
   1. Finance.   2. Money.   3. Banks and banking.
4. Economics.   I. Title.
HG173.D28   1987   332.1   87-4851
ISBN 0-673-15876-4

Cover photograph: © Andrew Moore.

Acknowledgments for all copyrighted material used are given on page.
Photos not credited on page are property of Scott, Foresman and Company.

Preface

Instructors in courses entitled *money and banking, financial markets and institutions*, and *money, financial institutions, and monetary policy* are faced with both a challenge and an opportunity. The challenge comes along with rapid change in the financial industry and its implications for designing and delivering courses. The opportunity comes with the increasingly interesting possibilities the change brings to the industry, and the scope and magnitude today's research and writing provide for detailed exploration of financial topics.

For authors of money and banking texts, the challenge is to develop a framework that allows analysis of current changes and still has applicability for the changes yet to come. The opportunities are many, but most important is the chance to introduce, with a new approach, the world of money and financial institutions. This new approach offers an analytical model of industrial organization that helps students understand the reasons for change, assess the impact of change, and make some judgments about what is yet to come. Developing such an approach is what this text is designed to do.

Who Should Use This Text?

Money, Financial Institutions, and Economic Activity is intended for use by undergraduates and MBA students in either economics or finance departments. The text presupposes no additional knowledge beyond that acquired in the economic principles course. Because the economic theory is presented as a separate section, and theoretical references in other parts of the text are self-contained, the book may be used without extensive reliance on the theory section. Students with an interest in financial markets, institutional development and behavior, or industrial organization analysis can benefit as much from this text as economics majors.

What's Different About This Text?

Probably the most important differentiating element of this text is its attention to the student. The book is written in an understandable fashion. An organization of the topic in each chapter-opening objectives section highlights important concepts and helps the student focus attention while reading the chapter. The objectives section also specifies the essential points of understanding which the student will have mastered after studying that chapter.

The text provides a unique integration of institutional policy analysis with a historical orientation. This allows analysis of the evolution of the financial system and depository institutions rather than just presenting a discussion of what exists at this point in time. If students are able to see how events have influenced the structure and functioning of the industry as it evolved, they will be in a better position to analyze the ongoing changes that will occur over the next decade.

The industrial organization approach lays a solid foundation for our analysis of the financial industry. The model is introduced to give students a basic framework upon which to assess changes in a market's structure, in a firm's behavior, and within a financial institution.

Policy analysis is also stressed in the text. In addition to studying more traditional models, a close look at the rational expectations model will give the students the benefit of new insights into monetary policy questions. This text uses the conclusions from rational expectationists' work to shed new light on macroeconomic policy issues.

Finally, because of the text's attention to the changes in institutions and financial markets, important new elements in the financial world are developed as an integral part of the text. These new elements include analysis of the "supermarket" approach to financial services, financial futures, and their impact on risk and interest rates, and the most up-to-date discussion of deregulation and its impact on institutions and markets. Attention to the structural changes in the industry allows analysis of the significant unresolved issues presented by deregulation, such as deposit insurance, the future of small banks, and the future of American banks in the global marketplace.

How Is the Book Organized and Why?

Money, Financial Institutions, and Economic Activity uses a developmental approach. It is organized to assist the student in acquiring a complete understanding of three interrelated topics: money, the financial industry, and economic activity. Students need clear components of information which they, after understanding each individually, can build into an integrated whole. The text's chapters are organized to allow students to put the various pieces of the financial industry puzzle together as cogently as possible.

Part I introduces money and its relation to the financial aspects of the economy. A bridge is built between money and the real sector of the economy by discussing the role of interest rates. Part II deals with financial institutions, establishing a continuity within the industry by exploring the origins and evolution of financial intermediaries, as well as their roles and benefits. The foundation for an industrial organization approach is laid by discussing banks as firms; a brief exploration of market structure and firm performance completes this concept. This section concludes with a chapter on deposit expansion as a transition to the theoretical discussion of money in macroeconomic models.

For instructors seeking to develop theoretical understanding, Part III incorporates an overview of macroeconomic theory, an adapted Keynesian model, a discussion of the controversy between the Keynesian and monetarist models, and a chapter on rational expectations. The theoretical model is given utility by discussing the contemporary economic problems of inflation and unemployment. Questions relating to the usefulness of these models for an understanding of current problems leads to an exploration of the rational expectations alternative.

Part IV is unique. With some background in institutional developments and theoretical issues, the student can now investigate the financial system from the industrial organization perspective. By looking at financial intermediation from an industry perspective, the students have a framework from which to assess change and evaluate its implications.

The first three parts, although self-contained, are building blocks. The institutional background and theoretical models combine with the industrial organization approach in the fourth part to give students a complete set of tools for analyzing monetary policy in the world today. All four parts have greater utility because they can be smoothly applied to Part V's assessment of monetary policy and its policy implications for institutions, individuals, and the macroeconomy.

References are made throughout the text to international issues, and those issues are explored in detail in an extensive chapter on the international aspects of money and financial institutions. No world is more "real" than that of the international realm, and the final chapter helps reinforce this understanding.

Over forty high-interest boxes enliven the book as they mine today's financial ground in our three main areas of study; they are titled *Money Today*, *Banking Today*, and *Economics Today*. These features give the student some practical applications annd the instructor the opportunity to explore current issues in detail by serving as springboards into more discussions.

Are There Alternative Ways to Organize the Material?

Since *Money, Financial Institutions, and Economic Activity* was designed to accommodate an array of economics and finance courses, instructors may find it useful to reorganize the chapters to suit their needs. Here are two suggestions. Instructors not interested in stressing economic theory may assign Parts I and II, skip part III, and proceed to Part IV. Then, before moving to a discussion of monetary policy, they may assign Chapter 11 on inflation and unemployment as a base for analyzing and assessing monetary policy in Part V. The final chapter on international issues would conclude this course.

Economics instructors may want to assign only Chapters 2 and 3 of Part I and then proceed to the theory section, Part III. Chapter 7 of Part II, on financial systems and deposit expansion, would provide a transition into a discussion of monetary policy in Part V. Chapter 5 and 6 might be added to Part IV to complete the course. The final chapter on international issues can be added if time permits.

What Are the Features to Improve Learning?

In addition to the developmental organization of the text, the use of learning objectives, and the incorporation of high-interest applications, the text and its support package offer many teaching and learning aids.

End-of-chapter questions are intended not only to help students check their understanding but to stimulate them to think about extensions of the textual material. Each chapter also contains annotated suggestions for further reading. A number of chapters include appendices, which are intended either to clarify basic material or to elaborate on issues ancillary to the text. An extensive glossary will also prove helpful.

In addition to text learning aids, a complete support package includes the following features:

- An *Instructors Manual* specifies the text's chapter objectives, provides multiple-choice test questions, and includes answers for the end-of-chapter questions from the text.

- The *Student Workbook* helps the student focus on the major objectives of each chapter, reviews key concepts, provides a vocabulary review, offers multiple-choice questions for self-testing, includes problems (both data-based and essays) to develop better understanding, and suggests additional educational activities for improved comprehension of the text material.

- An *Interactive Problem-Solving Computer Disk* aids problem-solving skills and reinforces basic principles introduced in the text.

Acknowledgments

The process of writing a book is long and arduous. There are scores of individuals who have assisted me in the project, and, although not all of them can be mentioned, their assistance is appreciated. In mentioning significant people I must first acknowledge N. J. Simler, economics department chair at the University of Minnesota, who started me on this project by encouraging me to accept the challenge. Then, of course, I must mention Scott, Foresman economics editor George Lobell, who was the first person to talk to me about writing the book, and who talked me through the project as well. I only hope this book makes his efforts worthwhile. All the professionals at Scott, Foresman were terrific. Developmental editor Trisha Nealon and project editor Nancy Siadek not only provided invaluable assistance in the technical aspects of the project, but did it with a good humor and sensitivity which made things so much more pleasant.

I want to thank my graduate assistants, Doh-Yeon Whang, Stacey Schreft, and Eric Olson, who didn't let me down despite my never-ending demands. The staff at the Center for Economic Education—Clare Gravon, Melody Mafi, and Lee Russo—provided encouragement and support as I rushed to meet deadlines. Most of all I want to thank them for putting up with me as I rode the emotional roller coaster of textbook writing.

The outside reviewers offered helpful suggestions throughout the writing process. I would like to acknowledge:

Susan Alexander	College of St. Thomas
Michael D. Bradley	George Washington University
Pamela J. Brown	Auburn University
Kevin Campbell	Staten Island College
Phillip P. Caruso	Western Michigan University
William A. Christiansen	Florida State University
Alan J. Duskin	Boston University
C. Alan Garner	University of Notre Dame
Charles M. Gray	College of St. Thomas
Beverly Hadaway	University of Texas at Austin
Bassam Harik	Western Michigan University
Michael T. Hutchins	University of North Carolina at Chapel Hill
Jon Innes	Lehigh University
Walter D. Johnson	Sangamon State University

Richard H. Keehn	University of Wisconsin, Parkside
Tim Krehbiel	Western Illinois University
James M. McGibany	Marquette University
Phillip W. Moery	Shepherd College
Richard C. Schiming	Mankato State University
A. Charlene Sullivan	Purdue University
Daniel Teferra	Ferris State College
John B. White	Old Dominion University
C. Frank Zarnowski	Mount Saint Mary's College

Above all I want to thank my colleague and best friend, my wife Kathy. She made extensive professional sacrifices to help me on this project. In every aspect of the process she was indispensable. Kathy offered solace and encouragement, served as my editor, typist, and most reliable critic, and functioned as my coauthor on the student workbook. This book would never have been completed without her; my gratitude and admiration are immeasurable and unending.

Bruce R. Dalgaard
Minneapolis, Minnesota

OVERVIEW

CONTENTS

PART II FINANCIAL INSTITUTIONS

PART III THE MACROECONOMIC MODEL

CHAPTER
TEN
Monetarism and the Keynesian-Monetarist Debate   239

PART IV THE CHANGING STRUCTURE OF FINANCIAL INSTITUTIONS

CHAPTER THIRTEEN **Financial Intermediation: An Industry Study**   318

PART V   MONETARY POLICY/MONETARY MANAGEMENT

PART VI INTERNATIONAL MONETARY SYSTEM

PART ONE

MONEY and the FINANCIAL SYSTEM

CHAPTER ONE

MONEY
and the
REAL WORLD

Money does not exist in a vacuum. It is not a mere lifeless object, but a social institution.

Paul Einzig, *Primitive Money*

What is money? How has it changed over time? How have people viewed money, described its properties and characteristics? How much more will money change? This chapter addresses these questions. Its purpose is to place the development of money into a historical context. This first chapter attempts to show that the sociopolitical environment interacts with economic factors to influence the evolution of money and the attitudes people have about money.

Few would debate the proposition that money influences economic activity. The precise nature of the relationship between money and the economy—how much money matters—is the subject of an ongoing debate among economists. This book explores the influence money has on the United States economy and analyzes the relationships between financial institutions and economic activity.

When one considers the evolution of money and the different attitudes relating to it at various stages in history, it is easy to understand how disagreements about the role of money in contemporary society occur. The sociopolitical environment influences society's views on money to no less an extent than money influences society.

Chapter Objectives

This chapter makes a broad sweep of the history of money and the evolution of a monetary system and discusses the properties and characteristics of money. You should use this chapter to acquire a perspective from which you can later make some judgments about economic issues and monetary policies. By the end of this chapter you should be able to:

- Give a general definition of money.
- Explain the connection between the evolution of the economy and the development of money.
- Identify the properties and characteristics of money.

As you read this chapter think about the changing nature of money and the monetary system. You should be able to explain the changing nature of money and how money may change in the future. By the end of this chapter you should be able to:

- Describe how the mercantilist, classicist, and monetarist positions on money evolved.
- Explain how the concept of value influenced changing attitudes about money.
- Relate the purposes of money to the forms money can take.
- Speculate about the form money might take in the future.

Keep these objectives in mind as you read Chapter 1. Achieving an understanding of these points will help you comprehend the more technical definitions of money given in Chapter 2 and the overall financial system presented in Chapter 3.

Origins of Money

Money is defined quite differently depending on the time period, its use or perceived role, and the person who defines it. For our discussion in this chapter, we may define money as a "unit or an object conforming to a reasonable degree to some standard of uniformity, which is employed for reckoning or for making a large proportion of the payment customary in the community concerned, and which is accepted in payment largely with the intention of employing it for making payments."[1]

---

[1] Each of the many definitions of money differs slightly from the others. This definition is from Paul Einzig, *Primitive Money* (Oxford: Pergamon Press, 1966): 317.

The use of objects as money can be validated probably as far back as the Stone Age (over 250,000 years ago). As furs were traded, they came to be accepted as an exchange medium; early people accepted furs in return for goods and then used those same furs to acquire other goods. We begin to see an object, as Einzig says, that is accepted as payment to be used in turn for payment rather than for consumption. Cattle were also an important exchange item for many peoples throughout early recorded history, including in Greek and Roman times. We can trace many monetary terms to the use of cattle as an exchange item—*pecuniary*, meaning monetary, is derived from a Latin word for cattle; and the Indian monetary unit, the rupee, can be traced to a Sanskrit word for cattle.

Shells represent one of the earliest recognizable forms of money. Ancient civilizations used cowrie shells (tiny sea shells) or tortoise shells in much the same way that American Indians later strung clam shells together to form wampum. Gold, bronze, silver, and iron were the principal metals that came into use as media of exchange. The three most ancient civilizations to leave records—Egypt, Babylon and China—all used bronze and other precious metals in exchange transactions. The Chinese exchanged precious metals as early as 2100 B.C. Bronze was formed into shapes resembling cattle and hides and exchanged as early as the fourteenth century B.C. But the earliest record of anything resembling coin money dates back to the end of the eighth or the beginning of the seventh century B.C. in the Eastern Mediterranean region and from at least the seventh century in China.

Weighing made it possible to dispense with identification of money by primitive measurement. This was an important factor in the development of coins and the expansion of monetary systems. The Latin word *pondus* from which the British monetary unit, the pound, is derived means weight. And *libra*, the word from which the Italian lira is derived, means balance and weight.

Coinage was never actually invented. Still, few debate the notion that coinage first began in the Aegean civilization of the Mediterranean. The Aegeans marked metal ingots to indicate weight and purity. The Greek civilization that followed refined the process of coinage.

From the beginning of the seventh century B.C., trade and invasion dispersed the use of coins. From Asia Minor the idea moved quickly through trade to continental Greece where it was well established by the middle of the sixth century B.C. The conquests of Alexander the Great in the latter half of the fourth century B.C. carried the custom of coin use to Egypt, Southern Asia, and India. Greek trade through Marsala, Italy, helped bring coins to Europe toward the end of the third century B.C. The Gauls, recognizing the advantages of coins, began using copies of the Greek coins; about a century later the Britons adopted the idea. By the beginning of the Christian era, coins were in use throughout the greater part of Europe and Asia.

Attitudes on the Importance of Money

The United States has a very sophisticated monetary system. Our monetary system and the attitudes we hold about money have their origins in earlier times. Today we use symbols as money, instead of inherently valuable items. A discussion of the historical development of money will help us understand both the type of system that has evolved and the attitudes people have developed toward money.

Much of what constituted the basis of knowledge about money in an economic system can be traced back to Aristotle. Aristotelian thought regarding money involved two basic ideas: 1) the fundamental function of money is that it serve as a medium of exchange, and 2) money must have some use beyond that of an exchange medium; money must have "intrinsic value." The second idea was later referred to as the *metallist* position. As we will see, history proved Aristotle accurate in his first proposition but inaccurate in the second. Centuries later, well into the nineteenth century, economists rejected the intrinsic value notion. Throughout modern times much debate about the role of money in the economy has revolved around this notion.

Money in the Middle Ages

While money in the form of coins existed during the Middle Ages, it was in short supply.[2] Much of the feudal community of the Middle Ages was self-sufficient, and peasants had little or no need for money. But there was a general understanding that money was necessary for increased economic activity. In the growing cities money was essential to sustain economic activity. Writers often referred to money as the lifeblood of the economic body. The demand for currency kept growing but the production of gold and silver did not keep pace until near the end of the fifteenth century. Since metallic money was in short supply, its value grew in terms of goods and services. This is the same as saying commodity prices fell. This drop in commodity prices, or deflation, hindered economic activity.

To get around the shortage of money, people tried alternative means of exchange, and debasement of the currency occurred. Because it was abundant, leather was used for "minting" coins but proved unsuccessful. More

---

[2] Charlemagne imposed a monetary reform during the eighth century which was quickly extended to all of Christian Europe. The system was based on a new silver coin, the *denarius*, or penny, which weighed approximately 1.7 grams. The system prescribed that 1 pound = 20 shillings = 240 pennies. This system prevailed on the continent until the time of the French Revolution and in Britain until the 1960s.

often the currency was debased by "clipping" coins; a very small amount of metal was scraped off the edges of coins, melted, and recoined.

The shortage of money and the desire for convenience influenced the development of paper money and a credit system. During the Middle Ages goldsmiths found they could augment their income by safeguarding precious metals of wealthy individuals for a fee. Owners of gold received paper receipts for the valuable metal they left with the goldsmith. Rather than returning to the goldsmith and reclaiming the gold each time they wanted to make a purchase, people began to exchange the receipts for commodities. These receipts circulated instead of the gold and represented an early form of paper money. Furthermore, the goldsmiths realized that not all the gold coins were withdrawn at the same time. Maintaining a portion of the total amount on deposit to cover withdrawals meant that the remainder could be loaned out to meet the increasing demand for currency. The origins of a system of credit, discussed in detail in a later chapter, often are traced to the ingenuity of the goldsmiths of the Middle Ages.

Mercantilists

The economic doctrine of mercantilism appeared in the period after the Middle Ages but before the rise of laissez faire economic thought. Mercantilist thought prevailed from around 1500 until 1776. During the early part of the mercantilist period, capitalism, and with it trade within and between countries, became dominant over the isolation of feudalism. With the rise of trade came the need for an increase in money. Mercantilists regarded gold and silver as the most desirable form of wealth. Bullion represented the means by which individuals and nations could achieve power.

Mercantilists understood that the increase in money (gold and silver) was necessary to facilitate production. Without a well-developed banking system to make funds available for production and trade, the inflow of precious metals was the only way to "quicken" output and trade. While mercantilists recognized that an increased money supply would influence prices upward, they believed that the increased economic activity would prevent prices from rising too quickly. An increasing money supply also would help keep interest rates low (the medieval concern about usury was passing) and this would stimulate production of exportable goods and further add to the country's accumulation of precious metals.

The mercantilists associated money with wealth. Money was intrinsically valuable because of what it represented—the means to augment power through monetary means and the acquisition of riches. In a sense the metallist view mentioned earlier by Aristotle dominated mercantilists' thinking. Money and wealth were the means and the end during the mercantilist period. These attitudes changed with the writings of the classicists.

Classicists

During the late eighteenth century, as Britain was moving through the industrial revolution, a new school of economic thought developed. Classical economists viewed money quite differently from their mercantilist predecessors. The classicists' attitudes on money held the seeds of what would later grow into the more sophisticated views on money expressed by contemporary monetarists. It is useful to explore briefly the classical views on money so we may subsequently compare and contrast them with some twentieth century ideas.

The classical school began in the late eighteenth century, more specifically around 1776 when Adam Smith published his book, *The Wealth of Nations*. This period of economic thought ended about a century later but has had a profound effect on economists to the present day.

Whereas the mercantilists had viewed the accumulation of metallic money as an all-important goal for nations, the classical thinkers deemphasized the importance of money. They saw money as important because without it the economic system would be forced to rely on barter for exchange transactions. Money itself did not add to the productivity of the system; it facilitated the circulation of goods. The classical view of the economy saw the production of goods, not the existence of money, as generating revenue and increasing economic activity. Classicists saw money as a veil over the system which needed to be pulled aside to allow examination of the real economic world.

Money was not considered unimportant; in fact, its role was often hotly debated. In 1797, during its war with France, England suspended the payment of gold for bank notes. A lengthy debate ensued over the need to back paper currency with precious metal. This "bullionist" controversy continued for decades. The heated debate primarily related to the influence of paper currency on price inflation (a debate which persists in the 1980s). One of the staunchest opponents of unbacked paper currency, economist David Ricardo, argued that "however abundant may be the quantity of money . . . [and] though it may increase . . . the prices of commodities, . . . nothing will be added to the real revenue and wealth of the country . . . ."[3] Classical economists like Ricardo were concerned about money's influence on prices but discounted the impact of money on production. This position was in stark contrast to the importance mercantilists placed on money in the promotion of economic activity.

---

[3] David Ricardo, "The High Price of Bullion," in J.R. McCulloch, ed. *The Works of David Ricardo* (London: 1886): 287.

From Classicists to Monetarists

The separation of money from real economic activity meant that money and prices were subordinate to more basic economic factors. The economic thinkers who followed the classicists began to integrate monetary analysis into general economic theory. With this new work, individuals began to see money as a more important factor in fundamental economic processes. While the ideas of economists were evolving, banking was expanding, the concept of credit was developing, and economic fluctuations were necessitating a better understanding of money and the real world.

The importance of money in the economy found expression in what we will later discuss as the quantity theory of money. Briefly, the quantity theory illustrates that changes in prices are related directly to changes in the quantity of money. This theory forms the basis for debates over the role of money. The integration of monetary and economic factors during the nineteenth century brought the role of money into prominence among economic theorists and policymakers. With the increase in economic activity and the severe fluctuations that Western capitalist economies suffered during this period, businesspeople as well as economists began to look at money and the economy quite differently. The customary idea expressed by the classicists' view, that money was like a veil over the economy, needed reappraisal.

In this reappraisal, economists directed more attention to the impact of money on the economy, not simply prices. Their efforts became the foundation for the renewed interest in money that began in earnest among contemporary monetarists during the 1970s. We can narrowly define contemporary monetarists as those who view changes in the money stock as the predominate factor explaining changes in money income. This renewed interest in the importance of money in the economy has been a significant factor in shaping attitudes toward money and monetary policies during the 1980s. We will look more closely at the impact of the monetarists' ideas in later chapters.

An Exchange System and Money

How is it that money came to be used? A discussion of its early evolution does not explain fully why it came into widespread use. Economic systems progressed from the point where individuals were totally self-reliant to where people exchanged goods. The exchange of goods or services without the use of money is called barter and, as we mentioned, a system of barter preceded the use of any form of money. In many cases barter continued long after money came into use. This is either because of resistance to change, because of a lack of money as a basis for exchange, or possibly as a result of a distrust of money. The distrust may occur during times of severe inflation as individuals try to avoid holding a depreciating currency. Although money can only develop in an exchange economy, all exchange economies do not need money.

It is commonly assumed that money evolved when the earlier form of exchange, barter, became too cumbersome. Nineteenth-century economist Stanley Jevons illustrated this concept about the shortcomings of barter in his classic story about a traveling singer.

> Mademoiselle Zelie, a singer, . . . made a professional tour around the world and gave a concert in the Society Islands. In exchange for ⟨singing⟩ . . . she was to receive a third part of the receipts. When counted, her share was found to consist of three pigs, twenty-three turkeys, forty-four chickens, five thousand cocoanuts, besides considerable quantities of bananas, lemons and oranges. ⟨In Paris⟩ this . . . might have brought four thousand francs, . . . good remuneration for five songs.[4]

Jevons points out that unfortunately the singer could not use all the payments and since there was no money on the island, she left without anything she considered fair compensation.

The people of the Society Islands used commodities as money. The people of Paris relied on a metallic-based currency system. Both functioned effectively. Mademoiselle Zelie's problem was the result of a confrontation between two different cultural systems more than a shortcoming of the barter system. In primitive communities barter was not as inconvenient as it was for Mademoiselle Zelie. The realization of what Jevons called "double coincidence" of wants (that is, one person finding another who has something the first wants and who wants what the first has to trade) was not terribly difficult in a small, agrarian community.

Barter did give way to the use of money due largely to the convenience of money. Over years of bartering, people undoubtedly established fairly well-defined *exchange ratios*, the relationships between generally accepted quantities of goods needed to trade for other goods. These ratios might change depending on the seasons and the quality of the harvest. But one can imagine that corn tended to be exchanged for potatoes in roughly the same ratio no matter who was trading. As the number of products and services expanded and specialization of occupations increased, the quantity of exchange ratios became too numerous for most people to manage. Negotiating a ratio for each exchange also was becoming awkward and time consuming. In other words, the transactions costs of the barter system were too high. A more efficient system was needed.

---

[4] Stanley Jevons, *Money and Mechanism of Exchange* (New York: Appleton and Company, 1875): Chapter 4.

An intermediate step between pure barter and the use of money as we know it was the identification of some widely accepted object that could be readily exchanged. In return for goods and services people accepted this object not for direct consumption but rather to obtain something which they desired. The consistent use of one product or item meant that a standard of value or unit of account, something which formed the basis for establishing relative values, had developed.

Taking a widely accepted item in return for goods or services was more convenient than seeking a double coincidence. As people used one favored item consistently in the bartering process and expressed exchange ratios in terms of this item, it became the medium of exchange. Since we know that early civilizations valued certain commodities, such as shells, we easily can imagine that people made comparisons using these valued objects as a unit of account or standard of value. Even before a numerical system evolved, the accumulated shells of one family might be compared to those of another based on size or weight.

The use of a medium of exchange, especially once it was identified as a unit of account, allowed for greater efficiency in the marketplace. The costs of bartering stemmed primarily from the time involved in the exchange process. In part because of the time reduction resulting from the use of a medium of exchange, the quantity of trade increased.

Properties of Money

Our discussion of the evolution of money so far has not specified the particular properties of money. Discussion of the development of a money system from a barter system illustrates two essential characteristics, namely that money is a medium of exchange and a standard of value or unit of account. Most economists point to these properties as the essential characteristics of money. Aristotle made passing reference to the advantages of certain commodities as mediums of exchange and he also observed that commodities that met the rule of equivalence in exchange also were to be used as a measure of value.

Money in the modern sense possesses two other properties. Money serves as a store of value and a standard of deferred payments. The identification of an item as money requires that it serve as a *store of value*. Individuals must have confidence that money will translate into goods or services of generally equal value when used immediately. Money also serves as a *standard of deferred payments*; it holds value for use days or months later.

However, throughout history price fluctuations have affected the value of monetary units. As a store of value, the United States dollar faired rather poorly during the double-digit inflation of the late 1970s and early 1980s. As we will discuss later, during periods of extreme inflation, called *hyperinflation*, people may abandon the conventional monetary unit in an attempt to find another item which will serve as a store of value. Only in extreme cases throughout history, where inflation was beyond control and persisted for an extended period, has a country abandoned its money unit. In these cases, for example in Germany in the early 1920s or Guatemala in the late 1920s, the money unit became so devalued that people had no confidence in it, would not accept it, and sought alternatives. The adoption of a second currency occurred not just because the initial monetary unit was no longer a store of value but because it no longer possessed the other properties of money. Today, when a currency becomes devalued rapidly, people often switch to American dollars, as they did recently in Argentina, or they quote all prices in terms of a stable currency, as Israelis did with the dollar in the early 1980s.

A final property of money is that it must serve as a standard of deferred payment. People must be able to specify future payments in terms of a monetary unit. During the nineteenth century, long-term contracts specified payments in terms of a certain quantity of gold. A widely accepted monetary unit can serve the same purpose as gold; it can be used to specify contract payments since it serves as a standard of deferred payment.

In summary, there are four functional properties of money. Money serves as a:

1. *Medium of exchange.* It is readily acceptable for exchange transactions.
2. *Standard of value.* It is used as a way of measuring values.
3. *Store of value.* It retains its purchasing power.
4. *Standard of deferred payment.* It is used to express debts or future obligations.

Characteristics of Money

Besides having functional properties, money needs to possess four additional characteristics. Money must be:

1. *Easily verifiable.* Verifiability contributes to general acceptability. People must feel confident that what they accept as money is what it appears to be. Biting gold coins (since gold is such a soft metal) was one way to verify that a coin was valid. Today, the difficulty in counterfeiting dollars and the constant surveilance virtually assure verifiability.
2. *Convenient.* Convenience includes easy transportation and storage. Coins were much more convenient than most commodity monies, but paper money is more convenient than coins. "Plastic money," or credit cards, seems even more convenient to some people today.

3. *Durable*. Durability, or lack of perishability, permits money to be held over long periods of time and helps ensure that it can function as a basis for deferred payments. Colonists often converted the commodity money corn into whiskey, not only because it was easier to transport but because it kept longer and was more durable. Paper dollars, although having a limited life expectancy (just over a year), are relatively durable when treated properly.

4. *Divisible*. Divisibility provides that money is available in a variety of denominations to allow large and small transactions.

Full-bodied versus Credit Money

Money has taken many forms. Virtually all monetary systems have settled on metal currency or metal-backed paper currency as the most efficient and effective type of money. All forms of money fall into one of two basic categories—full-bodied money and credit money.

Full-bodied money has value in and of itself, the "intrinsic value" to which Aristotle and the metallists referred. The value of full-bodied money is equivalent to its value when used as a medium of exchange. We can identify two kinds of full-bodied money—commodity money, including metallic currency, and redeemable paper currency.

Commodity money, such as cattle for the Greeks and tobacco or corn for Colonial Americans, is full-bodied money. Commodity money has value beyond its medium of exchange property. People sell tobacco or corn as a commodity in the open market.

Paper currency, which is redeemable in precious metals, possesses the same quality. Paper currency represents full-bodied money and was used because it was more convenient than coins. U.S. silver certificates, which circulated as redeemable paper notes until 1971, were the last full-bodied paper money in this country.

Credit money is an alternative type of money. It consists of unredeemable currency issued by the government (Federal Reserve notes) and deposits issued by financial institutions. Currency issued by the government has little or no inherent value (a dollar bill costs about three cents to produce) but it is valuable because it is accepted as a medium of exchange. During the American Civil War, the Confederacy issued *fiat money*. This was currency that the government printed and used to pay its war expenses. It was not readily accepted and lost value rapidly. Currency issued by the government is *legal tender*, that is, it must be accepted in payment for all debts (unless a contract prescribes an alternative form of payment). Deposits at financial institutions are not legal tender. Ultimately it is the public's acceptance of a circulating medium which determines whether it will retain its value.

Societies progressed from exclusive use of full-bodied money, initially commodity money and then gold or silver coins, to currency redeemable for gold or silver. There was no concern about the acceptability or value of money when it was full-bodied money. Until the use of coins and metal-backed paper, commodity money was sometimes inconvenient to use but it did fulfill the basic properties of money.

Today most modern societies use unredeemable or inconvertible paper money as the circulating medium. Token metal coins of small denominations also circulate widely. Some countries mint gold or silver coins; they are usually purchased by collectors. The United States began minting gold coins in late 1986 after a fifty-year hiatus (see Figure 1.1).

United States silver dollars, last minted in 1935, are still present. The more recent Susan B. Anthony dollar was not all silver. (Money Today 1.1 describes the problems that occur when a coin is not accepted.) Why aren't traditional American silver dollars used more extensively? They are a little heavier than other coins and they are not regularly minted any longer. These are primary factors but a more complete explanation is Gresham's law.

Sir Thomas Gresham was an English merchant who supposedly told Queen Elizabeth in 1558 that "bad money drives out good" when explaining to her why Henry VIII's debasement of the currency had caused gold to flow out of England. (Sir Thomas never actually said that bad money drives good out of circulation but the notion was attributed to him and it has taken on his name.) For centuries people have preferred to hold sound currency with less value as the circulating medium. To rephrase this, if two forms of money differing in value possess equal legal-tender power, then people will use the cheapest and the other will disappear from circulation.

Such a situation occurred in this country in the eighteenth century. Legislation passed in 1792 provided for the minting of a silver dollar and a ten-dollar gold piece based on the established mint ratio of 15:1 (that is, the value by weight of gold was fifteen times that of silver). But market forces altered the relationship and set the ratio at 15½:1. As a result, people melted down the ten-dollar gold pieces and traded them for silver, making a 3-percent profit in the process. The overvalued silver drove the gold piece out of circulation. In 1834 the official mint ratio was changed to 16:1 but the market ratio was unchanged; gold coins then drove silver coins out of circulation.

A similar situation occurred in the United States recently with silver-backed paper money and coins. Silver certificates were redeemable in silver coins. By the mid-1960s with the market price of silver rising, converting silver certificates into silver coins became profitable. The Treasury announced termination of redemption after June 30, 1968. As the price of silver rose even higher, the silver value of United States coins (which were composed of 90-percent silver) was higher than the exchange value of the coin.

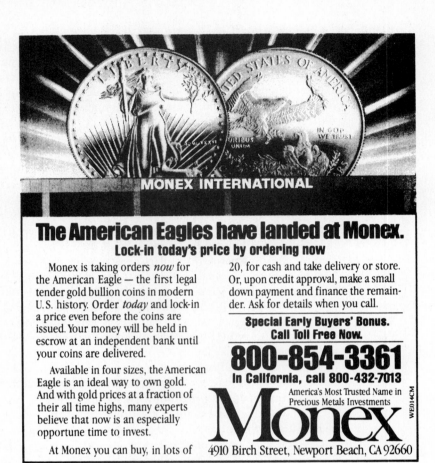

FIGURE 1.1   *Purchasing Gold Coins*   Certain countries, Canada and South Africa, and very recently the United States, sell gold coins. These coins do not circulate but are purchased for investment purposes.

These coins practically disappeared from circulation as people either held them for speculative purposes or sold them for their silver content. Congress permitted sandwich quarters and dimes—copper coins with a copper-nickel combination on the surface—to be coined to take up the slack.

The silver dollar is another example of the same phenomenon. The silver dollar is worth more than one dollar because of the increased value of silver and because it is becoming a collector's item. It no longer circulates with any regularity as a medium of exchange. Money Today 1.2 illustrates two very different reasons why some coins do not circulate.

Changing Nature of Money

The discussion to this point has concentrated on coin and currency as the components of money. Money has come to include much more than currency and coins. The most obvious additional component is checkable deposits. Until recently, economists would have described the components of money as coin, currency, and demand deposits. Demand deposits are deposits against which an account holder can "demand" payment by writing a check. Until 1980 in most of the country, only commercial banks could offer demand deposits; other financial institutions could offer only time deposits, that is, savings accounts. With legislation passed in 1980 all types of financial institutions can offer checking accounts. Beyond that, with the use of different instruments such as NOW (Negotiable Order of Withdrawal) accounts at savings and loans, share drafts at credit unions, and transaction accounts at commercial banks, the line between demand deposits and savings deposits is becoming very fine. For all practical purposes, people may draw checks against the money in their time deposit accounts as well as their demand deposit accounts. Table 2.1 in the next chapter provides a detailed analysis of the components of our money supply. Table 1.1 identifies the components considered as money based on the latest figures. As you will see

Every night, all across America, people empty the loose change from their pockets and purses into some recepticle or other in their bedrooms. Every bedroom seems to contain an ashtray or a fraternity mug filled with coins. A few people pick up their coins in the morning, but most of them don't. Some keep them for a vacation, or a night on the town, or give them to children or grandchildren, but most of the coins simply lie there as inflation cuts into their worth.

According to the United States Mint (the branch of the Treasury that makes the coins), 172 billion pennies have been produced since 1959, but it has been estimated that only about 40 billion are still in circulation. The higher the face value of a coin, the more likely it is to remain in circulation, but the story is similar when it comes to nickels, dimes, and even quarters. Some 17.2 billion nickels have been minted since 1956, and about 7.2 billion are in circulation. 22.5 billion dimes have been minted since 1965, but 14.1 are in circulation. 18.7 billion quarters have been minted since 1965, but 11.1 billion are in circulation. The unused coins have a face value of $4,260,000,000!

The following ad tells of another out-of-circulation coin—the one-dollar "IKE." Although out of circulation, this silver dollar remains in demand with a cost of $12.50 in 1986.

Source: Los Angeles Times article by Penny Pagano, March 10, 1984. Reprinted by permission.

Save America's Scarce "Ike" Silver Dollar

Minted in 5 years only — the "IKE" was the shortest lived U.S. regular-issue silver dollar minted since 1839. Now available for $9.95 each in mint-state rolls.

June, 1986, Montpelier, Vermont — International Coins & Currency, Inc., a national distributor of numismatic coins, is offering for sale a limited number of America's "IKE" silver dollars — the shortest lived regular-issue silver design minted since 1839. These mint state brilliant uncirculated coins were the first and only coins to honor America's historic lunar landing.

In 1976 a 200 year old U.S. tradition ended -- the U.S. Government stopped minting regular-issue one dollar coins containing silver. And the "IKES" became historic relics of a bygone era. Minted from 1971-1976, they bear the important distinction of being the *first* and *only* coins to symbolize America's historic lunar landing and portray our 34th president of the United States, Dwight David Eisenhower.

Source: Courtesy International Coins & Currency, Inc.

Less than 6% of all the "IKE" dollars minted were struck in silver. Because a significant portion of silver IKE's disappeared into the melting pot during the big melts of the 1970's, these coins are considered by some numismatists as modern "sleeping" classics. Each silver dollar is a big 39mm in diameter, 24.59 grams, .400 fine silver, dated 1971-1976, and are in absolutely mint state brilliant uncirculated condition.

Just $9.95 in investor rolls

Because of these coins' historical significance, relative scarcity and mint state quality you might expect to pay up to double what we charge. But while supplies last, they are available on a first-come, first-served basis as low as $9.95 each in investor rolls of 20 coins. Prices are as follows: 1 coin $12.50 (#7401) 2 coins $25.00 3 coins $37.50 10 coins $115 (save $10) 20 coin investor roll $199 (save $51).

	Billions of $	Percent
Currency	177.6	26
Traveler's Checks	6.4	1
Demand Deposits	288.3	43
Other Checkable Deposits	203.9	30
TOTAL	676.2	100.0

Note: Money supply figures are seasonally adjusted.

**Source: Federal Reserve Bulletin (October 1986): A-13.
Reprinted by permission.**

TABLE 1.1   *Money Supply Components, July 1986*

in a presentation of the theoretical and empirical definitions of money in the next chapter, economists disagree about exactly what counts as money.

Liquidity

Although economists and policy makers disagree about how to measure the supply of money, society considers as money those items or symbols which possess a high degree of liquidity. *Liquidity* refers to the relative ease with which an asset can be converted into a medium of exchange. Money, by definition, is completely liquid. Any number of items might be accepted as payment but not all can be counted as money. Assets, whether land, automobiles, or corporate stock, have value and therefore may be accepted as payment for goods and services. But they need not necessarily be accepted. They are not legal tender, and they are not very liquid—they cannot be converted into recognizable money quickly, easily and with a high degree of assurance about the conversion price. We generally would not consider these assets money.

Many items are certainly more liquid than corporate stock or real estate. Traveler's checks are generally thought as "good as cash" and some are classified as money.[5] However, anyone who has had car trouble in rural America can attest that traveler's checks are not *quite* as good as cash. Food stamps or other coupons are practically as good as cash but we probably

---

[5] Traveler's checks issued by non-bank companies are considered part of the money supply; bank traveler's checks are not.

would not classify them as money. Although food stamps are quite liquid, these coupons are not accepted everywhere, usually cannot be exchanged for cash, and cannot be used for any purpose other than food. We can refer to these highly liquid assets as *near monies*. They possess many of the characteristics of money and perform many of the same functions but are not nearly as readily acceptable.

The United States is moving from a currency system to an accounting system in financial transactions. Rather than exchanging currency, or even something representing currency, such as a check, for goods and services, people are making exchanges through bookkeeping transfers. No money changes hands; accounts are adjusted instead. For centuries, businesses and nations have operated this way, but widespread use by consumers is rather new. Why is this happening and what does it mean?

The quantity of checks used in the United States has increased significantly. The Federal Reserve Bank of Atlanta estimated that 18.5 billion checks were written in 1970; 32 billion were written in 1979. That is a 70 percent increase. And it means that in 1979, on average, each American wrote over 150 checks. Many contemporary transactions take place with checks. Processing and collection costs are between $.25 and $.40 for each check. That is a significant cost. Besides, as any financially squeezed college student knows, it takes time for the transfer of funds after a check is written. This time period, called the float, allows firms and individuals to make payments when no funds actually exist in their checking accounts. The day or two it takes for a check to clear allows time to transfer funds or deposit a paycheck to cover the check. Especially with large sums of money and high interest rates, time is money. Financial institutions try to reduce the float as much as possible so they have more control over the supply of money.

In considering the evolution of money you should realize one other key element of money. In a general sense, people decide what money is. This is an important point when you consider what our money will be by the turn of the century. This issue is also important in later chapters for discussions about attempts to control the supply of money and regulate financial institutions. Part of the problem in controlling the supply of money is that financial institutions, and people in general, can decide upon some new form of money, a form people might not even consider money today.

Cashless Society

Processing costs for checks are encouraging the application of microelectronic technology to the financial sector. Such technology not only reduces these costs but speeds up financial transactions. Some observers extrapolate this trend, which has been underway for the last decade, and predict the eventual achievement of a cashless society, one in which accounting transfers handled by computers totally replace currency transfers.

Many situations point to the movement toward a cashless society. For years individuals have used telegraphic (wire) transfers to move large sums of money quickly. Today instantaneous transfers can occur through the use of computers. The most visible example of the application of technology to personal banking is the electronic funds transfer (EFT). EFTs usually occur through remote terminals (terminals away from the bank itself) or automatic teller machines, ATMs. Plastic cards, similar to credit cards, allow individuals to access the machine and perform the desired financial operations. There are about 60,000 ATMs in use in the United States. Telephone fund transfers, often performed through computers, allow the movement of funds when automatic teller machines are unavailable. Money Today 1.3 illustrates the potential problem of deposit security in electronic banking.

These kinds of electronic payment systems are actually modern examples of the same principle involved in the use of checks. The only real differences are the speed and techniques involved in the transfer. Individuals may soon make all their payments at retail establishments through point-of-sale electronic transfers. Plastic bank cards, called debit cards, will allow the immediate transfer of funds from the payor's account to the payee's account. We discuss these in the next chapter. Although technologically superior to checks, the process is still the same. A continuation of the trend toward the application of electronics to banking may well result in a cashless society.

MONEY TODAY 1.3   Does Electronic Banking Threaten Deposit Security?

In the "old days" recognition by a bank teller or an authorized signature was necessary to cash a check or to access bank records. This was usually enough to prevent fraud. Today, with both small, individual, and large corporate transactions and data acquisitions occurring electronically, without the assurance of written approval, people are concerned about the security of their deposits and the confidentiality of their records.

How can transactions be protected? Most financial institutions use a series of controls and checks to prevent fraud or abuse. Both individual and institutional transactions include some sort of access key or card, a user ID or password and, sometimes, a code for each specific electronic transaction.

For added confidentiality in accessing institutional data, encryption devices scramble data so they cannot be understood without a similar device on the other end of the line (this is similar to the scrambling of television signals used by pay-TV companies).

Beginning in 1988 financial institutions will be required to provide electronic message authorization for all transactions involving the U.S. Treasury. Similar authorization may be applied to other transactions. For now, voice verification, which uses sophisticated recording systems, is used by many major financial firms.

In the future similar voice verification techniques or fingerprint tests may be applied to individuals as they use automated teller machines.

Chapter Conclusion

This chapter provided some background on the origins and evolution of money. The form of money people use has changed rather dramatically over the years; money evolved from concrete objects—cattle, cowrie shells, tobacco, or precious metals traded by weight—to precious metal coins, to paper money redeemable in metal coins, and on to more abstract symbols—irredeemable paper money—and now checkable deposits. These tokens have little or no value themselves, but they do allow the bearer to draw upon the system's output because other people are willing to accept these tokens as payment. Still, the properties and characteristics of money are not much different today than they were in Aristotle's time. The form money takes has changed for reasons of necessity and convenience. The monetary system of the country has changed too, for the same reasons.

Although people have a better understanding today of what constitutes money, the difficulty in clarifying what passes as money probably will continue. While you the consumer are able to adjust to coins, currency, checks, credit cards, and electronic transfers of funds, policy makers disagree about how to measure the quantity of money and what effect money has on overall economic activity. These issues are the focus of the next chapter. We'll look at the relationship of money to the economy and in the process see why a definition of money is important for economic policy-makers.

Consider These Questions

1. The mercantilists associated precious metals, gold and silver, with power and urged accumulation of them to augment national power. How did this attitude give way to a willingness to exchange money for goods?

2. Today the Soviet Union is reluctant to exchange its currency, the ruble, in international markets. Why do you think this is the case? Is it a vestige of mercantilist thinking?

3. Using money for transactional purposes is considerably more efficient than establishing numerous exchange ratios in a barter system. The formula to determine the number of exchange ratios (prices) given N goods is the following:

$$\frac{N\,(N-1)}{2}$$

Assuming even a simple barter economy, how many exchange ratios would exist with 10 goods? 50 goods? 500 goods? 1000 goods? How does this compare with the number of prices in a money economy?

4. In a classic article about economic life in a prisoner of war camp during World War II, R. A. Radford illustrates how cigarettes functioned as money. How could this happen? Which characteristics and properties of money do cigarettes fulfill? (See Suggestions for Further Reading for citation.)

5. How would you distinguish between the properties and characteristics of money? In a cashless society, how are these properties and characteristics satisfied? If there is no tangible evidence of money, does that mean there is no money in the system?

6. Throughout much of the 1970s, the U.S. Mint could not maintain an adequate supply of pennies. Pennies were not being lost, they simply weren't circulating. What might explain this peculiarity?

Suggestions for Further Reading

Burns, A.R. *Money and Monetary Policy in Early Times*. New York: Alfred A. Knopf, 1927.
> An early exploration into the evolution of money and its role in the economy.

Einzig, Paul. *Primitive Money in Its Ethnological, Historical and Economic Aspects*. 2d ed. Oxford: Pergamon Press, 1966.
> For the "monetary archeologist" this book has it all. It includes many photographs of ancient forms of money.

Nussbaum, Arthur. *A History of the Dollar*. New York: Columbia University Press, 1957.
> This book does the same thing for the American dollar that Einzig's book does for currency in general.

Pryor, Frederic L. "The Origins of Money." In *Journal of Money, Credit and Banking* 9 (August 1977): 391–401.
> A short but thorough summary of the economic origins of money.

Radford, R.A. "The Economic Organization of a P.O.W. Camp." *Economica* 12 (November 1945): 189–201.
> This interesting article illustrates that money is important in any society.

Schumpeter, Joseph A. *History of Economic Analysis*. New York: Oxford University Press, 1968.
> This is the classic book outlining the history of economic thought. It has everything you ever wanted to know about the origins of economic ideas but were too smart to ask.

Smith, Adam. *An Enquiry Into the Nature and Causes of the Wealth of Nations*. New York: Modern Library, Inc., 1937.
> The first great economic treatise.

CHAPTER TWO

RELATIONSHIP of MONEY to the ECONOMY

The definition of money is to be sought not on the grounds of principle, but on the grounds of usefulness in organizing our knowledge of economic relationships. . . .

Friedman and Schwartz, *Monetary History of the United States*

Chapter 1 explored the historical origins and contemporary conclusions about the characteristics of money. A clear definition of money is important because money is seen as affecting economic variables. Policy makers want to control money's influence on the economy. A generally accepted definition is necessary so policy makers have an accurate, promptly available measure for money. Without some common understanding of what money is, economists could hardly debate the question of how money affects the economy let alone undertake policies to stabilize the economy.

This chapter looks at what constitutes money in our economy today and explores how money affects the economy. The chapter also looks at the role money plays as the foundation for our financial system, and it explains how a well-developed financial system is important for an expanding economy. Also discussed are the ways in which financial resources are mobilized through financial markets and the essential role credit plays in a modern economy. The chapter concludes with an explanation of various financial instruments. The Chapter Appendix explains some of the measurement tools used in assessing economic activity.

Chapter Objectives

Your overall goal in reading this chapter should be to acquire an understanding of money and financial markets and their connection to economic activity. To do this you need to understand what constitutes money. By the end of this chapter you should:

- Know the difference between the theoretical and empirical definitions of money.
- Understand why the distinction between the theoretical and empirical definitions of money is important.
- Distinguish between the three basic empirical definitions of money which are used by the Federal Reserve System.

Beyond a knowledge of what money is and how it is defined, you need to understand why an accurate empirical definition of money is important. You should identify which money measures are most useful for policy makers, as well as understand the connection between money and economic activity. To do this you need a general notion of the association between movements of monetary aggregates and changes in output measures such as GNP.

Since money influences the economy and economic development through the financial system, you need to consider the structure and functioning of the financial system. You should be able to:

- Explain how financial resources are mobilized.
- Know what constitutes a financial market.
- Differentiate between surplus spending units and deficit spending units and understand the ways in which the two come together in financial markets.
- Understand the reasons why surplus units are willing to make funds available and what deficit units are willing to do to appropriate needed funds.
- Understand financial intermediaries and how they facilitate the flow of funds through direct and indirect intermediation.

The discussion of financial markets focuses on both the process by which funds are transferred from surplus units to deficit units and the price for this transfer. You should understand:

- The role interest rates play in the intermediation process.
- How the prices of funds are influenced by price expectations.
- The distinction between nominal and real interest rates.

Finally, you should realize that there are many different financial markets. You need to:

- Know the distinction between money markets and capital markets.
- Explain some of the most important money market and capital market instruments.

Empirical Definitions of Money

Money is defined in either a theoretical or an empirical manner. The discussion in the previous chapter relied primarily on a theoretical definition of money, specifically that money possesses the properties known as the *functioning four—medium, measure, standard*, and *store*. The properties are fairly clear and distinct, and by using this definition we were able to move through a brief history of money rather easily. But in trying to define money by identifying what items function as money, we encounter more difficulty. The job of specifying exactly what constitutes money prompts analysts to define it in the empirical manner. (Empiricism means relying on experience and observation rather than theory.)

An *empirical definition* of money specifies the measurable components (items) that are included as parts of money and that correlate to certain measures of economic performance. Some economists are most interested in transactions money—money that can be used for exchange purposes. Other economists are more concerned with a broader empirical definition of money, one that includes less liquid types of money, such as time or savings deposits. As the economic system changes and new legislation affecting the financial system is enacted, money must change. Monetary authorities have changed with the times and have adopted a series of technical definitions of money. This section will look at each of those, but first it will examine the relationship between money, credit, and liquidity.

Money, Credit, and Liquidity

When an individual makes a purchase on credit, is that purchase made with money? Does the extension of credit affect the quantity of money in the economy? This raises the issue to which we alluded in Chapter 1, namely the relationship between money, credit, and liquidity. The exact relationship depends in part on the initial definition of money.

The key issue is not so much whether the extension of credit influences the supply of money as much as it is *what quantity* of money according to *which* empirical definition. If transactions represent an important aspect of the things monetary economists look at, then credit purchases (transactions) must surely fit into our discussion of the quantity of money. Couldn't consumers undertake a transaction using some asset such as corporate stock or an automobile? Observers are much less willing to consider an automobile part of the quantity of money than corporate stock or a credit purchase, even though all may be used for transactions purposes under certain conditions.

This reinforces the point made earlier. Society considers as money only highly liquid items or symbols used in transactions. But adopting this approach to defining money results in a "money is as money does" concept. Practically anything can serve as a transaction medium and an almost equally broad set of items can serve as money even when using the functional criteria. An operational definition of money is needed.

Three Basic Definitions of Money

For much of American history the only instruments that performed all of the functions of money were publicly held coin and currency and commercial bank demand deposits. As late as 1971 the Federal Reserve System published only one measure of the nation's stock of money, which included the above components. Currently, the Federal Reserve uses three measures of the money supply, often called monetary aggregates, and one measure of liquidity.[1] Table 2.1 outlines these.

M1   M1 includes components of the money supply most often used in exchange transactions. Specifically, M1 consists of coin and currency held by the public, non-bank traveler's checks, and checkable deposits at financial institutions. Of these, demand deposits is the largest component, representing 50 percent of M1.

Transaction or checkable deposits are deposits which the depositor can transfer, usually by using a check. Using the Federal Reserve's terminology, we can define *transaction deposits* further as "all deposits on which the account holder is permitted to make withdrawals by negotiable or transfer instruments, payment orders of withdrawal, telephone and preauthorized transfers (in excess of three per month), for the purpose of making payments to third persons or others."

---

[1] The old and new measures of the money supply are discussed in Thomas D. Simpson, "The Redefined Monetary Aggregates," *Federal Reserve Bulletin* (February 1980): 97–113. There were four money supply measures adopted in February 1980—M1-A, M1-B, M2, and M3 and one liquidity measure, L. In early 1982, the M1-A measure was dropped and M1-B was relabeled M1. There are now three money measures and one liquidity measure.

Traditionally, demand deposits at commercial banks were the only transaction deposit. Beginning on a small scale in New England in the early 1970s and then expanding nationwide with the Depository Institutions Deregulation and Monetary Control Act of 1980, other types of depository institutions (that is, Savings and Loan Associations, Mutual Savings Banks, and Credit Unions) began to offer transaction deposits, which are substitutes for demand deposits. Today, commercial bank demand deposits are still the most widely used, but new types of transaction deposits also exist. These include negotiable order of withdrawal (NOW) accounts, automatic transfer service (ATS) accounts, and credit-union share-draft accounts.

M2   M2 is a broader money supply measure. It includes all the items of M1 plus some that are less transactions-oriented. M2 is defined as M1 plus savings and small-denomination time deposits at all depository institutions,

		October 1985 $ billions
M1	Currency and coin outside the Treasury, Federal Reserve Banks, and commercial bank vaults	168.8
	Traveler's checks of nonbank issuers	5.9
	Demand deposits at commercial banks	264.0
	Other checkable deposits—negotiable order of withdrawal (NOW) and automatic transfer service (ATS) accounts at banks and thrift institutions, credit union share draft accounts (CUSDs), and demand deposits at thrift institutions	172.4
	TOTAL M1	**611.1**
M2	Savings deposits	301.7
	Money market deposit accounts	496.7
(M1 plus:)	Small denomination (under $100,000) time deposits at all depository institutions	871.6
	Overnight repurchase agreements (RPs), money market market mutual funds (MMMFs), and overnight Eurodollars	243.3
	TOTAL M2	**2524.4**
M3	Large denomination (over $100,000) time deposits	428.6
(M2 plus:)	Term repurchase agreements at commercial banks and savings and loan asociations, institutionally held MMMFs	226.7
	TOTAL M3	**3179.7**
L (M3 plus:)	Other liquid assets such as savings bonds at outside banks, bankers' acceptances, commercial paper, Treasury bills and other liquid Treasury securities, and U.S. savings bonds	
	TOTAL L	**3781.7**

Note: Dollar figures are seasonally adjusted.

Source: Economic Report of the President (1986): 327–328.

TABLE 2.1   *Money Supply and Liquidity Measures*

money market mutual funds (MMMFs), overnight repurchase agreements (RPs), and overnight Eurodollar balances. Until recently, many of these components, especially savings deposits, were not very liquid. With the movement toward financial deregulation and the utilization of computer technology, savings deposits can be transferred easily to checking accounts.

M3   M3 expands the definition of the money supply. It consists of M2 plus large denominations time deposits (over $100,000) and longer-term RPs.

The Federal Reserve also publishes data on a broad measure of liquid assets. Referred to as L, this measure includes M3 plus longer-term Eurodollars held by individuals, bankers' acceptances, commercial paper, savings bonds, Treasury bills, and other liquid Treasury securities. Figure 2.1 illustrates the growth patterns of these money measures.

Economists disagree about which monetary aggregate is most important in policy decisions. Those who adhere to the traditional definition of money would stick with M1, while those adopting the empirical definition,

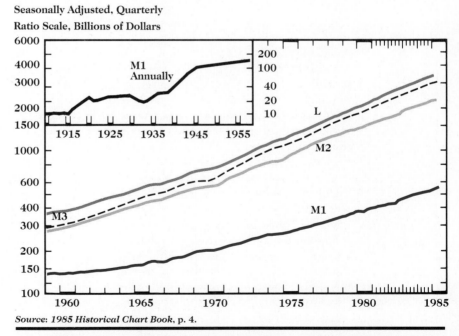

Seasonally Adjusted, Quarterly

Ratio Scale, Billions of Dollars

Source: 1985 Historical Chart Book, p. 4.

FIGURE 2.1   *Growth Paths for Money Measures*   While various money measures may have very different growth patterns in the short term, over time, the Federal Reserve's money measures show very similar growth paths. M1, M2, M3, and L have moved along similar growth paths for the past 25 years.

those who are concerned about general measures of liquidity, would look more favorably on a broader definition, perhaps M3. Some even argue that a measure as broad as L, or one that includes assets such as bonds and stocks, which may serve as a substitute for the components with a higher degree of "moneyness," should be considered since these assets may influence the supply of money or overall economic behavior.

In the short run (monthly), money measures exhibit patterns of change which at times are similar and at other times are different. But as Figure 2.1 shows, in aggregate, M1 and M2 tend to move in the same direction over time. This indicates that in the short run it is important to utilize one monetary aggregate that correlates closely with economic variables which policy makers want to influence. In the long run, since the monetary aggregates move together, the measure which is considered may not be so important.

Money and Economic Activity

Money and economic fluctuations are closely associated as are money and price level changes. Look at Figure 2.2. This figure illustrates changes in economic activity (percent change in Gross National Product) and changes in the supply of money (percent change in M1). Note that changes in the money supply measure are in real terms (corrected for inflation by the GNP implicit price deflator) and are lagged eight quarters (that is, the movements in M1 are shown two years after they initially changed).[2] These economic movements are often referred to as the business cycle—the general fluctuations around a trend rate of change of aggregate output, employment, and the rate of inflation.

Until very recently, the business cycle and the changes in real M1 were highly correlated (see Money Today 2.1 for a discussion). Few economists will question the long-term association between money and economic growth as illustrated in Figure 2.2. But economists will disagree over the interpretation of these data. Monetarist economists argue that excessive changes in the rate of growth of the money supply are the primary causes of the business cycle. Many Keynesian economists not only dispute this claim but argue instead that changes in the growth of monetary aggregates result in response to changes in the level of economic activity.

---

[2] Empirical evidence suggests that money supply changes begin to have an effect on economic activity six to nine months after policy implementation. The full impact takes nearly two years to work its way through the system.

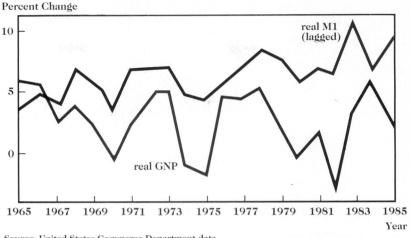

Percent Change

Source: United States Commerce Department data.

FIGURE 2.2 *Real Money (M1) and Real Output: Growth Rates* This figure reveals how GNP and lagged M1 (both adjusted for inflation) have changed over the past 20 years. These two indicators have moved in the same direction until the last few years. Money Today 2.1 discusses the recent divergence.

MONEY TODAY 2.1 Is M1's Impact on the Economy Waning?

Recent unpredictable growth of the nation's money supply is causing even die-hard monetarists to question the impact of the growth of M1 (the standard measure of money) on the nation's economy.

Monetarism is based on the relationship between money and economic growth. Simply stated, it proposes that the growth of the money supply determines the economy's future growth and rate of inflation.

From 1983 to 1987, the growth of M1 ran ahead of economic growth rates without any noticeable re-ignition of the rate of inflation. President Reagan's chief economist, Beryl Sprinkel, a noted monetarist, admitted recently, "Nobody knows where we are going."

The problem is that it has become difficult to know exactly what money is. The deregulation of banking has blurred the distinction between transaction money and other sorts of money measures and has made it difficult for the Federal Reserve to anticipate how the money supply will increase.

With all the changes in the financial system, people are handling their money differently than before. They move it from one account to another and it is not clear which of these accounts is really a transaction account—an account that allows the expansion of the money supply, which in turn churns its way through the economy, influencing growth and price-level changes.

Sprinkel and other prominent monetarists argue that monetarism isn't dead. They contend that better money measures are needed, perhaps the preEnglishderegulation M2, which does not include the various new types of checking accounts. Monetarists claim that this money measure (the old M2) continues to correlate with economic growth and price-level changes.

Beryl Sprinkel summed up the problem for monetarists and policymakers alike in stating, "The question is how best to measure money."

Source: "Monetarism Theory Runs Aground Amid Odd Growth in Money Supply," A *New York Times* release appearing in the *Minneapolis Star and Tribune* (July 5, 1986).

Percent Change (annual rate)

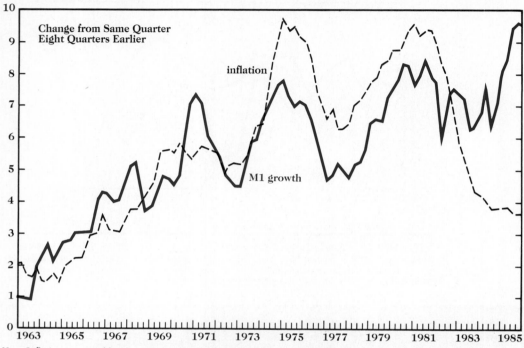

Note: Inflation measured by change in GNP implicit price deflator. Based on seasonally adjusted data.

Source: 1986 Economic Report of the President.

FIGURE 2.3 *M1 Growth and Inflation (M1 Growth Lagged Eight Quarters)* This figure shows that, like M1 and GNP growth in Figure 2.2, the growth of M1 has correlated highly with the rate of inflation. This relationship is the cornerstone of monetarism. In recent years, M1 and the rate of inflation have followed divergent growth paths. Money Today 2.1 discusses this.

Economists also disagree over the degree to which money influences prices. Changes in the supply of money and changes in the price level are strongly correlated. Figure 2.3 illustrates this point. The correlation between these changes was originally formulated years ago as the *quantity theory of money.* This idea is discussed in Chapter 10 along with an examination of monetarism. At this point, it is sufficient to note that a connection exists between money and prices.

The association between money, economic activity, and prices, illustrated by Figures 2.2 and 2.3, is further evidence of the importance of money in the economy. The question "does money matter?" has, of late at least, been replaced by the question "how much does money matter?" During the recession of 1981–1982, observers of Federal Reserve policies gave credence to the claim that money matters quite a bit. The Fed was criticized for causing the recession. In the years since, the Fed has received praise for containing inflation. The Fed's monetary policy actions are clearly perceived as important factors in American economic activity.

The recognition that "money matters" still does not resolve the issue of the direction or magnitude of the relationship between money and the economy. For example, monetarists believe in some form of the quantity theory of money, which says that changes in the supply of money affect prices. But these same monetarists argue that excessive changes in the supply of money cause business cycles. How can this be? This issue is not resolved here; it is deferred until a more detailed discussion on the record of monetary policy occurs in Chapter 19. Remember that money is related to real economic variables (for example, GNP and employment), not just prices. The details of that relationship may need further clarification, but for now, note that the relationship does exist.

Mobilization of Financial Resources

The financial system functions to mobilize financial resources (loanable funds and financial capital) and to allocate these resources to the highest return. This allocation process works through financial markets. To clarify this process we now turn to financial markets and the allocative process.

Financial Markets

The term *market* appears quite often in economics textbooks as well as in the nontechnical writing of economists. But, while markets are essential to the functioning of our economy, they represent an often misunderstood economic concept. It is difficult to explain the concept of a market in general for the simple reason that there are not many tangible examples. The same problem occurs in discussing the financial market.

A financial market is not represented by a single institution, nor is it a physical setting. A *financial market* refers to the widely dispersed needs of borrowers and lenders expressed through literally thousands of communication channels. The demand for and supply of loanable funds and financial capital translate into an array of "ask" and "bid" prices, which converge around a market clearing equilibrium in much the same fashion as the supply and demand of commodities determine the prices and quantities exchanged. The collection of offers to buy and sell, when taken together, represents the financial market. Financial resources are mobilized and allocated through market process.

The financial market provides a mechanism for surplus income units (SU) to transfer funds to deficit spending units (DU). A surplus income unit is an economic unit with total revenues exceeding total expenditures during a specified time period; a deficit income unit is an economic unit with total expenditures in excess of total revenues for a specified time period. Balanced budget units (BU) have revenues that just match expenditures. In summary,

$$SU = \text{current inflow} > \text{current outlays}$$
$$DU = \text{current outlays} > \text{current inflow}$$
$$BU = \text{current inflow} = \text{current outlays}$$

Economic units include households, nonfinancial business firms and nonprofit organizations, and all levels of government. Financial institutions will be considered separately.

Each of these economic units has a budget. Individual household units must work to bring revenues and expenditures into alignment. If income (wages/salaries and rental and investment returns) is not sufficient to cover expenditures across a period of time, revenues from borrowing must supplement earned income. The same may be said for business firms and all levels of government. Especially in recent years concern about the size of the federal government's deficit has drawn attention to the fact that government revenues (from taxes) have not kept pace with expenditures; the result is a need to borrow funds.

Across an economic system, some economic units within each of the three categories mentioned above have surplus funds which are not needed for current period expenditures. The SU defers expenditures and makes the surplus funds available to DU with the expectation of some return. This return is, of course, called the interest payment. The SU's funds are made available to DUs in exchange for an agreement to repay the borrowed funds plus some additional amount (the interest payment). The financial market exists to facilitate the movement of funds from the SU to the DU and to determine the price (rate of interest) associated with the movement of funds.

Remember the trade-offs involved here. The SU trades the opportunity for current period expenditures for additional funds available for expenditure in a subsequent period. The DU acquires funds for current period expenditures but only by trading this for claims against revenues from a subsequent period.

MONEY TODAY 2.2

Is "Plastic Money" Really Money?

Today many people carry so-called "plastic money" in their wallets and purses. This "plastic money" really represents the two different components of the financial system. One is a liability and the other an asset. As such, one is money and the other isn't.

Credit cards appear to function as money. People use them for transaction purposes. In this sense credit cards serve as a medium of exchange. But they do not fulfill the other functions of money. In fact, credit card purchases represent liabilities.

A credit card purchase is actually based on the extension of a loan. Whether using a department store revolving charge account or a major credit card like Visa or MasterCard, an individual is borrowing funds to make the purchase. These funds must be repaid; if they are not repaid promptly, an interest charge accumulates. In either case this credit card purchase means that the purchaser has incurred a liability. This type of "plastic money," although allowing for transactions, does not represent a store of value but rather a future claim against the purchaser's assets.

The other type of "plastic money" is a debit card. A debit card is used to make purchases much as a credit card is but the purchase with a debit card draws upon existing assets rather than placing a claim against future assets.

A debit card functions much like a check. A purchase with either is made with accumulated funds, assets. In this sense a debit card fulfills the store of value function as well as the medium of exchange function of money.

One type of "plastic money," credit cards, is not really money at all. It's actually a liability on the purchaser's account. The other type of "plastic money," the debit card, is money. When the Federal Reserve attempts to measure the money supply it includes the funds held in the account against which debit card purchases are made.

Money and Credit

Perhaps this is a good time to differentiate between money and credit. To the economic units receiving money and credit, money is an asset, while credit is a liability. Think about this from your own perspective. The money you possess, which you have received as payments or a gift, is an asset to you. The credit you acquire is actually spending power borrowed from someone else. Since you must repay this loan (you have provided the lender with some sort of I.O.U.), credit is a liability in a balance sheet sense. Credit is the rental of money. You pay (in the form of an interest payment) to use someone else's money. Consider the issue of credit and debit cards discussed in Money Today 2.2.

Transfer of Funds (SU to DU)

How is credit extended? To phrase this question differently, how are funds transferred from the surplus income units to the deficit spending units? Consider the simple circular flow diagram (Figure 2.4) depicting economic

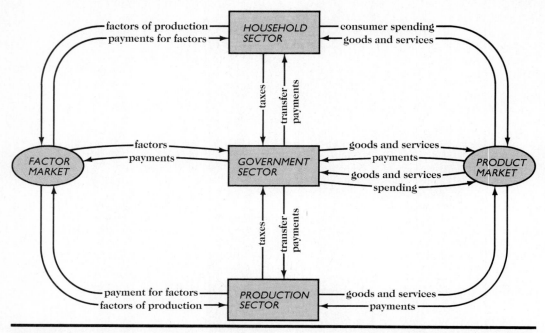

FIGURE 2.4 *The Circular Flow of the Economy* The basic sectors of the economy are depicted in this diagram. The household sector, which includes all members of society, interacts with the production sector in the two basic markets. The government sector is also shown interacting with the other two sectors both directly and through the product and factor markets.

activity. In the exchange of goods and services, or factors of production for pecuniary payments (wages, salaries, and expenditures), there is not an even flow of funds. In total, the household sector takes in more than it expends, while the nonfinancial production sector and the government spend more than they take in. These unexpended funds from the household sector are available for lending.

Realize before proceeding that this discussion is in aggregate terms. Many household units borrow funds and many nonfinancial business firms lend funds. Loanable funds flow not only from household units to nonfinancial business firms but also from the business firms to the household units. In actuality, individual units within each category probably function both as lenders and as borrowers. For example, most households borrow money (for home mortgages, car loans) while at the same time lending money (through direct stock and bond purchases, indirect purchases through retirement funds or by deposits with financial institutions). What is represented by the figures is a generalization, not a rule.

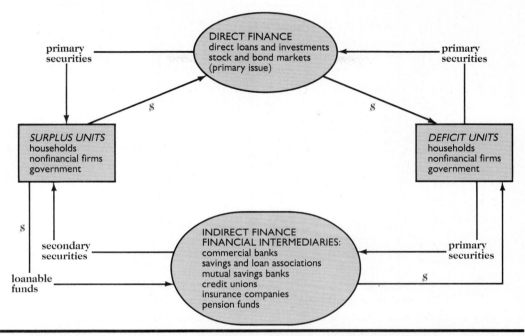

FIGURE 2.5 *The Circular Flow of the Financial System*   The relationship between Surplus Units, those supplying funds, the Deficit Units, those borrowing funds, is shown in this diagram. The interaction of the SUs and DUs can take place directly, such as through the direct sale of bonds by a corporation to an individual investor, or indirectly, such as the purchase of corporate stock by a pension fund manager on behalf of the fund's members.

Direct and Indirect Finance

Refer to Figure 2.5. Notice that funds flow from SU to DU through financial markets. In some cases this occurs directly when SUs transfer funds by the direct acquisition of promises to repay from DUs. A household unit may, for example, directly purchase securities offered by corporations or government. This is usually accomplished through a brokerage house dealing in stocks and bonds.

Loanable funds also flow through indirect channels. Again look at Figure 2.5. SUs make funds available to DUs via financial institutions. Financial institutions (ranging from commercial banks to insurance companies) accept funds from SUs and in turn loan these funds to DUs. These financial institutions offer SUs a variety of instruments to attract loanable funds (for example, certificates of deposits at commercial banks). The full array of instruments is discussed later in the chapter.

Motivation for Lending

As already indicated, SU funds are made available to DUs in exchange for an agreement to repay the borrowed funds plus some additional amount, called the interest payment. This interest payment is determined through market forces and serves to allocate available funds. Funds are allocated in two ways. First, supply and demand forces in financial markets affect the price of funds (that is, the market interest rate paid on borrowed funds) and in so doing serve to direct funds to the highest return. Interest rates also allocate funds across time. The trade-off between present consumption and future consumption for individual financial units is influenced by the rate of interest. By spending funds in the present, financial units forgo interest payments on those funds and therefore give up the additional income in a future period. By borrowing to make purchases in the present, financial units make claims against their future income amounting to the level of the expenditure plus the interest they pay as a price of the borrowed funds.

Individuals and institutions are willing to defer the present use of available funds because the rewards for doing so are greater than the costs of postponing the expenditure. In other words, SUs are motivated to supply loanable funds because the expected return exceeds the cost. This introduces an important factor into our discussion of financial markets—expectations. Expectations must be related to the earlier discussion of nominal and real values.

Simple demand and supply analysis explains the functioning of the financial market. Figure 2.6 illustrates the discussion to this point. Changes in the demand for funds or the supply of funds will change the price of loanable funds and the quantity of funds actually loaned to borrowers. The interest rate or price of funds is expressed in nominal terms. But the purchasing power of the repaid funds (the loan plus the interest income) is always in real terms. As long as nominal and real rates are the same, that is, there is relative price stability, then our financial market results in the actual return to the lender being equivalent to the expected return.

During a period of unanticipated inflation the actual return to the lender is less than the expected return. Why? Because the purchasing power of the funds returned to the borrower has declined with the rising price level. Lenders adjust to this situation. Anticipating that the actual return to them will decline due to inflation, they are willing to offer fewer funds at each price (nominal interest rate). This is the same as saying they are willing to offer funds but only at a higher price. Such a reduction in the loanable funds is reflected in a shift in the supply of funds curve (see Figure 2.7).

The result is an increase in the price of funds or, phrased another way, a rise in the nominal interest rate. (Anticipated inflation may also encourage

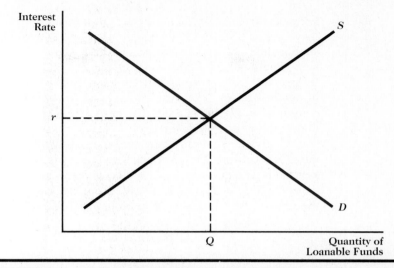

FIGURE 2.6 *Supply and Demand and the Interest Rate*   The traditional downward sloping demand curve and upward sloping supply curve apply in the determination of the interest rate in the financial market.

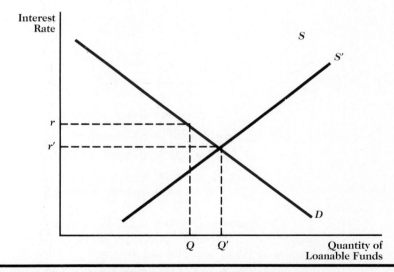

FIGURE 2.7 *Supply Shifts Influence the Interest Rate*   The shift to the left of the supply curve (that is, a reduction in the quantity of funds supplied at all rates of interest) results from a situation in which lenders are demanding a higher return for their funds. This may occur due to expectations about rising rates of inflation or changes in the tax laws which put interest income in a higher tax bracket.

borrowers to increase their demand for funds to cover increased costs; this may cause a shift in the demand curve, thus reinforcing the result of the supply shift and further raise the interest rate.)

The distinction between nominal and real again becomes important. Interest rates, along with most economic variables, are most often expressed in nominal terms. The difference between nominal and real rates often is considerable. Figure 2.8 reveals how widely these two measures varied during the period of high inflation rates in the 1970s.

Simple algebra can illustrate the distinction between nominal and real rates. Notice from the equations below that the rate of price increase is the key factor. When individuals project interest rates they come up with an expected price increase. Obviously, the higher the expected rate of inflation, the greater the difference between nominal and real interest rates.

$$(1 + R) = (1 + r) (1 + P)$$

or

$$R = r + P + rP$$

then

$$(1 + r) = \frac{1 + R}{1 + P}$$

or

$$r = \frac{R - P}{1 + P}$$

where

R = nominal rate of interest

r = real rate of interest

P = rate of increase in prices

$1 + R$ = payment due after one period for each unit of money borrowed

The discussion to this point has portrayed the financial market as though it is a single market. Furthermore, the discussion implies that the demand for loanable funds and the supply of loanable funds lead to a single price, one interest rate. In actuality the financial marketplace is made up of markets for many different financial instruments resulting in a variety of interest rates. This is easier to understand after looking at some of the more prominent financial instruments used in the major financial markets.

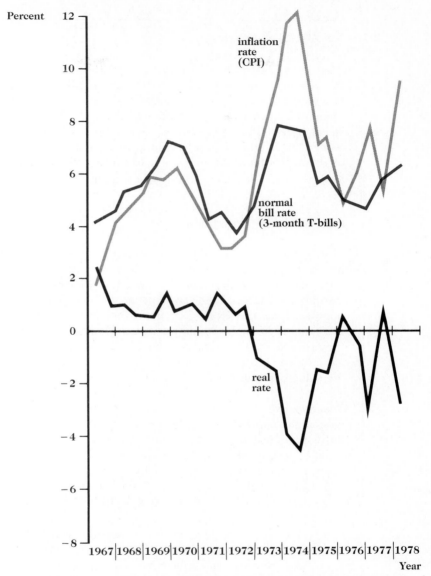

Source: Adapted from M. H. Willes, "Are Interest Rates Too High?" Federal Reserve Bank of Minneapolis, *Quarterly Review* (Fall 1978): 2–3.

FIGURE 2.8   *Nominal and Real Interest Rates*   Inflation cuts into the return on funds lent in financial markets. This figure shows that during a period of high inflation, the real interest rate (that is, the real return on a loan or investment after adjusting for inflation) may be very low or even drop below zero. This period was chosen to illustrate this phenomenon because it shows some extreme negative real rates of return even without the extraordinarily high inflation rates that followed just a few years later.

Financial Markets

A previous discussion divided financial markets into primary markets (where the financial claim was initially sold) and secondary markets (the market for resale of financial claims). Here financial instruments are discussed in terms of another financial market division. Financial markets are categorized into *money markets* and *capital markets*. Financial instruments are traded in one market or the other largely as a function of their maturity, that is, the length of time a lender must hold a financial instrument before receiving repayment.

Money Market Instruments

Money market instruments specify a fixed income, are highly liquid, and have a maturity of less than one year. Fixed income refers to the fact that the instrument specifically states the amount of the nominal payment when the instrument matures. The payment includes the repayment of the amount borrowed plus the interest payment for the use of funds. Money market instruments are highly liquid because they either function as money, that is, they are accepted in exchange transactions, or they are easily converted into money. The holder, therefore, has little possibility of loss. Table 2.2 shows the value of various money market instruments at one point in time.

Treasury Bills　Treasury bills, or T-bills, are promissory notes issued by the federal government. Maturities range from three months to one year. A T-bill is redeemable by the bearer for a specified amount, the bond's face value. The level of interest earned on a T-bill depends on how much below its face value it is purchased for in the money market. A $10,000 three-month T-bill sold "at a discount" for $9600 earns an annualized rate of interest of 16⅔ percent (400/9600 is .0416 × 4 = .166 or 16⅔ percent).

Negotiable CDs　Negotiable certificates of deposit are special time deposits issued by commercial banks. They usually have maturities of thirty to ninety days and pay an explicit interest rate. Negotiable CDs are sold by major banks in denominations ranging from $100,000 to $1 million. Because they may be resold before maturity in the secondary market, they are highly liquid. This resale capability is where they get the name "negotiable."

Commercial Paper　Well-established business firms, including corporations, finance companies, and banks, issue unsecured promissory notes in

Instrument	Value (billions)
Treasury Bills	$374
Negotiable Certificates of Deposit	$410
Commercial Paper	$240
Repurchase Agreements	$118
Bankers' Acceptances	$ 75
Federal Funds	$ 70

TABLE 2.2   *Value of Selected Money Market Instruments, March 1985*

denominations of $1000 and up. Commercial paper is sold on a discount basis; maturities range from a few days to nine months.

Repurchase Agreements   "Repos" are essentially very short-term loans (less than two weeks). An agreement between a lender and a financial institution results in the lender buying Treasury bills from the financial institution with the understanding that the financial institution will buy back the securities at a set time for slightly higher prices.

Federal Funds   Federal funds are the excess reserves on deposit with the Federal Reserve Banks that member banks lend to other banks. Federal funds are loaned for a very short time period, only one or two days, in large denominations, usually $1 million or more.

Bankers' Acceptances   Bankers' acceptances are promissory notes, issued by an individual or firm, that have been guaranteed by a bank. Usually the seller of goods, desiring payment before the buyer actually pays for the purchased goods, will issue a draft specifying the amount of the purchase and the time for payment. When a bank agrees to guarantee the payment, the draft is called a bankers' acceptance. Acceptances can be sold in the secondary market at a discount.

Capital Market Instruments

Capital market instruments are securities with a maturity of over one year. These instruments are less liquid than money market instruments although they can often be sold in the secondary market. Table 2.3 shows the value of capital market instruments at one point in time.

Instrument	Value (billions)
Corporate Stock (market value)	$2150
Mortgages (residential)	$1505
Corporate Bonds	$ 517
Treasury Notes and Bonds	$ 873
Commercial and Farm Mortgages	$ 517
State and Municipal Bonds	$ 404
U.S. Government Agency Securities	$ 260
Consumer Loans	$ 594

TABLE 2.3 *Value of Selected Capital Market Instruments, March 1985*

Corporate Stock   Stock represents the equity of corporations held by individuals and institutional investors (pension funds, mutual funds, and insurance companies). These are not debt instruments, have no maturity date, and pay no interest. Income (called dividends) accrues to stockholders depending on the profitability of the corporation.

Mortgages   Mortgages are long-term loans secured by real estate (the real estate is called collateral). Mortgages are extended for residential construction as well as for commercial and farm construction. These are debt instruments with a maturity and a specified interest payment. Recently some mortgages have been issued with provision for variable interest rate payments depending on market conditions.

Corporate Bonds   These are long-term (five to thirty year) debt obligations issued by corporations. Bonds may be secured by assets of the firm (property, equipment, or other securities) or may be unsecured (these are known as debentures and are usually issued only by firms with excellent credit ratings). Although there is a secondary bond market, it is not as active as that for stocks or for government bonds. Corporate bonds pay a specified interest rate.

Government Securities   This category includes Treasury notes and bonds and U.S. government agency securities. Notes are long-term obligations of the Treasury with maturities of one to five years; bonds have maturities of thirty years or more. Agency securities are long-term debt instruments issued by agencies such as the Federal Land Bank or the Federal Home Loan Bank. All these securities have fixed interest payments. There is an active market for notes and bonds and a less active market for agency issues.

State and Municipal Bonds   "Munis," as they are often called, are long-term debt instruments. They are tax exempt (interest payments are not subject to income taxes). There is a secondary market for some "munis" but they generally are not viewed as liquid investments.

Consumer Loans   These are loans to consumers made by banks, finance companies, and, with the financial reform legislation of 1982, savings and loan associations. These are the least liquid instruments because there is no secondary market for them.

Financial Futures

Besides the money and capital markets, called cash markets, there are noncash financial markets. These markets began in the mid-1970s. Financial futures include the *options market* and the *futures market*.

Financial options are a contractual arrangement providing for the right to buy (referred to as a call option) or to sell (called a put option) a financial instrument at a predetermined price, at some time before the expiration date of the option. Options exist for actual securities or for financial futures. Financial options are nonbinding. A depository institution portfolio manager may enter into an option agreement to buy a Treasury security at a set price within thirty days as a hedge against rising prices for such securities. If the price rises, the manager may exercise the option. In this case, the manager resells the securities at the higher prevailing price. If prices decline, the manager might want to allow the option to expire, paying only the small option fee.

The options and future markets are sometimes called derivative markets because prices on contracts are derived from actual commodity or financial instrument prices. These markets have arisen in response to the extreme volatility of interest rates. As interest rates fluctuated, especially during the mid-1970s and early 1980s, prices for interest-rate sensitive instruments, such as securities and mortgages, fluctuated greatly. These markets gave financial managers a mechanism to transfer the interest-rate risk. Individuals or institutions were willing to accept the interest-rate risk in exchange for the possibility of a high return. These speculators allowed risk-averse financial managers to hedge their positions.

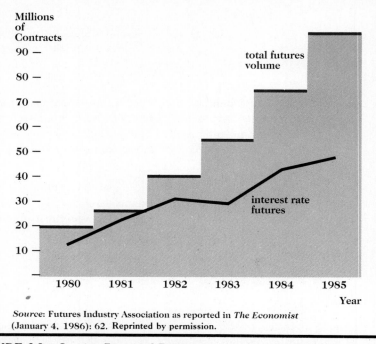

Millions of Contracts

Source: Futures Industry Association as reported in *The Economist* (January 4, 1986): 62. Reprinted by permission.

FIGURE 2.9 *Soaring Financial Futures* The volume of financial-futures contracts has soared since 1980. Financial futures include interest rate futures (shown separately by the line within the bar graph), foreign currency, and stock-index futures.

The notion of hedging has been widely applied to commodity markets, where speculators buy and sell futures contracts for all kinds of agricultural commodities. Trading in interest-rate futures has increased dramatically since the market first opened in 1975. Only about 129,000 contracts were traded that first year; more than 40 million were traded in 1984. Total futures trading for 1984 exceeded 100-million contracts (see Figure 2.9).

Six major instruments are currently traded in the financial futures markets: Government National Mortgage Association (GNMA) mortgages, United States Treasury bonds, United States Treasury bills, domestic bank CDs, Eurodollars, and United States Treasury notes. Whereas in early periods financial managers hedged interest-rate risk by matching maturities in the cash market, managers now can also hedge in the noncash futures market. A perfectly executed hedge would result in a futures gain to offset a loss in the cash market or vice versa. More recently, in 1982, a market developed for options on futures contracts. This combined the characteristics of an option contract with those of a futures contract.

These derivative markets expand the scope of risk management activities. Financial managers can include a wide range of financial instruments in their portfolios and reduce their interest-rate exposure by transferring risk to speculators in the futures market. Presumably these markets should reduce the overall level of risk exposure in the system. These markets certainly increase the liquidity of financial managers. Because it can use the futures market to hedge its position, a commercial bank can increase its fixed rate lending even though it needs to fund these loans with variable rate deposits.

Financial Markets and Interest Rates

Anyone who has glanced at the financial pages of a newspaper will realize that there are literally hundreds of interest rates on hundreds of types of securities. Why are there so many different interest rates? Is there any relationship between the interest rates on one type of security and those on another one?

We have indicated that the demand for and the supply of loanable funds will influence the price (interest rates on these funds). But what influences demand and supply? Why are lenders inclined to loan funds at a certain time to one borrower for, say, 8 percent and to loan funds to other borrowers at the same point in time for 10 percent. There are many factors that influence an individual borrower or lender. Different financial instruments have different rates of return, or prices, because of the risk involved, because of institutional factors, and because of the different maturities of the financial instruments.

Chapter 4 presents the concept of risk in more detail. But, briefly stated, the greater the chances of default, the greater the risk to the lender. Thus, risk refers to the credit-worthiness of borrowers, that is, the estimated likelihood that the loan to the borrower will be repaid in full and on time. A number of organizations, such as Moody or Standard and Poor for businesses and governments, and credit bureaus for individuals, evaluate borrowers and assign them a credit rating. Generally speaking, the better a borrower's credit rating, the lower the interest paid to the lender. To induce lenders to make funds available under risky circumstances, the rate of return on the funds they lend must be higher than it would be under normal circumstances. This helps explain why, for example, individuals are charged a higher rate of interest on revolving charge accounts than banks charge their best business borrowers.

Institutional factors influencing interest rates include tax considerations, administration costs, and information costs. For example, interest on many state and local government bonds is tax exempt. The interest income that individuals earn on these financial instruments is not subject to federal (or state) income taxes. The government agency issuing the bond, therefore, is in a position to offer a lower rate of interest because the after-tax return to the lender is the same as it might be for a higher yield, but taxable, investment.

Another important factor influencing the rate of return on financial instruments is the length of time for which the loan is made; this is called the maturity of the loan. The level and structure of interest rates is the topic of discussion in Chapter 3. Briefly stated, two financial instruments, alike in every way except maturity, will sell at different prices. To encourage savers to make funds available for longer periods of time (thus providing the seller of the financial instrument with more freedom to invest the funds), higher interest rates are offered. Prices on financial instruments tend to move similarly; that is, if the prices of short-term securities increase, the prices on long-term securities will also tend to increase. The relationship between prices of various securities is influenced by a number of factors, including alternative investment opportunities, overall economic conditions, and investor expectations.

Chapter Conclusion

This chapter investigated money and the economy by focusing on financial markets. It presented a discussion of what constitutes money and how it is measured. This is important because changes in the quantity of money and changes in the economy are related. Although this chapter did not develop a theoretical model to explain how changes in the supply of money are transmitted to other variables in the economy, it did demonstrate that money does matter.

Financial markets provided an opportunity to develop a better understanding of money and the economy. This investigation included a careful look at the process whereby purchasing power is transferred from those with surplus funds to those needing funds. The chapter also presented the specific instruments used in the money market and the capital market to effectuate the transfer of funds.

The purpose of this chapter has been to acquire a general understanding of the connection between money and the overall economy and a more detailed understanding of the structure and mechanics of financial markets. With this knowledge, you are now ready to take on the more complicated task of exploring the level and structure of interest rates.

Consider These Questions

1. The Friedman and Schwartz quotation at the beginning of this chapter indicated that a definition of money was important for "organizing our knowledge of economic relationships." Explain this statement by showing how different definitions might produce alternative views on money and economic activity.
2. Why does the Federal Reserve have different measures of the money supply (M1, M2, and M3)? Which one do policy makers use most often?
3. What is the difference between direct finance and indirect finance?
4. Kids and some adults are often skeptical about lending their money. Assuming the prospective borrower is a good credit risk, how would you convince someone that there are advantages to lending funds?
5. Many investors are upset. They argue that in 1981 they could earn a rate of return well over 12 percent on their money market mutual funds or even on government securities. By 1986 those rates of return were less than half what they had been five years earlier. What major issue do people fail to consider in comparing interest rates? How could you determine whether investors were doing better in 1981 or in 1986?
6. What differentiates money markets from capital markets from financial futures markets?

Suggestions for Further Reading

Duprey, James N. "How the Fed Defines and Measures Money." Federal Reserve Bank of Minneapolis. In *Quarterly Review* (Spring/Summer 1982): 10–19.
A careful explanation of monetary aggregates.
Friedman, Milton and Anna Schwartz. *Monetary Statistics of the United States.* New York: Columbia University Press, 1970.
The authors do a good job of discussing the problem of defining money but also present a strong argument for the empirical approach (see Chapter 3).
Humphrey, Thomas M. "The Early History of the Real-Nominal Interest-Rate Relationship." Federal Reserve Bank of Richmond *Economic Review* (May/June 1986): 2–10.
Koppenhaver, G.D. "Futures Options and Their Use by Financial Intermediaries." Federal Reserve Bank of Chicago *Economic Perspectives* (January/February 1986): 18–31.
A somewhat sophisticated discussion of futures markets. Section on the social value of such markets is useful.

Laidler, David. "The Definition of Money: Theoretical and Empirical Problems." In *Journal of Money, Credit and Banking* (August 1969): 508–25.

This article is very clear. If you want the single best, most comprehensive source on the subject, this is it.

Mason, Will E. "The Empirical Definition of Money: A Critique." In *Economic Inquiry* (December 1976): 525–38.

Friedman and Schwartz always provoke strong reactions. Mason presents an opposing view on the definition of money.

Rolnick, Arthur J. and Warren E. Weber. "Gresham's Law or Gresham's Fallacy." In *Journal of Political Economy* 94, 1 (1986).

Examines American and English coinage history to illustrate that Gresham's Law should be qualified.

APPENDIX

2. Measurement

We need to clarify the issue of economic measurement by explaining some economic indicators. One of the problems plaguing economists in their attempts to explain economic behavior is the confusion surrounding nominal and real measures. Economists are continually exasperated to see people misuse statistics.

A local newscaster reporting information released by the U.S. Commerce Department in January of 1983 was quoted as saying, "Gross National Product for 1982 was over $3 trillion for the first time in American history, rising from $2.9 trillion in 1981. Regardless of what economists say, the American economy continues to grow." Later in the report, it was announced that the GNP deflator for 1982 was 207.1 up from the 1981 level of 195.4—a 5.9 percent increase in prices.[1]

Price fluctuations always have complicated economic analysis. Whenever economic data are presented they are in terms of some base year, some reference point. When data from different years are compared they need to be expressed in similar terms. Let's use the data below to look more closely at the differences between GNP in 1981 and 1982 referred to by the newscaster.

	1981	1982
Nominal GNP	2938.0	3058.0
GNP Deflator	195.4	207.1
Real GNP	1503.0	1476.0

Note: GNP figures in billions of dollars

What does this mean? The table expresses expenditures in both nominal and real terms. We have introduced the concept of an index number to express nominal data in real terms. This is the same process involved in comparing income on a per capita basis or in considering the fact that a

---

[1] The GNP price deflator is the index most often used in determining real GNP. It is computed by determining a weighted average of the price indices for goods and services that make up GNP. It is discussed later in this appendix.

running back's performance should be on a per game basis since the National Football League season is now 16 games while it was only 12 games a few years ago. It is not accurate to compare the season performance of individuals now with those of the earlier period without accounting for the increased number of games. Whenever we compare economic indicators expressed in terms of a dollar value, for example, gross national product, defense expenditures, social security payments, we need to make sure that the indicators are expressed in comparable terms.

Indexes

To provide comparability, economists utilize index numbers. We can develop an index number for virtually any indicator that varies in value. An index number is determined using the following formula:

$$\text{index number} = \frac{\text{variable value in current period}}{\text{variable value in base period}} \times 100$$

For our purposes in this book, we are most concerned with price indices as we try to transform nominal measures into real terms. There are three major price index numbers—the consumer price index (CPI), the producer price index (PPI), previously called the wholesale price index, and the gross national product implicit price deflator (GNP Deflator).

Consumer Price Index

The most widely known price index is the CPI. Compiled by the Bureau of Labor Statistics (BLS) of the U.S. Department of Labor, the *CPI* is a statistical measure of changes in the prices of some typical consumer goods and services over some periods of time. The CPI uses a *market basket* of goods and services within categories such as food, housing, transportation, clothing, etc. The categories are weighted and adjusted from time to time to reflect typical household purchases. The CPI is geared toward urban consumers, using about 650 different products and services.

The CPI is used to assess changes in purchasing power. Often the CPI is the indicator used to adjust payments to account for price inflation and the associated decline in consumer purchasing power.

We can use the CPI to transform nominal values to real values. The nominal (or monetary) value is the dollar amount shown on a price tag or the amount which appears on your paycheck. To determine the real value of the dollars received in a paycheck, the amount must be adjusted to reflect price-level changes. We are thus able to determine the actual purchasing power of the money received. We can use the CPI to do this adjustment

$$\text{income real} = \frac{\text{income nominal}}{\text{CPI}} \times 100$$

By looking at Table 2A.1, we can see how income is adjusted for price level changes.

Year	GNP (Current Prices)	Price Index (1972 Base Year)	Real GNP (1972 Prices)	
1929	$ 103.4	32.76	$ 315.7	$\left(\dfrac{\$103.4 \times 100}{32.76}\right)$
1933	55.8	25.13	222.1	
1940	100.0	29.06	344.1	
1950	288.3	53.56	534.8	
1960	515.3	68.70	737.2	
1970	1015.5	91.45	1085.6	
1972	1212.8	100.0	1185.9	
1980	2732.0	177.45	1474.0	
1981	3052.6	195.50	1502.6	
1982	3166.0	207.21	1475.5	
1983	3401.6	215.34	1579.6	
1984	3774.7	223.38	1689.9	
1985	3992.5	229.82	1737.2	

Source: Economic Report of the President, 1985 and 1986.

TABLE 2A.1 *GNP and Real GNP for the United States, 1929–1980 (Billions $)*

Producer Price Index

The *PPI* measures price changes for intermediate goods, sold in bulk quantities at the wholesale level. Approximately 2800 commodities in some thirty subgroups form the base for the quantity-weighted producer price index. This index is compiled by the BLS and is reported monthly.

Implicit Price Deflator for GNP

The Department of Commerce, which collects data on national income, publishes the real value of GNP, sometimes referred to as GNP in constant dollars. The Commerce Department also publishes the GNP price deflator. The *GNP price deflator* measures the relative level of GNP prices. It is obtained by dividing nominal GNP by constant GNP and multiplying by 100. For example,

$$\frac{\text{GNP } 1985}{\text{GNP } 1972} \times 100 = \frac{3992.5}{1185.9} \times 100 = 336.66$$

This is not a price index per se. Prices are implicit within the ratio of current and constant GNP series. The current and constant GNP series determined by the Commerce Department utilize a broad base of price measures, for both consumer and producer products.[2]

Use of Indexes

The indexes we have discussed are used generally to determine the value of money by assessing its purchasing power. Aside from the uses these statistical tools have in economic analysis, indices have some very practical applications.

Price changes affect various groups differently. Inflation benefits debtors and hurts creditors. During periods of inflation, debts are paid with

---

[2] Price indices are designed to capture price changes. To do this accurately the quantity of goods, the market basket, must remain constant. We know from basic price theory that changes in prices affect the quantity purchased. A cost of living index measures changes in the cost of maintaining a constant standard of material well being. In a cost of living index, the quantity of goods or the mix of the market basket may vary.

money which has less value. Other groups are disproportionately hurt by inflation. Individuals with fixed incomes, whether retired people drawing a constant monthly pension check or disadvantaged people receiving a fixed income subsidy from the federal government, find their purchasing power eroded as prices rise while their incomes do not. Various groups have worked to reduce the erosion of purchasing power by adjusting incomes or subsidies to account for inflation.

Federal pensions, social security retirement benefits, and many private retirement programs adjust payments based on CPI changes. Many federal transfer programs are automatically adjusted for inflation. Such adjustments reflect public policies designed to reduce the unfair effects of inflation. Collective bargaining agreements have also provided for insurance against lost purchasing power due to inflation. Cost of living adjustments (COLAs), or escalator clauses, tie salary payments to the CPI or some other measure of price level changes.

During the 1970s and early 1980s, with inflation rates at historically high levels in the United States, adjustments for lost purchasing power were extended to many groups through the general application of indexation. Indexing is simply the formal adjustment of payments (made or received) to minimize or eliminate the effect of inflation. One of the more publicized types of indexing was tax indexation. To minimize "bracket creep," the inflationary-induced increase in nominal income that forces taxpayers into higher tax brackets, taxes were adjusted. Different formulas were used by various state governments, but the general effect was to use real income rather than nominal income as the basis for tax assessment.

Limitations

As we shall see in Chapter 11, inflation, along with our attempts to adjust to it, create problems for policymakers. Part of the problem relates to the limitations of the indexes we use to measure changes in the purchasing power of money.

With any price index that uses a representative market basket of goods and services there are problems. The market basket does not represent everyone's spending patterns. Consumer behavior changes in response to price changes and as a result of changes in tastes. The quality of products in the basket also changes. More specifically, critics argue that the CPI over-states inflation because of the makeup of its market basket. The single

53

largest consumer expense is for housing. The CPI includes home prices and financing costs. During inflationary times both rise, sometimes rather dramatically. (For the period 1972 to 1982 the price of the average home rose from less than $60,000 to nearly $80,000, while mortgage interest rates rose from 8 percent to over 17 percent.) But most consumers do not buy a home every year. The BLS is adjusting the CPI to remove this distortion. Instead of new home prices as the primary measure of housing costs, a rental equivalency measure will be used.

The PPI has its limitations, too. It includes only commodities, not services. With producer-used services accounting for a significant portion of the total output of this country, any index which overlooks services is seriously flawed as a measure of overall changes in purchasing power. Furthermore, the BLS does not use any scientific basis to weight the raw materials and intermediate goods used to determine the PPI. The GNP price deflator is also limited in its application. Since the deflator is derived from the ratio of current to constant GNP, it reflects some of the same problems as the CPI and the PPI which are used to deflate prices.

Of these three indices, the GNP price deflator is considered the best measure of price-level changes. This is primarily because it does not overstate price changes. The GNP price deflator reflects the smallest change in the price level. One might immediately ask, "If the deflator is the most accurate of the three, why isn't it used more extensively?" The best answer is a simple one: the implicit GNP deflator is not as readily available. The CPI, the most generally referenced price-level measure, is published monthly; the deflator is published only quarterly.

Despite limitations, indices such as these are important in reducing distortions of statistics. Real measures in economics are most significant during periods of dramatic price-level changes.

What we are really doing when we deflate GNP or adjust for inflation by using the CPI is trying to determine the value of money. In Chapter 1 we discussed the concept of value. We said that value is determined by an object's relative scarcity and its ability to provide utility to someone. The value of money is important ultimately because of its acceptance in exchange transactions. Money is the medium whereby we acquire other commodities or services that have some use value. The quantity of money and its purchasing power are closely related, a relationship that merits further discussion later.

CHAPTER THREE

INTEREST RATES: LEVEL AND STRUCTURE

The rate of interest is the reward for parting with liquidity for a specific period of time.

John Maynard Keynes
The General Theory of Employment, Interest, and Money

Chapter 2 explored the relationship of money to the economy. To understand money and economic activity, it is necessary to understand how interest rates work. The level and structure of interest rates are explained in this chapter. Here we will provide some additional pieces of the money and economic activity puzzle.

Specifically, Chapter 3 will present some of the basic mechanics of interest rates; we will look to answer questions such as, "What is present value analysis?" and "What are the various types of bonds in the system?" Then we will discuss the overall level of interest rates in the economy. What determines the level of interest rates in the economy? How can we explain interest rate movements? This technical definition of interest-rate levels will complement the theoretical discussion in Chapter 8 and provide background for the policy discussion in the last section of the book. This chapter presents prevailing explanations of the structure of interest rates. Why are rates on short-term securities lower than rates on long-term securities at some times, and why is the relationship reversed at other times? Finally, the chapter looks briefly at what causes interest rates to fluctuate.

Chapter Objectives

As you study this chapter think about the rate of interest in the same way you think about the price of other commodities or services. Interest is the price one pays to buy money, in other words, to acquire purchasing power. How do consumers acquire purchasing power? How has the financial system evolved to allow the transfer of funds from lenders to borrowers? What are the instruments that allow individuals to lend or borrow money? By the end of this chapter, you will:

- Understand the basic concepts of interest, structure of interest rates, and fluctuation of interest rates.
- Analyze the factors influencing interest.
- Relate the concept of interest to factors in the larger economic context.

You should understand why individuals forgo purchasing power in the present in exchange for greater purchasing power in the future. And to understand this, you need to understand the notion of the present discounted value of money. By the end of this chapter you will be able to:

- Explain how an individual determines whether a sum of money at some point in the future is worth more or less than an amount in the present.
- Identify factors that influence the level of interest rates.
- Describe what factors determine the interest rate that applies to a particular financial instrument.
- Use the liquidity preference theory and the loanable funds theory to explain the level of interest rates.

Although economists often talk about the rate of interest as though there is a single prevailing rate, daily observation reveals that there are scores of interest rates in the economy. You will be able to:

- Explain why so many different interest rates exist.
- Identify the factors that affect the structure of interest rates.
- Describe the influence of term to maturity, default risk, or marketability on the rate of interest for a security.

Finally, you will understand what causes fluctuations in interest rates. You will be able to:

- Explain the business cycle's effects on interest rates.
- Describe the importance of monetary policy actions to security brokers as they try to anticipate interest rate changes.

- Identify how government financing of deficits affects interest rates.
- Explain how inflationary expectations affect movements in interest rates.

If you keep these objectives in mind, you will gain a better understanding of interest rates and their movements by the end of the chapter.

Simple Mathematics of Interest Rates

Interest rates help allocate financial resources between present uses and future uses. Individuals may decide to forgo consumption in the present period and make funds available to others, in other words, lend their money. In so doing, the lender has increased his or her purchasing power at a time in the future. In making the decision to lend funds rather than to spend for current-period consumption, individuals need to consider the advantages and disadvantages of postponing consumption. (Most individuals use financial intermediaries to do the actual lending, but the process of saving in this discussion is synonymous with lending.) You have seen how price-level changes affect purchasing power. For this discussion let's assume that prices are relatively stable, and therefore purchasing power is not diminished as a result of inflation.

Present Discounted Value Explained

In deciding whether to spend or lend, individuals compare the purchasing power of money today with what those same funds, plus the return for lending (interest), will purchase at some future time. Underlying this discussion is the conclusion that a dollar in the present is worth more than a dollar will be at some future time. We can illustrate the process for making the comparison between present and future funds once we understand the relationship between funds available now, the interest rate, and accumulated funds (or earnings) in the future.

Let F_0 represent available funds at the present time; r represents the rate of interest; F_1 is the amount of money one year from now. Then:

$$F_1 = F_0 + rF_0 \tag{3.1}$$

We can also express this in words: the amount after one year is equal to the initial amount of funds plus the interest payment on those funds. This looks different when terms are rearranged.

$$F_1 = F_0 (1 + r) \qquad (3.2)$$

or

$$F_0 = \frac{F_1}{1 + r} \qquad (3.3)$$

F_0 represents the present discounted value of F_1 received one year from now and discounted at the interest rate, r. Given an interest rate of r, F_0 in the present is the equivalent of F_1 one year from now. That being the case, an individual would be indifferent between F_0 today and F_1 a year from now (remember we're assuming that the price level remains unchanged).

Consider this example. Bonnie Jackson has just received $5000. She can lend these funds for one year at the prevailing rate of interest, 9 percent. One year from now she would receive $5450:

$$F_1 = F_0 (1 + r) \qquad (3.2)$$
$$F_1 = \$5000 (1 + .09)$$
$$F_1 = \$5450$$

With 9 percent the prevailing rate, $5450 one year from now is identical to $5000 today, at least in terms of purchasing power. Given this option, Jackson would be indifferent between spending now and postponing consumption for a year and earning a 9 percent return on her funds.

What if Jackson were offered $5600 one year from now if she postponed consumption and lent her $5000? Consider the present discounted value of $5600:

$$F_0 = \frac{F_1}{1 + r} \qquad (3.3)$$

$$F_0 = \frac{\$5600}{1.09}$$

$$F_0 = \$5138$$

The present discounted value of $5600 is greater than $5000. This means that with the prevailing market rate, Jackson is better off with $5600 one year from now than with $5000 today.

The same process applies to longer periods of time:

$$F_2 = F_0 + \underbrace{rF_0}_{\substack{\text{interest for} \\ \text{year 1}}} + \underbrace{r(F_0 + rF_0)}_{\substack{\text{interest for} \\ \text{year 2}}} \qquad (3.4)$$

$$F_2 = F_0 + rF_0 + rF_0 + r^2 F_0 \qquad (3.5)$$
$$F_2 = F_0 (1 + r)^2 \qquad (3.6)$$

MONEY TODAY ③.1

Those High Salaries Aren't So High

In September, 1986, Jim Kelley, star quarterback from the defunct USFL signed a multimillion dollar contract with the Buffalo Bills of the NFL. It's not unusual for a star athlete to sign a big contract but this contract was noteworthy. While the exact terms of the agreement were not made public, the contract was reportedly worth $8 million. That sum made Kelley the highest paid football player in the NFL. Eight million dollars is quite a sum for any sports franchise to pay for a single athlete.

Long-term contracts, much the same as million-dollar lottery prizes, take advantage of the very same principle—present discounted value. In most instances the contract or the lottery prize specifies a sum of money to be paid each year over some extended period of time. The headlines may read: "Football star's contract costs team owner $8 million" or "Lottery winner takes $10 million from state's coffers." Such headlines are not exactly accurate. The football star, or the auto mechanic who won the lottery, will receive the specified amount (less federal and state income taxes of course) but this payment won't "cost" the team owner or the state lottery commission that much.

Most contracts call for payments that are spread out over years, sometimes many more than the life of the player's contracted services. Much of the athletic star's income comes in the form of "deferred payments." Let's assume that an $8-million contract specifies a payment schedule like this:

> Years 1 through 5
> $1 million/year ($5 million)
> Years 6 through 10
> $600,000/year ($3 million)

That's a total of $8 million. How much will it take to make those payments over the 10 years of the payment schedule?

Obviously, the precise answer to this question depends on the prevailing interest rate. At the time this particular contract was issued, interest rates were relatively high, at least by historical standards. Assuming an interest rate of 7 percent, and further assuming the football team's owner could come up with the necessary cash for investment purposes and take advantage of that interest rate and then make payments from the return on the investment, the actual outlay would be considerably less than most people might think. Using the present discounted value techniques, analysts estimate that Jim Kelley's contract would actually cost the team about $5.85 million.

This means that wise investments which take into account the present discounted value principle would allow the NFL franchise to buy $8-million worth of athletic talent for less than $6-million actual dollars!

$$F_0 = \frac{F_2}{(1 + r)^2} \tag{3.7}$$

The generalized version of this expression for F dollars made available for n periods is:

$$F_0 = \frac{F_n}{(1 + r)^n} \tag{3.8}$$

This indicates the present discounted value of F_n with interest rate, r, for n periods. To determine the funds generated from lending F dollars for n years with interest rate r, use the generalized version of equation (3.5):

$$F_n = F_0 (1 + r)^n \tag{3.9}$$

Relationship Between Bond Price and Rate of Interest

The purpose of this chapter is to explore the level and structure of interest rates. Interest is the price of money—either the price an individual pays for renting money or the price lenders charge for loaning money. Let's think about interest and interest rates in terms of one general type of liability instrument, the bond, before looking at some specific kinds of bonds.

Several terms are important to this discussion. A *bond* is an obligation of a borrower (usually a corporation or government) to repay the amount borrowed plus an interest payment to a lender on a specific date. This period of time is called the *maturity*. The interest rate the borrower is obliged to pay is called the *yield to maturity*, in some cases the coupon rate. The amount of money lent to the borrower, which is the amount to be repaid to the lender when the bond matures, is called the *maturity value* or *par value* (and sometimes is referred to as the *principal*).

For purposes of this initial discussion, consider an obligation such as a Treasury bill. You may recall from Chapter 2 that Treasury bills do not pay a stated rate of interest. Instead the T-bill is sold at a price below its par value. The difference between the purchase price and the par value determines the implicit rate of return to the bondholder. For example, consider a $10,000 T-bill with a maturity of one year. The security is sold by the Treasury for $9000. The rate of interest the bondholder would earn by holding the security to maturity can be determined by using equation (3.1) and rearranging the terms:

$$F_1 = F_0 + rF_0 \tag{3.1}$$

$$\therefore \quad r = \frac{F_1 - F_0}{F_0} \tag{3.10}$$

$$r = \frac{\$10,000 - \$9000}{\$9000} = 11\%$$

Consider the $10,000 T-bill with the one year maturity. Almost immediately after purchasing the bond from the Treasury, the initial bondholder re-sells the security in the open market for, say, $9200. The bond has traded at a premium since its original purchase price was $9000. What has happened to the bond's yield? Using equation (3.10) with F_0 being the new purchase price, we can figure the new implicit yield:

$$r = \frac{F_1 - F_0}{F_0} \tag{3.10}$$

$$r = \frac{\$10,000 - \$9200}{\$9200} = 8.7\%$$

The yield has dropped from 11 percent to 8.7 percent. On the other hand, what would happen to the yield if the bond had been sold for $8800 rather than $9200? Again, using equation (3.10) we can determine the yield:

$$r = \frac{F_1 - F_0}{F_0} \tag{3.10}$$

$$r = \frac{\$10,000 - \$8800}{\$8800} = 13\%$$

With the bond trading at a discount, the yield rises.

Perhaps you already have noticed the inverse relationship between bond prices and yields. In the secondary market when the price of a bond rises (it trades at a premium), the yield drops. When the price of a bond declines (it trades at a discount), its yield increases. This is an important relationship. Keep it clearly in mind during subsequent discussions of monetary policy.

Various Types of Bonds

The example above illustrates the inverse relationship between bond prices and yields using one particular type of bond called a *zero coupon bond*. (A coupon is the portion of the bond that is redeemed for payment; when a bond sells for less than its face value with the promise that it is redeemable for its face value at maturity, it is called a zero coupon bond.) Zero coupon bonds are usually short-term I.O.U.s. Besides T-bills, savings bonds and commercial paper can be categorized as zero coupon bonds. There are other types of bonds as well.

Perpetual Bonds   A *perpetual bond*, sometimes referred to as a *consol*, has no maturity date. It is an I.O.U. which promises to pay a stream of cash coupon payments in perpetuity, that is, forever. Given a stream of payments, the market price of a consol is determined as follows:

$$MP = \frac{C_1}{1 + r} + \frac{C_2}{(1 + r)^2} + \ldots + \frac{C_\infty}{(1 + r)^\infty} \tag{3.11}$$

where

$$MP = \text{the market price of the security}$$
$$C = \text{the coupon payment (in dollars)}$$
$$r = \text{the market rate of interest}$$

We can rewrite this expression as follows:

$$MP = \sum_{n=1}^{\infty} \frac{C_n}{(1 + r)^n} \tag{3.12}$$

If all coupon payments are identical, equation (3.12) reduces to:

$$MP = \frac{C}{r} \qquad (3.13)$$

This means that a bond making a fixed annual payment of $25 forever, given a market rate of interest of 8 percent, would have a market price of $312.50.

$$MP = \frac{\$25}{.08} = \$312.50$$

What would happen to the price of this bond if the prevailing market interest rate were to drop to 6 percent? It would rise.

$$MP = \frac{\$25}{.06} = \$416.67$$

Consols are common in England but not in the United States. Under special circumstances equities are similar to perpetual bonds. Equities are long-term I.O.U.s with no maturity date. Corporate stock is the best-known example of an equity. If the equity paid an annual dividend in perpetuity, it would be much the same as a consol. Unless the perpetuity of dividends exists, the equity is not similar to a consol and we would have difficulty finding such a bond in the United States.

Regular Bonds   I.O.U.s which pay the holder an interest payment at periodic times plus a payment at maturity are *regular bonds*. The interest payment is called the *coupon payment*. Treasury bonds, municipal bonds, and corporate bonds fit this category. The market price of a regular bond is influenced by the periodic coupon payments plus the par value or maturity value of the security:

$$MP = \frac{C_1}{1 + r} + \frac{C_2}{(1 + r)^2} + \cdots + \frac{C_m}{(1 + r)^m} + \frac{MV}{(1 + r)^m} \qquad (3.14)$$

This illustrates that the market price of a regular bond is the sum of the present values of the coupon payments plus the maturity value. We can rewrite equation (3.14) as:

$$MP = \sum_{n=1}^{m} \frac{C_1}{(1 + r)^n} + \frac{MV}{(1 + r)^m} \qquad (3.15)$$

What is the market price of a bond with a $4 annual coupon payment, a par value of $100, a maturity of twenty years, and a prevailing market interest rate of 8 percent? Look at the bond table shown as Table 3.1. Tables like this one make solutions of expressions such as equation (3.15) quite easy. Using Table 3.1 we can see that a $100 bond ($MV = \$100$) with a 4 percent coupon rate ($C = \$4$) and a twenty-year maturity ($m = 20$) has a market price of $60.41 when the prevailing market interest rate is 8 percent.

YEARS and MONTHS

Yield	18-6	19-0	19-6	20-0	20-6	21-0	21-6	22-0
2.00	130.80	131.48	132.16	132.83	133.50	134.16	134.81	135.46
2.20	127.24	127.83	128.42	129.00	129.57	130.14	130.70	131.26
2.40	123.79	124.30	124.80	125.30	125.79	126.27	126.75	127.22
2.60	120.46	120.89	121.31	121.73	122.14	122.55	122.95	123.34
2.80	117.23	117.59	117.94	118.28	118.62	118.96	119.29	119.61
3.00	114.12	114.40	114.68	114.96	115.23	115.50	115.76	116.02
3.20	111.10	111.32	111.54	111.75	111.96	112.16	112.37	112.57
3.40	108.19	108.35	108.50	108.66	108.81	108.95	109.10	109.24
3.60	105.37	105.47	105.57	105.67	105.76	105.86	105.95	106.04
3.80	102.64	102.69	102.74	102.78	102.83	102.88	102.92	102.96
4.00	100.00	100.00	100.00	100.00	100.00	100.00	100.00	100.00
4.20	97.45	97.40	97.36	97.31	97.27	97.23	97.19	97.15
4.40	94.97	94.89	94.80	94.72	94.63	94.55	94.48	94.40
4.60	92.58	92.45	92.33	92.21	92.09	91.98	91.86	91.75
4.80	90.26	90.10	89.94	89.79	89.64	89.49	89.34	89.20
5.00	88.02	87.83	87.63	87.45	87.27	87.09	86.92	86.75
5.10	86.93	86.72	86.51	86.31	86.11	85.92	85.74	85.55
5.20	85.85	85.62	85.40	85.19	84.98	84.78	84.58	84.38
5.30	84.79	84.55	84.32	84.09	83.87	83.65	83.44	83.23
5.40	83.75	83.49	83.25	83.01	82.77	82.54	82.32	82.10
5.50	82.72	82.46	82.19	81.94	81.69	81.45	81.22	80.99
5.60	81.71	81.43	81.16	80.90	80.64	80.39	80.14	79.91
5.70	80.72	80.43	80.14	79.87	79.60	79.34	79.08	78.84
5.80	79.74	79.44	79.14	78.86	78.58	78.31	78.04	77.79
5.90	78.78	78.47	78.16	77.86	77.57	77.29	77.02	76.76
6.00	77.83	77.51	77.19	76.89	76.59	76.30	76.02	75.75
6.10	76.90	76.57	76.24	75.92	75.62	75.32	75.03	74.75
6.20	75.98	75.64	75.30	74.98	74.67	74.36	74.06	73.78
6.30	75.08	74.73	74.38	74.05	73.73	73.42	73.11	72.82
6.40	74.19	73.83	73.48	73.14	72.81	72.49	72.18	71.88
6.50	73.32	72.95	72.59	72.24	71.90	71.58	71.26	70.95
6.60	72.46	72.08	71.71	71.36	71.01	70.68	70.36	70.05
6.70	71.61	71.22	70.85	70.49	70.14	69.80	69.47	69.16
6.80	70.77	70.38	70.00	69.63	69.28	68.93	68.60	68.28
6.90	69.95	69.55	69.17	68.79	68.43	68.08	67.75	67.42
7.00	69.14	68.74	68.35	67.97	67.60	67.25	66.91	66.58
7.10	68.35	67.94	67.54	67.15	66.78	66.43	66.08	65.75
7.20	67.56	67.15	66.74	66.36	65.98	65.62	65.27	64.93
7.30	66.79	66.37	65.96	65.57	65.19	64.82	64.47	64.13
7.40	66.03	65.61	65.19	64.80	64.41	64.04	63.69	63.34
7.50	65.29	64.85	64.44	64.04	63.65	63.28	62.92	62.57
7.60	64.55	64.11	63.69	63.29	62.90	62.52	62.16	61.81
7.70	63.82	63.38	62.96	62.55	62.16	61.78	61.42	61.06
7.80	63.11	62.67	62.24	61.83	61.43	61.05	60.68	60.33
7.90	62.41	61.96	61.53	61.12	60.72	60.33	59.97	59.61
8.00	61.71	61.26	60.83	60.41	60.01	59.63	59.26	58.90
8.10	61.03	60.58	60.14	59.72	59.32	58.94	58.56	58.21
8.20	60.36	59.91	59.47	59.05	58.64	58.25	57.88	57.52
8.30	59.70	59.24	58.80	58.38	57.97	57.58	57.21	56.85
8.40	59.05	58.59	58.15	57.72	57.32	56.92	56.55	56.19
8.50	58.41	57.95	57.50	57.08	56.67	56.28	55.90	55.54
8.60	57.78	57.31	56.87	56.44	56.03	55.64	55.26	54.90
8.70	57.15	56.69	56.24	55.81	55.40	55.01	54.63	54.27
8.80	56.54	56.07	55.63	55.20	54.79	54.39	54.02	53.66
8.90	55.94	55.47	55.02	54.59	54.18	53.79	53.41	53.05
9.00	55.34	54.88	54.43	54.00	53.58	53.19	52.81	52.45
9.20	54.18	53.71	53.26	52.83	52.42	52.03	51.65	51.29
9.40	53.05	52.58	52.13	51.70	51.29	50.90	50.53	50.17
9.60	51.96	51.49	51.04	50.61	50.20	49.81	49.44	49.08
9.80	50.90	50.43	49.98	49.55	49.14	48.75	48.38	48.03
10.00	49.87	49.40	48.95	48.52	48.12	47.73	47.36	47.01

Source: From *Comprehensive Bond Values Tables*, Third Desk Edition. Copyright 1953 by Financial Publishing Company. Reprinted by permission.

TABLE 3.1 *Bond Values Table*

What would happen to the yield on this security if it sold for $54 instead of $60.41? By looking at Table 3.1 we note that with the drop in the market price the market yield rises to 9 percent (again, reflecting the inverse relationship between the price of the bond and its market yield).

The Level of Interest Rates

This chapter so far has investigated the mechanics of interest rates. Perhaps more important, at least for subsequent policy discussions, is the level of interest rates. What determines the current level of interest rates? Chapter 2 briefly mentioned interest rate determination in the context of a discussion on financial markets and specific market instruments. It indicated only that interest rates are determined through the forces of supply and demand. Now the chapter will investigate two ways to explain the level of interest rates in more detail; both methods incorporate supply and demand analysis.

You are familiar with a variety of financial instruments. Each of these various instruments has a rate of interest. Instead of analyzing interest rate determination for each specific instrument, this discussion will generalize. Generalizing is possible because interest rates tend to move together and in the same direction. The discussion will center on *the* interest rate, a rate which is representative of interest rates in general. When talking about *the* interest rate, economists are referring to an approximation of the average of interest rates in the system. (An interest rate which is a good proxy for interest rates in general is the rate on short-term—three-month—T-bills but this discussion will identify a rate as an approximation of all interest rates.)

In Chapter 2 you learned that the financial sector of the economy functions to facilitate the movement of funds from surplus units (SUs) to deficit units (DUs). The discussion of interest rate determination will continue to concentrate on the financial sector. However, certain assumptions about the real sector of the economy underlie this discussion.[1] The real sector influences the financial sector, and the interest rates determined therein, as decisions about saving, spending, and investing are made. The flow-of-funds analysis revealed that lending and borrowing are influenced by these saving, spending, and investment decisions. There is a strong interac-

---

[1] Economists differentiate between real activity and monetary activity. Real economic activity refers to economic decisions of households, nonfinancial business firms and the government. These decisions about spending, saving, and investment influence the real economic measures of income, output, and employment. Refer to Figure 2.5 in Chapter 2 for a diagrammatic illustration of the real sector of the economy.

tion between the real and the financial sectors. For purposes of the present discussion, assume that the variables in the real sector which influence interest rates are constant; and assume that the real sector is in equilibrium. In a later chapter we can integrate the dynamics of the real and financial sectors. Until then we will have only a partial understanding of what determines interest rates.

Two theories aid the analysis of the level of interest rates: the *liquidity preference theory* and the *loanable funds theory*. These are not competing theories in the sense that only one is correct. Both approaches to interest rate determination can be used to illustrate a similar equilibrium interest rate. The liquidity preference theory looks at interest rates from a stock dimension; the loanable funds theory uses the flow dimension.[2] The former considers the demand for and supply of the stock of money. The latter considers the demand for and supply of loanable funds, a broader range of financial claims.

Liquidity Preference Theory

The liquidity preference approach identifies the public's demand for money (Dm) and the system's supply of money (Sm) as determining the interest rate. Identifying the factors influencing demand and supply illustrate how the equilibrium interest rate is determined.

Demand for Money   The demand for money is influenced by the level of income and the prevailing market interest rate. (Chapter 10 will explore in detail the factors underlying the demand for money.) This functional relationship takes the following form:

$$Dm = f(\overset{+}{Y}, \overset{-}{r}) \tag{3.16}$$

The signs above the variables indicate the direction of the change in the dependent variable (in the case Dm) resulting from changes in each of the independent variables (Y and r). Here the change in the demand for money is positively (directly) related to income ($\Delta Dm/\Delta Y > 0$) and negatively (inversely) related to the rate of interest ($\Delta Dm/\Delta Y < 0$).

Do not confuse the demand for money with the desire to have more income or wealth. Perhaps we can avoid this confusion by referring to Dm as

---

[2] *Stock* here refers to the fixed level of the money supply which is part of the liquidity preference theory; no time dimension is involved. *Flow* refers to the fluidity of the variables in the loanable funds approach; the demand and supply change over time.

the "demand for money to hold." To see how the demand for money to hold is directly related to income, consider this example. Government employees are paid every two weeks. Upon receipt of his paycheck a civil servant may immediately spend his pay, invest some or all of his money, or hold some or all of his money. This individual may need to hold on to some of his bimonthly income to cover day-to-day expenses. We know from macroeconomic theory that expenditures rise as personal income increases. When this civil servant receives a salary increase, his expenditures are likely to rise, thus his *Dm* will increase. We can apply this to the public in general and explain that the demand for money to hold will increase as income rises.

The demand for money to hold is inversely related to the rate of interest. Again, consider the government worker. Between paychecks he has a variety of payments to make. Not all of them come at the same time; an auto loan payment may be due on the tenth of each month, rent on the fifteenth, and utilities on the twentieth. This individual may hold on to all of his paycheck and make the payments when they are due. Or, he may put the money in a short-term, interest-bearing investment until he needs the cash. By holding the money until it is needed for expenditures, the civil servant loses the chance to earn some interest income; there is an opportunity cost associated with the holding of money in cash balances.

As long as interest rates are low, the opportunity costs of holding money are not very great. But, as interest rates rise, not investing available funds becomes more and more costly, even if for only a very short time.

This situation is perhaps best illustrated by the proliferation of interest-bearing transaction accounts (for example, NOW accounts) that developed in this country during the period of abnormally high interest rates of the late 1970s and early 1980s. Financial institutions realized that individuals were no longer holding money in liquid forms (such as normal checking accounts) until it was needed. Instead, individuals were finding short-term investments that generated some interest income. The interest-bearing checking accounts developed for the most part in response to individuals' desires to earn a return on their cash balances. (Legislation in 1980 also influenced the proliferation of interest-paying accounts.) Especially with high interest rates, the opportunity cost of holding money is great; people looked to reduce that opportunity cost. In so doing, they showed that the demand for money to hold is inversely related to the rate of interest.[3] Figure 3.1 represents this situation graphically. With increasing income, the *Dm* shifts outward to the right.

---

[3] Despite some controversy about the demand for money function, empirical research substantiates the significance of the demand for money's positive relationship to income and inverse relationship to the rate of interest. See, for example, David Laidler, *The Demand for Money, Theories and Evidence* (New York: Dun-Donnelly, 1977).

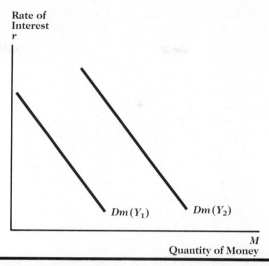

FIGURE 3.1 *Income, Interest Rate, and the Demand for Money* The demand for money is related to individuals' incomes. As the level of income rises, the demand for money curve shifts to the right [from $Dm(Y_1)$ to $Dm(Y_2)$].

Supply of Money A complete analysis of interest rate determination using the liquidity preference theory needs an explanation of the supply of money (Sm). The Sm is determined by the Federal Reserve, depository institutions, and, to a certain extent, by the public.[4] The Federal Reserve influences the supply of money through its monetary policy tools—buying and selling securities in the open market, its requirements regarding the reserves depository institutions must hold, and the rate of interest it charges for lending funds, the discount rate. We will investigate how monetary policy affects the supply of money in Chapter 17.

Depository institutions influence the supply of money through their ability to attract deposits (paying higher interest rates will attract more deposits) as well as through the quantity of reserves over and above the required level which they hold. Chapter 7 investigates how the expansion of the money supply occurs through the financial system. The public has some impact on the money supply via its decisions to borrow and lend funds. These influences are summarized by explaining that the Sm is related to reserves (R) in the financial system. While both the Federal Reserve and

---

[4] Here, we are using a narrow definition of the supply of money, namely currency and checkable deposits.

depository institutions determine the level of reserves, we can simplify our discussion by concentrating on the Federal Reserve as the dominant factor in the level of reserves in the system.

Some economists argue that the Sm is also influenced by the level of interest rates. The claim is that the interest rate influences financial institutions' willingness to lend funds. At high rates financial institutions are more eager to make loans. Via the money multiplier (explained in detail in Chapter 7) this willingness affects the overall supply of money. Recent research indicates that the interest sensitivity of the Sm is extremely low.

Without rejecting the interest sensitivity of the Sm or the degree to which depository institutions and the public affect reserves, we can explain the liquidity preference theory by stressing the Federal Reserve determination of R and thus of Sm. This being the case, we consider the Sm to be largely exogenously determined (that is, the Sm is set outside of our model). This functional relationship is expressed as follows:

$$Sm = f(\overset{+}{R}, \overset{+}{r}) \tag{3.17}$$

The larger the reserves in the system (again, in this discussion reserves are determined primarily by the Federal Reserve), the larger the supply of money. The extremely low interest sensitivity of the Sm is also shown here.

Figure 3.2 represents Sm graphically. It shows Sm with some interest rate sensitivity (left side) and with no interest rate sensitivity (right side). The following discussion concentrates on the interest insensitive Sm.

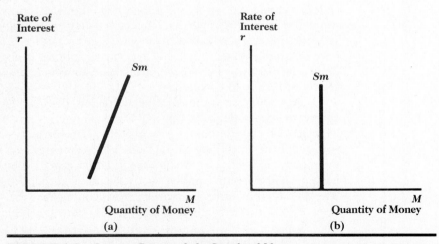

FIGURE 3.2 *Interest Rate and the Supply of Money*   If the supply of money is sensitive to the rate of interest, the Sm function will have a slight positive slope. This is the case in the left side of the figure. The right side of the figure shows an inelastic or unresponsive Sm function as a perfectly vertical line.

Equilibrium   Using the functional relationships expressed in these figures, we can derive the resulting equilibrium relationship:

$$Dm = f(\overset{+}{Y}, \overset{-}{r}) \tag{3.16}$$

$$Sm = f(\overset{+}{R}) \tag{3.17a}$$

$$r = f(\overset{+}{Y}, \overset{-}{R}) \tag{3.18}$$

Equation (3.18) indicates that the interest rate is positively related to the level of income and inversely related to the reserves in the system.[5] As income rises in the economy, the demand for money to hold rises and, all else being equal, this will result in a rise in the interest rate. Stated another way, with an increase in the demand for money, given a supply of money, more people are desiring purchasing power now rather than later. Only with higher interest rates will some people forgo consumption today and loan money to those who desire it today. On the other hand, as reserves increase, that is, as the supply of money increases, with all else remaining unchanged, there will be a downward pressure on the interest rate. Figure 3.3 represents this situation graphically.

---

[5] Our discussion has completely ignored the influence of price expectations. We mention the price expectations effect as it relates to interest rates later in this chapter.

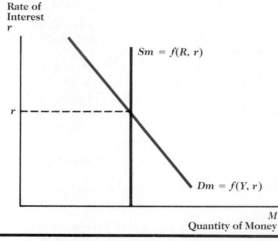

FIGURE 3.3   *Interest Rate Determination*   The intersection of the demand for money function, *Dm*, and the supply of money function, *Sm*, determines the prevailing rate of interest, *r*.

Loanable Funds Approach

The loanable funds approach identifies the demand for credit, or loanable funds (D_L), and the supply of credit (S_L) as determinants of the interest rate. Loanable funds are demanded by deficit units (DUs)—either households, businesses or the government—to cover personal deficits, business investment, and government deficits, respectively. Credit is provided by surplus units (SUs), again in all three sectors, from personal savings, retained business earnings, government surpluses, and the Federal Reserve, which can increase the stock of money through the addition of reserves. Keep in mind that the supply of loanable funds is the same as the demand for financial claims (I.O.U.s) by lenders, and that the demand for loanable funds is the same as the supply of I.O.U.s by borrowers.

The supply of loanable funds is determined by the interest rate and the level of income in the system:

$$S_L = f(\overset{+}{r}, \overset{-}{Y}) \qquad (3.19)$$

As interest rates rise, SUs are willing to make more funds available to borrowers. And, with an increasing level of income, SUs have more funds which can be lent to deficit units. The demand for loanable funds is determined by the interest rate:

$$D_L = f(\overset{-}{r}) \qquad (3.20)$$

As the price of borrowing (the rate of interest) rises, the demand for funds drops off.

Graphing the supply and demand functions illustrates equilibrium in the loanable funds approach. The equilibrium rate of interest is that rate which clears the credit market, that is, the supply is just equal to the demand. Figure 3.4 shows this graph. As income rises, the S_L increases (shifts outward to the right from S_L to S_L'). With demand remaining unchanged, the interest rate drops from r to r'.

The loanable funds (or credit market) functions like any other market as long as competition exists. The forces of demand and supply will always bring the market into equilibrium with a rate of interest just sufficient to clear the market and satisfy borrowers and lenders.

Remember that the liquidity preference and loanable funds theories are different approaches explaining the same phenomenon, the market mechanism which establishes the interest rate. As such, these two approaches result in the same market interest rate. The loanable funds theory currently is accepted more widely by financial market practitioners. This is

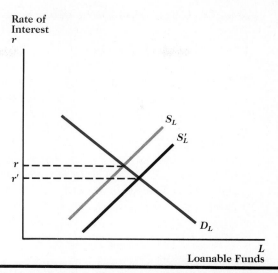

FIGURE 3.4 *Shifts in Supply of Loanable Funds and Changes in the Interest Rate* When income rises, the supply of loanable funds increases. This is shown by the shift to the right of the supply of loanable funds curve (from S_L to S_L'). When demand remains unchanged, such a shift results in a decline in the rate of interest (from r to r').

probably because financial market analysts are involved with demand and supply of funds in the personal, business, and government sectors; this is a more practical, institutional approach to interest rate determination. (Money Today 3.2 and 3.3, on pages 76 and 77, examine the interest rate on installment credit.)

Structure of Interest Rates

This discussion of the level of interest rates explored *the* rate of interest, that approximation of the average of all interest rates in the system. A perusal of the financial section of the newspaper reveals that there are, in fact, many different interest rates. Table 3.2 illustrates the diversity of interest rates. Observation of interest rates over time indicates a systematic relationship between the movements of the various interest rates. Analysts have identified a number of characteristics of securities as the primary factors influencing interest rates. These are *term to maturity*, *default risk*, *taxability*, and *marketability*.

Prime Rate	8.5%
Federal Funds	6.87%
Discount Rate	6.5%
Call Money Rate	7.75% to 8.0%
Commercial Paper (high grade)	6.85% for 30 days; 6.80% for 60 days
Certificates of Deposit	6.80% for 1 month; 6.85% for 6 months
Bankers Acceptances	6.75% for 30 days; 6.65% for 120 days
Eurodollars	7.12% to 7.0%
Treasury Bills	6.31% for 13 weeks; 6.39% for 26 weeks
Federal Home Loan Mortgage Corp.	10.43% fixed rate; 7.50% adjustable rate
Federal National Mortgage Assoc.	10.27% fixed rate; 8.30% adjustable rate
Merrill Lynch Ready Asset Trust	5.77%

Source: **Market Interest Rates from** *The Wall Street Journal*, **June 13, 1986. Adapted by permission of Dow Jones & Company, Inc.**

TABLE 3.2 *Market Interest Rates, June 13, 1986*

Term Structure

To investigate the structure of interest rates, we need to look at securities, which, except for term to maturity, are the same in all respects. Recall that *term to maturity* refers to the length of time until the loan's principal is repaid. The *term structure* of these securities is the relationship between the rates of interest on securities with different maturities. We can use government securities as an example because they are identical in all respects other than terms of structure (that is, they have no default risk, are all treated the same for tax purposes and are very similar in their marketability).

We can represent the relationship between interest rates and term to maturity by using a yield curve. A *yield curve* is a line which best fits the various interest rate-maturity combinations for a particular type of security when they are plotted on a graph. Figure 3.5 shows the yield curve for Treasury securities on October 10, 1986. This yield curve indicates that the rate of interest is greater for financial claims as the time to maturity increases. This is an ascending yield curve.

Not all yield curves are ascending like the one in Figure 3.5. Figure 3.6 shows the yield curve for Treasury securities for five different dates.

It should be clear from these two figures that yield curves take many different shapes and do not remain constant. Yield curves may take the specific shapes shown in Figure 3.7 on page 74. A variety of factors are used to explain changes in yield curves.

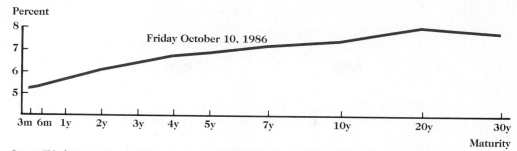

Source:"Markets at a Glance" from *Fed Fortnightly*, October 14, 1986. Reprinted by permission of Maxnews Financial Network, Inc.

FIGURE 3.5 *United States Treasury Yield Curve, October 10, 1986* A yield curve is a line which best fits the various interest rate–maturity combinations for a particular type of security at a particular point in time. The curve shown here is an ascending yield curve.

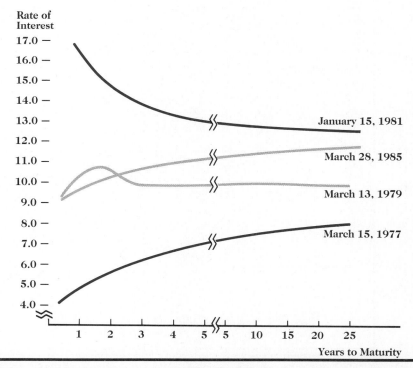

FIGURE 3.6 *Yields of Treasury Securities for Multiple Dates* Yield curves display varying patterns. Expectations about interest rate movements influence the behavior of buyers and sellers in the securities market. An ascending yield curve indicates that the public expects interest rates to rise whereas a descending yield curve indicates the opposite.

Economists have engaged in considerable debate over what causes yield curves to take on different shapes at different points in time. Three theories may help explain the shape of the yield curve and why it changes over time—*expectations theory*, *liquidity premium theory*, and *market segmentation theory*.

Expectations Theory The expectations theory attempts to explain the shape of the yield curve by relying on investors' expectations about future interest-rate movements. Investors, this theory assumes, have no preference between holding long-term securities and a series of short-term securities. Furthermore, investors are able and willing to move between short-term and long-term financial claims in an effort to achieve the greatest possible return

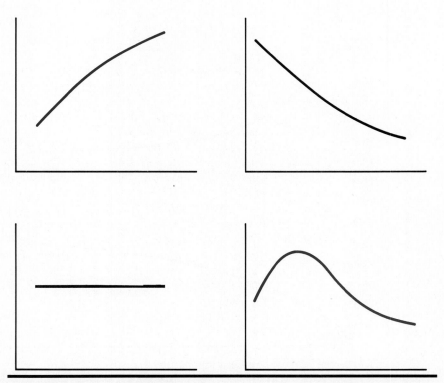

FIGURE 3.7 *Shapes of Yield Curves*   In most cases, yield curves take on one of the four shapes illustrated by this figure. The humped curve indicates that the public thinks rates will rise in the short term but decline in the long term.

on their investments. This attempt to maximize returns is not affected by transaction costs, which are assumed to be nonexistent or insignificant.

According to this theory, an investor will be indifferent between a long-term bond and a series of short-term bonds when the rate of return on the long-term bond is just equal to the return from a series of short-term bonds, where the return is based on the current short-term rate plus the short-term rates expected to prevail over the maturity of the long-term security. Confusing? We can express this relationship as:

$$(1 + R_n)^n = (1 + r_1)(1 + r_2)(1 + r_3) \ldots (1 + r_n)$$

where

$(1 + R_n)^n$ is the compounded value of a dollar invested

at an interest rate of R_n for n years,

r_1 is the current short-term rate, and

$r_2, r_3, \ldots r_n$ are the expected short-term rates each

year in the future

An example will illustrate this situation. An investor has $10,000 to invest for a two-year period. The investor may either invest for the full two years or invest in two 12-month securities, one year at a time. The expected rate of interest at the end of the first year is the determining factor in the investor's decision. If the current nominal rate for two-year investment securities is 10 percent, then that $10,000 will generate $12,100 after two years: $10,000 (1 + .10)^2 = $12,100. Let's assume the current nominal rate on one year loans is 8 percent. Investing the $10,000 for one year at 8 percent produces $10,800: $10,000 (1 + .08) = $10,800. If investors expect the nominal rate on one-year securities one year from now to be 12 percent, they will be indifferent between two one-year investments and a single two-year investment. This indifference results because the $10,800 earned the first year when invested for another year at the expected rate of 12 percent will generate the same total return as the $10,000 invested for two years at 10 percent: $10,800 (1 + .12) = $12,096, which is close enough to $12,100 for purposes of our discussion.

But if investors expect the rate for one-year loans one year from now to be higher than 12 percent (perhaps the increase resulted from anticipated inflation), they will prefer the two one-year loans. For example, if the anticipated rate of interest on one-year loans one year from now is 14 percent, then the $10,800 earned after one year when reinvested will generate $15,120. This is considerably more than what would result from investing the $10,000 for two years at the prevailing 10 percent rate. What results from

MONEY T●DAY 3.2

Do Credit Card Rates Defy the Laws of Economics?

Consumer credit card interest rates seem to defy the law of supply and demand. The figure shown here reveals how the prime interest rate (a good proxy for short-term rates in general) has declined but bank credit card rates (a good proxy for consumer credit rates in general) have remained very high. Why is this the case?

Maximum finance charges are set by state law. They range from a 12 percent rate in California for balances under $1000 (for balances over $1000 the rate jumps to 19.2 percent) to a high of 21 percent in Nevada. Since these rates are set by law, they tend to lag behind other market interest rates. When interest rates skyrocketed to nearly 20 percent early in the 1980s, many states had ceilings on credit card rates that kept these rates around 12 percent or 15 percent. Now, although most rates are falling, legislated interest rate maximums remain high and the ceiling has become the floor.

Most retail establishments and many commercial banks offer credit cards. In many instances, especially for retail establishments, the criteria for qualifying are well below those applied by financial institutions for conventional consumer loans. The risk on these loans is higher and the rate charged reflects this risk factor. Despite the credit worthiness of the borrower, all individuals pay the same finance charge for this type of consumer credit.

Finally, consumer spending in general and credit card spending in particular have remained very high. Consumer spending led the economic recovery after the 1981–82 recession and continued high even when the recovery began to slow down. The figure shows how credit card debt outstanding has risen over the last few years. This high demand for installment credit offered by retail establishments and commercial banks through their national credit cards has contributed to the apparent unresponsiveness of credit card interest rates.

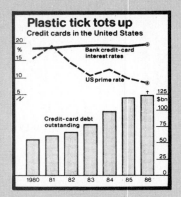

Plastic tick tots up
Credit cards in the United States

The high rate of interest on installment credit doesn't violate the laws of economics. State regulations, risk and high demand combine to keep interest rates on consumer credit cards well above other short-term rates.

Source: Figure from *The Economist* (May 17, 1986):93. Reprinted by permission.

this situation? The expectations of an increase in the one-year rate a year from now will convince some investors to shift to one-year loans and away from two-year loans. At the same time, if borrowers have the same expectation they will shift heavily into two-year securities. As a result the supply of two-year loans will decrease and the supply of one-year loans will increase while the demand for two-year loans will increase and the demand for one-year loans will decrease. Given the expected return of 14 percent on one-year loans a year from now, these shifts would occur until the rates on two-year loans and the current rate on one-year loans change so that the earnings generated from investing in a two-year loan or two one-year loans are the same.

MONEY T(3.3)DAY

Will Credit Card Rates Decline?

Credit card rates have resisted the overall decline in interest rates (see Money Today 3.2). There is increasing pressure on the major banks which issue credit cards to lower these rates. Interestingly enough, the pressure is coming from two very different sources: smaller competing banks and state legislators.

The large money center banks issue most of this nation's bank credit cards (the top 25 issue 75 percent of the credit cards). The volume of credit coupled with the high profit on credit cards (reported at five times that of other types of lending activities) encourages major banks to work very hard to maintain a large share of the credit card market. (Citibank generates as much as 25 percent of its earnings from credit card operations.) Because of the big spread between major bank credit card rates and rates on other types of consumer credit, some small banks are willing to take a lower profit spread associated with lower credit card rates in order to lure customers from the large money center banks.

Conneticut Bank and Trust, for example, cut its credit card rate from 18 percent to 12 percent during the summer of 1986. The bank admits it may raise the rate to 15 percent after it attracts some new customers but points out that 15 percent is still considerably lower than its larger competitors' rates (Citibank was charging 19.8 percent in July, 1986).

This competition by smaller banks may force the major money center banks to rethink their credit card pricing policies. If competition doesn't force rates down, legislation may. Consumer awareness of the discrepancy between credit card rates and other interest rates is being translated into pressure on state legislators to take some action. Some legislatures are lowering the interest rate cap for their states (this only applies to in-state institutions; out-of-state firms can charge whatever rate is allowed by their home states). Other legislatures are passing laws tying credit card rates to the discount rate or the prime rate.

Competition and legislation may give credit card customers some relief from high interest rates. But, the fact remains that borrowing continues at historically high levels despite high interest rates. Pressure for interest rate declines will have to come from somewhere other than reduced demand.

Liquidity Premium Theory The liquidity premium theory utilizes the basic assumption of the expectations theory, that is, that expectations of future interest rates influence investors' behavior. But the liquidity premium theory rejects the notion that investors are indifferent between short-term and long-term securities. Unlike the expectations theory, liquidity is afforded a premium by investors. The rate of return on long-term securities must be equal to the average of the current short-term rates and the expected short-term rate *plus* a liquidity premium to compensate investors for the loss of liquidity occasioned by holding long-term securities.

In this theory the normal yield curve is ascending, since a premium must be added to the long-term interest rate. A descending yield curve could result with the application of this theory, but only if short-term rates are expected to decline substantially below long-term rates and thus overcome the liquidity premium.

Market Segmentation Theory This theory differentiates, or segments, the short- and long-term markets. Market segmentation means that short- and long-term securities are not easily substituted; investors cannot move easily between short- and long-term securities. The primary explanation for segmented markets is institutional. Certain types of investors have specific needs, for example, life insurance companies try to match their long-term liabilities with long-term securities, while other institutional investors that have largely short-term liabilities, say commercial banks, purchase short-term securities. Investors do not move regularly between long- and short-term securities.

With segmented credit markets, the supply and demand for various types of instruments with similar term structures will determine the overall yield curve. Any type of yield curve is consistent with this theory.

Other Factors Influencing Interest Rate Structure

Although the term to maturity is considered the most important factor explaining the differences in interest rates, other factors also influence interest rate differentials. *Default risk*, *taxability*, and *marketability* are important influences on interest rates.

Default Risk Default risk refers to the possibility that a loan and/or its interest payment will not be paid to the lender. In some instances the riskiness of a loan is obvious to lenders. More often, lenders use an investor rating service, such as Standard and Poor or Moody, to determine the degree of risk. Investor rating services assign a quality rating to security issues (for example, Standard and Poor's AAA rating means the security is of highest quality, while a B rating indicates the loan is speculative).

Federal government securities carry no risk. Investor rating services evaluate state and municipal government securities just as they do corporate bond issues. New York City has had a very low rating because of its overall financial condition. Security issues with low default risk (those with high ratings) pay a lower interest rate than issues with a high default risk. In 1983 municipal bonds with a Standard and Poor's rating of "triple A" were paying approximately 12 to 13 percent while those with a "B" rating were paying around 1½ to 3 percent higher interest. When other factors are held constant, default risk can account for interest rate differentials on similar security issues.

Taxability   With the exception of certain tax-exempt bonds, the interest income from securities is taxable. Various types of taxes are levied on interest income (for example, federal and state income taxes). Securities that are taxed or taxed more heavily tend to pay higher rates of interest. All else being equal, investors require higher interest rates to allow an attractive after-tax return.[6]

Marketability   When all other factors are equal, interest rates will be lower on securities that are readily marketable (through a secondary market) than for obligations for which no secondary market exists. The degree of interest-rate differential attributable to marketability is not significant.

Fluctuations in Interest Rates

Interest rates fluctuate as a result of a number of factors. These factors include the business cycle, government deficit financing, monetary policy actions, and inflationary expectations.

Movements in interest rates follow the business cycle. Interest rates rise during periods of expansion, usually reaching their peak at about the same time that nominal income is cyclically high. Interest rates decline during periods when economic activity slackens. The close association between interest rates and the business cycle is easily explained. Consumer confidence rises with the business cycle, and borrowing increases. Businesses are borrowing also to finance investment spending (firms increase the supply of bonds faster than the demand for bonds increases, and this depresses bond prices while increasing bond yields). Figure 3.8 depicts this relationship, showing how interest rates declined with the recessions of 1960, 1974, 1979 and, most visibly, during the 1981–82 downturn.

Deficit financing also influences interest rates. The federal government can finance a deficit by selling bonds either to the non-bank public or through the Federal Reserve underwriting the security issue. In the first instance, the Treasury issues new bonds; the increased supply of bonds depresses bond prices while raising interest rates. Interest rates may decline

---

[6] The interest rate on taxable securities equivalent to that on tax-exempt bonds can be determined as follows:

$$\text{taxable bond rate} = \text{tax-exempt rate} \left(\frac{1}{\text{marginal tax rate}} \right)$$

initially when the Federal Reserve finances the Treasury's security issue. (The Fed actually buys bonds in the secondary market at the same time the Treasury is issuing new bonds; this stabilizes or reduces interest rates.) But the increase in the supply of money from the Fed's actions produces excess bank reserves. Under most circumstances these reserves are used for loans or investments and the money supply expands. The result of this increased activity is upward pressure on interest rates.

Monetary policy and inflationary expectations also influence interest rates. In discussing the effects of deficit financing, we have highlighted the effect of money supply expansion on interest rates. Whether the Federal Reserve is underwriting a Treasury security or not, expansionary monetary policy increases excess bank reserves and stimulates the expansion of credit. This is often called the liquidity effect. An expansion of the money supply

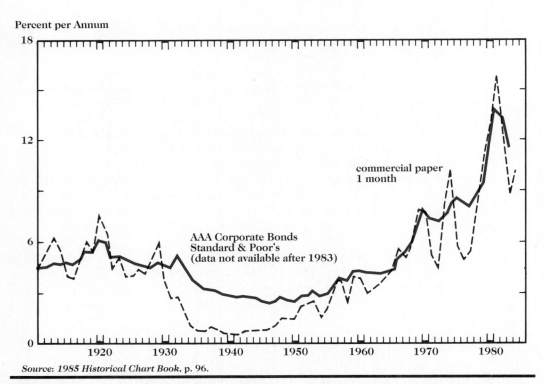

Percent per Annum

Source: 1985 Historical Chart Book, p. 96.

FIGURE 3.8 *Long- and Short-Term Interest Rates*   This figure illustrates the fluctuations in interest rates. Short-term rates (commercial paper) fluctuate more than long-term rates (corporate bonds). The business cycle and expectations for rate shifts cause interest rates to fluctuate.

(liquidity) leads to a decline in interest rates. (The opposite occurs when the money supply contracts.) The liquidity effect probably will not have a long-term effect on interest rates. The money supply expansion will lead to an increase in income, and the demand for bonds eventually will increase. This will moderate the original interest rate decline. The price expectations effect may prevent the movement of interest rates back toward their original levels.

The price expectations effect, often called the Fisher Effect because Irving Fisher popularized the explanation, results when borrowers and lenders expect the increase in nominal income to produce inflation. If inflation is anticipated, interest rates reflect an inflation premium on top of the real rate of interest. Thus, rates are higher than without any expectations of inflation.

This discussion of fluctuations has consistently referred to interest rates. While there are scores, maybe even hundreds, of interest rates in our economy (reflecting the many types of debt instruments), those rates tend to move together. The demands for loanable funds in different markets are interrelated. Both borrowers and lenders will attempt to get the best possible interest rate available. As a result, markets are linked together, and interest rates, although somewhat different, will tend to move at the same time and in the same direction.

Chapter Conclusion

This chapter investigated the level and structure of interest rates and the factors that cause interest rates to fluctuate. Interest rates are an important variable in the macroeconomy.

The level of interest rates means the overall composite rate or level received for making funds available or paid for borrowing funds. Interest rates are determined through market forces of supply and demand. The liquidity preference theory explains interest rate determination in terms of the demand and supply of money in the economy. The loanable funds approach focuses on the demand and supply of credit, or loanable funds.

The structure of interest rates refers to the various specific rates on different types of securities in the financial market. Maturity, risk, taxability and marketability help explain why the rate on one security is different from that of another. Yields on similar securities vary depending on the time to maturity. The yield curve, which reflects the interest rate-maturity combinations for a particular type of security, is watched carefully by financial analysts. Expectations theory and the liquidity premium theory are alternative explanations of why yield curves take on different shapes.

Yield curves, or the term structure of interest rates, are important because they correlate closely to other economic events. Fluctuations in interest rates relate to the business cycle, government financing patterns, monetary policy, and the expectations of individuals and institutional investors. These factors eventually affect other economic variables, such as aggregate income, the level of employment, or inflation. Because interest rates are sensitive and change more quickly than other economic variables, analysts follow interest-rate fluctuations and patterns of fluctuations to predict how the economy will behave.

Consider These Questions

1. Many states now have lotteries with very large payoffs. Assume you just won a state lottery. You have a choice of $500,000 now or $1 million ten years from now. Which should you choose to maximize your winnings? (Assume no inflation and a constant rate of interest of 8 percent.)

2. What role does inflation play in interest rate determination?

3. You will learn later that the Federal Reserve can influence the interest rate by buying or selling securities in the open market. How is it that this buying or selling (changing the demand or supply) affects the interest rate rather than just the price of securities?

4. Explain the difference between the liquidity preference theory and the loanable funds theory. How can two different theories result in an explanation of the same interest rate?

5. What is the difference between the level of interest rates and the term structure of interest rates?

6. How can you explain the fact that yield curves take on different shapes at different times?

Suggestions for Further Reading

Darst, David M. *The Complete Bond Book*. New York: McGraw-Hill, 1975.
Explains debt instruments and interest rates. Also shows how to use bond tables.

Fisher, Irving. *The Theory of Interest Rates*. New York: Augustus M. Kelley, 1965 (originally published in 1930).
Many consider this the "bible" on interest rate theory. Despite its age it has withstood the test of time.

Malkiel, Burton M. *A Random Walk Down Wall Street*. New York: W.W. Norton, 1981.
Provides some applied insights into returns on investments.

Nelson, Charles R. *The Term Structure of Interest Rates*. New York: Basic Books, 1972.
A complete analysis of interest-rate theory and application.

Trainer, Richard D. *The Arithmetic of Interest Rates*. New York: Federal Reserve Bank of New York, 1983.
   A clear explanation of the mathematics of interest rates.
———. *Handbook of Securities of the United States Government and Federal Agencies and Related Money Market Instruments*. Boston: First Boston Corporation, 1981.
   Short but sweet information on all types of securities. Does a nice job of explaining securities prices and their yields.

PART TWO

FINANCIAL INSTITUTIONS

CHAPTER FOUR

FINANCIAL INSTITUTIONS
in an
EXPANDING ECONOMY

Rags make Paper
Paper makes Money
Money makes Banks
Banks make Loans
Loans make Beggars
Beggars make Rags

Anonymous eighteenth-century writer

This chapter presents a closer look at financial institutions. The next four chapters investigate the origins of financial institutions, the structure and functioning of this nation's banking system, and ways in which financial institutions affect the economy through the deposit expansion process.

The first chapter in this section explores the "whys and wherefores" of financial institutions. The benefits of financial intermediaries, as they help explain the evolution of banks and other financial institutions, are outlined. A discussion of the types of financial institutions provides the perspective necessary to assess the institutional changes which will be described in subsequent chapters.

Chapter Objectives

The basic principles of financial intermediaries are the same today as they were years ago. Although purposes have not changed much, the process of intermediation is changing and all types of intermediaries are affected.

After exploring financial intermediaries you should be able to:

- Explain the underlying reasons for financial intermediaries.
- Discuss how these intermediaries have evolved.
- Identify and differentiate between the types of financial institutions.

As you proceed through the chapter, think about the contributions of intermediaries in terms of the functions they perform. When you have a thorough understanding of intermediaries, you will be able to:

- Explain why individuals turn to intermediaries rather than do their own lending and borrowing.
- Define risk.
- Describe how intermediaries minimize risk.
- Explain how financial intermediaries got started in this country.
- Identify the factors which shaped the structure of the financial industry.
- Explain why we have so many kinds of financial intermediaries.
- Differentiate among the roles of various intermediaries.

In a more general sense, you should consider financial institutions in a changing environment. Use this chapter to gain a working knowledge of how financial institutions developed so that you will be able to explore the many changes that are occurring within the financial industry. Part IV of the text will discuss those changes.

Financial Intermediation and Risk

Chapter 2 described financial markets and how they provide a mechanism for surplus units (savers) to transfer funds to deficit units (borrowers). This transfer can occur directly—an individual can buy a corporate stock or a government security—or indirectly—through a third party, an intermediary. Financial institutions provide this intermediation function. Questions arise as to why financial intermediaries exist in a competitive economy and what benefits they provide.

Benefits of Intermediaries

Intermediaries meet a need within the economic system. They originated in response to that need and have evolved and adapted to meet changing conditions. The basic reasons for intermediaries are that they provide *convenience*, *economies of scale*, and *risk pooling*.

One of the obvious reasons for intermediaries is *convenience*. Because of intermediaries, borrowers do not need to find able and willing lenders or vice versa. Beyond bringing savers and borrowers together, intermediaries actually attract surplus funds from economic units willing to give up current spending power in return for deposit receipts (the intermediaries' liabilities). Intermediaries then identify economic units seeking current spending power who are willing to sacrifice future power to get it. In other words, intermediaries sell claims on themselves and buy claims on borrowers. In so doing financial intermediaries also reconcile the conflict between short- and long-term consumption patterns and income flows. Consumption and income patterns for individuals and firms may differ. Young people often have more consumption needs than income, while older people often have more income and savings than they need to cover their consumption needs. Financial intermediaries allow young people to meet those consumption needs while giving older individuals the opportunity to earn a return on their surplus funds.

The convenience offered by intermediaries and the fact that they enhance the financial process do not adequately explain why they exist. Economic reasons for the existence of financial intermediaries include economies of scale and risk pooling.

Both costs and benefits are associated with financial intermediation, although many of the benefits are available only to large investors. Financial intermediaries can take advantage of their size to realize *economies of scale*. Intermediaries bear information costs—seeking out information about the credit worthiness of borrowers and keeping abreast of the returns on various investment opportunities—and transaction costs—redeeming coupons on bonds, securing collateral for loans, and arranging legal work for contracts. Financial intermediaries spread these costs over a large number of customers and therefore reduce the cost per customer. Intermediaries pool resources and take advantage of large-scale investment opportunities for which individual savers could not qualify. In so doing, the intermediary has the potential to earn greater returns than those available to an individual.

The other economic benefit for financial intermediaries relates to *risk pooling*. Risk pooling applies to both the asset and liability sides of financial intermediaries' balance sheets. Financial intermediaries can take advantage of the law of large numbers to minimize the risks in both cases. This pooling process helps assure maximum capital gains on assets and interest rate returns on liabilities because losses are small in relation to total investments.

A small percentage of loans is always bad (not repaid). Individual investors gamble that their loans will not be among that percentage. According to probability theory, the outcome of one or a few events is uncertain, that is, a lender making only one loan would be relatively uncertain of repayment. By increasing the number of occurrences (loans), the outcomes (repayment) of the group of occurrences is more certain. Financial intermediaries take advantage of the law of large numbers in that they make many loans, gain greater certainty about the number of bad loans and spread the risk (or loss from the bad loans) among the many depositors.

The same principle applies to the intermediaries' liabilities (deposits). By attracting a large quantity of deposits, the intermediary reduces the probability that deposits will be withdrawn in such large numbers that the intermediary cannot meet the demand. If the probability of a deposit being withdrawn on a given day is 10 percent, then with two deposits the probability of both being withdrawn on the same day drops to 1 percent ($.10 \times .10$), and for three the probability drops to .1 percent ($.10 \times .10 \times .10$). By reducing the uncertainty of deposit withdrawals at any point in time through the law of large numbers, financial intermediaries are able to issue highly liquid liabilities (deposits) and guarantee the return on them, yet take on a high proportion of illiquid assets (loans) with uncertain returns.[1]

Risk and Risk Aversion

The law of large numbers helps financial intermediaries reduce uncertainty about deposit flows and loans. Risk still exists with financial intermediation, but individuals and financial institutions can avert the results of high-risk situations.

Three types of risk are associated with the financial intermediation process. *Default risk* applies to bad loans; the borrower simply does not repay the principal or the interest. If Chrysler Corporation had not turned around its profit potential, it would have defaulted on the loans granted to it by the Federal Government.

Market risk relates to the value of the asset. An asset such as corporate stock may decline in value. Those who bought oil drilling company stocks when oil prices were high immediately following the OPEC embargo saw the value of their purchases decline as the petroleum glut developed in the mid-1980s.[2] There is also *inflation risk* because price-level increases may reduce or even eliminate the purchasing power of the return on an asset. Individuals who redeemed U.S. savings bonds in 1982 after holding them to maturity found that the money they received purchased less than what they had invested 7½ years earlier.

---

[1] For a complete discussion of the laws of probability, especially the law of large numbers, see any statistics text, for example, William Mendenhall and Richard Scheaffer, *Mathematical Statistics with Applications* (Duxbury Press, 1973):243–48.

[2] With the increasing importance of financial futures, market risk is taking on new significance. Chapter 13 contains a discussion of the financial futures market and its implications for investors and financial firms.

Some individuals are risk seekers; most are *risk averse*.[3] To deal with an uncertain world and to minimize the risk associated with investments, individuals may apply the expected return criterion to alternative investment possibilities, or they may seek to diversify their investments.

The *expected return criterion* dictates that an individual consider the expected return and the probability of receiving that return for all investment alternatives. The expected return (E) is the sum of the possible returns (X) weighted by their respective probabilities (P):

$$E_{(x)} = P_1X_1 + P_2X_2 + P_3X_3 + \ldots + P_nX_n$$

Consider a situation where you can purchase one of two securities. Each costs the same and is supposed to pay $100 at maturity. Table 4.1 shows the probabilities for various possible returns for the two securities.

Given these probabilities the expected return for each security is figured as follows:

$$E_{(Associated)} = .5(100) + .3(75) + .2(0) = 72.5$$
$$E_{(Balanced)} = .6(100) + .4(25) + .0(0) = 70.0$$

The expected return test indicates that Associated Dog Food is the better investment; its expected return is higher than that for Balanced Computers. This investment strategy calls for an individual to place all the funds in the asset generating the greatest expected return. Such a strategy tends to reduce the uncertainty about investment alternatives.

Individuals who are risk averse may look more favorably upon a *diversified portfolio approach* to investment decision making. Notice that while the expected return for Associated Dog Food is greater than that for Balanced Computers, there is also a higher probability that the former will generate no return at all. A risk-averse individual may seek a variety of investments to avoid or minimize these kinds of risks.

Again the law of large numbers comes into play. Even though each of a number of investments has some risk associated with it, the larger the number of assets in the portfolio, the less the likelihood that all will fail. Thus, an individual concerned about inflation risk and uncertain about what will happen with the price level may choose some assets that will gain with a high rate of inflation and some that will lose under the same circumstances. By portfolio diversification, investors can reduce uncertainty without reducing expected returns. In so doing investors reduce the likelihood of large losses but they also forgo the likelihood of ..rge gains.

---

[3] Even individuals who are normally risk averse may be risk seekers in certain instances, for example, the appeal of a large payoff in a state lottery may attract purchasers despite the very high odds against any one individual winning the prize.

Associated Dog Food		Balanced Computers	
Probability	Return	Probability	Return
.5	100	.6	100
.3	75	.4	25
.2	0	.0	0

TABLE 4.1 *Probabilities for Returns*

Because they attract large numbers of deposits, financial intermediaries can generate a broadly diversified portfolio. In this way they offer depositors a way to minimize risk that individual investors could not achieve on their own.

Because they can take advantage of economies of scale and because they can minimize risk, financial intermediaries have grown and prospered.[4] The next section reviews the evolution of financial intermediaries.

Evolution of Financial Institutions

Intermediation takes place through a variety of types of financial institutions. The most dominant type of financial institution through most of history has been the commercial bank. Some form of banking dates from ancient times, but banks as we know them evolved from the activities of traders during the Middle Ages. Rather than transferring money in the trading process, traders used bills of exchange. The exporters drew up an agreement for the sale to the importer. The importer signed, indicating that the bill for the exchange was acceptable and promising to provide payment. The bill of exchange became a negotiable instrument that could be sold and resold before actually being presented for redemption in gold. Financial merchants during the Renaissance continued this practice of facilitating the transfer of funds.

The activities of traders highlight the process of facilitating trade by issuing pay authorizations. Although pay authorizations do facilitate trade, the process does not actually increase the quantity of the exchange medium.

---

[4] Chapter 15 discusses the problems that deregulation have created as financial institutions try to balance profitability and the minimization of risk.

We can identify the source of one of the major distinguishing characteristics of commercial banks, the deposit creation process, by looking at the origins of banking in England. Goldsmiths in England charged a fee to provide for the safe storage of gold and other valuables. Often these goldsmiths were called upon to transfer gold from one customer's account to another as a result of some commercial transaction. In so doing they performed a bookkeeping function—they facilitated trade in much the same way that the early merchants did. But the goldsmiths did more than just facilitate trade. Goldsmiths issued receipts for the gold deposited with them. These receipts came to circulate as part of the payment mechanism existing at the time. The receipts were, essentially, paper bank notes fully backed by the gold on deposit with the goldsmith. The innovation came when goldsmiths realized that not all the receipts they had issued in return for gold deposited with them would be presented for withdrawal at the same time. The goldsmiths could actually lend some of the gold on deposit by issuing additional payable-on-demand receipts. In so doing the goldsmiths performed a major function of commercial banks—they were creating money through deposit expansion.[5]

The gold on deposit with the goldsmiths, provided the reserves against which the "money" was created. The gold reserves represented but a fraction of the total receipts created. The fractional reserves system is an important characteristic of American commercial banking and the key element of the deposit expansion process.

Early Banking in the United States

Early banking activities in the United States revolved around trade and commerce. In colonial times there were no banks *per se*. Merchants often performed some banking functions by issuing bills of exchange, which circulated as currency. The first formal American bank was the Bank of North America, chartered in 1781 (a year earlier its forerunner, the Bank of Pennsylvania, had begun operations). The Bank of North America was created to help the Revolutionary War effort; it accepted deposits of specie or bank notes and issued its own notes. In 1784 the Bank of New York and the Bank of Massachusetts were chartered.

---

[5] Until other financial institutions were allowed to issue transactions accounts (demand deposits), only commercial banks could create money through deposit creation. Chapter 7 discusses the deposit creation process.

The chartering of a bank in the United States required special legislation by the colonial (subsequently state) government. The only banks created by federal actions in the years before the Civil War were the 1st Bank of the United States, granted a twenty-year charter in 1791, and the 2nd Bank of the United States, which existed from 1816 to 1836. These central banks are discussed in some detail in Chapter 16 which explores the Federal Reserve System.

The 1st Bank of the United States (BUS) established eight branches in major cities. It followed very conservative policies and exerted pressure on state banks to do the same (for example, holding more reserves and restricting loans). The BUS could enforce these policies by collecting and presenting for redemption large quantities of notes issued by the state bank. The opposition of state-chartered banks to the BUS was one factor in Congress' failure to renew the bank's charter in 1811.

With the restraining influence of the BUS removed, the number of banks in the nation increased. From 1811 to 1816 the number nearly tripled. The federal government's reliance on state banks to help finance the War of 1812 encouraged a rapid increase in note issues. The suspension of convertibility and resulting inflation were factors which led the Madison Administration to establish the 2nd BUS in 1816.

By 1800 the nation had 28 state-chartered banks; by 1830 there were 329. The controversy surrounding the rechartering of the 2nd Bank of the United States revolved around whether the federal government should place its deposits in a single bank and concentrate so much financial power in one institution. President Andrew Jackson, a champion of states' rights, opposed the 2nd BUS and acted to reduce its influence even before the Bank's charter expired in 1836. The recharter issue was a confrontation between the established Eastern monied interests and the "upstarts" from the Western frontier. Within this atmosphere, Michigan passed the first free banking act in 1837. New York passed similar legislation one year later. (See Banking Today 4.1. for discussion of a present-day central-bank criticism.)

From 1837 until 1863, the so-called Free Banking Era, eighteen states passed legislation which made the process of starting a commercial bank easier. The 2nd BUS had provided banking services through its twenty-five branches. States recognized that with the demise of the 2nd BUS, additional banks would be needed. Under free banking legislation, any group which met certain specific conditions relating to sufficiency of backing for bank notes and redeemability of notes on demand at face value could open a bank. The alternative meant establishing a special legislative charter, and this was often done only through intense lobbying and occasionally through bribery. The free-banking laws ushered in a rapid increase in the number of banks in the United States. In New York, for example, the total number of banks doubled in the three years following the adoption of a free-banking law. By

BANKING T⓸DAY

Critics Call for Curbing of the Central Bank

The call for the elimination of the United States central bank was not only heard in the 1830s. Periodically since the formation of the current central bank, the Federal Reserve, critics have argued for its elimination.

The calls for elimination of the central bank in the 1830s revolved around concerns with the power the bank exerted and the fear that it represented narrow, special interests. Today, concern with the Fed is more likely to stem from its conduct of monetary policy than with charges of special interests.

Criticism of the Federal Reserve is usually most noticeable during periods of economic problems. During the late 1970s and early 1980s, when inflation was creating havoc with the American economy, there were loud cries for elimination, or at least reform, of the Federal Reserve.

Unlike the 1st and 2nd Banks of the United States, our current central bank does not have a time limit on its charter. It is a creature of Congress and that legislative body could pass a law abolishing the Fed just as it passed one creating it. That is unlikely, but when the economy isn't functioning smoothly, especially when inflation is a severe problem, criticisms of the central bank are given consideration by legislators. Although it will probably never eliminate the Federal Reserve, Congress has considered limiting the Fed's independence. Some have forcefully suggested that the Fed should be directly subservient to the Office of the President. By limiting the ability of the Fed to oppose the president, all blame or praise for the performance of the economy would be more readily directed to the president.

Beyond the conventional arguments for reducing the independence of the Fed, there are "fringe" groups which lobby for complete elimination of the central bank. Such groups, usually with libertarian connections, oppose all types of centralized authority. Their campaigns usually do not receive much attention but they promote the evils of the central bank through mailings and by lobbying elected representatives.

1860, over 1500 banks were operating, a number double that at the time Michigan passed the first free banking law.[6]

Although this discussion has focused on commercial banks, other types of financial institutions existed as early as the nineteenth century. In 1816 the first mutual savings societies opened in Philadelphia and Boston. (Both the Philadelphia Saving Fund Society and the Provident Institution for Savings are still in existence today.) The depositors at mutual savings banks owned the institution started by the saving society. These mutual savings banks evolved largely because commercial banks dealt almost exclusively with commercial businesses; they did not see the advantage of dealing with the small savings of working class individuals. The savings banks were

---

[6] Free banking achieved its goal—a rapid increase in the number of banks—but critics often challenged the safety and durability of the newly created banks. For a discussion of these issues see Rockoff, Hugh, "The Free Banking Era: A Reexamination," *The Journal of Money, Credit and Banking 6* (May 1974): 141–67; and Arthur J. Rolnick and Warren E. Weber, "Free Banking, Wildcat Banking and Shinplasters," *Federal Reserve Bank of Minneapolis Quarterly Review* (Fall 1982):10–19.

intended as a safe repository for household savings. These institutions served the small saver as their names often indicate, for example, the Dime Savings Bank in New York City and Boston's Five Cents Savings. By 1907, 678 mutual savings banks operated, mostly in New England. Their numbers today are relatively small, less than 500 in seventeen different states.

In 1831 the first savings and loan association (S&L) opened. Initially S&Ls were formed as cooperative home financing institutions. The first S&L was the Oxford Provident Building Association in Philadelphia. After the Civil War, S&Ls expanded to attract deposits from nonmembers. Where they did, their numbers and deposits grew rapidly. By 1890 every state had S&Ls, and over 5000 existed in total. The Great Depression hit S&Ls particularly hard; they did not recover completely until after World War II. In the early years members deposited funds until the pool was large enough to finance construction of a member's home. Even today S&Ls are strongly oriented toward the home mortgage market.

Not until 1909 did the fourth type of financial institution, the credit union, begin. In that year St. Mary's Cooperative Credit Association was started in Manchester, New Hampshire. CUs are cooperative self-help thrift and loan societies whose members have a common bond (for example, place of employment, union membership). Credit union growth was slow until after World War II. Since the 1960s, credit unions have grown in number faster than any other financial institution.

From Free Banking to the National Banking Act

From the elimination of the 2nd BUS in 1836 until the passage of the National Bank Act in 1864, the country's monetary system was not controlled centrally. This free banking era created a precedent for large numbers of bank charters and, following that, the experience of widespread bank failures and often-resulting financial panics. With no centralized money system, the present American system with a recognizable currency was nonexistent. Instead, hundreds of types of bank notes circulated. Merchants and bankers needed a bank note circular to check the quality of notes (much like the credit card list department stores use to check for bad credit cards). Bank currency that was not of high quality (that is, currency with some risk of not being redeemed) was either not accepted as a payment instrument or was accepted only at a large discount. Significant numbers of unstable banks had an image of "fly-by-night" operations out to obtain quick deposits before closing shop and disappearing with depositors' funds. (These banks were often called wildcat banks.) Also during this period, many banks failed. For the most part, though, the failure of banks in the eighteen free-banking states was caused by the lack of diversified investment portfolios rather than the action of unscrupulous wildcat bankers.[7] Excessive creation of bank notes and unsound bank practices caused or aggravated financial panics during this period. (See Banking Today 4.2.)

The outbreak of the Civil War accentuated the shortcomings of a financial structure that lacked a unified currency system and allowed abuses in banking. The Treasury needed support in its finance of war efforts and legislators recognized the limitations of the existing banking system. As a result Congress passed the National Banking Act of 1864, an amended version of the 1863 National Currency Act. This legislation had far-reaching implications for the structure of American banking.

The National Banking Act created the position of Comptroller of the Currency, with responsibility for issuing national bank notes (a central, unified currency) through newly chartered national banks. Any group could obtain a national bank charter by meeting certain capital requirements. The Comptroller issued national bank notes in exchange for Treasury securities. Newly chartered national banks seeking securities as backing for their note issues provided a ready demand for the Treasury's bond issues, which were needed to support the war effort. The federal government encouraged the system by accepting national bank notes as payment for taxes and by using them to pay for goods and services.

The National Banking Act addressed some of the deficiencies in the banking system by establishing reserve requirements, setting capital requirements, and requiring bank examination by the Comptroller of the Currency.[8] Initially few banks applied for national charters because of the additional restrictions on national banks which would interfere with profitability. Legislation in 1865 encouraged an increase in applications for national bank charters.

Primarily to further encourage a central currency, in 1865 Congress adopted legislation which imposed a tax on state bank notes. This essentially drove state bank notes out of circulation, but since state-chartered banks could issue transactions accounts (checks), state-chartered banks were not themselves driven out of existence. The number of state-chartered banks did decrease. More than 700 banks shifted to national charters in 1865. National bank charters continued to increase for at least the next decade; within two years of the passage of the National Banking Act, state banks totaled 325 and national banks 1612. But, the dual banking structure of state

---

[7] See Rolnick and Weber as cited in footnote 6.
[8] The precise requirement depended on whether the bank was in a major urban area, a smaller city, or in a rural community. The Act also established three classes of banks—central reserve city banks, which served as central repositories for funds; reserve city banks, which served as repositories and provided services to small banks, and country banks. The required reserve ratios imposed on banks varied depending on which class a bank fit into.

BANKING TODAY 4.2

Commercial Bank Notes—
A Solution for Inflation

During the nineteenth century, commercial banks printed and circulated their own bank notes. In smaller communities only one or two banks existed and the different kinds of bank notes were limited. In larger towns, or in small ones close to cities, the number and kinds of bank notes were quite extensive.

Bank notes were accepted as currency only as long as people had confidence that they were either redeemable for gold or silver or that they were easily circulated for purchases. To check on the credibility of bank notes, bankers and merchants subscribed to a Bank Note Circular which listed bank notes by quality. High quality notes were acceptable at face value; lesser quality notes were discounted.

Today some have suggested that we return to commercial bank notes rather than Federal Reserve notes as the circulating currency. The notion behind this suggestion is that, if a currency's value depends on its acceptability, commercial banks, unlike the Treasury, will not debase the currency by printing too much money.

What do you think of the idea?

Source: Bank note from "Money, Banking, and the Federal Reserve," Federal Reserve Bank of Minneapolis Instructional Unit (1982). Included courtesy of Federal Reserve Bank of Minneapolis.

and national banks was in place to stay. Although it created some regulatory problems (discussed in the next chapter), the structure was never seriously threatened. In fact, state-chartered banks made a comeback as the turn of the century approached, and by 1910 the number of state banks once again surpassed that of the national banks.

The National Banking Act did create a central currency. The state-bank note tax ended the confusion caused by having hundreds of different currencies. The Federal Government backed national bank notes. They had the confidence of the public. From 1879, when the United States restored the specie payments that had been suspended during the Civil War, until 1933, the United States functioned on a metallic-based single currency system. People could redeem paper money for specie, that is, gold or silver.[9]

Despite a unified currency and the redeemability of paper money for specie, the financial system continued to have problems. Prices declined throughout the 1880s and 1890s primarily because the supply of money did

---

[9] For all intents and purposes, the United States was on a gold standard during this period. Silver did not circulate largely because it was undervalued.

not keep pace with the increased demand fostered by economic expansion. This created hardships for debtors and for agriculture interests. During the latter part of the nineteenth century, the country experienced continual bank panics, some of which were serious enough to precipitate economic recessions. Bank panics resulted not so much from unsound bank practices as from an inelastic currency system.

The financial panics of 1873, 1884, 1893, and 1907 resulted largely from the unresponsiveness of the financial system to demands for credit. Money deposited in rural banks flowed to reserve city banks to take advantage of higher interest-earning opportunities. Funds from communities throughout the Midwest were drawn to the East coast money centers. When people in the Midwest heavily demanded funds, the system could not rapidly return monies to these communities. The fractional reserve system is based on the premise that not all depositors will demand their funds simultaneously. Depositors, hearing that a bank was slow in responding to a withdrawal request, would panic. Runs on banks followed. The system could not respond and banks closed their doors to buy time to call in loans; a contractionary process began.

A dramatic expansion of the number of commercial banks and total bank assets accompanied the tremendous growth of the American economy during the late nineteenth century. Table 4.2 illustrates this point.

A multiple banking system was evolving. Not only did the United States have state and national banks, but the number of small banks and the growth of large banks increased. Population shifts to the expanding Midwest and the need for large sums of money to finance America's industrial growth precipitated evolution of the multiple banking system. By 1900, 7,000 American towns had banks; the large majority of these communities had a population of less than 2500. At the same time the major New York banks were growing rapidly. Only six banks in 1900 had more than $50 million of loans and securities; by 1920 over seventy were in this category.

With this expansion, more of the economy became integrated through capital markets and financial institutions. Thus, without the benefits of a regulated, insured banking system, a bank panic in one part of the country could spread rapidly and produce serious deleterious consequences.

	1867	1880	1900
Banks	1908	2696	8100
Bank Assets ($ millions)	1494	2390	6700

Source: Historical Statistics of the United States, U.S. Government Printing Office, 1975.

TABLE 4.2 *Expansion of Commercial Banks*

The most serious bank panic occurred in 1907. Gold outflows, caused by an imbalance in the country's foreign trade account, prevented New York banks from meeting withdrawal demands. Many banks closed and some failed. Although the crisis was short in duration, it was severe. The crisis focused attention on the remaining deficiencies in the monetary structure created with the National Banking Act forty-three years earlier. As a result of this crisis, Congress created the National Monetary Commission to investigate the causes of the financial crisis and to recommend a way to eliminate the problems. The Commission recommended the formation of a central banking structure, the Federal Reserve System, which Chapter 16 describes.

Structure of Banking Since the Federal Reserve

The creation of the Federal Reserve System did not alter dramatically the structure of commercial banking in the United States. It did establish a mechanism to bring bank behavior and operations more fully into the sphere of influence of a central monetary authority. Supervision and regulation applied to all national banks, which were required to join the system, and to state banks, which chose to join the system. Federal Reserve monetary actions affected all banks. The Panic of 1907 and subsequent events reflected struggles within the banking industry that influenced the structure of the industry and resulted in formation of the Federal Reserve System.

Unit versus Branch Banking   The problems associated with financial panics prompted some states to create state-sponsored deposit guarantee funds. This response was due in part to the country-wide conflict between the unit and branch banking systems. *Unit banking* refers to each commercial bank being restricted to one facility. Banks cannot have branches or satellite banks. *Branch banking* allows a banking operation to open multiple offices.

Under the National Banking System, branch banking was relatively unimportant. After 1910, branch banking began to expand as more states allowed some form of branching. This was in response in part to a need states had for more security for depositors. Some unit banking states had tried to provide security through deposit insurance.[10] State insurance systems were doomed to failure. They allowed banks to substitute state insurance for their own careful avoidance of risky investments. Their success was predicated on

---

[10] Kansas, Mississippi, Nebraska, North Dakota, Oklahoma, South Dakota, Texas, and Washington all established some form of deposit insurance.

a healthy economy. When regional recessions occurred, the state system could not survive. By 1930 virtually all commercial bank state deposit insurance systems were abolished.

Unable to safeguard deposits through deposit insurance, more states reduced restrictions on branch banking. Branching was attractive because it allowed banks to realize some of the benefits of economies of scale. Many people put forth the argument that the consolidation of administrative duties, the opportunities for enhanced returns occasioned by larger deposit pools, and broader loan opportunities allowed branch banks to realize a fair return for two reasons. These were, first, a lower operating cost to deposit ratio and, second, avoidance of investments that were associated with many high interest opportunities. In 1909, 9 states and territories allowed branching, 4 provided for limited branching, and 35 prohibited branch banking. By 1980, 14 states allowed statewide branching, another 22 provided for limited branching, and only 14 states prohibited branch banking. The barriers to branching continue to decline.

The concerns about branch banking during the early part of the century eased somewhat in the post–World War II era, but some resistance continues. The major concern regarding branch banking always has been that branching would eliminate smaller, locally controlled banks while allowing major institutions to dominate.[11]

Consolidation and Failures   During the 1920s, bank assets continued to rise, while the number of banks in America declined. See Table 4.3. The decline resulted from suspensions and liquidations as well as from consolidations and absorptions. From 1921 to 1929 nearly 4000 banks merged. During this period 5400 banks suspended operations and over 4000 never reopened.

---

[11] This issue is addressed in the contemporary context in Chapters 14 and 15.

	1914	1920	1929
# of banks	25,510	29,086	24,504
% national	29.5	27.5	30.7
% state	70.5	72.5	69.3
Deposits ($ millions)	17,390	36,114	49,035

TABLE 4.3   *Banking Consolidations*

The number of banks in America declined from a maximum number around 30,000 to less than 24,000 at the onset of the Great Depression.

Although the formation of the Federal Reserve was played out against the backdrop of changes in American banking and by itself did not cause widespread changes, the depression was responsible for dramatic changes on the financial scene. The stock market crash in October, 1929, did not cause immediate widespread bank panics, but within a year bank panics did begin to occur, aggravated by a sharp economic decline. More than 500 banks failed by the early months of 1931. Although the rate of failures slowed somewhat later in 1931, bank failures were widespread again during 1932.

Almost immediately after taking office, Franklin Roosevelt declared a bank holiday; all banks closed until examiners could certify them as solvent. (See Banking Today 4.3.) Although most banks reopened, significant changes did occur. Between 1929 and 1933, the number of banks in the United States was cut almost in half to a total of about 14,700. In all, almost 9800 banks failed during this period, while other reductions occurred due to consolidation. Figure 4.1, on page 103, shows how unusual this period was in terms of the number of bank failures. Over the next few years New Deal legislation brought dramatic changes in the structure of the American financial system. The Banking Acts of 1933 and 1935 included far-reaching reforms. These reforms did the following:

- Resulted in the formation of the Federal Deposit Insurance Corporation.
- Separated investment banking (securities underwriting) from commercial banking.
- Prohibited interest payments on demand deposits.
- Created interest payment ceilings on savings and time deposits (what came to be Regulation Q).
- Eased restrictions on branch banking.

A concern about the need for safety and soundness in the banking system dominated the thinking of reformers over the next few decades. Those who had been adversely affected by the banking failures of the late 1920s and early 1930s influenced legislation that affected the structure of American banking for years into the future, definitely until the historic Depository Institutions Deregulation and Monetary Control Act of 1980.[12]

---

[12] The exceptions to the relatively unchanging legal structure for banking were the Bank Holding Company Act of 1956 and the amendments to that act passed in 1970. This legislation is discussed in terms of government regulation in Chapter 6.

Chapter 13 will examine the scope and structure of the financial industry in the post–World War II period. At this point you need only understand how American financial institutions evolved. You should keep several issues in mind as you move on to discussion of specific types of American financial institutions. First, throughout most of American history, competition has not existed between various types of financial institutions; they tended to attract different customers and to provide different services.

BANKING T⁴·³DAY   What's a Bank Holiday?

In 1932, just after taking office, President Roosevelt declared a national bank holiday. In March 1985 Ohio Governor Richard Celeste declared a bank holiday for seventy state-chartered savings and loan associations in his state. *Bank holiday* is a euphemism for temporary bank closing; the institutions' doors are shut and customers have no access to their deposits.

Both President Roosevelt and Governor Celeste took the action because public confidence had dropped so low that depositors were withdrawing their funds in near-panic proportions. Depository institutions cannot withstand massive withdrawals. A bank holiday is intended to halt withdrawals and give officials time to develop a strategy to salvage as many of the troubled depository institutions as possible.

In 1932 all banks across the country were closed until regulatory officials could certify them safe. In Ohio in 1985 the failure of a Cincinnati S&L threatened to exhaust the reserves of the Ohio deposit insurance program, the Ohio Deposit Guarantee Fund (Ohio was one of the state's with a state rather than a national deposit insurance program). Ohio officials needed time to work out arrangements to guarantee deposits either through federal assist-

Ohio S&L failure triggered runs at other associations backed by a state-regulated fund.

ance or through mergers of failing S&Ls with more stable institutions. The bank holiday gave them that time.

Bank holidays are serious business not just to the customers of the closed institutions but to financial markets in general. The closing of seventy Savings and Loans in a nation with over 20,000 depository institutions may seem like nothing more than a local news story. Despite such appearances financial markets

worldwide reacted to Governor Celeste's action by selling off some of their dollar holdings, thereby lowering (temporarily at least) the value of the dollar in international trade.

Source: Photo from G. Mathieson/ Sygma.

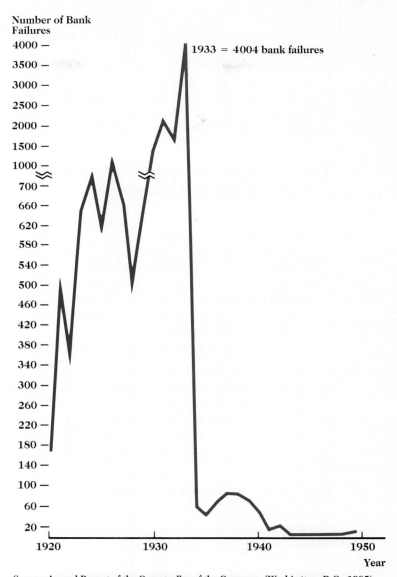

Number of Bank
Failures

1933 = 4004 bank failures

4000 —
3500 —
3000 —
2500 —
2000 —
1500 —
1000 —
700 —
660 —
620 —
580 —
540 —
500 —
460 —
420 —
380 —
340 —
300 —
260 —
220 —
180 —
140 —
100 —
60 —
20 —

1920   1930   1940   1950

Year

Source: Annual Report of the Comptroller of the Currency, (Washington, D.C., 1985).

FIGURE 4.1   *Number of Bank Failures, 1920–1950*   Beginning in 1929, and at an escalating rate during the first few years of the Great Depression, the number of bank failures was well above the rates of the previous years. After President Roosevelt's bank holiday, the number of failures declined, and in the years following the New Deal banking legislation, bank failures became very unusual.

Second, almost from the beginning of banking in the United States, a very large number of small banks have existed at the same time that a few large banks have grown to dominate the marketplace. Third, numerous financial panics in the nineteenth century and especially the Great Depression of the 1930s caused concerns about safety and liquidity; those concerns resulted in strict regulations on the behavior of financial institutions. Remember these points as you consider the types of American financial institutions described in the next section and commercial bank behavior described in Chapter 5.

Types of Financial Institutions

Commercial banks have had the greatest impact on the financial sector for most of United States history. Other types of financial institutions have come to play an increasingly important role in the country's financial structure. With the deregulation of financial services, begun most significantly with the 1980 Depository Institutions Deregulation and Monetary Control Act, the financial industry has become more of a free market. Understanding types of financial institutions is critical to understanding the financial industry, and current changes within it.

Four types of financial institutions are the following:

1. *Depository institutions*, including commercial banks, savings and loan associations, mutual savings banks, and credit unions.
2. *Contractual institutions*, made up of insurance companies and private and government pension funds.
3. *Investment companies*, consisting of closed-end and open-end investment firms such as money market mutual funds.
4. *Finance companies*, including commercial companies, mortgage companies, personal finance companies, and sales finance companies.

Table 4.4 illustrates the relative size of these types of financial institutions (using assets as the basis for comparison) and shows how their relative sizes have changed.

Depository Institutions

Depository institutions accept the savings of surplus units in the form of deposit accounts and then make loans using these deposits. Depository institutions' liabilities (deposits) take the form of savings accounts, time

| | 1950 | | 1960 | | 1985 | |
	$ billions	%	$ billions	%	$ billions	%
Commercial Banks	168.9	(56.7)	257.6	(43.1)	1,951	(35.8)
Savings & Loans	16.9	(5.7)	71.5	(12.0)	988	(18.2)
Life Insurance Cos.	64.0	(21.5)	119.6	(20.0)	694	(12.7)
Credit Unions	1.0	(0.3)	5.7	(1.0)	116	(2.1)
Private Pension Fund	7.1	(2.3)	38.1	(6.4)	634	(11.6)
Gov't. Employee Pensions	4.9	(1.6)	19.7	(3.3)	355	(6.5)
Finance Companies	9.3	(3.1)	27.6	(4.6)	292	(5.4)
Mutual Savings Banks	22.4	(7.5)	40.6	(6.8)	206	(3.8)
Investment Cos.	3.3	(1.1)	17.0	(2.8)	n.a.	—
Money Market Mutual Funds*	—	—	—	—	210	(3.9)

* The first money-market mutual-funds were established in 1971.

TABLE 4.4 *Relative Asset Size of Financial Institutions*

deposit accounts, certificates of deposit and transactions accounts (from which the depositor can withdraw cash on demand or make payment to a third party). There are four types of depository institutions: commercial banks, savings and loan associations, mutual savings banks, and credit unions.

Commercial Banks Commercial banks are the largest (in terms of assets) and the most diversified (in terms of services) type of financial institution. Chartered by the federal or state government, commercial banks accept savings, time, and demand deposits and other checkable deposits such as NOW and ATS accounts. There are over 14,000 commercial banks in the United States. The state's banking commissioner charters state banks and the Comptroller of the Currency supervises federally chartered banks.

Savings and Loan Associations Savings and loan associations accept deposits much like commercial banks. They can offer transactions accounts similar to commercial banks as well as other depository accounts. Historically savings and loan associations have been oriented toward the mortgage market for their assets. S&Ls primarily have dealt with long-term investments (20- or 30-year mortgages). The number of S&Ls grew slowly until the post–World War II housing boom began. Until the deregulation of financial services legislation provided S&Ls with greater flexibility, their well-being was tied to the level of activity in the construction industry. Approximately 2000 federally chartered S&Ls are regulated by the Federal Home Loan Bank Board and over 2500 state-chartered associations are supervised by state banking commissioners.

Mutual Savings Banks   Mutual savings banks are small in number (less than 500) and are located predominately in the states of New York, Massachusetts, and Connecticut. Designed to encourage savings by laborers, mutual savings banks have most of their assets in mortgages (about 66 percent) and in government and corporate bonds (about 20 percent). Mutual savings banks offer savings accounts and time deposits, and have recently offered NOW accounts. Historically states have chartered mutual savings banks (state banking authorities regulated them), but recent legislation allows these institutions to obtain federal charters.

Credit Unions   Credit unions are the fastest growing type of depository institutions. CUs are nonprofit cooperatives that pool the savings of members and make loans only to members. Credit unions are organized such that all members have a common bond, usually occupational, but sometimes fraternal. CUs accept savings and time deposits and now offer share drafts, which make interest bearing accounts into transactions accounts. The number of credit unions has risen to more than 20,000. CUs are chartered by either the federal government (in which case they are regulated by the National Credit Union Administration) or by state governments.

Contractual Institutions

Insurance companies (life, property, and casualty) and private and government employee pension funds receive a regular flow of funds from insurance premiums or from pension plan payments. By using actuarial tables these institutions can accurately predict the outflow of funds for death, property damage, injury, or retirement. A contract between the financial institution and the customer dictates payment and repayment arrangements.

Insurance Companies   Insurance companies accumulate funds from premiums. The insurance company agrees to absorb the risk of uncertainty from death, property damage or liability. By pooling resources from many policyholders and by spreading the cost of unexpected events out over a long period of time, insurance companies can provide financial security in the event of an untimely death, or "cover the losses" of the small number of policyholders who incur unexpected financial disaster.

Insurance companies are organized as either stock companies or mutual companies; the only significant difference is that mutual companies are owned by the policyholders. Approximately 2000 life insurance companies and over 3000 casualty insurance companies do business in the United States today. But life insurance companies dominate the industry in terms of assets.

Insurance companies invest their funds in long-term assets such as corporate bonds and mortgages—residential and especially commercial. Policyholders may also borrow against their insurance policies. The total amount of insurance in force has risen substantially over the years so that now the annual increase is more than $6 billion.

Pension Funds   Pension funds are designed to provide a vehicle for individuals to save for retirement. Since New Deal legislation created the Social Security system, the government has provided basic retirement income. Supplemental retirement plans have become increasingly popular, especially in light of the concern that the Social Security system may be in financial difficulty. In most cases pension funds are employer-sponsored, either by private employers or by the local, state, or federal government. The employer contribution to the employees' retirement account is part of the overall wage package (according to a 1949 Supreme Court ruling these contributions are viewed as deferred wages). Employees may use salary or wages to augment the employers' contributions; these augmented funds are usually not considered taxable income until the worker actually receives the funds at retirement. The number of workers covered by private pension plans has increased from 9.8 million in 1950 to almost 45 million in 1986.[13] Government pension funds, by local, state and federal employers, have also grown dramatically. Over 2000 separate plans with assets in excess of $275 billion currently exist. By the end of 1984 the total of individuals' "investments" in insurance and pension funds was roughly comparable to their time and savings deposits.

Pension plans are usually administered by a bank trust department or by a life insurance company. Since the number of workers involved in pension plans has increased faster than the number of retired workers, pension funds have revenue inflows well in excess of outflows.[14] The

---

[13] Beginning in 1962, self-employed individuals were able to contribute tax-deferred funds to a retirement plan, the so-called Keogh Plan; beginning in 1983, even workers covered by employer pension plans were allowed to contribute up to $2000 per year as tax-deferred funds to individual retirement accounts (IRAs). The tax-deferred nature of IRAs was eliminated for most taxpayers by the 1986 tax reform legislation.

[14] This situation is in contrast to the plight of the Social Security system where increasing benefits to recipients placed the system's continuation in jeopardy. A plan to revitalize the system was signed into law in March, 1983.

schedule of workers retiring is well established, so pension fund managers have a good idea of when and how many funds are needed in any period of time. These factors have influenced pension fund managers to invest in long-term assets, mainly corporate stocks and bonds.

Investment Companies

Investment companies are nondepository institutions. They raise money by selling stocks through brokers or issuing small denomination securities to individuals. Companies pool and invest the funds in a diversified portfolio of assets. Investment companies offer economies of scale, management expertise, diversification of risk, and the opportunity for divisible liabilities with competitive rates of return.

Closed-End Investment Companies   Closed-end investment companies sell stocks through brokers or investment bankers. They do not offer to buy back their stocks. Individuals hold the stocks to earn a return.

Open-End Investment Companies   Open-end investment companies sell shares to the public on a regular basis and offer to redeem the shares on demand. This type of investment company is called a *mutual fund*. The most visible and popular type of open-end investment company is the *money market mutual fund*. Since the mid-1970s the number of shares in money market mutual funds has risen dramatically (see Figure 4.2).[15]

The money accumulated through a mutual fund is invested in a variety of short-term assets—government securities, large denomination commercial bank certificates of deposit, and short-term business debts. Money-market mutual-funds gained popularity when the rate of interest offered to shareholders greatly exceeded what depositors could earn at other financial institutions; this was because of the ceiling on deposit account interest payments that existed until the early 1980s. When the money-market mutual-funds began to offer a high degree of liquidity, allowing shareholders to cash in shares and to write checks, individuals flocked to these high-yield investment alternatives even though their shares were usually not insured the way deposits are at depository institutions.

---

[15] The decline in MMMFs resulted from the removal of interest rate ceilings on other depository accounts.

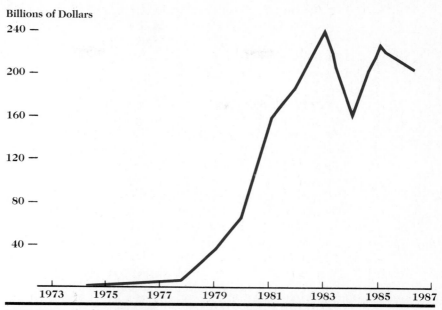

Billions of Dollars

FIGURE 4.2 *Growth of Money Market Mutual Fund Balances* With the accelerating interest rates of the late 1970s and early 1980s, a new financial instrument became very popular. Money-market mutual-funds were originally offered by non-bank financial institutions, aggravating the disintermediation process. As interest rates moderated and depository institutions were able to offer market interest rates on deposits, the rapid growth of these money-market funds slowed considerably.

Finance Companies

Finance companies are usually oriented toward a specific function. Four basic types are described below. In each case the finance company raises money by borrowing, usually by issuing its own commercial paper, but also with long-term bonds or by securing bank loans. The company then lends these funds.

Business and Commercial Finance Companies Business and commercial finance companies make loans to business firms in some cases using the firm's accounts receivable as a type of collateral. In other cases these finance companies may actually purchase the firm's accounts, for a discount of course, and service them until the loans are repaid.

Mortgage Companies   Mortgage companies concentrate on financing and servicing mortgages. The mortgages these firms issue are often sold to another institution (such as the Federal National Mortgage Association, or "Fanny Mae") to be held. In either case the mortgage company will continue to service the loan.

Personal Finance Companies   Personal finance companies make small consumer loans. Individuals are attracted to finance companies because of the relative ease of securing the loan. But, since the costs of servicing small loans are very substantial, interest rates charged by personal finance companies are high.

Sales Finance Companies   Sales finance companies are probably familiar to anyone who has thought about purchasing an automobile or a consumer appliance. Sales finance companies are usually associated with a retail outlet and make loans to faciliate product sales. Customers are able to repay the loans through installment plans. The General Motors Acceptance Corporation (GMAC) is one of the largest sales finance companies. Most department store credit is actually offered through a sales finance company, which is either part of the company owning the department store or which has worked out an agreement to offer credit in the name of the store.

Chapter Conclusion

United States financial institutions have gone through a continuous evolution. The instability of the financial system climaxed in the Panic of 1907 and the Great Depression of the 1930s. The Panic of 1907 resulted in the formation of our central bank, the Federal Reserve System. The Great Depression produced far-reaching legislation that dictated the structure and prescribed the rules of the game for the financial industry for four decades.

The basic structure of the industry provided for clear distinctions between the types of financial institutions, while at the same time it tended to dictate operating guidelines for these institutions. You should understand how financial institutions evolved and the distinguishing features of those institutions. Now you are prepared to look more closely at the behavior of the major types of financial institutions, commercial banks, and to analyze the structure, performance, and regulation of financial institutions.

Consider These Questions

1. What are the benefits of intermediation?
2. Banking is often described as the "grease" which allows the wheels of commerce to turn smoothly. Explain this statement.

3. In the early 1980s there was a popular television program, *Mork and Mindy*. As a visitor from another planet, Mork couldn't understand why he should give the local bank his hard-earned money in return for a book of apparently worthless checks. How would you have advised Mindy to handle this problem?

4. What role does risk play in the intermediation process? How can intermediaries reduce the risks for its customers?

5. How can you explain the evolution of four distinct types of depository institutions in this country?

6. How was the United States able to exist for so long without a central bank?

7. Why did this distinction between unit and branch banking develop? What is the impact of these alternative systems?

8. What might explain the increase in relative asset size of savings and loan associations in the post–World War II period?

9. Distinguish between depository institutions and the other type of financial institutions. Do they compete in the same market?

10. What explains the rapid rise of money-market mutual-funds?

11. With the increasing competition among financial intermediaries, does an institution's name mean anything in the marketplace? For example, is there any advantage or disadvantage in a name such as the Third Second National Bank as opposed to the First National Bank?

Suggestions for Further Reading

Aspinwall, Richard A. and Robert A. Eisenbeis, eds. *The Banking Handbook.* New York: John Wiley and Sons, 1985.
> Excellent reference source on banks, banking and the role of intermediaries.

Block, Robert P. and Doris E. Harless. *Non-bank Financial Institutions.* Federal Reserve Bank of Richmond, 1975.
> Takes a close look at the various types of financial intermediaries.

Gurley, John G. and Edward S. Shaw. *Money in a Theory of Finance.* Washington, D.C.: The Brookings Institution, 1960.
> Laid groundwork for a theoretical understanding of the role of financial intermediaries in an expanding economy.

Hammond, Bray. *Banks and Politics in America From the Revolution to the Civil War.* Princeton, N.J.: Princeton University Press, 1957.
> Although thirty years old, this is still the best history of pre–Civil War banking.

Krooss, Herman E. and Martin R. Blyn. *A History of Financial Intermediaries.* New York: Random House, 1971.

Another good book by Krooss. This one focuses more on the evolution of financial institutions.

Studenski, Paul and Herman E. Krooss. *Financial History of the United States*. New York: McGraw-Hill, 1963.
Weaves evolution of banking system into a general discussion of United States economic growth. Chapters 16, 21, and 28 are particularly appropriate.

CHAPTER FIVE

COMMERCIAL BANK BEHAVIOR

Neither a borrower nor a lender be;
For loan oft loses both itself and friend;
And borrowing dulls the edge of husbandry.

William Shakespeare, Hamlet

After looking in the last chapter at the evolution of financial intermediaries, we can now turn our attention to the functions of financial intermediaries. This chapter focuses on the behavior of commercial banks. Since commercial banks are the largest type of depository institution, and because historically commercial banks have performed the full range of services available at depository institutions, they merit very careful review. By looking closely at commercial banks, we will be in a position to understand how bank behavior has influenced the operation of other types of financial institutions and to observe how commercial bank behavior has changed over time.

Chapter Objectives

Later in this text (Chapters 13–15), we will analyze the entire financial industry. You will find it helpful at that time to understand how particular firms within the industry operate. Chapter 5 attempts to provide an understanding of the behavior of one type of firm, the commercial bank. Throughout the chapter you should think about the commercial bank in much the way you would any other business firm.

When you understand what motivates commercial bank behavior, you will be able to:

- Describe what prompts individuals to use entrepreneurial talents to organize and run a financial firm.
- Explain why managers of financial institutions need to consider liquidity and solvency.
- Decide whether high-profit margins are sufficient to insure the success of a bank or a savings and loan.

After gaining some insight into the factors which motivate commercial bank behavior, you will be ready to examine tools of a depository institution, its assets and liabilities. Analysis of commercial bank balance sheets requires you to:

- Identify the sources and uses of funds available to a bank manager.
- Describe changes in the composition of assets and liabilities.
- Explain how a bank manager uses assets and liabilities to make the bank profitable.

You should step back from the operation of a single commercial bank and consider the theories that explain bank behavior in general. In analyzing theories of bank behavior, you will be able to:

- Describe the traditional theories of bank management.
- Explain how these theories have changed and the possible reasons for these changes.
- Describe the difference between asset management and liability management.
- Explain why the contemporary marketplace requires attention to discretionary funds management.

Finally, you should also analyze the newest management theories so you can:

- Describe implications of the new management theories.
- Assess the effects of the new management theories on firms.

Keep in mind that this chapter is followed by one on the structure of banking. You will need to combine the information on bank behavior with that on the structure of banking in order to gain a complete picture of bank operations.

Financial Institutions as Firms

In previous chapters you gained insights into the benefits of financial intermediation from the viewpoint of the economy as a whole in terms of borrowers and lenders. But these discussions have only alluded to the motivation behind the formation of financial intermediaries from the point of view of the business people involved. It is time to look more closely at why financial firms exist within the private sector of our economy.

Financial intermediaries are formed as profit-making operations.[1] They have the same basic goal as all business organizations. Financial intermediaries attempt to maximize profits over time by generating more revenue than it costs to acquire funds and to operate their facilities. (Revenue in this case is essentially interest income and service charges, while banks pay to acquire funds by interest payments on deposits.) Financial intermediaries face the challenge of achieving profitability without abandoning the need for liquidity and solvency.

Liquidity refers to a financial institution's ability to meet withdrawal and loan requests, virtually on demand. *Solvency* refers to the need for a financial institution to be sure that liabilities do not exceed assets. Profitability, liquidity, and solvency are related. For example, the temporary closing of seventy-one Ohio savings and loans in early 1985 was prompted by liquidity problems (too many despositors trying to withdraw funds) resulting from concern over the solvency of one particular institution, Home State Savings Bank of Cincinnati. Home Savings absorbed tremendous losses when a government securities firm failed. These losses resulted in insolvency for Home Savings and caused a liquidity crisis for S&Ls doing business with Home Savings.

Add one more factor to the dilemma facing financial firms—risk. Financial institutions cannot risk losses on investments and/or loans for fear of a loss of customer (depositor) confidence even if the losses do not actually threaten the firm's solvency. Depositors need to feel secure in the knowledge that their funds are safe. Although only Home Savings was in trouble because of risky investments, depositors' lack of confidence in other S&Ls threatened their operations.

Financial firms need to make trade-offs between profitability, liquidity, and risk. While a bank or a savings and loan wants to maintain a highly

---

[1] Strictly speaking, among the depository institutions only commercial banks, savings and loans, and mutual savings banks are profit-making operations. Credit unions are cooperatives and maintain the position of nonprofit organizations.

liquid position, such a position costs the firm the opportunity to generate additional income through loans or investments. Banks or savings and loans can avoid investment or loan opportunities that carry any appreciable risk, but in so doing they forgo many reasonably secure investments and reduce their profit-making potential. A bank or savings and loan must balance profits against liquidity and risk but must achieve sufficient profits to maintain solvency and to attract investors.

All depository institutions are faced with the additional challenge of extensive regulations and controls of the type that do not "burden" other profit-seeking firms. In the last chapter we referred to the concern for safety, which was incorporated in legislation affecting the historical development of commercial banks. In the next chapter we will explore the regulatory structure which affects all depository institutions. In thinking about financial institutions as firms, consider as an example that commercial banks:

- are subject to minimum capital and reserve requirements.
- must allow withdrawals on demand (for demand deposits), virtually upon notice for time deposits, and upon maturity for savings deposits.
- are constrained regarding certain non-banking financial activities (for example, securities underwriting) and all non-banking activities.
- are restricted in the types and, in some instances, the sizes of loans they can make.

Thus the need to balance profits and risk with liquidity and solvency and the need to consider the various regulations force commercial banks, savings and loan associations, mutual savings banks, and credit unions into a position that is quite different from other profit-seeking firms.

Bank Balance Sheet

Looking at the components of a commercial bank balance sheet provides some insight into how financial institutions deal with the dilemma of profitability versus liquidity and safety. As with all firms, a bank's assets must equal its liabilities plus its net worth. A bank's goal is to acquire funds it can use to generate income by making loans and investments.

A bank's sources of funds include *deposits* (transactions accounts, savings accounts, and time accounts), *other liabilities* (for example, borrowing from other banks or the Federal Reserve), and its *net worth* (the capital invested in the operation by its owners). A bank has a number of uses for its funds. These include *cash assets* (for example, vault cash, deposits at the Federal Reserve), *loans* (business, real estate, and consumer), *financial in-*

vestments (securities issued by governments and government agencies), and *other assets* (for example, bank buildings and land).

Table 5.1 shows a simplified version of the combined balance sheet for all American insured commercial banks. Notice that time-accounts represent the single largest source of funds and that loans are banks' most significant use of funds. Notice also that the combined assets of American commercial banks exceed $2 trillion.

Looking more closely at the components of a commercial bank balance sheet gives a clearer picture of a bank's sources and uses of funds. Keep in mind that while bank balance sheets often look similar, not all banks behave alike. Banks give differing attention to various types of activities. For example, a major metropolitan bank will keep a small percentage of deposits as vault cash, while a small rural bank will hold a much larger percentage of deposits as vault cash. This difference is related to the time required for delivery of cash.

Sources of Bank Funds

Transaction Accounts or Demand Deposits Transaction accounts are deposited funds held by a bank which depositors can draw upon for cash transactions. Until financial reforms expanded these accounts, they were referred to as demand deposits. Individuals, firms, nonprofit organizations, and government agencies all hold demand deposits at banks. Depositors may immediately withdraw or transfer funds from transaction accounts. As shown

	12/31/80		12/31/82		12/31/85	
	$ billions	*%*	*$ billions*	*%*	*$ billions*	*%*
Assets						
Cash	202	13	207	11	181	8
Securities	526	35	373	20	459	20
Loans & related assets	811	52	1281	69	1629	72
TOTAL ASSETS	1539		1861		2269	
Liabilities & Net Worth						
Transaction Accounts	432	28	453	24	484	21
Savings Accounts	201	13	220	12	453	20
Time Accounts	559	37	1060	57	752	33
Other Liabilities	233	15	—	—	416	18
TOTAL LIABILITIES	1452		1733		2105	
NET WORTH	114	7	128	7	164	7
TOTAL LIABILITIES + NET WORTH	1539		1861		2269	

TABLE 5.1   Combined Balance Sheet for Insured Commercial Banks in the United States

BANKING T●DAY 5.1

The Trick to Banking Success

In his book on commercial bank management, Joseph Sinkey identifies five critical factors which will determine the level of success depository institutions will achieve in the deregulated environment. He incorporates these into the acronym TRICK.

T = TECHNOLOGY—the ability of firms to adapt to technology and use it to expand markets and increase productivity

R = REREGULATION— the extent to which the competitive, deregulated environment will give way to a renewed government presence

I = INTEREST RATE RISK—the degree to which firms can manage risk

C = CUSTOMERS—the ability of firms to keep existing customers and attract new ones

K = KAPITAL ADE- QUACY—the extent to which firms can maintain and expand kapital.

Sinkey says that TRICK represents the key factors which will determine the survival and prosperity of financial firms.

Source: Adapted with permission of Macmillan Publishing Company from *Commercial Bank Financial Management: In the Financial-Services Industry*, Second Edition by Joseph F. Sinkey, Jr. Copyright © 1983 by Macmillan Publishing Company.

---

in Figure 5.1, demand deposits as a percentage of bank liabilities have been declining. This decline is because of attractive interest rates on other accounts and non-bank financial institutions promoting their own transaction accounts.

Savings and time deposits represent the largest source of funds for commercial banks. *Savings accounts* include regular passbook accounts, automatic transfer service (ATS) accounts and negotiable order of withdrawal (NOW) accounts. Because depositors can earn interest without sacrificing the transactional nature of the account, ATS and NOW accounts make savings deposits more attractive than previously. Savings accounts have no fixed maturity. Although by law banks may require a 30-day notice of withdrawal on savings deposits, they rarely exercise that option.

Time Accounts Time accounts are fixed maturity deposits. Early withdrawal is allowed, but only with an interest penalty. The most prominent time accounts are certificates of deposit, or CDs. Money Market CDs are fixed in maturity date and denomination (usually $10,000). These accounts offer a higher interest rate to depositors primarily because they offer more certainty and greater flexibility to banks. Negotiable CDs are large denomination ($100,000 or greater) fixed-maturity deposits that are issued to corporations and institutional investors. A secondary market for large denomination CDs has developed, which makes these certificates negotiable.

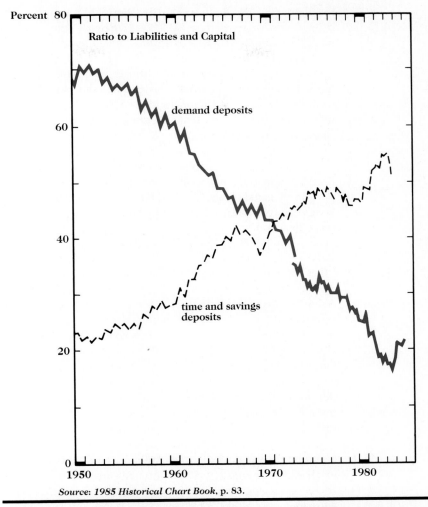

Percent 80

Ratio to Liabilities and Capital

60

demand deposits

40

time and savings
deposits

20

0

1950   1960   1970   1980

Source: 1985 Historical Chart Book, p. 83.

FIGURE 5.1   *Balance Sheet Ratios for All Commercial Banks*   Demand deposits as a percentage of liabilities and capital have dramatically declined at commercial banks. During the same period, time and saving deposits have increased. The sources of bank funds are changing in response to competition and new types of financial instruments.

Other Liabilities   Other liabilities include borrowed funds, funds borrowed from the Federal Reserve, repurchase agreements, and Eurodollars. *Borrowed funds* come from other commercial banks that have funds in excess of necessary reserves. Banks may lend these excess funds to other commercial banks. These are also called *federal funds*, because the transaction is usually handled through a district Federal Reserve bank. Funds are made available for short periods of time, usually overnight. A commercial bank may also have *funds borrowed from the Federal Reserve*; these are usually short-term loans. Through *repurchase agreements*, a commercial bank may sell a security to a depositor with an agreement to repurchase the same security for a set price at a specified point in the future. The bank has access to these funds between the sale and resale. Essentially the bank is borrowing for a short term. *Eurodollars* are deposits dominated by American dollars in financial institutions outside the United States.[2] An American bank may access these funds on a short-term basis.

Capital Account   A capital account is another source of commercial bank funds. Capital is the owners' equity in the bank. Although a very small portion of bank funds, the capital account represents a fund against which losses on assets can be charged. This is a protection for depositors against bank insolvency.

Uses of Bank Funds

A bank's uses of funds are its assets. Commercial banks either hold cash assets or use acquired funds to generate income. Banks generate income by investing their available funds or by extending loans.

Cash Assets   Commercial banks hold some deposits as cash to "cover" withdrawal demands. Banks also hold cash assets as reserves against their deposit liabilities. Reserves required by law or bank regulatory agencies have been declining as a percentage of deposits. In the 1930s the required reserve ratio against demand deposits was as high as 20 percent; after the Monetary Control Act of 1980 this ratio had declined to 3 percent (for transactions accounts totaling less than $30 million; the ratio is 12 percent when accounts exceed this amount). Cash assets may be deposited with the Federal Reserve, held as cash in a vault, or deposited at other banks to compensate correspondent banks for check collection or clearing.

Loans   Commercial banks generate the largest share of their revenues through interest payments on loans. Banks may make various types of loans. *Business loans* and *commercial loans* are either the more important short-term (one year or less) loans or term loans (up to ten years). Rates vary from the

---

[2] Originally, in the 1950s, most dollar-denominated deposits borrowed by U.S. banks were held in Europe. Although still largely based in Europe, dollar denominated deposits now are often borrowed from Asian or Caribbean banks as well.

lowest rate for the bank's best customers (called the prime rate) to higher rates for less qualified borrowers. Banks make *security loans* to individuals, brokers, or dealers to purchase equities or bonds. Commercial banks cannot acquire equity securities for their own portfolios and corporate bond purchases by banks are restricted by law, but they can lend funds to others for such purchases. The percentage of an equity security's purchase price that can be covered through a loan is regulated by the Federal Reserve. This so-called margin requirement originally was set in 1934 in response to banks' overextension of security loans during the stock market expansion preceding the Great Crash of 1929.

Financial Institution Loans   Commercial banks make financial institution loans to finance companies. These loans form the basis for the operation of finance companies (see Chapter 4). *Real estate loans* are extended by banks as mortgages for the purchase of new or existing commercial and residential structures. These long-term loans have become increasingly important to commercial banks. Through *consumer loans*, individuals borrow from banks to finance consumer purchases such as automobiles, home appliances, and vacations. These loans may be either single-payment or installment loans. Bank credit cards, although historically only a minor part of total loans, are included in this category and are increasing in importance. Banks that make loans to other commercial banks have *federal funds* (as described above) as assets. Although federal funds loans are usually only overnight loans, a bank may ease a weak loan demand by extending federal funds loans to different banks on a regular basis or by a continuing contract agreement whereby the one-day loan is rolled over on a regular basis.

Investments   Banks cannot hold equities although they can offer brokerage services. They can acquire securities issued by local, state, and federal governments and by federal government agencies. Included as investments are United States Treasury Bills (maturities of one year or less) and Treasury Bonds (maturities over five years). Banks may also purchase municipal bonds or government agency bonds such as those issued by the Federal Land Banks, the Federal National Mortgage Corporation (Fannie Mae), and the Federal Home Loan Bank Board.

Changing Composition of Liabilities and Assets

The commercial bank balance sheet has changed over the years. Figure 5.1 showed how the composition of total liabilities has changed. Figure 5.2 shows how the general balance sheet categories as a percentage of total assets have changed. Figure 5.2 illustrates how significantly cash and securities

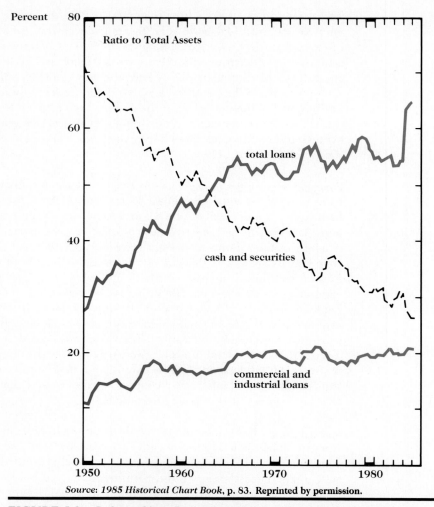

Percent

Ratio to Total Assets

total loans

cash and securities

commercial and
industrial loans

1950   1960   1970   1980

Source: 1985 Historical Chart Book, p. 83. **Reprinted by permission.**

FIGURE 5.2   *Balance Sheet Ratios for All Commercial Banks to 1985*
Commercial bank loans have been increasing while cash and securities have declined rather
significantly. Coupled with Figure 5.1, this figure shows that the portfolios of commercial
banks are quite different in the 1980s than they were as few as fifteen years ago.

have declined in importance relative to total bank assets. On the other hand,
the percentage of total loans to bank assets has risen significantly.

We can explain these changes through a number of factors, all of which
are discussed in the section on bank performance in Chapter 6. The need for
efficiency behavior prompted by competition, the increase in interest rates,
and banking reforms in response to these two factors have had profound

effects. For example, banks have turned away from demand deposits, at least relatively speaking, to take advantage of interest-bearing accounts and, more recently, to achieve the higher interest rates that new versions of time and savings accounts now offer.

What do these changes mean in terms of bank behavior? You can answer that question by looking at the theories explaining commercial bank behavior and by noticing how they have changed over time. We can contrast these theories with new strategies for bank management to see how bank behavior has been influenced by the changing financial structure.

Theories of Commercial Banking

Banks always have had to face the dilemma of maximizing profits while at the same time maintaining liquidity and insuring safety. Historically bank managers have tried to balance profitability against liquidity and soundness by relying on some generally accepted theories of bank behavior. Most of the early theories reveal that liquidity was the chief priority. These bank theories have influenced the way bankers have managed their assets and liabilities.

We will discuss these theories largely in historical order. You will see how bank management evolved from what was predominately passive deposit acquisition and asset management to active deposit acquisition with a blend of asset and liability management.

Commercial Loan Theory

The traditional theory of banking, which dates back to the eighteenth century, is *commercial loan theory*. This theory calls for the extension of short-term, self-liquidating loans only. A self-liquidating loan is extended for the production of saleable goods or the acquisition of goods in transit. Under this procedure the completion of the production process and the sale of the goods would generate the income necessary to repay the loan. Bankers considered these to be productive loans with a high probability of repayment. They typically made loans to allow firms to build up their inventories in anticipation of a busy sales season.

Commercial loans of this nature were also called *real bills loans* because they financed the acquisition of real goods. It was often argued that such real bills loans complemented the business cycle and accommodated the needs of trade. As business activity quickened and the demand for self-liquidating loans increased, banks would create funds by extending loans and thus would facilitate real economic expansion. These loans would contract as demand declined. Theorists thought such bank behavior not only facilitated trade and commerce but stabilized the economy.

Commercial loan theory is both flawed and impractical. It is flawed because no loan is truly self-liquidating. Loans to allow the completion of production or to build up inventory are self-liquidating only if sales actually occur. As for complementing the business cycle, such loans did not necessarily stabilize the economy. Since loan demand was based on the dollar value of goods in production or inventory, price inflation stimulated loan demand and the so-called self-liquidating loans would expand to fuel the flames of inflation. A second problem was that commercial banks could not continue to function by giving only short-term loans. An increasing demand for business term loans to finance capital goods acquisition and for mortgage loans required commercial bankers to adapt to the times.

Practicality, above all else, forced the abandonment of the commercial loan theory. Nevertheless, you will notice that this theory has influenced subsequent bank regulatory legislation and thus remains ingrained in much of commercial banking.

Shiftability Thesis

In the early twentieth century, critics argued against the real bills doctrine by claiming that bank liquidity was based not so much on the type of loan extended but on the shiftability or saleability of the assets the bank held. Such arguments, the increasing demand for different types of loans, and the development of an active securities market all led to an acceptance of an alternative theory of bank management. This *shiftability thesis* called for banks to hold a portfolio of shiftable assets, assets which could be sold easily or shifted to more liquid assets. The purpose was to secure liquidity. A result of this prevailing view was that banks held short-term investments, such as T-bills, for which an active secondary market existed.

By holding sufficient shiftable assets, a bank could achieve liquidity whenever deposits declined or the bank needed cash. This theory did not replace bank reliance on commercial loans, but rather suggested a more broadly based asset portfolio. With the growth of money market instruments, commercial banks were able to accommodate the need for liquidity without constraining their loan possibilities.

The shiftability thesis is sound only as long as a stable price remains in the secondary market. If widespread sale of T-bills forced the price of these securities down, bankers would have to assume a capital loss in order to maintain liquidity. A classic example: large numbers of banks moved into the secondary market following the stock market crash of 1929 and there were few buyers. As a result many banks faced a liquidity crisis.

Anticipated Income Theory

The limitations of the commerical loan theory and the shiftability thesis argued for an expanded definition of bank liquidity. Banking specialist Herbert Prochnow advocated establishment of a continuum of term loans whose periodic maturity would provide a bank with a regular and continuous flow of funds. The *anticipated income theory* met the requirement of liquidity while allowing bankers to meet the rising demand for long-term loans.

Proponents of this theory reasoned that commercial loans are repaid from borrowing firms' future earnings, or their anticipated income. Under the guidelines established by the anticipated income theory bankers would consider the borrower's overall ability to repay the loan, that is, the firm's credit-worthiness, rather than considering the self-liquidating nature of the loan or even the saleability of the assets held.

The anticipated income theory provided for an even broader conceptualization of the types of loans a bank might make. Short- and long-term business loans, mortgage loans, and even consumer loans were all quite acceptable if the borrower's anticipated income reduced or eliminated the riskiness of the loan. The regular payments, for example, payments on installment loans, and the continuous maturity of long-term loans provided the flow of funds necessary for normal liquidity needs. In the event of unusual liquidity demands, a bank's portfolio still needed some shiftable assets, for example, short-term money market instruments, which would be easily convertible into cash.

Asset Allocation Theory

Given the continuing desire for liquidity and the broadened definition of what would provide liquidity for commercial banks, the *asset allocation theory* was simply an adaptation of asset management to accommodate the attention to a bank's liabilities. Proponents of this theory argued that the maturity structure of bank assets should be determined by the maturity structure of its liabilities. Different liability structures dictated different asset mixes. For example, the greater the ratio of demand deposits to total deposits, the greater the need for a higher proportion of liquid short-term assets to total assets (since demand deposits have a higher rate of turnover). To a certain extent the theories of commerical banking had come almost full circle with the asset allocation theory. Liabilities would now strongly influence the bank's asset mix.

Summary of Theories

Acceptance of a new theory of asset management did not mean abandonment of the old. Instead, bank management has steadily broadened the consideration of loans that promote revenue flows without sacrificing liquidity.

Use of all of these theories has dealt with management of assets. Beginning in the early 1960s, attention (to the goal of liquidity) was directed to the liability side of the bank balance sheet in addition to the asset side. Because of the rise in importance of CDs, and commercial banks' declining ability to attract sufficient deposits relative to other financial institutions, banks looked to develop methods to attract new funds. For the most part, this meant developing new liability instruments. And with the increasing attention to new liability instruments came the need to manage the liabilities.

Liquidity Management in the Contemporary Setting

In the contemporary setting, bank managers do not rely on asset management exclusively in addressing the challenges of profitability and liquidity. Managers combine asset management with increasing attention to liability management.

Liability management prescribes that bank managers look to liabilities as a source of liquidity. Even more simply stated, this theory provides for bank liquidity through borrowing rather than through the sale of assets. Keep in mind that a commercial bank's primary source of income always has been from interest payments and loan fees on direct loans. Banks must be in the position to respond to loan requests, especially in the face of increasing competition. A bank's responsiveness to a loan request, especially from business borrowers, is a major factor in a firm's decision to use the services of a particular bank. The need for liquidity therefore extends beyond simply meeting withdrawal requests.

This rather significant change in the theory of bank management is tied to the development of certificates of deposit, the expansion of the Federal Funds market, and the acceptance of the Eurodollar and repurchase markets as a source of borrowed funds. These instruments allow banks to adjust short-term interest rates to attract interest-sensitive funds. Instead of having to rely on savings and demand deposits as the exclusive source of funds (neither of which was very responsive to the incentives banks could offer under the constraint imposed by Regulation Q), banks now can take advantage of interest sensitive markets and manage their liabilities.

Bank managers look to liability management to: 1) increase available funds for investment, and 2) secure liquidity in the event of deposit with-

BANKING T⬤DAY 5.2

"Securitization" Changes Bank Portfolio Management

The primary function of financial intermediaries is to facilitate the flow of capital from savers to borrowers. Banks perform this function by making loans and accepting deposits. Sometimes, however, a financial intermediary's demand for loans is greater than its supply of deposits, in which case it may purchase federal funds, sell securities under repurchase agreements, or sell assets such as government securities or loans. When an institution sells loans, it can sell whole loans or it can "securitize" a portfolio of similar loans.

Securitization is a recent innovation in asset sales. It involves the pooling and repackaging of loans into securities, which are then sold to investors. Securitization provides an additional funding source and eliminates assets from a bank's balance sheet. It is often used to market small loans that would be difficult to sell on a stand-alone basis. Most importantly, securitization can increase the liquidity of a bank; the ability to package and sell these otherwise illiquid assets in an established secondary market increases the bank's liquidity.

The asset used for securitization is the home mortgage.

Mortgage-backed securities began in 1970 when the Government National Mortgage Association (GNMA) developed "Ginnie Mae," a mortgage-backed security collateralized by FHA and VA mortgage loans. The GNMA, a direct agency of the federal government, guarantees the principal and interest on these securities. Subsequently the Federal National Mortgage Association developed "Fannie Mae" and the Federal Home Loan Mortgage Corporation developed "Freddie Mae." All these mortgage-backed securities sold very well in the secondary market. The chart below reveals how they expanded.

Subsequently, other types of assets have been pooled and used as a basis for securities. Bank of America issued the first private sector mortgage-backed securities in 1977. Automobile loans have been packaged and sold as se-

curities, computer leases, loans guaranteed by the Small Business Administration, and various types of trade credit have been used for securitized loans.

If the securitization of loans other than mortgages becomes as successful as mortgage-backed securities, the financial services industry will be transformed into a system in which banks have to compete with nonbanks in allocating credit. For now, securitization represents a way for commercial banks to increase their liquidity. In the process, it has changed the way they manage their portfolios.

Source: From "Securitization" by Christine Pavel in Federal Reserve Bank of Chicago *Economic Perspectives* X, 4 (July/August 1986): 16–31.

	Mortgage-based Securities ($billions)					
	1980	1981	1982	1983	1984	1985
Ginnie Mae Freddie Mae Fannie Mae	114	127	177	243	287	366

---

drawals or heavy loan demand. In either case it is not necessary to sell off assets. The generation of funds through liability management has focused on four types of managed liabilities.

Federal Funds   The federal funds market began to grow in the late 1950s. Federal funds are excess reserves of other financial institutions (commercial banks, federal agencies, savings and loans, mutual savings banks) that are made available for borrowing. Loans made through the federal funds market are short term, usually overnight or for a few days, normally large scale, $1 million or more, and unsecured. Typically the loan takes place via a wire transfer from the lending institution to the reserves of the borrowing bank at the Federal Reserve District Bank. The following day the borrowing bank transfers the funds plus interest by wire back to the reserves of the lending institution. These arrangements are made through federal funds brokers. In 1980 net federal funds purchases exceeded $20 billion; by mid-1985 the average weekly level of federal funds purchased by large commercial banks exceeded $50 million.

Large Denomination CDs   These represent the largest type of liability management instrument. The market for large denomination CDs became active in the early 1960s. In 1961 there was virtually no trading; by 1970 over $20 billion in large denomination CDs exchanged hands; in 1980 the total was around $100 billion, and in 1985 it surpassed $350 billion. Large denomination CDs allowed banks to adjust interest rates in response to market conditions. This allows banks to regularly and competitively tap funds from the nonfinancial sector.

Eurodollars   These are dollar-denominated deposits held outside the United States. If a foreign bank, or a foreign branch of an American bank, receives a U.S. dollar deposit that the depositor does not want converted into domestic currency, the bank may lend these funds to American banks. Caribbean banks are increasingly active in attracting dollar deposits which are in turn loaned to American banks. The quantity of funds borrowed in the Eurodollar market has averaged around $90 billion over the past few years.

Repurchase Agreements   These are similar to federal funds—in fact the two are reported together in most data on flow of funds. A bank may sell securities to a corporation with the understanding that the bank will buy back, repurchase, the securities at a higher price on a set date. Thus the bank borrows the funds, denominated by the selling price of the securities, and repays the loan with an interest payment, indicated by the difference between the original purchase price and the repurchase price.

Federal Discount Window Borrowing   In addition to the liability instruments, a bank may acquire short-term funds from the Federal Reserve. Total borrowing in this category amounts to less than $5 billion per year.

Liability management through the use of these markets allows banks some discretionary action in acquiring funds. This is in contrast to the more passive role that characterized the industry before the 1960s. We can look at the increase in purchased funds as an indication of the importance of the short-term borrowing of commercial banks (see Figure 5.3).

Discretionary Funds Management

In the contemporary setting we might describe bank behavior as less focused on asset management versus liability management issues and more concerned with discretionary versus nondiscretionary funds management. This reflects the fact that contemporary bank management combines what is essentially an anticipated income/shiftability thesis approach in asset acquisition with an active liability management policy.[3] United States banks behave quite differently in discretionary funds management than in the past when they simply accepted deposits and then loaned or invested deposited funds. Banks now solicit deposits and borrow funds from a variety of sources to provide flexibility for lending activities. To highlight this point, consider the fact that the percentage of total bank assets supported by transactions accounts has dropped from nearly 70 percent in the early 1950s to around 30 percent in the early 1980s.

---

[3] Some observers have expressed concern about this increasing reliance on liability management. The major concern revolves around the limitation of the entire financial system trying to increase liabilities; obviously there is only so much liquidity at any one point in time. Refer to Dudley G. Luckett and Steve B. Steib, "Bank Soundness and Liability Management," *New England Journal of Business* (Summer 1978):37–47.

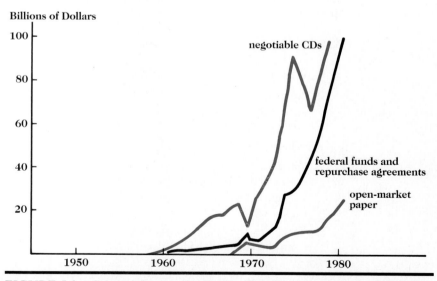

FIGURE 5.3 *Selected Commercial Banks Short-Term Borrowing, 1950–1980*
Since the early 1970s, commercial banks have expanded greatly their use of "purchased funds" (liabilities) as a source of funds for their portfolios.

The bottom line is that bank management is an active mix of asset and liability management. Computer models allow managers to more accurately forecast liquidity needs and loan requests. With this information they can access discretionary funds, whether managed liabilities or shiftable assets, to maximize profits while securing liquidity and insuring safety.[4]

Chapter Conclusion

This chapter began with an explanation of the motives behind the formation and operation of financial intermediaries. Intermediaries, whether commercial banks, savings and loan associations, or mutual savings banks, are motivated by the desire to maximize profits. Financial intermediaries face some constraints that dictate how they can function in attempting to achieve this goal.

Commercial banks' balance sheets provide a look at how banks seek profitability. And, knowing how our financial system has evolved historically helps you appreciate why commercial banks have adopted various theories of operation. The movement from profit-seeking behavior, based exclusively on asset management, to the more broadly conceived discretionary funds (assets and liabilities) management reflects the changing financial environment.

These theories of bank behavior will prove helpful as you move on to the next chapter to discuss the structure, performance, and regulation of commercial banks.

Consider These Questions

1. What motivates the pricing decisions of financial intermediaries?

2. How do profitability, liquidity, solvency, and risk fit into bank management decisions? Do you think the ranking of importance of these factors has changed over the years? How?

3. What is the difference between sources and uses of funds?

4. What factors influence a bank's decision on the composition of its assets and liabilities? Give an example of how the composition might change if bank managers think that the rate of inflation will increase dramatically.

5. What are the major components of the combined balance sheet for commercial banks? How have these components changed over time?

---

[4] Shiftable assets include government agency securities, federal, state, and local government securities, bankers acceptances and call loans.

6. How has liquidity management changed bank behavior? Does it have any implications for Federal Reserve control of bank reserves and bank lending?

7. What effect has the theory of discretionary fund management had on commercial bank behavior? Contrast behavior in light of this approach with behavior based on a more conservative strategy, for instance the commercial loan theory.

8. Assume you are considering investment possibilities. Stock in one of your local banks is a relatively attractive possibility. One bank executive tells you his bank has never called in a loan or needed to borrow to cover deposit withdrawals. The executive at the other bank admits to calling in loans, at times quite a few, and to borrowing to adjust her bank's liabilities. Based on this information, which bank would make the best investment? Why?

Suggestions for Further Reading

Baughn, W. H. and C. E. Walker, eds. *The Bankers' Handbook*. Homewood, IL: Dow Jones-Irwin, 1978.
An authoritative guide to the details of banking.

Havrilesky, Thomas M. and John Boorman. *Current Perspectives in Banking*. Arlington Heights, IL: Harlan Davidson, 1980.
Contains numerous articles, some presenting different perspectives, on bank management. See especially Parts I, II, and IV.

Hodgman, Donald R. *Commercial Bank Loan and Investment Policy*. Champaign, IL: Bureau of Business and Economic Research, 1963.
Interesting to compare analysis from twenty-five years ago to current loan and investment policies. Hodgman's framework is still useful.

Jessup, Paul F. *Modern Bank Management*. St. Paul: West Publishing, 1980.
Solid text on bank management.

Mayer, Martin. *The Bankers*. New York: Weybright and Talley, 1974.
Provides real insights into the world of banking in a very readable, interesting style.

Nash, Ogden. "Bankers Are Just Like Anybody Else, Except Richer." In *I'm A Stranger Here Myself*. Boston: Little, Brown, 1938.
A caustic yet humorous view of banks and bankers.

Sinkey, Joseph F., Jr. *Commercial Bank Financial Management in the Financial Services Industry*. New York: Macmillan Publishing Co., 1986.
Very thorough, innovative text on bank management in the changing financial services industry.

CHAPTER SIX

STRUCTURE, PERFORMANCE AND REGULATION OF FINANCIAL INSTITUTIONS

The stresses and doubts that have characterized recent financial experience are, however, bringing sharply back into focus the essential role of regulation and supervision in maintaining a sound system of banking.

Arthur Burns
Address to the American Bankers Association, October 1974

The name of the game within the financial industry in general and banking in particular is marketing. Deregulation has changed the rules of the game so that firms must market their products and services in an increasingly competitive environment. The changing environment is producing an altered structure for financial firms and greater attention to the performance of those firms.

This chapter reviews the structure and performance of financial institutions, with a concentration on the commercial banking sector of the industry. Bank holding companies, increased mergers within banking, and the press for interstate banking are resulting from the deregulation of the industry and are producing a very different structure for the banking sector.

Structural changes within banking may have been prompted by deregulation within the financial industry, but that industry is still characterized by a high level of government involvement. Regulations have changed to produce a more competitive environment, but the extent to which federal and state governments are involved has not lessened; rather, the nature of their involvement has changed. Analysis of the banking sector reveals more attention to government-funded deposit insurance programs and an increasing role for government agencies in supervising financial institutions and in minimizing disruptions by arranging mergers when banks are near failing.

The structure, performance, and regulation of the industry merit attention. Realizing that the industry is in a state of flux will prove why macroeconomic analysis and monetary policy are not exact.

Chapter Objectives

Your major goal for this chapter is to understand the changing nature of the banking sector in terms of its structure, the performance of the firms within it, and the extent of government intervention. To achieve this overall goal, you should be able to:

- Explain what is prompting the change in the structure of commercial banking.
- Analyze bank performance.
- Evaluate the impact of the increasing number of bank failures.
- Assess the reasons for and effects of government regulatory and supervisory agencies, especially in light of the industry's changing structure.

To achieve the chapter goal, you will need to consider some related issues. In terms of the structure of commercial banking, you will be able to:

- Analyze trends in numbers of banks.
- Describe implications of a dual banking system.
- Describe effects of changes in mix of unit versus branch banking states.
- Describe the size distribution of American banks.
- Explain the importance of holding companies.

To analyze bank performance and the effects of bank failures, you should be able to:

- Explain how mergers are a response to bank failures.
- Discuss interstate and regional banking.
- Assess measures of bank performance.
- Describe the need for bank profitability.

To assess government regulation and supervision, you will:

- Explain the motivation for government involvement in the industry.
- Outline the changing nature of government intervention.
- Identify agencies responsible for supervision, regulation, and insurance.

Structure of Commercial Banking

Since the industry is changing rapidly, you should consider how the trends up to this time can help you project what might happen in the future. This will prove particularly helpful as we move on to discuss how the industry structure, monetary behavior, and macroeconomic policy are interrelated and how they may change.

The structure of the commercial banking industry has changed significantly over the years, especially during the last decade. Deregulation, more than any other single factor, is altering the structure of the industry. This section looks at the industry structure. (A more detailed discussion is included in Part IV, which covers analysis of the changing legal and regulatory environment of the financial industry.) The industry structure provides necessary background for assessing commercial bank performance.

Number and Chartering of Commercial Banks

This country has approximately 14,500 commercial banks.[1] This number is significantly reduced from the number during the period before the Great Depression when there were over 30,000 banks. The number of commercial banks dropped annually until the mid-1960s; since then, the number has increased modestly each year (see Table 6.1).

The slight annual change in the number of commercial banks does not reveal the kinds of changes that are occurring within the industry. In any given year, banks fail, mergers occur, and new branch offices open. In recent years, the number of bank failures has increased, although it is a small number compared to the total number of commercial banks in operation. In 1983 almost fifty banks failed, and about 140 banks collapsed in 1986. Looking beyond the total number of banks reveals the dramatic increase in bank branches. Figure 6.1 illustrates how the recent modest change in the total number of banks is overwhelmed by the increase in bank branches.

This increase in branches is occurring in large part because of changes in chartering provisions. As you will recall from Chapter 4, banks are chartered by either the federal government (national banks, of which there are about 4700) or state governments. This dual banking system provides for some different operating rules. Regardless of which level of government

---

[1] As of the early 1980s, the *American Banker* reported a total of just over 22,000 banks worldwide. Over 60 percent are American banks.

Selected Years	Commercial Banks
1910	24,514
1920	30,291
1930	23,679
1940	14,534
1950	14,146
1960	14,147
1970	13,487
1972	13,930
1974	14,459
1976	14,672
1978	14,712
1980	14,836
1982	14,543
1983	14,473
1984	14,518
1985	14,481

TABLE 6.1   *Number of Commercial Banks in the United States*

charters a commercial bank, each state determines its own operating structure. Some states allow banks to operate branches throughout the state (*branch banking states*), while other states limit a bank to one facility (*unit banking states*). The remaining states allow some branching (*limited branch banking states*).

Figure 6.2 shows how the nation is divided into unit, branch, and limited branch banking states. The dominance of unit banking in the Midwest is a carryover from the era when this agriculturally dominated area feared the concentration of financial power among one or a few major banks. Citizens in this part of the country had experienced agricultural foreclosures and felt that many smaller, local banks would have greater sensitivity to local concerns. This situation is changing; since the early 1970s, three unit banking states have authorized limited branching while three others approved statewide branching. Other states have liberalized laws to allow more broadly based branching. Many of those states that continue to restrict branching have permitted various kinds of detached facilities that offer limited services (for example, drive-in deposit/withdrawal, loan production offices, and remote automatic teller machines).

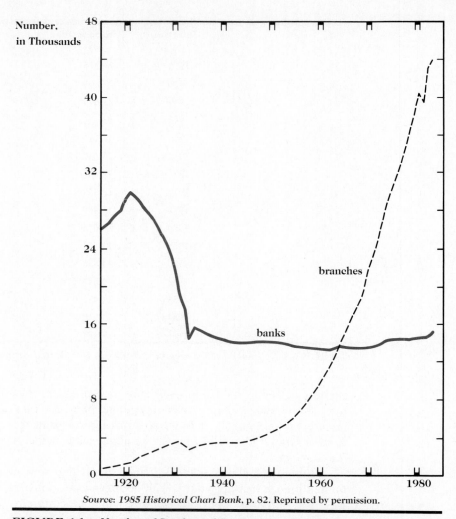

Number, in Thousands

48

40

32

24

16

8

0

branches

banks

1920   1940   1960   1980

Source: *1985 Historical Chart Bank*, p. 82. Reprinted by permission.

FIGURE 6.1 *Number of Banks and Branches* Although the number of banks has declined since the years of the Great Depression (leveling off during the last thirty years), the number of branches has increased markedly. Relaxed restrictions on branching have allowed this to occur.

Size and Distribution of Commercial Banks

Throughout its history the American banking industry has been characterized by a relatively modest number of very large banks and a very large number of modest-sized banks. The fifty largest American banks (about 4 percent of the total) have slightly over half of the total United States

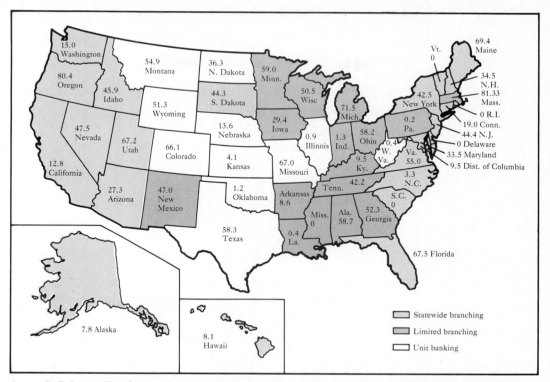

Source: D. T. Savage, "Development in Banking Structure, 1970–1981," *Federal Reserve Bulletin* (February 1982): 84. Reprinted by permission.

FIGURE 6.2 *Patterns of Branch Banking Restrictions* Although state laws are changing, especially since the deregulation legislation of 1980, this figure represents the differing state opinions on branching. The numbers of each state refer to the percentage of total commercial bank deposits held by banks in multibank holding companies in each state.

banking assets. The degree of concentration is further illustrated by Table 6.2, which shows the deposits and assets of the ten largest American banks. These ten commercial banks hold over 30 percent of total deposits. Therefore, despite the large number of American banks, assets and deposits are concentrated in a relatively small number of depository institutions.[2]

───────────────

[2] Bank concentration in the United States is overshadowed by that in other countries. And relative to the rest of the world, American commercial bank deposits are not significant given the large number of American banks. Even though over 60 percent of the banks in the world are located in the United States, the American Bankers Association estimates that only about 20 percent of total deposits are held in American banks. This same source reveals that only two American banks (Bank of America and Citicorp) are among the world's ten largest banks (measured in terms of total deposits). See the *American Banker* (July 27, 1983); and *The Economist* (March 22, 1986).

	Deposits ($ billions)	Assets ($ billions)
Citibank (New York)	94.38	138.62
Bank of America (San Fran)	88.17	106.15
Chase Manhattan (New York)	58.77	78.74
Manufacturers Hanover (New York)	46.20	60.67
Morgan Guaranty (New York)	41.33	67.39
Chemical Bank (New York)	35.69	53.04
Security Pacific (Los Angeles)	32.88	44.81
Bankers Trust (New York)	30.77	51.18
First National Bank (Chicago)	24.33	33.37
Wells Fargo (San Fran)	19.50	29.43
Top 10 Commercial Banks % of Total*	31.9%	34.5%
Top 50 Commercial Banks % of Total*	56.2%	59.8%

* refers to 1983 totals

TABLE 6.2 *Ten Largest American Commercial Banks (Deposits and Assets), End of 1985*

You can see from this table that most of the large banking operations are located in New York City or California. Commercial banks have grown rapidly in major cities, as you might expect. New York is regarded as the financial center of the world. The long-time prominence of Bank of America can be explained in part because California is a branch banking state. Bank of America has hundreds of branches in California. Branch banking states have fewer commercial banks per capita, and the ones that exist are larger than in comparable unit banking states. There are not fewer bank offices in branch banking states; more offices are simply part of the same bank.

Location influences bank size and to a certain extent dictates or limits bank operations. Banks in rural areas tend to be smaller and deal more with agricultural loans than do city banks. Beyond that, rural banks must rely on the time-consuming transportation of currency and coin from the district Federal Reserve Bank or from larger regional banks where funds may be deposited. As a result of the time involved in moving money, a rural bank may retain a larger portion of its deposits as vault cash to avoid delays in servicing customer demands. Even within urban areas, location may influence operations. To carve out a share of the market, banks may concentrate on particular services that appeal to a restricted clientele. These may include providing services through foreign branches, specializing in trust activity, or other focused activities.

Rural banks are not the only ones to rely on larger banks to supply specialized services; many suburban and city banks do so as well. The provision of specialized services to other banks is referred to as *correspondent banking*. Correspondent banks may accept deposits from other banks, provide accounting and computer services, facilitate federal funds market loans, offer trust department services, or clear checks.[3]

Bank Holding Companies and Bank Mergers

In recent years, states have been liberalizing their laws on branch banking. Until the laws changed, and even now in unit banking states, the bank holding company was one way to circumvent limitations on expansion. At the same time, bank holding companies allow banks to position themselves to take advantage of reforms in the interstate banking laws. A *bank holding company* is a corporation established to hold the stock of one or more banks.

Bank holding companies have their origin in the early 1900s. Union Investment Company, now part of Norwest Banks, began operations in Minnesota in 1903. Bank of America founder Amadeo Giannini used the bank holding company to create a financial empire. By 1927, less than twenty-five years after its founding, Giannini's Bank of Italy had 300 branches in California. In that year, Giannini set up a separate corporation to hold his bank's stock. The holding company then purchased New York-based Bank of America. Concern over the rapidly expanding banking industry resulted in several pieces of legislation over the next few years. The Clayton Act of 1914 gave the Federal Reserve the power to enforce its antitrust provisions amongst banks. This legislation slowed but did not halt bank holding company formation. The number of bank holding companies increased dramatically in the mid-1960s as firms sought to stabilize their sources of funds. Bank holding companies allowed a circumvention of the restrictions on interest rates on deposits (Regulation Q). As such, banks could offer higher interest rates to attract needed deposits. Bank holding companies also allowed firms to get around the restrictions on branching.[4]

Major legislation affecting bank holding companies was passed in 1956 and 1966. The intent was to control the expansion of multibank holding

---

[3] Until the Depository Institutions Deregulation and Monetary Control Act went into effect in 1981 banks that were not members of the Federal Reserve System had to use correspondent member banks for check clearing through the Federal Reserve.

[4] Our discussion about bank holding companies anticipates a subsequent discussion about bank size and performance. As with most industries banks have associated expansion with success. One way to achieve increasing profits is to grow; banks can grow by increasing deposits. Expanding the geographic region served is a sure way to enhance potential deposits.

companies by requiring registration and approval by the Federal Reserve, by restricting acquisitions to "bank-related" companies, and by prohibiting out of state bank acquisition except where permitted by state law.

This legislation did not cover one-bank holding companies (that is, a corporation that holds the stock of only one bank). Nothing prevented a one-bank holding company from acquiring non-bank firms. An amendment in 1970 extended the provisions of the previous legislation to the 1352 one-bank holding companies that were in existence.[5]

Despite increasingly tight restrictions, the number of bank holding companies has increased steadily. Table 6.3 highlights this increase. By the end of 1985 the number of bank holding companies had risen to over 6000; many of these were single bank holding companies. Not only has the number of bank holding companies increased, but the reach of bank holding companies is impressive. At the end of 1984, Citicorp operated 980 offices in 41 states. Perhaps more significantly, one-quarter of American banks are controlled by bank holding companies; these banks hold more than three-quarters of total deposits at American banks.

Bank Mergers

The bank holding company is not the only method of coordinating the activities of several banks. Historically, firms have merged to gain the benefits of increased size. A *merger* is the combining of two or more firms into a single operation. Usually, one firm acquires control over the other through an exchange of stock or the purchase of assets and assumption of liabilities.

Three waves of bank mergers have occurred in the United States— around 1900, during the 1920s and early 1930s, and from 1950 to the late 1960s. A bank may merge with another for a number of reasons:

- to expand into a new market,
- to achieve some economies of scale through a large operation,
- to allow the provision of broader or more specialized services, or
- to take advantage of better facilities or management personnel.

Mergers may occur in states where branch banking is restricted. Generally, a larger bank acquires a smaller bank, but sometimes two or more small banks may merge to compete more effectively.

---

[5] The same legislation provided that holding companies could acquire non-bank firms that were "determined to be clearly related to banking . . . and that can reasonably be expected to produce benefits to the public . . . ." An example of such an activity would be a bank holding company's acquisition of an armored car company.

	#BHC	#Banks	#Offices	%Total Commercial Bank Deposits Held by BHC
1965	603	1018	NA	12.8
1973	1533	3097	15,374	65.4
1975	1708	3674	18,382	67.1
1977	1913	3903	21,223	72.0
1979	2357	4280	23,765	74.1
1980	2905	4954	25,948	76.7

TABLE 6.3 *Bank Holding Companies and Banks*

Until 1960, mergers were approved by state regulators who generally assumed that antitrust laws did not apply to the banking industry. The wave of mergers in the 1950s led to passage of the Bank Holding Company and Merger Act of 1960. This regulation gave federal supervisory agencies (the Federal Reserve, FDIC, and the Comptroller of the Currency) the responsibility for approving or denying mergers. The act also required the Justice Department to review mergers to assess the competitive factors. This act was amended in 1966 so that the important factor was whether the expected benefits to the community outweigh the anticompetitive effects.

The number of bank mergers between 1950 and 1970 totaled about 4000. From 1970 to 1980, the number of mergers each year declined by about one-half.[6] The increased restrictions may have influenced this decline. Action by the Justice Department in the early 1960s certainly put the issue of mergers into a new light. The merger between the Philadelphia National Bank and the Girard Trust Bank of Philadelphia, the second and third largest banks in the city, had been approved by state and federal regulators when the Justice Department filed suit. The suit argued that the merger violated antitrust guidelines. In 1963, the Supreme Court ruled in favor of the Justice Department and against the merger. The Philadelphia National Bank case placed greater importance on the question of competition and indicated that the Justice Department would play a larger role in bank mergers. The Bank Merger Act of 1966 confirmed the importance of avoiding any merger that substantially reduced competition.

In recent years, mergers have been used by regulators to prevent an unsound bank from failing. Farmers and Merchants National Bank merged with Marquette National Bank in Minneapolis in 1982. The FDIC and the Federal Reserve arranged the merger. This process avoided the necessity of

---

[6] From 1960 through 1985, nearly 5000 bank mergers and acquisitions involved over $2750 billion in acquired assets.

BANKING TODAY 6.1

Interstate Banking without the "Interstate"

Some large New York banks are testing a personal computer terminal, no larger than a hand-held calculator, that would allow people to conduct banking transactions without stepping foot into an actual bank facility.

This kind of technology would allow regional and even nationwide banking without the establishment of expensive bank branch facilities. As such, it is one more technological breakthrough that may hasten widespread interstate banking.

This small, portable banking terminal accesses the main bank computer through telephone line connections. It is much less expensive than personal computers, so much so that the banks are considering offering it for a modest rental charge to customers.

The new banking terminal would allow customers to perform many of the functions now handled by automatic teller machines; other transactions, including funds transfers, would take place through the mail.

The question for banking regulators is whether such a technological breakthrough circumvents current prohibitions on widespread interstate banking.

Handheld computer terminal connects to telephone line and provides user with remote banking capabilities by pressing touch-sensitive LCD readout panels.

Source: Cameramann Int'l., Ltd. Courtesy of Kiel Corporation.

the FDIC covering insured deposits for a failed bank and allowed for continuity of service to customers. Even in the case of a merger arranged by regulators, the Justice Department must make a judgment based on competition and benefits to the community.

Perhaps in part because of greater effort by regulators to combine weak banks with stronger ones, the level of merger activity has increased again during the 1980s. From 1960 to 1983, 4805 bank mergers and acquisitions involved $206.3 billion in net worth; for 1985 alone, the total was $8.1 billion of mergers.

Interstate Banking

This discussion of bank holding companies and bank mergers has only touched on an issue of overriding concern: interstate banking. Throughout much of our history, commercial banks and savings and loan associations have been prevented from conducting operations across state lines. With the expansion of nondepository institutions, such as Merrill Lynch and Sears Roebuck, into financial activities generally regarded as the special province of banks and savings and loans, traditional intermediaries began to seek ways to address a national, or at least regional, market. Interstate expansion was believed to be necessary for survival.

Neither the growing pressure for Congressional action regarding interstate banking nor the increasing confusion within the financial industry has produced reform legislation. Nonetheless, the barriers to interstate banking have been coming down. Loopholes and regulatory agency disagreements have resulted in *de facto* interstate banking. Congress is faced with the challenge of bringing order to the confusing field of interstate banking.

Reasons for *de facto* expansion of interstate banking despite no national enabling legislation are several. First, banking companies that had interstate operations when interstate banking was outlawed were allowed to maintain their operations. This "grandfathering" proviso permitted a dozen bank holding companies to own about 130 out-of-state banks.

Second, the Edge Act, as amended by the International Banking Act of 1978, permits domestic and foreign banks to operate offices in more than one state for the purpose of financing the export of American products.

Third, both the 1982 Garn–St Germain Act (applying to commercial banks) and Federal Home Loan Bank Board provisions (for savings and loan associations) allow government-arranged mergers on an emergency basis to prevent a depository institution from failing.[7]

Fourth, the Douglas Amendment to the Bank Holding Company Act allows bank holding companies to acquire banks across state lines if acquisition is permitted by state law. By 1986 more than twenty states had passed some sort of interstate banking legislation. In many cases, this legislation allows for regional reciprocity agreements whereby banks within a well-defined area are allowed mergers or acquisitions across state lines.

Massachusetts, Connecticut, and Rhode Island, among other states, have enacted reciprocity laws. This regional compact paved the way for the approval in early 1984 of a merger between a bank in Massachusetts and one in Connecticut. Efforts were made to form a Southern regional compact. South Carolina and Florida passed regional banking laws during 1984; and Georgia's law became effective in 1985. This allows the union of Sun Banks of Florida and the Trust Company of Georgia, one of the biggest merger deals to date among U.S. bank holding companies. In lieu of national legislation, regional banking is an attainable option.

Finally, and most significantly, a loophole in Section 4c(8) of the 1970 amended version of the Bank Holding Company Act allows bank holding companies to operate "non-bank" subsidiaries on an interstate basis. This

---

[7] This provision was liberally interpreted in October, 1984, when Citicorp (a bank holding company) was allowed to acquire three ailing savings and loan associations (in California, Illinois, and Florida). This started a trend in bank holding company acquisitions of savings and loan associations.

loophole and the resulting circumvention of interstate banking provisions have generated acrimonious debate. The Bank Holding Company Act defines a bank as an institution that accepts demand deposits *and* makes commercial loans. Bank holding companies have interpreted this to mean that a facility that offers an array of services but that provides *either* direct deposit *or* makes commercial loans is not strictly a bank and is, therefore, exempt from the Bank Holding Company Act restrictions on interstate banking.

Although Congressional banking leaders pushed for a redefinition of a bank (to include, for example, all agencies insured by the FDIC), Congress has taken no action. As a result, the Comptroller of the Currency began approving applications for limited service banks.[8] During 1984, 53 of the largest bank holding companies had applied for 300 new limited service banks in 38 states and the District of Columbia. The Federal Reserve System must approve such expansion after the Comptroller of the Currency acts. Although opposing interstate banking through limited service facilities, the Federal Reserve Bank has had no legal basis for denying the applications.[9]

The large bank holding companies are moving rapidly to become national in their operations. Citicorp, the most agressive at forcing the issue, has moved to convert person-to-person financial offices in thirty-seven states to limited service banks. Many smaller banks, unable to expand to this extent, fear they will have difficulty competing. The issues of profitability and bank performance are what we will address in the next section.

Bank Performance

In considering bank performance, one must begin by recalling how a commercial bank is established. In most cases, shares are sold to investors to provide the capital to begin operations. On the bank balance sheet, this is referred to as the capital account or the bank's net worth. Part of this initial infusion of capital is used to acquire operating facilities and equipment; the rest is held as cash reserves. A bank then works to maximize a return on assets.

---

[8] "Non-bank" banks or limited service banks can offer either demand deposits or commercial loans. Beyond that they can offer a variety of services such as consumer loans, leasing, financial advice, management consulting, etc.

[9] The Federal Reserve has tried to slow the expansion by imposing a restriction which prevents any interaction between the limited service facility and the rest of the bank holding company. This prevents the bank holding company from performing many accounting and data processing services and makes operation of a limited service facility more costly.

To generate an enviable return on assets, a commercial bank needs to maximize the spread between the returns from its lending, investing, and servicing operations on the one hand and its cost of acquiring funds and doing business on the other. By far the largest portion of a bank's income, as much as 90 percent, comes from its net interest margin (that is, the difference between the interest it earns on funds and the interest it pays to acquire funds). Banks can increase this spread by earning a higher interest rate on the funds they loan or by loaning out more reserves. Bank managers need to consider risk in making loans and thus must balance interest income against security. A bank also needs to maintain enough liquidity to satisfy withdrawal requests. A bank cannot allow its cash reserve to drop too low.

With these considerations in mind, commercial bank behavior is as profit-maximizing as any other firm. The economic performance of a commerical bank is influenced by a number of factors. We could summarize this using a simple functional relationship:

$$P = g(f, r_p, u, r_e, d, c, e, y)$$

where

f = level of sources of funds (that is, deposits)
r_p = interest rates paid to attract funds
u = unborrowed reserves
r_e = interest rates earned on deposits
d = loan defaults
c = costs of complying with regulations (for example, insurance premiums, noninterest earning reserves at the Federal Reserve)
e = operating efficiency
y = overall economic conditions

Bank performance can be measured in any number of ways, and careful analysis of a bank's operations usually results in the application of many different performance measures. One commonly used performance measure is *return on assets*. This refers to net income as a percent of the average of beginning and end of year assets (not including loan reserves). Another performance measure is *return on equity*. This is net income as a percent of average annual equity capital. Table 6.4 shows returns for commercial banks over the past few years using both measures. To remain competitive, a bank's return on equity must be sufficiently strong to match or exceed similar investment opportunities within the financial industry and compared to investments of comparable risk in other industries. Evidence indicates that after about five years of declining performance, bank profits are rebounding. This is especially true for the large money center banks. In comparing profits for the fourth quarter of 1984 with the same period for

Return on Assets (%)	1979	1980	1981	1982	1983	1985
All Banks	.80	.79	.76	.71	.67	.70
>$100 million	1.15	1.18	1.15	1.08	.96	—
$100 mill–$1 billion	.96	.96	.91	.85	.84	—
$1 billion or more (money center banks)	.56	.56	.53	.50	.51	.49*
Return on Equity						
All Banks	13.9	13.7	13.2	12.2	11.2	11.4
>$100 million	14.1	14.2	13.6	12.7	11.2	—
$100 mill–$1 billion	13.9	13.7	12.8	12.0	11.9	—
$1 billion or more (money center banks)	14.0	14.4	13.4	12.3	11.9	9.8*

* These are preliminary figures.
Net income as percent of the average of beginning and end of year fully consolidated assets net of loan-loss reserves
Net income as a percent of the average of beginning and end of year equity capital

TABLE 6.4 *Profit Rates of Insured Commercial Banks, 1979–1985*

1983, major American banks showed increases in profits that ranged from 9 percent (Chase Manhattan) to 38 percent (Bank of America). For 1985, the picture was even better—bank profits rose 18 percent. Large banks accounted for the profit rise. The largest American banks, with $5 billion or more in assets, posted a 49-percent profit increase, while banks with assets below $100 million sustained a 16-percent decline in profits.[10]

Bank Failures

Banks traditionally have been viewed as bastions of security and stability. Their imposing facades and stately lobbies convey a sense of strength and permanence. During only one period in our modern history has reality clashed with this image. During the late 1920s (when the agricultural sector was experiencing problems) and the early 1930s (when the Great Depression struck the entire economy), banks failed at an alarming rate. Table 6.5 illustrates the average number of bank failures per year for selected time periods. The number of failures for the years 1921–1933 is drastically out of proportion when compared to the years before or since.

---

[10] Figures are based on FDIC data reported in *The Wall Street Journal* (June 19, 1986).

Period	Number of Bank Closings/Year	
1900–1920	85	
1921–1929	635	
1930	1350	
1931	2293	
1932	1453	
1933	4000	
1934–1940	64	
1941–1981	7	
1982	42	
1983	48	
1984	79	
1985	120	
1986	140*	* estimate

TABLE 6.5   *Bank Closings*

In recent years, though, the rising number of bank failures is drawing attention to the inability of some banks to perform satisfactorily. From the First Security Bank in Horseshoe Bend, Arkansas, with $11 million in deposits, to the Franklin National Bank of New York with $1445 million in deposits, the story was the same. Banking authorities stepped in to close the bank because of large loan losses and other related problems. In the case of First Security in Arkansas and Franklin National, the banks were reopened, but their problems and those of scores of other banks have called attention to the weakened condition of the American banking industry.

What causes a bank to fail? What are the implications of a bank failure? And, what issues are raised, especially for regulatory agencies, by bank failures?

A bank fails when it becomes insolvent—that is, its liabilities exceed its assets. This situation could be caused by loan defaults exceeding the bank's net worth, by a "bank run" drawing down reserves and forcing a call-in of outstanding loans, or because of illegal activity such as embezzlement. In any case, bank failures have always been seen as severe problems, more serious than failures of other business firms. The integral nature of a bank to a community, the relationship between banks and monetary policy actions and the fear of a snowball effect threatening to disrupt the entire financial industry are reasons that efforts are made to insure the well-being of banks.

BANKING TODAY 6.2   Are Bank Failures Bad?

The demise of any business operation draws attention. The larger the firm, the more newsworthy the story. The 1986 filing by LTV, the nation's second largest steel producer, for protection under Chapter 11 of the bankruptcy laws and the near-collapse of Continental Illinois National Bank in 1984, at that time the nation's seventh largest commercial bank, attracted international attention. But, small businesses fail every day with little more than local interest. Until recently, the number of bank failures was minimal, and the collapse of any bank drew widespread attention. Now, with over 100 banks collapsing in 1985 and 1986, considerable interest is focused on bank failures, not because of the novelty, but because there are so many.

In a dynamic economy, the failure of inefficient firms is as necessary as the creation of new businesses. Does this apply to banks as well? Most economists would agree that banks should not be insulated from failure. To do so would encourage inefficient operations. This is essentially what existed before the deregulatory reforms of the early 1980s. When a bank fails, its stockholders and officers "pay the price." This is part of the risk of capitalism.

On the other hand, most policy makers do not feel that depositors should suffer if a bank fails. Thus the United States deposit insurance program exists to safeguard depositors. To head off massive claims against the FDIC and its related agencies, government regulators attempt to have poorly performing bank portfolios assumed by more viable institutions when a bank is forced to close its doors. This protects depositors while at the same time making sure that banks are subject to the competitive forces of the market.

Banks are regulated from the time they apply for a charter until their last deposits are repaid after they close. A bank needs a government charter to begin operations. Its performance is supervised on a regular basis. Regulators oversee its demise and work to maintain continuity of service through merger or even government assumption of its operation. Banks are regulated to safeguard the public interest.

The issue of bank failures within the context of the changes in the financial industry is discussed at length in Chapter 15. The public's concern over bank failures provides a convenient point for us to begin exploring the method or madness behind regulation of commercial banking.

Regulation/Supervision

Commercial banks and all other depository institutions are subject to extensive government intervention. This intervention takes the form of regulation, supervision, and insurance protection. Government intervention in the depository institutions industry is based on two basic premises. First, depository institutions are unique because of their centrality to the national payments mechanism, due to the importance of demand deposits to the nation's money supply and because these institutions affect such a large proportion of the population. Second, the industry is perceived as inherently unstable, requiring regulation and supervision to protect the public welfare. These premises have evolved from our nation's financial history and the extent and magnitude of government involvement is best understood in terms of our financial history.

Origins of Government Intervention

Almost from the beginning of this country, banking has been seen as a responsibility of the state. Banks must have charters, government authorization, to begin operations.

People in this country have consistently mistrusted banks and bankers. Hamlet's admonition might be amplified by the concerns of Senator Thomas Hart Benton. During the 1830s, in lamenting the power of bankers, he commented,

> Are men with pens sticking behind their ears to be allowed to put an end to this Republic? . . . All the flourishing cities of the West are mortgaged to this money power. They may be devoured by it any moment. They are in the jaws of the monster. . . .[11]

People have a tendency to see banks as all powerful, and Americans have had this view reinforced by events in history.

In the early nineteenth century, Andrew Jackson struck out at the monopoly power of Eastern monied interests by refusing to allow the 2nd Bank of the United States to continue. Throughout the rest of that century, economic recessions were usually triggered by financial panics. The struggle to achieve a unified currency system based on gold and grounded in the National Banking Act of 1863 led many Americans to side with William Jennings Bryan in 1896 when he implored the country not to "crucify mankind upon a cross of gold."

The events that most significantly affected the degree and type of government control over banking occurred in the twentieth century. First, Congressional revelations following the panic of 1907 identified the tremendous concentration of financial power in the hands of a few New York bankers. Second, the stock market crashed in 1929 following years of rampant speculation fed by unjustified extensions of bank credit. Finally, many banking collapses of the 1920s and 1930s were attributed to unsound banking practices.

---

[11] Thomas Hart Benton, *Thirty Years' View* I (New York: T. H. Benton, 1856): 232.

Policy makers were concerned about the instability of the financial sector. Congress made efforts to insure safety and soundness within the banking system by controlling entry, regulating behavior, and supervising operations. Congress created a central monetary authority to control the nation's money supply and devised a nationwide insurance system to protect depositors.

Much of the legislation passed during this period was designed to create a noncompetitive structure for banking. That structure included extensive restrictions on bank behavior, but it also protected banking from the pressures of the marketplace. We will look next at the extent of government involvement and briefly explore its impact on the industry. We can contrast the controlled market environment with the deregulated environment we will discuss in Chapter 15.

Extent of Government Intervention

Government involvement with depository institutions is extensive and complicated. Three federal agencies as well as state agencies are involved in regulating, supervising, and insuring commercial banks. These agencies are described in Figure 6.3. For convenience, we can organize our discussion of government intervention into the categories of regulation, supervision, and insurance.

Regulation

Government agencies control banks' entry into the industry, their location and operations, and their impact on the supply of money. A government agency (either the state or the comptroller of the currency) *charters* the bank. The regulatory authority considers the initial capital position of the bank, the community's needs for a bank, potential adverse effects of a new bank, and prospects for success. In exercising their chartering responsibilities, the comptroller and the state authorities regulate entry into the industry. The presumption is that disruption created by a new bank starting operations but going out of business will be avoided by granting charters only when conditions warrant.

Regulators also exercise *controls on competition*. This is done in a number of ways. The Banking Act of 1933 essentially separated commercial banking from investment banking by prohibiting the former from underwriting securities and from purchasing equities. State agencies, the comptroller, and the Federal Reserve influence bank expansion through branching or mergers. Earlier in this chapter, the discussion of the structure of commercial

Federal Reserve. Established in 1913 to provide nationwide check-clearing, consolidate required reserves in the central bank, and set up a mechanism for lending to banks. Controlled by a seven-member Board of Governors. Operates through twelve regional banks with twenty-five branches. Supervises and examines state-chartered banks that are members of the Federal Reserve System. Supervises and examines all bank holding companies (the predominant form of bank ownership), regardless of charter. Administers certain consumer protection laws for all depository institutions.

Comptroller of the Currency. Established in 1863 as an office of the Treasury Department to charter national banks (only state charters until that time). Also examines and supervises national banks.

Federal Deposit Insurance Corporation. Established in 1933 to protect depositors in closed banks and, more generally, to promote a sound and viable banking system. Insures deposits at virtually all commercial banks and most mutual savings banks. Examines and supervises state-chartered banks that are not members of the Federal Reserve System.

State bank departments. Charter, regulate, supervise, and examine banks and thrift institutions where state chartering provided for under state laws. Have limited powers with respect to national banks and federal savings institutions. In practice, share authority over state-chartered institutions with federal deposit insurer.

Securities and Exchange Commission. Established, under 1933 and 1934 legislation, to restore confidence in capital markets by regulating broker-dealers and the exchanges on which stocks, bonds, and other financial instruments are traded. Authority extended to mutual funds in 1940. Specifies and enforces public disclosure requirements, sets rules of conduct for broker-dealers and exchanges, and assures that corporation rules permit adequate shareholder participation.

Department of Justice. With respect to financial institutions, may review proposed changes in industry structure and may sue to block them.

Federal Home Loan Bank Board. Created in 1932 to provide a credit reserve for savings institutions. Responsible for chartering, regulating, examining, and supervising federally chartered savings and loan associations. Federal Savings and Loan Insurance Corporation established in 1934 under control and management of Bank Board to insure accounts at member institutions, including state-chartered associations.

National Credit Union Administration (not shown). Established in 1970 to charter and supervise federal credit unions and to regulate, examine, and insure federal credit unions and insured state-chartered credit unions.

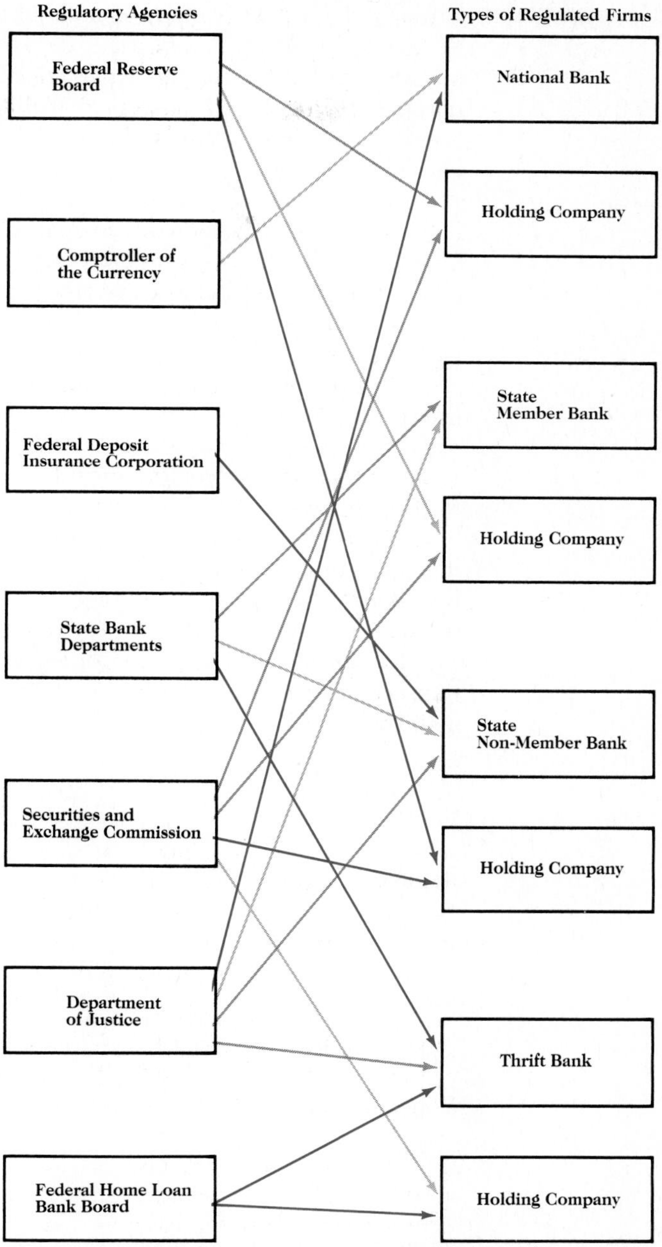

Source: From "Banking on Change: The Reorganization of Financial Regulation," *The Brookings Review*, Spring 1984, pp. 14-15. Copyright © 1984 by The Brookings Institution. Reprinted by permission.

FIGURE 6.3 ***The Current Regulatory Structure***

banking identified state laws regarding branching and the effects of the Bank Merger Act and Bank Holding Company Act on the expansion of banking activities within a state and across state lines and its effects on the type of non-banking activities allowed for bank holding companies. Beyond this, legislation has restricted the degree and type of competition between existing banks.

The concern over price competition (competing for funds by offering higher interest rates) and its adverse effects on the types of loans banks might make resulted in New Deal legislation giving the Federal Reserve the power to control interest rates on savings accounts and prohibiting interest payments on checking accounts. Both of these restrictions were eliminated by the financial reform act passed in 1980.[12]

Regulation also relates to *monetary control*. The Federal Reserve establishes reserve requirements against deposits, thus influencing the possible expansion of the money supply through loan extensions. The Federal Reserve also sets the interest rate banks must pay to borrow from the Federal Reserve's discount window.

Finally, government intervention relates to *consumer protection*. In passing the Truth in Lending Act in 1978, Congress established the Federal Reserve as the agency with power to write rules to keep the provisions of these acts up to date. As such, the Federal Reserve establishes rules requiring the disclosure of credit terms on loans and determines whether ATM transaction charges fall within the finance charge limits imposed on lending institutions.[13]

Supervision

Regulatory agencies monitor bank operations through regular examinations of bank records. The overlapping jurisdictions between federal and state regulatory authorities are very obvious in the area of bank supervision. Generally speaking, responsibilities are as follows:

Comptroller—all national banks
Federal Reserve—state-chartered member banks
FDIC—state-chartered nonmember banks
State Agencies—state-chartered banks

---

[12] The final interest rate restriction, called regulation Q, was phased out in March, 1986.

[13] For a complete discussion of the Federal Reserve's role in consumer protection see Lynn C. Goldfaden and Gerald P. Hurst, "Regulatory Responses to Changes in the Consumer Financial Services Industry," *Federal Reserve Bulletin* (February 1985):75–81.

Bank supervision takes the form of review of detailed financial statements that all banks must file on a quarterly basis. On-site bank examinations are conducted on a regular basis, usually annually. These unannounced examinations of bank records are not audits; those are done internally by the bank. Bank examiners look at the bank's financial condition, review its compliance with laws and regulations, and project its prospects for the

BANKING TODAY 6.3

National Bank Surveillance System (NBSS) and Bank Failures

To try to anticipate and avoid bank failure, the Office of the Comptroller of the Currency (OCC) has developed the National Bank Surveillance System (NBSS). This is the "early warning system" that detects operational problems among this country's national banks. The NBSS consists of four parts:

- *Bank Performance Report (BPR).* Specialists examine bank balance sheets, income-expenses statements, and bank examiners' reports to evaluate national banks' performance.
- *Anomaly Severity Rating System (ASRS).* This is a computerized scoring system designed to identify banks demonstrating unusual performance trends. It is applied quarterly to a sample of national banks. Problems are highlighted for specialists.
- *Review by Specialists.* NBSS specialists review and analyze the BPR and ASRS documents. Atypical cases result in more careful on-site investigations and usually lead to suggestions for operational changes to bank managers.
- *Action Control System.* This is a computerized monitoring

system that maintains information on all banks identified by the first three steps. The OCC reviews this system and only removes a bank from the list when reforms have resulted in a return to high operational performance standards.

The goal of the NBSS is to identify problems before they become too serious. Regional administrators for the Office of the Comptroller of the Currency use this sytem to provide information they need to advise bank managers on corrective actions.

Year	# Problem Banks	Failure Rate for Problem Banks
1970	215	2.79%
1971	239	2.51%
1972	190	0.53%
1973	155	3.87%
1974	181	2.21%
1975	347	3.43%
1976	379	4.22%
1977	368	1.63%
1978	342	2.05%
1979	287	1.95%
1980	217	1.47%
1981	223	3.14%
1982	340	10.00%
1983	642	7.01%
1984	848	9.32%
1985	1140	10.53%

future. Examiners hope to head off any problems by checking capital adequacy, asset quality, management practices, earnings, and liquidity.[14] In 1978, Congress created the Federal Financial Institutions Examination Council to establish procedures for consistent supervisory programs.

Bank supervision/examination is intended to spot potential problem areas and to recommend procedural changes to correct problems. In some cases, examination will reveal serious problems requiring the supervising agency to step in and take control of the bank to avoid bank failure.

Insurance

The collapse of hundreds of banks in the agricultural recession of the early 1920s and the depression of the 1930s highlighted the need to safeguard customers' deposits. After declaring a bank holiday in 1933, the Roosevelt Administration would allow banks to open only if they were financially sound. This was intended to prevent financial panic caused by bank runs. The Glass-Steagall Act of 1933 went one step further by creating the Federal Deposit Insurance Corporation. The FDIC provided insurance for depositors against bank failure. Initially, the federal government guaranteed only the first $2500 of deposits. That was soon raised to $5000. Now the guarantee is for $100,000.

Financed with a system whereby banks pay a flat fee based on the level of deposits, the FDIC has created confidence in the banking system and prevented depositors from losing their savings even if a bank closes.[15] To safeguard the insurance fund, the FDIC has authority to regulate and supervise all insured banks. In recent years, the FDIC has become actively involved in seeking buyers for failing banks or arranging mergers. These actions prevent bank failures and eliminate the need for the FDIC to tap the reserve fund to pay depositors.

During 1984, the failure of Ohio's Home State Savings and Loan brought to light the importance of deposit insurance. While most banks and S&Ls are insured by federal agencies (the Federal Deposit Insurance Corporation and the Federal Savings and Loan Insurance Corporation) guarantee-

---

[14] The Uniform Interagency Bank Rating System and Bank Performance Report standardizes the ratings in each category.

[15] Critics of the FDIC argue it insulates banks from market forces. Bankers know the FDIC will step in to safeguard deposits and they may behave with less restraint than they would without insurance. Beyond this critics suggest that insurance rates should be tied to the soundness of the bank. In this way individual banks, rather than the system, would bear the increased cost of unsound practices.

ing some $2.8 trillion worth of obligations, some states have their own deposit insurance. These state insurance funds often do not have the reserves to adequately cover customers' deposits.

Chapter Conclusion

The United States banking sector looks considerably different today than it did on the eve of the Great Depression. The widespread bank failures of the early 1930s did more than simply reduce the number of banks within the system. They created an attitude toward banks and the financial system that dictated the "rules of the game" and prescribed an industry structure that prevailed for nearly half a century.

The changes that are taking place, both legislatively and operationally, are creating a very different structure for the industry. Not only are these changes resulting in a breakdown of the barriers to interstate banking and an alteration of the traditional unit/branch banking mix, but the government's role in regulation and supervision is becoming more important.

Chapters 13 and 14 will analyze the financial industry in terms of a traditional industrial organization model. At this point, you can see that the financial industry is different because of the integral part financial institutions play within communities. Because of this integral role, government actively safeguards the public's well-being. This necessitates a visible presence by the government within the industry, regulating behavior, supervising operations, and insuring the public's financial deposits.

The financial industry is also important because it implements monetary policy actions. Depository institutions actually create money. This money creation process helps explain further the degree of government involvement in the industry and the integral place that depository institutions have within the macroeconomy. Before analyzing the functioning of the macroeconomy, you need to understand the money creation process. Chapter 7 introduces the role of financial institutions in the money creation process.

Consider These Questions

1. How would you explain the evolution of the dual banking system? Does it make economic sense?
2. Does your state allow branch banking? Has it always? Why is this system in place?
3. Who is the state banking officer in your state? How would you go about finding his/her name and determining responsibilities?

4. Is there an association of bankers in your state? Is it affiliated with the American Bankers Association? What role does this association play? Does it have a position on proposed laws that would allow interstate banking?

5. Why has the government historically required a bank to have either a state or a national charter? Should the government continue to exercise this kind of control? Try to explain what the financial system would look like if there was free and unregulated entry of banks into the system.

6. Compare and contrast operational restrictions placed on depository institutions with some other retail operation, for example, grocery or department stores. To what extent would operations of these retail outlets be affected by a regulatory structure like the one for depository institutions?

7. What is a bank holding company? Are there any in your area? How do the operations of the banks that are part of a holding company differ from those that are not?

8. Consider the boxed illustration about computer banking. How does this kind of technological advance affect regulations on interstate banking?

9. The American system of depository institution regulation and supervision is complicated. By referring to Figure 6.3 and the discussion on regulation and supervision, outline which organization has responsibility for which depository institutions.

10. What is the limit on FDIC-insured deposits? What happens to depositors with more than this amount when their bank fails?

Suggestions for Further Reading

Bentson, George J. *Bank Examination*. Rochester, N.Y.: University of Rochester Center for Research in Government Policy and Business, Reprint Series #C-16, 1973.
Best single source on bank examination—its purposes and operation.
Bentson, George J. "Federal Regulation of Banking: Analysis and Policy Recommendations." In *Journal of Bank Research* (Winter 1983): 216–244.
Discusses historical evolution of banking regulation.
Chase, Samuel and John Mingo. "The Regulation of Bank Holding Companies." In *Journal of Finance*, vol. 30 (May 1975): 281–292.
Provides survey of bank holding companies and the regulatory problems they present.

Golembe, Carter H. and David S. Holland. *Federal Banking Regulation, 1983–1984*. Washington, D. C.: Golembe Associates, 1983.
Comprehensive discussion of regulation of banks and the banking industry.

Langley, Monica. "FDIC Proposes Full Disclosure of Enforcement." In *The Wall Street Journal* (February 12, 1985): 2.
Outlines issues involved in FDIC investigation of financial institutions and the image problems created whether justified or not.

Robertson, Ross M. *The Comptroller and Bank Supervision*. Washington, D.C.: Office of the Comptroller of the Currency, 1968.
History of bank supervision.

Sinkey, Joseph F., Jr. "Identifying Problem Banks: How Do Banking Authorities Measure a Bank's Risk Exposure." In *Journal of Money, Credit and Banking*, vol. 10, no. 2, pp. 184–193.
Brief but clear and comprehensive analysis of most important factors considered by FDIC in trying to predict bank failures.

Volcker, Paul A. "The Burden of Banking Regulation." Washington, D. C.: Board of Governors of the Federal Reserve, October 14, 1980.
Remarks at the American Bankers Association Annual Meeting which highlight Fed's views on regulation of banking.

———. "Guide to Federal Reserve Regulations." Washington, D.C.: Board of Governers of the Federal Reserve, September 1981.
Outlines basic banking and other financial institution regulations set forth by the Federal Reserve.

CHAPTER SEVEN

FINANCIAL INSTITUTIONS and DEPOSIT EXPANSION

Money is such a routine part of everyday living that its existence and acceptance are ordinarily taken for granted. A user may sense that money must come into being automatically as a result of economic activity or as an outgrowth of some government operation. But just *how* this happens all too often remains a mystery.

Dorothy M. Nichols
Modern Money Mechanics, 1968

The first three chapters of this section investigated financial institutions from a microeconomic perspective. Now, after exploring the origins, structure, functioning, and performance of financial institutions, you will make a transition into macroeconomic analysis. The next part of the text discusses macroeconomic models and analytical frameworks. This chapter makes the connection between the micro world of financial institutions and the macroeconomy. It discusses financial institutions and the deposit expansion process. Because of our fractional reserve system and through the collective action of depository institutions, changes in the level of reserves at these institutions are multiplied several times to produce an increase in the economy's money supply.

Chapter Objectives

The deposit expansion process requires an understanding of the mechanics of the money multipliers but also an appreciation of the implications of this process for monetary policy decisions. You need to understand both.

Specifically, after you have studied the expansion and contraction process you should:

- Understand the roles that reserves and the monetary base play.
- Use balance sheet analysis to demonstrate the effect of an infusion of new funds.
- Understand the basic money supply multiplier and use it to estimate the potential expansion/contraction of the money supply.
- Identify leakages in the expansion/contraction process and explain their implications.

The implications of this process for monetary policy go beyond just being able to calculate a deposit multiplier and using it to estimate money supply changes. By the end of this chapter you will be able to:

- Explain who controls the supply of money.
- Evaluate the extent to which individual or institutional behavior influences the supply of money and monetary policy.
- Judge whether the multiplier is stable or changing by examining historical trends.

Keep these broader concerns in mind as you work to master the mechanics of the deposit expansion and contraction process.

Deposits in a Fractional Reserve System

The American financial system is based on the fractional reserve principle; thus, depository institutions can collectively create money through the deposit expansion process. Specifically, the fractional reserve system provides that a depository institution retain a fraction of deposits to cover daily withdrawals. The remaining funds are used for loans or investments.

Deposits at financial institutions are liabilities because the institutions are required to repay customers the money they have deposited. A previous chapter discussed various types of deposits. This chapter is primarily concerned with transactions deposits. These are demand deposits and other checkable deposits (NOW accounts, ATS accounts, and share draft accounts) at financial institutions. Remember also that these transaction accounts make up the largest component of our nation's money supply. Therefore, before proceeding to consider the money supply in the macroeconomy, you need to understand how actions by the Federal Reserve and depository institutions can increase or decrease transactions deposits and thus influence the money supply.

As far back as the goldsmiths, depository institutions have held a portion of all deposits as reserves. Institutions hold those reserves to cover deposit withdrawals. The remaining deposits are available for loans or investments. Chapter 4 pointed out that the probability of deposits being withdrawn drops dramatically as the number of depositors increases. The portion of total deposits that the goldsmiths or contemporary depository institutions need to retain is quite small. This percentage of deposits that financial institutions hold to cover withdrawals is sometimes called the natural reserve requirement. Regulatory institutions, especially the Federal Reserve, require depository institutions to retain a percentage of all deposits, but prudent financial management would result in depository firms holding reserves even without the regulation. The level of required reserves has changed over time. It also varies by state as some state regulatory agencies impose stricter requirements. Until the passage of the DIDMC Act of 1980, financial institutions were faced with a complex and often confusing array of reserve requirements.[1] In the years since deregulation began in March 1980, the Federal Reserve has phased in new reserve requirements. As of 1984 for Federal Reserve member banks and 1987 for all other financial institutions, the reserve requirements on checkable deposits are 3 percent for the first $25 million (with the first $2 million exempted to reduce restrictions on small institutions) and 12 percent for all deposits above $25 million.

Money Creation

Commercial Bank Balance Sheet

To begin, let's use conventional T-accounts to analyze a typical depository institution balance sheet. The focus could be any type of institution, but because commercial banks dominate, the focus here will be on a bank balance sheet. See Figure 7.1.

Keep in mind that assets must always equal liabilities. How will Community State Bank's balance sheet change if new deposits of $15 million are made as a result of a new factory opening? Refer to Figure 7.2. Notice that assets and liabilities have both increased by an amount equal to the new deposit. Furthermore, required reserves have increased (the level of required reserves is 12 percent of deposits) and excess reserves have increased.

---

[1] For example, there were five different reserve requirements for commercial bank demand deposits depending on the level of deposits. These ranged from 7 percent at the lowest level to 16-1/4 percent for institutions with demand deposits over $400 million. The reserve requirement for other types of financal institutions was different.

	Community State Bank		
Assets	(millions $)	Liabilities	(millions $)
Reserves	$10.0	Checkable Deposits	$50.0
Required reserves 7.5		Other Liabilities	15.0
Excess reserves 2.5		Capital	5.0
Loans & Securities	48.0		
Buildings, Equipment, and Other Assets	12.0		
TOTAL	$70.0	TOTAL	$70.0

FIGURE 7.1 *Typical Bank Balance Sheet for Period 1* This figure gives the simplified assets-liabilities statement (in the form of a T-account) for our illustrative bank. Notice the level of reserves available to cover deposit withdrawals.

	Community State Bank		
Assets	(millions $)	Liabilities	(millions $)
Reserves	$25.0	Checkable Deposits	$65.0
Required reserves 7.8		Other Liabilities	15.0
Excess reserves 17.2		Capital	5.0
Loans & Securities	48.0		
Buildings, Equipment, and Other Assets	12.0		
TOTAL	$85.0	TOTAL	$85.0

FIGURE 7.2 *Typical Bank Balance Sheet in Period 2* In this figure, deposits have increased by $15 million and reserves have jumped accordingly. The entire increase in liabilities from the new deposit is reflected on the asset side in the form of reserves.

Has the money supply increased as a result of these transactions? No! The increase in deposits occurred because the company that opened the factory transferred funds from its account in another city. Total deposits in the system have not changed.

The Money Creation Process

Let's look at the entire financial system and see how the collective action of financial institutions can "create" money. The strongest single force influencing changes in the nation's money supply is the Federal Reserve. As you will learn in more detail in Chapter 17, the Fed's major tool for changing the supply of money is open-market operations. By entering the open market or secondary market for government securities, the Fed can initiate the money expansion or contraction process that takes place through the nation's depository institutions.

Federal Reserve Open-Market Purchases   Once the decision is made to increase the money supply, the Fed, through its Open-Market Committee, purchases United States government securities. For discussion purposes, let's assume the Fed has purchased $10 million worth of securities. The Fed makes the purchase by using a check drawn against itself. This payment, when deposited in a financial institution (a bank, for example), immediately adds to the transaction account and reserves of the bank. The money supply has already jumped by $10 million.

The Multiple Expansion Process   Because this infusion of "new money" has increased bank reserves, funds are available for loans and investments. Assume that the $10 million received by the bond dealer in the sale of government bonds is deposited in the Community State Bank. Figure 7.3 shows how the bank's balance sheet has changed (compared to Figure 7.2). Notice that with the increase in deposits, both required and excess reserves also rise.

The majority of the $10 million deposit becomes available for loans or investments. Of the $10 million, $1.2 million or 12 percent must be held as required reserves; the remainder is available for loans or investments. If business conditions are good, the loan officers are in a position to use the entire new excess reserves, $8,800,000.

Assets	Community State Bank (millions $)	Liabilities	(millions $)
Reserves	$35.0	Checkable Deposits	$75.0
Required reserves 9.0		Other Liabilities	15.0
Excess reserves 26.0		Capital	5.0
Loans & Securities	48.0		
Buildings, Equipment, and Other Assets	12.0		
TOTAL	$95.0	TOTAL	$95.0

FIGURE 7.3   *Typical Bank Balance Sheet in Period 3*   The deposit of $10 million by the bond dealer, resulting from the Fed's open-market purchase has added to the reserves of Community State Bank (it now holds $26 million in excess reserves). The loan manager has some funds available for lending.

The Community State Bank extends loans in the amount of $8,800,000. These funds will in turn be deposited in the borrower's bank, adding to that institution's excess reserves position. The second bank, the Suburban National Bank, will seek to loan its excess funds rather than holding them as non-interest earning reserves. The 12-percent reserve requirement applies, but Suburban National still has $7,744,000 available for lending. Again assuming an active business climate, these funds can be loaned, at which point they will be deposited in the borrower's bank, Metropolitan Bank. Figure 7.4 illustrates this process through these three banks.

Remember, the process continues beyond these three stages whether the funds are loaned to someone dealing with a different bank or the same bank. As long as the loaned funds are reflected in new transactions deposits and excess reserves can increase, the expansionary process continues. Table 7.1 shows the collective impact of the multiple expansion process.

The process can continue until the entire original new deposit is held by various banks as reserves against deposits. The total potential increase in the money supply resulting from the Fed's infusion of $10 million in new funds is $83,333,333 (the original $10 million plus the expanded deposits from loans amounting to $73,333,333). Remember that this expansionary process resulted in an increase in the supply of money only because of the Fed's infusion of "new money." By drawing the original payment for the open-market purchase against itself (that is, basically increasing Community State Bank's reserve account at the Fed), the Fed began the multiple expansion of deposits. Had the original purchase been made with a check drawn against one of the banks in the system, no such expansionary process could have started. While this discussion has illustrated the expansionary

COMMUNITY			SUBURBAN			METROPOLITAN		
assets	liabilities		assests	liabilities		assets	liabilities	
reserves 35.0	deposits 75.0		reserves 8.8	deposits 8.8		reserves 7.74	deposits 7.74	
r.r. 9.0	liabil. 15.0		r.r. .929	liabil. 5.0		r.r. .818	liabil. 4.0	
e.r. 26.0	capital 5.0		e.r. 7.744	capital 2.0		e.r. 5.997	capital 1.0	
loans 48.0			loans 6.0			loans 4.5		
equip. 12.0			equip. 1.0			equip. .5		
TOTAL 95.0	TOTAL 95.0		TOTAL 15.6	TOTAL 15.8		TOTAL 12.74	TOTAL 12.74	

FIGURE 7.4 *Bank's Role in Deposit Creation*   This figure shows the beginnings of the expansion process triggered by the infusion of $10 million from the purchase of government securities by the Fed. The loan extended by Community is deposited in Suburban which uses part of its increased reserves to extend a loan which is deposited in Metropolitan. The multiple expansion process is underway. Refer to Table 7.1 for complete process.

	New Deposits	Required Reserves	Excess Reserves (for loans & invest.)
Bank 1 Community State	$10,000,000	$1,200,000	$8,800,000
Bank 2 Suburban Nat'l.	8,800,000	1,056,000	7,744,000
Bank 3 Metropolitan	7,744,000	929,300	6,814,700
Bank 4	6,814,700	817,764	5,997,000
Bank 5	5,997,000	719,700	5,277,300
Bank 6	5,277,300	633,300	4,644,000
Bank 7	4,644,000	557,200	4,086,800
Bank 8	4,086,800	490,400	3,596,400
Other Banks	28,969,500	3,596,340	26,373,160
TOTAL	$83,333,333	$10,000,000	$73,333,333

TABLE 7.1   *Total Possible Expansion in Deposit Creation Process*

process, the same scenario will unfold when funds are withdrawn from the system. The Fed's sale of securities in the open market is the most obvious example of how the contractionary process can begin. During the following discussion of the deposit expansion multiplier, keep in mind that the same process and multipliers apply in the contraction of the money supply.

The Deposit Expansion Multiplier   The infusion of "new money" by the Fed results in a multiple expansion of the nation's money supply. A few simple relationships determine this deposit expansion multiplier. Recall that the reserves (R) held against deposits (D) are a function of total deposits (where r is the reserve ratio):

$$R = rD \qquad (7.1)$$

Rearranging this equation leads to an equation for determining the total change in deposits resulting from an infusion of new reserves. Dividing both sides by r we have:

$$\frac{R}{r} = D \qquad (7.2)$$

Based on that equation:

$$\Delta D = \frac{\Delta R}{r} \qquad (7.3)$$

In the expansionary process example outlined in Table 7.1, the change of deposits would be:

$$\Delta D = \frac{\Delta R}{r} \qquad (7.3)$$

$$\Delta D = \frac{10,000,000}{.12}$$

$$\Delta D = 83,333,333$$

In other words, the deposit expansion multiplier here is:

$$8.33 \ (1/r = 1/.12 = 8.33.)$$

Leakages in the Expansion Process

The discussion of deposit expansion has been simplified to concentrate on the process. Not all loaned-out funds will find their way into transaction accounts. The public undoubtedly will choose to hold some of these funds as cash or may decide to place some in higher interest-bearing time deposits. Financial institutions may not choose to or may not be able to lend all available excess reserves. Each of these situations is a leakage from the deposit expansion process and results in a smaller deposit multiplier. A brief description of each leakage follows, and then they are incorporated into the deposit multiplier.

MONEY TODAY 7.1

When Can a Single Bank Create Deposit Expansion?

Our discussion of the multiple expansion process has distinguished between the actions of one bank, which we said could not create money through the deposit expansion process, and the banking system, which can. What about a situation where there is only one bank in a country? What about two or three? Does the multiple expansion process still work?

The quick answer to these questions is yes, the process still works. If there were but one bank in a country, it would be the banking system. Loans extended by this bank would return as deposits to the same bank. In a state like California where Bank of America dominates, or in a country like Canada where there are only a few major banks, the multiple expansion process works just the same way as it does in multibank states and countries.

The key factor in the deposit expansion process is whether the loans extended are redeposited. Knowing that the loans will be redeposited, our hypothetical monopoly bank can lend out a multiple of its excess reserves. A single bank that does not repre-

sent the entire banking system better not, because it has no assurance that the loans will be redeposited into its accounts. The loans may be deposited elsewhere, which means the original bank will have to cover payments on the loans. The single bank can only lend out a portion, not a multiple, of its reserves and therefore cannot create deposit expansion. The monopoly bank, acting as the banking system, can carry out the deposit expansion process.

Currency Held by the Public

For a variety of reasons, individuals may choose to hold some of their funds as cash rather than as transaction account balances. People find it convenient to hold more cash during the holiday season. Also, they are influenced by interest rates and may choose to hold money in anticipation of better investment opportunities. Proximity to a financial institution is also a factor. Individuals who cannot get to a bank and who do not have access to automatic teller machines may hold on to cash.

For whatever reason, these cash holdings serve as a drain on the expansionary process. The altered deposit creation equation representing this drain is:

$$\Delta D = \frac{\Delta R}{r + c} \tag{7.4}$$

where

$$c = \text{proportion of deposits held as currency } (cD)$$

Using a currency drain factor of 8 percent, the deposit expansion with this new multiplier is:

$$\Delta D = \frac{\$10,000,000}{.12 + .08}$$

$$\Delta D = \frac{\$10,000,000}{.20}$$

$$\Delta D = \$50,000,000$$

The deposit expansion multiplier is now:

$$5.0 \ (1/r + c = 1/.12 + .08 = 1/.20 = 5.0), \text{ rather than } 8.33$$

Excess Reserves

In the initial discussion, we assumed that banks were able to lend the full amount of their new excess reserves and that they wanted to be completely "loaned up." Business conditions might not permit institutions to extend loans to the maximum. An economic slowdown might be the reason behind the Federal Reserve's expansion of the money supply. Under these circumstances, insufficient demand may not allow the full expansion to occur.

We can incorporate these excess reserve holdings into the deposit expansion multiplier as follows:

$$\Delta D = \frac{\Delta R}{r + c + e} \tag{7.5}$$

where

e = proportion of deposits remaining as excess reserves (eD)

Assuming that 3 percent of deposits remain as excess reserves, the deposit expansion would be even less:

$$\Delta D = \frac{\$10,000,000}{r + c + e}$$

$$\Delta D = \frac{\$10,000,000}{.23}$$

$$\Delta D = \$43,478,260$$

The deposit expansion multiplier is:

$$4.35 \ (1/r + c + e = 1/.23 = 4.35)$$

Time Deposits

In addition to leakages due to currency holdings and excess reserves, the deposit expansion multiplier is also modified due to deposits into time accounts. Rather than placing all their funds into transaction accounts (whether regular checking accounts or money market checking accounts), individuals may choose to take advantage of time deposit accounts.

If individuals see high rates of return on time accounts and anticipate that interest rates will decline, they may want to "lock in" the higher rate by depositing some funds into the longer-term time deposit account. Time deposits require a different level of reserves than do demand deposits. This factor must be included in the deposit expansion multiplier:

$$\Delta D = \frac{\Delta R}{r_d + c + e + r_t(t)} \tag{7.6}$$

where

r_d = reserve ratio on demand deposits

r_t = reserve ratio on time deposits

t = proportion of demand deposits held as time deposits

Assuming that people hold 20 percent of demand deposits in time accounts and using a time account reserve requirement of 5 percent, the deposit expansion is now:

$$\Delta D = \frac{\$10,000,000}{.12 \, + \, .08 \, + \, .03 \, + \, .05(.20)} \qquad (7.6)$$

$$\Delta D = \frac{\$10,000,000}{.23 \, + \, .1}$$

$$\Delta D = \$41,666,666$$

The deposit expansion multiplier is now 4.16 ($1/r_d + c + e + r_t(t) = 1/.24 = 4.16$). This is only half of what the multiplier was without these leakages.

This discussion presumes that one can accurately estimate the leakages that occur in the expansion process. This is not always possible; conditions change and individuals and institutions may react differently than anticipated. Despite this constraint in estimating the exact magnitude of the expansionary process, the principle of the multiple expansion (or contraction) of deposits remains.

Who Controls the Supply of Money?

Thus far the discussion of expansion of deposits has assumed that the Federal Reserve has infused "new money" through its open-market operations. This implies that the Fed influences the money supply by affecting reserves. The Fed is certainly the dominant force influencing changes in the supply of money (Figure 7.5 shows the expansionary monetary action), but the actual conduct of monetary policy is somewhat more complicated. Determinants of the supply of money are more understandable in light of the concept of *monetary base* (sometimes referred to as *high-powered money*). The monetary base (MB) is equal to currency in circulation (C) plus depository instituton reserves (R). Thus:

$$MB = C + R$$

Through its open-market actions, the Fed can most assuredly influence the monetary base; its effect on reserves is not certain.

Consider open-market purchases that involve a bank. The Fed buys bonds from the bank by either crediting the bank's account at the Fed or providing the bank with payment the bank holds as vault cash. In both situations, reserves are increased. If, on the other hand, the Fed purchases securities from an individual (the non-bank public, in technical language) who cashes the Fed's check and holds the currency, reserves in the system have not changed.

In both of these scenarios the monetary base has increased (since the monetary base reflects currency in circulation and reserves). This points out

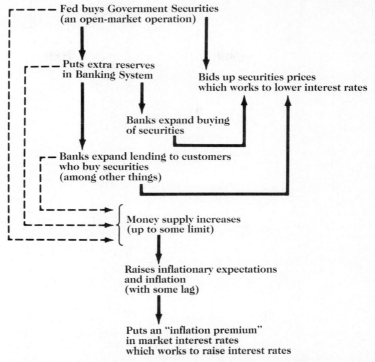

Fed buys Government Securities
(an open-market operation)

Puts extra reserves
in Banking System

Bids up securities prices
which works to lower interest rates

Banks expand buying
of securities

Banks expand lending to customers
who buy securities
(among other things)

Money supply increases
(up to some limit)

Raises inflationary expectations
and inflation
(with some lag)

Puts an "inflation premium"
in market interest rates
which works to raise interest rates

Source: Adapted from Federal Reserve Bank of Minneapolis Conference on "The New Dynamics: The Financial System, Economic Policy, and the Private Sector," (Fall 1984).

FIGURE 7.5 *Some Effects of Expansionary Monetary Action* The Fed's expansion of the money supply works through the open market in two ways—first, by increasing reserves and allowing depository institutions to expand loans and, second by lowering interest rates and stimulating borrowing.

why the monetary base is a more important variable for the Fed to consider in its monetary policy deliberations—the Fed has more direct control over the monetary base than it does over the level of reserves in the system.[2] Keep in mind that the Fed does not have complete control over the monetary base. Borrowing from the Fed, although influenced by the discount rate set by the Fed, is largely determined by demand by borrowing institutions.[3]

_____

[2] This scenario described Fed open-market operations, but a similar result occurs with discount window borrowing.
[3] The Chapter 17 appendix identifies other aspects of the monetary base that are not directly controlled by the Fed.

MONEY T⑦②DAY

Whenever reading about money supply growth, you will see the term "seasonally adjusted." This relates to a procedure the Federal Reserve uses to adjust data for seasonal factors.

The procedure the Fed uses to seasonally adjust the monthly money supply data is based solely on the behavior of the money series itself. Using both past and future data, the process attempts to separate the seasonal movement in the data from movements due to the business cycle, long-term growth, and irregular shocks. These four components multiplied together are assumed to comprise the total money supply. To keep up with trends in the components, the seasonal factors for each year are based on weighted moving averages of the data over several surrounding years. Future and past data are weighted symmetrically in the calculation, with the greatest weight given to the years closest to the year being adjusted.

The precision of the adjustment is enhanced by computing separate seasonal factors for the different components of the monetary aggregates. The adjusted components are summed to obtain the total seasonally adjusted series.

Since 1982, the Fed has used the X-11-ARIMA seasonal adjustment procedure. ARIMA stands for autoregressive integrated moving average, which is the statistical technique utilized in the forecasting model. Such models provide minimum mean square error forecasts based on the past values of the monetary series. The Fed's X-11 ARIMA is a slight variation of the Bureau of the Census' X-11 seasonal adjustment process.

The seasonal adjustment process may be modified if an unusual series of events is known to have affected money supply behavior. Before the seasonals are computed, the effects of such events are identi-fied and removed from the unadjusted money data with a statistical technique called intervention analysis. The seasonals calculated from the modified data are then applied to the unadjusted series.

The money supply data that you see reported by the Fed have undergone extensive statistical adaptations so that unusual economic factors are removed from the monetary aggregate series. This allows more accurate comparison of the monetary aggregates across time.

Source: Adapted from Diane F. Siegel and Steven Strongin, "M1: The Ever-Changing Past," in Federal Reserve Bank of Chicago *Economic Perspectives* X, 2 (March/April 1986): 3–12.

The Federal Reserve bases its decisions about open-market operations on the assumption that it can predict the money supply multiplier. The actual money supply multiplier can be determined by taking the ratio of the money supply (M1) to the monetary base. For M1, the money multiplier is:

$$MM = \text{M1}/(MB)$$

Figure 7.6 reveals that the money multiplier has been relatively stable over time, although it fluctuates from month to month.

Despite the relative stability of the money multiplier, the Fed cannot predict the effects of its actions perfectly because it is not the only actor in this monetary play. You have seen that actions by individuals, including their decisions about cash holdings, their allocation of funds between transaction accounts, time accounts, and even accounts outside of depository institu-

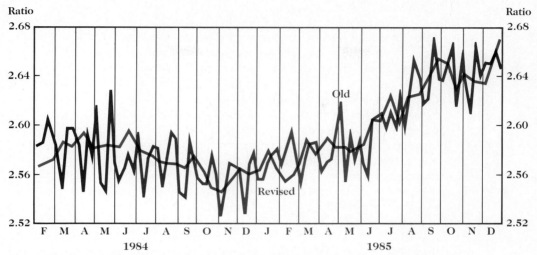

Note: The old series is weekly; the revised series is biweekly, covering reserve maintenance periods.

Source: Figure, "M1 Multiplier" from Federal Reserve Bank of St. Louis Review, December 1985, p. 32. Reprinted by permission.

FIGURE 7.6 *M1 Multiplier*   The money multiplier has been measured using two techniques. Using either technique, the M1 multiplier has been relatively stable, although showing some tendency to increase in recent months.

tions, and borrowers' and lenders' expectations about market conditions all influence the expansionary process. One additional factor is involved in the money supply process—the role of the financial institutions themselves.

We have already noted indirectly that decisions by depository institutions affect the multiple expansion and contraction of the money supply. These institutional decisions about the level of reserves they want to maintain will influence the magnitude of the expansionary and contractionary process. (Holding excess reserves essentially reduces the expansionary effect of high-powered money.)

Beyond this, the extent to which depository institutions utilize the Fed's discount window also influences the potential expansion of the supply of money. Borrowing from the Fed increases the monetary base.

In summary, the forces influencing changes in the supply of money are the following:

- the Fed—through open-market operations and discount window rates,
- individual institutions—through their decisions to increase lending,
- depositors—through the mix of deposits and their holdings of cash, and
- depository institutions—through their decisions on excess reserves and their borrowings from the Fed.

Chapter Conclusion

The deposit expansion/contraction process is important because it is the mechanism that translates the monetary authority's policy actions into money supply changes. The specifics of this process as presented in this chapter are clear and straightforward. In reality, the estimation of the various multipliers is complicated by individual and institutional behavior. The extent to which policy makers can accurately predict how their open-market actions will reverberate through the financial system will determine whether monetary policy will move the system in the desired direction. In subsequent chapters, the debate over the usefulness of monetary policy as a macroeconomic tool will be debated. Whether it is a useful, successful tool depends on theoretical considerations. Since the Federal Reserve continues to influence the supply of money through open-market actions, the accuracy of predicting the expansionary/contractionary process is crucial. Understanding the money multipliers will help you work through the macromodel in the next section and analyze and evaluate monetary policies in Part III of the book.

Consider These Questions

1. Using the money multiplier explained in this chapter, figure the maximum possible contraction of the money supply resulting from the Fed's sale of securities amounting to $10 million when the average reserve ratio across depository institutions is 10 percent.

2. Do the leakages in the money expansion process apply when the money supply is contracting as well as when it is expanding? Explain.

3. Why can't a single depository institution create deposits (expand the supply of money) while the entire system can?

4. What's the difference between the monetary base and a more conventional money measure such as M1?

5. Refer back to Chapter 2, especially Table 2.1 and Figure 2.1. Using this information and what you learned about the monetary base in this chapter, is the money multiplier for M2 larger or smaller than that for M1? Why? What are the implications for monetary policy?

6. Since the deregulatory legislation of 1980 and 1982, non-bank depository institutions have been allowed to operate just like banks. This means they can offer transaction accounts (essentially demand deposits). What effect has this had, if any, on the multiple expansion of the money supply described in this chapter?

7. What factors influence the degree to which the Federal Reserve can control the nation's money supply?

Suggestions for Further Reading

Burger, Albert E. *Money Supply Process.* Belmont, CA.: Wadsworth Publishing Company, 1971.

See Chapters 1–4 for a detailed discussion of the deposit creation process and money multipliers.

Gurley, John J. and Edward S. Shaw. *Money in a Theory of Finance.* Washington, D. C.: The Brookings Institution, 1960.

This early work presents a theory explaining the relationship between commercial banks and other non-bank depository institutions.

Johannes, James M. and Robert H. Rasche. "Predicting the Money Multiplier." In *Journal of Monetary Economics* 5 (1979): 301–325.

This is a somewhat sophisticated analysis of economists' ability to estimate the money multiplier.

Nichols, Dorothy M. *Modern Money Mechanics: A Workbook in Deposits, Currency and Bank Reserves.* Federal Reserve Bank of Chicago, 1982.

Title pretty much describes the book. It's a clear exposition of the deposit creation process and money multiplier determination with problems and self-guided study plans.

Tobin, James. "Commercial Banks as Creators of Money." In *Banking and Monetary Studies*, edited by Deane Carson, 408–419. Homewood, IL.: Irwin, 1966.

Nobel prize winner's classic analysis of deposit creation process in which he criticizes the simple approach to money expansion.

PART THREE

THE MACRO-ECONOMIC MODEL

CHAPTER EIGHT

AN OVERVIEW of MACRO-ECONOMIC THEORIES

There are no crucial experiments that instantly annihilate a theory. But theories do get nickled and dimed away until their adherents are ripe for seduction by different theories.

Paul Samuelson
"Succumbing to Keynesianism," *Challenge*
(January/February 1985)

So far in this text we have discussed the world of intermediation, banking, and interest rates. We have been studying what we might call the *microeconomics of banking*. Now we will shift gears and study money and monetary theory as we begin to examine the *macroeconomics of the financial system*. Your goal in the next four chapters is to understand the role of money in the economy and what policies can be used to stabilize the economy.

The models we will use to develop monetary theory are from macroeconomics. You most likely have explored the rudiments of these macro tools in the economic principles course. The theory that informs the first seven chapters of the text is generally shared by all economists. However, as you may know, the world of macroeconomics is full of disagreements about what is the "true, correct theory" of the macroeconomy. In fact, no single macro model is agreed upon by even a majority of economists. Thus the task is left to you to learn various competing models.

In the past, macroeconomics has been divided conveniently into two schools of thought, classical economics and Keynesian economics. The events of the 1970s and 1980s necessitate broadening this categorization somewhat. We will consider the classical school, Keynes and Keynesian economics, monetarism, and the *new classical* school, which includes supply-side economics and rational expectations. Despite the expanding list of relevant schools of thought and the explanation here of more recent macroeconomic theories, remember that quite often economics is discussed only in terms of classical and Keynesian theories.

The following quotation illustrates the approaches to economic problems taken by classical economists and Keynesian economic policy makers.

> Herbert Hoover recommended a big tax *increase* in 1931 when unemployment was extremely high and a large budget deficit was in prospect.
> John F. Kennedy recommended a big tax *reduction* in 1962 when unemployment was again a problem, although a much less serious one, and a large budget deficit was again in prospect.[1]

The approaches taken by presidents Hoover and Kennedy were markedly different. They characterize the divergence between pre-Keynesian and post-Keynesian economic policy. How can we explain such different responses to very similar predicaments? In the first part of the chapter, we will look at the basic tenets of the classical and Keynesian schools of thought and gain some insight into the policy prescriptions flowing from each theoretical framework. Then we can compare and contrast these schools with the monetarist and the new classical schools.

Chapter Objectives

Chapter 8 provides the foundation for exploration of a complete macroeconomic model in Chapter 9. You should consider how classical economics was challenged by the Keynesian view and what additional insights are provided by Keynes' ideas.

In particular, you should reflect on the basic tenets of classical economics and ask yourself what aspects of the classical model allowed the Keynesian alternative to become so widely accepted. By the end of this chapter, you will be able to:

- Explain Say's Law and its dependence on flexible prices.
- Assess the degree to which wages and prices are flexible.
- Outline the role of money in the classical model.

In exploring the basics of the Keynesian aggregate demand model, you should think about the ways you can use this model to explain economic

---

[1] Herbert Stein, *The Fiscal Revolution in America* (Chicago: University of Chicago Press, 1969): 3.

events. In order to use the basic Keynesian model effectively, you need to be able to:

- Explain why aggregate expenditures and income are always equal.
- Assess the effects that stimulation of expenditures will have on income.
- Explain the equality of investment and saving under conditions of equilibrium.
- Discuss the expenditure multiplier and illustrate its importance.

After outlining the basic Keynesian model, this chapter also gives you an introduction to the connection between money, income, and output. To understand this connection, you should be able to:

- Explain the factors that make up the demand for money.
- Illustrate the effect of changes in the demand and supply of money on interest rates.
- Discuss the influence interest rates have on income and expenditures.
- Identify the ways in which money markets and capital markets interact.

Finally, the chapter introduces monetarism and new classical economics. These economic models are important for the synthesis approach used later in this part of the text. To understand these models and their impact on macroeconomics, you should be able to:

- Explain the rise in popularity of monetarism.
- Identify the differences between the simple quantity theory and contemporary monetarism.
- Specify the components of the new classical economics.
- Discuss the basic premise of supply-side economics.
- Explain the origins and basic components of rational expectations.
- Contrast these models with the basic Keynesian model.

Above all you should be able to use these models to interpret and analyze macroeconomic events. Throughout the chapter think about how these models will apply to contemporary policy issues.

Classical Economics and its Implications

We will now briefly review the basic tenets of classical economic theory. With these in mind we can outline the classical view of the macroeconomy and how it works.

Overview of Classical Economics

The classical model is undergirded by Say's Law. According to J.B. Say, production creates a demand of equal value.[2] No glut of products can exist; markets will always clear. Crucial to the achievement of this equilibrium are flexible wages and prices. Prices adjust to ensure that demand is sufficient to absorb supply. With flexible wages the labor market is always in equilibrium; involuntary unemployment does not occur.

In the classical model money is a medium of exchange. Money is essentially neutral; it does not affect output or employment. Money does influence the price level, as the quantity theory of money explains. (For a detailed discussion of this theory, refer to Chapter 10.) Classical economists also explain interest rates rather easily. Interest rates influence the level of saving and the level of investment spending. Saving is the postponement of consumption and occurs only if interest rates are high enough to overcome the opportunity cost of abstaining from current period consumption.

Savings are loanable funds. Business people demand loanable funds for investment purposes. Their demand is inversely related to the interest charge for borrowing. Markets work to equate the supply of loanable funds with demand. Since markets always clear, whatever portion of aggregate income is saved is also borrowed by businesses to make investment expenditures. According to classical economists, interest rates are related to the levels of savings and investment and vice versa, but unrelated to the supply of money. On the other hand, the demand for money is related to income and the level of expenditures but unrelated to the rate of interest.

Implications of the Classical Economic Model

The classicists' view of the macroeconomy has a number of policy implications that we need to keep in mind, especially in subsequent chapters when we assess policy alternatives. In the classical world, money is neutral. Changes in the supply of money affect the price level but not relative prices. This implies that efforts to influence the economy through monetary policy are undesirable. Some neoclassicists admit that wage rates may not be perfectly flexible. They recognize that under certain circumstances the government may need to stimulate the economy to correct a disequilibrium; in these instances monetary policy is useful. Fiscal policy is not useful and is, in

---

[2] Personal savings did not interfere with this relationship since savings were used to allow producers to make investment purchases.

fact, often counterproductive. The belief that markets work, that they will adjust to changing economic conditions, is the most compelling justification classical economists use to argue against government intervention.

Keynes' Criticism of the Classicists

Keynes called into question the basic tenets of the classicists. He challenged the rigid interpretation of Say's Law. Keynes argued that the "short-run" validity of supply creating sufficient demand to maintain full employment was incorrect. The demand for labor might be insufficient to produce full employment and no automatic forces would intervene to restore it.

In part, Keynes' argument was based on the fallacy of flexible wages. Pointing out that wage rates are determined through contracts which were not easily changed, Keynes illustrated that wages did not move easily downward. Without flexible wage rates the automatic market clearing assumption of the classicists was not functional.

Beyond this, Keynes argued that savings and investment would not necessarily be equal at a level sufficient to produce full employment. Keynes pointed out that interest rates are not the sole determinant of the level of savings and investment. Savings is determined by the level of income; investment depends on expectations regarding sales potential. Therefore, even interest rates fluctuating freely and declining during slack periods might not prove incentive enough to stimulate investment. Therefore savings and investment might fall below the level required to produce full employment.

In criticizing the classicists' model, Keynes explained how the economy of the 1930s could "bottom out" and remain depressed. Beyond this, Keynes constructed an alternative macroeconomic model which stressed aggregate demand rather than supply. A simple Keynesian aggregate demand model will precede a closer look at Keynes' views on money and interest rates.

Keynes' Aggregate Demand Model

A macroeconomic model includes both the supply and demand sides of economic activity. Demand factors and a simplified explanation of supply factors are useful in understanding equilibrium and disequilibrium. The macro model has some of the same characteristics as a simple supply/demand price determination model. In a price determination model, the interaction of supply and demand produces an equilibrium price and quantity exchanged. Equilibrium occurs when there is no tendency for further change; nothing within the model will lead to an alteration of the price established by the market. Markets are not always in equilibrium; when markets do not clear we say they are in *disequilibrium*. In disequilibrium the market shows a tendency for change, for movement toward an equilibrium state.

The phrase "within the model" raises another point needing some clarification before we can proceed. Economists refer to factors "within the model" as *endogenous factors*. In this model endogenous variables are variables for which the model explains relationships and changes. Factors "outside the system" are called *exogenous*. We cannot determine the value of exogenous variables from any relationships described in the model. Exogenous variables are determined outside the model through some other process. *Exogenous variables may affect endogenous variables.*

Aggregate Expenditures and Income

The expenditure or demand portion of the real sector, as distinct from the monetary sector, includes the household sector (with consumption expenditures designated by C), the production sector (with investment expenditures designated by I), the government sector (with its expenditures designated as G), and the foreign sector (the difference between exports and imports designated as $X - M$). Aggregate demand (or total expenditures) equals aggregate supply or output (the same as GNP), designated as Y:

$$Y = C + I + G + (X - M) \tag{8.1}$$

At this point let's proceed with a more simple version of the model, one that ignores the government and international sectors and which focuses on the household and production sectors. In this simplified version of the world, the household sector receives income by selling the factors of production to the production sector. Members of the household sector either use their income for consumption or they save some portion of it. The production sector generates income by selling its products and spends its income to acquire the factors of production. In this situation aggregate demand consists of consumption expenditures (C) plus the production sector's expenditures for plants and equipment (I). Aggregate supply is the total of goods and services generated by the system. This model is in equilibrium when aggregate demand is equal to aggregate supply.

We can look at equilibrium in a different way as well. Aggregate income (designated by Y) generated in the system is used for either consumption (C) or saving (S). This relationship is represented as:

$$Y = C + S \tag{8.2}$$

Aggregate expenditures (designated by E) are composed of consumption and investment (I):

$$E = C + I \qquad\qquad (8.3)$$

Equilibrium occurs when expenditures equal income, $E = Y$; disequilibrium occurs when expenditures do not equal income, $E \neq Y$.
The equilibrium condition is:

$$E = Y \qquad\qquad (8.4)$$

Substituting equations 8.2 and 8.3 into 8.4, equilibrium occurs when:

$$\underset{\text{aggregate expenditures}}{C + I} = \underset{\text{aggregate income}}{C + S} \qquad\qquad (8.5)$$

Simplifying this by subtracting C from each side of the equation leaves:

$$I = S \qquad\qquad (8.6)$$

Thus, when the model is in equilibrium, investment equals savings. At this point the equality of S and I is definitional. This equality is also a condition for equilibrium within the system.

Why does the equality of aggregate demand and aggregate supply represent equilibrium within the system? And precisely what does equilibrium mean in this model? If aggregate supply exceeds aggregate demand, producers will find their inventories building up as they are unable to sell all that they produce. To compensate they will cut back production, that is, aggregate supply will decline. Producers will adjust output until aggregate supply is just sufficient to meet aggregate demand.

A similar but reverse process will occur if aggregate demand exceeds aggregate supply. Similarly, saving and investment explain disequilibrium and the movement toward equilibrium. If saving exceeds investment expenditures ($S > I$), income is withheld from the spending stream. This is equivalent to aggregate supply exceeding aggregate demand and will set into motion the same process. Equilibrium is the condition under which no internal forces move the economy away from the established level of activity. An external shock, such as a drought and the resulting crop shortages, could disturb equilibrium and force the system to readjust. In a sense equilibrium in the economy is like a perfectly balanced ecosystem, say a terrarium. When in equilibrium the system needs no external stimulation to sustain itself.

The consumption function is central to the Keynesian aggregate demand model. Keynes pointed out that consumption expenditures increase as income increases, but not by as much. One particular level of consumption expenditures is autonomous; that means it is fixed and unrelated to the level of income. We can express this relationship between consumption and income, as follows:

$$C = cY + \overline{C} \tag{8.7}$$

where

$C =$ total consumption

$Y =$ income

$c =$ the marginal propensity to consume, that is, the change in consumption caused by a change in income, $\dfrac{\Delta C}{\Delta Y}$

$\overline{C} =$ autonomous consumption (the bar over a symbol implies that the symbol's value is constant)

The consumption function is shown graphically in Figure 8.1. Notice that the slope of the consumption function $\left(\dfrac{\Delta C}{\Delta Y}\right)$ is the *marginal propensity to consume (mpc)*. In this case *mpc* = .8.

Business and government sectors are added to the model by including investment and government expenditures (in this discussion we assume both are *autonomous*, that is, they are determined exogenously rather than as a function of income).

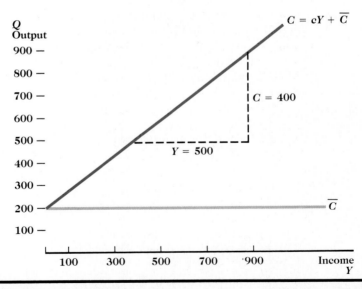

FIGURE 8.1 *The Consumption Function*   This is a simple consumption function showing how C responds to changes in Y. The slope of the line is the *mpc* (change in consumption resulting from a change in income, here equal to .8), and the intercept is the autonomous level of consumption ($\overline{C}$ = 200). The equation of this function is $C = .8Y + 200$.

Figure 8.2 illustrates the complete aggregate demand and aggregate supply diagram. Panel 8.2a incorporates a 45-degree line. Emanating from the origin, the 45-degree line is equidistant from the two axes. The line represents aggregate supply or aggregate output because all points on the line represent the equality of expenditures and income. In other words, aggregate supply is a 45-degree line because it shows all the levels of total output generated for every level of real income in the system.

Panel 8.2b illustrates equilibrium occurring where $S = I$. The saving function is derived from the consumption function.[3] Where $S = I$ there is no tendency for change in the system; both savers and investors are satisfied. At point E in Figure 8.2, equilibrium occurs because aggregate demand equals aggregate output. At this point savings is just equal to investment, Point E in 8.2.[4]

The Multiplier

An important aspect of the aggregate demand model is the expenditure multiplier. Changes in consumption, investment, or government expenditures have a multiple increase on the change in the equilibrium level of income.

In Figure 8.3 notice that investment expenditures have increased from 100 to 150. The equilibrium level of income also increased but by considerably more than the change in investment. In this case the change in the equilibrium level of income was five times the change in aggregate demand. This is the multiplier effect. Why does this occur?

The change in autonomous investment expenditures reverberates through the system. In each phase of this reverberation the expenditure

---

[3] Knowing $Y = C + S$, we can derive the saving function:

$$Y = cY + \overline{C} + S$$
$$S = Y - cY - \overline{C}$$
$$\text{so}$$
$$S = (1 - c) Y - \overline{C}$$

We call $(1 - c)$ the marginal propensity to save (*mps*).

---

[4] We can use algebra to illustrate the equality of saving and investment at equilibrium. Excluding the government sector to simplify our work, we represent equilibrium as:

$$Y = C + I$$

Subtracting C from both sides of this equation, we have

$$Y - C = I$$

Since $Y - C = S$, then $S = I$.

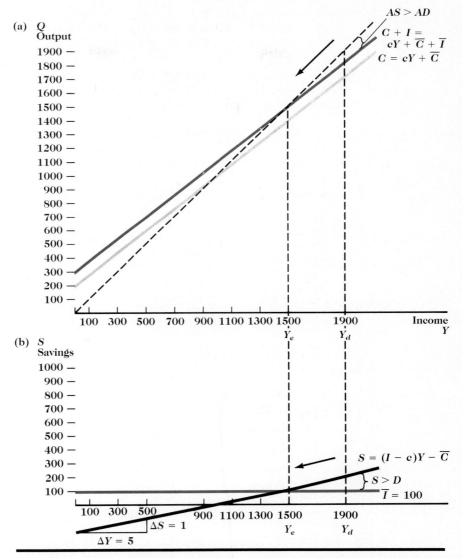

FIGURE 8.2 *Macroeconomic Equilibrium* This figure combines the aggregate demand function (consumption plus investment) and the aggregate supply line (the 45-degree line) in the top graph to produce equilibrium, which occurs at point *E*. The lower graph plots the savings function, which is derived from the consumption function, and the autonomous investment line to show that equilibrium occurs where *S* = *I*.

becomes income for someone who in turn spends part (the amount determined by the *mpc*) and saves part (determined by the *mps*). This secondary expenditure becomes income and again is partly spent and partly saved. Consider Figure 8.4.

The change in investment of 50 (movement from point A to point B) affects income in the next period (movement from point B to point C). This change in income produces an increase in spending (.8 × 50) in the next

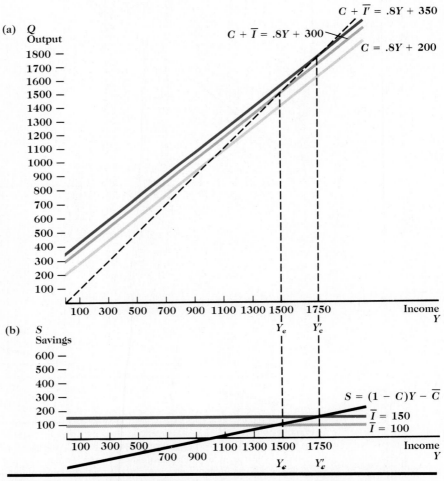

(a) Q Output

$C + \overline{I} = .8Y + 350$

$C + \overline{I} = .8Y + 300$

$C = .8Y + 200$

(b) S Savings

$S = (1 - C)Y - \overline{C}$

$\overline{I} = 150$

$\overline{I} = 100$

FIGURE 8.3 *Changes in Autonomous Investment* In this figure we see the multiple effect on income of an increase in one of the components of the aggregate demand function. In this case autonomous investment increases from 100 to 150 (shown in the lower graph) causing aggregate demand to increase (shown in the upper graph). This change of 50 in investment produces a five-fold increase in income, from 1500 to 1750.

period (point C to point D). This spending increase stimulates output and income (point D to point E), which calls forth an increase in spending again (point E to point F). This process continues and the total change approaches 250:

$$50 + .8(50) + .8(40) + .8(32) + .8(26.50) + \ldots = 250$$

We need to incorporate government into this simple aggregate demand model. Government expenditures are treated just as autonomous invest-

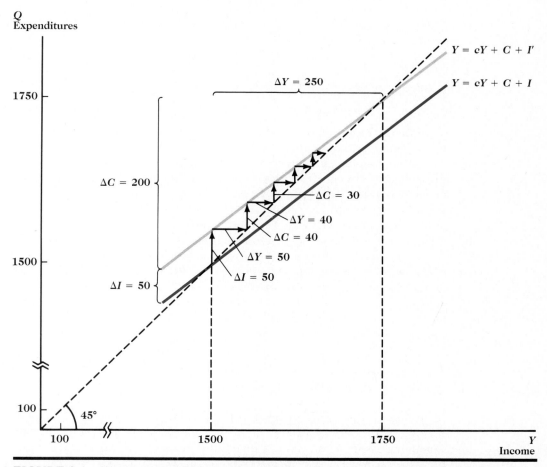

FIGURE 8.4 *The Multiplier Process*   The multiplier process occurs in stages. This figure shows how the change in investment of 50 sets into motion a continuous and almost instantaneous increase in income. The original increase of 50 causes income to rise by the same amount which, due to the marginal propensity to consume, results in an increase in consumption causing an increase in income, and so on and so on. The total change in income approaches 250.

ment expenditures.[5] This expands aggregate demand so that it includes $C + I + G$.

Now we can formulate a general rule regarding the multiplier effect by using simple algebra:

$$Y = cY + \overline{C} + I + G$$

or

$$Y - cY = \overline{C} + I + G$$
$$Y(1 - c) = \overline{C} + I + G$$

Solving for Y we get:

$$Y = \frac{1}{1 - c} (\overline{C} + I + G)$$

Whenever aggregate demand (represented by C, I and G) changes, Y will increase by that amount times $\frac{1}{1 - c}$. We call $\frac{1}{1 - c}$ the expenditure multiplier. The larger c is (the steeper the slope of the aggregate demand line), the larger the multiplier.

This simple expenditure model highlights how changes in aggregate demand can influence the economy. In the Keynesian system, aggregate demand is more important as a driving force than is supply. And, since government expenditures represent one component of aggregate demand, government intervention in the form of expenditures can have a powerful effect on the economy. This multiplier effect can work on the downswing as well as the upswing. If something causes producers, for example, to cut back on investment expenditures, a serious economic downturn may result. One of the essential conclusions of the Keynesian analysis is that when the economy turns down, the government needs to increase its expenditures to overcome the decrease in private spending and to stimulate economic expansion once again.

Money and Interest: A Keynesian View

In addition to viewing government expenditure policies as important, Keynes reevaluated the importance of money and interest rates. Before examining a complete income expenditure model, we need to understand the Keynesian view on money and interest rates.

---

[5] When the government sector is added (G representing expenditures and T for taxes), the equilibrium condition expands from $S = I$ to $(S + T) = (I + G)$.

Demand for Money

As you recall from Chapter 3, the two explanations for interest rate determination include the liquidity preference theory and the loanable funds approach. The liquidity preference theory identifies the public's demand for money (*Dm*) and the system's supply of money (*Sm*) as determining the interest rate. Now let's examine the factors underlying the public's demand for money with a more Keynesian interpretation.[6]

You'll also recall that we specified in our earlier discussion that the demand for money meant the "demand for money to hold." This point becomes particularly important to a discussion of the factors influencing the demand for money function. The main concern is the quantity of money the public desires to hold in very liquid forms (for example, cash or checkable deposits).

The liquidity preference approach is closely connected to the loanable funds approach. We assume that individuals have two choices for the money they do not spend; they may hold money in a liquid form or they may purchase bonds.[7] In this case, *ceteris paribus*, when the demand for money declines the demand for bonds will increase. You will read more details about this connection later.

Even with the simplifying assumption that individuals may only either hold money or purchase bonds, why would anyone hold money? Bonds provide a return; cash balances provide no return.[8] Distinct opportunity costs are associated with holding liquid cash balances. The need to hold money must be sufficient to overcome these opportunity costs or people would never hold cash balances.

Three components of the demand for money explain the desire to hold cash balances: the *transactions demand*, the *precautionary demand*, and the *speculative demand*.

Transactions Demand   Individuals need money to handle day-to-day transactions. For the teenager who carries a pocketful of quarters to the video arcade or for the business person who needs cash for taxicab fares or quick lunches, or for the young family paying bills that come due throughout the

---

[6] The loanable funds approach to interest-rate determination identified the demand for and the supply of loanable funds as the explanation for interest rates.

[7] Obviously people have many more investment opportunities than just bonds, but our discussion is simplified by using only two alternatives. The theory is not dramatically changed even when this assumption is relaxed.

[8] Our discussion here is not substantially altered by the fact that most checkable deposits today offer interest return. We are talking about a differential rate of return between liquid cash balances paying very low rates and less liquid deposits paying a higher rate of interest.

month, the situation is the same. Individuals need cash balances for daily transactions. Expenditures increase as income rises, so the transactions demand for money is positively related to income. For the most part the transactions demand for money is unrelated to the rate of interest. Moving money balances from high-interest earning deposits to a liquid form on a day-to-day basis is simply too costly for most people in terms of time and money.[9] Thus, the transactions demand for money is influenced only by income. The transactions demand for money is:

$$Dm = f(\overset{+}{Y})$$

Precautionary Demand Individuals also feel the need to have access to liquid funds in the case of emergencies. As a youngster this might have meant a dime (now a quarter) for a phone call. As an adult this may mean extra cash to handle an automobile breakdown on the expressway, or available money to cover more serious automobile repairs or replace essential home appliances, or money to purchase a cross-country airline ticket for a spontaneous trip.

The precautionary demand for money is also influenced by income. As income rises people feel the need to have access to larger sums of money. But, emergencies do not occur on a daily basis like normal transactions do. Individuals, therefore, are willing to reduce the amount of money they hold for precautionary purposes when the opportunity cost of holding money rises; that is, the precautionary demand for money is inversely related to interest rates. The precautionary demand for money is represented by:

$$Dm = f(\overset{+}{Y}, \overset{-}{r})$$

Speculative Demand Individuals' demand for money to hold is also influenced by the opportunities to earn a return on an investment. Since returns (interest rates) fluctuate, individuals may hold on to money temporarily in anticipation that interest rates will rise and they can earn a higher return. Over the past few years interest rates not only have reached historically high levels, they have fluctuated quite regularly. Consider how individuals have tried to anticipate the movements of interest rates in making decisions about

---

[9] Money market checking accounts allow people to earn a return on their deposits and still be in a position to pay day-to-day expenses by check. There are costs associated with these accounts (in some cases minimum balances) and despite earning a return individuals must accept a lower interest rate than that paid on other deposits.

whether to purchase a six-month certificate of deposit now or wait until next week when the rate of return may be higher. The speculative demand for money explains why people may hold cash balances anticipating rising interest rates.

Remember that in the Keynesian explanation people could hold either money or bonds. Recall from our discussion in Chapter 3 that when interest rates rise, bond prices fall. A fall in the price of a bond produces a capital loss for its holder. If individuals anticipate a rapid rise in interest rates, which might mean that the capital loss on the bond would exceed the interest return, they would want to hold on to money. Its return, although zero, would be greater than a negative return on the bond. But individuals also are less willing when interest rates are high to incur the opportunity cost of holding money on the chance rates might rise further. After observing interest rate fluctuations, individuals are not likely to expect interest rates to rise further when they are already very high or to fall rapidly when they are already low. Thus, the speculative demand for money is inversely related to the rate of interest. The speculative demand is:

$$Dm = f(\overset{-}{r})$$

Total Demand   The total demand for money is a combination of these components:

$$Dm = f(\overset{+}{Y}, \overset{-}{r})$$

Figure 8.5 shows the components of the demand for money in Panel 8.5a and total demand Dm, as a function of the rate of interest for various levels of income in Panel 8.5b.[10] The Keynesian view that the demand for money is influenced by interest rates is dramatically different from the classicists' view.[11]

---

[10] In explaining the speculative demand for money, Keynes developed the idea of the liquidity trap. He hypothesized that when the nominal interest rate drops to a very low level, individuals, realizing that nominal rates cannot decline below zero, will anticipate that rates will rise. Individuals will absorb money balances while waiting for rates to rise. The demand for money function would become horizontal, that is, the demand for money would become increasingly elastic in the liquidity trap. The notion of the liquidity trap was used to explain why monetary policy would not stimulate the economy during a depression. An increasing money supply would be absorbed in cash balances rather than entering the spending stream.

[11] In accepting that the Dm is influenced by interest rates, one must reject the assumption that velocity is constant. Instead it fluctuates in response to changes in interest rates. This is an issue of controversy which is discussed in Chapter 10.

Alternative Explanations

Before proceeding with a discussion of the supply of money, we need to acknowledge two alternative explanations of the demand for money. William Baumol has explained the demand for money by equating money to an individual's inventory, much like the inventory a business would accumulate. This is called the *inventory approach*.[12] Just as businesses allow invento-

---

[12] W.J. Baumol, "The Transaction Demand for Cash: An Inventory Theoretic Approach," *Quarterly Journal of Economics* 66 (November 1952): 545–56.

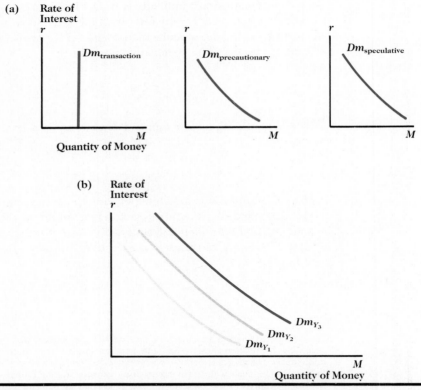

FIGURE 8.5 *Demand for Money and Its Components*   The upper three graphs show the individual components of Keynes' demand for money function. The precautionary and speculative components are sensitive to the rate of interest; the transaction component is not (determined by the level of income). By horizontally summing these three components we get the Keynesian demand for money function shown in the lower graph. This graph also shows that as income rises the demand for money increases (shifts to the right).

ries to increase during a period of economic growth and decline when interest rate costs rise, individuals hold larger cash balances as income rises and reduce their cash balances as opportunity costs rise with increasing interest rates. As in the Keynesian explanation, the inventory approach to the demand for money can be represented as a functional relationship:

$$Dm = f(\overset{+}{Y}, \overset{-}{r})$$

James Tobin developed a *portfolio approach* to explain the public's demand for money.[13] Tobin maintained that individuals hold a portfolio of financial assets so as to diversify the risk associated with any single asset. One of the assets in the portfolio is money. As income rises, the holdings in the portfolio rise. When interest rates rise, individuals shift their assets out of money, which generates no return, and into income-earning assets. The portfolio theory, although relying on a different explanation, leads to the same functional relationship as the inventory approach, namely that

$$D = f(\overset{+}{Y}, \overset{-}{r})$$

The Baumol-Tobin work demonstrates that the transactions demand for money, in addition to the precautionary and speculative demand, is influenced by interest rates. Consider for a moment how the Baumol-Tobin explanation of the demand for money is different from the dominant view before the time of Keynes. Since Keynes' analysis, economists have viewed money as filling more than just a transactions need. Money is considered an asset; as such the rate of interest (the price of borrowing money) influences the demand for money. Interest rates also influence the rate at which money "turns over." This is called *velocity*. We subsequently will examine how the changing notion about the Dm affected the thinking of monetarist economists. But for now, we'll complete our investigation of the money market by looking at the supply of money.

Supply of Money

Chapter 7 discussed deposit expansion and how this process influenced the supply of money. In considering the supply of money in this chapter, we will concentrate on two issues: the supply of money determined by the Federal

---

[13] J. Tobin, "Liquidity Preference as Behavior Toward Risk," *Review of Economic Studies* 25 (February 1958): 65–86.

Reserve System and the velocity of money.[14] Deposit expansion through the banking system is important, but to simplify the discussion we will assume that the Federal Reserve determines the supply of money. Consider the supply of money as an exogenously determined variable. In other words, the Sm is determined outside the model; nothing within the model automatically changes the supply of money. Without question the Federal Reserve is influenced by variables already addressed—the level of income and interest rates—but the decision to increase or decrease the supply of money is a discretionary decision of the Federal Reserve System, not an automatic one endogenously determined within our model.

With the Federal Reserve determining the supply of money, equilibrium is illustrated within the money market as is shown in Figure 8.6. The supply of money is a vertical line because it is assumed to be unrelated to interest rates (that is, it is an exogenous variable determined by the Federal Reserve). Equilibrium occurs where $Dm = Sm$. At this point a market rate of interest is established.

---

[14] Eventually we will investigate how the banking system also can affect the supply of money.

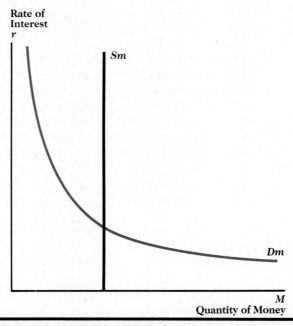

FIGURE 8.6 *Supply and Demand for Money* This figure combines the demand for money function with an interest insensitive supply of money function.

MONEY TODAY 8.1

The Cash-Balance Approach

The work of Baumol and Tobin, explaining that even the transactions demand for money has some interest sensitivity, is illustrated with the following description.

By assuming that the transactions demand for money is interest insensitive, we can illustrate the monthly expenditure pattern with Panel 8.1a. An individual receives income and holds the amount necessary to cover monthly expenses in cash balances. As expenditures are made, the cash balance dwindles to zero. The next month the same process is repeated.

The Baumol-Tobin explanation is represented with a slightly different diagram—Panel 8.1b. Upon receiving a paycheck at the beginning of the month, our hypothetical individual holds half the amount necessary for that month's expenditures in cash and puts the other half in an interest-bearing security, for instance government T-bills. As the middle of the month approaches and the cash balance dwindles, the T-bills are sold, providing the cash necessary to cover expenses for the rest of the month. The sale has also allowed the individual to generate some interest income.

According to this explanation, the higher the prevailing interest rates the larger the portion of cash balances placed into short term interest-bearing securities. Thus even the transactions component of the demand for money is sensitive to interest rates.

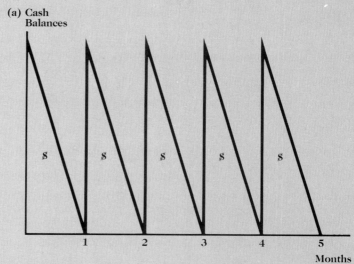

(a) Cash Balances

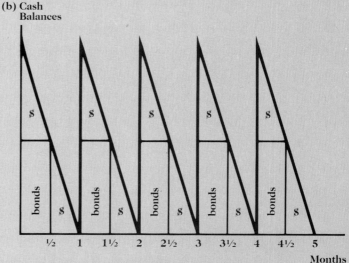

(b) Cash Balances

Interest-Rate Equilibrium: The Keynesian View

In the Keynesian view of the monetary sector, the demand for and supply of money interact to establish an equilibrium rate of interest. The rate of interest transmits the results of changes in the money market to the capital market and thus connects the monetary and real sectors.

The money market is somewhat different from other markets. All the money that is supplied must be held in cash balances or used to purchase bonds. The suppliers (the Federal Reserve System) cannot really build an inventory of money. Consider the connection between the money and bond markets, as shown in Figure 8.7.

Assume that the rate of interest is r. At r, $Sm = Dm$. What happens when the Federal Reserve increases the money supply to Sm'? The rate of interest drops (to r'). But why? The Federal Reserve can inject money into the system through the open market for bonds. When increasing the Sm, the Federal Reserve buys bonds, that is, it offers negotiable paper, dollars, to

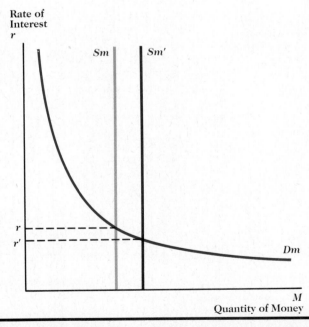

FIGURE 8.7 *Interest Rate Determination* The interaction of the demand for and supply of money functions determines the rate of interest in the simple Keynesian model. If the supply of money increases, while the demand remains unchanged, the rate of interest declines, in this case from r to r'.

individuals in return for non-negotiable paper, bonds.[15] In other words, the Federal Reserve buys bonds by injecting money into the system. This increased demand for bonds raises the price of bonds and lowers the rate of return (interest rate) on those bonds. Through this process the rate of interest will move toward the new equilibrium level, r'. Another way to think about this is that when the supply of money is increased, given the prevailing interest rate there is a surplus of money. Individuals use the surplus money to buy bonds, pushing bond prices up and interest rates down. A similar but reverse process occurs when the supply of money is reduced.

Money and Capital Market Interaction

Keep in mind that our discussion about interest rate determination in the money market has assumed that income is constant. In other words, we have undertaken only a partial analysis. To move to a broader analysis we need to provide for interaction between the money market (monetary sector) and the investment capital market (real sector). Interest rates provide the bridge we need.

Investment

The investment schedule, that is, what determines the level of investment, is important to the interaction between the monetary and real sectors. In an economic sense investment refers to expenditures for plant and equipment, sometimes called capital investment. A variety of factors influence the investment demand schedule. These include capital costs versus profitability (which subsumes sales potential), business expectations, government incentive and tax programs, and alternative investment possibilities. An investment schedule in which the quantity of investment funds is inversely related to the rate of interest can be built. As interest rates rise, the cost of capital rises. Higher costs must be covered by higher revenues. With higher costs, risks increase and business people are less likely to undertake these more costly investment expenditures. An investment demand schedule, often called the marginal efficiency of investment (MEI), is shown in Figure 8.8. Given a fixed set of circumstances (conditions are held constant), a level of investment is associated with each interest rate. When conditions

---

[15] We discuss open market operations as part of the section on Federal Reserve policies in Chapter 17.

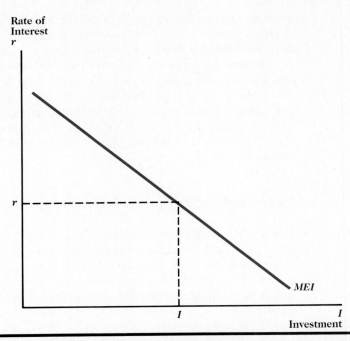

FIGURE 8.8 *The Investment Demand Schedule* Keynes' investment demand function is a simple downward sloping demand curve. Once the investment function is set, we can determine the marginally efficient level of investment for any given rate of interest.

change, for example, business tax rates change to encourage new investment or business expectations change, the *MEI* schedule will shift (any changes that encourage investment will cause the schedule to shift to the right).

By combining Figures 8.7 and 8.8 with Figure 8.2, we obtain Figure 8.9, which illustrates a simple relationship between the monetary sector and the real sector via interest rates.

In this simplified view, the rate of interest is determined in the money market. A given rate of interest determines the level of investment spending given the demand for investment funds. The level of investment spending is one of the components of aggregate demand that determines the equilibrium level of income in the system. This simple model illustrates how a change in the supply of money can set into motion changes that result in a higher equilibrium level of income in the system.

Don't become too attached to this model. Although the model is clear, it oversimplifies theory and reality. For example, while the model can illustrate how a change in the *Sm* leads to a lower interest rate, higher investment spending via the expenditure multiplier, and a higher equilibrium level of income, the model allows only a partial equilibrium analysis.

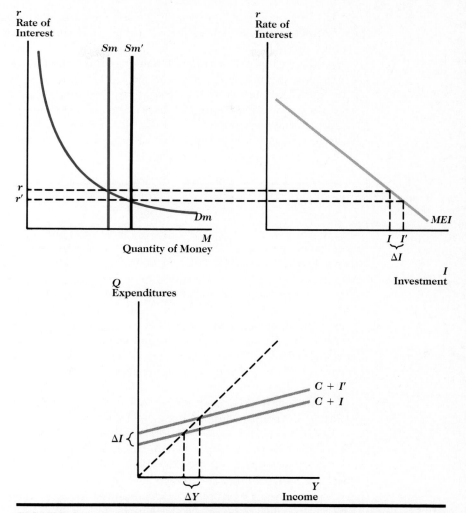

FIGURE 8.9 *Interaction of Money Market, Investment, and Aggregate Demand*
This figure combines Figures 8.7 and 8.8 with 8.2. It shows that the interaction of the demand for money and the supply of money set a rate of interest which determines the level of investment spending. That level of investment is reflected in the aggregate demand curve in the lower graph. The increase in the supply of money lowers the rate of interest which increases the level of investment spending. This, in turn, results in a multiple increase in the level of income in the system.

It has no provision for the increased level of income to feed back into the *Dm* schedule, and as such, the analysis has limited applicability. This model's explanation of the connection between money and the real world is limited also because it presumes that the monetary influence follows only one route. It ignores the monetarist view of the world. An expanded version of the model will be presented in Chapter 9. At this point, we will briefly explore the thinking of monetarists. This will set the stage for subsequent policy debate discussions between the Keynesian and monetarist approaches to the use of monetary policy which we will review in Chapter 10.

Monetarism

Until the rise of Keynesian economics most economists accepted the quantity theory of money as an explanation for price movements (the quantity theory was introduced in Chapter 1). In a very narrow sense, monetarism is a restatement of the old quantity theory—changes in the money supply are the major factor explaining changes in nominal income. In a broader sense monetarism stresses the underlying stability of the economy, the efficacy of the market mechanism, the influence of the money supply on nominal income and prices, the destabilizing effects of discretionary fiscal policy (and most government intervention into the economy), and the desirability of fixed rules (as distinct from discretionary actions) in the conduct of monetary affairs.[16]

Monetarism is most often associated with long-time University of Chicago economist Milton Friedman. In 1963, he and Anna Schwartz published *A Monetary History of the United States* in which they demonstrated a consistent relationship between fluctuations in the money supply and national income for the years 1867–1960. Friedman's prolific writing, along with the work of other economists such as Karl Brunner and Allan Meltzer, provided a core of theoretical and empirical research which brought monetarist thinking to the public's attention.

The inability of the predominant economic thinking (basically Keynesian thinking) to influence the economy positively during the late 1970s provided monetarists with the opportunity to urge reconsideration of reliance on fiscal policy as the major macroeconomic tool. The writings of academic economists, coupled with an array of empirical studies conducted by the

---

[16] A good outline of the basic tenets of monetarism can be found in Thomas Mayer, "The Structure of Monetarism," in a book by the same name which Mayer edited. (New York: W. W. Norton, 1978).

BILL SCHORR, 1982 LOS ANGELES HERALD

"... *First I was a Keynesian ... Next I was a monetarist ...
Then a supply-sider ... Now I'm a bum ...*"

Federal Reserve Bank of St. Louis, convinced many economic policy makers to reconsider the role of money in the economy.

Just as the early 1960s are often referred to as the period when Keynesian economics reigned, the early 1980s may be seen as somewhat of a triumph of monetarist thinking. Under the leadership of Chairman Paul Volcker, the Federal Reserve dramatically reduced the rate of growth of the money supply, from 1980 to early 1983. Undaunted by criticism that this policy was precipitating a recession, the Fed persisted to struggle against inflation with a tight monetary policy.

But a strict monetarist view contends that maneuvering of fiscal policy is destabilizing. Despite renewed interest in the role of money in the economy, macroeconomic policy in the late 1970s and early 1980s did not abandon the basics of fiscal policy that were influenced by decades of Keynesian economic thinking. When President Reagan urged adoption of a tax cut in 1981, he referred to the Kennedy-proposed tax cut enacted in 1964 as a precedent; Reagan was proposing the Keynesian policy of Kennedy. This illustrates that the lines between schools of economic thought often blur when those viewpoints become the basis for macroeconomic policy.

The blurring of lines distinguishing schools of thought also results from the general inability of policy makers to get the United States economy onto a stable growth path. The lack of a successful policy dominating economics, as Keynesian economics had done twenty years before, has prompted alternative views to develop. We will classify two such prominent views under the title of the *new classical economics*.[17]

---

[17] Kevin Hoover compares and contrasts monetarism with the new classical economics in "Two Types of Monetarism," *Journal of Economic Literature* (March 1984): 58–76.

The New Classical Economics

The United States economy in the late 1970s confounded economists. High unemployment levels, slow growth, high price levels, and high nominal and real interest rates presented an array of problems that before had seldom, if ever, confronted policy makers simultaneously. Consider that from 1975 to 1981 consumer prices rose an average of about 9 percent per year, while unemployment averaged approximately 7 percent. This resulted in a discomfort index (CPI + unemployment rate) of 16 percent, an unprecedented figure for any extended postwar period. Dissatisfaction with conventional macroeconomic policy (including Keynesian and monetarist programs) prompted consideration of alternatives.

A definition of the new classical economics includes two influential viewpoints—supply-side economics and rational expectations. These viewpoints evolved from models that contain some assumptions similar to those of the classical school of a century earlier. The most important assumption is that competitive markets produce wage and price flexibility resulting from forces of supply and demand. One major distinction between new classicism and the ideas of Keynesian and monetarist thinkers is the importance of aggregate demand versus aggregate supply. The new classicists place much less confidence in policies designed to influence aggregate demand. Instead these alternative views contend that demand-management policies are likely to have no beneficial results and possibly will have negative effects. Both the supply-siders and the rational expectations economists prefer to minimize barriers to natural economic activity on the demand side and, on the supply side, to create an atmosphere conducive to economic growth.

Unlike Keynesian economics, which adapted and refined a basic body of knowledge from Keynes, and unlike monetarist thinking, which has had its well-established proponents, supply-side economics is an amorphous blend of many different writers, many of whom disagree with one another. Rational expectations theory is a more clearly defined body of knowledge. Its roots can be traced to the writings of John F. Muth in the early 1960s, but its meaningful macroeconomic application date from 1972 with the work of Robert Lucas, Thomas Sargent, and Robert Barro.

Supply-Side Economics

In a narrow sense, supply-side economics is defined as tax policies that stimulate economic activity by increasing incentives to save, to invest, and to work. The Reagan administration's economic program, which took shape during the 1980 campaign and just after the inauguration, stressed tax policies as the dominant economic stimulus. Reagan advisors promoted the supply-side approach through the public press. Especially prominent was University of Southern California economist Arthur Laffer, whose name is often associated with the supply-side "Laffer curve."[18] Much of the Economic Recovery Act of 1981 was framed around supply stimulus through tax reform. The approach was to reduce inflationary expectations while increasing output and reducing prices through productivity gains. This narrow view of supply-side economics did not gain acceptance among economists; it also did not have a long honeymoon among policy makers.

In a broader sense, supply-side economics refers to the study of how potential output can be stimulated. In this sense it investigates ways to shift the production function within various economic sectors. Improvements in productivity can come from changes in tax policy which create incentives to produce, but they also can result from renewed research and development

---

[18] This is a proposition that economic disincentives may be so great with high tax rates that raising taxes actually will reduce government revenues while cutting taxes will stimulate the system and increase government revenues.

ECONOMICS T⑧⒈DAY

The Laffer Curve—A Component of Supply-Side Economics

In the first Reagan Administration, especially during the debate leading to the tax reform package of 1981, supply-side economics garnered considerable publicity. In almost every popular periodical article about supply-side economics, Arthur Laffer and his Laffer Curve were mentioned.

Laffer, a southern California economist, is said to have drawn the curve on a restaurant napkin in trying to explain his ideas to a colleague. The theory underlying the curve is said by many critics to have as much substance as a paper napkin. Despite such criticism the Laffer Cruve has gained widespread use.

The notion of the Laffer Curve is that tax receipts are a function of the tax rate and the tax base. If taxes are so high that they have stifled individual and corporate initiative, tax increases may actually reduce tax revenues. On the other hand, a tax reduc-

tion might lead to an expansion of the base and an increase in tax revenues.

To illustrate this idea, Laffer used a simple semi-circular curve. Supply-side proponents of a tax cut referred to this curve, claiming that the economy was somewhere on the curve before the peak, say Point A. From that point a tax increase would move the economy to point B, actually decreasing tax receipts. A tax reduction would move the economy to point C resulting in greater tax revenues.

Critics of the Laffer Curve argue that there is no way of telling where we are on the curve. If the economy is at point D a tax reduction will move the system to point E causing receipts to decline, just the opposite of what the supply-siders predicted.

The escalating federal deficit after the tax cuts of 1981 seemed to reinforce the critics. Still the idea of tax cuts to stimulate the economy are imbedded in both Keynesian and supply-side recommendations.

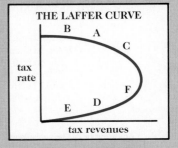

THE LAFFER CURVE

efforts, improved education and training for workers, industry deregulation, and a variety of cost-saving measures. Research into these aspects of production has resulted from renewed interest in the role of aggregate supply; or perhaps it is more appropriate to state that this is a reduced interest in the role of aggregate demand.

Supply-side economics is more closely related to the microeconomic orientation of the classical economists than to the approaches of Keynesian and monetarist economists. However, classicists always are concerned with the macroeconomic policy implications of their supply-side findings. This policy orientation makes the work of the supply-siders quite relevant to our investigation of macroeconomic theory, both because of its current prominence and because of its influence on macroeconomic theory in general and policy in particular.

Rational Expectations

Expectations have always played a significant role in macroeconomic theory. The rational expectations hypothesis makes some specific judgments about the rationality of expectations and the influence expectations have on economic policy. Rational expectations economists contend that economic actors (individuals and business decision makers) closely observe economic events and government policies. These economic actors do not make systematic mistakes in their expectations formation. Instead, based on observations, they form rational expectations about the future of government policies and economic activity, and then they act accordingly.

John Muth originally formulated the idea of rational expectations in the early 1960s. Muth applied the theory to commodity markets at the microeconomic level. Robert Lucas of the University of Chicago applied the theory to the macroeconomy. Other economists, such as Thomas Sargent of the University of Minnesota and Robert Barro of the University of Rochester have expanded the theory. The rational expectations literature is technically complex. This complexity has contributed to the confusion the theory has created among economists and to the disbelief it has generated among policy makers. Critics argue that the theory contains some unreasonable assumptions about the flexibility of wages and prices. The theory is new enough that debate over its validity continues. The basic ideas of rational expectations are fairly simple and its policy implications are significant.[19]

---

[19] An excellent nontechnical explanation of the theory of rational expectations can be found in Chapter 19 of *Principles of Economics*, 2nd Edition, by Roy J. Ruffin and Paul R. Gregory (Glenview, IL: Scott, Foresman, 1986). A discussion of the implications of the theory appears in B. T. McCallum's article, "The Significance of Rational Expectations Theory," *Challenge* (January/February 1980): 37–43.

According to the rational expectations hypothesis, all economic actors form expectations concerning monetary and fiscal policy actions by the government. Behaving in accordance with their self-interests, these actors try to anticipate government stabilization policies. Stabilization policies that are correctly anticipated by the public will have much less of an effect than policies that surprise the public. For example, if wage earners correctly anticipate that the Federal Reserve will increase the growth rate of the supply of money, they will act to benefit from such a policy. Such an increase in the money supply usually works to stimulate the economy. If wage earners rationally anticipate the inflation associated with monetary growth, they will act to protect themselves by exerting wage demands that will force up nominal wages. This will work to minimize or to neutralize the real stimulating effect of the monetary policy. Instead of employment, output, and possibly even real wages increasing, these variables are unaffected by monetary growth; only wage and price inflation will result.

Rational expectations economists thus argue that discretionary macroeconomic policy cannot be successful. The rational expectations of the public will undermine stabilization policies. Without interference, the economy will tend toward a natural equilibrium condition. The government should announce and maintain a realistic, stable policy for money growth and tax and revenue actions. With no price or policy surprises, inflationary expectations will decline and the economy will stabilize at some natural level for GNP and employment.

Rational expectations theory disputes the benefits of the interventionist policies of Keynesians. This theory further argues that even if interventionist policies are not anticipated by the public, the positive results will be only temporary. This view represents a direct challenge to those advocating monetary and fiscal policies for economic stabilization.

Macroeconomic Synthesis

Macroeconomic theory reflects a continually developing synthesis of ideas. Many of the principles of Keynesian economics, once considered revolutionary, are now integrated into some models with classical characteristics. By the same token, monetarist ideas have found their way into many Keynesian expositions.

What follows in the next few chapters is a presentation of a basic macroeconomic model. Grounded in conventional Keynesian notions, the model incorporates monetarist and new classical macroeconomic thinking. The purposes for developing a working macroeconomic model are to provide a theoretical base for investigating the interaction between the financial sector and the macroeconomy and to serve as a basis for evaluating monetary policy actions.

Chapter Conclusion

To understand the synthesis model presented in the next chapter, you first need to understand the basics of the classical and Keynesian models. Two foundations of classical economics covered were Say's Law and the classical view on money in the system. Most of this chapter explored the simple aggregate demand model and the concepts of the multiplier, the money market, and interest rates. Some of the newer economic schools of thought were mentioned because they, too, influence the synthesis model.

Now you are ready to understand a more sophisticated macroeconomic model. The synthesis model in the next chapter will assume the relationships identifed in this chapter and move beyond them to illustrate the connection between the money market, the goods market, and the labor market.

Consider These Questions

1. How does Say's Law relate to the notion of supply-side economics?

2. Summarize Keynes' basic criticism of the classical economic model. Is it a valid criticism?

3. What is the Keynesian expenditure multiplier? Does it really exist? Can you identify some examples of it from current events?

4. Why was Keynes' formulation of the demand for money function so important in light of the economic events of the 1930s? Using the insights gained from this type of economic model, what kinds of macroeconomic policies would you have recommended to President Roosevelt?

5. Why did Keynes' *General Theory* create such a stir within the economics profession?

6. Summarize monetarism in one sentence. Explain its policy implications.

7. What components of classical economic thought are incorporated into the new classical economics (both rational expectations and supply-side economics)?

8. Consider the cash-balance approach to the demand for money put forth by Baumol and Tobin. How is this explanation altered, if at all, by interest-bearing checking accounts?

9. What determines interest rates in the Keynesian model? What implications will this have for monetary policy decisions?

10. Which aspects of the Reagan economic program (both the first and second administration) would you categorize as classical? Keynesian? monetarist? and new classical?

11. How is the Laffer Curve analysis affected by the tax reforms instituted by Congress in 1986?

12. A major component of the supply-side approach to economics includes stimulation of investment spending. What do supply siders suggest as the best way to stimulate investment? Contrast that approach with the Keynesian approach.

13. Which aspects of monetarism and rational expectations are similar?

Suggestions for Further Reading

Breit, William and Roger L. Ransom. *The Academic Scribblers*. Hinsdale, IL.: Dryden Press, 1982.
    One of the many history of economic thought books; this one is easy to read and provides insights which apply to the contemporary application of economic theory.
Boyes, William J. *Macroeconomics*. Cincinnati: South-Western Publishing Company, 1984.
    Standard macroeconomic text which has a succinct explanation of Keynes' aggregate demand model in Chapter 3.
Goldfeld, Stephen M. "The Demand for Money Revisited." In *Brookings Papers on Economic Activity* 3 (1973): 577–638.
    Outlines empirical issues in the demand for money debate; includes econometric analysis.
Hansen, Alvin. *A Guide to Keynes*. New York: McGraw-Hill, 1953.
    Most authoritative analysis of Keynesian thought.
Heilbroner, Robert. *The Worldly Philosophers*. New York: Simon and Schuster, 1986.
    Provides a history of the great economic thinkers' contributions to the discipline but does so by highlighting the individuals so you feel you know and understand them. Easy to read.
Hicks, John. *The Crisis in Keynesian Economics*. New York: Basic Books, 1974.
    Chapters 1 and 2 highlight the classical-Keynesian debate.
Johnson, Harry. "Notes on the Transactions Demand for Cash." In *Essays in Monetary Economics*. Cambridge, MA: Harvard University Press, 1967, 179–191.
    Presents an excellent synthesis of issues related to the transactions demand for money.

Kantor, Brian. "Rational Expectations and Economic Thought." In *Journal of Economic Literature* XVII (December 1979): 1422–1441.

Summarizes the rational expectations view of the world, relates it to economic policy making and places it within the context of the history of economic thought. Sophisticated reading.

Mandy, David. "A Summary of Supply-Side Economics." In *Illinois Business Review* 41, 1 (February 1984): 1–9.

Clear, concise summary of the basic precepts of supply-side thinking.

Poole, William. *Money and the Economy: A Monetarist View.* Reading, MA: Addison-Wesley, 1978.

Provides a good, thorough introduction to monetarism.

Samuelson, Paul A. "Succumbing to Keynesianism." In *Challenge* (January/February 1985): 4–11.

One economist's view of how classical economics gave way to a Keynesian view of the world.

Schumpeter, Joseph A. *A History of Economic Analysis.* Oxford: Oxford University Press, 1954.

This monumental work provides the most thoughtful and integrative review of the evolution of economic ideas of any such volume.

CHAPTER NINE

INCOME DETERMINATION: BASIC KEYNESIAN MODEL

Macro Economics: a laudable attempt to explain how large parts (or the whole) of an economy work, without pretending to know how the component parts work.

Ralph Harris
"Everyman's Guide to Contemporary Economic Jargon," 1964

In the last few chapters we have begun to explore basic macroeconomic theory and a simple income determination model. We are now in a position to investigate a more complete income determination model, one that integrates the real and monetary sectors and introduces the price level. This approach allows us to analyze the effects of monetary and fiscal policy changes. It is a useful analytical tool we can employ in evaluating the impact of various macroeconomic policies.

The model developed in this chapter allows for the determination of joint equilibrium between the real sector (often called the goods market) and the monetary sector. In the previous chapter we were able to determine only partial equilibrium because we looked at the real and monetary sectors separately. We could not provide for feedback effects or the interaction of the two sectors. The synthesis model allows a general equilibrium solution. This model most often is referred to as the Keynesian *IS-LM* model. While the underlying model is Keynes', the diagrammatic approach presented here was developed by one of his contemporaries, J.R. Hicks. The *IS-LM* label is derived from the joint equilibrium in the goods sector—equilibrium occurs where investment (I) is equal to saving (S)—and the monetary sector—

equilibrium occurs where the demand for money, or liquidity (L), is equal to the supply of money (M). We label the equilibrium points in the goods market the *IS* curve and the equilibrium points in the money market the *LM* curve.[1]

The *IS-LM* model is appealing because it combines the real and monetary sectors in a simple graphical presentation. As such it is easy to use for analyzing the effects of various policy actions on the variables within the system. The model assumes that the price level is fixed, therefore real and nominal variables are the same.

Chapter Objectives

Your goals in exploring macroeconomic theory are to acquire some understanding of the precepts of economics and to develop a working model that can help you analyze contemporary economic policy actions. In earlier chapters of this section you acquired some insights into the basics of macroeconomics. By the end of this chapter you will understand a simple analytical model. Subsequently we will use this model in our policy discussions.

More specifically, by the end of Chapter 9, you should be able to:

- Explain a simple macroeconomic model.
- Describe uses of the model.
- Assess limitations of the model.
- Use the model to demonstrate the results of various policy actions.
- Evaluate the model's applicability to the macroeconomy.

Commodity Market Equilibrium

Equilibrium in the goods, or commodity, market occurs when desired (or intended) investment and saving are equal.[2] Equilibrium can occur at a variety of combinations of income levels and interest rates. We will derive an *IS* curve that represents equilibrium of investment and saving at all possible

---

[1] John R. Hicks, "Mr. Keynes and the Classics: A Suggested Interpretation," *Econometrica* 5 (April 1935): 147–159. A concise statement of the Keynesian general equilibrium model appears in Warren L. Smith and Ronald L. Teigen, "The Theory of Income Determination," in *Readings in Money, National Income and Stabilization Policy* (Homewood IL: Irwin, 1970).

[2] We distinguish between desired (or intended) saving and unintended investment. When producers misjudge demand and products go unsold, this is unintended inventory buildup or unintended investment.

income-interest rate combinations. This curve reflects the influence of interest rates on investment demand and the individual's marginal propensity to consume.

Deriving the *IS Curve*

In the last chapter we determined that investment demand was inversely related to interest rates.[3] We showed this with the downward sloping *MEI* schedule. We also showed that changes in the rate of interest produced a change in the level of investment spending, which resulted in a shift in the aggregate demand curve (refer to Figure 8.9).

To derive the *IS* curve, we use the investment demand schedule and the aggregate-demand/aggregate-supply graph we developed in the last chapter. Figure 9.1 presents these two graphs. The levels of investment spending shown in Panel 9.1a translate into the four aggregate demand curves in Panel 9.1b. The highest interest rate, r_1, resulting in the lowest level of investment spending, I_1, is associated with aggregate demand curve AD_1 and the lowest equilibrium level of income Y_1. The lowest interest rate, r_4, produces an investment level of I_4, which is associated with AD_4 and the highest equilibrium level of income, Y_4. We can illustrate the points representing these various interest rates and equilibrium incomes in Panel 9.1c. By connecting the four points, we have the *IS* curve.

The *IS* curve represents all the points of equilibrium in the goods market. It shows the level of income that will produce saving to match the level of intended investment given various interest rates. Although the *IS* curve reveals the various equilibrium points for interest rates and income levels, we cannot determine an equilibrium point until we know the interest rate. This is where the monetary sector and the *LM* curve come into play.

Money Market Equilibrium

Equilibrium in the money market occurs when the demand for money is equal to the supply of money. Equilibrium can occur at a variety of combinations of income levels and interest rates. The locus of points representing the equilibrium condition is called the *LM* curve.

---

[3] To explore a more detailed derivation and the equations of the *IS* and *LM* curves, see a standard macroeconomic text, for example, T.F. Durenburg, *Macroeconomics* (New York: McGraw-Hill, 1985): 201–206.

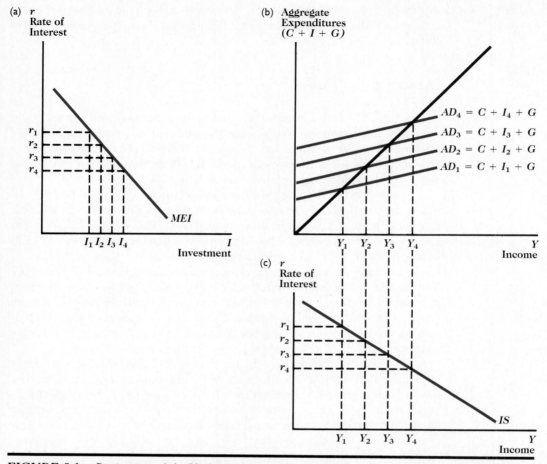

FIGURE 9.1 *Derivation of the IS Curve* The *IS* curve is derived from the *MEI* schedule and the aggregate demand/aggregate supply graph. Each interest rate produces a level of investment spending which, as a part of aggregate demand, is associated with a specific income level. The *IS* curve in (c) shows the relationship between these interest rates and income levels associated with equilibrium.

Deriving the *LM* Curve

Again picking up on the discussion about money and interest from the last chapter, we can determine the various equilibrium points within the monetary sector. The monetary sector is in equilibrium when the demand for money (Dm) is just equal to the supply of money (Sm). Since the Dm is determined by the rate of interest and the level of income (based on the Keynesian liquidity preference theory), we need to show $Dm = Sm$ for various interest rates and income levels.

Figure 9.2 shows the money demand and supply graph we derived in Chapter 8. As income rises the demand for money shifts. By holding the supply of money at a fixed level, we can identify the rates of interest associated with various income levels, each of which produces a different demand for money function. As income rises the Dm shifts, thus Y_1 produces the lowest demand for money, Dm_1, while Y_4 results in the highest, Dm_4. Remember that the Dm is inversely related to the interest rate (that is, it is a downward sloping curve), because as the interest rate rises the opportunity cost of holding money increases and vice versa.

Panel 9.2b shows the various points which result in equilibrium between the rate of interest and the level of income. By connecting these points we have the LM curve. The LM curve is a line representing all the points of equilibrium in the monetary sector. The LM curve shows the level of income which will yield equality of the demand for and supply of money given various interest rates. In other words, this curve tells us for each interest rate what the income level must be to make the demand for money equal to the supply of money.

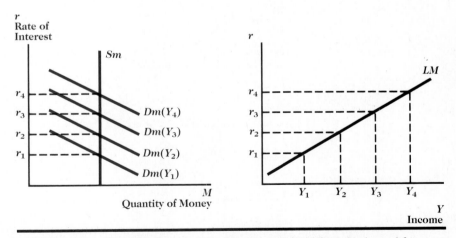

FIGURE 9.2 *The* **LM** *Curve*   The *LM* curve is derived from the demand for money curves associated with various income levels and the supply of money which interact to set interest rates. The *LM* curve in (b) shows the various combinations of interest rates and income levels associated with equilibrium.

Joint Goods and Money Market Equilibrium

Having derived the *IS* and *LM* curves, we have an array of equilibria in both the goods market and the money market. With a given set of circumstances only one rate of interest and income level will result in joint equilibrium. We seek this single equilibrium. We can determine joint equilibrium by combining the locus of equilibrium points from the goods market (the *IS* curve) and from the money market (the *LM* curve). We do this in Figure 9.3 by superimposing Panel 9.2b on Panel 9.2c.

The intersection of the *IS* and *LM* curves (point *E* in Figure 9.3) provides us with joint equilibrium.

What does joint equilibrium represent? *Joint equilibrium* means that the real sector and the money sector are in simultaneous equilibrium; a tendency for change does not exist within either of these markets. To help understand the equilibrium condition, consider a disequilibrium situation. In Figure 9.3, point *D* represents disequilibrium. The goods market is in equilibrium; point *D* is on the *IS* curve. But the money market is not in equilibrium. For the income level which point *D* represents, the demand for money here

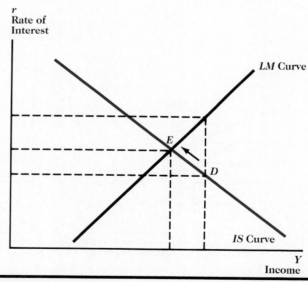

FIGURE 9.3 *Joint Equilibrium*   This figure combines the *IS* curve from 9.1 and the *LM* curve from 9.2 to produce the joint product market/money market equilibrium. It also identifies a point of disequilibrium, *D*; under this situation there is a tendency for interest rates to rise and income to decline to re-establish equilibrium at *E*.

exceeds the supply of money. Under these circumstances, the interest rate must increase and income must decline. The result of the adjustment is movement along the *IS* curve toward point *E* and a restoration of joint equilibrium.

Changes in *IS-LM*

Joint equilibrium in the monetary and product sectors indicates no tendency for change within the system. But exogenous changes may occur. The supply of money may change as a result of Federal Reserve action or the level of government spending may increase or decrease. These changes set into motion changes within the money and/or goods markets. *IS-LM* analysis allows us to see the results of these changes as they influence both the money and goods markets.

Consider first how an exogenous change influences the product market and the *IS* curve. Figure 9.4 is a basic duplication of Figure 9.1.

What would happen if the federal government increased expenditures? In Panel 9.4a the aggregate demand function would shift by the amount of increased government expenditures. This results in a shift outward and to the right of the *IS* curve in Panel 9.4c (to *IS'*).

What happens if a change occurs in the monetary sector, say the Federal Reserve System increases the supply of money? Figure 9.5 is a basic duplication of Figure 9.2. The increased supply of money shows up in Panel 9.5a by shifting the money supply curve outward to the right from *Sm* to *Sm'*. This money supply increase results in the *LM* curve moving to the right from *LM* to *LM'* in Panel 9.5b.

Figure 9.6 illustrates how these changes influence the joint product and money market equilibrium. Notice the original equilibrium condition with *IS* and *LM* producing equilibrium at point *A*. When the government increases expenditures, *IS* shifts to *IS'*, resulting in equilibrium at point *B* with a higher interest rate and a higher income level. The higher income level can be sustained despite the higher interest rate because of the greater level of spending in the system.[4]

Now look at what happens when the Federal Reserve increases the money supply, shifting the money market equilibrium points from *LM* to

---

[4] Note that the increased government expenditures do not generate as great a change in *Y*, as was the case in Chapter 8 when we introduced the expenditure multiplier. This is due to the influence of the higher interest rate.

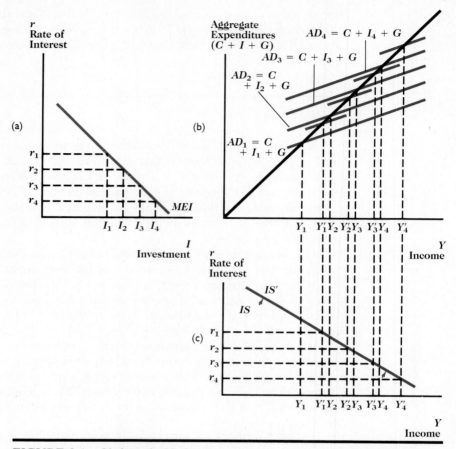

FIGURE 9.4 *Shift in the* **IS** *Curve*   An increase in one component of aggregate demand, say government spending, will increase the equilibrium level of income associated with various aggregate demand conditions. These new higher income levels result in an increase, a shift to the right, of the *IS* curve. What might cause the *IS* curve to decrease?

LM'. First notice that if this had occurred without any federal expenditure changes (that is, the *IS* curve had not shifted), the result would have been equilibrium at point *C* with the interest rate falling and the level of income rising. The increased money supply and the expenditure increase resulted in equilibrium at point *D* (*IS'* and *LM'*), with the interest rate unchanged from the original equilibrium and with an increased income level. The money supply increase complemented the expenditure change to stimulate economic activity and to generate a higher income level without a change in interest rates. The increased supply of money helped offset the upward

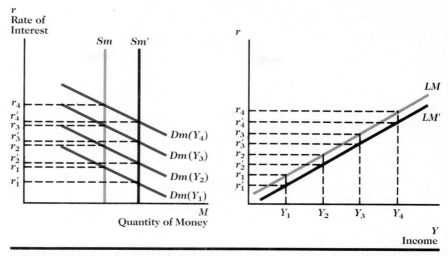

FIGURE 9.5 *Shift in the* **LM** *Curve*   An increase in the money supply will reduce the rates of interest associated with the various demand for money functions. These
new lower interest rates result in an increase, a shift to the right of the *LM* curve. What
might cause the *LM* curve to decrease?

pressure on interest rates resulting from the increased demand for investment capital.

This scenario illustrates how *IS-LM* analysis can assist in assessing the
impact of exogenous changes in the monetary and/or product markets. We
need to exercise some caution in our use of this analysis. Our discussion has
assumed a great deal. The shifts in the *IS* and *LM* curves were exactly the
same and the *IS* and *LM* curves we have used were both very "normal," that
is, they were linear and did not have extreme slopes. Consider the results
displayed in Figure 9.6 in contrast to those in Figure 9.7.

A similar expenditure increase shifts the *IS* curve in Figure 9.7, precipitating an equilibrium change from point *A* to point *B* just as it did in
Figure 9.6. But note that the steepness of the *LM* curve results in a higher
interest rate and virtually no change in the equilibrium level of income.
Why? The steep *LM* curve might be a result of a very steep (inelastic)
speculative demand for money curve. This implies that changes in the rate
of interest would not result in the normal change in the demand for money to
hold in speculative balances.

Normally a decline in the rate of interest would increase the demand
for speculative balances, and an increase would decrease the demand for
money to hold in idle speculative balances. A steep speculative demand for
money curve would produce a steep *LM* curve. In this case the expenditure

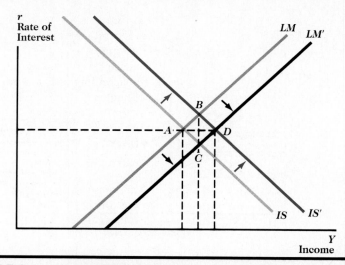

FIGURE 9.6   Changing Equilibrium   This figure illustrates the various points of equilibrium resulting from combinations of increases in the *IS* and *LM* curves. What caused the point of equilibrium to shift from *A* to *C*?

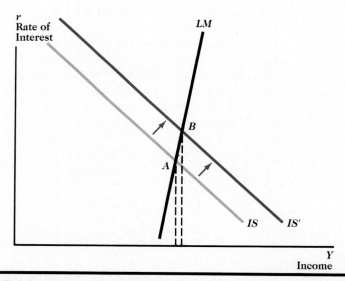

FIGURE 9.7   Slope of Curves Affects Changing Equilibrium   The change in the equilibrium level of income/rate of interest associated with a shift in the *IS* curve is influenced by the elasticity of the *LM* curve. Here a shift in the *IS* curve associated with an inelastic *LM* curve produces little change in income.

increase would force interest rates up without dramatically influencing the equilibrium level of income. Despite the change in interest rates, individuals would continue to hold large quantities of money in idle speculative balances. The expenditure increase would be absorbed in idle balances rather than finding its way into the spending stream and stimulating GNP.[5] The constant money stock in conjunction with a low interest elasticity of demand for money would prevent expenditures from increasing to any great extent.

We could describe other situations where the *IS* and *LM* curves are not "normal." In these cases the analysis becomes more difficult. The point of our discussion is that *IS-LM* analysis is helpful only if we have an accurate picture of the components of the curves. We need to know the slope of the *MEI* schedule and the saving function for an accurate *IS* curve. We need accurate slopes for the demand for money functions. To express this caveat in another way, when we use the *IS-LM* approach to analyze policy, we must be certain to note that our findings apply only under normal circumstances. We have to consider how our conclusions might change if circumstances were not normal.

Limitations of the *IS-LM* Model

The diagrams of the *IS-LM* model presented in the previous sections allow us to analyze the interrelated effects of changes within the monetary and goods sectors. As presented, this model has some limitations. These limitations do not mean that the model is not useful; they do indicate that we must take other factors into account in drawing conclusions about the effect of a particular policy action.

Slopes of the *IS-LM* Curves

As mentioned earlier, we have explored very normal-looking curves in each of the sectors. We did this to develop an understanding of the model. We need to consider the slopes of the *IS* and *LM* functions. In so doing our analysis becomes more sophisticated.

When we introduced the components of the demand for money function, we discussed issues such as the liquidity trap but we did not incorporate those issues into the formulation of the *LM* curve. At very low interest rates

---

[5] This is a situation where fiscal policy will not work. The increased government spending did not have the desired effect. We discuss some of the problems caused by abormally sloped *IS* and *LM* curves in the next section of this chapter.

individuals may assume that rates will fall no further. The speculative demand for money then becomes elastic (the *LM* curve is horizontal), because individuals absorb cash into idle balances waiting for interest rates to rise. At the other extreme, with a fixed supply of money the *LM* curve also might become vertical when interest rates become very high and individuals conclude that rates will rise no higher (security prices will fall no further). Individuals then will hold securities and no idle cash balances. In between these two extremes the *LM* curve may have a variety of slopes.

Figure 9.8 illustrates an *LM* curve with a horizontal section, due to the liquidity trap, and a vertical section. The horizontal section is called the *Keynesian range* because in this situation Keynesian demand stimulation policies are most effective. Notice that a shift in the *IS* curve produces a significant increase in income (from Y_1 to Y_2). On the other hand, monetary policy will have no effect since individuals will absorb any increase in the money supply into idle cash balances.[6] The vertical section is called the

---

[6] There is a counter argument to the claim that only fiscal policy stimulation will work in this situation. In the 1940s, A.C. Pigou argued that consumption depends on real money balances. Therefore, with declining prices, consumption would increase, shifting the *IS* curve to the right. The "Pigou Effect" has been the subject of considerable discussion. See A.C. Pigou, "The Classical Stationary State," *Economic Journal* (December 1943): 345–351.

ECONOMICS T●DAY   9.1   Economic Eclecticism Gains in Popularity

Monetarism, Keynesianism, classicism and eclecticism! The latest listing of economic doctrines may well need to include the *eclectic* approach. At a time when conventional economic models have come under severe criticism and new schools of thought can't seem to capture the attention of policy makers, many economists appear to be more eclectic than doctrinaire.

University of Rochester economist Karl Brunner, himself rather firmly rooted in the monetarist camp, has suggested that eclecticism means you believe the earth revolves around the sun one day and on the very next day you state the opposite.

More seriously, the eclectic approach borrows bits and pieces from many models and schools of thought. Federal Reserve Bank of New York President, E. Gerald Corrigan, popularized the eclectic approach while holding the Fed presidency in Minneapolis. He argued against hard rules for implementing monetary policy. Instead he favored a more common sense approach that selected ideas from various approaches or schools of thought. Monetary aggregates, interest rates and credit conditions all need attention in Fed policy-making according to the eclectic approach.

Macroeconomics in general has seen the emergence of a blending of schools of thought. Axel Leijonhufvud, a UCLA economist, argues that macroeconomic schools of thought actually "flip-flop" on many issues. As a result, a rational expectations economist today may sound more like an early Keynesian, at least on some issues, than do contemporary Keynesian thinkers.

Whether the rise of eclecticism is a result of a dearth of new economic theories or the blending of theories into a synthesis approach which has applicability in the 1980s is open to considerable debate. The point remains that prominent policy makers are looking to all schools of thought for guidance rather than restricting themselves to a more narrow approach.

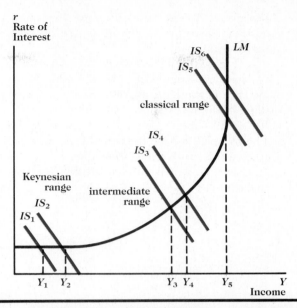

FIGURE 9.8   LM *Curve Slope Affects Equilibrium*   The slopes of the *LM* curve are illustrated in this figure and divided into three ranges—the Keynesian range where shifts in the *IS* curve have the greatest impact on income, the intermediate range where there is a moderate income change, and the classical range where shifts in the *IS* curve produce no change in income.

classical range because classical theory assumes that money primarily is held for transactions purposes (not speculative purposes). Thus, the speculative demand for money is zero. In this range demand stimulation through fiscal policy will have no impact on income. Interest rates are so high that investment demand cannot be stimulated. Notice that the shift in the *IS* curve (from IS_5 to IS_6) does not change income, which remains at Y_5. In this range monetary policy is effective since it lowers interest rates. In between these two extremes is the *intermediate range*. The slope of the *LM* curve changes, and shifts in the *IS* curve have varying effects on income (from a maximum impact in the more horizontal portion of the range to a minimum effect in the more vertical portion).

The *IS* curve also may have different slopes. The slope of the *IS* curve depends on the responsiveness of investment demand to interest rate changes. The *IS* curve is vertical when investment expenditures are unaffected by interest rate changes. This would result from an inelastic *MEI* schedule; investment demand is unresponsive to interest rate changes perhaps because of negative expectations about the future business climate.

During the 1930s, even extremely low interest rates would not encourage business investment; producers saw no prospect that consumer spending would pick up.

Figure 9.9 includes two *IS* curves within each range of the *LM* curve, one has a moderate slope and the other has a very steep slope. Notice how the shift in the *LM* curve has varying impacts on income, depending on the slope of the *IS* curve.

The slope of the *IS* curve also is influenced by the savings function. The *IS* curve is more horizontal if the marginal propensity to save is low. In other words, with a low *MPS* (thus a high marginal propensity to consume) demand stimulation through fiscal policy actions will have a greater impact on income.

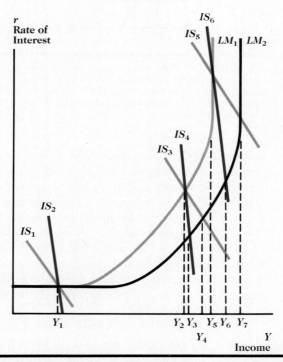

FIGURE 9.9   IS *Curve Slope Affects Equilibrium*   The slope of the *IS* curve affects the impact of *LM* curve shifts on income. With the steeper *IS* curve (that is, the more inelastic), the shift in the *LM* curve has less of an effect on income regardless of the range in which joint equilibrium occurs.

Aggregate Demand and Aggregate Supply

Ignoring for a moment the problems posed by slopes of the *IS-LM* curves, we can proceed to expand the expenditure model. One omission in our model is any reference to changes in the price level. We can use the aggregate demand and aggregate supply curves to integrate the price level into our expenditure model. This will also allow us to discuss the level of output in the system. Then we can combine the aggregate demand and aggregate supply curves with the *IS-LM* model to analyze the effects of monetary and fiscal policy actions.

Aggregate Supply

The aggregate supply curve illustrates the short-run relationship between aggregate output and the price level. The curve can be derived from the demand for and supply of labor (the chapter Appendix derives the aggregate supply curve). Economists have engaged in considerable discussion about the shape of the aggregate supply curve. Classical economists argued that it was perfectly inelastic, vertical, at the full employment level of output. An extreme Keynesian explanation of the aggregate supply curve reveals a perfectly elastic, horizontal, curve until full employment level of output is approached, at which point the curve begins to slope upward and becomes perfectly inelastic once the full employment level of output is reached. The extreme classical case assumes a world in which labor markets clear perfectly and the money wage rate is flexible downward. In the extreme Keynesian case, wages are assumed to be fixed and the marginal product of labor is held constant (that is, each additional unit of labor produces the same additional unit of output).

   We will describe a situation where prices and wages are less than completely flexible, in fact, wages are downwardly inflexible. Markets do not clear for one or a combination of reasons. These may include incomplete knowledge, a lack of worker mobility, the costs associated with job changes, or adjustment lags. The money illusion (where workers confuse nominal and real wages and offer more labor services when nominal wages rise during a period of price inflation) is another reason why markets may not clear.[7] Under these circumstances, and assuming diminishing marginal productivity

---

[7] Economists have attempted to explain why labor markets may be in disequilibrium. For a discussion of this issue, see R.M. Solow, "Alternative Approaches to Macroeconomic Theory: A Partial View," *Canadian Journal of Economics* 12 (August 1979): 339–354.

of labor, the aggregate supply curve becomes less than perfectly elastic at some level of output below full employment. Also keep in mind that the pricing policies of firms and resource price changes influence the divergence of wage and price movements.

Figure 9.10 shows an aggregate supply curve incorporating the Keynesian and classical cases. This curve is sometimes called the *intermediate case*. The horizontal portion of the curve represents the fact that initially firms are able to increase output with little or no change in prices. Note that this portion of the curve also coincides with economic conditions of excess productive capacity and much less than full employment. As the economy approaches full employment, output can increase only with some upward movement in prices. A critical question remains—when and how quickly does the aggregate supply curve begin to slope upward? This issue is under debate.

Aggregate Demand

We can discuss the impact of price-level changes on aggregate expenditures by introducing the aggregate demand curve, which relates aggregate expenditures to various price levels. We can derive the aggregate demand curve by using our *IS-LM* model.

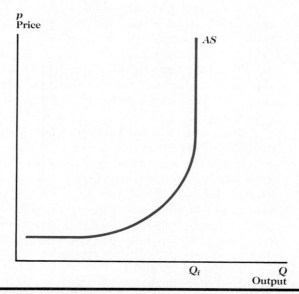

FIGURE 9.10 *Aggregate Supply Curve*   The aggregate supply curve illustrates the short-run relationship between aggregate output and the price level (see the appendix for derivation).

Figure 9.11 shows the *IS-LM* curves on the upper graph with the price level and aggregate income on the lower graph. *IS* and LM_1 intersect at point *A*; the price level is assumed to be p_1. There is an *LM* curve for each real money supply, and with price-level changes there is a different *LM* curve. Each price level is associated with a different *IS-LM* equilibrium. As the price level rises, the *LM* curve shifts further and further to the left and the equilibrium level of income declines accordingly. Since aggregate demand responds downward to declines in the equilibrium level of income, we have a downward-sloping aggregate demand curve.

The interaction of aggregate demand and aggregate supply shows the results of movements in either curve in terms of the price level and output in the system. We can combine the aggregate supply and aggregate demand curves to illustrate equilibrium between the system's output and price level. Figure 9.12 reveals an initial equilibrium at *p* and *Q*. Let's look at the case

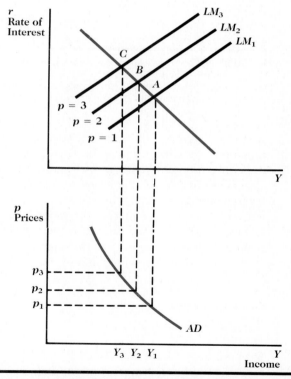

FIGURE 9.11   *Deriving the Aggregate Demand Curve*   The aggregate demand curve illustrates aggregate expenditures at various price levels. Derived from the *IS-LM* curves the aggregate demand curve shows that with higher price levels (causing the *LM* curve to shift to the left), the equilibrium level of income is lower.

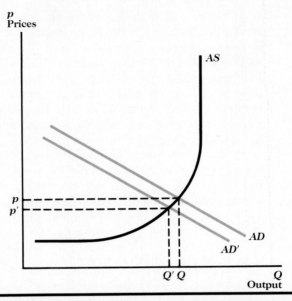

FIGURE 9.12 *Aggregate Demand—Aggregate Supply Equilibrium* This figure shows equilibrium between the system's output and the price level (at the intersection of the aggregate demand and aggregate supply curves) as well as the impact on the price level and output of a decrease in aggregate demand (they both decline).

where the aggregate demand curve declines, or shifts backward. Such a shift might occur as a result of massive tax increases imposed to reduce the federal deficit. Consumers would have less money to spend and total demand in the system would drop. With the shift in aggregate demand, from *AD* to *AD'*, the level of output generated drops from *Q* to *Q'*, while the price level falls from *p* to *p'*. This is consistent with our understanding of how supply and demand factors affect prices and output in the system. In the next section we will further discuss movements in the aggregate demand and aggregate supply curves in conjunction with shifts in the *IS* and *LM* curves.

Complete Expenditure Model

Keeping in mind the limitations of the expenditure model, we can use the model to illustrate changes resulting from policy actions. Consider the situation depicted in Figure 9.13. Notice that the *IS-LM* and *AD-AS* curves result in less than full employment, *Y* and *Q*. What might occur as a result of an increase in the money supply or increased government spending?

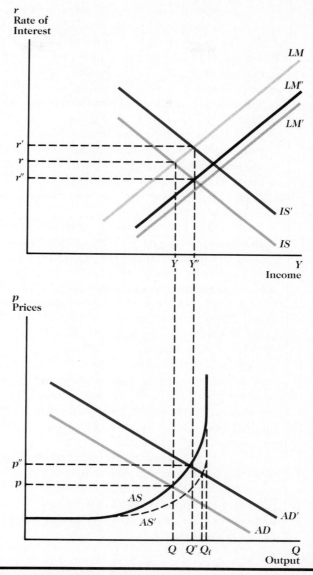

FIGURE 9.13 *Complete Expenditure Model* This figure combines the aggregate demand/aggregate supply with the *IS-LM* graph. By using both we can illustrate the changes in income, output, the price level and the rate of interest occasioned by various policy actions. Notice that with an expansion of the supply of money (from *LM* to *LM'* while *IS* remains unchanged), the rate of interest declines and the income level rises; this is associated with an increase in aggregate demand which causes the price level to rise as output increases.

Let's first consider an expansion of the money supply. An increase in the money supply would cause the LM curve to shift to the right (from LM to LM'). The money supply increase would lower the interest rate and stimulate investment expenditures. This would shift the aggregate demand curve to the right (from AD to AD'). Notice that this process results in higher prices (p has increased to p''). The rising price level means that the real money supply is reduced. A reduction in the money supply shifts the LM curve back (to LM''), although not all the way back to its original position. (The aggregate demand curve remains at AD'; it incorporates price changes so it is not affected.) This reduction moderates the expansion and produces an equilibrium condition represented by the intersection of the new aggregate demand curve and the existing aggregate supply curve (Q'') with the new LM and original IS curves (Y''). Notice the resulting higher prices (the price level increased from p to p'').

A second situation would consist of increased government spending. Perhaps the government would undertake a massive public works program, such as building high speed rail lines between major cities. In our model the increase in expenditures resulting from this government program would: (1) increase aggregate demand (from AD to AD'); (2) shift the IS curve (from IS to IS') because the investment demand curve would shift outward as a result of the changed investment environment; and (3) shift the aggregate supply curve as more resources flow into productive activities and labor productivity increases. The intersection of IS' and LM, and AS' and AD' produce an equilibrium condition which moves the economy closer to a full-employment level of output. Notice again that the price level rose (exactly how much would depend on the productivity increase that shifted AS). But with the expansionary fiscal policy, interest rates also rose to a point (r') above their original level (r) and well above the new level produced through monetary expansion (r'').[8]

These two scenarios indicate that the expenditure model is useful in analyzing policy actions. We will return to this discussion in Chapter 10 when we contrast Keynesian and monetarist policies. For now it is sufficient to have some appreciation of how the expenditure model works. While it is certainly not perfect, it provides a useful reference point for macroeconomic policy discussions.

---

[8] The increased expenditure for new equipment should eventually make the manufacturing sector more productive. Once this happens the price level may drop once again. Supply-side economists would argue that the demand for labor will not decline since workers are now more productive. The end result of this process may actually be a higher level of output and more employment without inflation. This is why supply-siders argue that expansion is best accomplished by using incentives to stimulate private sector output rather than government expenditure programs that do not influence worker productivity.

Feedback Effects

In considering the impact of policy changes using *IS-LM* analysis, we need to keep in mind some feedback effects. We can see the initial impact of a shift in the *LM* curve due to some monetary policy action, but in the long run there may be some additional effects which are not reflected in the graphical analysis.

One such effect, much discussed today in light of large federal deficits, is the *crowding-out effect*. In one version of crowding-out, government borrowing to finance deficits competes with private-sector borrowing, as it drives up the interest rate. Government borrowing crowds out private sector borrowing. In a more sophisticated version of this process, government borrowing is seen to deplete the nation's savings, leaving less available to finance private investment. Using either version, the result is the same. A demand stimulation policy by the federal government, for example through a jobs program, will increase income in the system. If the program is funded through deficit financing, interest rates will rise. The higher interest rate will choke off investment expenditures. The drop in private investment spending will reduce, or perhaps even counteract, the stimulatory effect of the government spending program.[9] In our expenditure model, the crowding-out effect would shift the *AD* curve back toward its original position after expansionary policy had shifted it outward and movement along the *IS* curve produced by the interest-rate rise would reduce private investment expenditures.

Three other effects of monetary policy tend to work in opposite directions. We cannot determine the overall results of these conflicting effects with simple *IS-LM* analysis, but we need to keep them in mind. When the government undertakes an expansionary monetary policy, it often does so through open-market operations. The Federal Reserve expands the supply of money by purchasing securities in the open market. The increased supply of money works to lower interest rates and this stimulates investment spending. Via the multiplier effect, aggregate income rises. This is called the *liquidity effect*. The increased liquidity stimulates the system. But the increased level of aggregate income produces an *income effect*. The increase in income is accompanied by an increased demand for money (the transactions demand certainly increases and the speculative demand may also increase). Increased demand for money puts upward pressure on interest rates. Unless

---

[9] There is debate over the validity of the "crowding out" effect. For an early discussion see Burton Zwick, "'Snap Back' and 'Crowding Out' in Monetary and Fiscal Policy: Explanation and Interpretation," *Journal of Money, Credit and Banking* VI (November 1974): 559–566. Recently Norman B. Ture has argued that it is taxation with or without a deficit, rather than simply interest rate rises, which crowds out private investment. ("What Really Does the Crowding Out?" *The Wall Street Journal* (September 14, 1983).

additional monetary expansion occurs, the income effect will push interest rates back up. This may partially or completely offset the initial effect of monetary expansion.

A third related result of expansionary monetary policy is the *price expectations effect*. If the money supply is increased at a time when the public is anxious about inflation such that prices once again begin to rise, individuals will come to expect higher rates of inflation. In such a circumstance the *LM* curve would shift backward. Once again, the initial stimulatory action may be moderated or offset by the effects of the price expectations feedback.

Chapter Conclusion

The model presented in this chapter is a convenient tool for assessing the effects of external shocks on both the monetary and product sectors. The *IS-LM* model offers a "snapshot" of the joint equilibrium condition and allows insight into the results of monetary and/or fiscal policy actions. When we add the aggregate demand/aggregate supply graph to the model we are able to see the effects of macroeconomic policy on all major economic variables— the price level, the interest rate and the level of aggregate income.

This model is useful for developing an understanding of the interaction between the monetary sector and the goods sector of the economy. We can use it to see the effect of policy actions or the results of changes in consumer or business behavior. As is the case with any model, there are limitations. It offers a more complete analysis than anything we have explored so far. Still, you should use the model only to gain some insight into the direction of changes within the system. By using this model in conjunction with an appreciation of the other factors which influence the economy, you can make some judgments about the effects of various policy actions.

Consider These Questions

1. *IS-LM* analysis shows how general equilibrium (in the money and goods markets) occurs. If one market, say the money market, is in equilibrium but the other market, the goods market, isn't, how can general equilibrium occur without disrupting the balance in the money market?

2. The simple *IS-LM* model determines output and the interest rate with a fixed price level. What determines the price level in an expanded model incorporating the *IS-LM* analysis?

3. Why do the slopes of the *IS* and *LM* curves have any bearing on their usefulness for analysis?

4. Why is the vertical portion of the *LM* curve called the classical range?

5. What is the crowding-out effect? If it applies as the government increases spending and borrowing, should the reverse scenario result as the government reduces spending? Explain what might occur during a period of reduced spending.

6. From where does the aggregate supply curve come? Why is it important for analysis?

7. Illustrate, using the complete expenditure model, the outcome if the Gramm-Rudman-Hollings bill forces a significant reduction in government spending during an economic recession.

Suggestions for Further Reading

Brown, Weir M. "Employment vs. Unemployment Data as Macro-policy Guides." In *Journal of Post Keynesian Economics* 1 (Summer 1979): 70–82.
  Presents discussion of unemployment data and its usefulness in prescribing economic policies.

Fischer, Stanley and Rudiger Dornbush. *Macroeconomics*. 3rd edition. New York: McGraw-Hill, 1984.
  Standard macroeconomics textbook; Chapters 3 and 4 present *IS-LM* model.

Friedman, Benjamin. "Crowding Out or Crowding In? Economic Consequences of Financing Government Deficits." In *Brookings Papers in Economic Activity* 3 (1978): 593–641.
  Interesting analysis of the effects of budget deficits on capital markets.

Heller, Walter W. "Activist Government: Key to Growth." In *Challenge* (March/April 1986).
  Prepared at the time of the 40th anniversary of the 1946 Employment Act. This is a tribute to the contribution of Keynesian theory and its effects on economic policy.

Hicks, John R. "Mr. Keynes and the Classics: A Suggested Interpretation." In *Econometrica* 5 (April 1937): 147–159.
  This is a classic itself. It introduced *IS-LM* analysis.

Johnson, Harry G. "The General Theory After Twenty-Five Years." In American Economic Association *Papers and Proceedings* 51 (May 1961): 1–7.
  Johnson's presidential address provides an interesting retrospective view on the durability of Keynesian economics.

Smith, Warren L. "A Graphical Exposition of the Complete Keynesian System." In *Readings in Money, National Income and Stabilization Policy*, edited by W. L. Smith and R. L. Teigen, 61–67. Homewood, IL.: Richard D. Irwin, 1974.
  The title says it all. Clear and concise.

APPENDIX

9. Labor Market and Aggregate Supply

To better understand the aggregate supply curve and to illustrate how the labor sector relates to the expenditure model, we need to take a moment to review some microeconomics pertaining to the production function and the labor supply and demand curves. In discussing the labor market we make a couple of simplifying assumptions. We assume competitive product markets, profit maximizing behavior by firms, diminishing marginal returns for labor, a fixed money wage, and circumstances which depict the short run rather than the long run.

Production Function

The output (Q) of the system (synonymous with aggregate supply) depends on a number of factor inputs—labor (N), capital (K), and raw materials (R). The output also depends on the level of knowledge, technology, and managerial ability in the system, all of which influence worker productivity. If we assume that these latter factors are held constant at any point in time, we can express a production function as follows:

$$Q = f(\overset{+}{N}, \overset{+}{K}, \overset{+}{R})$$

In the short run, only labor input is truly variable; workers can put in overtime or a second shift can be added. It takes time to alter the capacity to handle additional raw materials, and the technology to improve production evolves over time. Therefore, we will concentrate on labor as the variable input in the short run and express our simplified production function only in terms of the labor input (in other words we will hold capital constant and vary resources in accordance with increases in labor). In this simplified version the production function is:

$$Q = f(\overset{+}{N})$$

Under these circumstances, and recalling from microeconomics the principle of diminishing returns to labor, we can represent the production curve as is shown in Figure 9A.1.[1] Notice that output increases as the variable input, labor, is added but that the rate of increase declines (we can illustrate this by drawing tangents to the production function at various points and noting that the slope of the tangents declines as we move along the production curve).

Once we know the quantity of labor employed, we can use this production curve to determine output in the system. The quantity of labor is determined in the labor market through the interaction of the labor supply (S_N) and the demand for labor (D_N).

With the simplifying assumptions outlined at the beginning of this appendix, the demand for labor is determined by the wage rate, productivity, and the firm's ability to sell its products at a profitable price. In other words, an employer will continue to hire workers as long as the additional

---

[1] To review the details of the theory of production, refer to an intermediate level micro-economic theory textbook, for example, E. Mansfield, *Microeconomics: Theory and Application* (New York: W.W. Norton, 1982) Chapters 6–9.

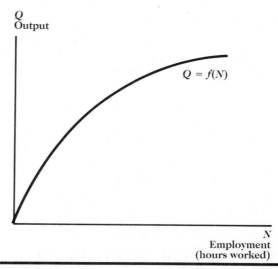

FIGURE 9A.1 *Production Curve* The production curve shows that output increases as the variable input increases but the rate of output expansion slows down as long as the capital stock remains fixed.

units produced can be sold profitably. We can summarize this by saying that the return to labor (the real wage) is equal to labor's marginal product.[2]

$$\frac{w}{p} = MP$$

Then the demand curve for labor becomes a downward sloping line because the marginal product of labor is a diminishing function.

$$D = f\left(\overline{\frac{w}{p}}\right)$$

The supply of labor is influenced by the real wage rate. Just as with the supply of other resources or products, when the returns to labor (that is, wages) rise, the quantity of labor offered increases. This occurs as a result of two factors: additional workers entering the labor force, and workers putting in longer hours or taking on second jobs. On the other hand, there are some indications that as wages rise and workers are able to achieve more easily their desired income levels, workers may respond by reducing the hours they work. Families may earn the income they need and want without continuing second jobs. Leisure may be of more value than extra income from additional work.

This second factor undoubtedly influences wage earners, particularly when pay rates are high. However, under normal circumstances the labor supply curve will be upward sloping.[3]

$$S = f\left(\overset{+}{\frac{w}{p}}\right)$$

Figure 9A.2 illustrates the demand for labor and supply of labor curves. Point *E* represents equilibrium in the labor market.

The market-clearing point in the labor market may or may not represent full employment. Remember, classical economists argued that there

---

[2] This reflects the equilibrium conditions that marginal costs (wages) must equal marginal revenues ($MP \times P$) or $W = MP \times P$; to put this another way, the real wage paid (w/p) for an extra unit of labor must equal its marginal product, $w/p = MP$.

[3] The labor supply curve may look "normal" until wages reach unusually high levels at which point it may begin to bend backward. We will only consider the upward sloping portion of the curve. For a more complete discussion of the backward bending labor supply curve, see R.G. Ehrenberg and R.S. Smith, *Modern Labor Economics*, 2nd edition (Glenview, IL: Scott, Foresman and Company, 1986) 157–162.

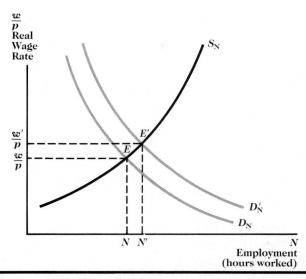

FIGURE 9A.2 *Labor Market Equilibrium*   The demand for and supply of labor determine the real wage rate. An increase in the demand for labor results in rising wages.

could be no involuntary unemployment. If the market-determined level of employment did not include all able-bodied workers, it was because they were unwilling to accept the market wage rate. Today this explanation is not widely accepted. The level of employment determined through market forces may result in involuntary unemployment. This may be because wages are inflexible downward such that the market cannot clear. At any rate, if this is the case we would say that the market-clearing level of employment represents disequilibrium. We analyze this issue more extensively in Chapter 11.

The interaction of supply and demand determines the quantity of employment (total work hours). Knowing this, we can determine the level of output in the system. Figure 9A.3 illustrates this point by combining the labor market with our labor-sensitive production function.

Notice in this diagram that an increase in the demand for labor from D to D' (perhaps stimulated by a federally sponsored program offering tax incentives for employers hiring new workers) results in a higher utilization of labor resources and, because output depends on the labor input, a higher level of aggregate output (Q' rather than Q).

235

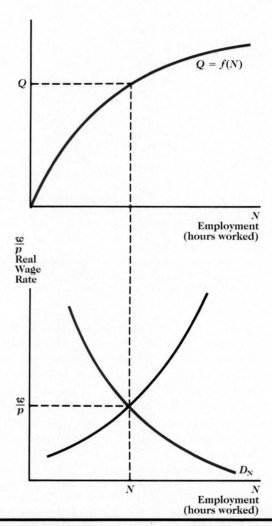

FIGURE 9A.3 *Labor Input Determines Output* This figure combines the production schedule and the labor market. Once demand and supply set a level of employment, we can determine the level of output.

Labor Market and Aggregate Supply

Derivation of the aggregate supply curve comes from the labor market. It is not appreciably different from an individual firm's supply curve. In fact, the aggregate supply curve really is the summation of the supply curves for all industries in the economy.

Figure 9A.4 illustrates the derivation of the aggregate supply curve. In Panel 9A.4a, we have the aggregate production function: the axes are reversed for convenience, otherwise it is the same as Figure 9A.3. Panel 9A.4b is the graph of the labor demand and labor supply curves, again with the axes reversed from what was illustrated in Figure 9A.2. Panel 9A.4c shows the various combinations of price and marginal product of labor, where their product ($p \times MP_L$) is equal to the wage rate. In other words, given a fixed wage rate, as the marginal product of labor declines, the price firms charge for their products must increase in order for the employment level to remain unchanged. Panel 9A.4d illustrates the aggregate supply curve that results from these circumstances. Notice that once output reaches Q_f, a condition that results from employment of N_f, the aggregate supply curve becomes perfectly elastic.[4] At this level of employment all workers who want to work are employed.

The expenditure model discussed in Chapter 9 incorporates the labor sector through that sector's influence on the aggregate supply curve. Changes in the labor sector, either through technological improvements that influence labor productivity, or labor management negotiations that influence the prevailing wage rate, will have an effect on the equilibrium in the expenditure model.

---

[4] For a more extensive discussion of the relationship between the labor market and the aggregate supply curve, especially the derivation of the aggregate supply curve, see E. Shapiro, *Macroeconomic Analysis*, 5th edition (New York: Harcourt Brace Jovanovich, 1982) 135–140.

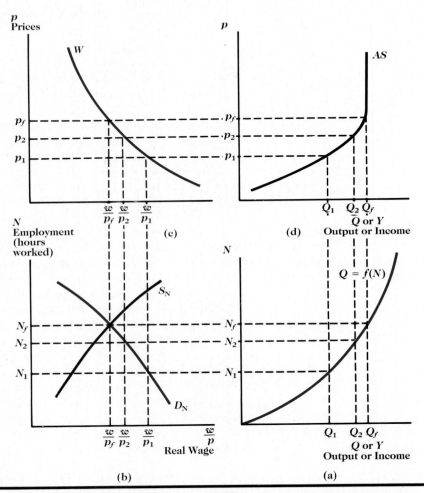

FIGURE 9A.4 *Derivation of Aggregate Supply Curve* This figure shows how the aggregate supply curve is derived from the labor market and production function.

CHAPTER TEN

MONETARISM and the KEYNESIAN-MONETARIST DEBATE

It is a capital mistake to theorise before one has data. Insensibly one begins to twist facts to suit theories, instead of theories to suit facts.

Sir Arthur Conan Doyle
A Scandal in Bohemia, 1891

The model outlined in the previous chapter does not give a complete explanation of monetarist views on the role of money in the economy. This chapter elaborates on the origins of monetarism, including factors monetarists see as affecting the demand for money, and concludes by contrasting monetarist and Keynesian views. The chapter appendix offers a more detailed explanation of the income velocity of money.

Monetarism is more than an updated version of the old quantity theory. Empirical research has helped make the case that money influences prices. But, beyond that, monetarism has come to represent a series of economic propositions. When these propositions are combined with the results of empirical research, monetarists make a strong case for eliminating wide swings in the growth rates of money supply. This strong case has forced Keynesians to refine their thinking. The result has been an evolving consensus on the role of money in the economy.

Chapter Objectives

In this chapter you will explore the forces behind the increasing prominence of monetarism in the late 1970s and early 1980s. As you read this chapter, be aware of the origins of monetarism and its proponents' efforts to build a strong case for the importance of money in the contemporary economy. By the end of this chapter, you should be able to:

- Define monetarism.
- Explain all aspects of the monetarist position rather than the simple money-influences-prices-and-income argument.
- Illustrate the importance of the specification of the demand for money function and the predictability of the velocity of money in the monetarist analysis.

Having acquired a solid understanding of the precepts of monetarism, you will then be in a position to contrast the Keynesian and monetarist models. Specifically, you should be able to:

- Outline the alternative transmission mechanisms for each model.
- Explain the implications of the money supply versus interest rates as the key monetary policy variable.
- Translate the basic Keynesian and monetarist approaches into working models which can be used for policy recommendations.
- Differentiate between the results in financial markets of relying on one model versus the other in policy deliberations.

When you finish this chapter, you will be able not only to explain monetarism but to analyze its usefulness for policy actions. You will also be able to assess the value of one model versus the other given various economic conditions.

Origins of Monetarism

Chapter 1 introduced the quantity theory of money; Chapter 8 discussed monetarism in the context of the evolution of macroeconomic theory. The quantity theory forms the original basis for monetarism, although contemporary monetarists are more sophisticated in their explanations of the connection between money and the economy than were the quantity theorists. The quantity theory of money holds that changes in the quantity of money generate proportionate changes in the level of prices in the same direction. Simply stated the quantity theory is:

$$M \times V = P \times T \qquad (10.1)$$

Or, money times velocity equals the price level times the quantity of transactions in the system. Stating this relationship in a dynamic form expressed in terms of percentage change in each variable the relationship is:

$$\%M + \%V = \%P + \%T \qquad (10.2)$$

In either case the relationship is an identity and is often referred to as the *equation of exchange.*

In 1911, using the results of his research into the velocity of money, Irving Fisher transformed this definitional identity into a theory of how the demand for money is determined. This more sophisticated version of the quantity theory transforms the equation of exchange identity into a functional relationship:

$$M_q = kY_P \qquad (10.3)$$

where

> M is the money stock
> k is the proportion of nominal income, Y_P,
>   that people want to hold as money

therefore,

> $k = 1/v$
> v being the velocity of money

With this version, equilibrium occurs where

$$M_s = M_q = kY_P \qquad (10.4)$$

Fisher and other classical economists believed the economy was operating at or near full employment, therefore income could not change in the short run. With that assumption, and after demonstrating that velocity was virtually constant, Fisher was able to argue that changes in the supply of money would result in proportional changes in the price level.[1]

Criticism of the quantity theory focused on the stability of velocity. Figure 10.1 shows the income velocity of money. It reveals that over time, the velocity of the broader money supply measures, M2 and M3, has remained fairly stable. However, M1 has increased noticeably over time.[2]

---

[1] Two versions of the quantity theory preceded the modern version. Irving Fisher's version of the theory viewed money as primarily a medium of exchange, that is, a transactions variable. Although distinguishing between the short- and long-run effects of changes in the money supply, Fisher pointed to short-run money supply variations as the primary factor responsible for business-cycle fluctuations. Fisher also described the velocity of money as fixed, determined largely by institutional forces. The Cambridge version evolved from the work of Cambridge University economists, most notably Alfred Marshall. This version interpreted money as an asset, rather than only as a medium of exchange, and hypothesized that velocity might not be stable.

[2] The appendix to this chapter elaborates on the concept of the income velocity of money.

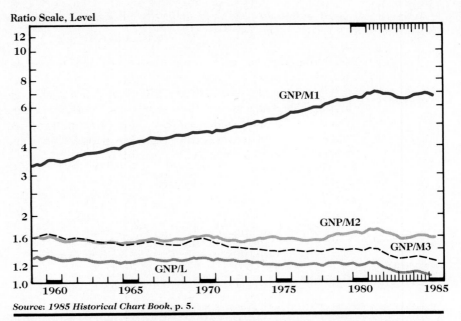

Ratio Scale, Level

GNP/M1

GNP/M2

GNP/M3

GNP/L

Source: 1985 Historical Chart Book, p. 5.

FIGURE 10.1 *Income Velocity of Money*   The velocity of the broader money measures, M2, M3, and L, has been fairly stable. On the other hand, the velocity of M1 has increased steadily until about 1982 when it began to decline. The income velocity reported in this figure is seasonally adjusted data reported on a quarterly basis.

Keep in mind that classical economists, who dominated economic thinking at the time the quantity theory evolved, described a world with full employment. They did not believe that interest rates affected velocity. As a result, they viewed velocity as constant (at least in the short run), or slowly changing (in the long run).

Monetarists' Response to the Keynesian Challenge

The most serious challenge to the quantity theory eminated from Keynes' notion of the *liquidity trap*. Prior to the 1930s, quantity theorists argued that a change in the supply of money had a direct effect on prices and nominal income. Keynes argued that the demand for money and thus velocity was a function of the level of income and the rate of interest. Changes in the supply of money might be offset by changes in velocity. In the scenario Keynes described, a depressed economy might result in a situation where interest rates were so low and expectations about profit potential so bleak that increasing the money supply would not stimulate economic activity. In this situation the velocity of money would decline to offset the increased money supply and individuals would absorb idle cash balances.

For those who believed that money influenced economic activity, the challenge was to address not only the impact of money on the economy but also the issue of the stability of the demand for money function and of velocity.[3] Rather than developing elaborate theoretical models, monetarists have relied on empirical evidence to make their points. Milton Friedman is largely responsible for generating a body of empirical research demonstrating the stability of the demand for money function.

Spearheaded by Friedman, monetarists have argued that the prevailing Keynesian approach could not adequately capture the influence of monetary phenomena.[4] Monetarists believe that an empirical approach is the only way to assess monetary influences. Monetarists have relied on the use of positive economics; they selected the most important, albeit simple, theoretical relationship that would permit the prediction of major macroeconomic variables, such as GNP, from the supply of money. Monetarists judge the chain of causation to be less important than the correlation between money and these variables.

Monetarists investigated the rate of money supply growth relative to movements in the business cycle. Friedman and Anna Jacobson Schwartz looked at nearly one hundred years of business-cycle fluctuations and money supply changes. They concluded that increases in the supply of money caused the business-cycle fluctuations, because, on average, the rate of money growth peaked about sixteen months before the peak of the business cycle.[5]

Friedman and more contemporary monetarists have argued not that the velocity of money is fixed, nor even that it is stable, but instead that it is a *stable function*. They argue that the demand for money is dependent on variables, for example, nominal income and the nominal rate of interest, in a fashion that is stable and predictable. Economists can predict the demand for money from observable variables. Based on this argument we have a variation of equation (10.4).

---

[3] Moderate monetarists do not hold as tightly to the Friedman view that velocity is unaffected by interest rates. Their views are not terribly dissimilar from some contemporary Keynesians. We might provide a more distinct contrast by comparing these moderate monetarists and Keynesians who look to macroeconomic policy as an effective stabilization tool with hard-line monetarists and the rational expectationists. We do this later in this chapter.

[4] Along with Friedman, Karl Brunner of the University of Rochester, Allan Meltzer of Carnegie Mellon University, Leonall Andersen of the Federal Reserve Bank of St. Louis, and Jerry Jordan of the University of New Mexico and formerly on the Council of Economic Advisors, are prominent members of the monetarist school.

[5] Milton Friedman and Anna Schwartz, "Money and Business Cycles," *Review of Economics and Statistics* 45 (February 1963): 32–64.

$$M_s = M_d = f(Y_P + r) \qquad\qquad (10.5)$$

or

$$M_s = M_q = a + bY + cr \qquad\qquad (10.6)$$

where

a, b, and c are coefficients that can be
statistically estimated. They are stable and
predictable based on historical behavior

Karl Brunner and Allan Meltzer attempted to assess whether the demand-for-money function has been stable over time. They estimated a demand-for-money function using data from the 1930s and investigated whether this function accurately predicted the demand for money in the 1950s. It did. This study suggested that the demand-for-money function is relatively stable.[6]

Monetarist made their case through historical studies, statistical tests on the stability of the demand-for-money function and on velocity, and eventually through the generation of econometric models. Monetarists documented the connection between the money supply and nominal income and prices by looking at the United States, and later the United States and Great Britain. In 1963 Friedman and Schwartz published *A Monetary History of the United States, 1867–1960*. In this volume the authors demonstrate a correlation between changes in the money supply and nominal income (see Figure 10.2). The authors highlight particular time periods of dramatic changes in the supply of money to justify their assertion that a causal relationship runs from money to income. They point to the "Great Contraction" (Friedman's name for the depression of the 1930s) as a situation in which the money supply contracted due to bank failures and a tight money policy by the Federal Reserve, and income and prices followed. Subsequently Friedman and Schwartz published another book, *Monetary Trends in the U.S. and the U.K.: Their Relation to Income, Prices and Interest Rates 1867–1975*, which further supported their contentions. Other authors argued similarly.[7] Figure 10.2 illustrates the relationship between money stock, income and prices which forms the foundation for arguments about the connection between money and economic variables.

Monetarists demonstrated another important construct—that the demand for money function (and thus velocity) was stable. To do this Friedman and other monetarists discussed the demand for money in more detail

[6] Karl Brunner and Allan H. Meltzer, "Predicting Velocity: Implications for Theory and Policy," *Journal of Finance* 18 (May 1963): 319–354.

[7] See as an example Philip Cagan, *Determinants and Effects of Changes in the Stock of Money, 1875–1960* (New York: Columbia University Press, 1965).

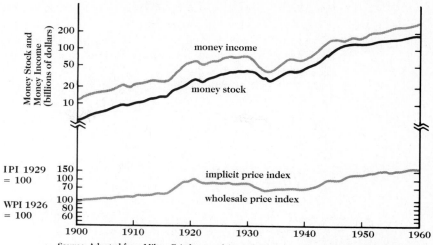

Source: Adapted from Milton Friedman and Anna J. Schwartz, *A Monetary History of the United States, 1867–1960* (Princeton: Princeton University Press, 1963) Chart 62. Reprinted by permission.

FIGURE 10.2 *Money Stock, Income, and Prices, 1900–1960* This figure shows the relationships which form the basis for Friedman's and Schwartz's argument that changes in the supply of money determine changes in the price level and, ultimately, income. Notice the similar movements of the money stock, income, and the price indices.

than did Keynes and his followers.[8] In its elaborate form the monetarist *Dm* function includes a number of variables:

$$Dm = f\left(\frac{r_B}{p}, \frac{r_E}{p}, \Delta p, \frac{Y}{p}, u, \frac{w}{p}\right) \qquad (10.7)$$

where

$$r_B = \text{rate of interest on bonds}$$
$$r_E = \text{rate of interest on equities}$$
$$p = \text{prices}$$
$$\Delta p = \text{changes in prices}$$
$$Y = \text{income}$$
$$u = \text{tastes of wealth holders}$$
$$w = \text{aggregate wealth held by individuals}$$

---

[8] For a detailed discussion of the D_m function, refer to Milton Friedman, "The Quantity Theory of Money: A Restatement," *Studies in the Quantity Theory of Money*, edited by M. Friedman (Chicago: University of Chicago Press, 1956): 3–21.

Friedman demonstrated that all these variables collapse into one measure, permanent income.[9] Permanent income is more stable and predictable than other more transitory measures. Furthermore, the monetarists argued, the relationship between money supply changes and nominal income, on average, is more stable and less influenced by institutional and historical events than the Keynesian multiplier relationship based on the consumption and investment functions.[10]

The Contemporary Case for Monetarism

In recent years monetarists, especially those at the Federal Reserve Bank of St. Louis, have used regression analysis to assess the impact of money supply changes on income.[11] Leonall Andersen and Jerry Jordan analyzed the degree to which changes in the money supply (M1) explained changes in income, and they compared this to the effects of government fiscal actions. Changes in M1 had a clear impact on nominal income in Andersen and Jordan's analysis, whereas fiscal policy had less of an impact.[12] Their work led to a lengthy debate between monetarists and nonmonetarists about the validity of the Andersen and Jordan econometric techniques.

Contemporary monetarists argue that the money market calls the tune for short-run economic changes. According to this group, real income and output are determined by basic forces within the economy, for example, the level of capital stock, education, and technology. In the long run the system will tend toward its natural employment level. The challenge, then, is to analyze how changes in the supply of money influence nominal variables.

Changes in the supply of money create a disequilibrium in individuals' desired money balances. If the money supply is increased, individuals will

---

[9] The notion of permanent income was developed by Friedman. Permanent income is a weighted average of expected future income receipts. It minimizes the impact of short-term changes in an individual's income flow and looks at the long-term trend of earned income.

[10] See Friedman and Meiselman, "The Relative Stability of Monetary Velocity and the Investment Multiplier in the United States 1877–1958," *Stabilization Policies: Commission on Money and Credit* (Englewood Cliffs, NJ: Prentice Hall, 1963).

[11] Regression analysis is a procedure in which the impact of independent variables on a dependent variable is statistically measured.

[12] See Leonall Andersen and Jerry Jordan, "Monetary and Fiscal Actions: A Test of Their Relative Impact in Economic Stabilization," Federal Reserve Bank of St. Louis *Review* 50 (November 1968): 11–23.

use excess money balances for consumption or investment in real or financial assets. Changes in the money supply influence aggregate demand. In spending their excess money balances, individuals drive up the price level and/or induce increased production.[13] This process continues until the demand for money rises to meet the increased supply and equilibrium is restored. Note that money balances drive the system in this process. Factors such as interest rates, the propensity to consume or the demand for investment capital (all very important in the Keynesian analysis) have little or no influence on the changes that occur.

Money and the Economy: The Monetarist Scenario

Let's look more closely at the monetarists' explanations for results of a money supply change. Assume the economy is dynamically stable:

- Unemployment has stabilized at about 5 percent.
- The economy is growing at a real rate of 3.5 percent.
- The Federal Reserve has maintained the growth of the basic money supply at 6 percent.
- Consumer prices are rising at an annual rate of 3 percent.
- Market interest rates average around 9 percent.
- The supply of money and demand for money are equal.

Now assume the Federal Reserve boosts the rate of growth of the money supply from 6 percent to 13 percent!

As individuals adapt to the increase in the money supply by purchasing financial assets and consumer goods and services, interest rates and unemployment levels drop and the rate of economic growth increases. The price level responds upward. Unfortunately the rate of unemployment, interest rates and real GNP do not remain at the new levels; real GNP and the rate of unemployment return to their long-term growth path, ultimately unaffected by monetary expansion. Also unfortunately, the price level and nominal interest rates continue to rise.

---

[13] Strict quantity theorists and most monetarists would argue that the interest elasticity of the demand for money is very low. Nonetheless, part of the excess supply of money goes toward the purchase of securities, forcing up the prices of these securities and lowering interest rates. With lower interest rates, the amount of money individuals are willing to hold rises (as the opportunity cost of holding money has declined).

Basic Monetarist Propositions

Monetarism, although grounded in the assumptions of the quantity theory, consists of a set of propositions that go beyond a simple relationship between money and the nominal level of income. Keeping these propositions in mind will help you understand monetarism and make a distinction between monetarist and Keynesian views.[14]

First, the antecedents of monetarism are found in the quantity theory of money. Monetary factors strongly influence nominal income and movements in the quantity of money are the most reliable guage of monetary impulses. Stated more precisely, changes in the supply of money are the primary determinant of changes in total spending. Closely related to this is the notion that a sustained increase in the nominal growth rate of money beyond the growth of output will result in a decline in purchasing power.

Second, monetarists argue that the private sector is inherently stable. But, erratic swings in the money supply disturb this stability and in turn lead to swings in the rate of inflation. Associated with this belief in the stability of the private sector is a dislike of government intervention. Third, prices and wages are relatively flexible, at least around the economy's potential output.

Fourth, monetarists argue that increases in the growth rate of the money supply designed to stimulate the economy will reduce the unemployment rate only temporarily. Because changes in the money supply do not influence real variables, using changes in the rate of growth of money to stimulate the system will lead to a rise in the price level. Therefore, monetarists argue for a monetary growth rule; the money supply should be allowed to grow at a constant rate roughly equivalent to the long-term rate of growth of the real GNP.

Fifth, the transmission process whereby monetary changes are transmitted to the real sector focuses on money balances and relative prices (the portfolio adjustment process) affecting an array of financial and real assets, not interest rates.

Monetarists share a basic proposition with Keynesians. Both view money as an asset. Monetarists see the demand for money being influenced by a wider range of variables (wider than the transactions, precautionary and speculative components). Individuals maintain a portfolio of assets, money among them. As we specified in equation (10.7), the demand for money is affected by real permanent income, real wealth, individual tastes, the rate of

---

[14] For a more detailed discussion of the precepts of monetarism see Thomas Mayer, "The Structure of Monetarism" (I) and (II) in his book by the same title published by W.W. Norton, 1978.

interest on bonds and equities and changes in the price level. Considering that all these variables influence the demand, you can see that the rate of interest is not as important here as in the Keynesian model.[15] This difference has important policy implications which are discussed in Chapter 18.

Keep in mind that monetarists explain money supply changes as affecting real variables only in the short term. In the long run, these variables, for example, employment, real income, and output, are determined by basic economic forces (technology, resource availability). In the long run, money affects only the price level and nominal interest rates. Monetarists see the demand for money as relatively stable. Changes in the supply of money beyond the normal growth rate destabilize the economy.

Summary of Monetarist Thinking

Contemporary monetarism has built on the nineteenth-century quantity theory to the extent that disproportionate changes in the growth of the money supply are seen as resulting in changes in prices. To demonstrate that excessive money supply growth rates will produce inflationary price increases, monetarists undertook historical and empirical studies that showed the velocity of money as a stable function. In doing this, monetarists have built an elaborate demand for money function in which interest rates play a much less significant role than they play in Keynesian analysis.

Within the context of some basic propositions, which stress price and wage flexibility and the destabilizing effects of excess monetary intervention, monetarists argue for predictable, perhaps even a fixed, growth rate for the money supply. This provides a contrast to the policy recommendations Keynesians suggest. It is this contrast to which we now turn our attention.

Contrasting Monetarism and Keynesianism

Our purpose in exploring macroeconomics and monetary theory is to develop an understanding of how money relates to the economic variables that are crucial to a prosperous economy. Eventually we will analyze the degree to

---

[15] To support their contention that the interest rate is not the most important variable determining the Dm, monetarists often point to empirical studies such as the one by David Laidler, "The Rate of Interest and the Demand for Money—Some Empirical Evidence," *Journal of Political Economy* 74 (December 1966): 545–555.

which monetary policy, implemented by our central bank, the Federal Reserve System, has been successful in helping the economy achieve its macroeconomic goals. Monetary policy responses are influenced by the policy makers' views on how the economy operates. These views are to a large extent determined by the macroeconomic models the policy makers use to interpret economic behavior.

This section contrasts the principles and implications of the Keynesian and monetarist views. It summarizes these alternative views by concentrating on the linkages between the monetary and real sectors inherent within each approach.[16]

Keynesian Transmission Mechanism

The Keynesian view explains that monetary changes transmit themselves to income through household portfolio adjustments with interest rates representing the crucial variable.[17] Keep in mind that this explanation regards money as a close substitute for financial assets. An example will illustrate the monetary transmission mechanism.

Assume that the Federal Reserve wants to increase the money supply. One way it can do so is by buying bonds in the open market. Individuals receive cash balances in return for the sale of their bonds. The money supply increases as a result of this step but the money does not affect income until it finds its way into the spending stream through expenditures for goods and services.

The increased cash balances which individuals now hold create an imbalance in their portfolios; cash balances exceed the desired amount relative to other financial assets. To restore portfolio balances, individuals purchase financial assets (stocks, bonds, etc.). This pushes the prices of the assets up, and the return (the rate of interest) drops. The higher asset prices encourage firms to issue new assets and to use the revenues to purchase capital goods. This increase in investment spending produces an increase in aggregate income via the expenditure multiplier. The expansionary monetary policy now has influenced income.

---

[16] An excellent, detailed analysis of these competing views can be found in Brian Morgan, *Monetarists and Keynesians—Their Contribution to Monetary Theory* (London: The Macmillan Press, 1978).

[17] This process is outlined in more detail in James Tobin, "Money, Capital and Other Stores of Value," *American Economic Review* (May 1961): 26–37.

Equilibrium is restored when consumer spending rises as a result of the rise in income. With this, demand for money rises (both the transactions demand and the speculative demand, which increases in response to the decline in interest rates) to absorb the increased supply of money.

Under normal circumstances (assuming, for example, no liquidity trap), expansionary monetary policy produces a higher level of aggregate income. The process occurs because interest rates respond and generate investment expenditures.

Monetarist Transmission Mechanism

The monetarist view explains that monetary changes transmit themselves into income directly through consumer spending. Monetarists agree with Keynesians that monetary changes are transmitted through portfolio adjustments, but they contend that these adjustments affect a broader range of assets and expenditures than in the Keynesian model. Monetarists do not view the world as restricted to a trade-off between holding cash balances and purchasing bonds. For example, the monetarists' explanation includes all durable goods owned by firms and households as capital assets.

Again consider an expansionary monetary policy. The infusion of money through open-market bond purchases creates portfolio imbalances. Households and firms make adjustments to their capital assets. These adjustments are in terms of real assets (durable goods such as appliances for individuals or machinery for firms), as well as financial assets (stocks and bonds). These moves to restore portfolio balance directly influence the level of expenditures in the system and the aggregate income.

Equilibrium is achieved similarly to the Keynesian process except that consumer goods prices increase along with capital asset prices. The response to higher prices for goods and services prompts increased output by the production sector and the associated increase in income.

Notice that interest rate changes are not crucial to the monetarist transmission mechanism. Real interest rates may change, temporarily, as a result of the expansionary monetary policy, but eventually they move back toward their original levels. Because of the relative unimportance of interest rates, monetarists argue that changes in the money supply are the best way to assess the effects of monetary policy. Furthermore, monetarists look more to the money supply as an indicator because they feel it can be measured more effectively than can interest rates. They argue that there is no accurately measureable counterpart to the theoretical interest rate discussed in Keynesian models.

Implications of the Differences in Keynesian and Monetarist Thought

Two prominent econometric models highlight the differences in the two transmission mechanisms. These econometric models illustrate how the Keynesian and monetarist approaches differ in their policy applications.[18] The Federal Reserve Bank of St. Louis developed an econometric model that is still in use.[19] The St. Louis model is an eight-equation monetarist model used to test stabilization policies. The Federal Reserve-MIT model, a more complex Keynesian model, was originally introduced in the early 1960s.[20]

The St. Louis model is designed so that money dominates spending. Although fiscal policy changes are included in the model, fiscal policy has only a limited and temporary effect. Money is the primary determinant of aggregate demand and changes in income. Figure 10.3 is a flow chart of the St. Louis model. It illustrates that changes in the money stock affect spending directly. Other variables, such as nominal GNP, prices, output, the rate of unemployment and interest rates, follow from changes in spending. Money is the most significant exogenous variable; changes in the supply of money are transmitted to the economic system through changes in spending.

With over 400 equations, the Federal Reserve-MIT model is considerably larger than the St. Louis model. The Federal Reserve-MIT model develops detailed channels through which monetary and fiscal policy changes affect spending. Figure 10.4 is a flow chart for this model. It illustrates the monetary sector of an early version of the model. Monetary policy affects the supply and demand for money as outlined in the Keynesian IS-LM model (described in Chapter 9).

---

[18] A more detailed discussion comparing the role of money in different econometric models may be found in Joseph M. Crews, "Econometric Models: The Monetarist and Non-Monetarist Views Compared," *Money Supply, Money Demand and Macroeconomic Models*, edited by Thomas M. Havrilesky and John T. Boorman (Arlington Heights, IL: Harlan Davidson, Inc., 1982).

[19] An original discussion of this model was by Leonall C. Andersen and Jerry L. Jordan, who were then at the Federal Reserve Bank of St. Louis, in "Monetary and Fiscal Actions: A Test of Their Relative Importance in Economic Stabilization," Federal Reserve Bank of St. Louis *Review* 11 (November 1968): 11–23. See also L.C. Andersen and Keith M. Carlson, "St. Louis Model Revisited," *International Economic Review* 15 (June 1974): 305–327.

[20] A widely known version of the Federal Reserve-MIT model is the MPS model (MPS refers to the institutions involved in the model's development—MIT, Pennsylvania, and the Social Science Research Council). A description of an early version of the model can be found in R. Rasche and H. Shapiro, "The F.R.B.-M.I.T. Econometric Model: Its Special Features," *American Economic Review* (May 1968): 123–149. For a discussion of the expanded model see D. Ballenberg, J. Engler, and A. Havenner, "MINNIE: A Small Version of the MIT-PENN-SSRC Model," *Federal Reserve Bulletin* (November 1975): 721–727.

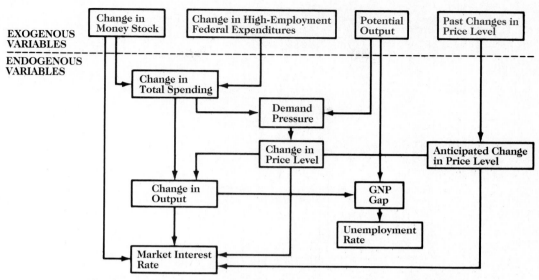

EXOGENOUS VARIABLES

ENDOGENOUS VARIABLES

Change in Money Stock

Change in High-Employment Federal Expenditures

Potential Output

Past Changes in Price Level

Change in Total Spending

Demand Pressure

Change in Price Level

Anticipated Change in Price Level

Change in Output

GNP Gap

Unemployment Rate

Market Interest Rate

Source: From "A Monetarist Model for Economic Stabilization" by L. C. Andersen and K. M. Karlson, Federal Reserve Bank of St. Louis *Review*, April 1970, pp. 9–10. Reprinted by permission.

FIGURE 10.3 *The St. Louis Econometric Model*   This figure shows the relationship of exogenous variables and endogenous variables in one of the basic monetarist econometric models. Especially compared to Figure 10.4, notice the relatively small number of variables.

Notice from Figure 10.4 that money supply changes affect interest rates for corporate bonds, mortgages, municipal bonds, etc. With the cost of capital altered, investment expenditures for plant and equipment as well as residential construction are changed. The changes in interest rates also influence the household sector's net worth and the availability of credit. These in turn affect consumption spending. Monetary policies affect interest rates, which become the vehicles for transmitting money supply changes to aggregate demand.

The eight-equation monetarist model and the 400-equation Keynesian model highlight another difference between the two approaches to policy discussions. Monetarists tend to rely on simple econometric models. This may be because monetarists see monetary changes as affecting the economy in many ways. Economists would find it difficult if not impossible to develop a model that includes all these structural influences. A simple, reduced-form approach is thus more reliable. On the other hand, Keynesians see monetary changes as influencing the economy through a limited number of channels; they address each of these channels in their structural models. The different foci of attention among the monetarists (specifically, money supply changes) and the Keynesians (interest rate changes) become very important in monitoring monetary policy actions.

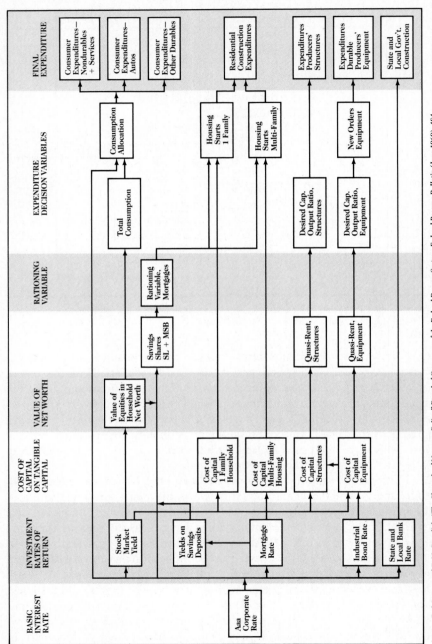

Source: F. deLeeuw and E. M. Gramlich, "The Channels of Monetary Policy," Board of Governors of the Federal Reserve System, *Federal Reserve Bulletin (June 1969)*: 484.

FIGURE 10.4 *The Channels of Monetary Policy in a Keynesian Econometric Model* This figure shows the greater complexity of a Keynesian-influenced econometric model. Compare the number of variables in this model with the number in the monetarist model shown in Figure 10.3.

The differences between economists adhering to a Keynesian approach and those espousing monetarist principles are many. In terms of the transmission of monetary policy influences, the groups differ in their opinions of which variables set and monitor monetary policy.

Debate between these two different approaches has been going on since the early 1960s and usually has taken the form of disagreements about the value of monetary versus fiscal policy.[21] A significant implication of this ongoing debate is the increasing importance given monetary policy in overall national stabilization policies. Monetarist arguments have gained increasing acceptability, especially among policy makers. Throughout much of the post–World War II era and until the late 1970s, macroeconomic policy tended to concentrate on the Keynesian approach. This situation has changed; November 1979 is often considered the watershed date.

We can underscore the distinction between monetarists and Keynesians on monetary issues by looking at the Federal Reserve's policy change that took place in November, 1979. Throughout the 1970s, the Federal Reserve had used interest rates as its target variable. The Fed undertook monetary policy changes to maintain interest rates within a predetermined range. This behavior reflected a Keynesian orientation in Federal Reserve policy. The Fed used the interest rate as the mechanism for transmitting changes in the money supply from the monetary sector to the real sector of the economy.

With its announcement in late 1979, the Federal Reserve shifted the focus of its attention from interest rates to the money supply. This was a clear change from a Keynesian to a monetarist orientation. Instead of aiming at achieving a target range for interest rates by changing the money supply in response to demands in the financial sector, the Federal Reserve now set growth targets for the money supply. As demand factors changed in the financial markets, interest rates would be allowed to fluctuate in response. Not only did the Federal Reserve alter its target variable, it also began looking more critically at the expansion of the money supply. The monetarist view that the money supply should not grow uncontrollably has influenced policy makers at the Federal Reserve. The Fed's policy actions are discussed in greater detail in Chapter 19.

The application of an alternative target variable and the renewed attention to money growth rates have been associated with a period of distinct changes in the economy. Consider the fact that the rate of inflation for the years 1978 to 1980 averaged nearly 12 percent per year; in the years 1981 to 1986 the rate averaged less than half that. On the other hand,

---

[21] Milton Friedman and Walter Heller carried on the public debate throughout much of the 1960s and 1970s. An example of this debate is Friedman and Heller, *Monetary vs. Fiscal Policy: A Dialogue* (New York: W.W. Norton, 1969).

measures reflecting the level of economic activity also have changed. For 1978 and 1979 the level of unemployment hovered around 6 percent; in 1982 unemployment peaked at over 10 percent; at the end of 1983 it was still above 8 percent; in early 1986 the rate was steady at around 7 percent. The rise and persistence of high real interest rates have evoked considerable discussion about the Federal Reserve's targets and its overall policies.

In considering the policy implications of the Keynesian-monetarist debate we also should mention the increasing market orientation in policies relating to the financial sector. The Depository Institutions Deregulation and Monetary Control Act passed in 1980 was a major piece of deregulatory legislation. We discuss the entire deregulatory movement in future chapters. Most important is the point that monetarists have argued for less government involvement in the economy. The increasing acceptance of some monetarist views was not the major force behind the financial reform legislation of 1980, but the legislation is surely consistent with the views of many monetarists.

Chapter Conclusion

Despite growing attention to the work of new classical economists, Keynesians and monetarists still dominate in economics texts and in the thinking of many policy makers. This chapter highlighted the monetarist view and some of the major policy-oriented differences between the two schools of thought.

We pointed out that, according to a Keynesian approach to monetary economics, the demand and supply of money determine the rate of interest. The rate of interest, given the marginal efficiency of investment schedule, determines the level of investment spending. Investment spending is one of the major determinants of the equilibrium level of income in the economy.

The basic propositions of monetarist thinking include the connection between money supply increases and the rate of inflation, which is a sophisticated version of the quantity theory of money. Also, monetarism holds a belief in the stability of the private sector of the economy, as well as the claim that changes in the supply of money have only temporary effects on factors such as employment. Finally, monetarism concentrates on the importance of monetary balances in changes in spending and income in the system.

Monetarists argue that the rate of interest is not a significant policy variable. Instead they emphasize the fact that changes in the supply of money only temporarily affect real variables; in the long run these variables are changed only by basic structural economic forces. Thus changes in the supply of money beyond that necessary to support economic growth will tend to destabilize the economy.

The monetary theory of income is therefore quite different for the Keynesians and the monetarists. The key is the transmission mechanism which each view emphasizes. The Keynesians rely on the rate of interest: $\Delta M \Rightarrow \Delta r \Rightarrow \Delta I \Rightarrow \Delta Y$. The monetarists look to monetary aggregates (some measure of the supply of money): $\Delta M \Rightarrow \Delta C \Rightarrow \Delta Y$. Note that in the Keynesian view the level of output is increased via increases in the level of investment following changes in the rate of interest. In the monetarist view this is not automatic. This distinction helps explain why monetarists see changes in the money supply as affecting the price level.

We concluded this chapter by illustrating the implications of these alternative views by looking at econometric models. Depending on the approach and the model one uses, policy makers either will concentrate on interest rates as the key variable, and let the supply of money fluctuate, or they will concentrate on the supply of money, and let the interest rate fluctuate.

Consider These Questions

1. What aspects of Keynesianism and which economic events combined to allow the monetarist counter-revolution?

2. How would you assess the empirical evidence used to support the monetarist position?

3. Monetarists argue there is much more to monetarism than the quantity theory of money. What do they mean?

4. Explain the alternative transmission mechanisms presented by the monetarists and the Keynesians.

5. How do econometric models reflect the alternative approaches of the monetarists and the Keynesians?

6. The St. Louis Federal Reserve Bank is famous for its monetarist approach to policy analysis. What is it about the St. Louis Fed which gives it this image?

7. Compare and contrast the effects of an expansionary monetary policy on prices and income under a monetarist model and a Keynesian model.

8. What is velocity? Why does it matter?

9. What might occur to change the growth path of velocity?

Suggestions for Further Reading

Fisher, Irving. *The Purchasing Power of Money*. New York: Macmillan, 1911. Comprehensive theoretical analysis which is responsible for the prominent role velocity has played in economic analysis.

Friedman, Milton. "Studies in the Quantity Theory of Money." In *Studies in the Quantity Theory of Money.* Edited by M. Friedman. Chicago: University of Chicago Press, 1956.

Friedman's classic, although rather sophisticated, article outlining the founding of modern monetarism.

Humphrey, Thomas M. "The Quantity of Money: Its Historical Evolution and Role in Policy Debates." Federal Reserve Bank of Richmond *Economic Review* (May/June 1974): 2–19.

Humphrey always provides understandable analysis of issues. This article is no exception; it provides a clear explanation of the historical origins and contemporary applications of the quantity theory of money.

Johnson, Harry G. "The Keynesian Revolution and the Monetarist Counter-Revolution." American Economic Association *Papers and Proceedings* LXI (May 1971): 1–14.

Outlines in nontechnical terms the social and intellectual conditions that make a counter-revolution possible.

Keynes, John M. *A Treatise on Money.* London: Macmillan Press, 1930.

This book gives the Cambridge version of the quantity theory.

Laidler, David E. W. *The Demand for Money: Theories and Evidence.* New York: Dun-Donnelley, 1977.

Excellent source for thorough, rigorous presentation of the various theories on the demand for money.

Poole, William. *Money and the Economy: A Monetarist View.* Reading, Mass.: Addison-Wesley, 1978.

Good overall review of monetarist view.

Purvis, Douglas D. "Monetarism: A Review." *Canadian Journal of Economics* XIII (February 1980): 96–122.

A very thorough review of the foundations and evolution of monetarism; includes an extensive bibliography.

McCulloch, J. H. *Money and Inflation: A Monetarist Approach.* New York: Academic Press, 1982.

A short (100 pages), understandable treatment of the monetarist views on the origins of inflation.

Thornton, Daniel L. "Does Velocity Matter?" Federal Reserve Bank of St. Louis *Economic Review* (December 1983): 5–13.

Examines role that income velocity plays in monetary decisions and evaluates problems that arise when policy makers attempt to offset fluctuations in velocity.

10. Income Velocity of Money

Chapter 1 introduced the quantity theory of money ($MV = PT$) and the concept of velocity as part of a discussion of money and economic activity. Velocity is important for any discussion of the quantity theory, money and economic activity, or the demand for money.

Velocity of money refers to the number of times money changes hands, or turns over, during a period of time. The quantity of money, regardless of how it is measured, that circulates over a period of time is less than the total value of goods and services generated during that same time period. The quantity of money must perform "double duty" to support the higher level of economic activity. Velocity is defined as the nominal value of income divided by the quantity of money:

$$V = \frac{Y \times p}{M}$$

Early quantity theorists, and even some contemporary monetarists, considered velocity to be stable. Most economists will explain that over the long term the income velocity of money may change slowly, perhaps even predictably. Figure 10A.1 shows the annual change in the income velocity of money. Since 1946, the growth rate of velocity has been about 3 percent per year. The rate of change of velocity will be different depending on which money measure is used. The broader the money measure, the less velocity changes over time.

In the short term, velocity changes often and quite dramatically. Figure 10A.2 illustrates the short-term changes in velocity. In 1984 nominal GNP was approximately $3680 billion. Using M1 as a money measure, which averaged about $550 billion, velocity was just over 6⅔ ($V = 3680/550 = 6.7$). The velocity of money declined throughout 1985 and into 1986. With disinflation and lower interest rates, the cost of holding money declined and individuals allowed their cash balances to build up. This caused the turnover of the dollar to fall. If interest rates stabilize or begin to rise and if there is any indication that inflation will accelerate, the decline in velocity will undoubtedly abate.

Generally speaking, velocity increases during periods of economic expansion. This is partly because interest rates usually rise during upswings and individuals are inclined to shift from holding money balances (including

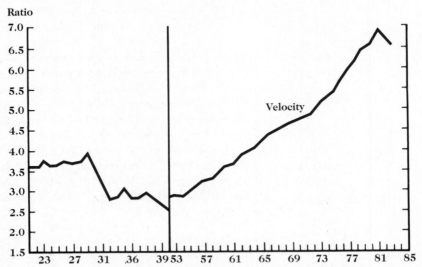

Source: From *Economic Review*, Summer 1984. Reprinted by permission of the Federal Reserve Bank of San Francisco.

FIGURE 10A.1 *Velocity of Money*   This figure illustrates the steady, almost pre-dictable growth of the income velocity of money from the early 1950s until 1982. Since 1982, velocity has been declining, to a degree not anticipated by analysts.

checkable deposits) into interest-bearing accounts. The existing supply of money must then "turn over" more often to support the rising level of economic activity. The reverse is true during economic contractions.

Velocity is higher today than during earlier periods in large part be-cause people can "economize" on money more easily today. The ready availability of credit, overdraft provisions, large negotiable certificates of deposit and commercial paper allow the conduct of business with less cur-rency and checkable deposits. For example, negotiable CDs facilitate the transfer of money from firms which do not immediately need funds to borrowers seeking funds. Idle money balances are used and the velocity of money rises. High interest rates during the late 1970s and 1980s, which raised the cost of holding money, have also contributed to a higher velocity of money.

The stability or predictability of the income velocity of money is important in determining an approach to monetary policy. If velocity is

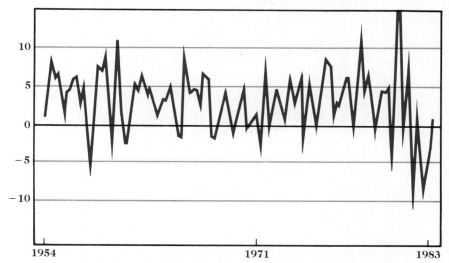

Source: Figure, "Rate of Change in Velocity (Quarterly)" from Federal Reserve Bank of St. Louis *Review*, December 1983. Reprinted by permission.

FIGURE 10A.2 *Rate of Change in Velocity* On a short-term (quarterly) basis, velocity fluctuates dramatically. Such a short-term measure is not useful except as an early indication of changes in the trend rate for velocity.

either stable or predictable, then monetary authorities can feel more confident about the linkage between money supply changes and changes in prices and/or the level of economic activity.[1] Monetarists argue that short-run fluctuations in velocity are not as important as the long-run trend. Non-monetarists argue that velocity is unpredictable. A change in velocity can result in monetary policy being too restrictive or too stimulatory.

---

[1] Daniel L. Thornton, "Why Does Velocity Matter," Federal Reserve Bank of St. Louis *Review* (December 1983), argues that velocity is important but that policy makers need to focus on long-term trends, rather than responding too quickly to changes in velocity.

CHAPTER ELEVEN

INFLATION, DISINFLATION and UNEMPLOYMENT

There are times I almost think I am not sure of what I absolutely know.

Puzzled Monarch
"The King and I"

The most perplexing economic problem facing the United States in the post–World War II period has been inflation. In the years before WW II, the United States struggled to overcome the scourge of high unemployment levels. And for thirty years after the Civil War this country was plagued by deflation. This is important to remember, not because it reveals how much difficulty we have faced, but because we need to keep in mind the fact that there is no all-time economic "public enemy number one." This country, as well as other industrialized and developing nations, is troubled by unemployment and price fluctuations.

This chapter reviews the causes and consequences of high levels of unemployment and uncontrolled price fluctuations.

Chapter Objectives

Over the last few chapters you should have developed an understanding of the essentials of macroeconomic theory. This theoretical background was complemented by discussions on the policy alternatives stemming from various macroeconomic theories. All of this will prove useful as you now investigate the challenges to a stable American economy, namely inflation and unemployment.

As you proceed through this chapter, try to envision how macroeconomic theory has influenced policy makers' understandings of and responses to inflation and unemployment. You should understand that the success of economic policy depends not only on the application of the proper tools but also on an accurate assessment of what is causing the problem. After reading this chapter you should be able to:

- Analyze the causes of inflationary price increases.
- Differentiate between demand factors, supply factors, and expectations as precipitators of inflation.
- Specify the consequences of inflation by identifying those who benefit and those who lose during periods of inflation.
- Analyze the effects of inflation on tax payments, output, capital formation and economic growth.
- Assess the relationship between inflation and unemployment by outlining the Phillips Curve notion and the Friedman-Phelps alternative.

Finally, you can use this chapter to examine this country's responses to the challenge posed by inflation. As you reflect on policy alternatives, you should consider the reasons for using various policies and the results of each. You should be able to:

- Determine which policies are better suited to deal with inflation.
- Assess the effectiveness of specific policies under different conditions.
- Specify the procedures policy makers should use to determine which policy alternative to follow.

You will have the opportunity in Chapter 19 to analyze specific monetary policy actions. After reading this chapter you should understand how and why inflation has been such an intransigent problem and why it continues to influence policies even when it is under control. With these understandings you will be in a position to move on to explore the financial system and monetary policy.

Price Fluctuations

We begin with an overview of the history of price fluctuations in the United States and with a brief investigation of some serious price fluctuation problems inside and outside this country.

Overview of Price Fluctuations

In Chapter 2 we discussed various measures of price movements. Figure 11.1 illustrates the changes in wholesale prices between 1800 and 1980.[1] (We now refer to wholesale prices as producer prices.) Notice that until the current period, price rises tended to occur—and definitely were most extreme—during wars. In reflecting on inflation during the major American wars (War of 1812, Civil War, WW I, WW II, Vietnam) we can use the simplistic definition of inflation to explain what pushed up prices—"too much money chasing too few goods." Notice from Figure 11.1 that wartime inflation always was followed by price declines (deflation). This pattern held until the WW II era. The business boom that accompanied the WW II military build-up slackened, and the economy subsequently experienced recessions. However, during the conversion to peacetime in the late 1940s and again in the early 1950s, prices did not decline to the prewar level.

What causes prices to rise and fall? Why didn't prices fall after WW II the way they had after previous wartime inflations? Why did prices stay so high from 1965 until 1982? We will address these questions in the pages that follow. To help us understand the causes and complexity of inflation, first we will explore instances of extreme price inflation.

American Civil War Experience

The most dramatic inflation in the United States occurred during the Civil War. When the war erupted in 1861, few people anticipated a long costly war. When funds became needed to support the Union war effort, Secretary of the Treasury Salmon P. Chase called for Congress to provide a source of revenue. No significant tax program existed. Instead of raising revenues through taxes, Congress authorized the creation of a fiat money system. The Legal Tender Act of February, 1862, provided for the issuance of $150 million of "greenbacks" (currency with green ink on one side). The treasury issued greenbacks to pay soldiers and to purchase military provisions. From 1862 until the end of the war, Congress passed legislation that resulted in the creation of $400 million in paper currency.

Government expenditures rose from about $606 million in 1860 to $1.2 billion in 1865. Debt issues and money creation were the primary sources of revenue to finance the war effort. Since specie payments (redemption of paper money for gold) had been suspended in late 1861, the large numbers

---

[1] For a more detailed view of price changes refer back to Figure 2.3.

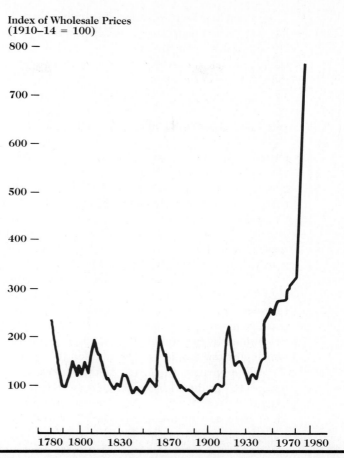

Index of Wholesale Prices (1910–14 = 100)

FIGURE 11.1 *Wholesale Price Movements, 1780–1985* The price level has fluctuated throughout American history. Wars have led to rapidly rising prices, but postwar periods have seen declining prices. This pattern was broken in the post–World War II period. Prices have risen steadily since that time.

of greenbacks had no backing. The money supply had increased from about $680 million in 1861 to about $1.6 billion in 1865, almost a 150-percent increase. This dramatic increase resulted in a rapid increase in the price level.

At the end of 1861 the index of retail prices was at 105; by the end of 1865 it had risen to 191. This was a 90-percent increase in four years. The worst inflation we have experienced in any recent four-year period was from 1978 to 1982 when consumer prices rose by about 43 percent, significantly less than the increase during the Civil War years.

The Civil War inflation reflected a common wartime practice of creating money to finance military expenditures. Following the Civil War, the United States went through a protracted period of deflation as the government reduced the money supply in an effort to resume the gold convertibility of the currency.[2]

German Hyperinflation

Perhaps the most startling and devastating inflationary period occurred in Germany after World War I, from 1919 to 1923. Germany was forced to pay exhorbitant reparations as a penalty for starting the war. More than anything, these payments were responsible for German hyperinflation. To dramatize the magnitude of Germany's hyperinflation, consider the fact that in January 1919 the wholesale price index stood at 262; in June 1924 the same index read 115,900,000,000,000! The currency printed by the government was worth more as scrap paper than as money.

The Weimar Republic was expected to pay reparations to the Allies in gold. The government responded with a spectacular money creation program in order to buy gold in the international market. In 1919 about 51-billion marks circulated in Germany. By the end of 1921, this figure stood at over 113 billion; by the end of 1922, 1280-billion marks circulated. A pair of shoes which cost ten marks in 1914 sold for 1000 marks in mid-1922.

The greatest expansion of the money supply and the worst inflation occurred after the French occupied the Ruhr Valley in January 1923. Workers struck in resistance to the French occupation and the German government tried to support the unemployed workers with cash payments. The quantity of marks in circulation rose to over 17 trillion by mid-1923. The government worked at a feverish pace to print enough money. In late 1923 the central bank had resorted to printing 100-trillion mark notes.

With the increase in the supply of money, consumer prices skyrocketed. In June 1923 the price index reached 7,478,700 and then went through the roof. In mid-1923 it took 3-million marks to buy a half-dozen eggs; by the end of the year Germans used 80-billion marks to buy one egg—the price index had reached 126,160,000,000,000.

In December, 1923, the supply of money peaked at 496,507, 424,772,000,000,000 (nearly 500-quintillion) marks. In late 1923 the govern-

---

[2] Wesley Clare Mitchell, *Gold, Prices, and Wages Under the Greenback Standard* (Berkeley: University Press, 1908).

ment created a new currency, the rentenmark (1 rentenmark equaled 1-trillion paper marks). The government also established a new central bank and placed a limit on the total quantity of the new currency which the central bank could issue.

Almost overnight the hyperinflation ceased and the horror which had plagued the German people for years came to a halt. Confidence was restored; as we discussed in Chapter 1, acceptability of or confidence in a currency ultimately determines its value and stability. Once the German people were confident the government would control currency expansion responsibly, they accepted money at its face value rather than discounting it.

The excessive inflation in the United States during the Civil War and the outrageous hyperinflation in Germany in the early 1920s were extreme cases of inflationary periods that have plagued economies throughout history. In both instances the economies recovered; in fact, Germany prospered in the years between 1924 and the Great Depression.

These two examples illustrate that excessive money creation is a major source of inflationary pressure. From our own experience we know that inflation is disruptive. We now must look closely at the causes and consequences of inflation.

Causes of Inflation

Earlier in this chapter, we referred to inflation as "too much money chasing too few goods." In addition to oversimplifying the inflation problem, this trite phrase overlooks a variety of possible causes. We will outline in somewhat more detail the causes of inflation. In so doing we will concentrate on demand factors and supply factors as well as inflationary expectations. We can employ the macro model developed in Chapter 9 to illustrate the various causes of inflation.

Demand Factors

Demand-induced inflation results from aggregate demand increasing beyond the economy's ability to respond with a sufficient supply of goods and services. Demand pulls up prices. This situation may occur when the economy is operating at or near full employment; in this case aggregate demand increases result predominately in the price level rising (as opposed to output increasing). We also may see a rise in the price level even though the economy is below full employment if the production sector does not or cannot increase output. Demand-induced inflation may result from real or monetary factors. We will look at both in the context of traditional excess demand (or demand-pull inflation).

Output excess demand is the classic situation where aggregate demand increases. It is most likely to result from an increase in government spending without an associated tax increase, or a tax reduction without any accompanying reduction in expenditures, or an increase in investment (or a shift in *MEI*). We can illustrate output excess demand by using our macro model, Figure 11.2.

In Figure 11.2, *AD* results from the intersection of IS_1 and $LM_{p=1}$, IS_2 and $LM_{p=2}$, and IS_3 and $LM_{p=3}$. AD_1 intersects *AS* to generate an output of Q_1 and a price level of p_1. Assuming that spending increases (via $\Delta \uparrow G$, $\Delta \downarrow T$, or $\Delta \uparrow I$), the *IS* curves will shift outward to the right (to IS'_1, IS'_2 and IS'_3) and shift the aggregate demand curve to AD_2. The result of this spending increase, given that the economy is near full employment, produces an increase in prices (from p_1 to p_2). Output increases slightly.

Input excess demand is a situation where the demand for labor or other factors of production forces up wages or intermediate product prices. This translates into increasing prices through both the increased purchasing power of laborers and the increased spending of business firms for investment goods. In either case the explanation associated with Figure 11.2 applies. If input excess demand persists and results in an increasing demand for workers, wage rates will begin to rise producing a situation where demand inflation is translated into cost-push inflation.

Money excess demand is again a situation where aggregate demand increases, causing prices to rise. In this case the increase in aggregate demand occurs because of an expansion of the money supply, which then produces increased spending by consumers.

In Figure 11.3, AD_1 and *AS* originally produced an output Q_1 and a price level of p_1. Assuming that the supply of money increases, the *LM* curves will shift outward to the right (to $LM'_{p=1}$, $LM'_{p=2}$, and $LM'_{p=3}$) and will shift the aggregate demand curve to AD_2. With the economy near full employment, the result of the increased money supply and the associated increased spending is an increase in prices (from p_1 to p_2). Output increases slightly (from Q_1 to Q_2).

Demand Related to Supply Factors

In addition to the traditional excess demand, prices may increase as a result of another demand factor, sectoral excess demand. This concept includes components of demand and supply factors. Demand in a particular market or sector of the economy may force prices up in this sector. Demand may result

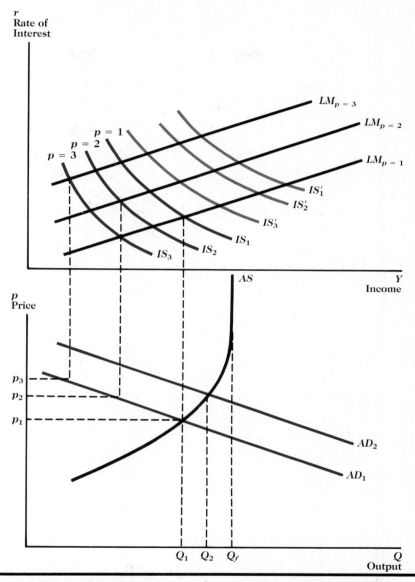

FIGURE 11.2 *Output Excess Demand* An increase in aggregate demand and a shift outward of the *IS* curves illustrate how prices are pulled upwards. As the economy approaches full employment, the price level effect of an increase in aggregate demand becomes greater.

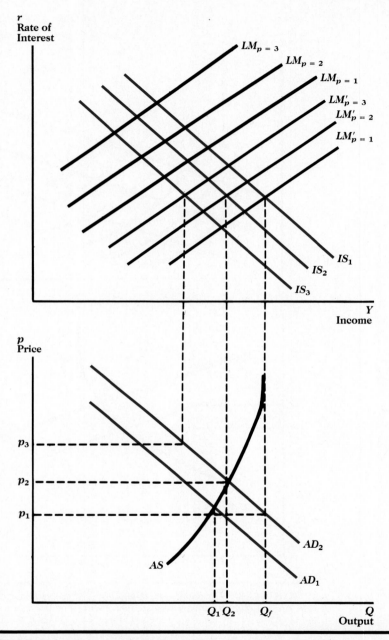

FIGURE 11.3 *Input or Money Excess Demand* An increase in the supply of money reflected in the shifting *LM* curves will cause aggregate demand to increase, pushing the price level up, from p_1 to p_2.

Inflation, Disinflation, and Unemployment

from seasonal labor shortages in one industry or shortfalls in production of another industry so that demand exceeds supply and forces prices to rise.

This alone does not translate into a general increase of the price level (except to the extent that the sector in question has a disproportionate impact on the consumer price level, which was the case with housing before the CPI was adjusted). But the reverberation caused by price increases in one sector may eventually cause prices in general to rise. A specific example is the increased demand for health care services over the past decade. As a result of population changes and expanding third party payment (insurance or government) arrangements, the demand for health care has risen and forced up prices. As prices in this sector continue to rise, related costs, such as insurance payments, also rise. In this sense the demand-induced situation in one sector translates into supply-based price increases in another sector. The result is a general increase in prices, that is, inflation.

Supply Factors

Supply-induced inflation results from cost factors pushing up prices. We can include *wage-push inflation* and *profit-push inflation* within this category. Supply-induced factors can cause inflation even when the economy is not at or near full employment. Labor unions or firms in imperfectly competitive industries exerting market power over prices may have effects on prices well beyond the initial wage/profit increase. These *long-lag effects* may also influence prices.

In recent years two other supply factors have been seen as influencing the rate of inflation. *Uneven productivity* is related to wage-push inflation. Of great interest throughout the 1970s was the influence of *market shocks*, both international and domestic.

Wage-push inflation occurs when workers are able to exert market power over wage determination. Such market power usually results from workers being organized into unions. Unionized workers may extract money wage increases without such increases being justified by productivity gains.[3] Figure 11.4 illustrates this situation. Increasing money-wage rates cause the aggregate supply curve to shift backward to the left, since producers must charge more for each unit of output. Instead of AS_1 and AD establishing a price level at p_1, AS_2 and AD result in the price level rising to p_2. Trade unions probably do not start the inflationary process. They do, however, contribute to its continuation.

---

[3] If the marginal product of labor increases (that is, workers' productivity rises) wages can increase without the product price increasing.

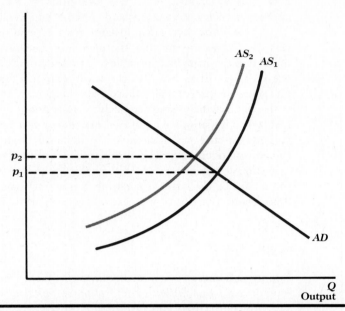

FIGURE 11.4 *Wage or Profit Push Inflation* Increasing wage rates cause the aggregate supply curve to shift to the left. This pushes the price level up. Excess profits produce the same result.

An example of wage-push inflation was the wage increases in the steel industry during the mid-1970s. These contributed to the continuing rise in the price of domestic steel at a time when imported steel was capturing an increasing share of the American market.

Profit-push inflation comes when prices rise from a firm's exercise of market power. With monopolistic or oligopolistic market conditions, firms may exact higher profits by pushing prices beyond those justified by resource or capital cost increases. This situation again results in the aggregate supply curve shift backward to the left as shown in Figure 11.4. The price level rises from p_1 to p_2.

An example of profit-push factors influencing the price level occurred during late 1983 and early 1984. Restrictions on the import of foreign automobiles gave American auto producers market power. Prices on American autos rose largely because producers sought higher profit levels.

In addition to these traditional supply constraint influences on the general price level, inflation may result from other supply factors. Uneven productivity, long lag contracts, and market shocks may contribute to inflation.

Uneven productivity exists between industries. This uneven productivity affects inflation in ways related to traditional wage-push inflation but has a slightly different origin. Throughout the period of double-digit inflation in this country, certain industries had productivity gains which justified wage increases. Firms within these industries could grant wage increases without increasing product prices. In a system where relative wage gains are important, these justifiable, noninflationary wage gains were often used as a reference point for workers in other industries where productivity would not justify wage increases. If workers in the industries with no productivity gains received money wage increases commensurate with workers in industries that had increasing productivity, inflationary price increases resulted. Uneven productivity has been particularly prevalent between manufacturing industries, such as the electronics industry, where productivity gains have justified wage increases, and service industries, where productivity gains have lagged but wage demands have kept pace with the manufacturing sector.

Long lag contracts are related to wage-push and uneven productivity problems. In this situation wage contracts extend over several years. When the contract is negotiated and settled, productivity gains or cost of living factors may justify or explain wage increases. But one or two years later, when neither of these factors is present, wage increases continue. We are left with a special case of wage-push inflation which is intractable in the short run.

Market shocks are similar to the traditional supply constraints already discussed, but they may or may not result from an intentional exercise of market power. Market shocks may cause even more problems than the other supply constraint causes of inflation. They may be beyond the control of policy makers.

Domestic supply shocks may result from crop shortages—either artificially induced by producers holding down supply or as a result of climatic conditions. The latter is certainly beyond human control; the former may stem from and cause further changes in political forces.

International supply shocks are troubling because they are usually beyond the control of the private sector or the federal government. The most obvious example here is the increase in the price of petroleum-based products resulting from OPEC raising oil prices in 1973–74 and again in 1978–79. The international oil cartel was able to exercise dramatic market power during the 1970s. The resulting price adjustments were felt throughout the economy. Estimates place the resulting increases in the American consumer price index between 6 percent and 10 percent.

Inflationary Expectations

The steady and irreversible increase in prices that occurred almost without interruption from 1965 until well into the 1970s created an atmosphere in which individuals, firms, and labor unions came to expect inflation. Because the price record showed regular increases in all price indices, rational economic behavior called for actions to anticipate price increases. Just as the situation described in an earlier chapter, where an individual might find it cheaper to borrow money to buy today rather than waiting a year when the product price would rise appreciably, firms, labor unions and consumers acted to protect themselves from inflation. The anticipation of inflationary price increases promotes behavior which in and of itself encourages inflation; to a great extent the expectation of inflation is a self-fulfilling prophecy.

An example of inflationary expectations influencing prices can be seen by considering the present discounted value notion we described in Chapter 3. In explaining present value we used the formula

$$\text{Present Value} = F_0 = \frac{F_n}{(1 + r)^n} \qquad (3.8)$$

ECONOMICS T⬤DAY Forecasting Inflation

Many economic transactions require a commitment to exchange money at some future time. Credit transactions are a good example of this. Since inflation reduces the future value of money, it pays people (both potential borrowers and lenders) to try to forecast inflation over the relevant time period. This forecast is called *anticipated inflation*. As the name suggests, anticipated inflation is forward-looking. It is the rate of change in the general price level that people *think* will occur during some specific future time period.

Of course, the accuracy of inflation forecasts depends on future events and circumstances that are unknown when each forecast is made. Consequently, these forecasts generally will be "wrong." Any difference between actual (or realized) inflation and anticipated inflation is call *unanticipated infla-*

tion. Unanticipated inflation is known only with hindsight. Because it is known only after the fact, it plays no role in people's decisions. It is important, however, in assessing whether the decisions produced profits or losses.

The nominal interest rates quoted in financial markets are formed in the process of contracting between borrowers and lenders. They indicate the number of dollars the borrower must pay to the creditor in the future in exchange for a given number of present dollars. If borrowers and lenders expect the value of the dollar to depreciate in terms of the goods it will buy over the life of the loan (that is, if they anticipate inflation), the nominal interest rate specified in the loan contract will take this into account. The interest rate will be

sufficiently high to compensate for the expected depreciation in the value of the dollar.

To illustrate, suppose the real interest rate is 3 percent and the anticipated rate of inflation over the coming year is 5 percent. People think that it will take $1.05 one year from now to purchase the goods that $1.00 will buy today. A loan of $1000 for one year will require a payment of $1081.50 at maturity (1000 × 1.03 × 1.05). This implies a nominal interest rate of 8.15 percent, that is, (1081.50/1000 − 1)/100. The anticipated real value of this amount at maturity is $1030 which is the sum of the principal and the real return.

The quality of inflation forecasts along with overall expectations about prices will have a lot to do with the cost of borrowing money.

If individuals come to expect inflation, they will incorporate that expectation into their plans. The effect of expected inflation (represented by π) on the present value notion is shown by an adaptation of equation 3.8.

$$\text{Present Value} = F_0 = \frac{F_n}{(1 + r)^n} \div 1 + \pi \qquad (11.1)$$

Using the same example we developed in Chapter 3 where a sum of $5600 one year from now given a prevailing interest rate of 9 percent was equivalent to $5138 today, notice how that sum is reduced assuming an expected inflation rate of 5 percent:

$$F = \frac{5600}{1 + .9} - 1.05 = \$4969$$

The extent to which expectations influence the rate of inflation is determined by the way people form their expectations. If individuals base their expectations about the future on what has happened in the past, expectations may lag somewhat. On the other hand, if individuals form expectations based on what they estimate prices will be based on policy actions, then expectations may lead to "defensive" actions which will precipitate inflation.

Relationship Among Causes of Inflation

One way to summarize the causes of inflation is to refer to a diagram presented by Thomas Humphrey of the Federal Reserve Bank of Richmond. Figure 11.5 shows how the various causes of inflation may interrelate. In this diagram, excess demand (either output-excess demand or money-excess demand) sets into motion a chain of events. Demand factors influence supply factors, and expectations interact with both. The inflationary process need not begin always with excess demand, but once underway, the various causes discussed above feed on one another and increase the duration or magnitude of price inflation.

Consequences of Price Fluctuations

Price fluctuations have different effects on different people. John Maynard Keynes summarized the situation:

> . . . [A] change in the value of money, that is to say in the level of prices, is important only insofar as its incidence is unequal. Such changes [produce] . . . social consequences because, as we all know, when the value of

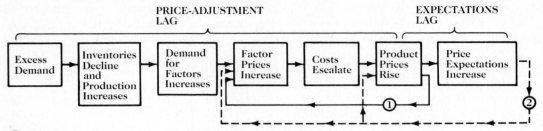

FIGURE 11.5 *The Inflationary Transmission Mechanism* The inflation process may be set into motion by a rise in spending. This will increase output, but at the same time increase the demand for factors of production. Prices will not respond immediately but the increased demand will cause factor prices to rise and this will cause consumer prices to increase. While it may take awhile for prices to respond, once they do expectations may serve to maintain high prices for some time.

money changes, it does not change equally for all persons for all purposes . . . . Thus, a change in prices and rewards as measured in money, generally affects different classes unequally, transfers wealth from one to another, bestows affluence here and embarrassment there and redistributes Fortune's favor so as to frustrate design and disappoint expectation.[4]

Price fluctuations help some individuals or sectors of the economy and hurt others. During the price deflation that followed the Civil War, farmers suffered. They borrowed to begin the season when prices were at one level but had to pay off the debt later in the year or the next year after prices declined. They had to pay off their debts with money which was becoming harder to earn. In general, debtors are hurt by deflation. Creditors benefit from deflation since the money they receive in payment of the loan is worth more (in terms of purchasing power) than the money they initially loaned.

During inflationary periods the tables are turned. Debtors benefit. During the course of the loan, prices and presumably wages rise. The money that is repaid is worth less in real terms (purchasing power). This was true especially during the 1970s when, despite rising interest rates, the price level continued to rise at a rate that exceeded expectations. Real interest rates

---

[4] John Maynard Keynes, "Social Consequences of Changes in the Value of Money," in *Essays in Persuasion* (London: reprint Hart Davis, 1951): 80–81.

were close to zero (in some cases they were negative). Millions of Americans who took out mortgages to buy homes when rates were at 5 percent, 6 percent, or 7 percent, benefited greatly when a rising price level pushed interest rates up to 12 percent, 14 percent, even 18 percent.[5]

Other consequences of inflation depend to a large extent on whether individuals can anticipate price fluctuations. Individuals or groups who can anticipate price changes, who know what action to take to protect themselves (or even to benefit), and who are able to exercise the options which will benefit them, will be better off than individuals or groups who can do none of those things. At the extreme, where inflation is a serious and ever present danger, everyone may anticipate price fluctuations and act to reduce or eliminate the impact. In Germany during the severe inflation of 1922–23, people often paid for a restaurant meal before it was served because prices rose so quickly that the meal would cost more at the end of the dinner. Menus and prices were recorded on chalkboards to accommodate frequently changing prices. The society under these circumstances may adopt a comprehensive indexing scheme. Under this arrangement everything, from interest rates paid and charged to mortgage payments or taxes, is automatically adjusted on a regular basis. A particular inflation index is used for adjustment purposes. Under these circumstances, assuming the indexing is comprehensive and fair, no one is disadvantaged disproportionately except those who hold large cash balances.

When a comprehensive indexing scheme is not in place or when inflation is unexpected, certain groups benefit at the expense of others. Generally speaking, those individuals whose income is flexible, or inflation-sensitive, will fare better than individuals with inflexible, or inflation-insensitive, income. For example, individuals whose salaries or income are tied to COLAs (cost of living adjustments—a form of indexing) will find that they do not lose purchasing power the way those on fixed incomes do.

To illustrate this point consider social security recipients. During the inflation of the Vietnam War period these individuals saw their purchasing power dwindle because prices were rising but their social security payments were fixed. Since the late 1970s, social security payments have been adjusted using an inflation index. Before this change, social security recipients were hurt by inflation because their incomes were unresponsive to inflation. Since the use of a cost of living adjustment these same people have inflation-sensitive income and their incomes keep pace with rising prices.

---

[5] In Chapter 14, we will discuss how lending institutions that primarily made mortgage loans (Savings and Loans) were seriously threatened during the period of rapidly rising interest rates.

Redistribution of Income and Wealth

When inflation is unexpected or when only certain groups are able to adjust to inflation, income and wealth are redistributed within society and the relative well-being of groups changes. To address the redistribution effects of inflation we need to specify how we are measuring individual and household well-being. Depending on whether we look at current income, some variant of income, or wealth, we get a somewhat different picture of the effects of inflation on individual or household well-being. Generally speaking, *income* refers to the direct or indirect flow of revenue to individuals, households, or corporations. *Wealth* is accumulated income and really is a measure of net worth.

Any discussion of the effects of inflation on income and wealth addresses the average individual or household. As such it masks individual differences. Still, in looking at the redistributional effects of inflation, the conventional interpretation (the rich get richer and the poor get poorer) may not be supported.

In looking at two periods of inflation during the 1960s, Albert Burger concluded that in the period of faster inflation (the years 1965 to 1968 versus 1960 to 1965), the real earnings of professional workers increased more than earnings during the period of lower price increases, and they increased more than the real earnings of unskilled and blue-collar workers.[6] Burger did not look at low income groups.

On the other hand, when considering wealth, Bach and Stephenson concluded that inflation transfers purchasing power from older to younger people and from the very poor and the very rich to middle and upper middle income groups.[7]

Joseph Minarik reported the results of an extensive study conducted by the Brookings Institution.[8] Using a Census Bureau survey of households and unidentified tax returns from the IRS, Minarik looked at inflation's effects on what he calls census income and accrued comprehensive income. Census income includes current direct revenues—wages, salaries, business income, interest, dividends, rent, pension benefits, and government transfers without taxes. Accrued comprehensive income, or ACI, reflects a broader range

---

[6] Albert E. Burger, "The Effects of Inflation 1960–1968," Federal Reserve Bank of St. Louis *Review* 51 (November 1969): 25–36.

[7] G.L. Bach and James B. Stephenson, "Inflation and the Redistribution of Wealth," *Review of Economics and Statistics* 56 (February 1974): 1–13.

[8] Joseph J. Minarik's work is summarized in "Who Wins, Who Loses from Inflation?" *Challenge* (January/February 1979): 26–31. A more detailed version of his study is reported in "The Size Distribution of Income During Inflation," in *Review of Income and Wealth* (December 1979): 377–392.

of household revenues—employee benefits, in-kind government transfers, depreciation of bonds, appreciation of home values, and taxes.

Minarik simulated a 2-percent rise in the rate of inflation over one year (1970). The results of his analyses are shown in Figure 11.6 as a ratio of real income after inflation to pre-inflation real income (a value greater than 1.0 implies a gain and a value less than 1.0 indicates a loss in real income).

When looking at the narrow income measure—census income—the results, although modest, support the common notion that the poor are disadvantaged by inflation while the rich benefit. Low income groups experience a slight loss in real income, largely because government transfer payments are slow to respond to inflation. Middle income groups hold their own primarily because their wages and salaries are income sensitive. Upper

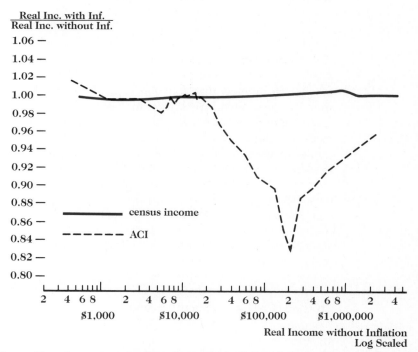

Source: Figure from "Who Wins, Who Loses from Inflation" by Joseph J. Minarik, *Challenge*, January/February 1979, p. 29. Reprinted by permission of M. E. Sharpe, Inc., Publisher, Armonk, NY 10504.

FIGURE 11.6 *Effects of Inflation on Various Income Groups* This figure reports results of one study that shows how low income groups are disadvantaged by inflation when a narrow income measure is used (represented by the slight deviation of the top line from 1.00 for low income groups). When a broader income measure is used, higher income groups are more greatly disadvantaged (illustrated by the serious deviation of the bottom line from 1.00 for high income groups).

income groups experience a rise in real income mostly because their revenues increase as interest payments rise.

When considering accrued comprehensive income, the broader income measure, the results are quite different. Using ACI as the measure of well-being, low income groups are virtually unaffected and middle income groups are only slightly disadvantaged. Because of greater real income taxes, lagging corporate earnings, and the depreciating value of interest-bearing securities, upper income households experience a severe drop in real income.[9]

We can conclude from empirical studies that inflation hurts most groups but it disproportionately affects higher income groups when a broad measure of income is used. Most researchers point out that the causes of inflation may influence the impact of inflation. For example, if inflation is caused primarily by rising prices of necessities, food and fuel, then those groups for whom expenditures on these products predominate, mostly low income people, will feel the pinch most intensely.

Tax Payments/Reserves

Many have argued that inflation is really a tax. With a progressive tax structure using nominal income for tax determination, inflation serves to push individuals into higher income categories and thus into high tax brackets. Since the rate of taxation rises in the higher brackets, inflation results in individuals and corporations paying more taxes. This so-called bracket creep reduces the real disposable after-tax income.

By the same token inflation represents somewhat of a bonanza for the tax collector. Bracket creep provides additional tax revenue to the government. And, since the government is such a massive debtor, inflation allows the government to pay back its loans with less valuable dollars. Recent adjustments in the American tax laws were, in part, designed to redress this problem.

Output, Capital Formation, and Economic Growth

Inflation is often seen as stimulating the economy and decreasing unemployment. We will investigate in some detail the tradeoff between inflation and unemployment in the following section. Then and now we need to keep in mind the distinction between the short-run impact of inflation, which we can

---

[9] Minarik also reports that the elderly, especially low and middle income, are adversely affected by inflation (largely because their income is derived from property).

see reflected in employment and output figures, and the long-run effect, which shows up more in rates of capital formation and real economic growth.

Certain industries do quite well during inflationary periods. Those industries that can pass along price increases without any associated cost increases (or in which the cost increases lag) will find profit margins increasing. Also, once inflation has set in and wages begin to rise, industries that can substitute capital for labor may do better than those industries that remain heavily labor intensive. Those industries able to adjust most easily to inflation will attract resources away from those industries that cannot. The regulated industries, such as utilities, which must have rate increases approved by public oversight bodies, are less able to adjust to inflation. The prices utilities charge generally lag behind their increasing operational costs.

In the short run, and assuming that the economy is operating below full capacity, modest inflation may stimulate output and with it employment. With prices rising ahead of wages and with firms being able to sell off inventories at the higher prices, firms may actually recall workers to increase production. Once wages begin to catch up with the higher price level, this stimulus is reduced. We will postpone further discussion on this issue until later in the chapter.

Analyzing the effects of inflation in the long run is more complicated. Some economists have argued that inflation had a positive effect on economic growth. Economic historian Earl Hamilton hypothesized that the origins of capitalism in Europe could be traced to the inflation produced by the Spanish discoveries of gold in the Americas. His argument was that the expansion of the bullion supply produced a long and large rise in the general price level, and that stimulated commerce and economic activity.[10]

The notion that inflation may stimulate economic growth has been incorporated into development strategies for Third World countries. The central bank can create money and loan it to the government. The government then has the funds to bid resources away from the private sector and direct these resources into capital formation. Accompanying this process are resource price increases and a general price rise as purchasing power is expanded. Once output increases as a result of the expanded capital stock, prices will decline. The inflation stimulated growth but was self-liquidating. Of course for this process to work the government must have considerable control to ensure that resources are used to expand the capital stock rather than for increased consumer goods.

More recently economists have looked much less favorably on the long-run implications of inflation. Inflation creates uncertainty about future

---

[10] Earl J. Hamilton, "American Treasure and Rise of Capitalism, 1500–1700," *Economica* (November 1929): 338–357.

prices, wages, and interest rates—and uncertainty increases risk. Increased risk requires a greater return for the investor, and this may raise the price of investment funds to the point that capital formation is severely restricted. At the same time inflation disrupts investment patterns. Rational investors seek assets for which the return or appreciation keeps up with inflation. In this connection, some argue that Americans have overinvested in residential real estate, because home prices have kept pace with inflation, rather than productive resources.

Unemployment and Its Consequences

Unemployment not only means that individuals are without work, it also means that the economy is operating at some point below its maximum level of production. Unemployment, therefore, hurts society as a whole, as well as those without jobs.

Arthur Okun, Chairman of the Council of Economic Advisors during Lyndon Johnson's administration, provided us with some empirical evidence on the output lost due to unemployment. Okun identified a GNP gap which is defined as the difference between the output associated with the full employment level of production and that generated by the actual level of employment. He then looked at the relationship between the GNP gap and the difference between the actual and natural unemployment rates (the natural rate is explained on page 290). We call this relationship Okun's Law:

$$\text{GNP gap} = B\,(U - U_N)$$

where

B is an estimated variable
U is the actual rate of unemployment
U_N is the natural rate of unemployment

Okun determined that B was a constant equal to approximately 3.0. What this means is that for each percentage point increase in the rate of unemployment beyond the natural rate, real GNP decreases 3 percent. Let's calculate the economic cost of unemployment using the 1985 unemployment rate and assuming the natural rate to be 6 percent:

$$\text{GNP gap} = \text{real GNP} \times (U - U_N) \times 3$$
or

$$\text{GNP gap} = \$3576 \text{ billion} \times (7.2\% - 6\%) \times 3 = \$128.7 \text{ billion}$$

Beyond the personal suffering felt by the unemployed and the cost of government transfer programs for those without work, society must absorb an opportunity cost which in some instances may reach monumental proportions.

Inflation and Unemployment—Are They Related?

Developed economies are intermittently faced with the problem of inflation or unemployment. Historically, these problems have come at different times—periods of inflation are usually accompanied by relatively low unemployment; periods of high unemployment usually are not accompanied by rising prices. Figure 11.7 illustrates this point. The lines representing inflation and unemployment usually move in opposite directions. One might reasonably conclude that inflation and unemployment are inversely related. The research of A.W.H. Phillips in the early 1950s apparently verified the trade-off between these problems.

But in more recent times, inflation and unemployment have simultaneously plagued the American economy. Figure 11.7 reveals that throughout the 1970s inflation and unemployment were both at historically high levels. The combination of a stagnating economy and rising prices, often called stagflation, called into question the trade-off between inflation and unemployment. Next we will investigate the relationship between inflation and unemployment.

The Problem of Unemployment

On an individual basis unemployment creates personal hardships. At the aggregate level unemployment costs the economy the opportunity to be more productive. Figure 11.8 shows the gap between potential output and actual output that results from the nation not fully employing its labor force.

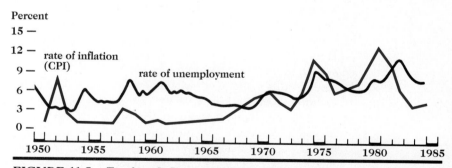

FIGURE 11.7 *Tracking Inflation and Unemployment*   For much of the post–World War II period inflation and unemployment have moved in opposite directions (illustrated by the spread between the two lines). Although there is still some evidence of this trade-off in the last fifteen years, it is not as distinct.

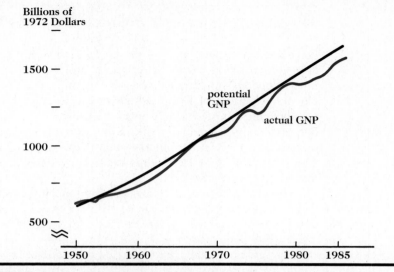

FIGURE 11.8 *GNP Gap Created by Unemployment* This figure reveals the gap between potential GNP and actual GNP that is created as a result of unemployment.

Technically the rate of unemployment is the ratio of individuals without jobs who are actively seeking work to the nation's total labor force. Data on unemployment are gathered and published by the Bureau of Labor Statistics.

Sources of Unemployment Economists divide the reasons for unemployment into four categories. *Frictional unemployment* refers to unemployment from market adjustments. Individuals may decide to change jobs and to go without work while they search for a new position. In a dynamic economy firms fail and new ones begin operations. The dislocations of workers from this process fits into the frictional unemployment category. *Structural unemployment* results from changes in the industrial structure which make a worker's skills inadequate or inappropriate. Individuals need time to adjust their skills to match the economy's needs. *Seasonal unemployment* is a consequence of the changing demand and supply factors which are produced by the changing seasons. Unemployment statistics are adjusted to account for these seasonal variations. *Cyclical unemployment* refers to unemployment occasioned by the economy's business cycle.

Economists have explained that "full employment" will fall somewhat short of a 100-percent labor force participation rate. Even during an economic upswing, frictional and structural changes will result in some portion

ECONOMICS TODAY

Are Deficits Related to Unemployment?

A federal government deficit is the excess of the government's annual spending over its total collected revenues. The government's current shortfall is huge. For FY 1985 (ending September, 1985) the government spent over $950 billion and collected under $750 billion resulting in a deficit of over $211 billion—that's slightly less than $1000 for every citizen of the country. For FY 1986, the deficit was only slightly less.

Where does the deficit come from? To answer this question we need to explain the components of the deficit. Economists divide the deficit into two parts, cyclical and structural. The cyclical part results from the economy running below par. The structural part is the basic excess of spending over tax revenues that occurs even when the economy is at its full capacity.

The cyclical deficit results when the economy slows down or, worse yet, moves into a recession. As a result, the government revenues drop primarily because as output drops and jobs are lost, incomes fall and people buy less. Thus, income taxes and sales taxes shrink. At the same time, government spending on transfer payments rises as people use more food stamps, unemployment compensation rises, and so on.

Throughout our history, the economy has moved in cycles of expansion and then recession. Although our economy has been expanding for over four years, it has not reached what economists consider "full employment." So, a part of our huge deficit is still cyclical. Most economists consider a 6-percent rate of unemployment about the best we can do without overheating the economy. In the 1980s we haven't come close to this figure. Even in 1985, unemployment averaged 7.2 percent.

That resulted in a sizeable gap between actual GNP and potential GNP. That gap accounted for about $50 billion of our deficit.

The structural deficit results from a basic imbalance in spending and revenue flow. It tells us what the deficit would be even if the economy were operating at its potential full capacity. For FY 1985 about $150 billion, or 75 percent of the deficit, was structural. The percentage was unchanged in FY 1986.

We can respond to the question, Are deficits related to unemployment? with a qualified "yes." The qualification comes about because, despite the relationship, the percent of the deficit that is caused by unemployment is minor (about 25 percent) compared to the portion caused by overspending.

of the labor force being unemployed. For years economists referred to a 4-percent unemployment rate as full employment level. With the increasing complexity of the production sector and the changing composition of the labor force, most economists today think that the full employment rate is closer to 6-percent unemployment.

Concern, Explanation, and Response Cyclical unemployment always has created the greatest problem for the economy. When a recession is prolonged or it becomes so deep we call it a depression, unemployment rates rise significantly. The most dramatic economic downturn occurred during the 1930s—the Great Depression. Unemployment rates rose from 3.2 percent in 1929 to nearly 25 percent in 1933. The unemployment rate averaged well over 10 percent for the decade of the '30s. Nothing of this severity or duration plagued the country before or since the Great Depression.

As we discussed in Chapter 8, the conventional view of economic fluctuations up to the 1930s was primarily one of acceptance, an attitude that the economy could only "ride out the storm." The theories presented by John Maynard Keynes challenged this attitude of acceptance. Keynes argued that the unemployment rate could be reduced by expansionary macroeconomic policies. The suffering of the 1930s made policy makers quite receptive to ideas which stressed that something could be done.

The belief that Keynes' theories had validity and the conviction that the federal government had the responsibility to do something to prevent another depression are evidenced in legislation passed in 1946. The Employment Act of 1946 stated:

> It is the continuing policy and responsibility of the Federal Government to use all practicable means . . . [to create and maintain] conditions under which there will be afforded useful employment opportunities, including self-employment, for those able, willing, and seeking to work. . . .

Since 1946, the federal government has had the responsibility to take action to promote high levels of employment. Especially with the post–World War II preoccupation with unemployment, politicians have sought ways to reduce unemployment.

The Inflation-Unemployment Trade-Off

A 1951 study by British economist A.W.H. Phillips provided the impetus for a body of empirical work which indicated a trade-off between inflation and unemployment. Phillips' study involved the relationship between the rate of unemployment and changes in the nominal wage rate.[11] Economists have subsequently explained the relationship in terms of the rate of unemployment and changes in the rate of inflation.[12] Figure 11.9 shows the original Phillips Curve which was based on data for the United Kingdom. Phillips fitted a curve to the points representing the rate of change in money wages and the rate of inflation for the years 1861 to 1957.

---

[11] A.W.H. Phillips, "The Relationship Between Unemployment and the Rate of Change of Money Wage Rates in the United Kingdom, 1861–1957," *Economica* 25, 4 (November 1958): 283–299.

[12] For a detailed review of the inflation-unemployment trade-off literature see A.M. Santomero and J.J. Seater, "The Inflation-Unemployment Trade-Off: A Critique of the Literature," *Journal of Economic Literature* 56 (June 1978): 499–544.

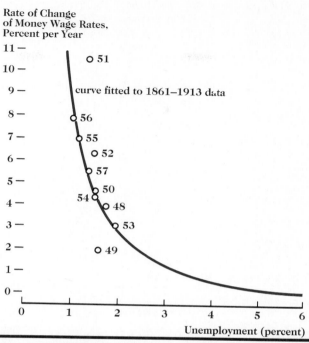

Rate of Change
of Money Wage Rates,
Percent per Year

11 —
10 —
9 —   curve fitted to 1861–1913 data

O 51

8 —   O 56
7 —   O 55
6 —   O 52
5 —   O 57
       O 50
4 — 54 O   O 48
3 —   O 53
2 —   O 49
1 —
0 —

0   1   2   3   4   5   6

Unemployment (percent)

FIGURE 11.9   *Original Phillips Curve*   This is the original Phillips Curve, plotting the change in money wages (as a proxy for price-level changes) against the level of unemployment. For the years 1861–1913 in Britain there was a clear trade-off.

American economists Paul Samuelson and Robert Solow studied the trade-off for the American economy.[13] They generated very similar results. Figure 11.10 represents the Samuelson-Solow work showing the trade-off for the United States for the years 1935 to 1960.

There is a very clear relationship which indicates that as the rate of unemployment declines, the rate of inflation increases and vice versa. The implication that the economy could "buy" more employment/lower inflation at the price of higher inflation/higher unemployment became the basis for policy research and extensive macro policy decisions.[14]

---

[13] Paul Samuelson and Robert Solow, "Analytical Aspects of Anti-Inflation Policy," *American Economic Review* 50, 2 (May 1960): 177–194.

[14] James Tobin, "Inflation and Unemployment," *American Economic Review* 62 (January 1972): 1–18. For a critical review of the importance of the Phillips Curve in policy decisions see Thomas Humphrey, "Phillips Curve Analysis," Federal Reserve Bank of Richmond *Economic Review*, (January 1978).

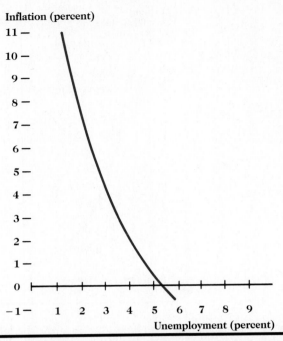

Inflation (percent)

Unemployment (percent)

FIGURE 11.10 *Phillips Curve for the United States, 1935–1960*   This is an early (1935–1960) Phillips Curve for the United States. The trade-off is clear during this period as well.

With an acceptance of the unemployment-inflation trade-off and the country's concern about a repeat of the Great Depression, it is not surprising that government critics have claimed that politicians have encouraged inflation to avoid unemployment. William Nordhaus argues that the political party in power manipulates the economy to produce low rates of inflation/ unemployment in election years.[15] More recently David Meiselman lodged a similar charge against the Federal Reserve.[16]

Explanation for Trade-off   Earlier in this chapter we discussed the possible relationship between inflation and economic activity. Some economists claim inflation stimulates economic growth because wages lag behind price

[15] William Nordhaus, "The Political Business Cycle," *Review of Economic Studies* 42, 2 (April 1975): 169–190.
[16] David Meiselman, "The Political Monetary Cycle," *The Wall Street Journal* (January 10, 1984). His points are discussed in Chapter 19.

increases (among other reasons). This differential encourages employers to increase employment. This same notion is at the core of the trade-off between inflation and unemployment. If workers don't expect inflation and push for compensatory increases in wages, employers can take advantage of the differential. Since employers can react more quickly to the changing price level they increase employment.

United States Record and Existence of Trade-off   Throughout the 1960s the Phillips Curve explained quite satisfactorily the relationship between inflation and unemployment in the United States. As a result of the stable Phillips Curve, policy makers were able to make some informed decisions about monetary and fiscal policies. The administration could decide to reduce unemployment by stimulating the economy and absorbing the increase in the price level. This appears to have been the decision by the Kennedy administration in 1961. Notice in Figure 11.11 how the unemploy-

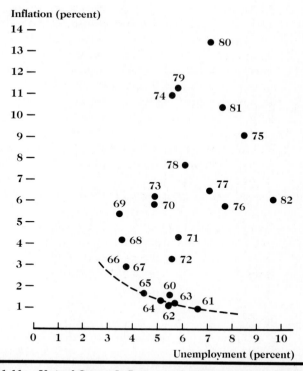

FIGURE 11.11   *United States Inflation and Unemployment, 1960–1982*   Since 1970, it became very difficult to fit a curve to the unemployment-inflation data. This is what led economists to challenge the applicability of the Phillips Curve.

ment rate dropped from 1961 to 1962. But, the stability of the Phillips Curve relationship between inflation and unemployment began to break down in the 1970s.

Figure 11.11 also shows the points representing the rate of unemployment and the change in the price level for the 1970s and early 1980s. The original Phillips Curve developed by Samuelson and Solow does not fit the new data.

In the early 1970s, when the rates of unemployment and inflation both began to increase, some economists hypothesized that the Phillips Curve relationship continued to hold but that the curve had shifted outward. Figure 11.11 also illustrates the difficulty of fitting curves to the new data. Economists explained the shifts in terms of structural and functional factors—the economy was going through some basic changes. Reasons for this included a movement from a predominately industrial to a service economy, the composition of the labor force changing as more second income earners entered the labor force, and technical sophistication required new skills.

Such changes increased the level of unemployment and the length of time workers stayed unemployed. Others explained the shift in the curves in terms of the causes of inflation. Instead of demand-induced inflation, which had characterized the United States in the post-war period, we were experiencing supply-induced inflation, for example, the rise in oil prices. With cost-push inflation, the policy makers could not reduce inflation by increasing unemployment. The causes of inflation were external to the American economy. These explanations maintained the existence of a trade-off but acknowledged that the "stakes had been raised."

Milton Friedman and, separately, Edmund Phelps had questioned the Phillips Curve trade-off even before the stable relationship began to break down.[17] This attack on the Phillips Curve had nothing to do with structural or functional changes in the economy. Friedman argued that there was a *natural rate of unemployment* which was caused by a frictional component (individuals between jobs) and by rigidities within the system or factors preventing labor mobility or wage flexibility. In the short run, policy makers could reduce unemployment by inducing inflation through supply expansion, but eventually the economy would return to the natural unemployment level.[18] Then, to reduce the level of unemployment, policy makers must

---

[17] Milton Friedman, "The Role of Monetary Policy," *American Economic Review* 58, 1 (March 1968): 1–17; and Edmund Phelps, "Money Wage Dynamics and Labor Market Equilibrium," *Journal of Political Economy* (July/August 1968): 687–711.

[18] The reason for the short-run trade-off is that economic stimulation, resulting in an increase in the rate of inflation, will reduce real wages and encourage employers to increase hirings. Eventually workers will demand wage increases to recapture their lost purchasing power, and real wages will rise and employment will decline.

increase the money supply more rapidly producing even higher rates of inflation.

Figure 11.12 illustrates the short- and long-run Phillips Curves as explained in the Friedman-Phelps alternative. According to Friedman and Phelps, policies to reduce unemployment will only result in permanently higher inflation as individuals come to anticipate price-level increases. Specifically, expansionary policy would move the economy from point *A* to point *B* (on the lower curve representing a 4-percent expected inflation rate). Eventually the system would move back to the natural unemployment rate, *C*. With acceptance of the new higher rate of inflation (the higher curve represents an 8-percent rate of inflation), attempts to lower unemployment will temporarily move the system along the higher short-run Phillips Curve to point *D*, but again the natural rate will prevail, point *E*, with a higher rate of inflation. The ultimate conclusion resulting from the Friedman-Phelps analysis is that demand-induced expansionary policies to deal with unemployment are counterproductive.

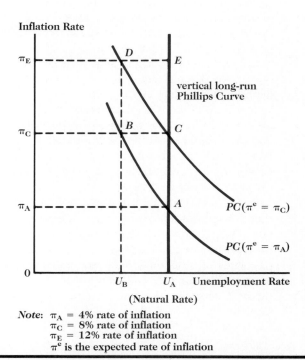

Note: π_A = 4% rate of inflation
π_C = 8% rate of inflation
π_E = 12% rate of inflation
π^e is the expected rate of inflation

FIGURE 11.12 *Short- and Long-Run Phillips Curves* This figure shows that in the short run a trade-off between inflation and unemployment may exist, but in the long run the Phillips Curve becomes a vertical line.

This new critique of the Phillips Curve also emphasized the role of inflationary expectations. Under this argument, if workers can correctly forecast current and future prices, there is no trade-off between inflation and unemployment. It is only when expectations are incorrect, when workers are fooled, that inflation will buy reduced unemployment. Under this circumstance we have the situation where prices rise faster than wages, and employees are stimulated to hire more workers. Unlike previous scenarios where the increased output brought prices back down, the Friedman-Phelps scenario has it that in the long run unemployment returns to its natural rate, but because of increases in the supply of money, inflation remains high.

Related to this explanation is the price expectations effect. Economists critical of the Phillips Curve trade-off explain its stability up to the late 1960s by the relatively rigid expectations about inflation that people held up to that time. Since prices had been relatively stable, or at least predictable, individuals did not expect persistently high inflation rates. They might have been fooled if rates rose to historically high levels and thus inflation would buy reduced unemployment. But starting in the 1970s, individuals came to expect inflation. They based their forecasts about future price changes on past rates of inflation—adaptive expectations. This resulted in what is often called the accelerationist Phillips Curve. The expectation of rising prices pushed the Phillips Curve out. The government could still buy some reduced unemployment but only with increasingly higher rates of inflation. Since expectations are constantly adjusted upward, the trade-off always happens in the short run.

The Phillips Curve trade-off debate led to a new theory, rational expectations hypothesis. Rational expectations is an outgrowth of the accelerationist Phillips Curve that evolved from the Friedman and Phelps work, but rational expectations will not concede that there is even a short-run trade-off between inflation and unemployment.[19] We will discuss this more fully in the next chapter.

As you recall, the entire basis for the inflation-unemployment trade-off was the assumption that workers did not foresee price increases and could not adjust to them as rapidly as employers. Even with the accelerationist hypothesis, workers may be wrong because they base price expectations on past rates of inflation. Policy that increases the inflation rate will, at least temporarily, produce an increase in employment. Rational expectations theory argues that there is no trade-off because price expectations are not incorrect.

---

[19] For a clear exposition of the rational expectations hypothesis as it relates to the Phillips Curve and macro policy issues, see Bennett T. McCallum, "The Significance of Rational Expectations Theory," *Challenge* (January/February 1980): 37–43.

Expectations are not based exclusively on past rates of inflation but instead through a rational process that incorporates consideration of a myriad of economic variables. As a result, in many cases workers' expectations for prices will be adjusted so that there is no lag. Without the different adjustment periods, employers have no advantage and gain nothing by increasing employment.[20]

United States Postwar Record on Inflation

Let's examine the record in the United States during the post–World War II era with special attention to the last twenty years. What have been the major causes of inflation? Considering the factors behind price inflation is important when suggesting policies to bring inflation under control. Inflation is not always caused by the same factor. A review of the United States record will reveal this. To facilitate our discussion we can divide the post–World War II experience into five time periods.

Korean War and Postwar Expansion, 1952–1965   After the removal of WW II price controls, consumer prices rose temporarily. By 1952 prices had stabilized. During the next thirteen years the American economy experienced a prolonged period of economic growth (the GNP expanded from $600 billion to $929 billion—over a 50-percent increase). Consumer prices increased during this period but at a very modest rate; the CPI rose at an average rate of about 1.5 percent per year. In terms of the more contemporary experience this hardly qualifies as inflation.

Vietnam War Inflation, 1966–1971   The next six years saw an increase in the rate of inflation. Figure 11.13 shows how the price level has changed. During this period the average annual rate of increase in consumer prices rose to just over 4 percent.

Most economists attribute this increase to demand factors. Vietnam War expenditures increased dramatically during this period; much of the increase was financed through government borrowing. Probably more than any period in our modern history the Vietnam War inflation was a classic case of too much money chasing too few goods. Neither public non-military expenditures nor private expenditures were reduced as military expenditures increased. The Vietnam War inflation fit with the conventional opinion of the period, namely that price-level increases were demand-induced.

---

[20] Even under these assumptions, there may be some lag due to the existence of contracts or the costs of acquiring sufficient information to make accurate predictions.

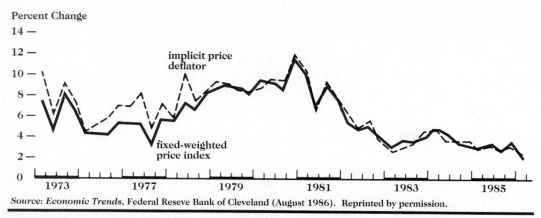

Percent Change

Source: *Economic Trends*, Federal Reserve Bank of Cleveland (August 1986). Reprinted by permission.

FIGURE 11.13   *Price Level Changes, 1975–1985*   This figure shows price-level changes (using the implicit price deflator and a weighted consumer price index) for the last ten years.

Wage and Price Controls, 1972–1973   The rate of inflation was increasing as the Nixon administration took office. For 1970–71 the rate was about 5 percent per year. The upward trend was temporarily halted when in August 1971 the president announced a wage and price control program. (Wage and price controls as a response to inflation are discussed in the next section of this chapter.) The inflation rate held steady during this period—the price level increase averaged just about 5 percent per year.

Supply Shocks, 1974–1975   Wage and price controls were removed in April, 1974. A strong demand for industrial raw materials coupled with an explosion in food and fuel prices created double-digit inflation. The biggest culprit in this price surge was supply shocks—crop failures in the United States and the U.S.S.R. pushed prices up and OPEC's crude oil price increase of almost 400 percent forced fuel prices upward. For 1974–75 the average annual price increase was over 10 percent.

Many economists point to supply shocks as the major cause of inflation during the late 1970s; there is little debate over the dramatic effects supply shocks had in 1974 and 1975.

Supply Shocks II and Expectations, 1976–1981   The United States experienced further supply shocks during the last half of the decade of the 1970s. By this time, price expectations and money supply growth were reinforcing the supply shock effects. The rate of inflation increased from about 5 percent for 1976 to 13 percent for 1979 to over 15 percent for 1981.

The price of oil doubled in 1979. Food prices rose as the reductions in cattle herds during crop shortages of a few years earlier resulted in meat price increases. Wage rates were rising (7.7 percent in 1977, 8.4 percent in 1978 and 9.9 percent in 1979) as workers tried to keep pace with inflation; productivity rates actually turned negative. Finally, monetary policy accommodated the expansion as the money supply (M1) increased from $310 billion to $440 billion—an average annual increase of over 6 percent.

Period of Disinflation, 1982–Present   The Reagan tax cut, which eventually served to stimulate economic output, and an aggressively tight monetary policy, which precipitated a recession, combined to dramatically reduce the rate of inflation beginning in 1982. The reduction in the growth rate of inflation has come to be called disinflation. For 1982 the rate of inflation dropped to 6.1 percent; in 1983 it was just over 3 percent. Inflationary expectations were reduced so that even an easing of the tight monetary policy did not rekindle the runaway inflation of the late 1970s and early 1980s. For 1984 to 85 the inflation rate averaged less than 5 percent. In 1986, it was just over 1 percent.

We can see that across the last twenty years the United States has experienced inflation stimulated by different causes: demand-induced inflation caused by excessive spending (during the Vietnam War and immediately thereafter) and money-supply expansion (throughout much of the period); supply-induced inflation during the early and late 1970s (caused by supply shocks, wage/profit push); and inflation stimulated by price expectations, largely from the mid-1970s.

Responses to Inflation

Responses to inflation are many and varied. Each has its proponents and all have been tried at one time or another. Although most anti-inflation programs have relied on monetary and fiscal policies, there are alternatives. The federal government takes the leadership role in combating inflation.

With the passage of the Employment Act of 1946, the federal government took on the responsibility "to promote maximum employment, production, and purchasing power." That responsibility was confirmed and its scope more clearly defined with the passage of the Humphrey-Hawkins Act in 1978. The president, Congress, and the Federal Reserve were charged with identifying national economic objectives and establishing goals based on these objectives. In an attempt to achieve price stability, policy makers have used one or more of the following programs.

Demand Management   Monetary and fiscal policies are vehicles for demand management. But since monetary restraint is often viewed as directly affecting prices, we will use demand management to focus on government

ECONOMICS TODAY
11.3

Is Deflation a Threat?

For years the American economy struggled with high and rising rates of inflation. During the last few years the rate of price increases abated; disinflation has been the name of the game. But, there is some evidence, albeit skimpy at this point, that disinflation may give way to deflation. For the first part of 1986 (January through April) the consumer price index actually declined (at a seasonally adjusted rate of about 4 percent). For the entire year, the price level increased by slightly over 1 percent.

Most consumers find the lower rate of inflation, and even declining prices, a real plus. With the price declines concentrated in energy, food and other basic commodities, American households translate the situation into lower gasoline prices or reduced food bills, which means they have more money for other types of expenditures.

Some sectors of the economy have suffered with the price declines. Oil drillers, domestic oil producers, farmers, and miners are hurting. Land prices in oil-producing and agricultural areas have also dropped, adding to the misery. The Federal Reserve estimates that farm land values declined by 30 percent from late 1983 to the end of 1985.

Declining prices and lowered land values raise the specter of generalized deflation—a downward spiral of prices across the entire country. Such a situation would probably throw the economy into a severe recession. The American economy experienced such a problem during the Great Depression. The price level declined by nearly 25 percent during the four years following the 1929 stock market crash. With this came unemployment; the rate of unemployment rose to nearly 30 percent of the labor force.

Few economists actually think that deflation is probable, but the unwillingness of some prominent economists to totally rule out the possibility is enough to give some policy makers cause for concern.

One prominent economist, former Council of Economic Advisers Chairman Alan Greenspan, pointed out in a PBS commentary during the summer of 1986 that although the "ominous scenario" of deflation doesn't seem likely "history warns of some unpleasant surprises."

Those who fear that the problem in oil and agriculture may drag the entire economy into deflation and recession are calling for more stimulatory Federal Reserve policies. For the first time in decades the Fed is receiving pressure to inflate the economy rather than to fight inflation. The question remains, "Can policy makers walk the fine line between renewed inflation and the recession that deflation may bring?"

---

spending and tax programs. Underlying demand management programs is the belief that slowing down the economy will reduce and eventually eliminate inflation. Adherents to this approach see a close connection between inflation and unemployment rates. Therefore, they acknowledge that monetary and fiscal restraint which reduce aggregate spending will increase the level of unemployment. Unless an administration and Congress are willing to absorb the criticism of precipitating a severe recession, demand management policies will only reduce inflation over an extended period of time.[21]

---

[21] This view was reinforced by Arthur Okun, who summarized estimates of the effects of demand managements from six econometric studies. A.M. Okun, "Efficient Disinflationary Policies," *American Economic Review* 68 (May 1978): 348–352.

The use of demand management programs is often seen as an appropriate response to demand-induced inflation. Whether through monetary or fiscal restraint, demand management programs are intended to reduce aggregate demand and, through the resultant economic slowdown, reduce the rate of inflation. Since the early 1970s, when inflation and unemployment both reached unacceptably high levels, much criticism has been directed at demand management as the primary anti-inflation program.

Monetary Restraint   In many instances demand management includes a tight monetary policy. The monetarist call for monetary restraint as an anti-inflation tool does not rely on changes in aggregate demand. Instead, as we have explained in discussing the monetarist position, an expansion of the money supply beyond that necessary to support real economic growth will create price inflation.

Milton Friedman repeatedly has said that the basic cause of inflation is a too high rate of growth in the quantity of money, and that the only cure for inflation is a slowing of monetary growth.[22] Those arguing for monetary restraint as an anti-inflationary tool point out that structural rigidities in the economy (the unresponsiveness of prices and wages due to imperfect markets) prevent demand management policies from having any effect on the price level.

The inability of demand factors to explain the inflation of the 1970s coupled with the Fed's expansionist policies during this period is often used to support the monetarist position that only monetary restraint will reduce inflation.

Reducing Expectations   The persistence of inflation, even in the face of high unemployment rates during the 1970s, reinforced the notion that Americans had come to expect inflation. In so doing the expectation of inflation became a self-fulfilling prophecy. William Fellner has argued that expectations played a major part in the inflation of the 1970s.[23]

Those adhering to the notion that inflation as ingrained in the expectations of Americans argued that the only way to halt price level increases was to break the inflationary psychology.

Since monetary and fiscal policies were seen as accommodating inflation, or when they were tight (not lasting long enough to affect the rate of inflation), something more dramatic was needed. Thus, those adhering to

---

[22] Friedman made his case when accepting his Nobel Prize in Economics. See M. Friedman, "Nobel Lecture: Inflation and Unemployment," *Journal of Political Economy* 85 (May/June 1977): 451–472.
[23] William J. Fellner, *Toward a Reconstruction of Macroeconomics* (Washington: American Enterprise Institute, 1976).

the view that expectations were the culprit did not speak with one voice in their calls for anti-inflation programs and are often associated with incomes policies, supply-side, or budget-deficit reduction programs.

Incomes Policies   The government has made numerous attempts to control wages and prices. An *incomes policy* is nothing more than government intervention to cause wages and prices to rise more slowly than would otherwise be the case. These interventions are either direct (for example, wage and price controls) or indirect (for example, a tax-based incentive program).

We saw mandatory wage and price controls during World War II and limited guideposts during the Kennedy and Johnson years. The most pervasive peacetime incomes policy was that imposed by Richard Nixon. Starting with a 90-day wage and price freeze in August 1971, the government controlled prices and wages until April 1974. The rate of increase in the price level was halted during the mandatory control period but intensified when controls were removed.[24]

The concern about inflationary expectations led to a series of tax based incomes policies (often referred to as TIP). Henry Wallich and Sidney Weintraub recommended a penalty program where taxes were imposed as wage guidelines were exceeded.[25] Arthur Okun recommended an incentive program whereby taxes were refunded if wage increases were kept under the guidelines.[26]

Incomes policies are intended to interrupt the wage-price spiral. In so doing inflationary expectations can be halted or moderated. Using the Phillips Curve analysis, an incomes policy has the effect of shifting the curve back and to the left. The desired result is reduced inflation without an extraordinarily high level of unemployment.

Budget Deficit Reduction   The federal deficit is perceived by many as the major cause of inflation. One could interpret this inflation as resulting from the increased spending which caused the deficit, the money creation process if the Federal Reserve underwrote the Treasury's securities issues, or the expectational effect whereby individuals and firms see the deficit pushing up interest rates. In any case, some have called for deficit reductions in order to eliminate inflationary pressures.

---

[24] For an analysis of the Nixon wage and price control program, see the series of papers in the *American Economic Review* (May 1974): 82–104.

[25] See H.C. Wallich and S. Weintraub, "A Tax-based Incomes Policy," *Journal of Economic Issues* (June 1971): 1–18.

[26] See A.M. Okun and G. Perry, "Innovative Policies to Slow Inflation," *Brookings Papers on Economic Activity* 2 (1978).

Supply-Side Stimulus   Especially with the election of Ronald Reagan, the supply-side effects on inflation have received attention. Those promoting a supply-side response to inflation argue that increased output/productivity and increased competition will work to reduce inflation.

Tax cuts to encourage saving and increase capital formation and tax incentives to encourage investment form part of the supply-side approach. Both are seen as stimulating production (supply). At the same time deregulation of key industries has been encouraged and accomplished. Deregulation will stimulate competition, which should help hold prices down. Those supporting a supply-side approach to fighting inflation see this program as complementing the anti-inflation fight on other fronts (for example, reducing the deficit and restraining monetary growth).

Rational Expectations   Belief in the rational expectations theory leads to the conclusion that short-run anti-inflation programs are untenable. Since workers make wage and price decisions based on the best information available and rationally act on this information, they are in a position to safeguard themselves against any macroeconomic stabilization policy. The rational expectations hypothesis, when coupled with the natural rate of employment hypothesis, leads to the conclusion that monetary policy must be stable and far sighted. Efforts to institute countercyclical monetary policy will not affect the level of unemployment but will instead be translated into aggravated inflation rates. As such, monetary and fiscal policies should focus on conditions that will foster long-run price stability.

Summary of Responses   Responses to inflation, at least in modern American history, have relied on programs to reduce expenditures. Whether through direct demand management, through tax increases or spending cuts, or indirect monetary restraint, policy responses have reflected the belief that excessive demand precipitates inflation. President Nixon tried to control inflation by freezing most wages and prices, while President Ford tried to break the back of inflationary expectations with his WIN campaign (Whip Inflation Now). More recently monetary restraint has been coupled with a supply stimulus. At least for the period 1982–1986 the program worked.

Chapter Conclusion

In this chapter we have taken a long, detailed look at the problems of inflation and unemployment. The approach included exploring two extreme cases of inflation and then investigating the causes of inflation. This chapter challenged you to use the model from Chapter 9 to analyze how these various causes were translated in price level changes. We then discussed the consequences of inflation. The review of the connection between inflation and unemployment and the consequences of unemployment served as a transition into a discussion of the inflation-unemployment trade-off controversy.

The disagreement over the existence of a trade-off between inflation and unemployment is at the heart of much of the controversy in macroeconomics. Policy makers have made many macroeconomic decisions on the presumption that either inflation or unemployment can be reduced by allowing the other to increase. You reviewed the record and you should have some opinion on this debate. In Chapter 19 we will take a careful look at monetary policy decisions. You can use the information from this chapter to help you evaluate the success of monetary policy. As you read about the institutional structure of the financial services industry and central bank operations, keep in mind that economists' abilities to explain the behavior of the economy are extremely important to policy makers who are trying to implement programs that will move the economy toward its economic goals. If policy makers can fight inflation and unemployment at the same time, they can help the system get closer to those goals.

Consider These Questions

1. Outline the major factors used to explain inflation.
2. Explain inflation, disinflation, and deflation. What are the effects of each on individuals, the government, and business decision making?
3. What role do expectations play in hyperinflations? What about the kind of inflation the United States experienced in the 1970s and 1980s?
4. Exactly what is the Phillips Curve and how was it developed?
5. Why is the simple Phillips Curve no longer accepted as an explanation of the relationship between inflation and unemployment? In answering this question, outline the Friedman-Phelps alternative.
6. In reviewing the American record on inflation, what would you identify as the major cause of price-level increases during the last thirty years?
7. What has been the major cause of declining inflation rates over the last few years?

Suggestions for Further Reading

Berman, Peter I. *Inflation and the Money Supply in the U. S.* Lexington, MA: D.C. Heath and Company, 1978.
    Packed with empirical evidence on the role of money in inflation.
Blinder, Alan S. and Robert M. Solow. "Does Fiscal Policy Matter?" *Journal of Political Economy* (November 1973): 319–337.

Two exponents of the power of fiscal policy present a compelling argument on its importance.

Blinder, Alan S. *Economic Policy and the Great Stagflation*. New York: Academic Press, 1979.

An understandable account of policy responses to the stagflation of the 1970s.

Humphrey, Thomas. "Changing Views on the Phillips Curve." Federal Reserve Bank of Richmond *Review* (July 1973).

Excellent explanation of development and changes in Phillips Curve analysis.

Lahiri, Kajal and Jung Soo Lee. "Rational Expectations and the Short Run Phillips Curve." In *Journal of Macroeconomics* (Spring 1979): 167–190.

Authors show how expectations affect the Phillips Curve and mitigate against the Keynesian view of the unemployment-inflation trade-off.

Okun, Arthur and George Perry (eds). *Curing Chronic Inflation*. Washington: The Brookings Institution, 1978.

This is a series of articles outlining fiscal policy approaches to ending inflation.

Ruffin, Roy J. and Paul R. Gregory. *Principles of Macroeconomics*, 2nd ed. Glenview, IL: Scott, Foresman and Company, 1986.

Chapters 14–16 provide a good basic discussion of inflation and unemployment and the Phillips Curve.

Sargent, Thomas. "The Ends of Four Big Inflations." In *Inflation: Causes and Effects*. Edited by Robert E. Hall, 41–98. Chicago: University of Chicago Press, 1982.

Illustrates how government commitment to holding the line on money expansion affected the end of inflations in four settings.

Tobin, James. "Inflation and Unemployment." *American Economic Review* LXII (March 1972): 1–17.

Tobin's presidential address analyzes the role of imperfect markets in explaining inflation.

CHAPTER TWELVE

RATIONAL EXPECTATIONS THEORY and IMPLICATIONS FOR POLICY

The Rational Expectations Hypothesis asserts that individuals do not make systematic mistakes in forecasting the future. In the last decade this innocuous proposition has transformed macroeconomics by [challenging] the old conventional wisdom on every front . . . .

David K. H. Begg
The Rational Expectations Revolution in Macroeconomics, 1982

The review of inflation, disinflation and unemployment in Chapter 11 revealed some serious disagreements among economists and policy makers about what sorts of policies to use to move the economy toward its goals. The lack of success of government intervention, often called activist macroeconomic policies, during much of the 1970s has led some economists to argue in favor of noninterventionist, nonactivist policies. The strict monetarists have offered this argument for years. They favor rules for the expansion of the money supply rather than discretionary intervention. More recently, another group of economists, those in the rational expectations camp, have generated research results that also lead to the conclusion that nonactivist policies are in the economy's best interest. Exactly what is the rational expectations revolution? How did it develop? What are its implications for policy makers?

This chapter answers those questions and provides insight into this latest revolution in macroeconomic theory and policy making.

Chapter Objectives

Your overall goal in reading this chapter is to develop a general understanding of rational expectations. You should be able to use rational expectations to analyze economic policy. This means understanding the foundations of rational expectations and applying the theory to contemporary economic issues. By the end of this chapter you should be able to:

- Differentiate the rational expectations approach from an adaptive expectations approach.
- Identify the basic assumptions in the rational expectations model.
- Explain the rational expectations economists' perception of the Phillips Curve and analyze their reasons for rejecting its actual existence.
- Analyze why adherents to the rational expectations approach argue that only unanticipated interventionist policies will have any effect on output and employment.
- Determine whether the assumption of flexible wages and prices is necessary for the basic conclusions of the rational expectations approach to hold.
- Explain the ways rational expectations have influenced economic policy decisions.

Origins of Rational Expectations

As mentioned briefly in Chapter 8, rational expectations originated with the work of John Muth. Although expectations were always very important in economics, until Muth's work was published economists interpreted expectations to mean that past events influenced views about the future. More specifically, *adaptive expectations* indicated that anticipated changes were essentially an average of past changes. People formed their expectations by looking back. Thus expectations changed slowly because the weight of past events overshadowed any current changes.

Muth developed the notion of *rational expectations*—the idea that expectations are based on an optimal forecast (that is, a best guess) of future changes using all available information.[1] This means that individuals con-

---

[1] John Muth, "Rational Expectations and the Theory of Price Movements," *Econometrica* 29, 2 (1961): 315–335.

sider not only what has happened in the past but what the evidence indicates may happen in the future. One of the key components of this view is that when any of the key variables change in the way they move, individuals change their expectations about those variables.

Building on Muth's ideas, other economists—namely Robert Lucas of the University of Chicago and Thomas Sargent and Neil Wallace of the University of Minnesota—have expanded the body of knowledge about rational expectations and, along with others, have used rational expectations to make some macroeconomic policy recommendations.

Rational Expectations and the Lucas Critique

The *Lucas Critique* is one of the major ideas evolving from the rational expectations revolution, specifically from the work of Lucas.[2] It has influenced policy makers whether they agree with the findings of the rational expectationists or not. The Lucas Critique calls into question the use of conventional econometric models for policy recommendations because those models cannot effectively assess the potential outcomes of alternative policies. A key reason for the Lucas Critique relates to the way econometric models make estimations using historical data. Going back to the difference between adaptive and rational expectations, recall that the way expectations are developed depends on the changes in behavior of forecasted variables. In other words, policy changes influence the way expectations are formed, and these expectations in turn affect economic behavior. Lucas argued that models using adaptive expectations will provide erroneous results because in reality the effects of a policy will depend largely on the public's expectations about and reaction to the policy.

The work of Muth led economists to consider both the formation and the impact of expectations on economic behavior. The Lucas Critique is one of the major insights to have evolved from the notion of rational expectations. But, rational expectations have had an impact well beyond the refinement of econometric models. We will now look more closely at the essential components of the rational expectations revolution.

---

[2] Robert Lucas, Jr., "Econometric Policy Evaluation: A Critique," in Karl Brunner and Allen H. Meltzer (eds.), *The Phillips Curve and Labor Markets*, The Carnegie-Rochester Conference on Public Policy, 1 (1976): 19–46.

The Rational Expectations Revolution

Exactly what is the rational expectations revolution in macroeconomics? It is a new way of thinking about macroeconomics. Rational expectationists hold many assumptions that are familiar to us, but the model of behavior they build is quite different from anything we have seen before, especially the basic Keynesian model.

The rational expectations view of the world is similar to that of the classicists in many ways. Classical economists could have easily accepted some of the conclusions drawn by rational expectations economists. (Recall from Chapter 8 that we categorized rational expectations under the new classical economics.) Two important assumptions in rational expectations are the following:

- Individuals use available information which influences them to act in their own best interest.
- Prices and wages are flexible, that is, prices and wages move quickly to bring supply and demand into equilibrium to clear commodity, factor and financial markets.

The first assumption, although somewhat more detailed because it incorporates the way individuals process economic information, is very much like Adam Smith's notion of "economic man" working for "his own self interest." The second assumption should remind you of the classical economists' explanation for why involuntary unemployment does not exist. In the same way, the rational expectations economists will argue that any level of unemployment above some full or natural employment level is not involuntary; it exists because real wages are not sufficiently high to attract people to jobs.

The central idea of the rational expectations hypothesis is that people not only make unbiased forecasts about the future (that is, there are no systematic errors in their forecasts) but that they understand economic variables and incorporate pertinent information into their expectations and behavior. When people fully understand economic conditions, they cannot be "fooled" by policy makers. An examination of the labor market provides a better understanding of how people's rational expectations work.

Rational Expectations and the Labor Market

The labor market described in the Chapter 9 will provide a basis for understanding the meaning of rational expectations. How would rational expectations economists interpret the Phillips Curve? Refer to Figure 12.1 as you read the next few paragraphs.

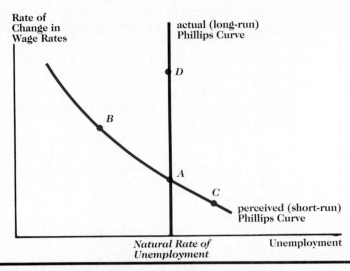

FIGURE 12.1 *Perceived vs. Actual Phillips Curve* This figure is essentially the same as Figure 11.12. It shows that initially, in the short run, workers respond to wage rate increases caused by inflation (movement from *A* to *B*) but when realizing that their real wages have not risen, workers adjust and unemployment increases (from *B* to *C*). In the long run, when workers understand the inflationary effects of expansionary policies, nominal wage increases result in no increase in employment, simply a movement to a higher nominal wage rate (from *A* to *D*)

Rational expectationists refer to the curve as the "perceived Phillips Curve." These economists offer an alternative explanation for the curve. Workers receive a raise (that is, money wages rise because of some shock to the system, such as the Fed significantly increasing the supply of money). Workers perceive that this is an increase in real wages. This entices workers to supply more labor causing unemployment to decline (a movement from point *A* to point *B* in Figure 12.1). But, when workers realize that wages in general rose because the price level increased and that they actually received no increase in real wages, a similar but reverse process is set into motion. The supply of labor declines (moving along the perceived Phillips Curve to point *C*).

These movements appear to provide the Phillips Curve trade-off between rising prices (and nominal wages) and the level of unemployment that Keynesians espoused and policy makers used to justify policy actions. But, the rational expectationists argue, these changes in the supply of labor occurred only because of misperceptions. Workers had been "fooled" into thinking their real wages had increased. Interventionist policies based on the perceived Phillips Curve will produce negative and not positive results.

Adherents to the rational expectations view argue that as people come to understand and anticipate that interventionist policies (whether the Fed increasing the money supply or the government expanding its spending) will occur, they act to protect their personal interests. In the case of the labor market, workers realize that the wage change was only a nominal wage increase; they understand that the price level rose as well as their wages. The nominal wage increase would call forth no increase in employment. It would instead produce only higher nominal wages, thus aggravating inflation. Under the rational expectations view such an expansionary interventionist policy would move the economy along the "actual" Phillips Curve to point D, resulting in the same level of unemployment but higher wages and prices. This result is similar to that outlined in the Friedman-Phelps alternative to the Phillips Curve but the process and reasons are different.

Do People Actually Anticipate Policy Actions?

Unless required to do so, few people would try to understand and interpret the kind of economic statistics published by the Department of Commerce, the Bureau of Labor Statistics, or the Federal Reserve. But, business firms, labor unions, pension fund managers, investment counselors and others do, or at least they hire economists to analyze data and assess policy alternatives. (Chapter 17 includes a discussion of the importance of "Fed watching" by financial market analysts.) These organizations have a major impact on public behavior. For example, labor unions advise their members on how policy actions will affect them and what they should do to safeguard their economic well-being. Beyond this, the level of economic analysis in the media provides the average citizen with sufficient information to make decisions about economic policy actions.

If one accepts the premise that people do form rational expectations and act on those expectations, then the rational expectations revolution will have some profound effects on macroeconomic policy. But before assessing the policy implications of rational expectations, let's look more closely at macroeconomics from the rational expectations perspective.

Macroeconomics from the Rational Expectations Perspective

Rational expectations have influenced more than just capital markets and labor markets. They have given economists a new perspective on macroeconomic analysis in general.

The Rational Expectations Model

Recall the basic assumptions underlying the rational expectations approach. One is that individuals use available information to make unbiased forecasts and then act in a manner that is in their best interest. The second is that prices and wages are completely flexible. These assumptions and the aggregate demand and aggregate supply curves from Chapter 9 are the basis for an investigation of the impact of macroeconomic policy actions from a rational expectations perspective.

Figure 12.2 illustrates the equilibrium condition of the economy (*AS* and *AD* produce equilibrium at *A*). The aggregate supply curve reflects an expected price level which is equivalent to the actual price level (p_1) at point *A*, generating income level Y_n. The output generated in this circumstance is sufficient to produce an employment level equal to the natural rate.

Let's introduce a shock into the system, namely an increase in the rate of growth of the money supply by the Federal Reserve. The result of this money supply increase will depend on whether it was anticipated or not. Figure 12.3 illustrates this shock.

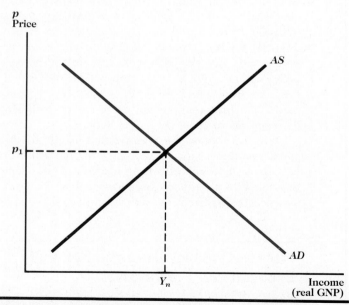

FIGURE 12.2 *Aggregate Demand and Aggregate Supply*   This is a simple aggregate-demand/aggregate-supply graph as introduced in Chapter 9. The interaction of aggregate demand and aggregate supply produces the price level and equilibrium level of income.

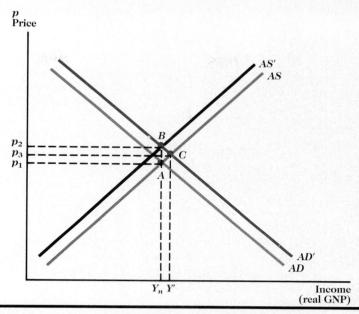

FIGURE 12.3 **Shifts in Aggregate Demand and Aggregate Supply**   This figure shows the results of an increase in the supply of money. If the monetary expansion is antici-pated, aggregate demand will increase because of higher spending and aggregate supply will decrease as workers attempt to protect themselves from the effects of inflation. The result is movement from *A* to *B*—no change in real GNP but a higher price level. The only way the monetary action will have its desired expansionary effect is if it is unanticipated. This results in aggregate demand shifting, moving the economy to a higher level of income; there is a slight increase in prices (movement from *A* to *C*).

If the Fed's action is *anticipated*, the economy will end up at point *B* in Figure 12.3. Why? With the money supply increase the aggregate demand will shift to *AD'*. Economic actors (workers and firms) behaving rationally will realize that this infusion of money will raise the price level. Workers will demand higher wages to compensate for the inflation and firms will incorpo-rate this increase into their costs, causing the aggregate supply curve to decrease (to *AS'*).

The aggregate supply curve shifts just sufficiently to return equi-librium to the natural employment rate because rational expectations argues that optimal forecasts result in actual prices being equal to expected prices (p_2). This new *AS* curve incorporates the higher expected price level. The new equilibrium position is point *B*, where neither firms nor workers are any better off but the price level has risen. Real GNP is unchanged and the employment rate remains at the natural level (Y_n). Rational expectations have caused automatic adjustments to occur.

If the Fed's action was *unanticipated*, the economy would end up at point C instead of point B. Why? The aggregate demand curve again shifts to AD' as a result of the stimulatory monetary policy. The Fed's action was unanticipated, so people do not expect prices to rise. The expected price level remains at p_1, and the aggregate supply curve does not shift. The Fed's unanticipated action resulted in a moderate increase in the price level (p_3), but a noticeable increase in the level of output (Y'') which increased employment beyond the natural rate.

The key factor determining whether the expansionary policy will have its desired effect is whether the stimulation is expected or unexpected.[3] Wallace and Sargent call this the policy ineffectiveness proposition.[4] Their findings suggest that macroeconomic policy can only work if it is unexpected. Discretionary policies do not produce the desired results, because such planning is not a game against nature, but a game played by rational economic agents.[5]

Monetary policy is anticipated when economic actors foresee the rate of change in the nation's money supply. When this happens rational consumers, producers, and workers expect that prices and wages will increase at a rate identical to the rate of change in the supply of money. Since all involved realize they are no better off, aggregate demand does not increase. Anticipated increases in the money supply will result in rising interest rates, as lenders incorporate an inflation premium into the rates they charge. Nominal interest rates will rise to keep pace with the price level (real interest rates remain unchanged).

When the monetary stimulus is unanticipated, rational expectations acknowledges the results are very similar to those outlined in the Keynesian model. Under such circumstances, when the Fed undertakes a stimulatory policy consumers actually increase real spending, interest rates decline, and investment spending accelerates. The rational expectations approach points out that rational actors learn from the past, and policy makers have increasing difficulty fooling the public. The public adjusts to policy actions. A good example is the period after 1979 when the Fed shifted from interest rate targets to monetary aggregates. The growth of the money supply contracted dramatically in 1980. Such an unanticipated action eventually resulted in a

---

[3] In the rational expectations analysis, if the stimulus is less than what was anticipated the result may be a decrease in the equilibrium income and employment levels.

[4] See Thomas Sargent and Neil Wallace, "Rational Expectations, The Optimal Monetary Instrument and the Optimal Money Supply Rule," *Journal of Political Economy* 83 (April 1975): 241–254.

[5] For an elaboration of this point refer to Finn E. Kydland and Edward C. Prescott, "Rules Rather Than Discretion: The Inconsistency of Optimal Plans," *Journal of Political Economy* 85 (October 1977): 473–489.

noticeable change in the velocity of money. As the Lucas Critique would predict, people began to behave differently when the policy variables were changed.

Is the Rational Expectations Revolution Realistic?

To decide whether the rational expectations revolution is realistic, we can look at the two basic assumptions of the approach: (1) individuals use available information to act in a way that is in their best interest, and (2) prices and wages are flexible. One of the most often cited examples in support of the rational expectations viewpoint is the public's response to the hyperinflation following World War I. The rates of inflation experienced by Germany, Austria, Poland, and Hungary were unprecedented and almost unimaginable (refer to Chapter 11 for a discussion of the German hyperinflation). Thomas Sargent has argued that each of these inflationary spirals was halted, with minimal cost in terms of GNP, once the public believed that the government was serious about implementing anti-inflationary policies.[6] The establishment of a second currency to replace the badly depreciated existing currency can serve as a signal that changes the public's expectations.

Many have criticized the rational expectationists for their assumptions regarding the flexibility of wages and prices. Wage rigidities, especially due to long-term union contracts, and price stickiness, especially regarding rapid downward movements, seem to undercut the rational expectations arguments. While some rational expectations economists hold to these strict assumptions, other economists reject these assumptions but still believe that expectations play an important role in the effects of macroeconomic policy actions. Economists including John Taylor of Stanford and Stanley Fisher of MIT have analyzed macroeconomic policies with a rational expectations approach but with a more realistic view on the flexibility of wages and prices.[7] They conclude that unanticipated policies have a greater effect on output and employment than do anticipated policies, but they reject the ineffectiveness proposition because they find that even when policies are anticipated they can produce the desired results in terms of output and economic activity.

What the continuing research seems to be saying is that the notion of rational expectations needs to be considered in the formulation of macroeconomic policies. We now turn to this last point.

---

[6] See Thomas Sargent, "The Ends of Four Big Inflations," in Robert E. Hall (ed.), *Inflation: Causes and Consequences* (Chicago: University of Chicago Press, 1982): 41–98.

[7] See for example John Taylor, "The Role of Expectations in the Choice of Monetary Policy," in *Monetary Policy Issues in the 1980s* (Federal Reserve Bank of Kansas City, 1982): 47–76.

Implications for Policy Makers

As economic policy makers reflect on the potential effects of their actions, they need to consider the rational expectations revolution. While economists still disagree about the overall value of the rational expectations approach, most economists agree that the rational expectations revolution has produced consensus on two important points.

First, the rational expectations revolution has forced economic forecasters and policy makers to incorporate a more carefully structured view of expectations into their models and projections. This recognition of the role of expectations includes the admission that the old adaptive expectations approach is inadequate and that economists need to pay greater attention to rational expectations. Recognition of the roles of expectations also means that macroeconomic policy makers need to consider the public's reactions as they formulate policies. Policy makers should not try to outguess the public but rather should realize how changes in policy will influence the way the public behaves (that is, the Lucas Critique). Understanding that the public will adjust when new policies are announced means that traditional stabilization policies may not work.

Second, the contrast between the effects of anticipated versus unanticipated policies is having an influence both on the way policies are formulated and how those policies are implemented.

Beyond these two points, economists disagree. A strict interpretation of the rational expectations approach leads one to conclude that interventionist policies may do more harm than good. Recall that anticipated intervention did not affect real output or employment but caused inflation. This strict interpretation leads to the conclusion that policy makers should eliminate uncertainty and adopt clear rules regarding intervention rather than using the discretionary approach. This conclusion is the same as that which strict monetarists would draw.

The less strict (some would say more realistic) rational expectations approach results in different conclusions. This approach acknowledges that wages and prices are not perfectly flexible. Factor and commodity markets do not clear automatically and instantaneously. This approach concludes that interventionist policies may be beneficial, especially if they are unanticipated, but policy makers need to recognize the expectations of the public and the effect policies have on these expenditures.

Our conclusions about the rational expectations view need to be adjusted to differentiate between policy actions designed to offset major disturbances (such as oil price increases resulting from the actions of OPEC) and stabilization policies aimed at fine tuning the economy. Both the strict and less strict rational expectations views would agree that intervention aimed at fine tuning is likely to create more harm than good. The less strict view would allow that, despite the uncertainty associated with intervention, there may be beneficial results. When economic conditions are worsening, intervention to counteract the disturbance may be worth the risk.

A good example is the anti-inflation program undertaken by the Federal Reserve during 1980–1982. The initial reduction in the growth of the money supply was undoubtedly unexpected and had the desired result. But because the rate of inflation was so high and the likelihood of its continuing so ingrained, it took more than the initial policy change to reduce the rate to a manageable level and to eliminate the inflationary expectations. Since the Federal Reserve did not have the reputation of being able to sustain a tight money policy it took a concerted effort to maintain the war on inflation. The less strict rational expectations view of Taylor and Fisher seems to apply here. By sustaining the policy, even though it was anticipated after its initial thrust, the Federal Reserve was able to reduce the inflationary rate. Keynesians, monetarists, and perhaps even rational expectationists will all find some evidence from this experience to support their contentions. But, the situation in the United States from 1980 through 1982 was in part similar to that in the countries experiencing hyperinflation after WWI. Once the public was convinced that the Fed would sustain the anti-inflationary program, the inflationary expectations subsided.[8]

In the short term, Keynesian-type macroeconomic models are unlikely to disappear as forecasting tools of policy makers. The rational expectations revolution, however, is likely to force modifications in these models and policy makers are likely to incorporate the conclusions of rational expectations researchers into their policy decisions.

Chapter Conclusion

The theory of rational expectations, originally developed as an alternative to the adaptive expectations approach, has been expanded through the work of numerous macroeconomists. Their work has resulted in the recognition by mainstream economists of the importance of expectations in econometric models. Beyond these points, there remains considerable debate over the validity and applicability of the rational expectations revolution to policy making.

An acceptance of certain aspects of the rational expectations is evolving, especially the Lucas Critique and a modified version of the policy

---

[8] This view is not universally accepted. For an opposing view see Oliver Blanchard, "The Lucas Critique and the Volcker Deflation," *American Economic Review* 74 (May 1984): 211–215.

ineffectiveness proposition. These insights are significant enough to make rational expectations revolution an important force in the rethinking of the traditional Keynesian approach to macroeconomic policy making.

Consider These Questions

1. What is the Lucas Critique? Why is it so important for policy implication?
2. Why is it that unanticipated macroeconomic policies will have the desired effect on the economy while anticipated macro policies will not?
3. Most people argue that they know very little about economics and probably couldn't care less that they don't. This being the case, how can rational expectations economists claim that people anticipate macroeconomic policies and take corrective actions?
4. Differentiate between the strict and the less strict rational expectations arguments.
5. Why might a rational expectations economist argue that large budget deficits are problematic?
6. The Federal Reserve was successful at bringing inflation under control. How might this success affect the public's expectation? Does this mean that subsequent monetary policies will have a better or worse chance of succeeding?

Suggestions for Further Reading

Attfield, C. L. F., *et al*. *Rational Expectations in Macroeconomics: An Introduction to Theory and Evidence*. New York: Basil Blackwell, 1985.
  Despite word introduction in the title, this is a very rigorous analysis. Important for serious student.

Begg, David K. H. *The Rational Expectations Revolution in Macroeconomics: Theories and Evidence*. Baltimore: The Johns Hopkins University Press, 1982.
  A very comprehensive, understandable explanation of rational expectations; best single source available.

Forman, Leonard. "Rational Expectations and the Real World." *Challenge* (November/December 1980): 36–39.
  A criticism of rational expectations based on its attention to risk.

Kantor, Brian. "Rational Expectation and Economic Thought." *Journal of Economic Literature*, XVII (December 1979): 1422–1441.
  Explores rational expectations in the context of history of economic thought.

McCallum, Bennett. "The Significance of Rational Expectations Theory." In *Challenge* (January/February 1980): 37–43.
Excellent review.

Maddock, Rodney and Michael Carter. "A Child's Guide to Rational Expectations." *Journal of Economic Literature*, XX (March 1982): 39–51.
An amusing but illuminating discussion of rational expectations done in the form of a two-person play.

Sargent, Thomas J. "Rational Expectations and the Reconstruction of Macroeconomics." In Federal Reserve Bank of Minneapolis *Quarterly Review* (Summer 1980): 15–19.
Does good job of explaining Lucas Critique.

Sheffrin, Steven. *Rational Expectations*. New York: Cambridge University Press, 1983.
Readable survey of applicability of rational expectations for microeconomic and macroeconomic analysis.

Willis, Mark H. "The Future of Monetary Policy: The Rational Expectations Perspective." Federal Reserve Bank of Minneapolis *Quarterly Review* (Summer 1980): 1–7.
Then-president of Minneapolis Fed gives overview of importance of rational expectations for Federal Reserve policies.

PART FOUR

THE CHANGING STRUCTURE OF FINANCIAL INSTITUTIONS

CHAPTER THIRTEEN

FINANCIAL INTERMEDIATION: INDUSTRY STUDY

The nature of the relationship between the number and size distribution of competitors in a market (market structure) and their performance is of crucial importance to bank regulators and others responsible for evaluating the competitive effects of bank and bank holding company mergers and acquisitions.

Gary Wahlen
Economic Commentary
Federal Reserve Bank of Cleveland, November 1, 1986

The financial industry is changing rapidly. For the last decade, and especially since the passage of the DIDMCA of 1980, the industry has been undergoing a transition from what was a series or collection of geographically limited firms to a regional or even a national market structure. The author of a 1967 book on American industrial structure classifies banks, along with barber shops, as service industries which sell in limited local markets.[1] Contrast that with the current situation in which major commercial bank holding companies, such as Citicorp, and non-banking financial newcomers, such as Sears, are positioning themselves to become national firms. To understand such changes and their causes, to assess their policy implications, and to evaluate their effects on the marketplace, use the economist's approach to studying an industry—industrial organization (IO).

For a long time, the world of depository institutions has been limited to local or state markets. This may help explain why analysts have not applied

---

[1] See Richard Caves, *American Industry: Structure, Conduct, Performance*, 2nd edition (Englewood Cliffs, N.J.: Prentice-Hall, 1967): 12.

an industrial organization approach to the study of financial institutions to the same extent as they have to other industries. Nevertheless, an industrial organization approach will help you understand the changing financial industry.

The chapter begins with a review of the industrial organization model for analysis. The review will provide background on what IO economists refer to as the structure, conduct, and performance paradigm. This model is then adapted to the special conditions of the financial industry, and the discussion points out the model's usefulness in dealing with the kinds of policy issues the industry has faced. Finally, an analysis of the American financial industry includes some empirical studies which use an industrial organization approach.

Chapter Objectives

In this chapter you will explore a procedure for analyzing industrial structure, adapt the procedure to fit the financial services industry, and then apply the procedure to that industry. By the end of the chapter you will:

- Understand the industrial organization approach.

    Describe what is meant by market structure.

    Explain the importance of an industry's structure.

    Outline the way in which economists assess industrial structure and behavior.

    Describe the connection between structure and performance.

    Explain the effects of performance on societal welfare.

- Apply the IO approach to the financial services industry.

    Explain structural changes of the financial services industry (number of firms, size of firms, conditions of entry, degree of concentration).

    Identify factors causing the structure to change.

- Analyze the financial services industry.

    Describe research findings on the connection between structure and performance.

    Decide whether or not a basic model of firm behavior exists in the industry.

    Identify trends in the financial services industry.

These objectives will help focus your attention and give a framework for analyzing the financial services industry.

The IO Model and the Financial Industry

The industrial organization model is a systematic way of looking at a market—assessing its basic conditions, determining the structure which evolved from those conditions, analyzing the conduct of the firms which must exist within the market, and evaluating the firms' and the industry's performance.

Basic Definitions

In general, a *market* refers to the concept of buyers and sellers interacting for the sale of goods or services. Observers of the financial industry have the problem of defining the boundaries of the market in terms of both function and geography. Should they use a narrow definition, including only depository institutions, or a broad definition, encompassing all firms which provide financial services? Should they divide the industry into local markets or consider regional and national markets? To a great extent the market is defined through legislation and court action; this is particularly true for the financial marketplace. The definition used for the market will influence the scope of the industry which serves that market. For now, an operational definition of the *financial marketplace* will include all financial services provided by institutions which accept demand deposits or offer commercial loans.

The *basic conditions* are the characteristics inherent in the product or service exchanged in the marketplace. These might include price elasticity of demand or the state of technology. The *market structure* refers to the economically significant features of a market which affect the behaviors of the firms in the industry supplying that market. The main elements of market structure include the number of buyers and sellers, the degree of product or service differentiation, conditions of entry into the market, and the size distribution of firms.

Conduct is the behavior of the firms in the marketplace, the strategies which they employ in pricing, production, promotion, and legal tactics. *Performance* refers to measurable results or achievements. These might include technical efficiency, economies of scale, profitability, and product or service quality. Regulators also consider whether the needs and convenience of customers are accommodated.

Figure 13.1 illustrates the industrial organization model. Notice that structure and conduct address the *how* of the marketplace, given its basic conditions, while performance deals with *how well* the market functions through the firms operating therein. The arrows in this diagram indicate direct relationships (solid lines) and indirect relationships (dotted lines)

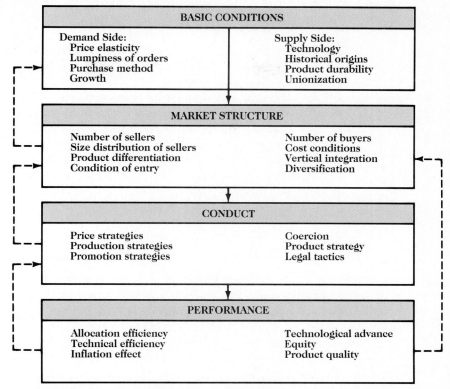

BASIC CONDITIONS

Demand Side:	Supply Side:
Price elasticity	Technology
Lumpiness of orders	Historical origins
Purchase method	Product durability
Growth	Unionization

MARKET STRUCTURE

Number of sellers	Number of buyers
Size distribution of sellers	Cost conditions
Product differentiation	Vertical integration
Condition of entry	Diversification

CONDUCT

Price strategies	Coercion
Production strategies	Product strategy
Promotion strategies	Legal tactics

PERFORMANCE

Allocation efficiency	Technological advance
Technical efficiency	Equity
Inflation effect	Product quality

Source: Reprinted with permission of Macmillan Publishing Company from *Industrial Organization and Public Policy*, Second Edition by Douglas Greer. Copyright © 1984 by Macmillan Publishing Company.

**FIGURE 13.1   *A Model of Industrial Organization Analysis*   The Industrial Organization model relates basic market conditions (demand and supply factors) to the structure of the market and to the conduct and performance of firms in that market.

between the components of the industrial organization model.[2] Two final definitions will complete the list of terms. In this analysis, the *industry* refers to the group of firms which produce the same or similar goods and services. *Firms* are the operating units which arise to serve a particular marketplace. The corner pharmacy is a firm within the retail pharmaceutical industry, just as your local savings and loan is a firm within the financial industry.

---

[2] This discussion relies on the basic introduction to industrial organization provided by Douglas F. Greer in *Industrial Organization and Public Policy*, 2nd edition (New York: Macmillan Publishing Co., 1984): Chapter 1.

Importance of Industry's Organization

The fact that structure influences the conduct of firms in an industry, which, in turn, determines the performance of the market helps to explain why an industry's organization is important. The ability of the market to deliver services efficiently and equitably to consumers is important to the survival of our economic system. The industrial organization approach provides a procedure for analyzing and evaluating market performance.

Economic theory tells us that seller concentration in the marketplace (monopoly or oligopoly) affects an industry's contribution to economic welfare. Economists have traditionally argued that industries with higher seller concentration generate higher product or service prices and greater corporate profits than industries with low seller concentration.

This analysis can be applied to the financial industry to help provide answers to broad questions such as these.

- Do government regulations benefit general welfare?
- Will deregulation of the financial industry enhance or improve general welfare?

The same approach can help to answer more specific questions.

- Does interstate banking enhance operational efficiency?
- Are there economies of scale for depository institutions?
- Will consumers be adversely affected or benefited under conditions of competition or concentration?

This section of the textbook addresses these questions. First, you need more detail on the industrial organization approach.

Industry Structure and Conduct

Economists typically have looked at the structure of an industry by examining numbers of firms, size of firms, and degree of concentration. Economists often use the government's Standard Industrial Classification (SIC). The SIC code divides markets by industry types and then specifies the breadth of the market with numerical codes. Table 13.1 illustrates the SIC code system using food and kindred products.

Using this system, economists are able to examine concentration within industries. They establish concentration ratios using some measure of market activity (for example, the dollar value of sales). The total sales of four and eight firms are compared to total sales within the industry. The higher the number, the greater the concentration.

SIC Code	Number of Digits	Designation	Name
20	2	Major industry group	Food and kindred products
203	3	Industry group	Canning, preserving
2037	4	Product group	Frozen fruit and vegetables
20371	5	Product class	Frozen fruit and juices
2037135	7	Product	Frozen strawberries

TABLE 13.1 *SIC Groupings*

Economists then classify and label markets depending on their degree of concentration. While no universally accepted classification scheme exists, we can gain some perspective by using the following as general reference points: in monopolistic markets a single firm's market share is at or near 100 percent; oligopolistic markets have a four firm concentration ratio above 60 percent; for monopolistically competitive markets the eight-firm ratio is probably around 50 percent; and perfectly competitive markets have very low concentration ratios. An industry may have a low degree of concentration at the national level but high concentration at the regional or local level. For most service industries (the financial industry included) little market concentration exists at the national level but evidence indicates concentration in local markets. Table 13.2 reports on concentration in terms of bank deposits. The first column lists the number of banking organizations in various American standard metropolitan statistical areas (SMSAs). The second column shows how many SMSAs have that range of banking organizations. The third column reports the average four firm concentration ratios for those SMSAs. Note the large number of SMSAs with less than twenty banking organizations and the high four-firm concentration ratios in those regions.

Having identified the degree of market concentration within an industry, analysts must determine its causes. Factors which have influenced concentration include market conditions of entry (excessive start-up costs, economies of scale, or scarce resources), government policies (legislation limiting new entrants, patents, or tariffs), and business policies (mergers, collusive practices, or product differentiation).

The structure of the market influences the conduct of the firms in that industry. Recall that conduct refers to firms' policies toward their products or services and their actions toward other firms in that market. Policy makers have traditionally criticized corporate policies which take decisions about products or services out of the hands of consumers. Such coercive practices include predatory price cutting, collusive pricing, operating agreements preventing new firms from entering or operating freely, and kickbacks. These practices have resulted in antimonopoly legislation.

Banking Organizations in SMSA	Number of SMSAs	Four Firm Concentration Ratio (Average) for SMSAs
101 or more	7	54.4
61–100	7	52.0
41–60	14	58.4
31–40	15	64.8
26–30	16	67.5
21–25	22	61.1
18–20	26	68.1
15–17	32	69.9
12–14	44	74.0
9–11	60	80.7
6–8	57	89.1
5 or less	18	97.9

Source: Jim Burke, "Antitrust Laws, Justice Department Guidelines, and the Limits of Concentration in Local Banking Markets," Board of Governors of the Federal Reserve, Staff Study (1983): 11.

TABLE 13.2 *Concentration Levels for SMSAs*

Some legitimate factors may allow one or a few firms to dominate the market. These factors include superior quality, effective product differentiation, or economies of scale.[3]

Consequences of Structure and Conduct: Measuring Performance

The issue of performance usually dictates the extent to which public policy affects market structure and firms' conduct. Market performance is the evaluation of the results of firms' behavior in a particular industry. Economists evaluate performance by assessing the extent to which economic results of firms' actions deviate from the optimum result or by comparing the benefits and costs of existing conditions with alternative conditions.

In evaluating performance, economists look at the operations of individual firms within an industry and at the industry as a whole. They evaluate

---

[3] The issue of economies of scale which gives preference to existing firms was essentially challenged in the case of telecommunications. In breaking up AT&T, the Justice Department made it clear that a firm's presence in a market could not be used to exclude competition.

BANKING T🄳DAY

Diversification in the Banking Industry

In many industries, diversification has been the key to success. For example, some tobacco companies have expanded into food products (R. J. Reynolds now owns Nabisco Brands) and some manufacturing firms have moved into new areas (U. S. Steel is now called USX Corporation reflecting its movement into plastics and other lines of production).

Depository institutions, usually large bank holding companies (BHC), have turned to diversification also. Their motivation is not unlike that for manufacturing firms—they hope to reduce their total risk and to increase their profit potential in the face of increasing competition. The diversification of BHCs is into lines of business that are not unrelated to banking (1970 amendments to the Bank Holding Company Act allowed diversification into closely related fields). Areas of new business activity for banks include discount brokerage (Bank America bought Charles Schwab and Company) and data processing (MCorp in Dallas has a technology subsidiary, MTech, which is the largest data processor for financial institutions).

What are the implications of this type of diversification in banking?

At least one recent study seems to indicate that without tight regulation and supervision, diversification is associated with greater risk of failure on the part of the BHC rather than a reduction of risk.* With careful scrutiny, a "go slow" policy on approving diversification on the part of regulators (which translates into less freedom for investment by the BHCs into new lines of business), the risk of failure declines.

As the financial services industry continues in its transition the structure of the industry will likely change not just through consolidation or interregional expansion, but through diversification of large BHCs. In an environment of increasing competition, but with a continuing concern for banking safety, such diversification will probably force regulatory agencies (the Federal Reserve being chief among them) to exercise greater control over the expansion by banks into other business endeavors.

* For a more extensive discussion of diversification and risk, see John H. Boyd and Stanley L. Graham, "Risk, Regulation, and Bank Holding Company Expansion into Nonbanking," *Federal Reserve Bank of Minneapolis Quarterly Review* 10, 2 (Spring 1986): 2–17.

individual firms in terms of operating efficiency—how their products or services meet standards of quality, safety and availability—and in terms of their overall performance—if their profit levels fall within normally acceptable ranges. The industry as a whole is also evaluated. Economists ask, "Does it meet market demands in terms of allocative efficiency, product quality, equitability, responsiveness to consumer demand, and technological advances, and does it contribute to overall economic stability?"

Societal norms influence conclusions about the performance of firms and industry groups. Policy makers react differently given changing circumstances. For example, the level of bank mergers we are seeing in the 1980s would never have been approved by regulators during the 1950s. But the procedures which economists use to assess market performance are important because the results of these assessments influence public opinion. With greater emphasis on efficiency today, rather than simply customer convenience which dominated evaluations of the industry thirty years ago, there is wider acceptance of consolidations among depository institutions.

Figure 13.2 summarizes the economists' basic market types categorized by structure, conduct, and performance. You will find the chart helpful as you look more closely at the applicability of the industrial organization model to the financial industry.

Financial Industry: Applying the IO Model

The basic information about the industrial organization approach serves as a basis for examining the financial industry. Even though the financial industry does not yet have firms which are as dominant nationally as General Motors in the auto industry or Coca-Cola in the beverage industry, the industrial organization model still applies and provides insights into the factors affecting the financial industry.

The Production Firm and the Finance Firm

In applying the industrial organization approach to the financial industry, keep in mind the distinctions between the production firm, to which economists usually apply the IO model, and the financial firm. The production firm uses capital, labor, and managerial talent to transform raw materials into intermediate or final products. Microeconomic analysis of the production firm reveals that pricing and output decisions for products offered in the market derive from the marginal-cost–marginal-revenue procedure. Economists can evaluate the production firm by measuring its profitability which is driven by competitive market forces and the firm's operational efficiency.

The financial firm, although a service rather than a production firm, uses the same factors of production. Deposits represent the raw material of the financial firm, which uses its productive resources to transform these deposits into interest-earning assets. The firm makes its pricing decisions in its attempts to acquire the deposits it needs to operate. It must decide how much to pay in order to attract the deposits needed to acquire interest earning assets. Financial firms do make decisions about pricing their services. For example, institutions charge varying rates for checking accounts and safe deposit boxes; but these services are not their primary sources of revenue. Financial firms obtain revenues primarily from the spread between what the firm pays to acquire deposits and what market forces determine as the firm's earnings on the assets it acquires.[4] A simple model of firm behavior is presented later in this chapter (Figure 13.7).

---

[4] This distinction is made, in part, because the acquisition of currency is still done primarily on a local or regional basis while earnings on assets are determined largely through national or even international markets.

Market Type	STRUCTURE			CONDUCT			PERFORMANCE		
	Number of Firms	Entry Condition	Product Type	Price Strategy	Production Strategy	Promotion Strategy*	Profits	Technical Efficiency	Progressiveness
PERFECT COMPETITION	Very large number	Easy	Standardized	None	Independent	b	Normal	Good	Poor perhaps
MONOPOLISTIC COMPETITION	Large number	Easy	Differentiated		Unrecognized interdependence	a	Normal	Moderately good	Fair
OLIGOPOLY	Few	Impeded	Standardized or differentiated		Recognized interdependence	a, b, c	Somewhat excessive	Poor perhaps	Good
MONOPOLY	One	Blocked	Perfectly differentiated		Independent	$a \equiv b$ c	Excessive	Poor perhaps	Poor perhaps

*Key: a = promotion of firm's brand product; b = industry or market wide advertising and promotion; c = institutional or political advertising.

Source: Douglas F. Greer, *Industrial Organization and Public Policy* (New York: Macmillan Publishing Company, 1984): 12. Reprinted by permission.

FIGURE 13.2 Basic Market Types Economists divide markets into perfectly competitive, monopolistically competitive, oligopolistic, and monopolistic. It is convenient to refer to this figure to compare the aspects of structure, conduct, and performance for firms in each type of market.

The success of the financial firm can be measured by determining its profits, which depend on the spread mentioned earlier plus the firm's operating efficiency. A key question is, "To what extent does the structure of the industry influence this spread and a firm's operational efficiency?"

A major distinction between the production firm and the financial firm, one which may influence the latter's operational efficiency, is that the financial firm does not own the "raw materials" it uses to acquire interest-earning assets. Consider that some financial firm's factors of production, its deposits, may be withdrawn at any time. Therefore, financial firms, especially depository firms, must forgo higher returns to maintain liquidity. This need for liquidity becomes an operating cost (really an opportunity cost) not faced by the production firm.

With these similarities and differences in mind, you are ready to investigate the features of the financial market which affect the industry's structure. That discussion will provide a basis for examining the industry's performance more closely. Because a link between conduct and performance in the financial industry is not intuitively obvious, this discussion will concentrate on establishing the structure-performance link.

Financial Market and Industry Structure

Remember that *structure* refers to the significant features of the market which affect the behavior of firms. These features determine firms' market power. Since economists consistently have linked structure to performance within production industries, we can begin to gain some insight into performance by analyzing structure. Later we will be in a position to speculate about what sort of performance we can expect given the structural changes occurring in the industry. To gain an overall view of the industry we can look at some structural characteristics.

	1965	1975	1985
Commercial Banks	13,818	14,654	14,481
Savings & Loan Associations	6185	4931	3391
Mutual Savings Banks	506	476	267
Credit Unions	22,119	22,703	15,144

TABLE 13.3 *Number of Financial Firms*

Country	Number of Commercial Banks	Number of Bank Offices	Population Per Bank	Population Per Bank Office	Share of Deposits at 5 Largest Banks
United States	14,451	54,235	15,676	4177	19.2%
W. Germany	243	41,000	254,156	1506	61.8
Canada	11	7425	2,221,636	3296	77.7
United Kingdom	35	14,000	1,601,914	4004	56.8
Japan	86	13,420	1,378,825	8835	34.5
France	206	40,200	262,913	1347	76.1
Italy	1170	11,970	48,987	4787	35.1
Switzerland	432	5501	14,682	1153	46.7

Source: From "The 'New England Experiment' in Interstate Banking" Richard F. Syron, *New England Economic Review*, March/April 1984. Reprinted by permission of the Federal Reserve Bank of Boston.

TABLE 13.4 *Bank and Branch Density and Deposit Concentration, 1982*

Number of Firms Most analyses begin with this characteristic. A study by the accounting firm of Arthur Andersen & Co., completed in late 1984, estimated that the number of commercial banks in the United States would drop below 10,000 by the end of the decade, a decrease from the more than 14,000 commercial banks in 1986. Observers of the other types of financial firms suggest similar reductions. Table 13.3 provides an indication of the changes in numbers of firms.

Even if the numbers of firms declined in line with the Arthur Andersen projections, a significant number of depository firms would remain in the financial industry. This point is reinforced by Table 13.4 which compares the United States with other Western economies.

Size Distribution of Firms A second structural measure of an industry is the size distribution of firms. A tally of the total number of firms may prove misleading if the industry includes a few large firms and a large number of small firms. Although there is some deposit concentration in the financial industry, no firms dominate the industry at the national level (there is evidence of local dominance, particularly in rural areas).

Economists measure the size of firms in a number of ways. For financial firms the dollar value of assets or deposits is a convenient measure. Table 13.5 provides an analysis of firms by assets. Table 13.5 reveals that a small number of firms hold a very large percentage of total assets, with the

Asset Size	Insured CBs	S & Ls	Mutual SBs	Credit Unions
Less than $250,000	} 2.5(0.1)	} 2.1(2)	} 6.6(z)	22.0(0.6)
250,000–999,000				30.1(3.2)
1.0–4.9 million		4.0(2)		29.9(13.5)
5.0–9.9 million	9.0(0.5)	4.1(0.1)	.3(z)	7.7(10.6)
10–24.9 million	28.8(3.5)	15.4(1.2)	2.0(0.1)	6.1(17.9)
25–49.9 million	25.9(6.6)	18.2(3.0)	4.8(0.4)	2.4(16.4)
50–99.9 million	18.1(8.9)	19.5(6.3)	21.1(3.4)	1.3(16.6)
100–499.9 million	12.7(17.1)	28.5(27.6)	48.6(23.2)	0.5(17.2)
500 million or more	3.1(63.3)	8.2(61.7)	18.3(72.9)	z(4.0)

z = less than .05%

Figures shown are percentage of institutions (percentage of assets).

Source: Statistical Abstract of the U.S., 1986.

TABLE 13.5 *Depository Institution by Asset Size, 1985*

BANKING TODAY 13.2

Commercial and Investment Banking: Will the Twain Meet?

Dating from the New Deal banking reforms, commercial banking and investment banking have been separated. The theory behind the separation was that the risky investment-banking business should not jeopardize the need for safety in commercial banking.

Although the barriers between the two types of banking have not legally come down completely (See Banking Today 14.1, page 352), some major commercial banks are making moves toward investment banking activity.

Investment banks extend long-term loans or provide equity capital to industry; this is called underwriting securities issued by corporations. Goldman Sachs and Salomon Brothers are two large investment banking houses that underwrite security issues by major corporations in this country and abroad. Investment banks also advise corporations on security transactions and acquisitions.

As investment houses, such as Merrill Lynch, begin to infringe on commercial bank activities, some commercial banks are returning the favor.

By the spring of 1986 some commercial banks were considering actual movement into investment banking despite the legal prohibition. Morgan Guaranty Trust, a major New York commercial bank, even considered getting rid of its bank charter if legal barriers restricting its investment banking activities were not removed.

At this point some major money center banks have developed or acquired merger and acquisition units which advise corporate clients on securities issues. Advising clients can be very lucrative. In 1985 Citibank advised on five transactions that yielded more than $1 million in fees each. The next step is to actually underwrite, rather than just advise, those securities issues. Such a step would certainly increase the level of competition on Wall Street as well as making some big banks even bigger.

exception of credit unions for which many small firms hold a significant percentage of total assets.

Another way to illustrate the size distribution of firms is to use the Lorenz Curve. You may recall from your economic principles course that the Lorenz Curve measures the deviation from absolute equality. In this case *equality* means that the cumulative percentage of firms is the same as the cumulative percentage of the industry assets held by those firms. Figure 13.3 is the Lorenz Curve for commercial banks showing percentage of assets on the vertical axis and percentage of firms on the horizontal axis. The 45-degree line represents absolute equality. The greater the deviation from the line, the greater the degree of inequality. Although no firms dominate the industry, the Lorenz Curve illustrates that the asset distribution among commercial banks is nowhere near being equal.

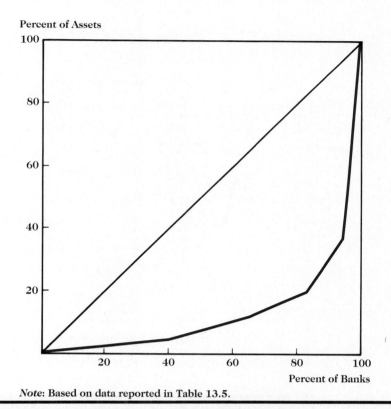

Note: Based on data reported in Table 13.5.

FIGURE 13.3   *Lorenz Curve for Commercial Banks*   This figure uses a Lorenz Curve to illustrate the uneven distribution of assets among commercial banks. The further the curve diverges from the 45-degree line, the greater the inequality. The results are similar, although not as extreme, for other types of depository institutions.

Conditions of Entry The ease with which a firm can enter an industry helps to guarantee sufficient firms to provide competition and fair market-established prices. Economic theory indicates that if the price determined by market forces is above each firm's average cost (economic profits are accruing to firms in the industry), new firms will enter the industry, pushing the price down. In a competitive market, this assures that the long-run price will tend toward average cost.

This, of course, assumes that firms can enter the industry. For financial institutions, entry is restricted through chartering provisions. A recent study indicates that from 1936 to 1962 entry rates for commercial banks were restricted at a rate below that which prevailed before 1935. Since 1962 the number of entrants has increased (see Figure 13.4). This fact does not contradict evidence presented earlier that the total number of commercial banks today is less than fifty years ago because the entry rates shown above

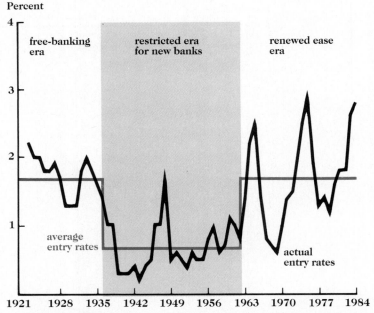

Note: The vertical axis shows new entrants as a percent of the total number of firms.

Source: From "The Regulation of Bank Entry" by Michael C. Keely, *Economic Review*, Summer 1985. Reprinted by permission of the Federal Reserve Bank of San Francisco.

FIGURE 13.4 *Entry Rates for Commercial Banks* This figure shows that in the thirty-year period following the massive bank collapses of the Great Depression, regulators restricted the entry of new commercial banks below what had existed before 1935 and what has occurred since the mid-1960s.

take into account the opening of branch offices. Restrictions on branch banking have been eased considerably over the past two decades. The point here is that ease of entry is influenced by regulators as well as by economic conditions. Since financial reform in the early 1980s, savings and loans have begun competing with commercial banks. When one considers this, the picture is even more startling. Figure 13.5 shows the total number of banking and savings association offices from 1920 to 1985.

The liberalization of branch restrictions has encouraged entry into the industry. This is particularly important from the perspective of customer service. It is still unclear whether the multiple offices of large bank holding companies actually compete or whether it is the number of national or regional firms which is important when assessing competition.

Concentration   Concentration within an industry tells a great deal about firms' market power. Despite the increasing number of branches of commercial banks and savings and loan associations, data indicate that concentration is increasing.

This discussion of concentration must include an important distinction. The firms in the financial industry do not function in a national market. They are certainly not local, the way they once may have been when

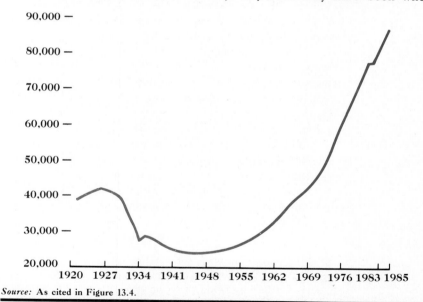

Source: As cited in Figure 13.4.

FIGURE 13.5   *Total Banking and Savings Association Offices, 1920–1985*
This figure reveals the increase in bank and savings association offices. Since the 1960s, the number of offices, including new depository institutions and branches of existing institutions, has increased dramatically.

financial firms could be compared to barber shops. Rather, they are firms with local and statewide markets. In this discussion concentration is considered for Metropolitan Statistical Areas, for urban areas and non-MSA counties, for rural areas, and for states. Bank holding companies are the focus rather than independent banks and bank offices.

Economists measure concentration by using a ratio comparing the size of the largest firms in a market to all firms in the market. An often used measure of concentration is the *Herfindahl Index*. The H-index equals the sum of the squared market shares (measured in percent of output) for every firm in the market. The maximum H-index value is 10,000. This occurs if one firm has 100 percent of the market share ($100^2 = 10,000$). A smaller Herfindahl Index indicates more firms in the market or the size distribution of the existing firms becoming more equal.

Examining concentration at the local level reveals a decline in concentration. Charles Morris studied concentration in the Tenth Federal Reserve District (the seven states served by the Federal Reserve Bank of Kansas City). He found that compared to 1973, the H-index for 1983 declined for every MSA and non-MSA county in the seven district states. He found similar results when considering banking organizations and savings and loan associations. Figure 13.6 illustrates his findings. Other studies indicate that the differences in bank holding company and geographic branching restrictions among states have had little effect on the degree of local market concentration.[5]

When the geographic region considered is the entire state, analysts are inclined to agree that concentration has been increasing recently.[6] New England has been on the cutting edge of the regional interstate banking movement (that is, the breaking down of state barriers within a specific region). In that region, the statewide Herfindahl indexes are above the national median (except for New Hampshire). See Table 13.6.

The discussion so far has focused on the structure of the financial industry. The questions of policy which have arisen over the past decade and which will continue to arise throughout the 1980s revolve around industry performance. Having acquired some insight into the structure of the financial industry, you are ready to study market performance.

---

[5] See for example John T. Rose and Donald T. Savage, "Bank Holding Company De Novo Entry and Banking Market Decentralization," *Journal of Bank Research* (Summer 1982): 96–100; and Stephen Rhoades, "National and Local Market Banking Concentration in an Era of Interstate Banking," *Issues in Bank Regulation* (forthcoming).

[6] See, for example, Thomas M. Havrilesky, "Increases in Statewide Banking Concentration in Anticipation of Regional Banking Compacts" (Duke University Working Papers in Economics, April 1985): 85–92.

				Median	**721**			
Alabama	721	Indiana	143	Nebraska	157	S. Carolina	1018
Alaska	1370	Iowa	181	Nevada	3332	S. Dakota	1234
Arizona	2703	Kansas	64	New Hampshire	699	Tennessee	509
Arkansas	132	Kentucky	229	New Jersey	425	Texas	467
California	1579	Louisiana	166	New Mexico	928	Utah	1602
Colorado	782	Maine	1210	New York	805	Vermont	1051
Connecticut	1438	Maryland	958	N. Carolina	1212	Virginia	800
Delaware	1142	Massachusetts	1103	N. Dakota	583	Washington	1525
Florida	485	Michigan	708	Ohio	493	W. Virginia	89
Georgia	676	Minnesota	1186	Oklahoma	165	Wisconsin	314
Hawaii	2840	Mississippi	343	Oregon	2482	Wyoming	647
Idaho	2199	Missouri	417	Pennsylvania	452		
Illinois	434	Montana	863	Rhode Island	2827		

Source: From "The New England Experiment in Interstate Banking" Richard F. Syron, *New England Economic Review* March/April, 1984. Reprinted by permission of the Federal Reserve Bank of Boston.

TABLE 13.6 *Herfindahl Indexes for the Fifty States*

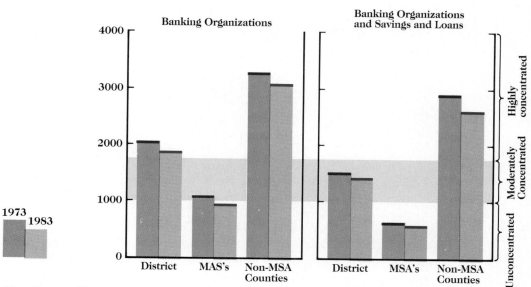

Note: Degree of concentration based on June 1982 Department of Justice merger guidelines

Source: Charles S. Morris, "Banking Market Structure in the Tenth District, 1973–1983," Federal Reserve Bank of Kansas City *Economic Review* (July/August 1985): 26. Reprinted by permission.

FIGURE 13.6 *Banking Concentration in Kansas City District* Using the Herfindahl Index (a measure of market concentration), this figure shows that at least in one market (the seven-state area around Kansas City), the degree of local market concentration declined from 1973–1983.

Financial Industry: Connections Between Structure and Performance

Considerable research in industrial organization has focused on the structure-performance hypothesis. Despite some challenges to the hypothesis, it continues to influence policy decisions.

The structure-performance hypothesis dictates that the degree of concentration influences competition. The hypothesis presupposes that a heavily concentrated market structure is more likely to result in collusion. The related supposition is that collusion results in higher prices/profits than would occur under competitive conditions. To test the structure-performance hypothesis, we need to estimate measures of firm performance and determine the degree to which those are influenced by structural factors, especially concentration.

The measures of performance which economists most often cite as indicators of the degree of competition or concentration for financial firms are profit rates, interest rates charged on loans, and interest rates paid on deposits.

Structure-Performance Hypothesis and Recent Challenges

The theoretical basis for the connection between structure and performance provides the rationale for much government regulation of business. Remember, economic theory indicates that competitive markets generally result in the lowest price for consumers that will allow producers to generate "normal profits." Concentration, or the lack of competition, results in higher prices, lower output, and higher profits for the firms in the industry.

Over the past decade some new perspectives on industrial organization have challenged the traditional theoretical link between structure and performance. Whether these new theories will alter the way economists look at industrial organization remains to be seen, but these views have generated considerable discussion.

The *differential efficiency*[7] argument suggests that the link between concentration and above-normal profit rates in an industry may result from greater operating efficiency in the industry's large firms rather than from collusion or market power. In the same vein, the *contestable markets*[8] literature

---

[7] See Harold Demsetz, "Industry Structure, Market Rivalry, and Public Policy," *Journal of Law and Economics* 16 (April 1973): 1–9; or Yale Brozen, *Concentration, Mergers, and Public Policy* (New York: Macmillan, 1982).

[8] William J. Baumol, John C. Panzar, and Robert D. Willig, *Contestable Markets and the Theory of Industrial Structure* (New York: Harcourt Brace Jovanovich, 1982).

presents a challenge to the structure-performance hypothesis. According to this view, barriers to entry may influence performance, but market structure is determined by industry characteristics. As such, the market structure is not in and of itself an independent determinant of competition. Some empirical studies have attempted to apply the differential efficiency argument and the contestable markets approach to the financial industry, but most empirical studies explore the structure-performance hypothesis.

Basic Model of Financial Institution Behavior

Before looking at the results of the empirical studies measuring the connection between performance and structure, it will be useful to see a simple model for bank behavior (Figure 13.7). This model demonstrates how a profit-maximizing strategy affects interest rates charged on loans and rates paid on deposits.[9]

This model is for a single depository firm. It assumes the following:

1. The single source of funds for the firm is deposits (d) which the firm attracts with an interest rate (r_d).

2. The firm's options for uses of its funds are loans (l) which earn a return (r_l) and government securities (s) which pay a rate (r_s).

3. The firm is a profit maximizer where profits (π) are the difference between revenues and costs:

$$\pi = r_l\,(l) + r_s\,(s) - r_d\,(d)$$

subject to the balance sheet constraint:

$$l + s = d$$

and market constraints:

$$l = l\,(r_l)$$
$$d = d\,(r_d)$$

In Figure 13.7b the source of funds—deposits—are shown as an increasing function of the interest rate on deposits. The marginal cost curve for the deposit supply curve is shown as the dotted line (MC_d).

Figure 13.7a shows the uses of the firm's funds. The loan demand function (D_l) is a decreasing function of the rate of interest. The marginal revenue curve associated with the loan demand function is shown by the

---

[9] The model discussed here is adapted from a model presented by John H. Wood and Norma L. Wood in their book, *Financial Markets* (New York: Harcourt Brace Jovanovich, 1985): 32–7.

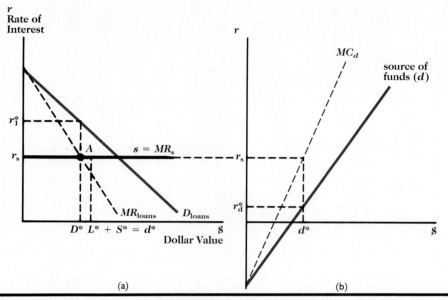

FIGURE 13.7 *Simple Model of Bank Behavior* This simple diagram represents a useful model of depository firm behavior. A firm, in choosing between the extension of loans and the purchase of government securities, will be influenced by market conditions establishing the interest rate in the competitive securities market (shown in 13.7b as r_s). This rate, combined with the demand for loans (D_{loans} in 13.7a), determines the interest rate on loans (r^*). As with any firm, the depository firm equates the marginal revenue of various services—the firm will extend loans until the marginal revenue from loans (MR_l) is just equal to the marginal revenue from securities (MR_s). This occurs at point A in 13.7a and represents a profit maximizing behavior which results in the quantity of loans (l^*) with the residual of funds available being used for securities (S^*).

dotted line (MR_l). The other use of bank funds is government securities. Since the firm may purchase as many or as few securities as it desires, and since the rate of interest on these securities is determined in the perfectly competitive securities market, government securities are illustrated as the horizontal line (s) at the prevailing market interest rate on securities (r_s). This line represents the marginal revenue from government securities (MR_s).

This firm has control over the rate of interest it charges on loans, the quantity of loans it extends, the rate it pays on demand deposits, the quantity of deposits it attracts, and the quantity of securities it buys. Its decisions are subject to the constraints mentioned above and these decisions are closely related.

In this model the overall market sets the interest rate on securities. This rate combines with the demand for loans function (and its associated marginal revenue curve) to determine the interest rate on loans and quantity of loans which will maximize revenues. The firm is willing to extend loans until the marginal revenue from loans (MR_l) is just equal to the marginal revenue from securities (MR_s). This occurs at point A in 13.7a, indicating loans of l^* and the associated interest rate of r^*_l. Any reduction or increase in the loan/securities mix will generate less revenue for the firm.

The prevailing market interest rate on securities influences the level of deposits this firm needs to attract. The rate paid on securities (r_s) becomes the driving force behind the firm's decision on the deposit rate. The firm determines the optimal quantity of deposits by equating MC_d to MR_l which is equal to r_s. In so doing, the firm decides to extend loans equal to d^* which will occur by paying a deposit rate of r^*_d.

Having determined its level of deposits, the firm allocates funds to the optimal level for loans (l^*) and places the remaining funds in securities such that $l^* + s^* = d^*$.

This simplistic model does not translate perfectly into the real world but it reveals some of the factors constraining depository firm behavior. It is useful as we think about the connection between industry structure and firm performance because it reveals that the competitive market (in this case the securities market) is the driving force in interest rate determination, and indicates that with limited investment opportunities (only loans and securities) the firm's ability to attract deposits is really determined by market forces. It cannot unilaterally raise the interest rate on deposits without jeopardizing its chances of maximizing profits.

What we need to consider is the extent to which such a model—essentially a market driven model—applies to the behavior of firms in the financial industry. We can use the results of some empirical studies to assess the link between structure and performance.

Bank Market Structure and Performance: Conclusions

The final portion of this section reports on the results of a survey of empirical studies related to structure and performance.[10] Studies of market structure in the financial industry have not changed much over the past two decades. Despite increasing criticism of the structure-performance hypothesis as it applies to the financial industry (especially since it does not explicitly account for regulatory changes), most empirical work continues to address the connection between concentration and performance from a very traditional theoretical perspective; namely, that concentration will produce anti-competitive results.

---

[10] This discussion is based on the survey of empirical studies by R. Alton Gilbert, "Bank Market Structure and Competition," *Journal of Money, Credit and Banking* 16, 4 (December 1984, Part 2): 617–645.

After reviewing 44 studies which tested the influence of market structure on bank performance, R. Alton Gilbert reported that 32 found evidence of a small but significant association between market structure and performance. More specifically, these studies report that a rise in market concentration results in higher loan rates. To illustrate this point, three studies reviewed by Gilbert revealed that banks in regions with relatively high concentration engaged in "expertise preference behavior." In other words, they hire more employees and incur higher costs than other banks. These higher costs keep profit rates from reflecting the higher operating costs which result in higher interest rate charges. The connection between concentration and service charges was not significant.

Gilbert concludes, "the better studies report a significant influence of market concentration on the performance measures . . . ."[11] He hastens to point out that this does not mean the structure-performance relationship reflects collusion among firms. An association between concentration and performance does not necessarily mean market concentration caused the performance. Some observers argue that the higher profits of large firms in concentrated markets actually result from economies of scale (called the *differential efficiency* argument). Others claim that the use of book profits as the measure of performance masks the firm's use of revenues to achieve objectives other than maximizing shareholder profits.

Precisely why the connection exists between structure and performance is not clear from the empirical studies. Some connection does emerge from the research, and this connection may be the basis for policy decisions. We will explore this issue in the next two chapters.

Chapter Conclusion

This chapter introduced an approach for analyzing the financial services industry. Although most often used with production firms rather than service firms, the industrial organization approach provides a mechanism for analyzing the structure of the financial services industry and the behavior of financial firms, especially depository institutions.

The utilization of the industrial organization approach and some empirical studies revealed a connection between structure and performance in the financial industry. This will help explain legislative actions over the years and set the stage for policy discussions.

Across industries, the influence of structure on performance has led policy makers to enact legislation ensuring that firms in an industry perform

---

[11] Ibid., 636.

in a socially desirable fashion. In the minds of most analysts, the economic model of competition—one which prescribes low market concentration—comes closest to achieving the socially optimum performance by firms in an industry.

The next chapter reveals how legal and legislative measures led to the deregulation of the financial services industry. Chapter 15 explores some implications of this deregulation.

Consider These Questions

1. Consider some highly visible American manufacturing industries, for example, steel or automobile production. What has been the trend over time in these industries in terms of structure? How would you assess the performances of these industries in recent years? Do you think there is any connection between these industries' structures and their performances? Explain.

2. Now consider some other types of industries, for example, retail food or clothing. Answer the same questions posed in question number 1.

3. Using the industries identified in the first two questions, what are the similarities/differences between these industries and the financial services industry? Can you draw any conclusions about the financial services industry and its structure and performance by comparing it to these other industries?

4. The contestable markets theory argues that market structure is determined by specific characteristics of an industry rather than by barriers to entry. Identify some industries where you think this explains the performance of firms within the industry. To what extent does this theory apply to the structure of the financial services industry in your region of the country?

5. What might banking, or the entire American financial services industry, look like if only one major firm existed in the industry? How could you determine whether the country would benefit under such conditions?

6. Describe the trend in the American financial services industry in terms of number of firms and degree of concentration. Does this description apply to your region? Why or why not?

7. Refer to the model of firm behavior depicted in Figure 13.7. What would happen if the demand for loans curve was perfectly inelastic (a vertical line) rather than somewhat elastic as is shown in the figure?

8. Try to make a case for and against the structure-performance argument in the financial services industry.

Suggestions for Further Reading

Baumol, William J., John C. Panzar and Robert D. Willig. *Contestable Markets and the Theory of Industrial Structure.* New York: Harcourt Brace Jovanovich, 1982.

This sophisticated but readable book introduced an alternative to the structure-performance approach in industrial organization.

Bain, Joe S. *Industrial Organization.* 2nd edition. New York: John Wiley and Sons, Inc., 1968.

This is one of the best conventional IO texts.

Fisher, Gerald C. *American Banking Structure.* New York: Columbia University Press, 1968.

This is one of the early works on bank structure. It is particularly useful for comparison with contemporary studies.

Greer, Douglas F. *Industrial Organization and Public Policy.* New York: Macmillan Publishing Company, 1984.

This is a conventional IO text in terms of the approach utilized but it devotes considerable attention to the policy aspects of industry structure and performance.

Heggestad, Arnold A. "Market, Structure, Competition and Performance in Financial Industries: A Survey of Banking Studies." In *Issues in Financial Regulation*, edited by Franklin R. Edwards, 449–490. New York: McGraw-Hill, 1979.

Excellent survey of banking studies up to the deregulation legislation of 1980 and 1982. Good source for summary of empirical studies.

Heggestad, Arnold A. and William G. Shepard. "The 'Banking' Industry." In *The Structure of American Industry*, 7th edition, edited by Walter Adams, 290–324. New York: Macmillan Publishing Company, 1986.

Places banking industry into overall review of structure, conduct, and performance of American industries.

Scherer, F. M. *Industrial Market Structure and Economic Performance.* Chicago: Rand McNally, 1970.

A best-selling IO text. Author has had major influence on use of industrial organization in assessing industry performance.

Scott, Kenneth E. "The Dual Banking System: A Model of Competition in Regulation." In *Issues in Financial Regulation*, edited by Franklin R. Edwards, 490–509. New York: McGraw-Hill, 1979.

Good analysis of the impact of regulation on the competitive behavior of commercial banks.

Searle, Philip F. "Alternative Organizational Structures." In *The Bankers Handbook*, edited by W. H. Baughn and C. E. Walker, 26–47. Homewood, IL: Dow Jones/Irwin, 1978.

Provides a "banker's eye view" of various organizational structures in the financial services industry.

CHAPTER FOURTEEN

ENVIRONMENT FOR CHANGE: LEGAL, REGULATORY and COMPETITIVE

These [financial reforms] . . . represent returns to practices that were well established by the 1920s or the resumption of trends that were underway in that decade but were interrupted by the Great Depression.

Randall C. Merris and John Wood
Federal Reserve Bank of Chicago
Economic Perspectives, September/October 1985

erception is as important as reality, especially when it comes to the legislative process. Evolving from the economic collapse of the 1930s was the perception that competition between banks had led to unsound practices which were largely responsible for the banking failures of the 1930s. This perception, and the legislative actions which it engendered, created an anticompetitive environment in the financial services industry; that environment has persisted until very recently.

Unlike many other industries in which legislation, regulatory actions, and court rulings combine to encourage competition between firms, legislation safeguarded the financial industry *from* competition. This prevented depository institution failure, and, as such, restored stability to the system. But it also prevented the kind of innovations expected from competitive industries.

Much of the initial motivation for change in the industry came from the courts which, before Congress, began to restore competition. National commissions kept recommending legislative reforms for the financial services industry, but only a crisis among thrifts in the industry prompted Congress to enact reforms. The legislative reforms of 1980 and 1982 provided for a deregulation of the financial services industry. These reforms are having far-reaching effects on the industry.

This chapter explores the attitudes which protected the industry for the half-century after the Great Depression. It looks at court rulings which interpreted legislation and established the guidelines for industry behavior. The chapter outlines the reasons for change—first, the analytical reasons which Congress ignored and second, the crisis of the thrifts which forced reform. The chapter concludes with a discussion of the provisions of the deregulatory reform legislation.

Chapter Objectives

As you review the process that led to financial reform and then investigate the components of that reform legislation, remember that the industry is still changing. To understand that change and its implications, you will find it helpful to understand how reality and perceptions of reality have changed and what the prevailing attitudes are now.

To help you develop this understanding, consider the overall objectives of this chapter. By the end of the chapter you should be able to:

- Describe the attitudes which resulted in "protection" of the financial industry.
- Explain how this protection provided for the safety of the industry but prevented innovation.
- Explain the role of the courts in the movement toward deregulation.
- Illustrate how the thrift crisis prompted a reassessment of competition in the industry.
- Outline the essential elements of the deregulation legislation.

You should also be able to analyze the financial industry. Specifically, by the end of the chapter, you will:

- Explain the role competition plays in an industry.
- Identify the effects that lack of competition had on the financial services industry.
- Predict possible effects of deregulation on the situation.
- Recommend goals for policy makers as they consider changes in the financial services industry.

The issues implied in these objectives continue to confront the industry. The approaches that develop over the next few years will have a strong influence on the structure of the financial services industry.

Environment Dictates Industry Structure

The events of the 1920s and 1930s shaped attitudes regarding the financial industry that would persist for years. Congress translated these attitudes into legislation which essentially dictated the industry's structure, conduct, and performance for the next few decades.

The "Overbanked" 1920s

During the years following World War I, the American economy experienced sustained growth. The Roaring Twenties brought rapid industrial and agricultural expansion without the uncertainty of an escalating price level or rising interest rates. In addition to these economic forces the newly formed Federal Reserve System created a sense of financial security and confidence. The environment was conducive to the growth and expansion of financial institutions. Figure 14.1 reveals that the number of depository institutions was growing. The number of firms peaked in 1925 and then declined slowly over the next two years as some consolidation began to occur.

These consolidations, which were part of a nationwide wave of business mergers, also occurred through bank holding company formation, and chain banking arrangements. Bank holding companies numbered nearly one hundred by the end of the 1920s. Some have claimed that the contraction in the number of depository institutions was a result of "overbanking" (the too rapid expansion of banks) and deteriorating profit margins. Others have argued, more convincingly, that the urbanization of America and improved transportation (for example, all-weather roads) made firms in hundreds of small rural communities unnecessary.

The Great Depression hastened the decline in the number of depository institutions. Insufficient liquidity and the drying up of deposits because of declining economic activity spelled doom for many firms. As described in Chapter 6, thousands of commercial banks, savings and loan associations, mutual savings banks, and credit unions failed during the early 1930s. Figure 14.1 documents these failures. From the peak of 40,660 depository institutions in 1925 the number of firms declined to 25,611 by the end of 1933.

Lessons of Depression

The widespread failure of financial institutions, caused by both illiquidity and insolvency during the early 1930s, opened the door for government intervention. In place of policies which liberalized restrictions on the financial industry, the federal government adopted legislation to protect consum-

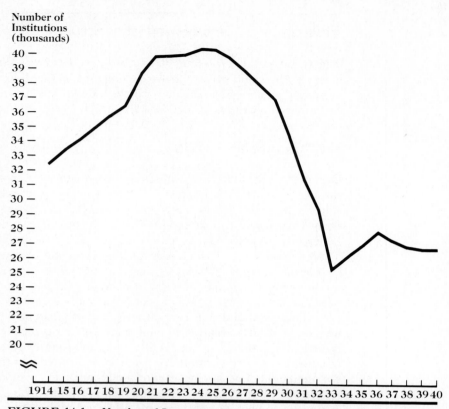

Number of
Institutions
(thousands)

FIGURE 14.1 *Number of Depository Institutions, 1914–1940*   This figure illustrates how the number of depository institutions declined from the peak of over 40,000 in 1925.

ers by limiting competition, regulating operations, and insuring deposits. This arrangement was intended to protect those firms which survived and to prevent such failures in the future.[1]

Much of what motivated the legislation of the 1930s stemmed from a fear that competition in the financial industry threatened a sound and secure system. The structure created during this period replaced the vagaries of the marketplace with the safeguards and controls of the regulators. The firms

---

[1] For a detailed discussion on this period, see Lewis J. Spellman, *The Depository Firm and Industry: Theory, History, and Regulation* (New York: Academic Press, 1982).

that survived the financial system's collapse were protected from failing but prevented from competing to earn high profits. Thus, through the political process, Congress made the decision to forgo the kinds of innovation prompted by competition in favor of the security and solvency that status quo maintenance would provide.

Structure, Conduct, and Performance

Under the regulatory arrangements the government restricted the entry of new firms and controlled the expansion of existing firms. Table 14.1 illustrates how the number of depository institutions and their offices stabilized.

Beyond this, asset markets were essentially divided among the various types of depository institutions. Commercial banks specialized in collateralized business loans, savings and loan associations concentrated on home mortgages, and credit unions extended the bulk of consumer credit. This segmentation of depository institution activities has been a major source of industry problems which continue in the 1980s despite reform legislation.

Constraints on new entrants and branch restrictions protected markets by region. Restrictions on activities protected markets by asset type. In addition to controlling the competition in these ways, the new legislation prevented competition for deposits through interest rate ceilings (Regulation Q) and eliminated price competition.

Year	Depository Institutions	Offices	Year	Depository Institutions	Offices
1935	26,780	----	1945	24,631	29,156
1936	27,508	----	1946	24,622	29,356
1937	26,872	----	1947	24,657	29,512
1938	26,780	----	1948	24,822	29,792
1939	26,273	----	1949	25,317	31,165
1940	26,227	----	1950	25,825	31,926
1941	26,316	----	1951	26,054	31,905
1942	26,939	31,247	1952	26,546	32,736
1943	25,187	29,544	1953	27,142	33,726
1944	24,804	29,302	1954	27,673	34,933

Source: From *The Depository Firm and Industry: Theory, History, and Regulation* by Lewis J. Spellman. Copyright © 1982 by Academic Press, Inc. Reprinted by permission of Academic Press, Inc. and the author.

TABLE 14.1 *Depository Institutions, 1935–1954*

To supervise the industry's structure and conduct, the government created a variety of supervisory agencies such as the Federal Home Loan Bank Board to oversee federal savings and loan associations and the Federal Credit Administration for federal credit unions. In addition, agencies designed to safeguard deposits through a federal insurance plan also supervised and regulated firms. The Federal Deposit Insurance Corporation supervised commercial and savings banks, the Federal Savings and Loan Insurance Corporation supervised savings and loans, and later, the National Credit Union Share Insurance Fund watched over credit unions.

Legislation essentially dictated the structure of the industry and the conduct of the firms in that industry. Beyond this, government-imposed restrictions on operations influenced performance of depository institutions. Financial firms were protected from failing; given such a safeguard, supervisory authorities had the important task of keeping profit rates in line with those in similar industries.

The industry structure dictated by New Deal legislation would form the basis for ongoing disputes between those sectors of the industry which benefited from the structure and those that the legislative and legal environments constrained. To a great extent challenges to the structure and inter-

ECONOMICS T●DAY 14.1

Football Wars and the Courts Affect the Structure of an Industry

In July, 1986, the upstart United States Football League (USFL) "won" its antitrust lawsuit against the established National Football League (NFL). In a jury trial the court ruled that the NFL did have a virtual monopoly in the professional football market but that it did not use its power to prevent the USFL from gaining the television contract it needed to survive.

The jury awarded the plaintiff damages in the amount of $1 (which were tripled according to antitrust statutes). Without monetary compensation in an amount sufficient to overcome the revenues the USFL would lose without a television contract, the league suspended operations.

In this case the court ruling essentially sanctioned the dominant position of one league over the other. As long as that dominant position is not used to exert pressure on contractors to keep competitors out of the marketplace, the dominant organization is not in violation of antitrust statutes, at least not in any practical sense.

The courts interpret antitrust legislation. In this instance the court reaffirmed the status quo in professional football. The court refused to provide a weak competitor with the financial resources it could not garner in the marketplace. A monopoly, without unfair competitive practices, is not really illegal. In this ruling, the court sanctioned the existing structure of a particular industry. In other industries the courts have been the agents for changing the industrial structure.

How do you think the courts might respond if a similar lawsuit were brought by one depository firm against another? What if the small commercial bank in your area sued the major regional bank claiming the latter's power prevented the former from succeeding? How do you think the court would rule? What about a situation where one or two major money center banks come to dominate a region of the country? In a suit do you think the court will rule to maintain competition in the financial services industry or will it allow certain firms to dominate? Will the football wars of 1986 become the bank wars of 1996?

pretation of the legislation were left to the courts. Court actions over the next decades had a profound effect on the industry structure.

Legal Actions Affect Structure

The anticompetitive structure which emerged from the financial reform legislation of the 1930s resulted from the pervasive view that the system had failed because of excessive competition. The New Deal legislation embodied the interpretation that the system was unsound because too many banks competed too aggressively. This competition encouraged high interest rates to attract deposits which led to high-risk investments and loans, particularly in the expanding stock and bond market and in real estate. When these sectors collapsed the banks' investment portfolios collapsed, too.

The legislation which followed the collapse of the industry tried to rectify these problems by restricting interest rate competition, separating investment banking from commercial banking, limiting competition by restricting the entry of new firms, granting commercial banks virtual monopoly over demand deposits, and restraining the uses to which banks could put their funds.

The new structure for the financial industry accomplished its stated purpose—a stable system. The relative stability is measured by number of bank failures and number of new entrants as well as the profitability of existing firms. Using these measures, relative stability soon gave way to renewed disputes over the appropriate structure for the system.

The regulated environment which evolved from the 1930s remained in effect with only slight modifications until the changing attitudes of the 1970s. The crisis of the thrifts in the late 1970s prompted the deregulation legislation of the 1980s. However, some changes occurred prior to this period. Regulators, policy makers, and the courts all became involved. Regulators and policy makers began to move away from their adherence to restricting competition through controlled access to the industry. They began to adopt the position that competition was important. The courts began applying antitrust laws to the financial industry. These factors combined with economic conditions to alter the structure of the industry.

The Bank Merger Act of 1960 specified that the maintenance of competition in the delivery of services was an important consideration for regulators when they ruled on mergers. The Comptroller of the Currency further signaled a shift toward encouraging competition by dramatically increasing the number of new bank charters granted. Between 1962 and 1965, the Comptroller granted 513 new national charters and 502 new state charters. These numbers were well in excess of those granted during the 1950s.

Some have argued that the apparent change in attitude about the importance of preserving competition actually resulted from the profitability of financial institutions. The postwar economic expansion brought increasing profit levels to most financial institutions. Regulators had difficulty justifying limitations on entry into the industry when the demand for services was resulting in rising profits for existing firms.

Regulations designed to prevent the failure of financial firms by restricting the entry of new firms tended to accentuate rates of return, especially during periods of economic expansion, and reduce risks for firms in the industry. As with any industry, rising rates of return increase the pressure for new entrants. Table 14.2 illustrates the situation in the financial industry leading up to the changing policies of the 1960s. The columns reveal that the

| | Commercial banks | | | | Moody's AAA |
Year	Federal Reserve members	FDIC members	Mutual savings banks	Savings and loan associations	long-term interest rates
1947	10.74	11.13	7.05	3.89	2.61
1948	9.70	10.04	6.70	3.90	2.82
1949	10.47	10.86	6.09	3.97	2.66
1950	11.86	12.09	6.37	4.06	2.62
1951	12.19	12.30	7.44	3.95	2.86
1952	13.35	13.38	4.98	4.09	2.96
1953	13.76	13.66	5.76	4.41	3.20
1954	15.56	15.51	6.00	4.67	2.90
1955	13.11	12.99	5.86	4.87	3.06
1956	12.77	12.68	6.14	4.94	3.36
1957	14.17	13.88	5.85	5.10	3.89
1958	16.85	16.34	6.04	5.23	3.79
1959	12.49	12.33	6.83	5.39	4.38
1960	16.83	16.39	5.45	5.66	4.41
1961	15.89	15.37	6.44	5.78	4.35
1962	14.12	13.72	5.04	6.04	4.33
1963	13.82	13.34	5.33	6.05	4.26
1964	12.75	12.50	5.89	6.19	4.40
1965	11.96	11.85	6.83	6.19	4.49
1966	11.73	11.71	4.45	6.15	5.13
1967	12.87	12.70	3.18	6.42	5.51
1968	12.83	12.81	5.41	6.66	6.18
1969	17.05	14.75	5.76	6.69	7.03
1970	16.77	15.74	5.05	6.77	8.04

Note: rates of return calculated as ratio of net income before taxes to capital account and expressed as percentage

Source: From *The Depository Firm and Industry: Theory, History, and Regulation* by Lewis J. Spellman. Copyright © 1982 by Academic Press, Inc. Reprinted by permission of Academic Press, Inc. and the author.

TABLE 14.2 *Depository Institution Rates of Return* vs. *Market Interest Rate*

rates of return for depository institutions exceeded the long-term market interest rate by a considerable margin. This helps explain the pressure on regulators and policy makers to ease restrictions on entry into the industry to restore some competition.

The typical response to a situation of rising profits, increasing the number of firms, occurred partly by adding new firms, but more through relaxed restrictions on branches. Largely because of a loophole (providing that existing bank holding companies could expand), the Bank Holding Company Act of 1960 allowed the addition of firms primarily through new branches. Figure 14.2 shows this situation for commercial banks and savings

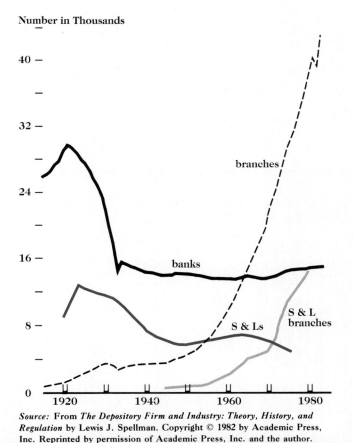

FIGURE 14.2   *Growth of Banks, S & Ls and their Branches, 1920–1985*
After the adjustments of the Great Depression era, the number of commercial banks and S & Ls leveled off. But, beginning in the early 1960s, the number of branches increased markedly.

and loans. A similar, but not so extreme, expansion was taking place for other types of depository institutions.

Regulators exhibited a somewhat relaxed attitude regarding mergers during this expansion in number of firms and branches. The Bank Merger Act of 1960, while specifying that competition was an important consideration in approving mergers, provided some legislative guidelines allowing mergers. The courts resolved the contradiction of encouraging competition with new entrants while at the same time allowing mergers.

The Department of Justice filed several suits to counteract the impression that the Bank Merger Act provided less stringent standards for bank mergers than those previously existing. The application of antitrust laws to the financial industry was something new. For years the industry was perceived as being exempt from the provisions of the Sherman and Clayton Acts.

The criteria for review in considering mergers were at issue. Regulators had concentrated on issues related to convenience of service and effects on bank performance. In the case *United States* vs. *The Philadelphia National Bank* (1963), the Supreme Court clearly stated the strict standards of the antitrust laws applied to bank mergers. Factors affecting competition were more important than convenience or performance.

BANKING TODAY 14.1 Court Allows Bank Expansion into Discount Brokerage

A January 1987 U.S. Supreme Court decision overturned an appeals court ruling that discount brokerage services in national bank branch operations violated the 1927 McFadden Act. (Discount brokers trade securities but do not offer investment advice to clients in the way full-service brokers do.) The McFadden Act limited the types of business that can be conducted by branch banks.

This ruling gives impetus to increased competition by national banks with brokerage firms although it does not eliminate the legal separation of commercial and investment banking (refer to Money Today 13.2). Bank holding companies have been permitted to operate discount brokerage subsidiaries since the 1984 Supreme Court ruling, but this more recent decision makes it less expensive for banks to establish such subsidiaries (since they no longer need to set aside a specified amount of capital for each brokerage subsidiary).

The case leading to the January 1987 decision resulted from a 1982 Comptroller of the Currency decision approving entrance by a California bank into the discount brokerage business. The Comptroller had concluded that brokerage operations were not bank branches because they did not accept deposits, issue checking accounts, or make loans. A challenge to this decision led to a 1985 circuit court ruling against the Comptroller's actions.

The 1987 decision affirmed the Comptroller's actions. The Supreme Court concluded that discount brokerage offices are not bank branches. Since the McFadden Act limits only "core banking functions," the Act "need not be read to encompass all the business in which the bank engages."

The ruling allowed national banks to compete more vigorously on a national basis with brokerage houses. The Court's action was another in a series of legal decisions blurring the distinction between commercial and investment banking. It gave banks the opportunity to offer more complete financial services at a time when brokers, such as Merrill Lynch, were encroaching on financial activities traditionally reserved for commercial banks.

Amendments to the Bank Merger Act passed in 1966 did not modify the Court's position; in *United States* vs. *The Provident National Bank* (1967) the Court again ruled that bank mergers are subject to the standards of antitrust legislation, specifying that the anticompetitive effect of a merger cannot be overlooked simply because the combined bank might render better customer services. The anticompetitive effects can be outweighed only if the public interest could not have been furthered without the merger.

The Court even overruled the notion that specific types of banking services constitute the appropriate market. In *United States* vs. *Phillipsburg National Bank* (1970), the Court determined that commercial banking in general was the relevant market.

The courts had clearly favored maintenance of competition. Whether to expand competition by reducing regulations was the responsibility of legislators. A growing body of evidence and the thrift crisis of the 1970s led to efforts at deregulation.

Changing Attitudes Prompt Reassessment

The changing attitudes about competition in the financial industry, whatever the motivation, led to the formation of national commissions to investigate the industry and recommend reforms. These commissions overwhelmingly supported deregulation and structural reform, but they resulted in no legislative action. It was the financial crisis faced by thrifts that prompted reform.

Industry Studies Recommend Changes

Throughout the 1960s more policy makers and economists realized that the institutional structure of the financial system and its overarching regulatory framework were grossly outdated. The system's structure and regulatory framework had evolved from the financial reforms of the 1930s. Designed to meet the perceived need for stability and security, these reforms had created a system which was not compatible with the changing scope of financial services or with the economic events that were challenging the system.

The June, 1970, Penn Central Transportation Company bankruptcy sent shock waves through the financial markets and made the financial system's limitations all the more visible. People began to question whether the financial system was flexible and responsive enough to handle the kinds of financial problems that an event like this might set into motion.

Growing out of those concerns was the formation of several national commissions to study parts of the financial system and to recommend reforms.[2] These commissions included:

- the Presidential Commission on Financial Structure and Regulation (the Hunt Commission, 1971),
- the Securities and Exchange Commission's "Institutional Investor Study Report on the SEC" (1971),
- the National Commission on Consumer Finances "Report of the NCCF" (1972),
- the House Banking Committee's "Financial Institutions and the National Economy (FINE) Report" (1975), and
- the National Committee on Electronic Funds Transfers' "EFT in the U.S.: Policy Recommendations and the Public Interest" (1978).

Although these studies each had a somewhat different focus, they reinforced one another's conclusions that the system needed reform. It could not adapt to changing economic conditions, to technological breakthroughs and their implications, to the economic condition of stagflation, or to the development of new financial instruments.

The Hunt Commission explicitly stated an attitude that had been developing throughout the 1960s. At the heart of this attitude was the philosophy that competitive markets are essential for an efficient financial system. The Commission's report stated that the United States should move toward free functioning financial markets with all types of financial intermediaries possessing the powers which would allow them to compete in these markets. This reform recommendation was intended to reduce the functional segmentation in place since the 1930s. The Hunt Commission concluded that the system needed general restructuring; to initiate reforms in ways other than as a complete package would result in failure.

The Congressional FINE Report enumerated over three dozen basic principles for an effective and efficient financial system. This report emphasized equity considerations for all types of financial intermediaries and the need for more effective implementation of monetary policy.

Some of the most important recommendations included in both the Hunt study and the FINE Report were the following:

1. removal of interest rate ceilings (Regulation Q),
2. elimination of commercial banks' monopoly over checking accounts,

---

[2] For an excellent discussion of these issues from which this section is adapted, see Thomas F. Cargill and Gillian G. Garcia, *Financial Deregulation and Monetary Control: Historical Perspective and Impact of the Act* (Stanford, CA: The Hoover Press, 1982).

3. expansion of the range of investment opportunities (uses of funds) available to depository institutions,

4. relaxation of barriers to entry restrictions,

5. expansion of intrastate and interstate branching, and

6. elimination of overlap of regulatory supervisory functions by reducing the number of agencies and combining authority.

These recommendations resulted in no immediate changes in the financial system. Congress incorporated many of them into the Financial Institutions Act which members introduced into Congress in 1973 and again in 1975. Opposition to the reforms prevented the legislation from being enacted into law; however, many of these recommendations did eventually find their way into law.

Financial Crisis Stimulates Reform

Although national commissions recommended changes, various factors conspired to prevent reforms from becoming law. Many observers of the actions of legislators and regulators have noted that financial institution reform in this country is crisis-oriented. Awareness alone is not sufficient to prompt change; significant malfunctions or near financial collapse are the only factors which will result in legislative reform. This was certainly the case with the reforms of 1980 and 1982.[3]

Thrift institutions (savings and loan associations, credit unions, and mutual savings banks) were particularly hard hit by the changing economic conditions of the 1970s. Since the restructuring of the financial system as a result of the Great Depression, the thrift institutions had been the primary repositories for household savings and the major sources of home mortgage credit. Legislation in the 1930s that was intended to provide a secure market for the thrifts had actually become a straitjacket. Thrifts generated funds through short-term deposits while making long-term investments. Throughout most of the post–World War II period the spread between mortgage interest rates and the regulated interest rates on deposits gave the thrifts a profitable operating margin. Rising interest rates caught the thrifts with assets that were long-term investments paying low interest rates while they were forced to pay higher rates to attract deposit liabilities. Thrifts could not sell these mortgages because the market for them had collapsed. To make

---

[3] For a detailed discussion of events leading to these legislative reforms, see *Leveling the Playing Field: A Review of the DIDMCA of 1980 and the Garn-St Germain Depository Institution Act of 1982* (Chicago: Federal Reserve Bank of Chicago, 1983).

matters worse, government ceilings on deposit interest rates resulted in massive disintermediation so that short-term funds were not available in sufficient quantity.

Rising interest rates during the late 1970s and early 1980s hurt all types of depository institutions. Interest rate ceilings prevented them from competing for funds (see Figure 14.3). All types of nondepository financial institutions, such as brokerage houses, began offering higher interest rates through instruments not subject to ceilings. Money market mutual funds are the best example. The disintermediation process accelerated as interest rates rose.

This combination of economic forces hit the thrifts particularly hard because of the maturity imbalance between their assets (invested long term) and their liabilities (deposits made for the short term). Beyond this the thrifts' reliance on mortgage lending meant that the collapse of the housing industry resulted in fewer investment opportunities. New home construction was at the lowest level since the end of World War II.

Increasing disintermediation, a downward sloping yield curve meaning the cost of funds exceeded revenue from investments, and declining new investment opportunities because of low rates in residential construction, all combined to put thrifts in a severe crisis. Thrifts experienced a net outflow of funds in this period. Figure 14.4 reveals how savings and loans' returns-

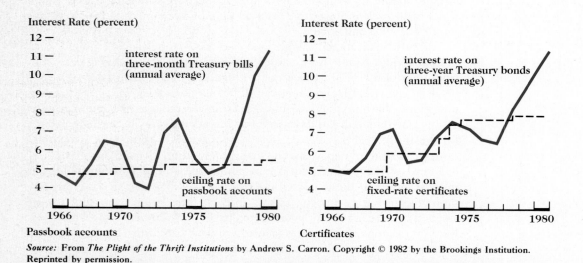

Source: From *The Plight of the Thrift Institutions* by Andrew S. Carron. Copyright © 1982 by the Brookings Institution. Reprinted by permission.

FIGURE 14.3 *Deposit Rate Ceilings at Thrift Institutions and Market Interest Rates, 1966–1980* These figures illustrate the problem deposit rate ceilings (the ceilings imposed by Regulation Q) caused for depository institutions, especially the thrifts. Despite the rise in other interest rates, the passbook rate and the fixed rate certificate rate of return lagged causing serious disintermediation.

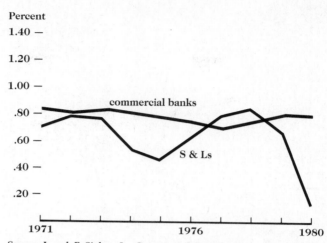

Percent

Source: Joseph F. Sinkey, Jr., *Commercial Bank Financial Managment*, 2nd edition (New York: Macmillan Publishing Company, 1986): 134. Reprinted by permission.

FIGURE 14.4   *S & Ls and Commercial Bank Return on Assets, 1971–1980*
This figure reveals the serious problem S & Ls faced as a result of disintermediation. Commercial banks were able to maintain their return on assets rate but S & L rates declined precipitously.

on-assets declined precipitously in the late 1970s. The thrift industry incurred losses in 1980 for the first time since the Great Depression.[4]

Regulators made some attempts to deal with the situation. In early 1978 regulatory authorities had authorized activities such as automatic transfer accounts at commercial banks and share drafts at credit unions (essentially allowing the payment of interest on demand deposits). In 1979 the Court declared these activities illegal because they had not been specifically authorized by Congress. The Court delayed its ban until the end of the year to give Congress time to enact legislation.

Regulatory authorities authorized new deposit instruments such as large denomination certificates of deposit and money market certificates. These new instruments helped depository institutions compete for funds by paying higher interest rates. Although reducing disintermediation and helping commercial banks, these actions further aggravated the plight of the thrifts. They were now forced to pay even higher rates to attract funds, thus accentuating the negative spread between rates paid and rates earned on their existing home mortgages.

---

[4] For a thorough analysis of the problem of the thrifts, see Andrew S. Carron, *The Plight of the Thrift Institutions* (Washington: The Brookings Institution, 1982).

BANKING TODAY

14.2

The Thrift Industry Faces Another Crisis

The 1981–82 recession, combined with disintermediation caused by the period of high interest rates, dealt the thrift industry a serious blow. In the years since then the number of thrift institutions shrunk from around 4000 to just over 3200. With economic recovery after the recession, financial reform legislation, and fewer institutions, many predicted the thrift industry would rebound (in some states commercial banks were changing to S & L charters to take advantage of greater flexibility in investment opportunities).

Despite early optimism for a return to profitability, the thrift industry is facing another crisis. This one may require more than financial reform legislation to save the industry.

A large portion of the thrift industry received only marginal benefits from the lower interest rates and the increased operational flexibility. The Government Accounting Office reported in early 1986 that 471 thrifts (15 percent) have seen their condition worsen or, at best, remain unchanged.

Another 800 thrifts (26 percent) are profitable, but their long-term viability is questionable. FSLIC Chairman, Edwin Gray, estimated that 130 thrifts, with $47.6 billion in assets, needed attention by the end of 1986.

The Reagan administration proposed legislation in the spring of 1986 to bail out the thrift industry's insurance fund (FSLIC) so that depositors need not worry about the safety of their deposits. The funds for the FSLIC would assure that troubled thrifts could be salvaged with little or no disruption to the industry. That legislation was "bottled-up" in the 99th Congress in fall 1986 by a dispute between the Federal Home Loan Bank Board and House Majority Leader Jim Wright of Texas.

Analysts estimate that the FSLIC would incur losses of at least $29 billion (some say $50 billion) if it were to liquidate the currently troubled thrifts. Such losses would jeopardize the insurance system.

Critics of this approach argue that the government should not subsidize inefficient operations. They argue for liquidation of the unstable thrifts, sale of other unprofitable ones, and a merger of all thrifts into the more solvent Federal Deposit Insurance Corporation program. Without such a program these critics charge that the Administration's bailout will just cost the taxpayers and the solvent thrifts a lot of money; it won't solve the current thrift crisis.

Note: For more details on the thrift crisis, see Thomas M. Buynak, "The Thrift Industry: Reconstruction in Progress," Federal Reserve Bank of Cleveland *Economic Commentary* (June 1986); and Bert Ely, "This Savings and Loan Mess Won't Go Away," *The Wall Street Journal* (July 17, 1986).

The Federal Savings and Loan Insurance Corporation worked to prevent massive failures by providing financial assistance to struggling savings and loans, and encouraging mergers, even across state lines, to maintain the operations of many hard-pressed firms. Congress permitted all depository institutions to attract deposits through the "all savers certificates"; the first $1000 in interest on these certificates was tax-exempt.

Such piecemeal attempts at changing the conditions under which the thrift institution operated could not prevent the decline in the number of thrifts. For example, the number of savings and loans declined by one-quarter between 1980 and 1984. The situation required a basic structural change in the industry. This came with the passage of two major pieces of reform legislation, the Depository Institution Deregulation and Monetary Control Act of 1980 and the Garn-St Germain Act of 1982.

Legislative Actions Create Different Market Structure

The legislative actions of 1980 and 1982 created a new structure for the financial industry. The acts provided for a more "level playing field" for all types of financial institutions. Commercial banks, savings and loan associations, mutual savings banks, and credit unions competed for deposits and observed similar reserve requirements. Eventually they competed with nondepository institutions as other types of financial institutions began to perform many of the functions traditionally reserved for banks, savings and loans, and credit unions. Although the legislation enacted in the early 1980s was very complex, this summary provides the background necessary to analyze the implications of a deregulated financial industry.[5]

The Depository Institution Deregulation and Monetary Control Act, 1980

The economic conditions previously described forced Congress to restructure the country's financial system. Beyond the pressure of the thrift crisis, the Federal Reserve System was also pressuring Congress. The Fed was facing declining membership because of its strict reserve requirements. In part because of declining membership the Fed was having difficulty managing the nation's money supply.

Congress responded to these pressures by passing a far-reaching financial reform act. The Depository Institutions Deregulation and Monetary Control Act (DIDMCA) was rushed through Congress in February and March of 1980 as interest rates soared to record high levels. President Carter signed the legislation into law on March 31. As its name implies, this act has two categories of reform—the financial system deregulation provisions and the monetary control provisions. The act's provisions are summarized in Table 14.3. The monetary control aspects are discussed in Chapter 19.

---

[5] *Financial Deregulation and Monetary Control* by Thomas F. Cargill and Gillian G. Garcia (Stanford, CA: The Hoover Press, 1985) provides a detailed discussion of the orgins, content, and impacts of these reform measures.

Deregulation provisions	Effective date
1. Permits nationwide NOW accounts for all deposit institutions	December 31, 1980
2. Phases out deposit interest rate ceilings	Over a 6-year period
3. Expands the lending powers of credit unions, savings and loan associations, and mutual savings banks	September 1, 1980
4. Eliminates state usury ceilings on first mortgage loans for residences. Raises loan rate ceiling for credit union loans	March 31, 1980
5. Increases level of federally insured deposits	March 31, 1980
Monetary control provisions	
1. Establishes reserve requirements for transactions accounts at all deposit institutions. Removes reserve requirements on personal savings accounts	Four-year phase-in for member banks; eight-year phase-in for non-member banks and other deposit institutions, both beginning September 1, 1980
2. Allows borrowing from the Fed for all deposit institutions	March 31, 1980
3. Makes Fed services available to deposit institutions on a fee basis	September 1, 1981

TABLE 14.3 *Summary of Financial Reform Act*

Policy makers intended the deregulatory provisions of the DIDMCA to increase competition in the financial system by (1) increasing the scope of deposit-taking (expanding the sources of funds), (2) expanding the lending activities (increasing the uses of funds for depository institutions), and (3) returning pricing activities to the marketplace by removing or modifying interest-rate constraints.

Observers were correct when they called the DIDMCA the most important piece of financial legislation since the reforms of the 1930s. The primary purpose of the deregulation provision was to restore a competitive environment to the financial industry. The act does not refer to banks or savings and loan associations; it refers to depository institutions.

Despite its contributions to reform of the financial system, conditions persisted which would require further reform initiatives. Specifically,

- high interest rates prevented a rapid phase-out of Regulation Q ceilings,
- the disintermediation process continued; money market mutual funds continued to grow,

- deteriorating conditions, perhaps aggravated by competition for funds, forced more depository institutions to fail and regulators did not have sufficient power to deal with these problems, and
- thrift institutions, especially savings and loans, were still tied to long-term, fixed rate mortgages as assets and to often volatile short-term liabilities.

Congress saw that additional restructuring of the system was necessary. It responded with a second major piece of reform legislation, the Garn-St Germain Act, 1982.

Garn-St Germain Act

The 1982 legislation is much more narrow in its focus. The stated objective of the legislation is to support the thrift sector of the financial industry. The act itself is lengthy and complicated, but it includes three categories of provisions.

1. *Expanded Sources of Funds.* The act makes it easier for depository institutions to compete for funds by allowing them to offer the equivalent of money market mutual funds (called *money market deposit accounts—* MMDA) and by setting January 1, 1984, as a deadline for eliminating Regulation Q differentials between banks and non-bank depository institutions.

2. *Expanded Uses of Funds.* The Garn-St Germain Act gives thrifts more options, such as authorizing them to offer commercial loans, invest in state and local government obligations, and make consumer and educational loans.

3. *Emergency Powers.* The act gave federal agencies expanded powers for dealing with failing institutions. (Those powers expired October, 1985.) As a result of these provisions the FDIC and FSLIC could issue guarantees, assume an institution's assets and liabilities, make loans to troubled firms, and arrange mergers and acquisitions (including purchases of savings and loans by banks and mergers across state lines).

The Garn-St Germain Act enhanced the deregulatory provisions of the DIDMCA by increasing competition within the financial industry. Taken together these reform acts eliminated many barriers to competition, for example, the market segmentation restricting the thrifts to the home mortgage market. Furthermore, they allowed market factors to establish deposit and loan rates and to dictate the types of services offered and the fees attached to those services. Finally these reforms enhanced the choices available to consumers.

Chapter Conclusion

The financial services industry has undergone major changes in the last fifty years. Attitudes on competition in the industry have changed during that period of time too. The issue of safety and soundness of the system is not of paramount concern today as it was in the years after the major banking collapse of the 1930s. Perhaps the safety net of deposit insurance and careful supervision has eliminated the need for such concern. Or perhaps the new attitude emphasizing the vitality of deregulated industries has pushed the concern for safety into the background. Attitudes, and with them rules of behavior, have changed.

Gaining some understanding of these attitudes, their effects on industry structure, both before 1980 and after, and the role of policy makers in the oversight of the financial services industry will help you analyze the ongoing policy issues discussed in the next chapter. The process of change in the financial services industry continues.

Consider These Questions

1. Why was it the consensus of policy makers following the banking failures of the 1920s and 1930s that entry into the industry should be restricted?

2. Are there any explanations for the decline in the number of financial institutions during the 1920s and 1930s beside the "evils of competition" argument?

3. What economic theory did policy makers utilize in their decision to restrict competition?

4. What role have the courts played in the changing structure of the financial services industry?

5. Why were the rates of return for depository institutions, illustrated in Table 14.2, a factor in the easing of restrictions on entry into the industry?

6. Summarize the findings of the commissions that studied the financial industry during the 1960s and 1970s. Why do you think it took so long for their recommendations to become law?

7. What caused the crisis for the thrift institutions? Why couldn't they adjust?

8. What role did the thrift crisis play in the passage of deregulatory reform?

9. How did the DIDMCA and the Garn-St Germain Act change the structure of the financial services industry?

10. What economic theories underlay the deregulatory legislation of 1980 and 1982?

Suggestions for Further Reading

Bennett, Robert A. "Another Crisis Engulfs the Thrifts." In *The New York Times*, July 22, 1984.

Provides a thorough update on the problems faced by the thrifts despite some recovery after 1982.

Benston, George J., ed. *Financial Services: The Changing Institutions and Government Policy.* Englewood Cliffs, N.J.: Prentice-Hall, 1983.

One of the authorities on financial services provides an overview of the changing institutions and the role of government in the process of change.

—————, Robert A. Eisenbeis, et al. *Perspectives on Safe and Sound Banking: Past, Present, and Future.* Cambridge, Mass.: MIT Press, 1986.

Study commissioned by the American Bankers Association includes articles by major banking analysts. See especially chapters 1, 2 and 11 for a review of the issues discussed in this chapter.

Bush, George, chairman. *Blueprint for Reform: The Report of the Vice President's Task Force on Regulation of Financial Services.* Washington, D.C.: U. S. Government Printing Office, 1984.

Title provides explanation of document. Many of the recommendations, although thoughtful, have not found their way into either legislative or regulatory statutes. Interesting reading nonetheless.

Cargill, Thomas F. and Gillian G. Garcia. *Financial Reform in the 1980s.* Stanford, CA: Hoover Institution Press, 1985.

Probably the best single source for an overview of the issues relating to financial reform from both a historical and contemporary perspective.

Carron, Andrew S. *The Plight of the Thrift Institutions.* Washington, D.C.: The Brookings Institution, 1982.

Short booklet outlining basic problems faced by thrift institutions before Garn-St Germain Act of 1982.

Garcia, Gillian, et al. "The Garn-St Germain Depository Institution Act of 1982." In Federal Reserve Bank of Chicago *Economic Perspectives* VII, 2 (March/April 1983): 3–31.

Excellent article providing an explanation of forces behind this legislation, its composition and intended effects.

Heggestad, Arnold E. "Fundamentals of Mergers and Acquisitions." In *Handbook for Banking Strategy*, edited by R. C. Aspinwall and R. A.

Eisenbeis, 703–24. New York: John Wiley, 1985.

Interesting analysis of mergers and acquisitions from bankers perspective.

Hester, Donald D. "Innovations and Monetary Control." In *Brookings Papers on Economic Activity* 1 (1981): 141–89.

Illustrates that a return to controls would not improve condition of thrift institutions in long run.

——————. "Depository Institutions Deregulation and Monetary Control Act of 1980: A Summary." Federal Reserve Bank of Chicago, 1980.

Brief account of landmark legislation.

——————. "Assessment of Business Expansion Opportunities for Banking." In a study prepared by Arthur Young and Company for the American Bankers Association, 1983.

Interesting analysis of opportunities for diversification.

CHAPTER FIFTEEN

THE DEREGULATED FINANCIAL INDUSTRY

The plain truth is, the American banking industry has arrived at a crossroads . . . and there's nobody out there directing traffic.

Edward R. Telling, CEO, Sears, Roebuck and Company
Address to Economic Club of Detroit, March 11, 1985

The deregulation legislation discussed in the last chapter hastened changes in the financial services industry. By restoring competition to the industry, this legislation gave efficient firms an opportunity to succeed but also removed safeguards against inefficient firms failing.

Deregulation resulted in both short-term and long-term changes. Short-term changes include new sources and uses of funds, great differences in performance across firms, and increasing consolidation. A transforming industry structure and challenges to depository institutions by other types of financial firms are among the longer term changes. But the legislation passed in the early 1980s did not address all of the issues confronting the financial services industry. This chapter describes continuing efforts to eliminate gaps in the DIDMCA and the Garn-St Germain Act.

The impact of competition deserves particular attention. The discussion of the new competitive environment describes competition's effects on depository institution performance and its significance for the structure of the industry. The interstate banking debate is one of the major issues arising in this new competitive environment. This chapter analyzes the degree to which interstate banking already exists, the implications of increasing interstate activities, and the likely outcome of the interstate banking debate.

The chapter concludes with an exploration of some other important policy issues: the crisis in deposit insurance, the prospects for small banks in the new environment, and the effects of deregulation for monetary control.

Chapter Objectives

Your overall goal in reading this chapter is to develop a basic understanding of the current conditions in the deregulated financial industry. Specifically, by the end of this chapter you will:

- Understand the results of the deregulation legislation on financial firms.
    Describe effects on depository firms' sources and uses of funds.
    Identify the effects of new operating procedures on firms' performance.

- Analyze the ongoing changes in the industry.
    Describe how deregulation augmented competition.
    Explain how innovation, such as transfer of risk and enhanced liquidity, has dictated increased competition.

- Analyze the causes and effects of competition.
    Summarize the important principles of industrial organization as applied to the financial services industry.
    Explain how restrictions on product offerings and limitations on geographic expansion still exist.

- Relate changes in the early 1980s to a continuing trend in the industry.
    Predict future changes from legislative initiatives since 1982.

- Analyze alternative views on the implications of competition.
    Explain whether increasing firm failure and greater consolidation are inevitable.
    Describe conclusions implied by examining other recently deregulated industries.

- Analyze issues related to interstate banking.
    Explain the current status of interstate banking.
    Relate interstate banking to market concentration.

- Evaluate unresolved policy issues facing lawmakers.
    Give reasons for the problems of deposit insurance.
    Explain alternative reform recommendations for deposit insurance.
    Use criteria to justify whether small banks have a place in the new financial services industry.
    Explain whether continuing change will threaten or enhance the Fed's monetary control function.

The Deregulated Environment

The legislation passed in 1980 and 1982 is having far-reaching consequences for the financial industry. Deregulation is a major, but not exclusive, factor causing change in the financial services industry. Financial innovations and increasing competition, although interrelated with deregulation, are separate forces that affect the industry. To understand the industry you need to understand the immediate effects of the DIDMCA and Garn-St Germain Act. This understanding is a basis for analyzing the longer term implications as well as the interrelated forces which are shaping the industry.

Immediate Effects of Deregulation

The last chapter made the point that the financial crisis facing the thrift industry produced the deregulatory legislation. One of the major purposes of this legislation, especially the Garn-St Germain Act, was to rescue the thrift industry.

After suffering widespread losses during 1981 and 1982 because of high market interest rates, the thrift industry became marginally profitable during the next few years. The provisions of the legislation which gave thrifts greater flexibility to attract deposits (namely their ability to offer market interest rates on deposits and to offer transactions accounts) helped overcome the revenue outflow. Authorization for expanded powers in the areas of commercial and consumer lending and the ability to offer long-term mortgages with adjustable rates reduced the thrifts' reliance on interest-rate-insensitive mortgages. Legislative provisions allowing emergency rescue operations through mergers helped to prevent many thrifts from failing.

Still, despite these measures, the stabilization of the thrift industry resulted more from the decline in interest rates than anything prompted by the Garn-St Germain Act. The thrifts continue to face challenges that are being met by the merger of marginal institutions with stronger, more competitive ones. For example, from December 1979 to June 1984 the number of FSLIC institutions decreased by more than 20 percent, almost the entire decrease resulting from mergers.

Beyond addressing the emergency situation facing the thrifts, the deregulation legislation prompted new operating arrangements. The DIDMCA and Garn-St Germain Act combined with the technological advances and increasing pressure from nondepository institutions to create a very different *modus operandi* for firms in the industry. The legislation gave depository institutions great freedom to compete; it almost completely eliminated pricing restrictions. The increased competition has reduced margins of earnings on many conventional financial activities. This has forced depository institutions to innovate within the financial industry. For example, banks have begun to offer discount brokerage services, and to provide customers data processing and electronic transmission services.

While these legislative initiatives corrected some of the imbalances in the industry, they created the "problems" which accompany a competitive environment. Thrift institutions competed for new deposits but they had to pay market rates rather than regulated rates for these funds. The effects of deregulation are complex and require careful analysis.

Implications of the New Operating Environment

Industry observers have difficulty specifying exactly what aspects of the new operating environment stem from the deregulatory legislation rather than from economic conditions or technological advances. However, observers identify passage of the DIDMCA in 1980 as the watershed in the financial services industry. With this act, and the Garn-St Germain Act two years later, have come changes in the industry's sources, cost of funds, and changes in use of funds for depository institutions. These have combined to influence the performance of banks and thrifts over the past few years.[1]

A major purpose of the deregulatory legislation was to promote competition among depository institutions. In terms of sources of funds (deposits), the legislation gave banks and thrifts greater flexibility over the types of accounts they could offer to customers (for example, the Money Market Deposit Account). This resulted in noticeable changes in the composition of depository institutions' liabilities. Figure 15.1 illustrates how savings accounts have declined and how MMDAs, and to a certain extent Super NOW accounts, have increased.

Closely related to these changes in the composition of bank and thrift liabilities portfolios is the cost of funds. Depository institutions compete for funds with one another as well as with nondepository financial firms. With interest rate ceilings eliminated, depository institutions must pay market competitive rates. The changing nature of these firms' liabilities means that they have more funds in market rate accounts, which has raised their overall cost of funds. In 1959, noninterest bearing deposits accounted for 41 percent of depository institution liabilities. By 1983 this percentage was down to 10.5 percent. The increased cost of funds has forced depository institutions to

---

[1] For a thorough review of these issues, see Diana Fortier and Dave Phillis, "Bank and Thrift Performance Since DIDMCA," Federal Reserve Bank of Chicago *Economic Perspectives* IX, 5 (September/October 1985).

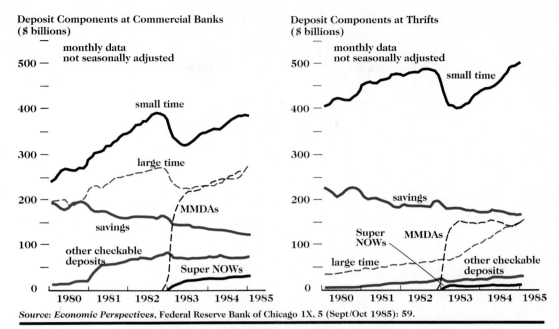

Deposit Components at Commercial Banks
($ billions)

Deposit Components at Thrifts
($ billions)

Source: *Economic Perspectives*, Federal Reserve Bank of Chicago 1X, 5 (Sept/Oct 1985): 59.

FIGURE 15.1 *Changing Composition of Depository Institution Liabilities* One result of the deregulatory legislation was to give banks and thrifts greater flexibility in the types of deposit instruments they could offer. These figures reveal how, after the 1982 legislations, both types of depository institutions began utilizing money market deposit accounts (MMDAs) and Super NOW accounts. Small time deposits declined initially but have recovered.

control other expenses (for example, salaries). Despite cost control measures and declining interest rates, data indicate that operating expenses as a portion of assets have risen for both banks and thrifts.[2]

The increasing cost of funds has stimulated depository institutions to adopt more systematic and explicit pricing policies for loans and for services. For example, free checking is virtually a thing of the past and safe-deposit charges now reflect the full cost of that service. Furthermore, firms have sought ways to "manage" interest rate risk by hedging the risk in the futures market. Packaging and selling mortages and other loans allow banks to shift interest rate risk.

The deregulation legislation also provided new uses of funds, especially for thrifts. Legislation allowed thrift institutions to expand into

---

[2] Fortier and Phillis found that between 1980 and 1984 the ratio of operating expenses to assets rose by 20 percent for banks and 15 percent for thrifts.

commercial and consumer loans. All depository institutions were able to reduce interest rate risk by offering variable-rate loans.

The new sources and uses of funds along with the new competitive environment have affected the performance of depository institutions in the years since 1980. Banks and thrift institutions have performed differently in one respect; banks maintained relatively steady net income whereas thrifts performed erratically. These institutions have performed similarly in another respect; small institutions for both groups are performing poorly.

When comparing net income for the four years following the beginning of deregulation with the period before the passage of the DIDMCA, commercial banks in every size class except the smallest maintained their level of net income. Because the smallest size class contains over 80 percent of all banks, net income for banks as a whole actually declined. This chapter will provide a closer look at the prospects for small banks in the deregulated environment.

Ongoing Forces for Change

The deregulation legislation was, by all accounts, hastened by the financial crisis facing thrifts during the late 1970s. This was not the only force moving the financial system toward the less restrictive environment. Deregulation, innovation, and competition interacted to create a financial industry which is much different today than it was ten years ago; those forces will continue to interact to guarantee that the industry will change over the next decade.

Deregulation legislation was, and continues to be, the necessary factor for change in the financial services industry. The DIDMCA and Garn-St Germain Act granted rights to depository institutions designed to create a "level playing field." Policy makers intended the acts to allow all types of depository institutions to compete on a fair and equal basis. The motivation behind the acts included a desire to restore safety and stability to an industry which was experiencing serious disruptions. Beyond this, Congress designed these acts to produce a more efficient system, one which provided customers with higher returns and lower costs.

Deregulation legislation attempted to achieve these goals primarily by removing price (or rate) restrictions. This encouraged competition, which fostered cost cutting and innovation. The legislation did not adequately address the issue of segmented markets. Neither act dealt with restrictions on branching or chartering. The acts did not resolve the issue of interstate banking or the question of expansion of bank holding companies. Depository institutions were encouraged to compete with one another within geographic regions. Competition beyond these geographic borders was left unresolved, as was the degree of allowable competition with nondepository institutions.

The degree of competition fostered by the deregulation legislation was sufficient to stimulate an accelerating rate of innovation and increasing competition.

Financial innovation had been under way before passage of the DIDMCA and Garn-St Germain Act. For example, in 1981 the Bank of California offered a money market fund type account through its London branch thereby claiming it was not subject to interest rate ceilings then in effect. In the same year the Dreyfus Corporation established "sweep accounts," moving money from bank savings accounts into money market funds on a daily basis. The needs of depository institutions prompted these kinds of innovations. Firms needed to broaden their access to the supply of funds and take advantage of technological breakthroughs that would allow the development of new instruments with complex financial structures. Generally speaking, financial innovations accomplish the following:

1. *Transfer risk.* With the increasing volatility of asset prices (because of exchange rate fluctuations and interest rate variability), firms have sought to develop instruments which allow them to transfer the price and credit risk. Examples of transferring risk include interest rate and foreign exchange options, currency swaps, and futures options.

2. *Exchange liquidity.* The shift from highly liquid savings deposits to less liquid capital market instruments and the movement out of demand deposits because of high interest rates created a desire to restore some liquidity through other instruments. Financial firms developed new instruments which would provide greater liquidity. Examples of exchange liquidity include cash management accounts and money market mutual funds.

3. *Generate credit.* The increasing demand for credit (borrowing by all economic sectors continues to increase) has led financial firms to develop new ways to meet credit demands. Examples of generating credit include providing a line of credit equal to increased home equity and the growing use of so-called junk bonds.

Economic pressures were moving the depository institutions toward financial innovation but the deregulation legislation and the competition it produced sped up the process.

Perhaps the greatest driving force behind changes in the industry is competition. With the deregulation legislation, depository institutions compete more strenuously against one another. Some of the performance problems cited earlier stem from pricing structures which cut into income and profitability. Such intra-industry competition will continue. It should produce better opportunities for consumers but it may produce some industry dislocations.

The deregulation legislation did not address competition between depository firms and non-bank financial firms (such as Merrill Lynch or Sears), nor did it provide any direction regarding international financial competition. Both of these areas will generate increasingly intense competition over the next few years.

Increasing Competition

By creating a more competitive environment, the deregulation legislation achieved one of its major goals. The motivation behind this movement toward increased competition stems from the lessons developed by the industrial organization approach to the financial services industry. Despite the far-reaching nature of the DIDMCA and the Garn-St Germain Act, Congress left numerous issues unresolved. The changing nature of the industry is forcing policy makers to consider new legislative initiatives to complete the job done by the early deregulatory acts.

Lessons From the IO Approach

As mentioned in Chapter 13, most industrial organization studies, including those in the banking industry, conclude that the industry's structure is related to the performance of firms within the industry. More specifically, an industry structure which encourages competition, through pricing policies and ease of entry into the market, is associated with lower product prices, greater assurance of normal, rather than excess, profits, and the greatest impetus for innovation and improved productivity.

This sort of model underlies the deregulation movement. Some financial industry observers argue that the movement toward more competitive markets in the 1980s is a return to the policy orientation of the 1920s. The movement toward competitive markets was interrupted by the massive bank failures during the Great Depression. This event changed policy makers' views on competition. Instead of seeing competition as the mechanism to provide the best possible product at the lowest price, they focused on increased risk and a less stable financial system as the results of competition. As described earlier in this chapter, this attitude led to the highly regulated financial industry structure that existed until the 1980s.

The changing attitudes about the value of competition and the movement to create a competitive industrial structure in the financial services industry are consistent with attitudes and policy actions in other industries. Most notable among these are the airline, telecommunications, and long-haul trucking industries. These industries are continuing to undergo changes, but already we can see that the economists' competitive model is accurate in predicting falling product prices. In the airline industry, the fares for routes in demand have declined because demand dictates competition. The same results are occurring in other industries.

In order to see the predicted results of this competitive model, deregulation must affect all aspects of the market. The initial deregulatory legislation restored price and product competition to the financial services industry. Competition in the demand for funds has raised interest rates on savings deposits and added interest rates to demand deposits. Competition for deposits and freedom from constraints in offering financial instruments have led to a myriad of new deposit accounts. A fully competitive financial industry would include freedom for geographic competition—the ability of firms to enter markets wherever demand exists. Beyond this issue, policy makers need to address other conditions necessary for a competitive financial industry.

Issues Unresolved by Deregulatory Legislation

The DIDMCA and Garn-St Germain Act removed many of the barriers to competition in the financial services industry. For example, commercial banks can compete with savings and loan associations in terms of types of deposit accounts as well as interest rates paid and charged. Nonetheless, this legislation left some major issues unresolved. The most apparent related to product lines, geographic expansions, and bank holding company activities.

Segmented product lines persist despite some major changes since 1980. The deregulatory legislation created a level playing field among depository institutions, providing the greatest possible expansion of activities for the thrifts. The continuing plight of the thrifts results partly from their inability to move quickly to take advantage of their new powers. The legislation did not provide the opportunity for depository institutions to expand beyond the product lines traditionally reserved for them. A major occurrence challenging the position of depository institutions is the expansion of nondepository institutions into the banking business.

The expansion of nondepository firms into territory traditionally reserved for banks and savings and loans has created considerable concern on the part of traditional depository firms. The initial disintermediation came when Merrill Lynch, and subsequently other brokerage firms, began offering money market mutual fund accounts. The deregulatory legislation helped depository institutions compete in this arena but other incursions have ensued. Retail firms, such as Sears Roebuck, began offering a full array of financial services. Sears Financial Centers combined insurance (Allstate), brokerage services (Dean Witter), depository services (Sears Savings Bank), and real estate (Coldwell Banker).

In 1986 Sears began issuing its Discover Card, a multipurpose money card. With retail outlets throughout the country, Sears is positioned to become a national financial operation. Table 15.1 reveals that a number of non-banking firms already dominate the market of consumer lending. As these firms expand their financial services, they represent an even greater challenge. Other examples of nontraditional banking firms competing with commercial banks, savings and loan associations, mutual savings banks, and credit unions are General Motors, offering home mortgages through its GMAC division, and brokerage firms offering traditional depository services on behalf of depository institutions.

Depository institutions argue that since these nondepository firms are expanding into the banking business, they should have the right to compete in other types of financial services. Some erosion of restrictions is already occurring. The long-time separation of investment and commercial banking (stemming from the Glass-Steagall Act) is breaking down. Claiming that offering discount brokerage services is distinct from actually underwriting securities issues, many commercial banks have begun to compete with brokerage houses. For example, Bank of America acquired Charles Schwab and Company. A 1987 Supreme Court ruling provided impetus to this type of competition (see Banking Today 14.1). Other depository institutions have acquired real estate firms. And, while the restrictions on insurance services still exist, some commercial banks have furnished office space to insurance

General Motors	40.2
Citicorp	15.4
Sears	13.8
Ford Motor	11.9
BankAmerica Corp.	11.4
American Express	7.7
Prudential/Bache	6.7
Merrill Lynch	6.1
J. C. Penney	5.5
Security Pacific	5.5

Source: Christine Pavel and Harvey Rosenblum, "Banks and Non-banks: The Horse Race Continues" Federal Reserve Bank of Chicago *Economic Perspectives* (May/June 1985): 15.

TABLE 15.1 *Top Consumer Lenders ($ billions)*

firms to provide one-stop service. South Dakota is trying to lure financial firms by lowering its restrictions on commercial bank insurance activities.

A second area left unresolved by the early 1980s deregulation legislation related to geographic market expansion. the Garn-St Germain Act technically allowed acquisition of a troubled firm by another even if located across state lines, assuming state law did not prohibit such an acquisition. However, the deregulation legislation was silent on the issue of branching/chartering and interstate banking. Major depository institutions argue that to compete with national firms such as Sears, they need the right to expand operations within a state and across state lines. To a certain extent, such expansion is already taking place through bank holding companies.

The deregulatory legislation did not expand or clarify the powers of bank holding companies. Some bank companies function across state lines. A dozen were "grandfathered in" when the Bank Holding Company Act was passed in 1966. These and other bank holding companies are taking advantage of a loophole in the definition of a bank as provided by the Bank Holding Company Act. According to that legislation as amended in 1970, a bank is "any institution. . .which (1) accepts [demand] deposits. . . , and (2) engages in the business of making commercial loans." By abandoning one of these functions, major banks are applying for charters allowing them to expand across state lines claiming such "nonbank banks" are not subject to restrictions against interstate banking. Sometimes called "limited service banks," these operations give large commercial banks the opportunity to establish a presence in states throughout the nation.

Since the DIDMCA and Garn-St Germain Act left these issues unresolved, the result is a financial industry in confusion, relying in many cases on the courts to clarify the issues. Legislative initiatives since 1982 point to the unresolved issues in the industry. Before looking at the negative effects in the industry occurring despite further legislative reform, this chapter explores some of the legislation proposed over the last few years.

Legislative Initiatives Since 1982

The confusion and disarray, which has charcterized the financial services industry throughout the 1980s, is matched by the disagreement within Congress on further financial reform. During legislative sessions in 1983 through 1986, Congress considered additional legislation; none was passed. All agree that confusion exists over issues such as:

- the definitions of banks and thrifts and the precise scope of their powers (see Banking Today 15.1),
- provisions of the Bank Holding Company Act which allow "nonbank banks" to expand across state lines,

- inconsistencies between regulations applying to thrifts and commercial banks, especially regarding branching,
- ability of depository institutions to engage in real estate activities, securities sale and underwriting, and insurance business especially when state and federal laws conflict, and
- the extent to which financial firms, other than depository institutions, need supervision, especially relating to monetary control issues.

The problem in Congress is the lack of consensus on any of these issues. For years Representative St Germain, chairman of the House Bank-

BANKING TODAY 15.1

Is It a Bank or a Thrift? Only the Board of Directors Knows

No one could see the television commercial for Sun Bank of Orlando and think it's a savings and loan. Sun emphasizes the word "bank" in its name and glorifies its banking image.

But the largest savings and loan association in central Florida, called The First, also looks a lot like a bank in its ads. And it's promoting itself as a kind of money supermarket that offers a wide range of financial services just like a traditional bank.

Since deregulation, the distinction between what banks and thrifts do has become blurred. In fact, what they do really isn't so different. But, with increasing competition, some banks are trying to reclaim the image of being uniquely experienced and trustworthy. Meanwhile, thrifts are just as actively trying to obscure the differences.

Many thrifts have eliminated the words *thrift* or *savings and loans* from their titles. Some even call themselves *banks*. Just about any title is better than *thrift*, according to market analysts. To many, *thrift* is a Depression-sounding word.

Meanwhile the American Bankers Association is running national advertising to promote the notion that thrifts and other financial institutions just don't measure up to commercial banks.

There are a few real differences between banks and thrifts. Thrifts must have a majority of their assets in home mortgages, their mortgage rates tend to be more competitive, and they tend to offer higher returns on savings instruments and accounts. CBs generally have more capital and more experience with a range of financial products.

The battle in central Florida between The First and Sun Bank shows how banks and thrifts are aggressively marketing themselves in areas that used to belong almost exclusively to the other.

For example, Sun, which already has more branches, automated teller machines, and drive-in lines than The First, is training branch managers to make home mortgages and is paying them $25 for each completed loan application. Sun is so aggressive on

personal loans that it automatically sends out invitations to renew loans as soon as they are half paid.

The thrifts are fighting back. The First is promoting checking accounts, a service that only banks could offer before deregulation. It recently began offering cash rewards to employees who bring in new customers.

Last year, The First spent $1.5 million in "image" advertising; that's more than five times the amount it used to spend. Dropping "Savings and Loan" from its name is only part of the campaign. It calls its offices "Financial Centers" to reinforce the multiple services they can provide.

The competition will continue. While it may be more difficult for consumers to know exactly what type of institution they are going to, the services may be better as all types of depository institutions try to be that "hometown" institution that can best serve the public.

ing Committee, has blocked further financial deregulation while Senator Garn, chairman of the Senate Banking Committee, has resisted piecemeal legislation in favor of a broad-based bill to address the issues left unresolved by earlier legislation. The Reagan administration has argued consistently for broader bank powers. The Federal Reserve chairman has supported clarifying legislation but only if it would facilitate the Fed's monetary control responsibilities.

As a result of these disagreements, no legislation can gain a sufficient amount of support. Without the pressure exerted by an event such as the crisis of the thrifts at the end of the last decade, no stimulus is sufficient to force action. In the absence of any new legislation, the financial services industry, aided in many instances by regulatory authorities and the courts, moves further toward increasing competition in all areas including interstate banking.

Part of the reason no consensus has developed is that policy makers continue to disagree over the possible consequences of increasing competition for the industry. The near failure of Continental Illinois National Bank in 1983, at the time one of the largest commercial banks in the country, triggered renewed concern about the safety and soundness of deregulated industry.

Impact of Competition

The goal of the deregulation legislation was to improve the financial system by creating a competitive environment. Competition can take place only in a relatively laissez-faire environment. Without the security of regulation, some questions have arisen about the impact of competition on the safety and soundness of the financial services industry.

Since the deregulation legislation, and especially since the near failure of Continental Illinois National Bank, some industry observers are expressing concern about competition. The rescue of Continental Illinois focused attention on the problems facing the industry. Only the $4.5 billion federal bailout kept this institution from failing. If Continental could nearly fail, could other institutions? In the years since the Garn-St Germain Act, financial firms have behaved much as one would expect of firms in a deregulated, competitive industry. More new firms have entered the industry (for example, an average of 336 new banks per year since 1980, over 450 in 1984, compared with 239 banks per year during the 1970s). At the same time the failure rate is increasing.

The increasing number of bank failures in the last few years is alarming to many industry analysts. Consider the statistics on the next page.

- Forty-eight banks failed in 1983, 79 in 1984, 120 in 1985, more than 140 failed in 1986.

- A 1985 Government Accounting Office study reported that 465 of the nation's 3100 savings and loans were insolvent.

- For 1985, the FDIC listed 1141 problem banks, those needing special attention to fend off failure.

- In early 1986, the top 10 American banks held $55 billion in foreign loans with little likelihood that repayment would amount to more than fifty cents on the dollar.

The problems of firms within the financial services industry have been aggravated by the farm financial crisis, the collapse of the real-estate market in many geographic regions, and the decline in oil prices which devastated energy companies, drove down the value of energy stocks and threatened repayment of loans to these firms. Despite these causes, or maybe because of them, analysts are expressing concern over escalating failure rates for banks and savings and loans, and over the industrywide consolidation that may result.

An examination of another recently deregulated industry may provide insight into the longer term effects of deregulation and the competition it spurred. (See Banking Today 15.2 for an interesting parallel between banking and brewing.)

The airline industry was regulated much like the financial services industry—routes and prices were controlled, and new firm formation restricted. After deregulation, competition increased on the heavily traveled routes and prices dropped precipitously. New firms, such as the now-struggling People Express and Texas Air, rose to prominence. Major carriers abandoned low profit routes and commuter airlines prospered by filling the void. The intense competition caused problems for some carriers whose profits had been safeguarded during the period of government control. Some carriers collapsed, such as Braniff; others consolidated, such as Northwest and Republic; and others limped along facing difficult problems, such as Eastern and Continental.

The pattern is easy to summarize. Competition brings lower prices for products and services in heavy demand. The competition results in lower profits and firm failure for some companies. Marginal firms struggle to survive. While some small firms thrive by serving specialized markets, mergers represent a way for many firms to reduce their vulnerability to market pressure. The extent of consolidation and the degree to which competition is increased or decreased seems to vary from one industry to the next. All this leads one to wonder what will happen in the financial services industry. The interstate banking issue is key because expansion and consolidation will ultimately transcend geographic boundaries.

BANKING T●DAY   Bankers, This Bud's for You

Last summer, I was interviewing executives of Stroh Brewery for a banking client when it struck me that the way the brewing industry expanded and rapidly consolidated after the repeal of Prohibition was something bankers ought to think about as they consider their approaches to an expected wave of mergers and acquisitions. Federal regulation in both industries led in different ways to an excessive number of participants who eventually, as free competition emerged, had to face alternatives of expanding, internally and through acquisition, or selling the business.

Other similarities, including local ownership, customer loyalty and economies of scale, suggest that history might, in fact, repeat itself in some ways. If banking does track a similar course to brewing as it deregulates, then small banks may need to move toward sales more quickly than they have been, money center banks will acquire fewer regional banks than predicted, and the regionals will have a limited window of time in which to make deals. A very large number of regionals will disappear, just like regional brewers.

Very few of them survived consolidation of the brewing industry, which occurred in clear stages. Initially, small brewers were purchased by other small breweries and by regionals. Regionals were then purchased by larger regionals and eventually some nationals were formed.

Between 1980 and 1983, acquisitions included Schlitz, Schaefer, Olympia, and Pabst. Between 1971 and 1974, in con-trast, acquisitions included Associated Brewing, Duquesne Brewing, Rheingold, Jackson Brewing, Hamm, and a consolidation of Falstaff and General Brewing.

The same pattern seems to be starting in banking. As recently as 1981 there were only two bank mergers of more than $50 million. That rose to 14 in 1982 and more than 30 in 1983.

If banks want to compete successfully following deregulation, how do they use the expected pattern of mergers and acquisitions? The brewing industry shows several very different ways of proceeding.

Heileman started as a small regional brewery serving the upper Midwest. As industry overcapacity grew, small brewers began to close. Heileman apparently saw this trend as an opportunity to build a multi-regional family of brewers that could compete with the national brands. Its strategy was to purchase assets at distressed prices, take advantage of scale economies in distribution and production, but still keep the local branded image and tailor the product mix.

By 1981 the company had acquired more than 40 beer brands and 10 regional breweries. Its fixed asset cost per barrel of beer was less than Anheuser-Bush.

Unlike Heileman, Anheuser-Bush expanded through internal growth rather than acquisition. Phillip Morris did something similar when it acquired Miller and developed it into a national brand through investment rather than further acquisition.

Most small brewers were either acquired or gradually died, but some still exist. They either make a high-quality product and compete with foreign brews or are located in isolated geographic markets. A good example is Anchor Steam beer on the West Coast, which sells for three times the cost of most beers.

Similar to these small brewers, many community banks will survive, located in isolated markets and passed over by the initial wave of consolidation. Those that successfully resist early acquisition won't likely be acquired later.

Such at least are the lessons from brewing. It's unlikely that the banking industry will ever be identical to the structure of the brewing industry. It has fewer economies of scale and may be less susceptible to mass distribution. But good strategies rarely come from obvious parallels, particularly when an industry is in turmoil. There were once 750 breweries in this country. There are now 50. A few years ago there were 14,000 commercial banks. How many will there be at the turn of the century? Perhaps as many as there are now in Europe. In Germany, France, Great Britain, and Switzerland, four or fewer banks control more than half of all deposits. In the United States, 150 control less than half.

Source: "Bankers, This Bud's for You" by Joel Bleeke, *The Wall Street Journal*, January 13, 1984. Reprinted by permission.

Interstate Banking

One of the most significant results of the deregulation of the financial services industry is the breakdown of the geographical restraints on banking operations. The movement of banking operations across state lines, although not technically legal, is proceeding at a breakneck pace. How is it that banking firms can operate across state lines without specific entitlement legislation? What are the implications of this movement toward interstate banking? Will we end up with a full-blown interstate banking system? These questions merit some attention.

Interstate Banking Already Exists

Widespread interstate banking is prohibited by the McFadden Act and the Douglas Amendment to the Bank Holding Company Act. The McFadden Act constrains the geographic areas in which banks can operate while the Douglas Amendment restricts bank holding companies from acquiring banks across state lines. In spite of these acts, interstate banking is already here. The inability or unwillingness of Congress to pass comprehensive national banking legislation has resulted in state governments taking the initiative and financial organizations forcing the issue by finding loopholes in existing laws.

Depository institutions currently have six ways to operate on an interstate basis.

1. In 1970 Congress passed the Douglas Amendment to the Bank Holding Company Act. This legislation outlawed bank holding companies from acquiring banks across state lines. The law had a "grandfather clause" which allowed bank holding companies with branches in more than one state to retain those institutions. As a result, 12 legally sanctioned holding companies own a total of 139 out-of-state banks and over 1100 branches in 21 states.

2. Because of the way banks are defined, non-bank banks, or limited service banks, are exempt from the prohibition on interstate facilities. In early 1986 about 40 limited service banks operated across state lines. Table 15.2 shows the scenario of events that has resulted in hundreds of applications to the Comptroller of Currency for the establishment of such limited service banks in 38 states.

3. According to Section 4c(8) of the Bank Holding Company Act, holding companies can operate non-bank subsidiaries in more than one state. Thus, activities such as consumer and commercial lending, data processing, financial counseling, and leasing are conducted outside the home

December 1970	Congress amends regulatory definition to say a *bank* is an institution that both accepts demand deposits and makes commercial loans.
August 1980	Associates National Bank, a unit of Gulf & Western, chartered by Comptroller of the Currency as first true limited-service or "non-bank" bank.
March 1983	Comptroller of Currency declares moratorium through March 31, 1984 on new national charters for limited-service banks.
April 1983	J.C. Penney sidesteps moratorium by taking control of a Delaware bank and turning it into a limited-service bank.
May 1983	Dimension Financial Corp. applies to charter 31 such banks in 25 different states.
January 1984	Fed tries to hamper limited-service banks. Dimension sues.
March 1984	Fed permits a bank holding company to open a limited-service bank in Florida to dramatize need for Congressional action. Other bank holding companies flood the Comptroller with applications.
May 1984	Comptroller declares a new moratorium on charters until end of Congressional session.
October 1984	Comptroller lifts moratorium and begins to grant charters.
February 1985	Federal court enjoins Comptroller from charter approvals.
January 1986	Supreme Court rules against Fed's ruling in Dimension case.

TABLE 15.2   *The Impasse for Limted Service Banks*

state of many bank holding companies. In 1983, 139 bank holding companies operated 382 non-bank subsidiaries through over 5500 offices.

4. The Bank Holding Company Act Amendment allows acquisitions across state lines if such acquisitions are permitted by state law. In early 1986, 24 states had some sort of interstate banking legislation allowing such mergers or acquisitions. These arrangements are called regional compacts.

5. The Edge Act allows interstate operations to promote international trade. About 6000 Edge Act offices are located around the country.

6. The Garn-St Germain Act contained an emergency provision allowing banks and savings and loans to acquire failing institutions across state lines. Some major banks, such as Citicorp, have taken advantage of this provision to acquire troubled savings and loans in major market areas. Between 1982 and 1984, when savings and loans were having serious difficulty, more than 40 interstate acquisitions took place.

As a result of these special provisions or loopholes, interstate banking exists on a limited scale. The major money center banks (for example, Citicorp, Chase Manhattan, Bank of America) and non-bank financial firms (for example, Sears, J.C. Penney) continue to press for Congressional action on national legislation. Congress has been slow to act, but the move toward banking across state lines seems inevitable. The interstate banking issue heightens the debate about the implications of interstate banking on concentration in the financial services industry. There is concern, especially in rural areas, that, once these banking giants are allowed to expand nationally, they will force small, regional banks out of business.

Implications for Concentration

Although federal law technically prohibits interstate banking, financial institutions have discovered innovative ways to circumvent this prohibition. Without national enabling legislation, innovations by nondepository institutions will accentuate the inequities which currently exist. One of the issues which confronts policy makers, and which will continue to generate debate even after enabling legislation, is the extent to which interstate banking will affect competition and concentration. Underlying this debate is the economists' notion that competition produces the greatest social welfare. This raises the question of what effect a more liberal approach to interstate banking will have on the industry.

Those arguing against interstate banking claim the result would be market concentration. Major banking operations would expand into new markets, using their size to gain an advantage over smaller local and regional banks, and capture a large market share so they could either drive smaller competitors out of business or gain a position of oligopolistic price leadership. Competition would give way to market concentration and the detrimental price and service implications associated with imperfect markets. Figure 15.2 represents this line of reasoning.

FIGURE 15.2 *Pattern of Market Concentration, I* This figure outlines one scenario which might result if interstate banking is authorized. In this case consumers are disadvantaged.

Proponents of interstate banking see a different end result. They argue that competitive pressure from major firms will actually improve industry performance and enhance consumer welfare. Whether the entry of new firms leads to some increase in local market concentration or to more firms in each market, the firms in these markets will compete more vigorously than firms in locally protected markets do with prohibitions on interstate banking. Figure 15.3 illustrates this view.

Analysts will not know which argument is right until some time well after Congress acts to authorize interstate banking, if it ever does. Empirical work will lend some insights. While no conclusive results exist, there is a growing body of research which indicates that concentration is unlikely to produce monopoly profits for firms in local markets.[3]

Recall from Chapter 13 that a quick review of studies on concentration indicated little change in local market concentration but some indication of increased concentration at the state level when regional compacts allow firms to expand across state lines. Studies continue and there is no clear-cut answer (in part because the studies cover relatively short time periods, because they might not compare equivalent markets, or because measures of concentration may be inappropriate).

Despite the disagreements, many industry analysts conclude that interstate banking will result in some increase in concentration, at least on a regional basis.[4] The industry has experienced a slight increase in concentra-

---

[3] A recent summary of the literature appeared in the Federal Reserve Bank of Cleveland's November 1, 1986, *Economic Commentary* in an article by Gary Whalen entitled, "Competition and Bank Profitability: Recent Evidence."

[4] Two studies with contrasting results are Charles Morris, "The Competitive Effects of Interstate Banking," Federal Reserve Bank of Kansas City *Economic Review* (November 1984): 3–16; and Stephen A. Rhoades, "Concentration in Local and National Markets," Federal Reserve Bank of Atlanta *Economic Review* (March 1985): 28–30.

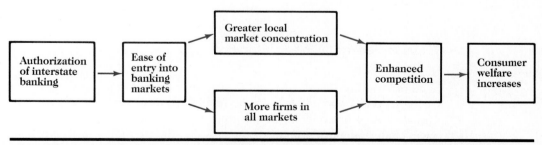

FIGURE 15.3   *Pattern of Market Concentration, II*   In contrast to Figure 15.2, this scenario results in consumer welfare increasing.

tion since 1980. But, statewide concentration, as measured by 5-firm deposit concentration ratios, is greater for states with statewide branching (72.4 percent) than those with limited branching (51 percent). The question facing policy makers is whether the cost of some increase in concentration is outweighed by the apparent benefits.

An expanding system of regional interstate banking has developed. Most observers conclude this trend will continue in the short run. State legislatures are approving reciprocal agreements, mostly on a regional basis. Under such arrangements, banks from one or more states may expand into the other and vice versa. These agreements are creating limited interstate banking. Figure 15.4 shows one possible regional interstate banking arrangement.

One of the results of this approach to interstate banking is that regional banks can grow, through merger, acquisition, and expansion. They will be in a better position to compete with the major money center banks in New York and California. (Note that Figure 15.4 shows both New York and California without any regional compacts.) By delaying a movement to full interstate banking, Congress may have created a situation with more strong banks capable of competing on a national level.

The issue of interstate banking is just one of many confronting policy makers as a result of deregulation. The financial services industry is in transition, some would say turmoil. Changes will continue. In the process of change, problems will need attention.

Additional Issues for Policy Makers

Whether deregulation continues or reregulation gains momentum, certain important issues need consideration by policy makers. In fact, these issues may have a strong influence on the direction financial industry reform takes over the next few years.

Crisis in Federal Deposit Insurance

The rise in commercial bank and thrift institution failures over the past few years has put a severe stress on the federal deposit insurance system. The near-failure of Continental Illinois drew attention to some of the problems facing federal deposit insurance programs, but the steady rise in smaller bank or thrift institution failure rates will be more likely to force action.

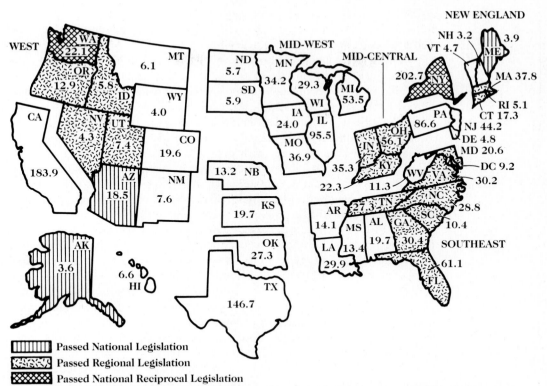

WEST

NEW ENGLAND

MID-WEST

MID-CENTRAL

SOUTHEAST

| | Passed National Legislation
| | Passed Regional Legislation
| | Passed National Reciprocal Legislation

Note: This map does not indicate states with limited purpose, grandfathered or troubled institution laws. The numbers refer to 1984 commercial bank deposits in billions of dollars.

Source: From "Regional Interstate Banking: New England Experiment Spreads" by Richard F. Syron, Economic Association 1985 Annual Meeting. Reprinted by permission of the Federal Reserve Bank of Boston.

FIGURE 15.4 *Principal Interstate Banking Regions, September 1985* Interstate banking may well result in regional rather than national banking. This is one possibility for banking regions.

Deposit insurance, remember, had its origins in the post-Depression desire to restore confidence in depository institutions by guaranteeing individual deposits. Congress intended the system to safeguard deposits against bank failure because of sudden withdrawals or bank illiquidity. By insuring depositors against bank illiquidity, the plans also provided depositors with protection against a bank's poor loan portfolio performance, bank insolvency. This is one of the problems with the current system.

A second closely related problem is the mechanism for funding these federal deposit insurance programs. From the beginning, insured firms have paid a fixed rate for insurance; the premium is determined by deposit levels, essentially one-twelfth of 1 percent of total deposits. Unlike most insurance premiums, which are related to risk, the deposit insurance premium bears no relationship to the behavior of depository firms.

These two aspects of the deposit insurance systems are basically unchanged since the beginning of the system. For years they presented no problems. Now, with the failure rate increasing and some very large commercial banks facing difficulties, the system is in trouble.

The FSLIC is facing the greatest challenge. It assisted the Federal Home Loan Bank Board in taking over about 85 ailing thrifts during 1985 and faced the same prospect with over 200 troubled thrifts in 1986. The FSLIC facilitates these circumstances either by paying off depositors, assisting in mergers, or guaranteeing deposits. With such demands, the FSLIC's reserves have dwindled. The FSLIC insures nearly $800 billion in deposits with reserves of less than 1 percent of that amount.

The FDIC, whose reserves are not so seriously threatened as those of the FSLIC, has come under sharp criticism. Table 15.3 shows the largest commercial bank failures in FDIC history. Six have come in the last few years. The rescue of Continental Illinois was, potentially, the most serious and has prompted many questions. Perhaps the most serious is the differential treatment of depositors at large banks versus depositors at small banks. Regulators have been reluctant to impose losses from failure on uninsured depositors (that is, foreign depositors and those with deposits over $100,000), particularly at large institutions.

This policy gives the impression that large banks are guaranteed against failure, at least as far as depositors are concerned. As Congress originally designed it, the system shifts the risk of insolvency from the depository institution and its creditors to society (taxpayers) and conservatively managed institutions. The deregulation of interest rates on deposits prompts some firms to compete vigorously with high interest rates on deposits. In light of this, analysts are concerned that depository institutions are pursuing high-risk strategies in order to maximize asset return.

Since insurance premiums are not related to portfolio risk and because of the perception that regulators and insurers will bail out failing firms, some people are concerned that depository institutions, especially large ones, may increase their questionable loans. The problems at Continental Illinois, as well as those faced by the failing thrifts in Ohio (Home State Savings Bank) and Maryland (Old Court Savings and Loan), stemmed from poor loan decisions.[5]

---

[5] These latter firms were insured through state deposit insurance. Their problems underscored the limitations of state-run insurance programs.

Bank	Year Failure Resolved	Total Deposits at Resolution Date (millions)	Deposits Adjusted for Interim Inflation (millions)
Continental Illinois Bank and Trust Co., Chicago	1984	$30,000 (approx.)*	$30,000
Franklin National Bank, New York	1974	1445	2769
United States National Bank, San Diego	1973	932	1943
Banco Credit y Ahorro Ponceno, Ponce, Puerto Rico	1978	608	892
United American Bank, Knoxville, Tennessee	1983	585	599
First National Bank of Midland, Midland, Texas	1983	574	587
Penn Square Bank, Oklahoma City	1982	470	501
Hamilton National of Chattanooga, Chattanooga, Tennessee	1976	336	560
Abilene National Bank, Abilene, Texas	1982	310	331
American City Bank, Los Angeles	1983	255	261

Notes: The largest pre-FDIC failure was the over $200-million Bank of United States in 1930. This failure would be the fourth largest on an inflation-adjusted basis. The inflation adjustment uses the implicit price deflator for GNP and the flash estimate for May 1984, as published in *Business Cycle Developments* (June 1984 and August 1983 issues).

* The Continental Illinois banking corporation did not fail. Rather, most of its stock was effectively nationalized. Also the institution's size would be recorded as 50-percent larger if we included nondeposit borrowing (for example, federal funds purchases, repurchase agreements, and borrowing from the Fed and FDIC).

Source: **Edward J. Kane, *The Gathering Crisis in Federal Deposit Insurance.* Copyright © 1985 by The Massachusetts Institute of Technology. Reprinted by permission of The MIT Press.**

TABLE 15.3 *Ten Largest American Commercial Bank Failures*

The Garn-St Germain Act called for each federal deposit insurance agency to produce a plan for reform. From these plans and the suggestions of industry analysts have come the following suggestions.

1. Create a risk-related private insurance system.
2. Require 100-percent reserves against deposits (essentially eliminating the need for external insurance).
3. Reduce insurance coverage and let the market determine sound and secure institutions.
4. Create a risk-related government insurance system.
5. Provide a system of public-private co-insurance.

The first three suggestions are either not viable or hold little prospect of acceptance. Reform of the deposit insurance system will probably involve some aspect of suggestions four and five.

The key to reformed deposit insurance is tying premiums to risk. This would eliminate some of the problems from poor loan decisions. Of course, even this system could not guarantee competent management; it would make the firm pay for its incompetencies through higher premiums.

The FDIC has already suggested a plan to classify firms as representing normal or above-average risk. This system would use factors such as primary capital, nonaccruing loans, net charge-offs for bad loans, and loans more than ninety days past due to assess risk. The insurer would set rates based on the level of deposits and risk. Private insurance firms might cover depositors not included in the federal insurance program.

Reform is crucial to the continuation of deposit insurance. The rate of failure has averaged one savings and loan and one commercial bank per week for the last few years. This rate and the questionable loan practices prompted by the present system make reform important. Policy makers need to consider equity and fairness as well as safety and soundness in devising a reform plan.

Prospects for Small Banks

Over 33,000 depository institutions operate in this country. Most of them are relatively small. With deregulation and change in the financial sector comes the inevitable question of their ability to survive.

Most commercial bank and thrift failures in recent years have occurred among the smallest class of depository institutions. This situation is heightened by the farm financial crisis and the trouble many small agriculture banks are facing. Despite these problems, profit levels for small commercial banks have remained fairly stable over the last decade. For thrifts, after the problem years of 1978–1982, profit levels have recovered.

The challenge for small depository institutions relates to the cost of operations and provision of high-demand products and services. Most studies indicate that economies of scale are not a factor in the competition between small and large firms. Evidence on the impact of economies of scope is not sufficient to draw conclusions. Much of the literature on economies of scale is based on markets not yet affected by computer and telecommunication technology. Results may change as firms utilize these technologies more extensively. To compete, small firms will have to acquire or gain access to cost-saving technologies. The same situation applies to the provision of new products and services. The route for many small depository institutions may be to link up with larger institutions, and through this cooperation, to provide new products and services.

The alternative to competing with larger firms is to create a market niche. Geography or customer service are two factors favoring this approach. In isolated regions, small firms may face little or no competition, and if it comes, customer loyalty may prove sufficient to make a difference. Even in competitive markets, the provision of special services (catering to groups such as senior citizens) will allow some smaller institutions to thrive. Again, links with larger firms will be necessary.

In *The Future of Small Banks in a Deregulated Environment*, a recent book on the future of small banks, the authors concluded that, despite turmoil in the industry, "problems will be no greater for small than for large banks."[6] As with other industries, innovation and managerial commitment will allow small firms to survive even amidst giants.

Deregulation and Monetary Control

Although the DIDMCA gave the Federal Reserve expanded power, namely bringing all depository institutions under the Fed's reserve requirements, central banking authorities are facing challenges as the financial services industry undergoes changes. These challenges relate to monitoring the composition of monetary aggregates and actually controlling the money supply to have the desired effect on the economy. The extent to which the Fed's ability to perform these functions is affected by the changing financial environment will determine whether additional monetary control reforms are necessary.

---

[6] Donald R. Fraser and James W. Kolari, *The Future of Small Banks in a Deregulated Environment* (Cambridge, MA: Balinger Publishing Company, 1985).

The composition of monetary aggregates has changed during the deregulation period. Traditionally the Fed has monitored M1 as an intermediate or operational target. But M1 excludes private sector financial innovations which function as quasi-money, that which is usually included in M1. Repurchase agreements and money-market mutual funds are examples of these innovations.

Beyond simply influencing the composition of monetary aggregates, financial innovations may affect the relationship between money and economic activity. The Fed has relied on a predictable velocity of money function in setting monetary targets. The downturn in velocity in 1982 was most likely caused by financial innovations (NOW and Super NOW accounts turn over at a much lower rate than demand deposits). Such a deviation disrupts the Fed's ability to use changes in monetary aggregates in order to affect the desired modification in real economic variables.

Along these same lines, the M1 connection with economic indicators may be breaking down. During the first half of 1985 the money supply was growing at a 10.4 percent annual rate while nominal GNP expanded at a mere 5-percent pace. This deviation continued in 1986. The income velocity of money may be changing, creating greater difficulty in predicting the relationship between money growth and nominal GNP growth. More empirical work on the M1-growth–GNP-growth relationship is necessary but there is a basis for questioning the traditional connection.

Another issue is the central bank's control of monetary aggregates. Traditionally, the Fed influences the availability of funds for borrowers by affecting depository institution reserves through open market operations. The increasing presence of nondepository institutions, beyond the direct control of monetary authority, means that these financial firms can make funds available despite a Federal Reserve policy of monetary restraint. In the same vein, the phaseout of deposit interest-rate ceilings means that depository institutions can gain access to additional funds for lending through liability management.

Federal Reserve authorities and policy makers will need to monitor the continuing changes in the industry to determine the Fed's monetary control capabilities. These unresolved issues imply that since Congress has added momentum to changes in the financial industry with its deregulatory legislation, Congress must determine whether further deregulation or reregulation legislation is necessary.

Chapter Conclusion

The deregulation of the financial services industry fits into a pattern of deregulation across production and service industries. The major result of deregulation is the restoration, or enchancement, of competition. Virtually all financial industry analysts applauded the removal of archaic regulations and the creation of a "level playing field" for depository institutions. Lawmakers did not enact additional legislation clarifying portions of the initial legislation and addressing gaps in those laws. As a result, the industry continues to change but with considerable uncertainty.

The major issues facing regulators and policy makers are bank/thrift failures and consolidations, the crisis in deposit insurance, and the push for interstate banking. Each of these issues relates to the safety, soundness, and efficiency of the financial system. Regional or interstate banking seems inevitable. Deposit insurance reform is imperative. Consolidations continue. The precise implications of these changes depend on subsequent actions by regulators and lawmakers. Thus, even though the industry was deregulated, its structure and performance, as well as its ability to meet consumer needs while assuring safety and soundness, ultimately rests with regulators and legislators.

Consider These Questions

1. What was the immediate intended purpose of the Garn-St Germain Act? Was it realized? Why or why not?

2. Give some illustrations of the ways the deregulatory legislation created a "level playing field" for depository institutions.

3. What is meant by *segmented markets*? To what extent does this situation still exist among financial firms?

4. Identify some examples of the effects of increasing competition among depository firms in your area. In what specific ways has deregulation affected you?

5. Do you consider the Sears Savings Bank to be as sound as a regular commercial bank? Why or why not?

6. How have non-banks, such as Sears, J. C. Penney, and even General Motors, begun to compete with traditional banking firms? Is this good or bad?

7. Why have bank failures increased in the last few years?

8. What is interstate banking? To what extent does it currently exist? List some of the advantages and disadvantages attributed to interstate banking.

9. Outline the arguments that result in more concentration and less concentration from interstate banking. Do other industries offer any signals for determining what might result if interstate banking is authorized?

10. Do you see any evidence of regional consolidations among medium-sized commercial banks in your area? This is happening in some regions. Why?

11. Can small banks survive?

Suggestions for Further Reading

Bentson, George, et al. *Perspectives on Safe and Sound Banking: Past, Present and Future.* Washington, D.C.: American Bankers Association, 1986.
Some of the most respected analysts of banking in America present their views. See especially Chapter 3 (government deposit insurance), Chapter 9 (risk-related premiums) and the Appendix (recommendations).

————. "Deposit Insurance and Bank Failures." In Federal Reserve Bank of Atlanta *Economic Review* 68 (March 1983): 4–17.
Thorough analysis of issues surrounding bank failures and deposit insurance.

Corrigan, E. Gerald. "Are Banks Special?" In Federal Reserve Bank of Minneapolis Annual Report (1982).
Makes compelling case for maintaining separation of commercial banks and other financial institutions. Easy to read and understand.

Council of Economic Advisors. "Financial Market Deregulation." In *Economic Report of the President, 1984.* Washington, D.C.: U.S. Government Printing Office, February 1984.
Major section of report is devoted to issues surrounding deregulation. Presents clear, consise overview.

Di Clemente, John J. "What is a Bank?" In Federal Reserve Bank of Chicago *Economic Perspectives* (January/February 1983).
Issue devoted to issue of the distinctiveness of commercial banks.

Fraser, Donald R. and James W. Kolari. *The Future of Small Banks in a Deregulated Environment.* Cambridge, Mass.: Balinger Publishing Company, 1985.
Solid analysis of deregulation's impact on small banks.
Combines analytical and descriptive approaches.

Nowesnick, Mary. "The FSLIC at 50: Time to Unwrap a New Plan." In *Savings Institutions* (December 1984): 44–60.
Identifies the major problems with the FSLIC. Anticipated some of the issues confronting the FSLIC at the present time. Good recommendations.

Rosenblum, Harvey, Diane Siegel and Christine Pavel. "Banks and Nonbanks: A Run for the Money." In Federal Reserve Bank of Chicago *Economic Perspectives* (May/June 1984): 3–12.

Outlines key issues relating to the competition between commercial banks, other depository institutions and non-banks. Clear and understandable.

————. *Federal Deposit Insurance Corporation: The First Fifty Years*. Washington, D.C.: FDIC, 1984.
Good history of FDIC and its contributions to industry. Represents agency's perspective but contains good data.

PART FIVE

MONETARY POLICY/ MONEY MANAGEMENT

CHAPTER SIXTEEN

THE FEDERAL RESERVE SYSTEM AS CENTRAL BANK

"There have been three great inventions since the beginning of time: fire, the wheel, and central banking."

Will Rogers

The financial industry is changing rapidly and dramatically. The Federal Reserve System, America's central bank, works with and through this evolving industry to provide monetary stability and economic growth. While Will Rogers may have thought central banking was one of the three great inventions of humankind, there are many who would not agree. The Federal Reserve regularly comes under careful scrutiny and, more than occasionally, severe criticisms.

This section includes an investigation of the Federal Reserve System—its origins, structure, functions, goals, and operations—and an evaluation of its performance. After studying the system, you can decide whether you agree with Will Rogers.

The beginning of the chapter will lend some insight into what the Federal Reserve System was intended to do and how it is structured to carry out its functions. The chapter conclusion discusses some major issues facing the Federal Reserve System. Throughout its history, the central bank has faced challenges. The rapid changes in the financial industry prompted by the deregulatory movement have presented the Fed with more, and perhaps greater, challenges than ever before.

Chapter Objectives

The Federal Reserve evolved as a compromise between those seeking a strong central bank and those fearing such centralization of power. As a result, our central bank looks much different from those in European countries.

Use this chapter to understand the role of a central bank and why events in this country led to the Federal Reserve System's unique structure. As you investigate the origins, development and structure of the Fed, you need to keep in mind your goals for this chapter. After reading the first three parts of the chapter you should:

- Understand the purposes of a central bank and how those are different from large private depository institutions.
- Understand the reasons why previous central banks in the United States failed.
- Analyze conditions that led to the establishment of the Federal Reserve System.
- Understand how the conditions which prompted formation of a central bank influenced its structure.

With this background information, you will be ready to study the functions of the Fed and the challenges it is facing. The last two parts of the chapter will help you understand:

- The Fed's multiple functions, including
  money supply control
  bankers' bank
  service to Treasury
  regulation and supervision.
- The challenge of independence.
- How changing conditions prompted by deregulation are influencing the Fed.
- Whether the changing environment will affect the Fed's ability to control the nation's money supply.

The chapter appendix provides a detailed look at the Fed's balance sheet—its assets and liabilities. When you read the appendix, think about how the Fed can manage its assets and liabilities to achieve the goals we discussed in the last chapter.

Role of a Central Bank

What is a central bank and why does it exist? A central bank is often described as the bankers' bank. This is accurate, although not particularly illuminating. A central bank serves the same functions for banks (actually all depository institutions) that commercial banks perform for customers. Namely, it:

- Establishes deposit accounts for commerical banks.
- Provides for securities transfers.
- Assists in the check clearing process.
- Makes loans to commercial banks (serving as lender of last resort).

Although the Federal Reserve System is relatively young (it began in 1913), central banks have been around for many years. Sweden's central bank began operations in 1668 and the Bank of England was originally established in 1694. The Bank of England began as a private operation serving the needs of the British government, but in almost all cases, central banks are public institutions. (The Bank of England was nationalized in 1947.) As public institutions working toward the general good rather than for shareholders' profits, central banks act as the banker for the government, providing many of the institutional mechanisms necessary for the government and its treasury department to function. Most people think of a central bank in this way.

A central bank functions to help achieve the generally accepted macroeconomic goals of stability and growth. It seeks to accomplish these goals by:

- Establishing and enforcing sound banking rules.
- Serving as the fiscal agent for the government.
- Controlling the supply of bank reserves and through them the nation's supply of money and credit.[1]

This second category of responsibilities provides the answer to the question of why a central bank is needed. Governments have relied on a central banking authority to help eliminate, or at least minimize, the disruptions caused by monetary instability.

---

[1] The Federal Reserve System also serves as the country's major international banker. Its purpose here is to manage international exchange rates. This function of the Fed is discussed in Chapter 20.

This answer may lead to another question—if central banks are so useful, why did the United States wait so long to establish one? Perhaps a discussion of the origins of central banking for the United States will provide an answer to this question.

Origins of the Central Bank in the United States

The legislation establishing the Federal Reserve System was signed into law in December, 1913. The Fed began operations in early 1914. This was not the United States' first central bank. You may recall from Chapter 4 that on two separate occasions during the nineteenth century, the United States established central banks.

Shortly after the formation of this country, our first central bank was formed. Congress chartered the *1st Bank of the United States* in 1791.[2] This bank evolved from a desire on the part of Secretary of the Treasury Alexander Hamilton to have a bank for the government. Hamilton felt that a central bank would provide the institutional mechanism necessary to allow the newly created federal government to promote economic growth through a stabilization in the value of the currency (which was "not worth a Continental" as a result of the Revolutionary War inflation).

To stabilize the value of the currency, the 1st Bank of the United States attempted to control bank-note creation by the state-chartered commercial banks. The 1st BUS used its reserves to acquire state bank notes and then presented them for redemption when it felt the state banks were too rapidly expanding the supply of currency. This primitive form of monetary policy brought the 1st BUS few friends. In 1811, when the Bank's charter was up for renewal, the state-chartered banks, seeking greater independence of action, led the fight against the BUS. Among other things, the state banks argued that the BUS exerted monopoly power and was influenced by political factors. The charter was not renewed.

Only five years later, sentiment was somewhat changed in the United States Congress as a result of the rapid increase in bank-note issues, the suspension of convertibility, and the run-away inflation associated with the War of 1812. Congress granted a charter to the *2nd Bank of the United States*. The 2nd BUS was intended not only to facilitate the fiscal activities of the Treasury but to regulate the value of money. As the exclusive collector and

---

[2] One of the many fine studies on this subject is Richard H. Timberlake's *The Origin of Central Banking in the United States* (Cambridge: Harvard University Press, 1978).

depository of government revenues the 2nd BUS was a powerful institution. Its bank notes were full legal tender for all government transactions.

Although the Bank seldom exercised its power in domestic money markets, its sheer size and potential power served as a constraint on the unregulated activities of the nation's many state banks. This conflict between the forces seeking a laissez-faire economic environment and those looking to regulate the value of currency by controlling credit became the basis for the so-called Bank War.[3] President Jackson opposed the rechartering of the 2nd BUS and vetoed the recharter bill. Attempts to override his veto highlighted the intense and bitter feelings surrounding America's "central bank."

Opposition to the 2nd BUS was, in part, based on ideology—states' rights versus federal control—but to a greater extent it stemmed from a desire to remove a major constraint on the expansion of credit. Agrarians and entrepreneurs who favored easy credit were supported by state-chartered bankers who opposed any restraint on free banking. The charge of monopoly power won out and the rechartering of the 2nd Bank of the United States failed.

From 1836 when the charter of the 2nd BUS expired, until 1914, when the Federal Reserve began operations, the United States had no central bank. The establishment of the National Banking System in 1863 was intended to rectify some of the country's financial problems, the most notable being excessive bank-note creation. This legislation was designed to create a unified national currency which the comptroller of the currency could control. Legislation passed in 1865 taxed state bank notes and essentially drove them out of circulation. Nonetheless, no effective mechanism existed to regularly and quickly influence the nation's money supply and no agency existed to dictate or influence the utilization of sound banking procedures. Therefore, while a laissez-faire banking system went unrestricted, the economy continued to experience severe financial panics and recessions.

The experiences of the 1st and 2nd Banks of the United States are illuminating. The reasons for the formation of these early central banks are not at all dissimilar to those behind the formation of the Federal Reserve. Furthermore, the issues which formed the basis for attacks on these banks are at the heart of much of the contemporary debate about the financial industry. What degrees of intervention and regulation should exist in the financial industry? How actively should the central bank intervene in credit markets? Who should make the decisions about central bank policy?

---

[3] Robert V. Remini has written an interesting and very readable account of this conflict, *Andrew Jackson and the Bank War* (New York: W.W. Norton, 1967).

These are important questions. Before attempting to answer them, you need more information on the origins and structure of the Federal Reserve System.

Origins and Development of the Federal Reserve System

The establishment of the National Banking System did help the country achieve a unified currency but many other problems remained. During the four decades after the Civil War, the United States experienced the growing pains of an economy in the throes of the industrial revolution. Credit and the banking system expanded in response to increasing demands from agriculture, industry, and commerce.

Throughout this period, financial panics often prompted economic recession. The Panic of 1907 illustrates the shortcomings of the National Banking System and helps explain why the United States finally established a central bank.

Two particular problems characterized the financial system at the turn of the century—the rigidity or inelasticity of the currency and the pyramiding of reserves. The nation's money supply did not respond to seasonal needs of the economy, for instance, the money and credit needed in spring as farmers began planting. Without sufficient currency to meet demand, the public questioned the liquidity and safety of banks. A fractional reserve system cannot withstand dramatically increased withdrawals.

Compounding this problem was the pyramiding of reserves. Small banks relied on larger banks to handle many banking functions. Small banks deposited reserves with these correspondent banks to take advantage of better interest rates. Correspondent banks, in return, deposited reserves with the major money-center banks in New York. When the demand for funds increased in the Midwest, reserves could not be mobilized fast enough to respond to withdrawal requests. Bank panics resulted and a general economic contraction occurred.

In 1907, liquidity demands led to the suspension of payments by the Knickerbocker Trust Company, New York City's second largest trust company. Existing reserves were not sufficient to respond to depositors' demands for funds and even a special reserve fund established by the Treasury and supported by financier J.P. Morgan could not halt bank closures. A full-blown panic resulted.

The Panic of 1907 led Congress to pass an emergency currency bill. This legislation also created a National Monetary Commission. The commission's report formed the foundation for the legislative package that created the Federal Reserve System.

Although people generally agreed that the banking and financial system needed reform, they disagreed considerably over what Congress should do. The fear of centralized control that had surfaced during the Jacksonian Bank War persisted. People were concerned that a central bank might come under the influence of monopoly money interests in New York. The ongoing competition between state-chartered and nationally chartered banks further complicated reform efforts.

Evolving out of this turmoil was legislation establishing not a European-style central bank, but a system. Regional interests and those of commercial bankers were addressed with the formation of regional banks controlled by bankers. A coordinating board, based in Washington and appointed by the president, provided some government control. The disparate parties involved felt satisfied that the Federal Reserve System safeguarded their interests and corrected the shortcomings of the existing structure. The regional banks provided a ready pool of reserves to meet the needs of member banks in the district. The system was "owned" by its member banks and they elected the officers of the regional banks. Guidelines were established for reserve requirements and operating procedures. The Federal Reserve was created out of the democratic process of compromise and concession. While people did not universally agree on the system, they generally accepted it.[4]

Structure of the Federal Reserve System

Dual concerns existed over large banks' domination and the federal government's allowance of political concerns to control banking. This resulted in a decentralized central banking system. The Federal Reserve System today looks much different that it did when it began operating in 1914. (President Wilson signed legislation creating the Fed in December, 1913.) This is more because of functional changes rather than structural ones.

---

[4] Some have argued that the Federal Reserve System was a cartelizing device conceived by the bankers to restrict competition. According to this argument, the system was but one of many government imposed agencies (such as the FTC and the ICC) which allowed large firms to expand (in this case by expanding money and credit) without the restraint of competition. See Murray N. Rothbard, "The Federal Reserve as a Cartelization Device," in Barry N. Siegel, editor, *Money in Crisis* (San Francisco: Pacific Institute for Public Policy Research, 1984): 89–136.

Centralized/Regional Structure

The Federal Reserve System consists of a Board of Governors located in Washington, D.C., and twelve Federal Reserve banks, some of which have branch facilities. Figure 16.1 shows the twelve districts and the locations of the Federal Reserve banks and their branches.

The Federal Reserve banks are corporations. Their stockholders are member banks within their districts. These member banks elect the majority of members of the boards of directors for their district banks; the remaining

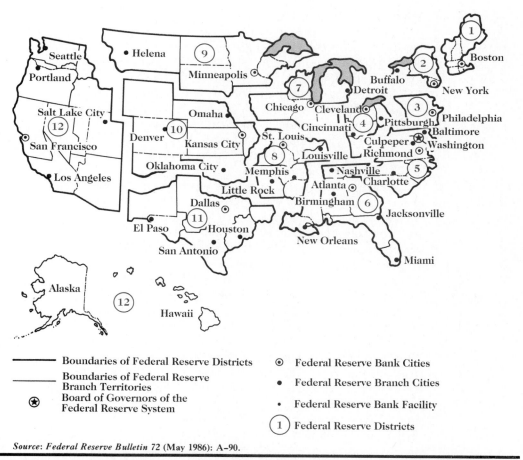

——— Boundaries of Federal Reserve Districts	⊙ Federal Reserve Bank Cities
——— Boundaries of Federal Reserve Branch Territories	• Federal Reserve Branch Cities
⊛ Board of Governors of the Federal Reserve System	· Federal Reserve Bank Facility
	① Federal Reserve Districts

Source: Federal Reserve Bulletin 72 (May 1986): A-90.

FIGURE 16.1 *The Federal Reserve System: District Boundaries and Branch Territories*
The country is divided into twelve federal reserve districts, each of which has a Federal Reserve bank.

directors are appointed by the Board of Governors. Regional control over the district bank is maintained through this arrangement. Although established as corporations owned and controlled by members, the Federal Reserve banks do not generate "profits" for their owners. The banks receive no funds from Congress, but turn over any operating surplus to the Treasury. They exist to serve the public interest.

The twelve district banks are "locally owned and locally controlled," but the members of the Board of Governors are appointed by the president and subject to Senate approval. Members of the board serve fourteen-year terms to remove any hint of influence by the administration.

Governance The balance between regional and centralized control is maintained in the system's governance and control. The Federal Reserve System is an autonomous federal agency with strong regional connections. Figure 16.2 provides a useful diagram of the system's structure and illustrates the blending of centralized and regional control.

Member banks and the Board of Governors jointly determine the directors of the Federal Reserve banks. The combination of directors from banking, business, and the public sector prevents domination of the board of directors by any one group. The president of each Federal Reserve bank is appointed by the board of directors but must receive approval from the Board of Governors.

Perhaps the clearest indication of the central-regional balance is the *Federal Open-Market Committee* (FOMC). While the Board of Governors sets overall Fed policy, the Federal Open-Market Committee establishes specific monetary policy targets and directs the open-market operations designed to achieve these targets. Figure 16.2 shows that the FOMC is made up of seven members of the Board of Governors and five Federal Reserve bank representatives (usually the presidents).[5] This mix is intended to ensure that regional interests are incorporated into monetary-policy decisions.

The Board of Governors, through its open-market committee, establishes and implements monetary policy. The Federal Reserve banks function as bankers' banks to provide for an efficient and smoothly functioning financial system. In the early years of the system, the regional banks, especially the New York Fed, exerted considerable influence over the Board of Governors. The most powerful central banker during the pre–World War II era was Benjamin Strong, the president of the New York Fed. This situation has changed. The Board of Governors, and especially its chairman, has become the dominant force in monetary policy decisions.

---

[5] The president of the New York Fed always sits on the FOMC because open-market operations are conducted through that bank. Four other Federal Reserve bank representatives serve on a rotating basis.

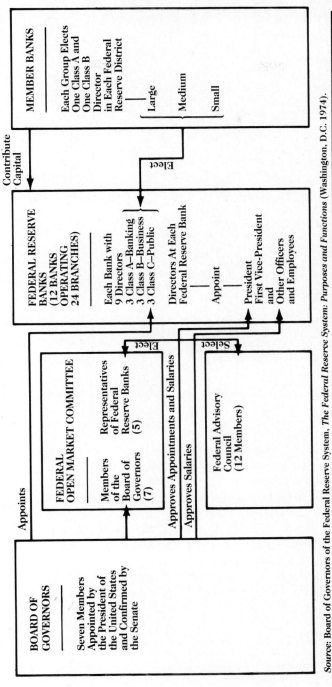

Source: Board of Governors of the Federal Reserve System, *The Federal Reserve System: Purposes and Functions* (Washington, D.C. 1974).

FIGURE 16.2   *The Structure of the Federal Reserve System*   The organization chart of the Fed shows the relationship between the Board of Governors and the Federal Reserve banks. Notice that the regional balance influences the FOMC and the Advisory Committee.

BANKING T⬤DAY 16.1   Stacking the Fed

In 1937, President Roosevelt got into real trouble when he tried to expand membership of the Supreme Court to allow the appointment of additional justices who were favorable to his point of view. President Reagan hasn't been forced to expand membership of the Board of Governors to make his appointments. Resignations and the expirations of terms have given the president the opportunity to appoint five new governors, each of whom represents views consistent with his own.

In his first term, President Reagan named Preston Martin and Martha Seger to the Board of Governors. During the recession of 1981–82, when the Fed followed a very restrictive monetary policy and was criticized by the administration, Martin and Seger often dissented from the board's decisions and called for a less restrictive policy. At that time, the Reagan appointees were only two in number and were consistently outvoted.

During 1986, President Reagan appointed three more governors (one, H. Robert Heller, was appointed to replace Preston Martin who resigned). Wayne Angel and Manuel Johnson immediately established their presence on the board. They combined with the previous two Reagan appointees to outvote Chairman Volcker on a symbolically important interest rate cut decision in February, 1986. Although a compromise was arranged to allow the chairman to achieve his goals and not "lose face," the vote was quite significant.

Some have described these presidential appointees as supply-siders. They are, at the very least, less concerned about inflation than Chairman Volcker and the members of the board who vote with him.

In early 1987, President Reagan was leaning toward appointing Edward Kelley, and investment counsellor Leif Olson, former chief economist at Citibank, to fill vacancies created by the resignations of Emmett Rice and Henry Wallich. These men are more monetarist than supply-side in their orientations.

These appointments, combined with the prospect that Reagan will not reappoint chairman Volcker when his term expires in August 1987, mean that the president will be able to name all seven governors. This may give the president the support he needs for a monetary policy that supports economic expansion. President Reagan was able to achieve a Board of Governors which was sympathetic to his economic ideology without having to expand the membership as Roosevelt attempted to do.

Membership   When Congress initially established the Federal Reserve System, membership was required of all nationally chartered banks and was optional for state-chartered banks. Membership carried with it special benefits. The member banks' privilege to borrow funds from the regional Federal Reserve bank was the chief benefit. The Fed also handled all check processing, at no charge for its members.[6] But member banks had capital requirements, had to adhere to stricter reserve requirements, and were under the scrutiny of Federal Reserve supervision.

Since many smaller state-chartered banks could access Federal Reserve services through correspondent banks, they concluded the costs of mem-

---

[6] As you will see, the entire membership question was altered with the financial reforms initiated in 1980.

bership outweighed the benefits. In the early 1920s, less than 10 percent of the nation's nearly 22,000 state-chartered banks were members of the Federal Reserve. Because many large state-chartered banks voluntarily joined with the nationally chartered banks that were required to be members, the Fed was able to influence banking and monetary affairs.

Not until the post–World War II era did declining membership cause Federal Reserve officials some consternation. The Fed's ability to "control" the money supply was, in the opinion of many, jeopardized by defections from its membership ranks. Much of this concern was eliminated when the DIDMC Act of 1980 extended reserve requirements to all depository institutions.

Policy Implementation   The Federal Reserve System has become a major macroeconomic policy force in the United States. Monetary policy decisions are made and carried out by the Board of Governors. The specific tools of monetary policy are discussed in detail in the next chapter. For now, it is sufficient to point out that the Board implements its policies through open-market operations, by setting the discount rate and with reserve requirements. Figure 16.3 illustrates the relationship of the Federal Reserve organization to the implementation tools for monetary policy. The Federal Reserve banks have direct input into monetary-policy decisions through the FOMC,

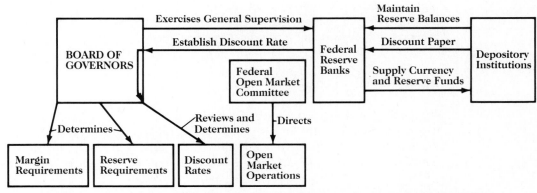

Source: Board of Governors of the Federal Reserve System, *The Federal Reserve System: Purposes and Functions* (Washington, D.C., 1974).

FIGURE 16.3 *Relationship of Federal Reserve Organization to Instruments of Credit Policy*
The Board of Governors, with input from the Federal Reserve banks, is responsible for implementing monetary policy through the instruments of margin requirements, reserve requirements, discount rates, and open-market operations.

and indirect input regarding discount rates and reserve requirements through the *Federal Advisory Council*. Composed of one representative from each of the twelve district banks' boards of directors, the Council meets at least twice a year to confer with the Governors.

The question of who controls the Fed remains. For an institution as powerful as a central bank, this question is quite important. The issue of control usually centers on one particular Federal Reserve function, money supply control.[7] This question is addressed in Chapter 19 when we examine the Fed's monetary policy record.

Functions of the Federal Reserve System

The legislation passed into law in 1913 provided for "the establishment of Federal Reserve banks to furnish an elastic currency, to afford a means of rediscounting commercial paper, to establish a more effective supervision of banking in the United States, and for other purposes." Although the policy functions of the Fed are the most visible, and often most controversial, the Fed serves many functions in the economy. The need to provide for a stable currency has evolved into the Fed's most prominent function—controlling the money supply. This function has taken on an importance far beyond that envisioned by the framers of the system. The role of today's Federal Reserve ranges from the day-to-day mechanical duties of check clearing and currency replacement, to the implementation of domestic and international monetary policies. We will look briefly at each area and discuss the Fed's policy function in greater detail in the next two chapters.

Money Supply Control

Originally, Congress established the Fed to overcome the rigidities of the American money supply. In the years after World War II, largely because of the Banking Act of 1935, the Fed moved toward a very active monetary policy role with the Federal Open-Market Committee making far-reaching

---

[7] In the years since deregulation began in 1980, this issue has also been directed toward the Fed's role as a regulatory agency. Federal Reserve Board Chairman Paul Volcker has taken a very cautious approach to deregulation and, in the process, has been criticized for exercising too much control by those who favor further deregulation. This issue of who controls the Fed was addressed by Sherman Maisel, *Managing the Dollar* (New York: W.W. Norton, 1973). He estimated the distribution of power within the Fed and identified the chairman as exerting the most influence over Fed policy.

decisions. Earlier chapters have discussed the importance of the money supply to overall economic activity. With a central bank, movements in the money supply are controlled, or at least strongly influenced, by a decision-making body rather than being left to chance. Controlling the supply of money is the Fed's most important function.

Bankers' Bank

Within this category, the Fed serves two functions. The first, *lender of last resort*, stems from concern over a ready supply of reserves to meet depositor demands on commercial banks. The second and less dramatic function includes the performance of some mechanical operations for commercial banks.

For member banks only, until 1980, and for all depository institutions since then, the Federal Reserve serves as lender of last resort. Through their *discount windows* (so called because member banks originally presented commercial paper, that is, corporate bonds, at these teller windows for rediscounting) the twelve Federal Reserve banks make loans to depository institutions. Such loans may be made to head off a financial shortfall for a particular bank or to provide for an influx of funds into a region in response to situational needs. As you will see in the next chapter, the rate of interest that the Fed establishes for these discount loans influences the creation of bank reserves and the overall supply of money.

The Fed also assists banks by buying, selling, and transferring government securities, maintaining reserve accounts, transferring reserve funds, clearing checks,[8] and providing for the replacement of worn-out currency. These *mechanical functions* help the financial system run smoothly.

Regulation and Supervision

As you learned in Chapter 6, the Federal Reserve is one of several agencies charged with supervision and regulation. The Fed sets operating rules, for example capital requirements, which it administers through examination of member banks. The Federal Reserve also regulates certain bank activities, such as mergers and acquisitions. (Refer to Figure 6.3 for a complete summary of the Fed's supervisory and regulatory responsibilities.)

---

[8] Until 1980, the Fed cleared the checks of its member banks as a no-charge service. Now there is a charge for check clearing and the Fed competes with private firms in providing this service.

Service to Federal Government

Central banks are often the government's bank. In the United States, the Federal Reserve does cooperate with the Treasury, provide formal and informal advice to the government, and serve as the fiscal agent for the government. This latter function includes receiving deposits and issuing checks for various government agencies. The Fed also issues American government securities and redeems them for brokers and the public. The Fed processes food stamps for the Department of Agriculture and postal money orders for the United States Postal Service. The Board of Governors and each district bank conduct research and undertake public information programs to keep citizens and organizations aware of monetary issues.

Cooperation with Foreign Central Banks

The Fed, through the New York Federal Reserve Bank, conducts the government's official reserve transactions with other countries. The New York Fed also acts on behalf of the Board of Governors in the implementation of international exchange-rate stabilization policies. These actions may be part of ongoing FOMC policies or they may result from unusual circumstances that could disrupt international markets and adversely affect the value of the American dollar. When President Kennedy was assassinated and when President Reagan was shot, the New York Fed used its foreign currency reserves to buy American dollars and prevent a precipitous fall in the value of the dollar. The New York Fed also holds the reserves, dollar deposits, securities and even gold, of foreign governments. The Federal Reserve plays a major role in all international exchange-rate negotiations and may be called upon occasionally to provide advice to foreign governments. During the Iranian hostage crisis in 1980, the Federal Reserve "froze" Iranian assets in the United States and participated in the process that led to the freeing of those assets.

Issues Facing the Federal Reserve

From its inception, when it was charged with responsibilities but accorded few powers, until today, when a deregulated financial industry is changing the rules of the game, the Federal Reserve has faced challenges. The final verdict on the Fed will come after we evaluate its monetary policy record. As a backdrop for that more detailed discussion, this section outlines some issues challenging the Fed.

During 1986, there was considerable upheaval within the Federal Reserve's Board of Governors. Aside from the resignations or retirements of Lyle Gramley, J. Charles Partee, and Emmett Rice, which were not totally unexpected, vice-chairman Preston Martin stepped down after a much publicized power struggle with Chairman Volcker. All these changes might imply significant policy shifts, especially since President Reagan appointed new Governors who hold a supply-side orientation (see Banking Today 16.1).

There always seems to be a great deal of continuity within the Federal Reserve. Much of it can be explained by the staffing arrangements at the Board of Governors. The senior staff at the Board demonstrates considerable permanence despite the turnover among the governors themselves. Staff Director Steven Axilrod has been with the Board of Governors since 1952; Donald Kohn, deputy staff director, came to the Board in 1976; and, Director of Research James Kichline came to the Fed just out of graduate school in 1971 and has held his present position since 1977.

These senior staff members have considerable influence over the information that flows to the governors. Most governors do not have economists on their private staffs so they rely on the research provided by the general staff members. The senior staff, closely identifying with Chairman Volcker, provides information to the governors at the twice weekly briefings. Staff director Axilrod structures these briefings very carefully—he sets the agenda with Chairman Volcker, organizes the presentations by junior staff economists, and handles most of the questions.

As a result of these arrangements, the generation of information is tightly controlled. Unlike a university, where diverse viewpoints are encouraged, there is only one acceptable among Fed staffers, and junior economists with an eye to their careers dare not displease their supervisors. The orthodox position does not always prevail when it comes to policy decisions but the continuity of the staff means there is less change within the Board than one might expect given the turnover among the governors.

Role of the Federal Reserve in Macroeconomic Policy

Today the Federal Reserve is perceived as one of the most powerful actors in the macroeconomic policy play which is continually unfolding. Through its open-market operations, the Fed exerts tremendous influence over the nation's money supply. That was not always the case.

The Federal Reserve Act did not mention open-market operations. The open market for securities was not even seen as a vehicle for monetary policy until the 1920s. And then, even though the FOMC was organized in the early 1920s, the Fed did not receive the legislative mandate necessary to implement a concerted monetary policy through the FOMC until the Banking Act of 1935. The debate over the usefulness of the Fed's open-market activities during the 1930s is still under debate today.[9] Most economists will agree that the Fed had little opportunity to pursue an independent monetary policy until after World War II.

Independence

During World War II, the Fed felt responsibility to assist in the country's war effort. Specifically, the government wanted to keep interest rates low so that the cost of borrowing to finance the war could be kept to a minimum. The Fed, using its reserves, entered the open market to absorb government securities. By maintaining demand for securities, prices remained high but interest rates were kept low. This process is called *pegging the interest rate*. As long as the Fed was "required" to peg the rate of interest, it could not pursue an independent monetary policy.

This situation changed in 1951. In that year, the Fed and the Treasury came to an agreement, called the *Accord of 1951*, which freed the Fed from pegging the interest rate. Without this constraint on its open-market actions, the Federal Reserve could establish monetary policy goals and undertake open-market actions to achieve them.[10]

The Accord of 1951 meant that the Fed was no longer required to pursue a low-interest-rate monetary policy. The question of the Fed's independence has not been eliminated. Historically, central banks have functioned as independent agents. To a large extent, this goal is pursued to prevent the government from using the central bank to inflate the money supply, allowing easier debt repayment. During the 1970s and 1980s, some have argued that monetary policy must be coordinated with fiscal policy and the only way to do so is to bring the Fed under the control of the president. Others have argued that the Federal Reserve does respond to political pressure from the administration and, especially in election years, undertakes policies to help the party in power.

The cries for reform to "control" the Fed are loudest during periods when the Fed is undertaking tight monetary policies, and economic sectors are adversely affected by high or rising interest rates. Most recently, such

---

[9] Milton Friedman, among others, argues that the Fed helped cause the "Great Contraction." For a discussion of this issue see Peter Temin, *Did Monetary Forces Cause the Great Depression?* (New York: W.W. Norton, 1976).

[10] For an excellent discussion of the Accord of 1951, see G.L. Bach, *Making Monetary and Fiscal Policy* (Washington, D.C.: The Brookings Institution, 1971): Chapter 4.

criticisms were heard during 1981–82 when Federal Reserve Bank Chairman Paul Volcker openly stated that the Fed would pursue a tight money policy to bring down the rate of inflation despite rising unemployment and declining economic growth.

Role in Deregulation

Since the DIDMCA of 1980, the Federal Reserve has been involved in the challenges posed by a deregulated financial industry. These challenges include the degree to which the Fed will exercise its regulatory authority in the expansion of commercial banks across state lines, and the responsibility the Fed must assume when commercial banks are in danger of collapsing.

Throughout the 1980s, the Fed has exercised caution in the movement toward interstate banking. The Fed has used its authority to restrict or slow the movement of commercial banks into the securities, real estate, and insurance businesses while at the same time restricting bank holding companies from expanding operations too rapidly. The Fed has assisted in resolving various financial crises, ranging from the near collapse of Continental Illinois Bank to the supervised reopening of Ohio thrift institutions which closed during the near panic in the Spring of 1985. While some applaud the Fed for its position and the actions it has taken, others argue that the Fed is exercising undue power in the financial system.

Competing in the Marketplace

For years, the Federal Reserve was the nation's largest check processor. By 1980 the Fed was clearing 40 percent of all checks. From its inception, the Fed had performed this service at no cost for all its member banks. Beginning in August 1981 the Fed began processing checks for any depository institution, but with a fee attached. Almost immediately, the Fed lost business to private firms. This drop in activity prompted the Fed to compete more aggressively to recapture some of its lost business. This bothered many banks which had benefited from the Fed's loss of business.

Much of the furor stems from the float. *Float* is the value of checks which have been written but not yet collected. Observers estimate the magnitude of the float for checks processed by the Fed alone at more than $1.7 billion a day. Banks and large corporations use the float to their advantage. As the Fed works to speed up its operations as a major competitor

BANKING TODAY 16.3   Reducing the Fed Float

Since the early 1800s, an invoice has been considered paid from the moment it's postmarked. That policy has allowed everyone to take advantage of the mail system, to "float" the check for a few days without having to worry about the funds being withdrawn to cover the check.

Taking advantage of this system, "playing the float," is a well-established cash management strategy. Stretching out the float can allow corporations to significantly increase their interest earnings. For a large corporation, disbursing upwards of $5 million each day, stretching the float for a few extra days could generate as much as $1 million in additional interest earnings per year.

While everyone tries to use the float, companies have learned how to stretch the float to its maximum. They can criss-cross payments, drawing checks on banks in one part of the country

and mailing them from another part. Doing this can extend the float from a few days, which is the normal time for checks to move through the system, to well over a week.

The Federal Reserve is concerned about the float. The "Fed float," funds the Fed makes available to banks before their deposited checks clear, has been increasing. It more than doubled from the daily average of $3.2 billion in 1969 to $6.5 billion in 1979, just before some action was taken.

As a result of the increasing float, the DIDMCA of 1980 included provisions for eliminating the float. The Fed was directed to charge for its check clearing services and to move toward an electronic check clearing plan. The motivation for such a move is more than just the float. People

are necessary to process checks, and labor costs are rising. It's estimated that for 1985 it took 1.5-trillion individual check handlings to keep the check payment system in operation. These costs apply to all aspects of the business system, but weigh most heavily on the Fed.

An electronic payments system is coming but the advantages of the float are keeping many corporations from moving too fast. What firms are doing is instituting electronic payments systems for their customers to reduce the consumer float. Some firms allow payment by home computer. Once the customer or retail payments system is in place, corporate wholesale payments systems will follow. Then the Fed can achieve its goal of reducing the float.

in the check clearing business, it threatens not only the revenue banks receive from processing checks but the advantages they receive from manipulating the float. With the financial industry changing, the Fed will face other similar issues as it competes more actively with private institutions.

Control over Money Supply

Before the DIDMCA, the Fed exercised control over the money supply through the reserve requirements it imposed on member banks and the involvement of banks in open-market operations/reserve creation. Leading up to 1980, the Fed expressed concern over its dwindling membership. With fewer member banks, Federal Reserve authorities felt they had less control over the money supply process. To a certain extent, this issue was resolved with the financial reforms of 1980. All depository institutions are now required to adhere to the reserve requirements established by the Fed.

The Fed is facing a related issue. As the financial industry changes and more non-banks (institutions which do not accept deposits and issue commercial loans) become involved in attracting funds, the Fed must consider how this will affect its monetary control policies. Some experts are concerned that the expansion of unregulated financial firms, such as insurance companies and retail firms such as Sears, into the financial marketplace may interfere with monetary control measures implemented by the Fed.

Chapter Conclusion

The structure of the Federal Reserve reflects the concern of early twentieth-century legislatures with a centralization of power. The existence of district banks provides the opportunity for regional views within the Federal Reserve System but the central authority resides with the Board of Governors. Since its inception in 1914, the Fed has taken on an increasingly important role in macroeconomic policy.

You will see the evolution of the Fed's power and responsibility when you review the goals and tools of Fed policy (Chapter 17), the strategies of monetary policy (Chapter 18) and especially the implementation of policy in recent years (Chapter 19). The functions and responsibilities of the Fed are rooted in its origins. The services it provides and the way it responds to challenges are, to a great extent, determined by the powers it received initially and the way it handled those powers in earlier periods.

Consider These Questions

1. Explain what is meant by a bankers' bank.
2. Why did the first attempts at central banking in the United States fail? Did the absence of a central bank have any influence on the various financial panics suffered by the United States during the late nineteenth and early twentieth centuries?
3. What factors led to formation of the Federal Reserve System?
4. Why does the American central bank have twelve separate banks in addition to the Board of Governors?
5. How might you account for two Federal Reserve banks in one state (Missouri)?

6. Why does the Fed rely so heavily on open-market operations for its policy implementation?

7. Outline some arguments on both sides of the independence issue.

8. Do you consider the Fed's regulatory function or its monetary policy function more important? Why?

Suggestions for Further Reading

Burns, Arthur F. "The Independence of the Federal Reserve System." In *Challenge* (July/August 1976): 21–24.
  A strong argument in favor of an independent Fed by the then-chairman of the Board of Governors.

Duprey, James N. and Clarence W. Nelson. "A Visible Hand: The Fed's Involvement in the Check Payments System." In Federal Reserve Bank of Minneapolis *Quarterly Review* X, 2 (Spring 1986): 18–29.
  Offers a unique, historical perspective on the Fed's role in the check payments system.

Evanoff, Douglas F. "Priced Services: The Fed's Impact on Correspondent Banking." In Federal Reserve Bank of Chicago *Economic Perspectives* IX, 5 (September/October 1985): 31–44.
  Provides a good overview of the Fed as a competitor since passage of the DIDMCA in 1980.

Friedman, Milton. "The Case for Overhauling the Federal Reserve." In *Challenge* (July/August 1985): 4–12.
  Nobel-laureate provides a far-reaching plan for restructuring the Fed which includes an end to its independence.

Kemmerer, Edwin W. and Donald L. Kemmerer. *The ABC of the Federal Reserve System*. New York: Harper, 1950.
  Originally published in 1932, this book provides interesting reading because it outlines the structure of the Fed (which hasn't changed much) and the policy orientation of the Board (which has changed quite a bit).

Maisel, Sherman. *Managing the Dollar*. New York: W.W. Norton, 1973.
  An easy to read and understand account of the Fed's policy actions and the role of power blocs in determining that policy.

Timberlake, Richard H. Jr. *The Origins of Central Banking in the United States*. Cambridge, Mass.: Harvard University Press, 1978.
  Concise history of American attempts at central banking in the nineteenth century and formation of the Federal Reserve in the early twentieth century.

Weintraub, Robert E. "Congressional Supervision of Monetary Policy." In *Journal of Monetary Economics* (April 1978): 325–86.
Offers alternative to independence of Fed argument.
———. *The Federal Reserve: Purposes and Functions*. Washington, D.C.: Board of Governors of the Federal Reserve, 1984.
Short but comprehensive booklet providing the essential elements of Federal Reserve organization and operation.

APPENDIX

16. The Federal Reserve Balance Sheet

Chapter 7 outlined the multiple expansion of credit and showed how, by changing depository institution reserves, the Federal Reserve can influence the total supply of money in the economy. In this appendix, you'll see a clearer picture of where those reserves fit into the overall Federal Reserve System balance sheet.

Keep in mind that reserves form the basis for the changes in the supply of money through the expansionary/contractionary process described previously. The level of reserves is influenced by the Fed's assets and other liabilities—reserves vary directly with Fed assets and inversely with other Fed liabilities. Government securities represent the largest category of assets in the Fed's balance sheet. Through purchases or sales of government securities in the open market, the Fed changes the level of reserves and sets into motion changes in the supply of money. When the Fed purchases government securities in the open market it has increased its assets and its reserves. These increased reserves allow the extension of loans and may result in an expansion of the money supply.

Balance Sheet and Account Entries Descriptions

Before proceeding, look at a recent Federal Reserve balance sheet. Table 16A.1 is a consolidated balance sheet for the entire Federal Reserve System. Notice the primary entries under assets and liabilities. Government securities represent the largest asset. Federal Reserve notes represent the largest liability. These are two important entries because they have significant influence over the degree of expansion and contraction of the money supply via changes in depository institution reserves. For example, an increase in the public's holding of currency resulting in an increase in Federal Reserve notes (a liability in the balance sheet) will cause bank reserves to drop and thus lead to a contraction of the overall money supply. Under circumstances where the Fed is seeking to maintain or increase the supply of money, it will sell securities in the open market to increase reserves.

Before continuing with a discussion of the Fed's control over factors influencing the supply of money, the entries on the consolidated balance sheet must be clarified. *Gold certificates* represent Fed claims against gold

Assets	June 1985
Gold certificates	11,090
Special drawing rights certificate account	4718
Coin	570
Loans	
to depository institutions	818
other	0
Acceptances	0
Federal agency obligations	
bought outright	8303
held under repurchase agreements	0
United States government securities	
bought outright (includes bills, notes and bonds)	176,620
held under repurchase agreements	0
Cash items in process of collection	5495
Bank premises	
Other assets	15,017
Total Assets	223,133
Liabilities	
Federal Reserve notes	177,189
Deposits	
to depository institutions	30,782
United States Treasury—general account	3280
foreign official accounts and others	785
Deferred availability cash items	4935
Other liabilities and accrued dividends	2184
Total Liabilities	219,155
Capital Account	
Capital paid in	1821
Surplus	1781
Other	376
Total Liabilities and Capital Account	233,133

Source: Federal Reserve Bulletin (June 1986): A–10.

TABLE 16A.1 *Federal Reserve Banks: Consolidated Condition ($millions)*

held by the United States Treasury at Fort Knox, Kentucky. The Fed previously was required to hold gold to support its Federal Reserve note issues; this requirement no longer exists, but the Fed still holds a claim against some Treasury gold reserves.

Special Drawing Rights are Fed claims against the international currency which has replaced gold. These special drawing rights, created by the International Monetary Fund in 1970 as a substitute for gold, can be used to obtain foreign currency. This entry represents the SDR certificates owned by the Fed. (The value of SDRs is based on a weighted basket of five national currencies.)

Loans to Depository Institutions are short-term borrowing by depository institutions. Depository institutions borrow from the regional Federal Reserve banks through the discount window at the discount rate established by the Fed.

Acceptances are bills of exchange (discussed in Chapter 5 as a means of credit in international trade) which have been purchased by the Fed or which are held under repurchase agreements.

Federal Agency Obligations and United States Government Securities are by far the largest entry among Fed assets. They represent an array of government issued securities, some emanating from government agencies and others from the Treasury, which the Fed either owns outright or is holding under repurchase agreements. These securities form the basis for the Fed's open-market operations.

Cash Items in Process of Collection (CIPC) is the value of checks currently being collected and cleared by the Fed. The Fed credits reserve accounts of depository institutions presenting checks and, after processing the checks, the Fed debits the accounts of the institutions on which the checks were drawn. During the process, the Fed lists the dollar value as an asset in this account entry. The Fed also lists a liability, Deferred Availability Cash Items (DACI) for checks in process. The difference between CIPC and DACI is the Fed float.

Bank premises refers to the Fed's brick and mortar assets, and *Foreign currency assets* are the Fed's foreign currency holdings as well as United States government securities held under repurchase agreements originally bought with foreign currencies. *Other* assets include equipment and similar holdings.

On the liability side, *Federal Reserve Notes* represent the value of paper currency in circulation. These Federal Reserve Notes are claims against the Fed. Each Federal Reserve bank issues its own notes and, while these notes are not backed by anything but the public's trust in the system, the regional banks must maintain collateral that is equivalent to the notes it issues. Collateral might include government securities, SDRs or gold certificates.

Deposits come from several sources. The *Depository Institutions* entry represents deposits from commercial banks and other depository institutions. Institutions must meet reserve requirements by holding vault cash or making deposits with the Fed. The *United States Treasury* entry represents funds from the Treasury. The Fed functions as the government's principal banker. Treasury payments are made from this account. The Treasury transfers funds to this account from its tax and loan accounts at depository institutions around the country. *Official foreign accounts* refers to deposits at the Fed from foreign central banks or the IMF, which represent the working balances these institutions have in the United States.

Deferred Available Cash Item (DACI) is checks in the clearing process. The Fed must debit reserve accounts as soon as it clears these checks. *Other Liabilities and Accrued Dividends* includes Fed obligations (for example, operating expenses) not yet paid and serves as the account reflecting the revaluation in dollars of the Fed's foreign exchange holdings for foreign central banks.

Balance Sheet and Money Supply Expansion

In looking at this balance sheet, specifically in terms of the Federal Reserve's impact on the money supply, notice that the Fed has only indirect or perhaps even no control over a number of entries. Specifically, these include the following:

- gold certificates which are determined by the United States balance of payments
- loans which are influenced by the discount rate, the prevailing market rate of interest on securities, and the demand for securities
- the Fed float which is influenced by everything from individual, corporate, and bank payment patterns to technological advances, to factors affecting the transportation of checks
- currency in circulation which is to a large extent dictated by the level of economic activity and the income velocity of money

- Treasury deposits which are controlled by the United States Treasury and depend on revenue inflow and government expenditures and transfer flows
- foreign deposits which depend on the actions of foreign banks, which in turn are influenced by international economic events.

The Fed has complete control only over the level of United States government securities. The Fed has some influence on the level of bank borrowing through the discount rate which it establishes. This reinforces the point made in Chapter 7 that the Fed is not the exclusive force controlling the supply of money. Still, in light of the dominance of government securities in the consolidated balance sheet, you can see how the Fed is the strongest force influencing the level of reserves and, ultimately, changes in the money supply. The Fed can use its dominant position vis-à-vis the open market to offset many of the changes brought about in the other account entries.

Analysts often refer to that portion of the Fed's balance sheet which has the greatest impact on the nation's money supply as *high-powered money*. High-powered money consists of Federal Reserve notes and depository institution deposits. If the Fed wants to affect notes and deposits, it does so through open-market operations. You can see the relationship between high-powered money and the money supply by referring to the Chapter 17 appendix.

CHAPTER SEVENTEEN

GOALS AND INSTRUMENTS of MONETARY POLICY

Actually, our nation sometimes expects more from the Federal Reserve than we can reasonably expect to accomplish, in view of the imperfect tools with which we work and the complex problems our nation faces.

Arthur M. Burns
Address at dedication of Minneapolis Federal Reserve Bank
September 8, 1973

Having developed an understanding of the origins, structure, and functions of the Federal Reserve System, you are now in a position to examine the operations of the Fed. This chapter explores the country's overall economic goals and how the Fed's monetary policy ties in with efforts to achieve these goals. Before the discussion of monetary policy strategies (Chapter 18), and an evaluation of the Fed's record (Chapter 19), this chapter reviews the tools of monetary policy. The chapter also describes the Federal Reserve's role in international monetary affairs. Since international events have an effect on domestic monetary policies, understanding the relationship of the Fed to international markets is a necessary prerequisite to evaluating the Fed's record.

This chapter concludes with an appendix entitled "Budget Deficits and the Federal Reserve," a topic that merits your attention. The actions of the Federal Reserve are intimately related to the deficit and attempts to reduce it.

Chapter Objectives

As you read this chapter consider the following questions: What is the Fed trying to accomplish? What mechanisms or tools does it use? What role does the Fed play in international financial markets?

In previous chapters, you learned that this country has stated clear economic goals. By the end of this chapter you should be able to:

- State the four major economic goals for the United States.
- Identify the goals of the Federal Reserve System.
- Explain whether attempts to maintain a secure and efficient financial system complement or interfere with the Fed's efforts at macroeconomic stability.

Although small in number, the Fed's monetary policy tools are large in their potential effect on the economy. You should understand these tools and why some of them are more important than others. By the end of this chapter you will be able to:

- List the Fed's monetary policy tools.
- Explain why the Fed relies so heavily on open-market operations.
- Differentiate between defensive and dynamic open-market operations.
- Describe "Fed Watching" and explain why it has become so important.
- Explain why changes in reserve requirements are used so seldom although they are a powerful tool.
- Identify reasons that the discount rate and reserve requirements may become more important policy tools.

Domestic monetary policy does not take place in a vacuum. Federal Reserve decisions are influenced by events in the rest of the world. This chapter will lead you to consider the Fed and its relationship to the international sector. You should be able to:

- Explain how financial markets influence the value of the American dollar.
- Discuss the role of the central bank in changing the value of the dollar.
- Describe relationships between domestic and international monetary policies.

Keep these objectives in mind as you read Chapter 17. Remember that your goal is to use the information from this chapter and the previous one to analyze monetary policy in Chapter 18, and then to evaluate it in Chapter 19.

Goals of the Economic System

Chapter 16 pointed out that our central banking system was created to provide for a safer and more flexible banking and monetary system. Specifically, the Fed was designed to provide an elastic currency, improve bank supervision, and create a mechanism for discounting commercial paper. But, the Federal Reserve System moved beyond these goals to address broader objectives for the economic and financial system.

The basic macroeconomic goals were enunciated in legislation passed into law at the conclusion of World War II. The Employment Act of 1946 stated that

> . . . it is the continuing policy and responsibility of the Federal Government to use all practicable means . . . to foster and promote . . . maximum employment, production and purchasing power.

Also included among the basic macroeconomic goals is a balance in international trade and finance. Subsequent legislation, most recently the Full Employment and Balanced Growth Act of 1978 (sometimes called the Humphrey-Hawkins Act), reinforced these goals.[1] This legislation requires the Board of Governors to report to Congress twice each year (February and July) regarding the

> . . . objectives and plans . . . with respect to the ranges of growth or dimunition of the monetary and credit aggregates. . . .

At various times, especially in the immediate postwar period, questions have arisen as to the applicability of the Employment Act to independent federal agencies such as the Federal Reserve. Although Fed critics sometimes will question the usefulness or timing of monetary policy actions, the Federal Reserve is a key partner in the conduct of macroeconomic policy. The Full Employment and Balanced Growth Act of 1978 underscored the importance of Fed monetary policy when it required the chairman of the Board of Governors to report to Congress twice each year on economic developments and monetary policy targets.

The goals of the Federal Reserve System can be lumped into two general categories:

1. maintenance of a secure and efficient financial system
2. attainment of macroeconomic stability

---

[1] Amendments to the Federal Reserve Act have been designed to enable the Fed to work toward the attainment of these goals in a more effective manner. Key legislation includes the Banking Act of 1935, 1970 amendments to the Bank Holding Company Act, the International Banking Act of 1978, and the Depository Institutions Deregulation and Monetary Control Act of 1980.

The first category includes the Fed's efforts relating to regulation and supervision, service to the United States Treasury, and the "housekeeping" functions (such as check clearing and distribution of coin and currency) performed for depository institutions. These activities were discussed in the last chapter. While extremely important, they are not part of Federal Reserve monetary policy. The second category, consisting of monetary policies to attain "maximum employment, production and purchasing power," defines the scope for our discussion in this chapter. The Fed serves as a partner with fiscal policy makers in working for macroeconomic stability by influencing the nation's supply of money and credit. The Fed does this through the use of its monetary policy tools.

Monetary Policy Tools

The Federal Reserve relies upon a set of general tools and a few specific, selective tools as it seeks to provide sufficient money and credit to encourage long-term, stable economic growth with reasonable price stability. In the short term, the Fed attempts to respond to seasonal conditions and unforeseen events by providing necessary liquidity to the financial system and to adjust its policies to prevent inflation or deflation.

The Fed's general monetary policy tools consist of open-market operations, setting the discount rate, establishing reserve requirements, and exercising some moral suasion. Selective policy tools include regulations relating to the stock market and consumer credit.

Open-Market Operations

Throughout much of its history, as well as today, the Fed has relied on open-market operations as its most important monetary policy tool. During the first decade of operations, the Fed used discounting as its primary policy tool. Before the early 1920s, the Fed relied largely on open-market purchases to generate interest revenue. Beginning in the early 1920s, the Fed saw the potential in using open-market purchases as a powerful monetary-policy tool. In 1923, the Federal Reserve began using open-market operations to effect changes in bank reserves and, through them, bank lending and the money supply.

Decisions regarding the Fed's purchase or sale of securities on the open market are made by the Federal Open-Market Committee. This committee, consisting of seven members of the Board of Governors and five Federal

Reserve bank presidents (the New York Bank president and four others who serve on a rotating basis), meets eight times a year and holds weekly conference calls. The committee makes decisions about Federal Reserve actions in the open market and directs the FOMC Manager for Domestic Operations at the New York Bank to carry out these actions. The Manager makes day to day decisions based on the directives received from the FOMC. The process involved in open-market operations is described in Banking Today 17.1.

The Fed's actions in the open market influence the level of nonborrowed reserves available to depository institutions. These reserves form the basis for depository institutions' loans, and, through this credit creation process, they provide the impetus for changes in the overall supply of money in the system.

As will be discussed in greater detail in the next chapter, the Fed has followed varying approaches to monetary policy over the years. The Fed consistently uses open-market operations as the vehicle by which it implements monetary policy. However, economic conditions, the composition of the board, and prevailing attitudes about monetary policy influence the philosophy which drives open-market decisions. For example, before October 1979, the FOMC considered monetary market and reserve conditions. To gauge these conditions, the committee observed the federal funds rate. The committee decided on open-market sales or purchases depending on whether the members wanted the federal funds rate and other short-term interest rates to rise or fall. In October, 1979, the Fed announced a change in procedure. The Fed would establish a goal for money supply growth and target reserves to achieve this growth. Monetary aggregates, rather than interest rates, were the key variables.

The FOMC releases its open-market directives to the public at the conclusion of the meeting following the one where they were delivered. In an era where expectations are as influential as policy actions themselves, Fed watching has become important and the minutes of the FOMC meetings are the best regularly published source of information. The FOMC minutes include a summary of the committee's assessment of conditions, the votes of its members, and discussion regarding the votes. Through the minutes, observers can gain insights into possible subsequent Fed actions.

Fed watching is a dynamic guessing game. Fed observers, usually employed by major banks, savings and loan associations, and insurance companies, look at all available information regarding Federal Reserve actions. Observers study the public policy pronouncements of Fed officials, Fed statistics, and Treasury data, and the actions of other institutions watching the Fed. These highly paid specialists help big financial institutions anticipate the effects of Federal Reserve intervention in the open market. Correctly anticipating Fed actions gives bond traders and brokers dealing in

The time is early afternoon on a Wednesday in mid-June. The place is the trading room on the eighth floor of the Federal Reserve Bank of New York. The manager of the Open-Market Account for Domestic Operations gathers with his trading room officers to reaffirm the judgment reached earlier to buy $1¼ billion of Treasury bills. The banking system has a clear need for additional reserves to meet the increased public demand for currency and deposits expected as the end of the quarter and July 4 approach. The markets for bank reserves and Treasury securities are functioning normally with prices moving narrowly. After a brief discussion, the manager gives final approval to the planned operation.

The officer-in-charge at the Fed's Trading Desk turns to the ten officers and securities traders who sit before telephone consoles linking them to three dozen primary dealers in United States government securities. "We're going to ask for offerings of all bills for regular delivery," she says. Each trader knows this means delivery and payment will take place the next day. Each picks up the vertical strips on which the offerings will be recorded for the four dealers he will call.

Bill, one of the group, presses the button on his telephone console, sounding a buzzer on the corresponding console of a government securities dealer.

"John," Bill says, "we are looking for offerings of bills for regular delivery."

John replies, "I'll be right back." He turns and yells, "The Fed is in, asking for all bills for delivery tomorrow." Moments later information-screens around the country and abroad flash the news. Salespeople begin ringing their customers to see if they have bills they want to offer. Meanwhile, John checks with the trading manager of his firm to see how aggressive he should be in pricing the firm's own securities.

Twenty minutes later John rings back. "Bill, I can offer you $15 million of bills maturing August 9 at 9.20 percent, $40 million September 13 bills at 9.42, $25 million of September 20's at 9.46 and another 25 at 9.44. I'll sell $75 million December 13's at 10.12 and another 100 at 10.9. I can offer $20 million of March 21's at 10.25 and 50 May 16's at 10.28. All for delivery tomorrow."

Bill reads back each of the offerings to double check, then says, "Can I have those firm?" "Sure."

Within 10 or 15 minutes each trader has written the offerings obtained from his calls on pre-printed slips. The officer-in-charge arrays the individual dealer strips on an inclined board placed atop a counter. A quick tally shows that dealers have offered $7.8 billion of bills for regular delivery.

The officer and a colleague begin comparing rates across the different maturities, seeking those that are high in relation to adjoining issues. She circles any special bargains with a red pencil. With an eye on heavy existing holdings, she circles other propositions that offer yields on or above a yield curve she draws mentally through the more heavily offered issues.

Her associate keeps a running total of the amounts being bought. When the desired volume has been circled and cross-checked, the individual strips are returned to the traders, who quickly ring up the dealers.

Bill says, "John, we'll take the $25 million of September 20's at 9.46, the 75 of December 13's at 10.12, and the 50 of May 16's at 10.28 for regular delivery. A total of $150 million. No, thanks on the others."

Forty-five minutes after the initial entry, the follow-up calls have been completed. The Trading Desk has bought $1,304 billion of Treasury bills. Only the paper work remains. The traders write up tickets, which authorize the accounting section to instruct the Reserve Bank's Government Bond Department to receive and pay for the specific Treasury bills bought.

On Thursday, the Federal Reserve will take delivery of the purchased securities from the banks that handle deliveries for the dealers—the clearing banks for non-bank dealers. As authorized by these banks, it will deduct these securities from the book entry list of their holdings at the Federal Reserve Bank. The Federal Reserve's credits to those accounts will add about $1.3 billion to the reserves maintained by United States financial institutions at the Reserve Banks.

Source: "The 'Go-Around'" from *Open-Market Operations* by Paul Meek (Federal Reserve Bank of New York, 1985). Reprinted by permission.

BANKING TODAY 17.2 — Fed Watching

It's a daily occurrence at all major banks. Fed specialists gather to brainstorm about Federal Reserve policy actions. Since the Fed's actions are so important in financial markets, correctly anticipating Fed announcements or actions, and acting accordingly, can help the firm increase its investment returns.

The official "Fed Watchers" are often former Fed employees. These specialists are in particularly heavy demand. Commercial and investment banks will pay upwards of $200,000 per year to land such a prized commodity. Since correct anticipation of Fed actions can generate significant dollars for the firm, Fed Watchers can more than pay their salaries with just a few correct predictions.

Information on Fed decisions is public information, but only after the fact. Many Fed Watchers study the FOMC minutes to try and discern patterns or trends. Others watch the public statements made by Fed officials to catch any indication of upcoming decisions for monetary policy. It's important for Fed Watchers to be able to differentiate between an actual policy move, an attempt to influence credit or the money supply, and a routine technical adjustment.

Chairman Volcker's influence is so significant that his statements can cause major movements in financial markets. He is literally "hounded" by reporters whenever he appears in public. In response to a reporter's question about foreign market intervention, Volcker is reported to have responded, "We did what we did, and we didn't do what we didn't do."

Despite such guarded comments, Fed Watchers are able to gain insights into Fed actions. Using their recommendations, banks will make decisions about rates on overnight loans and the weighted average maturity for their certificates of deposit. With demand for good advice pushing consulting fees for Fed Watchers up to the $2000-per-hour level, there are ample opportunities for former Fed staff members to make it big in the private sector.

interest-sensitive commodities and options the advantage in these fast-moving markets. Fed watchers' recommendations also influence banks' decisions on the interest rates they establish for instruments such as certificates of deposit with adjustable rates and overnight loans between banks.

Rational expectations economists argue that Fed watching reflects increased attention to Fed policies by the public, especially large institutional investors. As these institutions anticipate Fed actions or react to signals from the Fed, they can take actions which may diminish or counteract the effects of Federal Reserve policies. For this reason, some economists argue that the Fed should not intervene in the open market to respond to short-term changes in credit conditions. Instead the Fed should announce long-term money growth goals and stick to them.

In many instances, Fed watchers are trying to determine whether Fed actions are technical in nature, that is, short-term adjustments, or whether they signal a major policy decision which will have important long-term implications for interest rates.

The Fed implements open-market operations weekly or even daily. The policy directives driving the actions of the New York open-market desk are either proactive or reactive in nature. The Fed may react to conditions by undertaking *defensive open-market operations*. For example, a dramatic drop in the value of the dollar on international exchange markets may force the Fed to sell securities to keep interest rates up, preventing widespread movement of funds out of the United States.

The Fed also uses open-market operations in a proactive way, more commonly referred to as *dynamic open-market operations*. These actions are designed to achieve some overall long-term goal. The Fed may undertake open-market purchases regularly in order to increase reserves along the way toward the goal of expanding the supply of money and stimulating economic activity. A good example of dynamic open-market operations is the Fed's establishment of narrow money supply growth rates in the early 1980s and the regular use of open-market operations to achieve these monetary targets.

In either case open-market operations are the most often used policy tool. The Fed can enter the open market on a regular basis at whatever level it wants, either in response to particular events or to adjust reserves on a continuous basis. Furthermore, because the Fed can enter the open market so easily, actions can be intensified or reversed at any time. But while open-market operations are the most important policy tool, the other policy tools are also significant.

Discount Policy

A second monetary policy tool is the discount mechanism. Depository institutions may borrow from the Federal Reserve.[2] When first established, the Fed's only real monetary policy tool was setting a discount rate which would either encourage or discourage borrowing through the discount window. Subsequently, open-market operations became the primary tool of monetary policy. Discount rate policy is still important and, as will be discussed later, some argue it is becoming increasingly important.

Discount rate decisions pertaining to the administration of the discount windows at district reserve banks are made by the Board of Governors, but discount rate changes are initiated by the district banks. The boards of directors of the district Federal Reserve banks meet at least every two weeks to make recommendations about discount rate changes. Implementation of discount rate policy is coordinated by district bank lending officers and Board of Governors staff so that regional policy differences are minimized.

---

[2] A bank or other depository institution "borrows" from the Fed in one of two ways. First, it may discount or sell to a Reserve Bank loans or similar assets that carry the institution's endorsement. Second, it may receive an advance on its promissory note which is secured by adequate collateral (for example, United States mortgage notes or state/local government securities).

The Depository Institutions Deregulation and Monetary Control Act of 1980 instituted changes in discount policy. Before 1980, only Federal Reserve member banks were eligible to borrow through the discount window. With passage of the DIDMC Act all depository institutions subject to Fed reserve requirements are eligible to use the discount window.[3] Borrowing from the Fed is intended to help depository institutions, and the system as a whole, adjust to fluctuations in deposit and loan demand. Institutions may borrow from the Fed on either a short-term or long-term basis. Short-term borrowing, called *adjustment credit*, is intended to provide temporary relief to unanticipated reductions in reserve accounts. Longer term borrowing, called seasonal or *extended credit*, is designed to assist institutions experiencing more sustained liquidity demands. Table 17.1 illustrates the level of borrowing in each category.

The Board of Governors establishes a discount rate, or interest rate on borrowed funds, which is consistent with its overall monetary and credit objectives. Borrowing from the discount window is intended to fulfill the Fed's responsibility as "lender of last resort" for the financial system or an individual institution. The discount window is not intended to encourage "for profit" borrowing or to fund speculative investments. The Federal

---

[3] Institutions now eligible are member and nonmember commercial banks, American branches of foreign banks, savings banks, savings and loan associations, and credit unions. The act does specify that the Fed should not be the lender of first resort for noncommercial banks. For example, savings and loan associations should rely on the Federal Home Loan Bank before turning to the Fed.

Year	Adjustment Credit	Seasonal and Other Credit	Total
1975	144	52	195
1976	64	20	84
1977	405	56	461
1978	750	121	871
1979	1187	151	1339
1980	1153	163	1416
1981	1073	288	1361
1982	746	206	1052
1983	554	485	1039
1985	496	825	1321

TABLE 17.1 *Discount Window Borrowing*   (annual average in $millions)

Reserve discount officer has the responsibility for determining whether a loan request is necessary and appropriate. The officer may have difficulty deciding whether an institution's temporary need could have been anticipated. Since the discount rate is often below the prevailing market interest rate, the Fed sometimes takes action to assure that discount window borrowing is necessary. For example, on occasion, the Fed has imposed a discount rate surcharge for large banks using the discount window on a frequent basis. This policy allows the Fed to restrict borrowing selectively without adversely affecting small institutions.

Despite the ready availability of funds on an "as needed" basis from the discount window, many financial firms choose not to borrow from the Fed. Total borrowing from the Fed is relatively small, generally less than .1 percent of total loans and investments of the institutions eligible to use the discount window. Reluctance on the part of some firms to borrow from the Fed may stem from a desire to use the discount window only in an emergency situation or from a perception that such borrowing might reflect negatively on the institution's image. Other firms may want to avoid the pressure that the Fed applies for quick repayment.

The discount rate is an important part of Federal Reserve monetary policy. To those watching Fed actions, changes in the discount rate signal a possible policy shift by the Board of Governors. To many, the most important aspect of discount rate policy is the announcement effect. Attempts to interpret the reasons behind a discount rate change may be difficult, but an observation of the movements of the discount rate and short-term interest rates reveals a close correlation. In addition to the effect the discount rate has on depository institution reserves, the announcement effects of discount rate changes may influence expectations and market behavior. Others argue that discount rate changes actually respond to market conditions rather than influencing them. Figure 17.1 reveals the close connection between the discount rate and short-term interest rates. It also shows that changes in the discount rate lag behind changes in short-term interest rates.

Reserve Requirements

The Fed received authority to set reserve requirements, at least within broad ranges set by Congress, from the initial central banking legislation and subsequent amendments. The 1980 financial reform legislation greatly expanded the scope of reserve requirements and made them an even more powerful monetary control tool.

As you learned in the discussion on monetary expansion and contraction in Chapter 7, the level of depository institution reserves dictates the

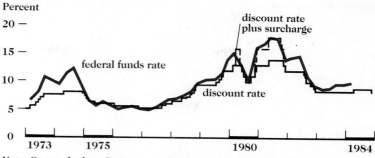

Percent

Note: Quarterly data. Data on reserves are seasonally adjusted.

Source: Board of Governors of the Federal Reserve System, *The Federal Reserve System: Purposes and Functions* (Washington: D.C., 1974): 32.

FIGURE 17.1   *Discount Rate Signals Interest Rate Changes*   The discount rate is a signal to money and capital markets. Short-term interest rates follow closely the movement of the discount rate.

degree of change in the nation's money supply. While the Fed uses open-market operations most often to effect changes in reserves, most economists agree that reserve requirements are the most powerful tool.

Before 1980, Fed-established reserve requirements applied only to member banks. For a number of years, the structure of reserve requirements was outdated. Changes in the financial system during the 1970s, especially the rise in new interest-bearing transactions deposits, necessitated a change in the structure of reserve requirements and in the scope of institutions affected by reserve requirements.[4] Effective monetary control by the Fed led to the need for the application of reserve requirements to a broader array of institutions. With passage of the financial reform act, all depository institutions must adhere to the reserve requirements set by the Fed and must hold these reserves as vault cash or deposits at Federal Reserve Banks. Table 17.2 shows the reserve requirements that apply to various deposit liabilities.

The new reserve requirement structure is designed to enhance the Fed's control over the M1 money supply measure. The highest reserve requirements apply to transaction accounts, the largest component of M1 (reserve requirements applying to components of M2 and M3 have been

---

[4] Because of the high interest rates nonmember institutions could earn on their reserves, member banks had increasing difficulty competing in an era of rising interest rates. This situation encouraged many member banks to withdraw from the Federal Reserve System and this, in turn, reduced the effectiveness of the Fed's monetary control actions.

Type of Deposit and Deposit Interval	Member Bank Requirements Before Implementation of the Monetary Control Act		Type of Deposit and Deposit Interval	Depository Institution Requirements After Implementation of the Monetary Control Act	
	Percent	*Effective Date*		*Percent*	*Effective Date*
Net demand			*Net transaction accounts*		
$0 million–$2 million	7	12/30/76	$0–$28.9 million	3	12/29/83
$2 million–$10 million	9½	12/30/76	Over $28.9 million	12	12/29/83
$10 million–$100 million	11¾	12/30/76	*Nonpersonal time deposits*		
$100 million–$400 million	12¾	12/30/76	By original maturity		
Over $400 million	16¼	12/30/76	Less than 1½ years	3	10/6/83
Time and savings			1½ years or more	0	10/6/83
Savings	3	3/16/67	*Eurocurrency liabilities*		
Time			All types	3	11/13/80
$0 million–$5 million, by maturity					
30–179 days	3	3/16/67			
180 days to 4 years	2½	1/8/76			
4 years or more	1	10/30/75			
Over $5 million, by maturity					
30–179 days	6	12/12/74			
180 days to 4 years	2½	1/8/76			
4 years or more	1	10/30/75			

Source: Federal Reserve Bulletin (January 1984): A-7.

TABLE 17.2 *Reserve Requirements of Depository Institutions* (percent of deposits)

reduced or eliminated). This indicates that policy makers see monetary control as most effective when it focuses on the more narrow money measure rather than on the broader monetary and credit aggregates. This implies that the linkage between reserves and money is most predictable when M1 is considered and when the same reserve ratio applies to various types of deposits included within that money measure. The current required reserve regime contributes to the Fed's control of M1. Shifts in funds from member to nonmember institutions, the movement of funds between various types of transaction accounts or transfers among institutions do not alter the reserve requirements and thus do not increase excess reserves, the basis of money supply expansion. Note also that reserve requirements apply more to large institutions than to small ones.

Beginning in early 1984, Fed policies required depository institutions to maintain reserves behind transactions deposits on the basis of average daily balances over a two-week period. This is called *contemporaneous reserve requirements* and contrasts with the previous policy allowing institutions to maintain reserves on the basis of deposits two weeks earlier (called lagged reserve requirements).[5] The new procedure is designed to improve monetary control; institutions now must stay up to date by acquiring reserves to support growing transactions deposits.

Despite the changes in reserve requirements and the accelerated reserve accounting procedure, most economists would argue that reserve requirement changes are not viable as a monetary policy tool. Compared to open-market operations and discount rate policy, reserve requirement changes are not consistent with a flexible approach to monetary control. In a period when Federal Reserve policy requires fine tuning of the money supply, reserve requirements are equivalent to using a blunt axe when a sharp surgical scalpel is needed. Reserve requirements apply to all institutions and may disproportionately affect some more than others. Frequent changes in reserve requirements complicate depository institutions' asset and liability management decisions. Because the Fed does not use reserve requirements on a regular basis, the announcement effect of reserve requirement changes may have disruptive effects on money and capital markets.

Discount Rate and Reserve Requirements in Contemporary Settings

Contrary to the prevailing view that the Fed's relatively infrequent use of the discount rate and reserve requirement changes means that these policy tools are unnecessary, some contemporary analysts argue just the opposite.[6] Legislative and institutional changes coupled with the Fed's shift from a concentration on interest rate targeting, to money and reserve targeting make

---

[5] For a detailed discussion of the mechanics of this process, see R. Alton Gilbert and Michael E. Trebing, "The New System of Contemporaneous Reserve Requirements," Federal Reserve Bank of St. Louis *Review* (December 1982): 3–7.

[6] A well-stated and concise argument on this point of view is put forth by Gordon H. Sellon, Jr., "The Instruments of Monetary Policy," Federal Reserve Bank of Kansas City *Economic Review* (May 1984): 3–20.

the use of the discount rate and reserve requirements more viable policy tools. More specifically, the application of reserve requirements and the discount rate to all depository institutions makes these tools more useful as instruments of short-term monetary control.

Evidence of the increased value of these tools is already appearing. The Fed's willingness to apply a discount rate surcharge (utilized in March, 1980, and again in November, 1980) allows the targeting of discount policy to specific institutions, based either on size or frequency of borrowing. By using the surcharge, the Fed can make discount policy more focused and can enhance its control over the money creation process.

On occasion, the Fed has also focused more narrowly on reserve requirement changes. It has changed reserve requirements on large denomination CDs and Eurodollar deposits. In being selective, for example, affecting large denomination CDs only, the Fed can influence some of the major financial institutions that use managed liabilities to fund credit expansion.[7] Although provisions of the financial reform act limit the Fed's flexibility in using reserve requirements on a differentiated basis, reserve requirements may become more valuable in the control of broader monetary aggregates.

Moral Suasion

The Federal Reserve may use *moral suasion*, its influence to urge depository institutions to adhere to a particular policy stance. This policy tool, although not mentioned in any Federal Reserve legislation, proves quite useful. Either because the Fed has such an array of expertise or because the Fed is such a dominant player in the money markets, financial institutions may take direct or indirect advice from the Fed. This may come in the form of policy statements by the Federal Reserve chairman or through suggestions from regional Federal Reserve bank officials. Beyond this, the Fed does possess considerable latent power through regulation of bank holding companies, supervisory authority, involvement with institutions considering mergers or by necessity facing liquidation, and decision-making authority over use of the discount window.

---

[7] Some institutions, especially during periods of tight money, shift from transactions deposits to lower required reserve managed liabilities and are thus able to expand credit even though the Fed is trying to restrict credit.

Selective Tools

In addition to the more general tools of monetary policy, the Federal Reserve in the past, and to a limited extent currently, has used some selective tools to influence the supply of money or to ensure a smoothly functioning financial system.

Stock Market Credit   The most visible selective tool is the Fed's control of stock market credit. Stemming from the excessive expansion of credit used to purchase securities in the years preceding the stock market crash of 1929, the Congress passed the Securities and Exchange Commission Act of 1934. This legislation and its subsequent amendments gave the Board of Governors responsibility for setting *margin requirements*, the portion of securities purchases which can be made with credit. Specifically, the Fed sets limits on the maximum credit a lender may provide when the purpose of the loan is the purchase of stocks.

   The portion of the stock price provided as a down payment is called the margin. The Fed sets limits on the amount of credit that lenders can provide for down payment on stocks. All lending agencies are affected: brokers (through Regulation T), banks (Regulation U), and other lenders (Regulation G). Borrowers themselves must comply with margin requirements (Regulation X).

   Through these limitations, the Fed prevents undue credit expansion to finance stock purchases. The Fed varies the limit depending on perceived level of speculative activity and economic conditions. These margin requirements also help prevent unnecessarily wide fluctuations in stock prices. In recent years, the Fed has taken an active role in preventing corporate takeovers through the use of *junk bonds*, bonds issued by companies whose ratings are below those normally accepted by the market.

Consumer Credit Controls   The Federal Reserve has at various times been responsible for enforcing consumer credit controls. The Credit Control Act, which expired in June 1982, provided that the president could authorize the Board of Governors to regulate and control credit. President Carter did so in 1981 as part of the administration's efforts to fight inflation. The Fed imposed reserve requirements against consumer loans which restricted bank lending. The Fed administered more extensive consumer credit controls during World War II and the Korean War.

   Until the DIDMC Act eliminated interest ceilings, the Fed enforced interest rate ceilings for savings and time deposits. Regulation Q had established the ceilings. The final stages of a gradual elimination of such controls were completed in 1986. Before market conditions forced Congress to reform the financial system, the Fed dictated the maximum interest rate that member banks could pay on savings and time deposits.[8] The notion behind these limits was that customer deposits would be safer if depository institutions did not have to compete for funds.

The Federal Reserve and the International Sphere

International economic and financial conditions and legislation related to international banking have had a noticeable effect on the United States in recent years. During the last decade, the interdependence of this country and the rest of the world has become more apparent as a result of the rise and then the fall in oil prices, the international recession and the world debt crisis. At the same time, the U.S. Congress, pushed into action by foreign and domestic bankers, has taken steps to internationalize banking and finance. These events and actions have made the Federal Reserve an even more important force in the maintenance of international financial stability.

The Fed is involved in international issues in a variety of ways. Although international finance is not discussed in detail until the final chapter, the Fed's role in exchange rates, the internationalization of banking, and cooperation with other central banks is important in understanding the operations of the Federal Reserve.

Financial Markets and Exchange Rates

Since the early 1970s, market conditions have determined the rates of exchange between currencies. This process for establishing the value of one nation's currency in terms of another is called a floating exchange rate system. The previous fixed exchange rate system required a central bank to take actions to maintain the agreed-upon value of its currency in relationship to others. With the floating rate system central banks enter the international exchange markets only to prevent disorder.[9]

The Federal Reserve, acting through the New York Fed's manager for foreign operations, enters into exchange markets on behalf of the United

---

[8] The Federal Home Loan Bank Board did likewise for savings and loan associations as did the FDIC for insured nonmember commercial and savings banks.

[9] For a good discussion of foreign exchange markets, see either Roger M. Kubarych, *Foreign Exchange Markets in the United States* (New York: Federal Reserve Bank of New York, 1983) or K. Alec Chrystal, "A Guide to Foreign Exchange Markets," Federal Reserve Bank of St. Louis *Review* 66, 3 (March 1984): 5–18.

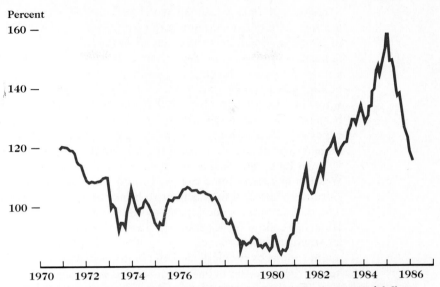

Percent

Note: The exchange rate shown here is based on a trade-weighted average of dollar exchange rates against the currencies of Germany, Japan, France, the United Kingdom, Canada, Italy, the Netherlands, Belgium, Sweden, and Switzerland. The weights are shares of each country's total trade in the trade of all ten countries from 1972 through 1976.

Source: *Economic Commentary*, Federal Reserve Bank of Cleveland (March 15, 1986). Reprinted by permission.

FIGURE 17.2 *Fluctuation in Dollar Exchange Rate* The American dollar exchange rate (that is, units of foreign currency units per dollar) rose rapidly from 1980 to mid-1985 when interest rates in this country were high. Since then, the dollar's value has declined.

States. The New York Fed may also act as the agent for foreign monetary authorities which maintain accounts with the Federal Reserve. The value of the American dollar relative to other currencies rose rather dramatically from 1980 to mid–1985 while high interest rates and generally favorable investment opportunities made the American dollar an attractive and stable currency. Then, in 1986 the value of the dollar dropped rapidly. Figure 17.2 reveals the historically high levels to which the dollar rose and the decline that followed.[10] (For a complete discussion of exchange rate movements see Chapter 20.)

---

[10] International supply and demand determines the value of the dollar. As foreign investors seek to exchange their country's currency for dollars to facilitate investment in this country, the demand for the American dollar rises. This makes the price of the dollar, in terms of other currencies, rise.

The Federal Reserve, along with the United States Treasury which acts through its Exchange Stabilization Fund, has responsibility for intervening in exchange markets to prevent disorder. The United States was under increasing pressure to do something to bring the dollar's value back down to a more reasonable level. Some estimates described the American dollar as being overvalued by one-third. Figure 17.2 shows one source of this pressure. The high value of the dollar makes American exports less attractive because they are more expensive in terms of other currency. American exports declined, while imports increased, putting the American international trade account in a seriously imbalanced condition.

In 1986, following a meeting of the central bank leaders from the major Western powers (United States, United Kingdom, Japan, France and West Germany), the Fed took actions to bring the value of the dollar back down. The dollar plunged, too far and too fast in the view of many, indicating the effects of central bank actions in financial markets. The continuing decline in American interest rates was a major factor in the dollar's decline. Subsequent actions by the Federal Reserve in conjunction with other central banks helped stabilize the dollar's decline (see discussion in Chapter 20).

The predicament facing the Fed in the 1980s raises two questions. How actively should the Fed intervene in foreign exchange markets? And, to what extent is domestic monetary policy affected by the Fed's posture in the international sphere? Governments of all the Western industrial nations are seeking ways to bring greater stability to financial markets.

The Fed generally attempts to separate its exchange intervention from its domestic monetary policy. For example, if the Fed purchases Deutsche marks, increasing the dollar reserves of the German Bundesbank held by the New York Fed, it might also sell securities in the domestic market to offset this action. Nonetheless, Fed actions in the international market may be used to complement domestic policy. For example, in 1979, the dollar's value was declining because of severe inflation; the Fed not only undertook a tightening of domestic monetary policy but used its holdings of foreign currencies to purchase American dollars, thus raising its value but also absorbing foreign central bank dollar reserves.

When the dollar is overvalued, requiring intervention, while at the same time domestic conditions require monetary stringency to prevent inflation (as was the case during the first part of the 1980s), policy makers are confronted with a decision about which actions will prevent international intervention from disrupting domestic monetary policy. This issue is raised again in Chapter 20. The point here is that the Federal Reserve is an active player in the international money game and that domestic and international monetary policy actions and financial conditions interact.

Internationalization of Banking

Although for centuries international bankers have functioned in all corners of the globe, the 1970s and 1980s have seen an acceleration of the internationalization of banking. Two acts before 1920 encouraged international links. The Federal Reserve Act of 1913 allowed nationally chartered banks to establish foreign operations but few American banks did so until very recently. The Edge Act of 1919 permitted American financial firms to open offices across state lines for the express purpose of encouraging American exports by providing credit. Foreign banks have maintained a presence in the United States but only recently have they come under Federal Reserve supervision.

The United States Congress has sought to make American firms competitive abroad and has instituted controls over foreign banks in the United States. The Federal Reserve has primary regulatory, supervisory, and policy responsibilities for international banking. The Federal Reserve

1. has responsibility for authorizing American member banks to establish branches abroad and then regulating their activities.
2. charters and regulates Edge Act corporations.
3. regulates the American operations of foreign banks.
4. supervises the foreign lending of American member banks.

BANKING TODAY ⒘③ The Swap Network

The Swap Network is a system of reciprocal currency arrangements between central banks. Specifically, a swap is the simultaneous purchase and sale of a currency for different maturity dates (usually about 90 days apart). Under this arrangement, any central bank can borrow the foreign currency it needs from a central bank in the network so it can intervene in the international financial market to support its own currency. In return, the borrowing central bank provides its own currency. The arrangement comes with an agreement to swap the currencies back. The Federal Reserve has swap arrangements with 14 foreign central banks and the Bank of International Settlements.

It's not only central banks which engage in swap arrangements. Commercial and investment banks and businesses do, too. They are more inclined to engage in interest rate swaps (there is even a newly formed International Swap Dealers Association). Interest rate swaps are simple. One corporation has access to fixed-rate financing at an attractive rate. Another corporation can get a good rate on a floating rate financing package. The two corporations issue the debt (borrow the funds) and then swap their interest payments. It's a simple concept. Complications arise when dozens of firms are involved.

Thus, although central banks originated the idea of swaps, private firms have refined the idea by applying it to interest rate exchanges. Estimates of the total volume of interest rate swaps for 1985 range from $150 to $200 billion; for 1986, the total volume exceeded $220 billion.

Cooperation with Foreign Central Banks

Throughout much of its existence, the Federal Reserve has cooperated with the central banks in other countries. The assistance the Fed provided to Britain in its efforts to return to the gold standard during the 1920s has generated much discussion and criticism. More recent Fed cooperative efforts are perhaps less controversial but equally significant.

The Fed is in regular contact with other central banks, especially those of our major trading partners, regarding the fluctuating values of currencies. This cooperation facilitates the financial market intervention discussed earlier in this section. For example, beginning in September, 1985, the United States, Japan, Germany, Britain, and France have coordinated their intervention actions to devalue the American dollar. To facilitate such actions, the Fed is part of a network of central banks which agree to swap currencies when intervention is necessary.

The Federal Reserve is also involved in negotiations with developing countries which have borrowed heavily from American financial firms. The International Lending Supervision Act of 1983 gave the Fed responsibility for negotiating with authorities in other countries to finalize consistent policies for loan arrangements and repayment plans so as to encourage American lending abroad. The Fed's efforts are intended to prevent massive defaults by foreign borrowers, a situation which would seriously threaten American financial stability, while encouraging continued sound lending and preventing risky loans by American lenders.

Chapter Conclusion

The Federal Reserve has tremendous power and authority, both domestically and internationally. It uses its policy tools, especially open-market operations, to achieve its established growth rates for monetary aggregates in order to move the economy closer to its desired macroeconomic goals. Internationally, the Fed, in conjunction with the U.S. Treasury, works with other central banks to maintain or restore stability in international financial markets.

With some understanding of the overall operation of the Fed, you are now ready to consider in more detail the policy strategies that are employed by the Board of Governors.

Consider These Questions

1. What are the major goals of the macroeconomic system? How can the Federal Reserve help achieve these goals?

2. Explain the functioning of the FOMC and the usefulness of open-market operations. Why is this tool used more extensively than the other tools of monetary policy?

3. What is "Fed Watching"? Why is it becoming so prominent? Does "Fed Watching" have any relationship to the rational expectations revolution?

4. If the discount rate is often below the prevailing market interest rate, why is borrowing from the Fed not greater than it is?

5. What's been happening to the discount rate lately? What effect has this had on other short-term lending rates? Give specific examples.

6. What role does a central bank play in the international exchange market? Does its international activity have any effect on domestic monetary policy?

7. The appendix addresses the federal budget deficit and monetary policy. How does monetary policy relate to the deficit? What would happen if the Fed did not "monetize the debt"?

8. If the monetary base is such a useful measurement tool for monetary authorities, why isn't it used instead of the conventional M1 measure?

Suggestions for Further Reading

Bach, G. L. *Making Monetary & Fiscal Policy*. Washington, D.C.: The Brookings Institution, 1971.
> Old book but its chapter on policy goals (Chapter 2) is still worth reading.

Cook, Timothy Q. and Bruce J. Summers, eds. *Instruments of the Money Market*. 6th edition. Federal Reserve Bank of Richmond, 1986.
> A compilation of articles on money market instruments including Treasury bills and the discount window.

Eccles, George S. *The Politics of Banking*. University of Utah School of Business, 1982.
> Section V, "The Struggle to Govern," outlines issues behind Federal Reserve goal setting and the influence of politics on monetary policy.

Meek, Paul. *Open Market Operations*. Federal Reserve Bank of New York, 1978.
> Excellent description of practical aspects of open-market operations.

Mengle, David L. "The Discount Window." In Federal Reserve Bank of Richmond *Economic Review* 72, 3 (May/June 1986): 2–10.
> Excellent overview of the mechanics and policy implications of the discount window.

Wooley, John T. *Monetary Politics: The Federal Reserve and the Politics of Monetary Policy*. New York: Cambridge University Press, 1984.
Interesting analysis of political factors involved in Federal Reserve goals setting and policy implementation.
———. "Is Central Banking Obsolete?" In *Manhattan Report on Economic Policy* IV, 3 (1984).
Provocative monograph which explores goals and utility of central bank operations.

APPENDIX

17. Budget Deficits and the Federal Reserve

The federal budget deficit has generated increasing concern on the part of economists and politicians. The budget deficit, simply stated, is the difference between inflow, government revenues, and outflow, government expenditures. Figure 17A.1 shows the magnitude of the federal deficits from 1963. The federal debt (the accumulated annual deficits) exceeded $1.4 billion at the end of 1983 and is estimated at almost $2.1 billion for fiscal year 1986. The United States Treasury is responsible for generating the revenues so the government can operate; it is also responsible for covering any shortfall and for servicing the debt. The government budget constraint illustrates the limited ways the Treasury can finance a deficit.

$$\text{DEFICIT} = G - T = \text{BONDS} + ME$$

where

DEFICIT = federal budget deficit

G = government expenditures

T = tax revenues

BONDS = new government securities purchases by the public

ME = additions to the monetary base

Additions to the monetary base are what tie the federal deficit to the Federal Reserve and monetary policy. You will see, as the monetary base and the Treasury's techniques for financing the deficit are explained, why so many people express so much concern about the Federal Reserve's role vis-à-vis the deficit.

The potential scenario that generates this concern goes as follows. The United States Treasury is forced to enter the financial markets to borrow funds to finance the government's deficit. Following the conventional loanable funds approach to interest rate determination, discussed in Chapter 3, this increases the demand for funds, and interest rates rise. To head off the negative effects of rising interest rates, the Fed will increase the supply of money (loanable funds). The increasing supply of money may then set off a new round of inflation.

What are the Treasury's options in financing the federal deficit? What role does the Federal Reserve play in these financial efforts? Finally, how does the deficit affect Fed policies and the supply of money?

445

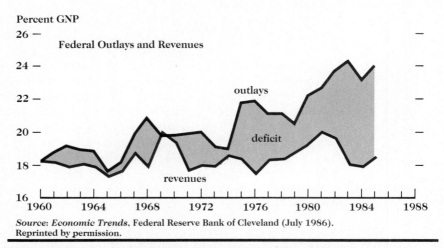

Percent GNP

FIGURE 17A.1 *Federal Budget Deficit* Federal budget deficits are not new. The magnitude of the deficit since 1980, even in the face of economic recovery after 1981–82, *is* new. It has prompted Congressional action, namely the Gramm-Rudman-Hollings Balanced Budget Act.

The Fed, the Treasury, and the Monetary Base

The *monetary base* refers to depository institution balances held by the Federal Reserve and currency in circulation, essentially liabilities of the Fed and the Treasury. We can represent this as:

$$MB = C + R$$

where

$$MB = \text{monetary base}$$
$$C = \text{currency in circulation}$$
$$R = \text{reserves}$$

Currency and reserves are made up of the following:

$$MB = C + R = \text{Federal Reserve notes} + \text{Bank deposits at Fed}$$
$$+ (\text{Treasury currency outside Fed} - \text{coins held by Fed})$$

Recall from the discussion of the multiple expansion of the money supply that bank reserves form the basis for the expansionary process.

(Currency serves the same purpose when it is translated into bank deposits.) The monetary base, sometimes referred to as high-powered money, determines the degree to which the money supply can expand.

The appendix to Chapter 16 described the Federal Reserve's balance sheet. If you have not read that appendix you may want to refer to it in the course of this discussion.

The monetary base is affected by a number of factors: Federal Reserve purchases of securities, loans through the discount window, the Fed float, Treasury currency outstanding, the Fed's assets, its gold and SDR accounts, and the Treasury's account with the Fed. Increases in the first five increase the monetary base while a decrease in the last results in the monetary base increasing. The most important of these for purposes of our discussion is the Fed's purchases of securities.[1]

The Federal Reserve and monetary policy are affected by the way the Treasury finances government operations, especially the way it funds the deficit. Tax collections, federal expenditures, and even deficit financing through securities sales to the public will have no effect or only a small impact on the monetary base. When the Treasury sells securities to the Federal Reserve or issues new currency or coins, the monetary base is increased. Laws place limits on the former, and the latter generally occurs only in response to increased demand for coin.

Deficit and Monetary Policy

The major relationship between Treasury deficit financing and dynamic monetary policy hinges on the extent to which the Fed responds to the Treasury's entrance into the securities market. Because the Fed is constrained in buying securities directly from the Treasury, what usually occurs is that the Fed purchases these securities on the open market after the Treasury has sold its original issue to the public. When the Fed purchases Treasury securities through this procedure we say the Fed is *monetarizing the*

---

[1] Keep in mind that the Treasury uses the Fed as its fiscal agent. That is, the Fed receives deposits in the Treasury account through tax payments and issues checks on this account to pay Treasury bills. The Fed monitors the Treasury account and may undertake defensive open-market operations to offset fluctuations in this account and the associated effect on the monetary base.

debt. Essentially, negotiable currency (that is, high-powered money) was substituted for the non-negotiable, publicly held government debt.

The question is, to what extent does the deficit influence Fed policy? Or, putting this another way, does the Fed accommodate deficit spending by the government? People hold differing views on this issue. One view is that Federal Reserve monetary policy is independent of the federal deficit. Richard Sheehan argues that from 1958 to 1970, when deficits were nonexistent or modest, rising deficits correlated somewhat with money growth. From 1971 to 1984, when deficits were large and increasing, he finds no relationship between deficits and money supply growth.[2]

An alternative view is that the Fed does respond to the large deficit. In an early study, Alan Blinder found that Fed policy is more expansionary when deficits are higher.[3] More recent theoretical research indicates that the question is not whether the Fed responds but when and to what extent. Thomas Sargent and Neil Wallace, as well as Preston Miller, have argued that only by increasing the supply of money and precipitating inflation will tax revenues rise fast enough to finance higher deficits.[4] Under these circumstances, the Fed cannot control the supply of money.

---

[2] Richard G. Sheehan, "The Federal Reserve Reaction Function: Does Debt Growth Influence Monetary Policy?" Federal Reserve Bank of St. Louis *Review* 67, 3 (March 1985): 24–33.

[3] Alan Blinder, "On the Monetarization of Debt," National Bureau of Economic Research, Working Paper 1052.

[4] Thomas J. Sargent and Neil Wallace, "Some Unpleasant Monetarist Arithmetic," Federal Reserve Bank of Minneapolis *Quarterly Review* (Fall 1981): 1–17; and Preston J. Miller, "A Monetarist Approach to Federal Budget Control," Federal Reserve Bank of Minneapolis, Working Paper 210.

CHAPTER EIGHTEEN

STRATEGIES AND IMPLICATIONS of MONETARY POLICY

A single monopolistic governmental agency can neither possess the information which should govern the supply of money nor would it, if it knew what it ought to do in the general interest, usually be in a position to act in that manner.

Friedrich A. Hayek
Denationalization of Money, 1976

The last chapter described the Federal Reserve System's responsibility for maintaining a stable financial system and, especially after more recent legislation, its responsibility for working to achieve the overall macroeconomic goals of the system. The Humphrey-Hawkins Act of 1978 requires the Fed chairman to present a report on monetary policy objectives to the Congress (in February) and then report on its progress toward achieving those goals (in July). Inherent in these requirements and the policy actions the Fed undertakes is the assumption that monetary policy has an effect on the economic goals of maximum employment, price stability, and economic growth. Most economists accept this assumption, and the discussions in this chapter are predicated on just such an assumption.

Still, the connection between Federal Reserve monetary policy actions and the overall macroeconomic goals is unclear. Furthermore, the mechanisms by which the Fed's day-to-day actions affect the real variables in the system are the subject of continuing debate. Despite the uncertainty of the economic world, Fed officials have some clearly defined paths to follow in implementing monetary policy.

This chapter presents an overview of alternative monetary transmission mechanisms which influence specific policy recommendations. Because of the delay between their actions and the results, Fed officials need to gauge the effects of their actions over time. This chapter will help you understand what policy makers consider as they monitor the monetary transmission process. Finally, because of the ongoing debate over operating strategies, we will look at evidence about which target is best. Although the evidence is inconclusive, you will have some background information to help you evaluate specific monetary policy actions.

As you read through this chapter, recall the distinction between dynamic and defensive monetary policy. Although the discussions that follow apply to both types of monetary policy, most of the chapter relates to dynamic policies, those where the Fed establishes a target to achieve a goal and then takes action to move the system toward that goal.

Chapter Objectives

Your overall goal for this chapter is to understand the connection between the Fed's selection of target variables—operating, instrumental, and intermediate—and the conduct and results of monetary policy. This is a rather large challenge but you will find it easier to achieve this goal if you think about some intermediate targets of your own.

As you proceed through this chapter, think about how the use of a particular set of target variables can influence economic performance. By the end of this chapter you should be able to:

- Understand the transmission mechanism whereby monetary policy actions affect real economic variables.

    Explain how policy actions influence intermediate targets in the short run along the way toward changing economic variables in the long run.

- Analyze the influence of the rational expectations approach on Federal Reserve policy.

    Describe how the policy ineffectiveness proposition applies to monetary policy.

- Integrate an understanding of the interest rate and the money supply hypotheses as alternative targeting procedures.

    Explain the differences between the two approaches.

    Identify the different targets used in each approach.

    Explain the relationship between these targets and the final economic goals.

- Understand the Fed's recent targets and operating procedures.
  Describe the three approaches used since 1970.
- Evaluate the various views about which target is best.
  Describe the existing opinions about the various targets.
  Analyze each approach in light of theoretical tools and empirical studies.
  Draw conclusions about whether one target is better than others.

Factors Affecting Policy

The conduct of monetary policy, as well as the debate surrounding its effectiveness, is grounded in the alternative theoretical models which depict the relationship of money to real variables in the economy. Chapter 10 described differences between Keynesian and monetarist explanations of how changes in the supply of money affect the system. Accepting the notion that money does matter in the system still leaves considerable room for disagreement about how it matters. Through what channels does money affect consumer and investment spending, output and employment, and prices? The view that policy makers hold on the channels through which money affects the economy will influence, maybe even dictate, the way in which monetary policy is implemented.

The Keynesian and Monetarist Views

In the Keynesian view, money influences interest rates which, in turn, drive investment spending, and through that, income and employment.

$$\Delta M \Rightarrow \Delta r \Rightarrow \Delta I \Rightarrow \Delta Y, \Delta N$$

The monetarist view is a portfolio balance explanation. Changes in the supply of money affect individual and business portfolios and this drives consumption and investment decisions which, ultimately, affect income.

$$\Delta M \Rightarrow \Delta C, \Delta I \Rightarrow \Delta Y$$

Even before proceeding to discuss how the monetary authorities monitor their actions, you can see that interest rates are important in the Keynesian view whereas the monetarist view does not include them. This difference will become more obvious in the discussion of goals and targets.

Transmission Mechanism for Monetary Policy

Policy makers need to have some way of assessing whether their actions are "on target." This holds true regardless of the theoretical model which influences their decisions. Monetary policy does not instantaneously affect income and employment. Therefore, policy makers identify some intermediate target which provides a clear signal as to whether their policy actions will have the desired effect. The Fed establishes realistic economic goals, for example, a level for GNP growth or a rate of inflation. It decides what changes in its intermediate target are necessary to achieve its ultimate goals. Finally the Fed selects policy tools and decides to what extent to use those tools. The Fed will also monitor some money-sensitive indicator to determine the degree to which its policies are working. Figure 18.1 illustrates a generalized version of the monetary policy transmission mechanism.

What differentiates one set of Federal Reserve operating procedures from another is the intermediate target. Monetary policy tools are fixed and the Fed's reliance on open-market operations is well established. But the intermediate target will have considerable influence on the variables affected by monetary policy. Later, this chapter describes two alternative transmission mechanisms. At this point, a brief review of factors affecting money markets is helpful.

Factors Affecting Money Markets

Keep in mind that market forces play an important, even dominant, role in the monetary arena. The Federal Reserve is an influential participant in money markets but it cannot dictate specific levels for monetary variables. One reason is that the connection between Federal Reserve tools and

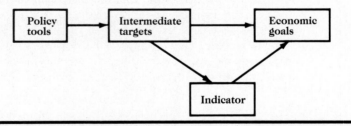

FIGURE 18.1 *Generalized Monetary Transmission Mechanism* Regardless of the theoretical model that underlies monetary policy transmission to the real sector, the Federal Reserve monitors intermediate targets and indicators to determine whether policy actions are achieving the desired economic goals.

economic variables is not known precisely. Second, many exogenous forces, over which the Fed has no control, intervene in the monetary process.

The loanable funds notion (discussed in detail in Chapter 3) applies here again. Figure 18.2 is Figure 3.4 with a slight modification. The Fed influences the supply of loanable funds. The supply of funds curve is perfectly inelastic (vertical) up to a point (interest rate r) at which time it becomes interest elastic. The Fed essentially dictates the level of loanable funds through its provision of depository institution reserves via open-market operations (and discount window borrowing). At some interest rate, financial intermediaries tap other sources of funds, perhaps through liability management. These funds allow the supply of loanable funds to increase. The precise point at which this occurs, as well as the degree of interest elasticity of the supply of loanable funds, are not known. In fact, they are not important for our purposes. The aim of Figure 18.2 is to illustrate that supply factors beyond those controlled by the Fed influence the rate of interest and the money expansion process.

Demand factors also influence both interest rates and money expansion. Notice that as the demand for funds shifts from D_1 to D_2, the rate of interest and the quantity of loanable funds in the system both increase.

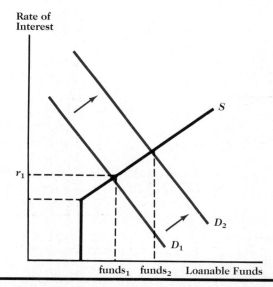

FIGURE 18.2 *Demand and Supply Set Interest Rates for Loanable Funds*
This figure illustrates that the demand for loanable funds and the supply of loanable funds interact to determine the rate of interest. The supply of loanable funds is interest inelastic until the interest rate is sufficiently high to attract additional funds to the market.

Admittedly the Fed can take actions to counteract the demand influence but, as we will discuss later, it cannot hold down interest rates and the growth rate of the supply of funds at the same time.

Exogenous factors, such as commodity price hikes, trade deficits, financial market innovations, inflationary expectations, and budget deficits, all intervene to affect both the demand for funds and the supply of funds. In addition, the velocity of money is a factor. Figure 18.4 (page 459) illustrates some of the interrelated factors affecting monetary policy.

Rational Expectations and Policy

Expectations play an important role in economic activity in general and monetary policy in particular. Although still representing a minority view-point, the work of rational expectations economists tells us a great deal about the effectiveness of monetary policy and is beginning to have a major influence on the conduct of that policy.[1]

According to the strict rational expectations view—the policy ineffec-tiveness proposition—monetary policy has no effect on real variables unless it is completely unanticipated. This contrasts sharply with the Keynesian view, in which changes in the supply of money affect real output and usually prices, and the monetarist view, in which changes in the supply of money have no effect on real variables in the long run although they may influence output in the short run. The policy ineffectiveness proposition results from the behavior of firms and individuals. They anticipate money supply changes and undertake actions which offset the policy action such that no changes in real variables occur.

The rational expectations proposition does agree that unanticipated money growth will have an effect on real variables. As we discussed in Chapter 12, rational expectationists explain that when the supply of money increases at an unanticipated rate, consumers mistakenly see an increase in their real wealth. Being better off, they increase their purchases of goods and services (following the portfolio balance theory). This results in an unex-pected rise in prices which producers mistakenly perceive as an increase in relative prices. Accordingly, they step up production and the associated output and employment variables respond. This occurs only when the increase in the money supply was unanticipated.

---

[1] Two excellent articles on the policy implications of the rational expectations proposition are A. Steven Holland, "Rational Expectations and the Effects of Monetary Policy: A Guide for the Uninitiated," Federal Reserve Bank of St. Louis *Review* 67, 5 (May 1985): 5–11; and R. Maddock and M. Carter, "A Child's Guide to Rational Expectations," *Journal of Economic Literature* XX (March 1982): 39–51.

In most cases, individuals and firms correctly anticipate money supply changes. Under these conditions, monetary policy is ineffective in terms of real variables. What may prove more disruptive is that monetary policy will not necessarily have the desired effect. Public expectations and the economy's institutional structure will adjust to Fed policy but not always in the same way. Similar monetary policy actions may have very different results, and models which do not incorporate rational expectations may produce inaccurate results.[2]

The implications of the rational expectations policy ineffectiveness proposition are twofold. First, whether the Fed chooses to control interest rates or monetary aggregates does not matter. Regardless of the choice, public actions mitigate against any effects on real variables. Second, since monetary uncertainty interferes with the efficient functioning of markets, the Fed should establish a well-publicized and predictable monetary policy and stick to it. Trying to implement policy actions which fool the public in an attempt to achieve short-run goals may actually create greater macroeconomic imbalances in the long run.

Setting Goals and Targets

The Federal Reserve's role in macroeconomic policy has become increasingly important in the post–World War II period. The importance of the Fed was underscored by the Humphrey-Hawkins Act of 1978 which recognized the Fed as a major macropolicy actor in requiring the Fed chairman to report to Congress twice each year. And under Chairman Paul Volcker, the Fed moved to a position of prominence in the domestic and international policy arena.

This recognition of the importance of the Fed has not stemmed from nor eliminated the controversy about how the Fed conducts monetary policy. The debate does not concern the goals of monetary policy. Economic growth, price stability, maximum employment, and a favorable international trade and payments balance (and in many instances low real interest rates) are seen as the Fed's and the nation's primary economic goals. The controversy, within the Fed and among policy analysts, relates to the Fed's operating procedures, more specifically the Fed's selection of target vari-

---

[2] This is the famous "Lucas Critique." See R.E. Lucas, "Econometric Policy Evaluation: A Critique," in K. Brunner and A. Melton, eds., *The Phillips Curve and Labor Markets* (New Holland Press, 1976): 19–46.

ables. A discussion of alternative transmission mechanisms and the Fed's recent experience with target variables will highlight this controversy and lead into a discussion about which target variable is best.

Alternative Targeting Procedures

Historically, the Federal Reserve has considered three general targets in assessing the impact of its monetary policy actions. These are interest rate, monetary aggregates, and credit. Although some people are calling for the Fed to give more attention to an overall credit measure (such as total domestic nonfinancial debt), most analysts come down in favor of some interest rate or monetary aggregate measure and the Fed has relied on one or the other of these measures.

Inherent in the choice of a targeting procedure is a transmission mechanism connecting Fed policy actions to overall macroeconomic goals. This chapter outlined a general transmission mechanism. At this point more detail is in order.

The Fed needs to monitor the effects of its policy actions as they work their way through the system. The variables the Fed chooses depend on the implementation philosophy prevailing within the Board of Governors and the FOMC. Figure 18.3 illustrates the two alternative transmission mechanisms and the target variables used by the Fed at various stages.

The left side of the diagram reveals the money supply hypothesis. This transmission mechanism is consistent with the monetarist proposition that the money supply influences economic performance in the short run. The right side of the diagram is the interest rate hypothesis, more consistent with the Keynesian viewpoint that interest rates provide the vehicle for the changes in real economic variables. Each approach includes different variables to monitor.

Once the FOMC decides on its goals and a strategy to achieve these goals, it undertakes operating procedures (open-market operations, discount rate policy, etc.). To determine whether its procedures are on target, the Fed observes target variables which respond almost immediately (operating tartets), some of which take a month or two to respond (instrumental targets) and variables which begin to change after three to six months (intermediate targets).[3] Once the intermediate target begins to respond to the Fed's operating action, the economic indicator signals the degree to which the final variables will change. In six to twelve months, the Fed's actions begin to result in changes in output, income, employment, and prices.

---

[3] Federal Reserve Governor Henry C. Wallich discusses this approach in "Recent Techniques of Monetary Policy," Federal Reserve Bank of Kansas City *Economic Review* (May 1984): 21–30.

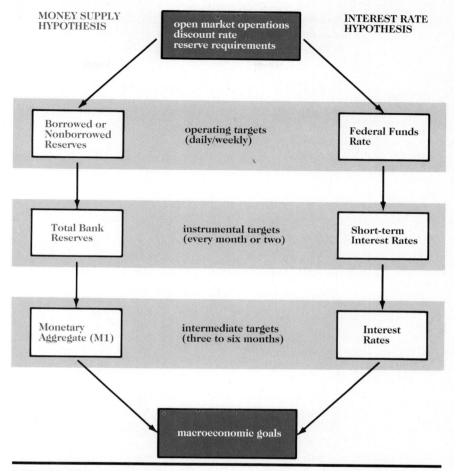

FIGURE 18.3 *Alternative Transmission Mechanisms*   There are two alternative monetary transmission mechanisms illustrated in this figure. The *money supply hypothesis* focuses on banks reserves and a monetary aggregate measure. The *interest rate hypothesis* focuses on short-term and long-term interest rates.

In choosing its target variables the Fed considers a number of factors:

Measurability—Can the FOMC collect accurate, reliable data for its chosen targets?

Controllability—Can the FOMC actually influence, in a predictable manner, the chosen targets?

Relationship to Goals—Do the chosen targets have a causal influence on the ultimate economic goals?

Opinions on these issues vary as do philosophies about the transmission of monetary policy. These factors, as well as exogenous forces, have resulted in numerous recent changes in the Fed's operating procedures.

Recent Fed Targets and Operating Procedures

Throughout its history, and especially in recent years, the Fed has changed its operating procedures. Procedural changes are influenced by a number of factors:

- Opinions within and outside the Fed[4]
- Exogenous forces, for example, oil prices, financial innovation, budget deficit, trade deficit
- Improved or changing economic models

Figure 18.4 illustrates the monetary transmission mechanism with numerous intervening variables. At different times, one or a number of these factors will influence Federal Reserve operating procedures.

The Fed has employed three distinctly different operating procedures since 1970. They merit some attention because they reveal the factors which influence Fed decisions, the variability of monetary policy and the need for a clearer, more predictable relationship between monetary policy and real economic variables.

Targeting Interest Rates, 1970 to September 1979 Specifically, the FOMC targeted the federal funds rate, the interest rate applied to overnight borrowing among depository institutions. Under this procedure, the FOMC would set a target range for the federal funds rate and the Open-Market Desk would provide reserves through open-market operations to maintain the federal funds rate within this range. This approach fits the interest rate hypothesis transmission mechanism shown in Figure 18.3. By monitoring the federal funds rate and adjusting its monetary policy to maintain sufficient reserves to keep this rate within the designated target range, the Fed was providing an overall supply of funds to keep market interest rates from rising too rapidly. This approach assumed that the demand for money was fairly stable and rejected the monetarist proposition that an increasing money supply would lead to inflation. Figure 18.5 shows that this assumption was not holding true.

---

[4] In his book *Managing the Dollar* (W.W. Norton, 1973), Sherman Maisel estimates the distribution of powers within the Fed (Chairman 45 percent, Staff 25 percent, other Governors 20 percent, and Regional Banks 10 percent) and outside the Fed (Administration 35 percent, Congress 25 percent, and the Public 20 percent). Events in the 1980s would indicate that Chairman Volcker is more powerful than was the case ten years ago.

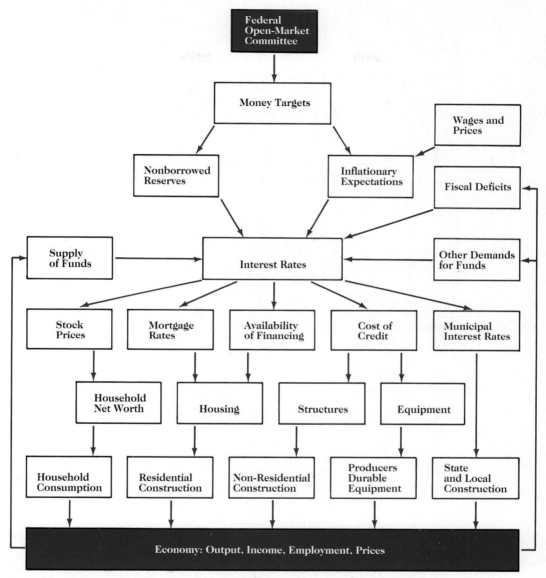

FIGURE 18.4 *Transmission of Monetary Policy*   The FOMC's actions, aimed initially at money targets, influence a wide range of nominal and real variables throughout the economy along the way toward effecting the overall macroeconomic goals.

Monetary policy is based on the changes in the rate of growth of the money supply, M1, and its relationship to the real sector of the economy. The money supply data that are released by the Fed are watched closely by the Fed itself and other agencies both public and private. It is the Fed which observes these data changes as it makes its adjustments in monetary policy actions. Are these data accurate? Should they form the basis for monetary policy decision?

In examining M1 data for every year between 1965 and 1981, two Federal Reserve Bank of Chicago economists found that M1 growth often appeared to be significantly more variable when recent data (the past two years) were used than when longer range

money supply changes were considered. The error in the most recent data, they found, may well cause money supply growth to appear more variable in the current period than in past periods. Policy makers are thus led to believe that the monetary environment has suddenly become more volatile when in fact they are merely observing a statistical problem.

The reasons for the misleading initial report all relate to the statistical procedures used for collecting and analyzing the data. As more data become available, the variance between reported and actual figures is reduced.

This finding has some important implications for monetary

policy. First, it would seem to indicate that long-run monetary growth trends are more important than short-run changes in the supply of money. Policies should not be geared to short-run swings in reported data. Second, it would seem that the Fed should set long-term targets and monitor them rather than using intermediate targets as a gauge for FOMC actions.

Note: For the complete study, see Diane F. Siegel and Steven Strongin, "M1: The Ever-changing Past," in Federal Reserve Bank of Chicago *Economic Perspectives* X, 2 (March/April 1986): 3–12.

Targeting Nonborrowed Reserves, October 1979 to September 1982
Figure 18.5 graphically reveals why the Fed changed its operating procedures in the fall of 1979. Interest rates had been held within the target range, but the money supply growth rate was escalating and the rate of inflation was increasing at an alarming rate.

In October, 1979, the Fed announced that it was shifting its intermediate target from interest rates to the money supply, namely M1. To achieve its goals for money supply growth the FOMC focused on nonborrowed reserves—despository institution excess reserves minus borrowing from the Fed. In announcing the switch, newly appointed Fed Chairman Paul Volcker stressed the importance of bringing money growth rates under control in order to break inflation.

The Fed's operating procedure during this period, sometimes referred to as the reserve-targeting method, had dramatic effects on the alternative target variable, interest rates. As Figure 18.5 reveals, beginning in early 1980, interest rates not only rose but fluctuated greatly.

Observers argued that the Fed had adopted a monetarist approach to monetary policy. The Fed adhered to its money supply growth targets rather

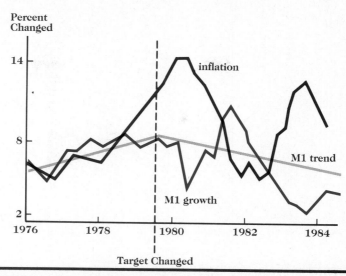

FIGURE 18.5 *Money Growth and Inflation Before and After October, 1979*
This figure illustrates the change in the trend rate of growth for M1 after the Fed changed
its operating target in October, 1979. The rate of inflation declined along with the rate of
money growth.

strictly. The inflation rate responded, after an appropriate lag, by declining.
This period of disinflation was accompanied by recession.

From 1979 to 1982, instead of controlling the growth of money by
influencing the quantity demanded via the interest rate (again, this had
assumed a fixed demand for money), the Fed more directly controlled the
supply of money by influencing reserves. Market forces took the interest rate
where they would. Figure 18.6 shows that the Fed was successful in keeping
M1 growth within its target cones (the range of the growth rate of the supply
of money).

Targeting Borrowed Reserves, 1982 to Present Three years after abandoning its interest-rate approach in favor of a monetary aggregate approach,
the Fed again modified its position. The change was not as dramatic as in
1979. Starting in 1982, the Fed has focused less on the short-term movements of M1. Economists were concerned that the relationship between M1
and the final economic goals (specifically, total spending) was changing
because of events in financial markets. These events included the maturing
of a large quantity of All Savers Certificates and the introduction of money
market deposit accounts and Super NOW accounts. Economists expected

Billions of Dollars

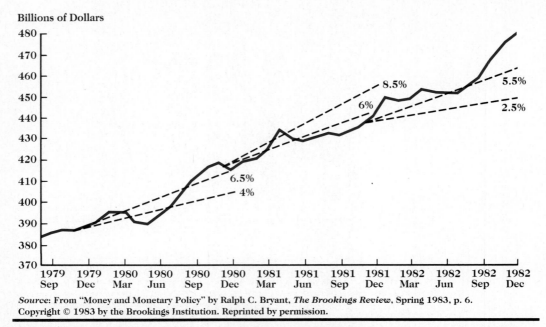

Source: From "Money and Monetary Policy" by Ralph C. Bryant, *The Brookings Review*, Spring 1983, p. 6. Copyright © 1983 by the Brookings Institution. Reprinted by permission.

FIGURE 18.6   *M1, Actual Path, and Target Cones, Monthly Data*   After changing its operating target in October, 1979, the Fed was successful in keeping the money growth rate within the established ranges (called cones). Data shown are seasonally adjusted monthly averages.

these events to produce a surge in M1 which would distort the transmission mechanism.

Instead of relying exclusively on M1 by monitoring nonborrowed reserves, the Fed began focusing on borrowed reserves. By using the discount window and open-market operations the Fed would work toward a specified degree of reserves ease or restraint.

Federal Reserve Governor Wallich has described this procedure as "an indirect method of influencing the funds rate and other short-term rates which, in turn, affect the demand for money."[5] Thus the Fed seems to have adopted what may be called an eclectic approach. The Fed is responding to market forces, not relying exclusively on M1 but not rejecting interest rates.[6] Put another way, the Fed is searching for a reliable target variable.

[5] *Op. cit.*, p. 22.
[6] Some have argued that this approach is reminiscent of the 1950s and 1960s when the Fed targeted free reserves.

MONEY T(18.2)DAY

Monetary Policy Objectives for 1986: Midyear Review

Note: Twice each year, the Chairman of the Board of Governors is required to appear before Congress to review the economy's performance and outline the Fed's policy objectives. The following is taken from Paul Volcker's testimony on July 18, 1986.

Sharp contrasts among sectors and regions of the economy characterized economic developments during the first half of 1986. Because of strong competitive pressures from abroad and large spending cutbacks in the oil industry in response to sharply declining prices, industrial and investment activity was restrained. In contrast, activity continued to expand rather strongly in housing, the financial sector, and the broad service area of the economy.

Although there are substantial uncertainties about the degree and timing of a pickup in overall economic activity, a number of positive economic and financial developments have occurred that should provide a basis for somewhat faster economic growth and some reduction in unemployment over the year ahead. Interest rates have moved lower, and, reflecting the decline of the dollar on foreign exchange markets, American industry is in a stronger competitive position internationally. In addition, inflation has remained subdued, reflecting not only declines in the prices of energy and other basic commodities but also continued restraint on wages in many sectors. Much of the uncertainty about a pickup in growth turns on the strength of economic performance in other industrialized countries, and there also is some concern over the transitional effects of tax reform legislation.

A reduction of the large deficit in the nation's external accounts is of critical importance over time, and this will be difficult to achieve in an orderly way without faster growth in key foreign economies. Agreement on tax reform also would remove a major source of uncertainty that probably has inhibited growth in the first half of the year. In addition, substantial progress toward eliminating federal budget deficits is essential to achieving better balance in the United States and world economies. Overall, prospects for the economy appear to be favorable, but much will depend on the evolution of policy, both in this country and abroad.

The FOMC reaffirmed the 1986 target ranges of 6 to 9 percent that had been established in February for growth in the broad money measures—M2 and M3.

For 1987, the Committee decided that the target growth ranges for both M2 and M3 would be lowered by one-half of one percentage point, to 5½ to 8½ percent, to achieve money growth at a rate consistent with maintaining reasonable price stability and sustainable economic expansion.

The rapid rise in M1 over the first half of the year underscored the degree of uncertainty surrounding the behavior of the aggregate and, in particular, about its behavior relative to GNP. The nature of the relationship among M1, income, and interest rates appears to have been significantly altered by the changed composition of the aggregate in recent years, as well as by the prospects for greater price stability. The Committee decided that growth of M1 in excess of the previously established 3 to 8 percent range for 1986 would be acceptable and growth in that aggregate over the balance of the year would continue to be evaluated in light of the behavior of the other monetary aggregates.

With respect to 1987, the Committee expressed the preliminary view that the current range for M1—3 to 8 percent—should provide for adequate money growth to support continued economic expansion, assuming that greater stability reemerges in the link between M1 and income in a more stable economic, price, and interest-rate environment.

Source: Monetary Policy Objectives for 1986: Midyear Review of the Federal Reserve Board, July 18, 1986, Publications Services, Federal Reserve Board, Washington, D.C. (FRB 10-48000-0786).

Which Target Is Best?

The Fed's experience since 1970 raises questions about the applicability of the targeting procedures used in recent years. Which target is best?

Recall that we identified three criteria for a good target variable— measurability, controllability, and relationship to goals. Most target variables achieve all or most of these criteria to one degree or another. Economists disagree as to which variables are best. We can gain some insight into opinions on the matter by referring to two surveys conducted in 1983 and by looking at *IS-LM* analysis.

Congressman Fernand St Germain surveyed academic economists for the House Banking, Finance, and Urban Affairs Committee and a private consulting firm did the same with financial analysts. Table 18.1 summarizes the results of these surveys. In both surveys, the single most chosen intermediate target was a monetary aggregate (such as M1). A majority of the

Target	Percentage of Academic Economists Who Prefer	Percentage of Financial Analysts Who Prefer
Monetary aggregate	30.8	56.6
M1		(37.7)
M2/M3		(18.9)
Other:	62.6	39.5
Monetary base	(15.5)	(5.6)
Credit aggregate	(3.3)	(9.4)
Interest rate	(7.7)	(1.9)
Mix of indicators	(24.3)	(7.5)
International variables	(1.1)	(0.0)
Other	(1.9)	(0.0)
Nominal GNP	(8.8)	(13.2)
Reserves	(0.0)	(1.9)
Final goals directly	2.2	3.7
Real GNP	(1.1)	(0.0)
Inflation	(1.1)	(3.7)
Don't Know/Unclear	4.4	0.0
	100.0	98.8

Source: Survey results reported in Gillian Garcia, "The Right Rabbit: Which Intermediate Target Should the Fed Pursue?" Federal Reserve Bank of Chicago *Economic Perspectives* (May/June 1984): 15–31.

TABLE 18.1 *Results from Two Surveys of Preferences Regarding Intermediate Targets*

Is the FOMC Violating the Law?

The FOMC implements the overall monetary policy goals set by the Board of Governors. In making decisions about changes in the supply of money, the FOMC exerts more power than most economic agencies in the government. Up until now, the FOMC membership has been, at least partly, an internal matter. Five of the twelve FOMC members are representatives of the district Federal Reserve banks, appointed by those banks' boards of directors. A lawsuit filed in 1984 by Senator John Melcher challenged the constitutionality of the FOMC, claiming that the district bank representatives are not subject to the "advice and consent" function of the United States Senate.

Senator Melcher's lawsuit was not frivolous. It challenged the operating procedures of the Fed. The chairman of the Board of Governors has considerable influence in the appointment by the district banks of presidents and vice presidents (the individuals who sit on the FOMC on a rotating arrangement). He therefore has a group of allies for his approach to monetary policy. Changing this arrangement, for example, by giving the power of appointment of district Federal Reserve bank presidents and vice presidents to the President or to Congress, would dramatically alter the monetary policy decision-making process.

Two previous lawsuits by members of Congress preceded his; both were dismissed on technical grounds. In 1983, the Committee for Monetary Reform, a group of private individuals and corporations, filed suit claiming the Fed operated unconstitutionally. That suit was dismissed as ultimately, Melcher's suit was. Beyond those who have actually taken court action, there is a significant number of individuals who question the constitutional and operational basis of Federal Reserve actions.

economists responding to the survey identified something other than M1 as their preference and some mix of indicators was the most preferred among these choices.[7]

Research into the most appropriate intermediate target for monetary policy produces no more definitive results than did the surveys. In the same article in which he reports on the survey results, Gillian Garcia assesses the various intermediate target variables by reviewing recent empirical research. He concludes that no target produces consistently better results (using the criteria mentioned earlier) than M1. He concedes that other variables provide valuable supplemental information.

---

[7] A mix of indicators refers to the use of a number of variables in the derivation of an index number. The process is much the same as that used in determining a consumer price index. A variety of indicators (for example, M1, credit measure, MMMF, and Super NOW accounts), each of which receives a weight in the determination of an index number, is used to develop the index. See Garcia article for more detailed discussion and references.

IS-LM Analysis

Perhaps we can gain some insight into the difficulty of choosing a target variable by using the *IS-LM* analysis introduced in Chapter 9. Consider two scenarios, one in which the *IS* curve is unstable and the other where the *LM* curve is unstable.

For this simple analysis, we will assume the price level is constant and that no inflation/deflation is expected. Therefore, we can use real income/output and consider nominal and real interest rates are identical.

Consider first a situation where the *IS* curve is unstable. This is produced by a number of factors, for example, a very unstable marginal efficiency of investment curve, perhaps resulting from uncertainty about tax reform of investment credits. Assume the *LM* is stable. Figure 18.7 depicts this situation.

If the Fed follows an interest rate strategy, that is, keeps interest rates fixed or stable, it will have to adjust the supply of money. Since the *IS* curve is unstable (shifting to *IS'* and *IS''*), to maintain *r* at the desired level the Fed

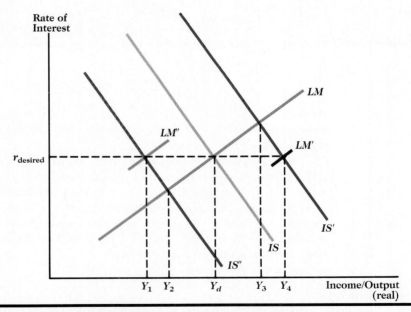

FIGURE 18.7 *Shifting* IS *Curve Presents Policy Dilemma*   This figure uses *IS-LM* curves to show the difficulty monetary policy makers have in choosing a target variable. Here, the *IS* curve is unstable, that is, it shifts. Under these circumstances, the Fed will have to constantly adjust the money supply in response to the *IS* shift to keep the interest rate stable. But, in so doing, income/output will fluctuate. A monetary aggregate approach under these circumstances will reduce the income/output fluctuation.

will have to increase or decrease the money supply. Notice that in so doing the income/output level will fluctuate between Y_1 (with IS'' and LM'') and Y_4 (with IS' and LM').

On the other hand, under these same circumstances, a monetary aggregate strategy will result in much less fluctuation in income and output. The Fed will maintain a fixed supply of money, so with a stable LM curve, even with an unstable IS curve, income will only fluctuate between Y_2 (IS'' and LM) and Y_3 (IS' and LM).

If the primary goal of monetary policy is stable income and output, then when IS is unstable, the money supply strategy appears best. Note that under these circumstances the stable income and output is achieved at the cost of fluctuating interest rates (r' to r'').

Now consider the situation where the LM curve is uncertain but the IS curve is stable. The fluctuating LM curve could result from a changing demand for money function. Figure 18.8 depicts this situation.

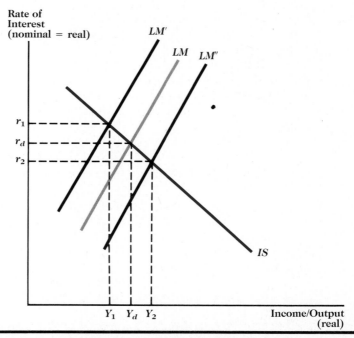

FIGURE 18.8 *Adjustable* **LM** *Curve Requires Money Supply Adjustment*
This figure shows that with an unstable *LM* curve an interest rate strategy will require the Fed's intervention to adjust the money supply to keep the *LM* curve in a range that will produce the desired interest rate, r_d. Following a monetary aggregate strategy the Fed would allow the *LM* curve to shift but this would cause income/output to fluctuate.

When the *LM* curve is fluctuating and the Fed is following an interest rate strategy, the Fed is forced to undertake dynamic policies to anticipate the *LM* curve shift or defensive policies to adjust to the shift. In either case, in order to keep *r* fixed, the Fed will take action to move the *LM* curve back to its original position. Income and output will not fluctuate.

On the other hand, if the Fed were following a monetary aggregate strategy, under these circumstances it would allow the *LM* curve to shift (remember it is the changing *Dm* which prompts the *LM* shift, even when *Sm* is constant) and income/output would fluctuate between Y_1 (*IS* and *LM″*) and Y_2 (*IS* and *LM′*). Besides the fluctuation in income, interest rates would fluctuate (from r_1 to r_2). Therefore, if stability in income/output is again the goal, the interest rate strategy seems best when the *LM* curve is unstable.

These scenarios reveal only that we cannot make a definitive choice. Policy makers cannot be certain when *IS* and *LM* curves are stable or fluctuating. The underlying theoretical and empirical premises seem to dictate which position a policy maker will take. For example, since monetarists claim the *Dm* function is stable or predictable, they would argue that scenario 1, and not scenario 2, holds. Keynesians, on the other hand, are concerned about the changing *Dm* while demonstrating confidence in the behavior of the *IS* curve. They would select the interest rate strategy depicted in scenario 2.

Empirical research reveals no more definitive results. A review of research into the most appropriate intermediate target for monetary policy concludes that no single variable stands out.[8] Various approaches produce different insights. This seems to argue for an eclectic approach where various targets are considered.

Chapter Conclusion

The conduct of monetary policy is by no means simple. Debates over the mechanisms by which money influences the economy continue even during periods of relative economic stability. Keynesians, monetarists, and rational expectationists all have strongly held viewpoints on the manner and extent of money supply changes on real economic variables. As we consider these viewpoints and look at the procedures utilized by the Fed, we need to keep in mind that demand factors, as well as supply factors, influence money

---

[8] The survey results are reported in Gillian Garcia, "The Right Rabbit: Which Intermediate Target Should the Fed Pursue?" Federal Reserve Bank of Chicago *Economic Perspectives* (May/June 1984): 15–31.

markets. Beyond this, the Fed is not the only actor influencing the money supply.

To provide the background necessary for evaluating monetary policy in the next chapter, we looked rather carefully at the goals, targets and operating procedures of the Federal Reserve. Alternative approaches were highlighted by looking at the changes in operating procedures utilized during the 1970s and early 1980s. We tried to gain some appreciation of the reasons behind these changes by assessing the usefulness of one target variable (interest rates) versus the other (monetary aggregates). We could conclude only that economic conditions and opinions about the transmission mechanism for money supply changes will determine the strategy recommended.

Although monetary policy is complicated, more so as a result of financial deregulation, the analysis of transmission mechanisms, policy targets, and operating procedures gives us the knowledge we need to evaluate the conduct of monetary policy. Chapter 19 addresses this issue.

Consider These Questions

1. What difference does it make for monetary policy whether one accepts a Keynesian or monetarist approach to the transmission of monetary policy?

2. Why is the supply-of-funds curve kinked? (Refer to Figure 18.2.)

3. What are the implications for monetary policy of the policy ineffectiveness proposition put forth by some rational expectations economists?

4. Explain the differences between the money supply hypothesis and the interest rate hypothesis. What are the implications of each for the conduct of monetary policy?

5. In general, what might prompt the Federal Reserve to change its target variable?

6. Describe in specific, the factors leading to the target variable change in October 1979.

7. Is there a general consensus as to which target variable is best? Why or why not?

8. Use *IS-LM* analysis to illustrate the difficulty in selecting a most appropriate target variable.

9. What issues does the Federal Reserve chairman address in his biannual report to Congress?

10. Which target variable has the Fed been using lately? What explanation is given for the use of this variable?

Suggestions for Further Reading

Batten, Dallas S. and Daniel L. Thornton. "Are Weighted Monetary Aggregates Better Than Simple-sum M1?" In Federal Reserve Bank of St. Louis *Review* 67, 6 (June/July 1985): 29–39.
> Sophisticated article but it points out that even when one target variable is chosen there is disagreement about measurement.

Gavin, William T. "The M1 Target and Disinflation Policy." In Federal Reserve Bank of Cleveland *Economic Commentary* (October 1, 1985).
> Good analysis of Fed targeting in a period of disinflation. Short and easy to read.

Hamburger, Michael T. "Financial Innovation and Monetary Targeting." In Federal Reserve Bank of St. Louis *Financial Innovations* (1984): 105–119.
> Discussion of changing financial sector and its implications for monetary target strategies.

Kane, Edward J. "Selecting Monetary Targets in a Changing Financial Environment." Federal Reserve Bank of Kansas City *Monetary Policy Issues* (1982).
> Reviews Fed's targeting strategies amidst financial services revolution.

McMillin, W. Douglas and James S. Fackler. "Monetary vs. Credit Aggregates: An Evaluation of Monetary Policy Targets." In *Southern Economic Journal* 5, 3 (January 1984): 711–723.
> Presents arguments that current Fed targets may be inappropriate in light of financial deregulation. Contains good list of references.

Wallich, Henry C. and P. M. Keir. "The Role of Operating Guides in U.S. Monetary Policy: A Historical Review." In *Federal Reserve Bulletin* 65 (September 1979): 679–691.
> Places ongoing debate about most appropriate monetary target variable into historical perspective.

———. "Monetary Policy Report to Congress." In *Federal Reserve Bulletin* (March and September of each year).
> Summary of chairman's report to Congress. Contains clear enunciation of Fed's evaluation of current economic conditions and explanation of targeting strategy for next six months.

CHAPTER NINETEEN

EXPANDING THE RECORD of MONETARY POLICY

Like fire, money is useful under control: but running wild, it can do great harm.

Sherman J. Maisel, *Managing the Dollar*

This chapter is the third part of the monetary policy discussion. Chapter 17 described economic goals and the *tactics or tools* the Fed uses to achieve those goals and Chapter 18 explored the *strategy or framework* for monetary policy. This chapter considers and examines the *effectiveness* of monetary policy and the issues such an evaluation brings to the forefront.

Recall that policy makers, and specifically monetary authorities, set forth clear macroeconomic goals: economic growth and maximum employment, price (and in some instances interest rate) stability, and a secure and stable financial system. Fed officials did not always have these goals uppermost in their minds. Legislation after World War II enunciated the goals for our system. The discussion of the effectiveness of monetary policy focuses on the period since Congress established these goals, with only a brief look at some earlier strategies that the Fed employed.

Chapter Objectives

To understand and evaluate Federal Reserve policies, you need a basis for assessing policies (provided in the last chapter) and a bit of a historical perspective on Fed actions. The Fed's early strategies included the real bills doctrine, interest-rate pegging, and the bills only approach. These strategies influenced subsequent policy actions. The Fed's success, or lack of it, in early years has affected its strategies in later years.

By the end of this chapter you should be able to:

- Evaluate specific past Fed strategies and the effects of those actions on contemporary Federal Reserve policies.

  Determine whether the Fed overreacted to inflationary pressures during the Recession of 1960.

  Describe the effects of the Fed's cutback on credit availability during the Credit Crunch of 1966.

  Assess the Fed's policy following wage and price controls during the Money Restraint of 1974.

- Analyze Fed actions over the last decade.

  Identify actions and consequences that led to changes in goals and ultimately to establishment of contemporary goals.

  Describe the effects of actions on public confidence in the Fed.

- Evaluate the conduct of monetary policy.

  Describe criteria for evaluating the Fed's actions.

  Assess how lags affect the Fed's ability to achieve its goals.

  Identify ways that coordination of monetary and fiscal policies affect the economy's performance.

  State conclusions about who actually controls monetary policy.

Reviewing Fed actions in the last few years with these objectives in mind should allow you to evaluate the success of monetary policy. In doing this you need to consider whether the United States structures its monetary policy in the most effective way and whether some reforms will improve the conduct of monetary policy.

Previous Strategies

In Chapter 16 you learned about the origins and early development of the Federal Reserve System. In its early years, the Fed relied primarily, if not exclusively, on discount policy as its tool. But the Fed's major responsibility in its early years was helping the government finance World War I. Essentially, the Fed and any goals it may have established independently were subordinated to the Treasury's goal of financing the war effort.

In addition, throughout these early years, the guiding principle behind Fed actions was the commercial loan theory or *real bills doctrine* (discussed in Chapter 5). This theory predicted that the extension of loans to facilitate production would stimulate economic activity without encouraging inflation. The Fed used the discount window to encourage member bank lending according to this real-bills doctrine. The financing of Treasury debt issues and the extension of loans through the discount window led to a doubling of the money supply in the years 1914 to 1919.

The Treasury's reliance on the Fed, establishing it as the fiscal agent for the government, gave the Fed increased prominence. After inflating the money supply and contributing to the wartime price inflation, the Fed abandoned the real bills doctrine and raised the interest rate, assisted in a large decline in the supply of money, and contributed to the recession of 1921–22.

The Fed's role as fiscal agent and its part in the recession of 1921–22 led, at least indirectly, to its discovery of open-market operations. During the early 1920s, the Fed tripled its holdings of government securities from $193 million to $603 million. This helped to propel the economy out of recession and into the boom years of the Roaring 20s. During this period, the first debate over strategies and targets ensued. New York Fed President Benjamin Strong argued that the Fed should offset the large gold inflows by using open-market sales to absorb bank reserves, thus maintaining some stability in lending and prices.[1] The Board of Governors wanted to stick to the "real bills doctrine" and make funds available to meet loan demand for productive purposes. The goal of both approaches was economic prosperity. The issue was whether to strive for stable expansion or to allow the system to progress at its own pace.[2]

Much of the Fed's policy during the late 1920s can be classified as moral suasion. The Fed professed the notion that credit should remain cheap for legitimate business activities but restrained for speculative stock market activity. The Fed could only undertake efforts to convince banks to follow

---

[1] Scholars attribute the early importance of the Fed to Benjamin Strong. The Board of Governors was not as powerful in the early years of the Fed as it is now, so Strong dominated monetary policy. Lester Chandler wrote an excellent biography of Strong, *Benjamin Strong: Central Banker* (Washington: The Brookings Institution, 1958).

[2] Much of what the Fed did during the middle to late 1920s was directed at helping Britain return to the gold standard. See Stephen V.O. Clarke, *Central Bank Cooperation 1924–31* (New York: Federal Reserve Bank of New York, 1967).

such a policy because it did not yet have the power to control margin requirements. The Fed's efforts were unsuccessful and the availability of credit for business expansion helped fuel stock market expansion.

Economists and historians have engaged in considerable debate over Federal Reserve actions in the early 1930s. Friedman and Schwartz call this period the Great Contraction because the nominal money supply contracted so precipitously—by more than one-third from August 1929 to March 1933. They argue that this aggravated the economic downturn. Peter Termin has challenged this view asserting instead that the drop in investment and consumption demand led to a drop in the demand for money and that the supply of money followed from this.[3]

The Depression did produce important banking reform legislation, described in Chapter 4, as the Fed struggled to provide some stability and security for financial institutions. For the most part, the 1930s represent an era when the Fed was without a consistent policy strategy. Whether or not its actions in 1929–30 precipitated the Depression, its misreading of signals in 1936–37 aborted economic recovery and sent the economy into another tailspin.

World War II resulted in another period when Fed policies were subordinated to the Treasury's need to finance a war. Specifically the Fed underwrote the Treasury's bond issues. The Fed would step in to purchase government securities not purchased by the public. Pegging the interest rates in this way did keep the interest rates low, and as such minimized the cost of financing the war effort. Continuing to peg interest rates after the war prevented the Fed from exercising any independent monetary policy and threatened another inflationary spiral. In March 1951 the Fed and the Treasury came to an agreement, the Accord of 1951, which freed the Fed from its pegging responsibility and allowed the Board of Governors to pursue monetary objectives consistent with the economic goals enunciated by the Employment Act of 1946.[4]

Shortly after the Accord was reached William McChesney Martin was appointed chairman of the Fed. As a Treasury official, Martin had helped negotiate the Accord. He was the most forceful monetary policy maker since

---

[3] See M. Friedman and A. Schwartz, *A Monetary History of the United States, 1857–1960* especially Chapter 7; and Peter Termin, *Did Monetary Forces Cause the Great Depression?* (New York: W.W. Norton, 1976).

[4] Although the Accord eliminated mandatory intervention by the Fed to control interest rates, the Fed has, to a greater or lesser extent, continued to intervene in money markets to achieve interest-rate targets. This is what makes the monetary aggregate strategy announced in November 1979 so dramatic.

Benjamin Strong. Throughout much of the post-Accord period the Fed pursued what we described earlier as a bills-only strategy. The Fed concentrated on short-term securities (Treasury bills) using free reserves as the operational target and short-term interest rates as its instrumental target. Free reserves are depository institution reserves in excess of those required minus borrowings from the Fed. Proponents of the bills-only approach argued that controlling free reserves provided the Fed with the maximum influence over money market conditions. According to this approach, increasing free reserve levels pointed to a ready availability of credit, an easy money position, whereas declining levels of free reserves, or negative free reserve levels, showed tight credit conditions. The Fed used open-market operations to achieve the desired target level for free reserves.

Federal Reserve critics and other respected analysts concluded that the free reserve strategy was flawed. Monitoring free reserves provided misleading signals. A negative free reserve position, signaling tight money, might actually coincide with a monetary expansion. Borrowed reserves could fuel the extension of loans and the expansion of the money supply. As such, the free reserve approach was actually procyclical.

Some examples of Federal Reserve policy actions during the 1950s and 1960s will demonstrate how these events influenced the evolution of more contemporary policy strategies.

Differential Effects of Fed Actions

Throughout the 1950s and into the 1960s, the Fed's policy was one of "leaning against the wind." The Fed attempted to use open-market operations to head off any deviation from a stable, noninflationary growth path. A fear of inflation had a major influence on Fed actions in this period. Equating monetary policy to an inexperienced and somewhat fearful newly licensed driver, the Fed jammed on the brakes whenever the economy, especially prices, began moving ahead too rapidly.

1960 Recession Concern about a too rapid economic expansion and the resultant inflation led the Fed to slow down money supply growth during 1960. The Fed had been cautious during the 1950s. M1 grew at a 1.9 percent annual rate from 1952 to 1959. The Consumer Price Index had risen slowly from 79.5 in 1952 to 81.5 in 1956. Then beginning in late 1957 and continuing into 1959, the CPI began to rise more rapidly, about 3 percent per year, which at the time was considered unacceptable. The Fed's concern with rising prices prompted a restrictive monetary policy. The money supply fell at an annual rate of 2 percent during the last half of 1959 and the first half of

1960. This helped produce the recession of 1960 when real output declined by 1.5 percent during 1960 and unemployment rose from 5 percent in early 1960 to 6.6 percent by the year's end.[5]

Credit Crunch, 1966 Increasing American involvement in Vietnam and the Great Society programs of President Johnson helped produce increased government spending, largely through debt issuance. The budget deficit increased from $1.6 billion in 1965 to over $2.5 billion in 1968. The Fed had cooperated in sustaining economic expansion after the recession of 1960–61 by holding down interest rates through its purchases of government debt instruments. The money supply had increased at an annual rate of less than 4 percent from mid-1962 to mid-1965; then it almost doubled in the next year, accelerating to a 6.9 percent growth rate from mid-1965 to mid-1966.

This money supply expansion was followed by rising prices. The CPI had been fairly stable, rising only about 1.5 percent from early 1961 to mid-1965. It rose rapidly to a 3.5 percent annual rate by early 1966.

The Fed's concern about inflation prompted a tightening of monetary policy. The Fed raised the discount rate in December 1965. Largely due to White House pressure, the Fed took no additional action. The Fed continued to provide ample bank reserves through open-market purchases. In May, 1966, the Fed moved to restrict money supply growth. The FOMC, instead of focusing only on money market conditions (interest rates), directed its attention to monetary aggregates. The result was dramatic. During the last half of 1966, money supply growth dropped to zero. From April to October the money supply actually declined at an annual rate of 1.5 percent.

The Fed's tight money policy coupled with the government's continuing credit needs to finance military expenditures led to a real credit crunch. Interest rates rose to levels that had not been seen since the 1920s. Market rates rose to a level where they surpassed the Fed-imposed ceiling on interest rates paid on time deposits. Figure 19.1 illustrates the short drop in the money supply and the rise in short term interest rates during 1966. The events in 1966 were a harbinger of things to come during the high interest rate period of the 1970s. Individuals moved funds from deposit accounts with interest ceilings to accounts which could earn market rates. Savings and Loans were particularly hard hit. Their net flow of funds declined to one-fourth of the 1965 level. This dried up mortgage funds for residential

---

[5] The recession may have cost Richard Nixon the election in 1960 and influenced subsequent policy. Nixon's economic advisor in the election was Arthur Burns (who would succeed Martin as Fed chairman). He warned that the Fed's monetary restraint would bring on recession. Despite requests from candidate Nixon, President Eisenhower refused to interfere with the independence of the Fed. Nixon has stated that the ensuing recession cost him enough votes to allow John Kennedy to win the 1960 election.

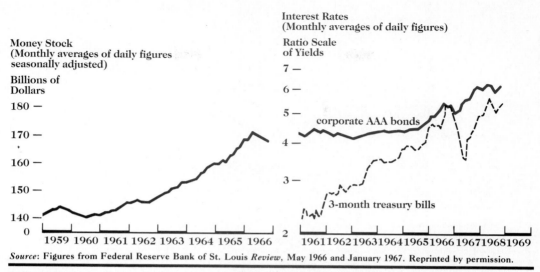

Money Stock
(Monthly averages of daily figures
seasonally adjusted)

Billions of
Dollars

Interest Rates
(Monthly averages of daily figures)

Ratio Scale
of Yields

corporate AAA bonds

3-month treasury bills

Source: Figures from Federal Reserve Bank of St. Louis *Review*, May 1966 and January 1967. Reprinted by permission.

FIGURE 19.1 *Interest Rates Rise in Response to 1966 Credit Crunch* When the Fed "slammed on the brakes" in 1966, the money supply took a quick drop and interest rates rose.

construction. The home building industry collapsed and other durable goods industries also suffered.

The Fed's tight money policy of 1966 not only created a crunch on credit markets but produced stress within the S & L and residential construction industries. This experience demonstrates that hitting the money growth brakes too hard can precipitate a severe economic downturn. The 1966 crunch also shows that Fed policies have a disproportionate effect on interest-sensitive industries.

The Fed countered its tight money policy of late 1966 with an excessive money creation in 1967–1968. M1 grew by over 7 percent from January 1967 to mid-1968. Interest rates responded by falling (see Figure 19.2). But the increase in the money supply contributed to the rising rate of inflation (the inflation rate rose to 5.6 percent by late 1969).

Monetary Restraint After Wage and Price Control Period President Nixon's wage and price controls, announced in August, 1971, directly attacked the inflationary spiral which began during the Johnson administration. The various phases of this control program ranged from a complete freeze in Phase I, to the transition to a free market in Phase IV; the program lasted until 1974. During the price control period, the administration used fiscal policy to stimulate the economy by increasing federal expenditures, extending tax exemptions, and expanding investment tax credits. The Fed,

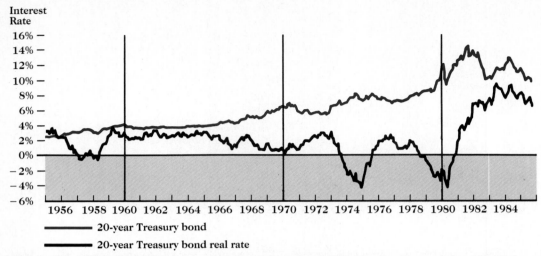

Source: "After Adjusting for Inflation, Interest Rates Remain Near Record Highs" Reprinted by permission of *The Wall Street Journal*, December 2, 1985. Copyright © Dow Jones & Company, Inc., 1985. All Rights Reserved.

FIGURE 19.2 *Interest Rates Remain Near Record Highs* Even though interest rates have declined sharply in the last two years after the extraordinarily high levels of the early 1980s, real rates are still very high by historical standards. This is particularly noticeable in contrast to the negative real rates of the 1970s.

under new Chairman Arthur Burns, accommodated the fiscal expansion to a large extent in order to prevent interest rates from rising while prices and wages were controlled. The economy responded with a noticeable spurt of growth. As the 1972 election approached, unemployment was declining and real GNP was rising.[6]

Even during the later stages of wage and price controls, the economy began to experience a rising price level. The increase in the money supply in 1972 coupled with the negative supply side effects of the strict early price controls put pressure on prices. Rapidly rising agricultural prices, aggravated supply problems from the price controls, and the OPEC oil embargo all added to an accelerating price level.

Realizing that the controls were threatening to cause long-term disruptions to our market economy, the Nixon administration gradually removed the controls during early 1974. But with the controls removed, prices sky-rocketed—rising to an unheard-of 11 percent during 1974.

The Fed was the last bulwark against the inflationary spiral. Burns argued that inflation could "threaten the very foundations of our society." Thus, the money supply which had grown by 5.7 percent from the second

---

[6] Recall Nixon's concern, prompted by then economic advisor Burns, that the recession had cost him the 1960 election. Obviously actions were undertaken that would assure that no recession would threaten election in 1972.

quarter of 1973 to the second quarter of 1974, grew at an annual rate of just 1.3 percent over the next six months. At the same time, the Fed raised the discount rate. Responding to this monetary restraint, the federal funds rate rose to a record 13.5 percent by June.

With nominal interest rising (real interest was declining because the price level was rising so rapidly) and the oil price shocks disrupting economic activity, the nation was plunged into the worst recession since the end of World War II. (The recession of 1981–82 would prove to be worse.)

The Fed had reacted to a worsening inflationary spiral and acted to prevent rising prices from totally disrupting market conditions. The economy recovered very slowly from this recession. Unfortunately, with recovery would come an accentuated inflationary period which would lead to a dramatic policy shift by the Fed in 1979.

Was Monetary Policy Procyclical?   Throughout these periods, the Federal Reserve was generally using nominal interest rates as the target variable. Although freed from a normal pegging of interest rates by the 1951 Accord, the Fed pursued a policy which, with a few exceptions, was designed to keep interest rates at moderate levels. Figure 19.2 reveals that the Fed was quite successful in achieving this goal. But, the nominal interest rate strategy may have precipitated or accentuated the post–World War II recessions.

The Fed's policy of maintaining nominal interest rates within target ranges was actually a procyclical policy. Consider what happens to interest rates during the business cycle. During a downturn with a declining demand for credit, interest rates drop. As rates decline below the target range, the Fed enters the open market to maintain interest rate stability; it sells securities to decrease depository institution reserves. This policy actually contributes to the downturn.

During an upturn when the expansion puts pressure on credit markets, interest rates rise. As the rates rise beyond the target range the Fed increases depository institution reserves through open-market purchases to ease credit conditions. This policy contributes to the expansion.

The procyclical nature of monetary policy with interest rates as the target variable results in part from policy lags. When monetary policy is reactive, rather than proactive, the time required to formulate a policy response coupled with the time for the policy action to work its way through the system, may well result in procyclical rather than countercyclical outcomes.

Table 19.1 provides some evidence of the procyclical nature of monetary policy from 1956 through 1981. The left-hand column lists the years with tight monetary policy and the right-hand column lists recessions. In each case where a recession occurs, it was preceded or accompanied by a period of tight money.

Years with Tight Monetary Policy*	Years with Recessions**
1956†	1957–58
1960†	1960–61
1966	1966–67
1969†	1970–71
1974†	1973–75
	1980
1981	1981–82

* Monetary policy is measured by four-quarter average rate of change of M1 minus the 20-quarter average rate of change. Deviation of more than one-half standard deviation from mean establishes relative tightness.

** As determined by NBER; 1966–67 was officially labeled a "credit crunch."

† Indicates fiscal policy was also tight according to Carlson's analysis.

Source: **Keith M. Carlson, "The Mix of Monetary and Fiscal Policies: Conventional Wisdom vs. Empirical Reality," Federal Reserve Bank of St. Louis** *Review* **(October 1982): 7–21. Reprinted by permission.**

TABLE 19.1   *Monetary Policy and Economic Recessions, 1956–1983*

Recent Policy Strategies

Recall from Chapter 18 that the Fed has followed three different targeting strategies in the period since 1970:

1970–September 1979	Targeting Interest Rates
October 1979–September 1982	Targeting Nonborrowed Reserves
October 1982–present	Targeting Borrowed Reserves

You can gain insight into the factors which prompted these various targeting strategies by reviewing events over the last ten or twelve years. In the process, you can acquire the information you need to evaluate the Fed's performance.

Events Leading to 1979 Targeting Shift

During the 1970s, the Fed came under increasing criticism. The economy was floundering. After the Fed cracked down on money supply growth, helping to push the economy into the 1974–75 recession, the Board of Governors adopted a more moderate monetary strategy. From early 1975 through the third quarter of 1976, the money supply grew at an annual rate of

5.5 percent. Unemployment remained at historically high levels (over 8 percent) even with the recovery from the most recent recession. In light of that level of unemployment, 5.5 percent was indeed modest monetary growth. Perhaps after receiving so much criticism for pumping money into the system just before the 1972 election, Chairman Burns was especially cautious as the 1976 election approached.

After the election, with the rate of inflation dipping under 5 percent but with unemployment hovering near 8 percent, President Carter declared unemployment public enemy number one. Despite continuing public pronouncements about holding the line against inflation, the Fed's policies showed increasing ease during 1977. Carter replaced Burns with G. William Miller in early 1978 and the monetary ease continued. Throughout 1977 and 1978, M1 increased at over 8 percent per year. Carter's war on unemployment was having positive results—the rate of unemployment dropped under 6 percent by late 1978—but inflationary pressures were intensifying. Table 19.2 illustrates trends in consumer prices over that time period. Prices received a severe commodity shock when OPEC oil prices rose almost 50 percent during early 1979. Analysts began to question whether interest rates were an effective target variable. Beyond this, public pressure was mounting. Opinion polls consistently reported inflation as the public's main concern. President Carter recognized the burgeoning problem. In the middle of this term he announced that his administration would orient itself toward fighting inflation. Perhaps as an indication of the severity of the inflation problem, Carter replaced G. William Miller as chairman of the Board of Governors. Paul Volcker, who was familiar to New York banking and financial interests from his years as Treasury undersecretary and New York Fed president, was named chairman in the summer of 1979.

Shift in Targeting Strategy

With domestic conditions worsening, Volcker wasted no time leading the Fed toward a new approach to monetary policy.[7] In October, 1979, the Fed announced it would control the money supply directly through changes in bank reserves rather than indirectly through manipulation of the federal funds rate.

The rapid acceleration of prices in the late 1970s was accompanied by rising interest rates. These factors served as the background to and the

---

[7] A critical analysis of the Fed's policy change in 1979 can be found in Karl Brunner and Alan H. Meltzer, "Strategies and Tactics for Monetary Control," *Carnegie-Rochester Conference Series on Public Policy* 18 (Spring 1983): 59–116.

Year	CPI	% Δ
1970	116.3	
		4.3
1971	121.3	
		3.3
1972	125.3	
		6.2
1973	133.1	
		11.0
1974	147.7	
		9.1
1975	161.2	
		5.8
1976	170.5	
		6.5
1977	181.5	
		7.7
1978	195.4	
		11.3
1979	217.4	
		13.5
1980	246.8	
		10.4
1981	272.1	
		6.1
1982	289.1	
		3.2
1983	298.4	
		4.3
1984	311.1	
		3.6
1985	322.2	
		1.1
1986*	325.9	

* preliminary estimates

TABLE 19.2   *Consumer Price Index (1967 = 100)*

stimulus for changes in the Fed's monetary targeting strategies. Volcker's primary reason for the change was to demonstrate the Fed's commitment to fighting inflation. His case within the Fed was bolstered by the continuing deterioration of financial markets. The dollar's value was falling as investors refused to hold the depreciating currency.

The Fed's policy shift created great uncertainty which was accentuated by world events. For example, in November, the United States Embassy in Iran was occupied and in December, the Soviets invaded Afghanistan. The public and the financial markets seemed unconvinced about the Fed's willingness to adhere to a more controlled money growth policy. Inflationary expectations persisted, adding to the uncertainty premium. Interest rates rose dramatically and inflation escalated. The Federal Funds rate went to 17.6 percent in April of 1980; the CPI hit an annual growth rate of 18 percent in the first months of the year.

In the early spring, with the inflation rate high and still rising despite the high interest rates, the administration, with reluctant support from the

Fed, announced the imposition of credit controls. The public stopped using credit, spending slowed and the economy weakened further. With these declines, the basic money supply declined such that its growth was well below the Fed's target. This situation, coupled with the administration's desire to get the economy moving again, encouraged the Fed to pursue a too expansionary monetary policy. The economy responded more quickly than expected and Fed critics charged that once again the Board of Governors had responded to political pressure and had abandoned the inflation fight. Therefore, even though the 1980 election was only five weeks away, the Fed announced a discount rate increase to demonstrate its resolve to fight inflation. This was just the beginning of a protracted period of monetary stringency designed to halt the rise in prices and to break the inflationary psychology.

Restoring the Fed's Credibility

Within the Fed, individuals were increasingly concerned that the inflationary expectations generated by a decade of rising prices were becoming ingrained in attitudes of Americans. An analysis of the 1970s indicated that one-third to one-half of the inflation in the middle of the decade resulted from oil and other commodity price shocks. The fact that the price level did not revert to lower growth ranges after the initial OPEC price increases had worked their way through the system indicates that inflationary expectations were quite strong. Even the 1974–75 recession did little to diminish these expectations. Accelerating prices in late 1978 and a rapidly expanding money supply reinforced those inflationary expectations.[8] The Fed was losing credibility because actual money growth regularly exceeded its target ranges. These factors undoubtedly influenced the Fed's decision to change its targeting strategy and to implement a tight monetary policy during 1980–81.

Ronald Reagan's inauguration seemed to signal White House support for the Fed's tight money policy. But when the stimulating results of the 1981 tax cut predicted by supply-siders did not come to pass, the Fed came under attack from administration officials for not accommodating the supply-side stimulus. The Fed certainly had not accommodated the tax cut with easy money but the increasing criticism did not change the Fed's strategy.

---

[8] Alan Blinder provides a thorough analysis of these issues in "The Anatomy of Double-Digit Inflation in the 1970s," which appears in Robert E. Hall, ed., *Inflation: Causes and Effects* (Chicago: University of Chicago Press, 1982).

Figure 19.3 reveals the extent to which interest rates increased during this period. The basic money supply growth rate in 1981 was the lowest in nearly two decades; it was below the Fed's originally announced target range.

The target money policy had the desired effect on inflation. As was shown in Table 19.2, the rate of growth of consumer prices slowed dramatically—from 13.5 percent in 1979 to 10.4 percent in 1980, to 6.1 percent in 1981 and finally to 3.2 percent in 1982. The cost of this reduction in inflation was the worst recession in the postwar era.

The 1979–1982 policies achieved the specified goals—restored confidence in the Fed and a reduced rate of inflation. The Fed altered its tight money policy in late 1981 and adopted a new operating policy in late 1982 resulting in an annualized M1 growth rate of over 9 percent from October 1981 to April 1982 and an actual growth rate of just over 11 percent from mid-1982 to mid-1983. After this alteration, inflationary expectations did not return and long-term interest rates declined. This outcome is evidence that the Fed had restored confidence in its ability to control inflation.

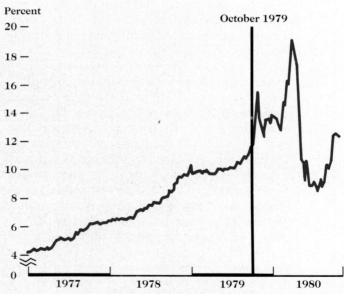

Source: From *Economic Review*, Summer 1984. Reprinted by permission of the Federal Reserve Bank of San Francisco.

FIGURE 19.3 *Federal Funds Rate Fluctuations After 1979* This figure illustrates how erratic interest rates have been in the recent past. Fed policy and deregulation have contributed to these fluctuations.

Monetary Control Act and 1982 Targeting Shift

Financial reform legislation and the resulting effects on monetary instruments and bank behavior contributed to the Fed's decision to alter its targeting strategy in October 1982. The Fed de-emphasized M1 as a target variable and adopted a broader, more flexible approach to monetary policy. This consisted of targeting borrowed reserves—directing the Open-Market Desk to act to increase, decrease, or maintain reserve levels—placing more weight on the broader monetary aggregates (M2 and M3), and monitoring nonfinancial debt.

In announcing the Fed's decision on October 9, Chairman Volcker insisted that the Fed was not abandoning its efforts to control money supply growth and was most assuredly not giving up its fight against inflation. He pointed out some technical and institutional reasons behind the switch, for example a rigid policy of monitoring monetary aggregates and adjusting money growth to market conditions as reflected in reserve levels.

Some significant events were behind the Fed's decision. Some people within the FOMC believed that the economy needed some relief from the tight money policy. Inherent in the targeting change may have been a desire to provide some monetary stimulus without appearing to have abandoned M1 growth-range targets. Events provided the Fed with a good excuse for shifting away from M1.

First, a large quantity of all-savers certificates would mature in October 1982.[9] Policy makers could not predict what the public would do with these funds. This could easily result in a large distortion of M1, something the Fed officials feared would confuse observers of money supply trends. Second, regulatory changes from the 1980 reform legislation were affecting depository institutions and money market instruments. The rise of NOW accounts (essentially permitting interest payments on checking accounts) and the fact that depository institutions could offer money market accounts would alter the way the public held money and therefore affect the money measures. Third, with interest rates declining, the velocity of money might well change, making monetary aggregates less reliable as a policy variable.[10]

---

[9] These certificates were authorized by Congress one year earlier. They carried a favorable yield and a one-year maturity. A large number were sold during the first month they were available. Those matured in October and reinvestment in the certificates was not an option for most holders.

[10] At the time the Fed was changing its targeting procedure, it was redefining the basic money supply measures. For a complete discussion of this, see "The Redefined Monetary Aggregates," *Federal Reserve Bulletin* 66 (Feb. 1980): 97–114.

MONEY TODAY 19.1

Effects of Financial Deregulation on Monetary Policy

There have been some major developments in the past decade which have greatly influenced the making of monetary policy in this country. One of the most significant is the deregulation of the banking system.

The deregulation of interest rates paid by depository institutions has had several positive results. It has increased competition for funds and opened up an array of new financial instruments offering market rates of return. Unfortunately, deregulation also has had two adverse consequences for the conduct of monetary policy.

First, in a deregulated system, larger interest rate changes will be required to produce a given impact on the domestic economy than was the case in the regulated system. In the 1960s, the Fed was able to influence the economy with relatively modest interest rate changes. Whenever market interest rates rose above the regulated ceiling rate, funds would flow out of depository institutions and widespread nonprice rationing of credit would take place. Borrowers who did not have access to the money markets were not able to obtain credit.

In the deregulated environment, nonprice rationing of credit is largely eliminated. Mortgage money will always be available at some price. Almost the entire burden of adjustment is thrown on the price rationing of credit. Inevitably, larger interest rate swings will be required than in the previous environment. In an era of widespread financial fragility, when changes in American interest rates have more international ramifications than ever before, this might be viewed as an unfortunate structural change. An additional burden is placed on American policy makers to avoid economic conditions that might lead to wide interest rate swings.

The second adverse consequence of deregulation is the blurring of the line between money and other liquid assets. In the 1960s, the line was very clear. Payments could be made only by demand deposits and currency. In addition, since no interest could be paid on demand deposits, there was a strong incentive to re-

strict assets held in this form to an amount needed for transaction purposes. Neither of these conditions exists today. Payments are being made from a variety of accounts paying a market rate of interest. The line between money and other liquid assets is irrevocably lost in the United States. It is one of the ironies of economic history that monetarist doctrine found its most widespread support at the very time that it became impossible to measure the money stock.

A reasonable response to this situation would be to move from targeting "money" to targeting liquid assets, an idea which has not received much support from the Federal Reserve. It seems likely that the Fed and other central banks as well will be groping in the years to come for some financial variable that can be used in place of "money" as a guideline for monetary policy.

Over the next eight or nine months, the Fed did ease up on its tight money growth policy. From the fourth quarter of 1982 to the second quarter of 1983, M1 growth was 12.4 percent. This undoubtedly contributed to the economic recovery which began at the end of 1982. The Fed's monetary ease gave way to a renewed monetary stringency by mid-1983. The increasing size of the federal deficit and the danger that renewed inflationary expectations would push interest rates up, aggravating the world debt crisis, led the FOMC to keep money growth rates at the lower end of established target ranges.

During 1984 and 1985, the Fed maintained a policy to keep prices from rising and achieved a steady decline in interest rates. The economy continued to grow although GNP did not increase at the anticipated rate. The Fed did not achieve its M1 growth target but was quite successful in maintaining M2 and M3 growth rates (see Figure 19.4). Through these years, the Fed directed much of its attention to cooperative arrangements to reduce the value of the dollar. The dollar did drop, faster and further than Chairman Volcker wanted. But the Fed's reputation for monetary stabilization spread as economic growth without inflation continued.[11]

There was little criticism of Fed policies during 1986. With the inflation rate under control, the CPI rose by only 1.1 percent for the year. And with interest rates declining, and economic growth continuing, albeit at a sluggish pace, the only shortcoming in domestic economic performance was the persistence of high unemployment. Despite some disagreements among members of FOMC, the Fed maintained what Chairman Volcker referred to as a "broadly accommodative" policy during 1986. Although M1 growth

---

[11] This lends some credence to the observation that the M1-GNP relationship is no longer very strong. Chapter 18 presented the money-to-GNP relationship and Chapter 20 addresses the Federal Reserve and the international sphere.

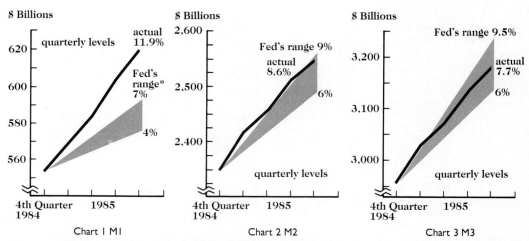

*This is the range the Fed announced in February 1985. In July 1985, the Fed announced a new range of 3–8% growth for the second half of the year. M1 outgrew that range too.

Source: Charts 1–3 "Money Growth vs. the Fed's Ranges in 1985" from Federal Reserve Bank of Minneapolis *1985 Annual Report*, p. 9. Reprinted by permission of the Federal Reserve Bank of Minneapolis.

FIGURE 19.4 *Money Growth versus Fed's Ranges in 1985* The Fed's success at achieving its monetary targets, using "cones," or ranges of money growth as the assessment technique, is shown by this figure. The range expands as we move further out in time because it is more likely that the rate will vary over time.

exceeded FOMC target ranges during most of the year, there was no indication that this would lead to an acceleration of the price level. In fact, the Fed's accommodative policy was generally credited with sustaining economic growth.

Evaluating Monetary Policy

Asking the question, "Can monetary policy work?" evokes considerable debate. Whether or not monetary policy works depends greatly on the criteria one uses to evaluate policy. The Federal Reserve's primary role in its early years was to facilitate a smoothly functioning financial system. Most observers would agree that the Fed is successful in this regard. More re-

MONEY TODAY 19.2   Isn't M1 the Propellant to Growth?

After a period of sustained economic growth, the American economy seemed to reach a plateau in 1986. Real growth slowed to almost a standstill and a low rate of inflation persisted. How could that be? many analysts asked. The Federal Reserve was pumping money into the economy at a rapid rate. The money growth rate for 1986 was in double digits. Shouldn't that have produced some greater increase in GNP? Perhaps not if we consider velocity and the rate of growth of money other than that measured by M1.

Velocity is the rate of money turnover. It has declined since 1985. Thus the connection between money growth and economic growth just isn't what it used to be. Even Paul Volcker, in his testimony before Congress in July 1986, acknowledged this by saying that M1 "is not today a reliable measure" of inflation or growth.

Some economists claim we're in a liquidity trap. People are holding money rather than spending or investing it. We're not in a liquidity trap but people *are* holding onto money. This makes sense; with declining interest rates and innovative financial instruments, it's possible to hold money without losing interest income.

This is one explanation for the declining velocity of money and the breakdown of the connection between money and GNP. Because M1 is more broadly defined to include interest-bearing NOW accounts, it captures the increasing money balances in checking accounts. Another explanation is that people are spending just as they used to but more of those expenditures are for imported goods. This situation worsens the trade balance and reduces GNP. Thus, with less GNP for the supply of money the velocity is lower.

Other economists, such as consultant A. Gary Schilling, claim that the supply of money hasn't grown fast enough to stimulate the economy. He points out that the Fed sets money growth targets based on the inflationary period of the 1960s and 1970s when velocity was understandably high and M1 was a narrower money measure. Now, with inflation at a more reasonable level and with technological improvements for transferring funds between accounts, velocity is lower and M1 is a much broader money measure. By concentrating only on M1 growth rates in setting policy at a time when velocity is dropping, the Fed has set a tight money course.

Following this line of thinking, one can't argue that money no longer propels economic activity. On the contrary, it does but there has been too little money to effectively stimulate the economy.

Perhaps the Fed agrees. In his 1986 report to Congress, Chairman Volcker indicated that the Fed would deemphasize M1 in setting its credit policies. Perhaps we will see an easier money policy.

cently, after World War II, the Fed has intervened in the system to achieve economic stabilization. Concensus on whether the Fed has been successful in this regard is harder to reach. Several issues are important in evaluating monetary policy.

Lags in Monetary Policy

Monetary policy changes take time to work their way through the economy. When contrasted with fiscal policy actions, monetary policy takes much longer. Recall from earlier in this chapter the discussion of target variables and the elapsed time between FOMC action and changes in the variables. This time is called an *outside lag*. *Inside lags* refer to the time involved in the Fed decision to implement a policy. Lags include the following:

Inside Lags:

recognition—noticing need for policy action

diagnosis—analyzing the problem

prescription—determining appropriate responses

instrumentation—deciding which tools to use

Outside Lags:

implementation—executing policy action

evaluation—assessing effects

The inside lag varies depending on the degree of unanimity within the FOMC. Compared to the outside lag, it is quite short. Estimates vary as to the time from implementation of a policy until its full impact is felt. Most observers agree that sixty to ninety days pass before initial results are observable and at least two quarters go by before any significant impact begins. A year or more may pass before a monetary policy has its full effect.

Unfortunately, economists also disagree about whether outside lags are of the same duration from one time to the next. The FOMC must correctly recognize the need and implement the proper policy in the right dosage. It also must take that action at the correct time. To many economists, this indicates that the usefulness of monetary policy for short-run stabilization is highly questionable.

Beyond timing issues, the Fed must attempt to coordinate its policy actions with fiscal policy decisions. Appearing before Congress twice each year, the Fed chairman gives clear indication as to what the Fed intends to do. This allows the legislative and executive branches to have full knowledge of monetary policy.

Who Controls Monetary Policy?

The Federal Reserve is an independent agency. Although it is required to report its policy objectives to Congress, the Fed is not subject to the authority of Congress or the president. The provision for independence was designed to provide the Fed the greatest possible freedom for implementing an objective, nonpartisan, nonpolitical monetary policy.

The Fed is variously accused of exerting too much independence, thus undermining the congressional/administration economic agenda, and of succumbing to pressure from the administration, thus allowing politics to influence policy.

Robert Weintraub argued in a 1978 article that presidents have actually controlled Federal Reserve policy.[12] Looking at the period 1950–1977, Weintraub concluded that "much of the history of monetary policy can be explained by noting who the president was. . . ."

Recall Meiselman's presidential year "political monetary cycle."[13] Meiselman argues that in Phase I of the cycle, about a year-and-a-half before the election, money growth slows down markedly in order to slow inflation in the election season. Then in Phase II, generally two or three quarters before the election, money growth increases so as to stimulate output and employment as November approaches. Meiselman uses the information in Figure 19.5 to illustrate his point.

Meiselman concludes that "these exquisitely timed cycles cast serious doubts on the policy independence of the Federal Reserve." His analysis seems to support Weintraub's conclusions.

On the other hand, if one observes the criticism that presidents level against the Fed, it is difficult to see that the Fed is following the wishes of the administration. President Reagan was particularly vocal in his criticism of Fed policies during his first term in office.

Results of Monetary Policy

The debate will continue about the degree of political influence exerted over Federal Reserve policies. So, too, will discussions regarding the effectiveness of monetary policy. Differential results of monetary policy and the Fed's record since it announced its war on inflation in 1979 contribute to an evaluation of monetary policy effectiveness.

---

[12] Robert E. Weintraub, "Congressional Supervision of Monetary Policy," *Journal of Monetary Economics* 4 (April 1978): 341–362.
[13] David I. Meiselman, "The Political Monetary Cycle," *The Wall Street Journal* (January 10, 1984).

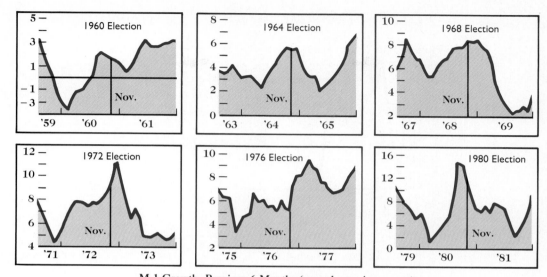

M-1 Growth, Previous 6 Months (annual rate, in percent)

Source: David I. Meiselman, "The Political Monetary Cycle" *The Wall Street Journal* (January 10, 1984). Reprinted by permission.

FIGURE 19.5 *The Political Monetary Cycle*   This figure shows how the money supply expansion correlates with presidential elections. In advance of the November election, usually by about six months, the money supply begins to expand. David Meiselman argues that this demonstrates the effect of political considerations on Federal Reserve policy.

Monetary policy can have dramatic effects. When money growth rates outstrip the productive capacity of the system, inflation results. When the Fed reduces that growth rate, it can choke off economic expansion. Monetary policy comes under the greatest criticism and seems to have the most disruptive effect when the Fed either jams too hard on the money supply brakes or stomps down for too long on the money supply accelerator. The credit crunch of 1966 and the recessions in 1974–75 and 1981–82 are examples of the former. The money supply expansion of the late 1970s is an example of the latter.

Many people point to the Fed's fight against the inflation of the late 1970s as its finest hour. The results of monetary policy actions to combat inflation were felt most acutely in the early 1980s but remain into the middle of the decade. Figure 19.6 illustrates how the war on inflation affected interest rates, unemployment, dollar value, and price level movements.

In early 1987, the rate of inflation was under control and inflationary expectations appeared nonexistent. The Fed was able to counteract the inflation of the 1970s and help to create more certainty about the price level. If a reduction in the rate of inflation is considered the goal of monetary policy in the 1980s, then the Fed, under Paul Volcker, has been successful.

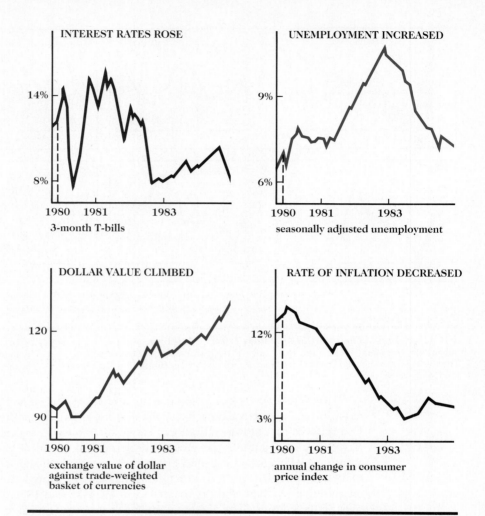

FIGURE 19.6 *Results of Fed's War on Inflation* These figures reveal the results of the Fed's attempts to combat inflation. Using October 1979 as the watershed, we can see that interest rates and unemployment rose as the Fed cut back on the growth rate of the money supply. In response to rising interest rates, the dollar's exchange value rose in the international market. The tight money policy worked as the rate of inflation decreased.

Is There a Better Way?

An article in *The Wall Street Journal* at the end of 1984 concluded with this observation,

> The Fed's success in restraining inflation, costly as it was in terms of lost jobs and output over the past five years, raises the question whether there is any alternative to letting the central bank maintain its tight, almost dictatorial power over the money supply and interest rates.[14]

Since the abandonment of the gold standard, the establishment of economic goals and the use of discretionary intervention to achieve those goals have driven domestic monetary policy. Unlike the gold standard years, when the money supply was adjusted automatically in response to international gold flows, the years since the early 1930s, and especially since the Accord of 1951, have seen the Fed intervene in the system to achieve economic stability.

Many people are critical of the Fed because of its manipulation of the money supply and the destabilizing effect this manipulation has had on the economy. Milton Friedman commented recently that "no major institution in the United States has so poor a record of performance over so long a period. . . ."[15] Analysts from across the philosophical economic spectrum argue that money can facilitate real economic growth, but not cause it. Excessive money creation will advance nominal GNP, not real GNP. Those critical of the Fed's interventionist policies point to excessive money creation as the major causal factor in the post–World War II inflation. These critics, and even some who are not so critical, have proposed reforms to either eliminate the destabilizing effects of monetary policy by restricting the Fed's freedom or to improve the conduct of the Fed's policies under current operating procedures.

Tactical Reform: Rules versus Discretion

Tactical reform refers to changes that alter the way the Fed conducts monetary policy. Currently the Fed uses discretionary monetary policy. One reform suggestion would replace this discretion with a *fixed growth rule*.

---

[14] Paul Blustein, "How Federal Reserve Under Volcker Finally Slowed Down Inflation," *The Wall Street Journal* (December 7, 1984).

[15] Friedman's comment was contained in an article outlining his reform recommendations. See M. Friedman, "The Case for Overhauling the Federal Reserve," *Challenge* (July/August 1985): 4–12.

Those promoting a growth rule for money expansion may differ on the specific rate for money growth, but they agree that the predictability of monetary expansion is most important. In most cases, the suggested rate for money growth is the average growth rate for the economy over some set period of time, for example, real GNP grew at an average annual rate slightly over 2 percent from 1980 through 1985. Using this as a gauge, the fixed growth rate would require the Fed to set an M1 target of approximately 2 percent and to use its policy tools to achieve this target. (The longer run increase in real transactions is closer to 3.6 percent.)

Other growth rule suggestions allow the Fed to select a target, rather than being constrained by some fixed number, but once it is set, the Fed must stick to it. Friedman has suggested setting a six-month growth target, determining the change in Fed securities holdings necessary to achieve this target, dividing that number by 26, and requiring the Fed to purchase that amount each week in addition to the amount needed to replace maturing securities. Under such an arrangement, the Fed performs a custodial function. It is no longer involved in discretionary intervention but instead serves as the technical agent for the creation of high-powered money. Important to the fixed rule approach is public awareness of the target and the Fed's steadfast adherence to the target.

Inherent in such an approach to policy reform is an assumption that the velocity of money is fairly constant over time and that the Fed is the major determinant of money-supply changes. If the velocity of money changes in an unpredictable manner, the fixed-rate money growth will have differential results. For example, during 1982–83, the income velocity of M1 declined well below the anticipated trend growth rate. See Figure 19.7.

Critics of the fixed-growth rule argue that under these circumstances, money growth would not have been sufficient to stimulate economic recovery. Critics also point out that a tight money policy by the Fed does not ensure slow money growth. Financial institutions may use liability management strategies to maintain higher levels of credit creation.

Those arguing against any fixed rule approach claim that flexibility is necessary to respond to exogenous shocks to the system, such as the OPEC price hikes, the rise in agricultural commodity prices occasioned by poor harvests, the failure of a major financial institution, or the default by a major foreign borrower.

The suggestion to eliminate discretion by adopting a fixed-growth rule has received some support from the *rational expectations* revolution. Rational expectationists have argued for the elimination of uncertainty and variability in monetary policy but they do not accept the fixed-growth rule simply because it minimizes intervention. Rational expectationists urge the adoption of a procedure or operating rule which is widely known and predictable. The procedure will ensure certainty of action under specific circumstances.

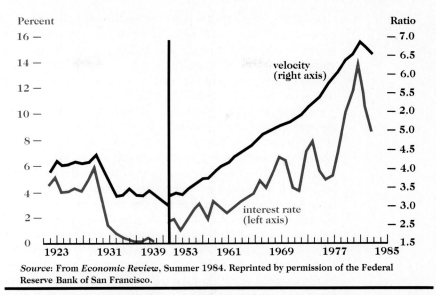

Source: From *Economic Review*, Summer 1984. Reprinted by permission of the Federal Reserve Bank of San Francisco.

FIGURE 19.7 *Recent Decline in Velocity* The velocity of money has been growing at an annual rate of approximately 3 percent per year throughout most of the postwar period. Since 1982, the velocity of money has declined rather precipitously causing controversy among policy makers and monetary analysts.

At different points in time with different circumstances, the exact monetary action may be different—as opposed to fixed at all times—but it is known that the Fed will act in a particular way. If across time the circumstances are the same, the policy will be the same. Rational expectations economists argue against activist policies and in favor of stable, predictable policies. The distinction between the monetarist fixed-growth rule for money growth and the rational expectationists' stable, predictable monetary policy procedure may be a fine line, but an important one.

Structural Reform

A tactical reform of the conduct of monetary policy, the fixed rule approach being the best example, is moderate compared with some structural reform suggestions. Whereas tactical reforms would alter the way the Fed conducts monetary policy, structural reforms would change the entire system.

One such suggestion is a return to a *metallic-based currency system*. For centuries, gold was the foundation of domestic currency systems and international financial relations. Plans for a return to some sort of gold standard arrangement vary greatly. What is consistent across all these plans is an arrangement whereby the dollar is readily convertible into gold or some other metal at a fixed price. The notion behind a gold or metallic-based currency system is one of controlling the money supply. If citizens can redeem paper currency for gold, the government faces a constraint on the degree to which it can expand the supply of money. Advocates of a "return to gold" contend that such a constraint would have prevented the wild inflation of the 1970s.[16]

Another suggested structural reform would *separate the regulatory from the monetary function*. Under this plan, the Fed would give up all supervisory and regulatory responsibilities; existing or newly created financial regulatory agencies would absorb these functions. The private sector would provide functions such as check clearing, the discounting of paper, and the lender of last resort. The Federal Reserve would exist to perform the technical operations associated with changes in the supply of money.

Rather than totally eliminating the discretionary monetary policy of the Fed, some suggest *combining the Fed with the Treasury Department*. This would allow a closer coordination of monetary and fiscal policies and would bring the Fed under the political scrutiny that the administration now receives.

A rather dramatic proposal suggested by many over the years is the *privatization of money issue*. This would eliminate the legal-tender privileges that government currency holds. Financial institutions could issue money in whatever form was acceptable by the public. In one variation of this reform, the government would continue to issue currency but it would have no legal tender privilege and would have to compete with privately issued currencies. Such competition, proponents argue, would prevent the debasement of money through inflation. Under this arrangement, the Fed's role is dramatically reduced.

For centuries, economists (such as Stanley Jevons and Alfred Marshall) have suggested *linking currency to an index*. The government would retain responsibility for issuing currency but fluctuations in some index, for example, a financial futures index, would determine the currency's purchasing power. This is somewhat similar to the variable interest rate concept. Money, and all financial arrangements, would exist on a price-level adjusted basis. Presumably, this would help eliminate inflation and maintain a more constant value for currency.

---

[16] In the fall of 1981, President Reagan appointed a Gold Commission to investigate the possibility of returning to a gold standard. The push for such a standard subsided as the rate of inflation and the high interest rates subsided. For a discussion of the Commission and the return to gold see, "A Return to the Gold Standard," *Business Week* (September 21, 1981): 114–120.

Operating Conditions Reform

Most of the suggestions presented above stem from a dissatisfaction with the conduct of monetary policy and, perhaps, a distrust of the value of discretionary stabilization policy. Those who are not so suspect of the Fed, but who desire greater stability in macroeconomic policy, argue for greater coordination between monetary and fiscal policies. As you noted from this chapter's review of monetary affairs and as the effects of large budget deficits demonstrate, the monetary authority is often the scapegoat for policy actions initiated by the administration and/or Congress. Congress has, through the 1978 Humphrey-Hawkins Act, required the Fed to become more explicit in setting its goals. The biannual reports to Congress by the Fed chairman provide the legislators and the public with more information about the conduct of monetary affairs. Perhaps the next step is to require the administration and Congress to work more closely with the Fed in planning and conducting macroeconomic policies.

The idea of long-term economic planning, called an *incomes policy*, has gained little acceptance. The coordination of monetary and fiscal policies is not an incomes policy. It is simply a rational and efficient way to make sure that strategies for achieving economic goals are not in conflict. An incomes policy moves beyond this and dictates specific actions for all policy arms of the federal government. Incomes policies garnered considerable attention as a policy option during the stagflation of the 1970s. This approach receives little discussion now.

While people have suggested many reforms, some dramatic and some simply procedural, the recent success of the Fed in slowing run-away inflation seems to have eliminated major reform as a viable option. Modest changes may continue, but unless the inflationary spiral gets out of hand again, the Fed's role or its operating procedures will change very little.

Chapter Conclusion

The Fed has a very checkered record in using monetary policy to achieve macroeconomic goals. The Fed did not have the autonomy to act as an effective agent of macroeconomic stabilization until 1951. Once the Fed achieved independence, it demonstrated an ability, although not always a willingness, to restrain inflation: often this was at the expense of economic growth.

More recent policy strategies demonstrate a closer connection between stated goals and outcomes. Especially during Chairman Volcker's tenure, the Fed has served as a bulwark against inflation. Despite this success, the "stop and go" nature of American economic performance has led Fed critics to suggest that monetary policy can be used in better ways to achieve economic goals. Critics have proposed means to reform the Fed or its conduct of monetary policy. Nonetheless, Congress appears to have little interest in initiating major reforms. The Fed itself, although adjusting its strategies from time to time, seems capable of fending off criticism so it can pursue an independent monetary policy.

Consider These Questions

1. Why is the Accord of 1951 considered an important milestone in Federal Reserve policy making?

2. What's the difference between the pegging of interest rates before the 1951 Accord and the policy of maintaining low-interest rates that the Fed pursued almost continuously until 1979?

3. How would you characterize Federal Reserve monetary policy during the 1960s? Cite examples to support your characterization.

4. What is the difference between procyclical and countercyclical monetary policy?

5. How would you evaluate monetary policy in terms of its ability to counteract economic extremes?

6. Outline Fed policy changes from 1970 to 1985. More recently, what position has the Fed taken on the usefulness of monetary aggregates, specifically M1?

7. What were the results of the Fed's 1979 policy switch? How would you evaluate these results?

8. How has financial deregulation affected the conduct of monetary policy?

9. Explain the notion of inside and outside lags in monetary policy. Why are they important in attempting to evaluate the success of monetary policy?

10. How would you assess the Meiselman argument on the political monetary cycle?

11. Explain the difference between tactical, structural, and operating conditions reform of the Federal Reserve.

Suggestions for Further Reading

Burns, Arthur F. "An Economist's Perspective Over 60 Years." In *Challenge* (January/February 1985): 17–25.
    An interview with the former chairman of the Board of Governors. Provides interesting perspective on approaches to monetary policy.

Hetzel, Robert L. "Monetary Policy in the Early 1980s." In Federal Reserve Bank of Richmond *Economic Review* 72, 2 (March/April 1986): 20–32. Readable account of monetary policy in 1980s. Contains an excellent list of references.

Hoehn, James G. "Monetary Policy Debates Reflect Theoretical Issues." Federal Reserve Bank of Cleveland *Economic Commentary* (May 1, 1986).
Good analysis of relationship between current monetary policy debates and their theoretical origins.

Kilborn, Peter T. "How the Big Six Steer the Economy." In *The New York Times* (November 17, 1985).
Analyzes Reagan administration's economic inner circle and how it relates to the Federal Reserve.

Minsky, Hyman P. "Money and the Lender of Last Resort." In *Challenge* (March/April 1985): 12–18.
Analyzes how the changing nature of money and the evolving structure of the financial services industry have raised the Federal Reserve's profile as the lender of last resort.

Maisel, Sherman J. *Managing the Dollar*. New York: W. W. Norton, 1973.
An insider view of Federal Reserve policy by a recent governor. Very readable.

Morris, Frank E. "The Changing World of Central Banking." In Federal Reserve Bank of Boston *New England Economic Review* (March/April 1986): 3–6.
Describes changed environment in which monetary policy objectives are now set.

Reich, Cary. "Inside the Fed." In *Institutional Investor* (May 1984): 136–162.
A real "gossipy" look at the working of the Federal Reserve.

Siegel, Barry N. *Money in Crisis: The Federal Reserve, the Economy and Monetary Reform*. Cambridge, Mass.: Ballinger Publishing, 1984.
Collection of essays on money and the Fed. See especially Chapter 7 on Fed policy since 1945.

Wallich, Henry C. "Recent Techniques of Monetary Policy." In Federal Reserve Bank of Kansas City *Economic Review* (May 1984): 21–30.
Member of Board of Governors provides interpretation of Federal Reserve policy actions during late 1970s and early 1980s.

————. "The Fed's Money Supply Ranges: Still Useful After All These Years." Federal Reserve Bank of Minneapolis *1985 Annual Report*.
Evaluates monetary policy in light of stated economic goals and specific monetary targets.

PART SIX

INTERNATIONAL MONETARY SYSTEM

CHAPTER TWENTY

INTERNATIONAL ASPECTS OF MONEY AND FINANCIAL INSTITUTIONS

No inconvenience can arise by an unrestrained trade, but very great advantage; since if the cash of the nation be decreased by it, those nations that get the cash will certainly find everything advance in price, as the cash increases amongst them. And . . . our manufacturers will soon become so moderate as to turn the balance of trade in our favour, and thereby fetch the money back again.

Jacob Vanderlint, *Money Answers All Things*, 1735

Although we have alluded to international aspects of money, financial institutions, and monetary policies, we have not explored the international financial system. This last chapter examines the functioning of the international financial system and relates it to the United States economy.

The international system is, in many respects, an extension of the domestic financial system. The most obvious difference relates to the existence of different currencies. The *procedures* countries use to relate currencies to one another so they can exchange freely is the first topic in this chapter.

Once we understand how currencies exchange and what influences the changes in these rates of exchange, we can examine the *structure* of the international system and operating rules that govern relations between the various financial systems around the world. While the intricacies of the procedures and the structure of the international system are not inconsequential, they are the means to an end. The end is an understanding of the *operations* of financial institutions in the international sector.

This is where the international system bears the most striking relationship to the domestic financial system and where we explore increasing overlap between the two systems. This process presents challenges to the United States financial system. We will explore these challenges and their implications.

Chapter Objectives

Your overall goal for this chapter is to understand the procedures and structure of the international financial system so that you can explain the operations of financial institutions within the international sector. The chapter is divided into three parts; the first two parts will help you to analyze the third.

The first part of the chapter explores the foreign exchange market. After completing this portion of the chapter you should be able to:

- Explain the role money plays in international trade and investment.
- Describe the foreign exchange market in terms of its origin and structure.
- Identify the theory behind exchange rate determination.
- Differentiate between spot and forward markets.
- Explain the movements of exchange rates in terms of spot and forward markets.
- Illustrate adjustments in the exchange market by discussing the recent American balance of payments experience.

The second part of the chapter focuses on the financial system itself, the structure that has evolved to facilitate international financial relations between countries. By the end of this part you will be able to:

- Explain the gold standard and the gold exchange standard.
- Identify the reasons behind the movement from a gold-based exchange system to the fixed exchange rate system of Bretton Woods.
- Discuss factors which contributed to the breakdown of the Bretton Woods system.
- Differentiate between a fixed exchange rate and a floating exchange rate system.
- List criteria for evaluating the present exchange rate system.
- Discuss various proposals for reform of the international financial system.
- Assess the role of the United States in movement toward a new financial system.

The final part of the chapter looks at the financial institutions which operate in international banking markets. After reading this portion you will be able to:

- Explain what is meant by the internationalization of banking.
- List some of the reasons for the expansion of international banking.
- Discuss efforts to allow American banks to compete in the international arena.
- Identify some of the potential problems arising from the linking of domestic markets.
- Explain the Eurocurrency market and the instruments used in this market.
- Assess the magnitude of the international debt crisis.
- Assess the implications of the international debt crisis for American banks.
- Evaluate American banks' competitive position compared to major banks in Japan and Europe.

Foreign Exchange Market

Countries need to establish a basis for trade in the same way that individuals do. We explored how a money exchange system evolved from a barter economy. Money facilitates exchange in the international economy just as it does in domestic economies. To understand the international financial system, you need to understand the role money plays in international transactions and what explains the exchange arrangements which countries have developed. In a more technical sense, we will explore the *international payments mechanism,* the arrangements that ensure the coordination and interaction of economies separated in the geographic, political, and monetary dimensions.

Countries have different currencies that they use in exchange transactions. Countries also engage in trade and investment with one another. To facilitate trade and investments, countries need some mechanism that relates their currencies to other currencies. The foreign exchange market provides the mechanism. How does it function? What influences the relationships between currencies? Does the foreign market have equilibrium? If not, how is disequilibrium rectified? The first concern is understanding why the market exists.

Money in an Open Economy

Our discussions to this point have focused on the domestic, or *closed economy*, with no attention to external trade or investment. The term *open economy* refers to an economic system where trade and investment take place with other countries. The simple macroeconomic model in Chapter 8 showed aggregate income (Y) as determined by total spending in the economy [consumption (C), investment (I) and government (G) spending]. For an open economy, the model expands such that:

$$Y = C + I + G + (X - M)$$

where

$$X = \text{foreign spending on domestic goods}$$
$$M = \text{domestic spending on foreign goods}$$
$$(X - M) = \text{net of exports and imports}$$

In recent years ($X - M$) in the United States has been negative; we have been spending more on imports than we generate through exports.

One aspect of an open economy, then, is trade with other countries. Another aspect is foreign investment in our economy and American investment abroad. Economists refer to the trade sector and the investment sector of an international account.

The price differential between domestic goods and foreign goods will drive American exports and imports (assuming no quality differences). Interest rate differentials between American markets and foreign markets will drive investments. The foreign exchange market becomes the mechanism which allows efficient international trade and investment. Simply stated, the *foreign exchange market* is the interaction of buyers and sellers of world currencies who together establish the price of one currency in terms of another.

While the foreign exchange market exists to facilitate trade and investment between countries, just like any other financial market, it is also a haven for financial speculation. The relationships between currencies provide an opportunity for investors to make money on the ebb and flow of those relationships themselves. As a result, three forces work in the foreign exchange market: traders entering the market to acquire foreign currency, investors doing the same for investment abroad, and speculators relying on shifts in currency values to make a profit.

The major centers for foreign exchange transactions are in London, New York, Frankfurt, and Tokyo. The financial centers of all countries participate in foreign exchange operations. Connected through telecommunications, these various centers combine in the worldwide foreign exchange market. The volume of foreign exchange transactions is astronomical. Estimates vary, but a fair assessment would place the daily volume at over $150 billion. Next, we examine the institutional arrangements which allow that volume of transactions.

Details of the Foreign Exchange Market

The need for the foreign exchange market dates back to times when individuals with different currency systems first attempted to trade goods or services. The key feature of the foreign exchange market is that it provides the basis for international transactions by establishing a relationship between currencies. The *exchange rate* is the price of a foreign currency in terms of a domestic currency.

The exchange rate between currencies is allowed to fluctuate (this was not always the case). *Flexible* or *floating exchange rates* mean that market forces determine the value of one currency in terms of another. At various times in modern history, countries fixed the relationship between their currencies. The next part of this chapter addresses that topic. *Fixed exchange rates* mean that countries agree to exchange their currencies according to a fixed schedule. The value of one currency relative to another is set by agreement, and countries commit to maintaining the established ratio.

The number of currencies is virtually as large as the number of countries on the globe. Figure 20.1 lists countries, their currencies, and the exchange rates in terms of American dollars.

Additional detail about the foreign exchange market will help. Like most financial markets, the foreign exchange market is a linkage of financial traders in major money centers via telephone and telex hookups. Individual customers work through their local banks, or perhaps brokers, to express their needs. For example, a firm based in Philadelphia wants to acquire German marks (DM) to purchase a precision die-casting machine made in Frankfurt. The price is 375,000 marks. Figure 20.2 outlines the process, and how the American manufacturer's action combines with similar actions by German traders, in both cases through a local bank, in the foreign exchange market. Given the exchange rate at the time of the exchange transaction, the Philadelphia manufacturer will pay a certain amount in American dollars (actually bank deposits denominated in American dollars) to acquire the necessary marks (bank deposits denominated in marks) to purchase the die-casting machine. Using the exchange rate shown in Figure 20.1, the American firm will need $182,000 to purchase the machine (DM375,000 × .4854 $/DM = $182,025).

Keep in mind that the exchange rates determined in the foreign exchange markets are those which apply to major transactions, usually in excess of $1 million. You can think of these as the "wholesale prices" of

FOREIGN EXCHANGE

Friday, August 15, 1986

The New York foreign exchange selling rates below apply to trading among banks in amounts of $1 million and more, as quoted at 3 p.m. Eastern time by Bankers Trust Co. Retail transactions provide fewer units of foreign currency per dollar.

Country	U.S. $ equiv. Fri.	Thurs.	Currency per U.S. $ Fri.	Thurs.
Argentina (Austral) ...	1.0858	1.0858	.921	.921
Australia (Dollar)	.6237	.6233	1.6033	1.6044
Austria (Schilling)	.06906	.06897	14.48	14.50
Belgium (Franc)				
Commercial rate	.02346	.02346	42.62	42.62
Financial rate	.02322	.02326	43.05	43.00
Brazil (Cruzado)	.07262	.07262	13.77	13.77
Britain (Pound)	1.4955	1.5033	.6687	.6652
30-Day Forward ...	1.4911	1.4990	.6706	.6671
90-Day Forward ...	1.4828	1.4906	.6744	.6709
180-Day Forward ...	1.4714	1.4785	.6796	.6764
Canada (Dollar)	.7200	.7213	1.3888	1.3863
30-Day Forward ...	.7189	.7202	1.3911	1.3885
90-Day Forward ...	.7159	.7173	1.3968	1.3941
180-Day Forward ...	.7108	.7124	1.4068	1.4038
Chile (Official rate) ...	.005182	.005182	192.97	192.97
China (Yuan)	.2707	.2707	3.6943	3.6943
Colombia (Peso)	.005073	.005073	197.14	197.14
Denmark (Krone)	.1292	.1290	7.7425	7.7525
Ecuador (Sucre)				
Official rate	.009153	.009153	109.25	109.25
Floating rate	.005970	.005970	167.50	167.50
Finland (Markka)	.2031	.2029	4.9225	4.9275
France (Franc)				
	.1493	.1492	6.6990	6.7020
30-Day Forward ...	.1492	.1491	6.7035	6.7075
90-Day Forward ...	.1489	.1488	6.7150	6.7190
180-Day Forward ...	.1293	.1484	7.7340	6.7390
Greece (Drachma)	.007052	.007463	134.40	134.00
Hong Kong (Dollar) ...	.1285	.1287	7.7820	7.7700
India (Rupee)	.07937	.07943	12.60	12.59
Indonesia (Rupiah)	.0008842	.0008842	1131.00	1131.00
Ireland (Punt)	1.3430	1.3470	.7446	.7424
Israel (Shekel)	.6702	.6702	1.492	1.492
Italy (Lira)	.0007052	.0007052	1418.00	1418.00
Japan (Yen)	.006499	.006504	153.87	153.75
30-Day Forward ...	.006509	.006513	153.64	153.54
90-Day Forward ...	.006524	.006529	153.28	153.17
180-Day Forward ...	.006549	.006554	152.69	152.57
Jordan (Dinar)	3.1066	3.1066	.3219	.3219
Kuwait (Dinar)	3.4400	3.4400	.2907	.2907
Lebanon (Pound)	.02212	.02212	45.20	45.20
Malaysia (Ringgit)	.3828	.3759	2.6120	2.6600
Malta (Lira)	2.6351	2.6351	.3795	.3795
Mexico (Peso)				
Floating rate	.001532	.001532	652.80	652.80
Netherland(Guilder) ...	.4309	.4305	2.3205	2.3230
New Zealand (Dollar) ...	.4950	.5040	2.0202	1.9841
Norway (Krone)	.1364	.1358	7.3325	7.3625
Pakistan (Rupee)	.05917	.05917	16.90	16.90
Peru (Inti)	.07168	.07168	13.95	13.95
Philippines (Peso)	.04909	.04909	20.37	20.37
Portugal (Escudo)	.006849	.006873	146.00	145.50
Saudi Arabia (Riyal) ..	.2666	.2666	3.7510	3.7510
Singapore (Dollar)	.4638	.4617	2.1560	2.1660
South Africa (Rand)				
Commercial rate	.3860	.3865	2.5907	2.5873
Financial rate	.2025	.20	4.9382	5.0000
South Korea (Won)	.001130	.001130	884.60	884.60
Spain (Peseta)	.007482	.007485	133.65	133.60
Sweden (Krona)	.1445	.1445	6.9200	6.9225
Switzerland (Franc) ..	.6020	.6026	1.6610	1.6595
30-Day Forward	.6035	.6037	1.6569	1.6565
90-Day Forward	.6051	.6054	1.6527	1.6517
180-Day Forward	.6077	.6079	1.6455	1.6450
Taiwan (Dollar)	.02649	.02649	37.75	37.75
Thailand (Baht)	.03828	.03828	26.12	26.12
Turkey (Lira)	.001452	.001452	688.52	688.52
United Arab(Dirham) ..	.2723	.2723	3.673	3.673
Uruguay (New Peso)				
Financial	.006766	.006766	147.80	147.80
Venezuela (Bolivar)				
Official rate	.1333	.1333	7.50	7.50
Floating rate	.05128	.05128	19.50	19.50
W. Germany (Mark) ..	.4854	.4854	2.0600	2.0600
30-Day Forward ...	.4862	.4862	2.0567	2.0566
90-Day Forward ...	.4876	.4876	2.0510	2.0510
180-Day Forward ...	.4894	.4894	2.0434	2.0432
SDR	1.20904	1.20992	0.827105	0.826502
ECU	z	1.02331	....	....

Special Drawing Rights are based on exchange rates for the U.S., West German, British, French and Japanese currencies. Source: International Monetary Fund.

ECU is based on a basket of community currencies. Source: European Community Commission.

z-Not quoted.

Source: Reprinted by permission of *The Wall Street Journal*, August 18, 1986. Copyright © Dow Jones.

FIGURE 20.1 *Foreign Exchange* The rates of exchange between currencies are quoted in two ways. "U.S. dollar equivalent" indicates how many dollars there are per unit of foreign currency. "Currency per U.S. dollar" indicates the units of the foreign currency per dollar. These rates change constantly.

foreign currencies. When individuals acquire a foreign currency for a trip they go to a bank or to an American Express agency office. In such a case, the retail price, somewhat higher than that quoted in the exchange market, would apply.

Figure 20.2 points out that, in addition to customers like the American manufacturer, brokers, institutional investors, and central banks enter into the market. They may do so through a regional market such as the Philadelphia Stock Exchange which engages in limited foreign exchange transactions or through major banks which participate in the interbank foreign exchange market. The larger banks, sometimes called "market bankers" set the tone for the exchange market. With so many dealers working in such

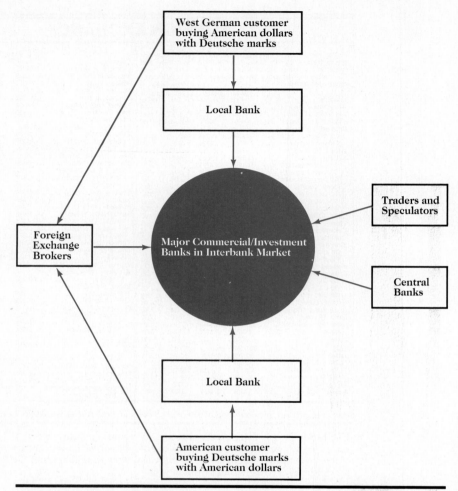

FIGURE 20.2 *The International Exchange Process* This figure illustrates how customers, working through their local banks or brokers, provide the supply and demand to make the international exchange market function.

close contact, the foreign exchange market is very competitive. Because so many exchanges take place around the world, the prices may vary slightly from one regional market to another. Overall, the collective actions of buyers and sellers combine to produce the total demand for and supply of currencies in the market. This interaction of demand and supply determines exchange rates.

Exchange rate determination is a function of the constantly changing forces of demand and supply. A demand and supply graph illustrates the price of one currency in terms of another (the exchange rate). Figure 20.3 shows the demand for a foreign currency, French francs, in terms of American dollars and the supply of francs. The original price, p_1 ($.14 = 1 franc), rises as a result of an increase in the demand for French francs in terms of American dollars. *Appreciation* of a currency refers to an increase in its value. *Depreciation* is just the opposite; it refers to a decrease in value, p_3 ($.13 = 1 franc), and shows a depreciation of the franc.

How can we explain exchange rate determination? One explanation is the law of one price. According to the *law of one price*, when two countries produce an identical good, the price of that good, not including transportation, should be the same throughout the world regardless of who produces it. According to the notion, the production costs in two countries establish a relationship between the currencies of those countries, which we call the exchange rate. Consider this example. The cost of lumber in the United States is $550 per 1000 board feet. In Japan, the cost is 90,750 yen. Lumber is lumber; the product is identical. According to the law of one price, the exchange rate between the dollar and the yen must be 165 yen/dollar (or $.0006/yen) if the product is to sell for the same price in each country. If the lumber did not sell for the same price, the opportunity for profit would exist. If the price were twice as much in Japan, people would buy the American

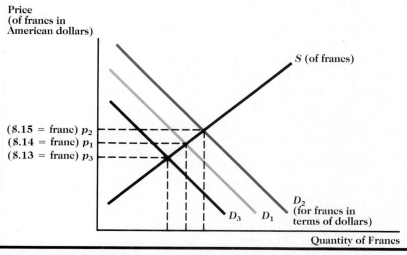

FIGURE 20.3   *Supply and Demand Determine Exchange Rates*   The interaction of demand for a currency and supply of a currency determines the price of that currency. Since demand for a currency can only be expressed in terms of another currency, the price always appears in terms of a particular country's currency. Notice that the price of French francs rises or falls depending on demand.

lumber and sell it in Japan. Such a process would continue until the exchange rate adjusted to make the prices in the United States and Japan the same.

The law of one price depends on *arbitragers*, individuals who seek to profit from exchange rate differentials. The actions of arbitragers will eliminate price differentials for identical products, or at least will reduce those differentials to the point where no profit exists if transportation costs, information costs, and government trade barriers prevent the prices from being identical.

Extending the law of one price to an environment with many products, one in which we refer to price levels rather than single prices, results in the theory of purchasing power parity. The *theory of purchasing power parity* states that exchange rates between two countries will adjust to reflect changes in the price levels of those two countries. Stated another way, the exchange rate between two currencies will reflect the relative purchasing power of those currencies.

To illustrate this theory, assume the world consists of two countries, both of whose goods are traded, and for which no transportation costs or trade barriers exist. Assume further that the market basket of goods from country A (the United States) sells for $100 and the same market basket sells for 150 pounds in country B (Britain). The exchange rate is $1 = 2 pounds. Under these circumstances the basket of goods is much cheaper in Britain; in other words, the purchasing power of the pound is greater than the dollar. Arbitragers will attempt to profit from this situation by using pounds to purchase dollars. Arbitragers speculate that dollars will increase in value. In so doing, they will cause the value of the British pound to fall (depreciate) until equilibrium is restored at $1 = 2 pounds.

According to this theory, the exchange rate of one currency in terms of another should rise when the inflation rate of the former exceeds that of the latter. Figure 20.4 illustrates the change in the exchange rate (American dollars per unit of foreign currency) and the changes in price indices for selected countries relative to the United States.

The purchasing power parity theory that held during the 1970s has broken down during the 1980s. The theory works best when the inflation rates between the countries are large. Economists explain the inability of the purchasing power parity theory to fully explain exchange-rate movements in terms of a number of factors. Not all goods are traded. Not all goods are identical: lumber may be lumber but the new Yugoslavian car appearing in the United States is not the same as the Japanese Honda. The existence of nontraded goods and product differences as well as government intervention mean that price rises in one country may not result in exchange rate changes. Despite these limitations, the theory of purchasing power parity does help explain exchange-rate determination.

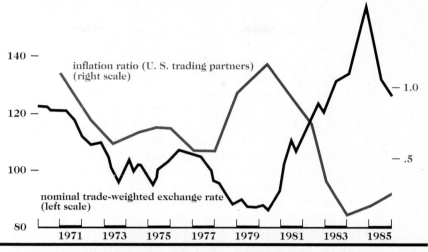

Index, March 1973 = 100

FIGURE 20.4 *Exchange Rate Movements and Inflation* The purchasing power parity theory explains exchange-rate movements in terms of the relative price level changes between two countries. This figure shows that the theory does not hold at all times, but nonetheless it forms the basis for at least partially explaining exchange-rate movements.

Several factors other than price level changes influence exchange rates. The most powerful are the following:

- *Productivity differences*—Productivity gains mean products are relatively less expensive, which may cause the country's currency to appreciate in value.

- *Tariffs and quotas*—Assuming no retaliation by other countries, the imposition of trade barriers will cause a country's currency to appreciate in value because such barriers essentially raise the prices of imported goods.

- *Tastes and preferences*—A preference for imported goods will cause the importing country's currency to depreciate in value.

This discussion of exchange-rate determination has focused on long-term movements in rates. A quick perusal of the daily newspaper's financial page reveals that exchange rates fluctuate tremendously, hour by hour and day by day. What causes these short-term fluctuations in exchange rates?

Exchange rate movements, whether long-term or short-term, are determined by the forces of demand and supply. To understand short-term movements, we need to examine two types of foreign exchange transactions.

Exchange transactions in the *spot market* involve immediate exchanges of bank deposits, taking about two days. Transactions in the *forward market* involve an exchange of bank deposits at some time in the future. Figure 20.1 shows foreign exchange quotations from August 15, 1986. Spot exchange rates exist for all currencies. Major currencies have both spot rates, the first rate quoted, and forward rates, listed beneath the spot rate and shown for 30, 90, and 180 days.

Exchange quotations sometimes show both a "bid" and an "ask" price. The difference between the buying and selling price, the "bid-ask spread," partly reflects cost margins associated with major bank transactions.

Do not be confused by the quotation in Figure 20.1. Two exchange rates exist for each currency. One, under the heading "U.S. $ equivalent," is American dollars for the foreign currency. For example, for the British pound it is $1.4955/pound. A second, under the heading "Currency per U.S. Dollar," is the quantity of the foreign currency per American dollar. For example, for the British pound it is .6687 British pounds/American dollar. The first version is the preferred form outside the United States, called "European terms" of exchange. The second is the version used in this country, the exchange rate in "American terms."

Demand and Supply in Exchange Markets

Fluctuations in exchange rates result from activities in the spot market. Individuals and institutions enter the exchange market in response to the needs associated with trade and investment abroad but also, especially in the short run, when they anticipate an increased return on the currencies of one country relative to others. This explanation of exchange-rate movements is called the asset approach. The *asset approach to exchange rate movements* specifies that short-term exchange market intervention is driven by the profit motive, the opportunity to benefit from expected return on one asset, in this case currency, relative to the expected return on another asset.

Using this approach, we can return to our simple supply-demand curves and analyze what would affect each, and how these factors will influence exchange-rate movement. The demand curve for one currency, for example dollar-denominated deposits, is a function of the exchange rate relative to another currency, for example German marks, DM. The demand for dollars is inversely related to the value of the American dollar. That is, as the exchange rate, DM/$, rises, fewer exchange market participants are willing to trade an increasing quantity of DMs for $s. The supply of dollar-denominated deposits in the international exchange market is ultimately fixed by the total quantity of assets in the American economy, which means

ECONOMICS T⊙DAY 20.1 — Exchange Rates and Tourism

Most Americans think about the effect of exchange-rate shifts in terms of the purchasing power of the dollar, either in terms of the foreign goods it will buy or for their travels abroad (1983 and 1984 were good years for foreign travel; 1986 was disastrous). Some countries, whose economies depend on tourism to generate much needed income, look at exchange rates as an important factor in their economic well-being.

Consider the Caribbean Basin countries where tourism is the number-one industry. Jeffrey A. Rosensweig at the Federal Reserve Bank of Atlanta measured the impact of exchange rate fluctuations on these countries in terms of tourism.* Most Caribbean countries peg their currencies to the dollar. During the period when the dollar's value rose, mid-1980 to early 1985, it was increasingly more expensive for non-American tourists to visit these countries.

Rosensweig determined that tourists have a very noticeable elasticity of substitution among holiday destinations with different exchange-rate movements (which essentially translates into different price structures). Countries in the Caribbean whose currencies were pegged to the dollar and which did not take corrective action, suffered a loss of tourist income (Barbados is a prime example). Other Caribbean countries which severed their currencies' ties to the dollar and devalued their currencies actually gained tourist income at the expense of the others (Jamaica and the Dominican Republic are examples).

While Rosensweig hastened to point out that other factors also influence tourism, namely natural catastrophes and political unrest, he concluded that exchange-rates can have an effect on tourist income. As a result, nations need to consider the actions they might take to minimize the effects of exchange-rate movements when their currencies are tied to the American dollar.

* Jeffrey A. Rosensweig, "Exchange Rates and Competition for Tourists," Federal Reserve Bank of Boston *New England Economic Review* (July/August 1986): 57–67.

---

the supply curve is vertical. Figure 20.5 illustrates the demand for dollars in terms of German marks.

Since the demand for American currency is a function of the expected return on holding that currency, other rates of return, specifically interest rates in the United States and in foreign countries, will help to explain shifts in the demand. If the United States interest rate rises, the demand for American currency will increase. Foreign investors will want to acquire dollar-denominated deposits to take advantage of the higher interest rates. This will shift the D curve in Figure 20.5 to D_2, pushing the exchange rate up. The opposite will occur if American interest rates drop, shifting the demand curve to D_3. If foreign interest rates rise, the demand for dollar-denominated assets declines as investors shift to currencies where they can take advantage of the higher returns. This will cause the demand curve to shift to D_3. The opposite will occur if foreign interest rates decline; the demand curve will increase to D_2. The same analysis applies to expected, as well as actual, interest rate changes.

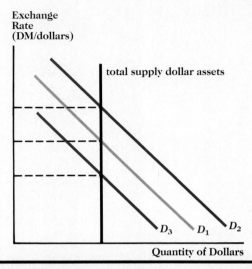

Exchange
Rate
(DM/dollars)

total supply dollar assets

D_3 D_1 D_2

Quantity of Dollars

FIGURE 20.5 *Shift in Demand for Dollars Affects Exchange Rate*   This figure shows shifts in the demand for American dollars in terms of German marks. To focus attention on the demand shifts, the supply-of-funds curve is considered in the broadest sense to include the total quantity of assets in the American economy. It is therefore a vertical line.

The supply curve in this scenario is only affected by central bank intervention in foreign exchange markets. When the central bank purchases its domestic currency in the international exchange market, using its international currency reserves to do so, the overall supply of dollar-denominated assets declines, shifting the supply curve to the left. The opposite results if the central bank sells its domestic currency. Obviously, central banks can have a major effect on exchange rates.

Just as movement into and out of a particular currency by international exchange market brokers and bankers is influenced by interest-rate movements, long-term exchange-rate movements are determined by the same factors that influence interest rates, namely the economic vitality, domestic macroeconomic policies, and international trade and investment patterns of one country relative to other nations. A closer look at the American situation will show the effects of these factors.

Exchange-Rate Movements and Balance of Payments

The value of the American dollar in exchange markets over the past few years provides an excellent case study of factors affecting exchange-rate movements. Figure 20.6 illustrates the significant change in the exchange rate of the American dollar relative to a market basket of foreign currencies

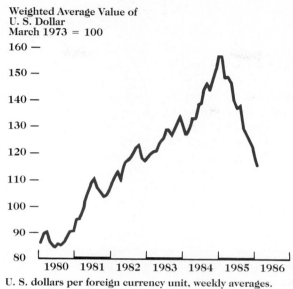

Weighted Average Value of
U. S. Dollar
March 1973 = 100

U. S. dollars per foreign currency unit, weekly averages.

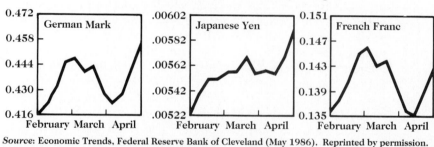

Source: Economic Trends, Federal Reserve Bank of Cleveland (May 1986). Reprinted by permission.

FIGURE 20.6 *Value of American Dollar in Exchange Markets*   The value of the dollar rose steadily from 1980 until early 1985. The value of the dollar just before it began to decline marked one of the highest values for the dollar in the postwar period. Since early 1985, the dollar has declined in value. The inset graphs show how the mark, yen, and franc rose against the dollar during this period.

(top graph). The American dollar has declined in value. Therefore, other currencies are worth more relative to the dollar; note the rise of the mark, yen, and most recently even the franc. To understand the change we need to incorporate a discussion of the American balance of payments account.

The *balance of payments* is an accounting record of a country's trade and investment activities with other nations for a particular period of time. Two general categories of international transactions by a country include:

• *Current account*—The value of the flow of goods, services and other current receipts and payments between one nation and other nations.

• *Capital account*—One country's assets invested abroad and foreign assets invested in that country, essentially the net of capital flows.

A country's balance of payments is recorded using double-entry bookkeeping showing inflow and outflow. International transactions must balance inflow and outflow at the end of an accounting period. If transactions do not balance, official reserves must be used to settle the account. For example, by receiving a deficit in its balance of payment account, the United States is forced to sell gold or foreign exchange to offset the deficit.

Historically, the United States has experienced a favorable balance of payments. Although our current account might show a deficit due to imports exceeding exports, the capital account surplus always exceeded the trade deficit because the United States was a net-creditor nation, lending funds abroad and receiving interest income.

The picture has changed in the last few years. The United States not only has continued to run a deficit in its trade relations, but it has become a net-debtor nation. The United States is borrowing more than it is lending to other nations. Figure 20.7 shows the current account portion of the American balance of payments.

What explains this situation and how does the American economy's performance relate to exchange rate fluctuations? Recall from the discussion on monetary policy in Chapter 19 that interest rates in the United States rose to historically high levels in the late 1970s and early 1980s. These high interest rates generated a very high demand for dollar-denominated deposits, helping to push up the value of the dollar. The high value of the dollar made imported goods more attractive, the dollar bought more in terms of foreign currencies, but made exports more expensive, more foreign currency was needed to acquire American dollars. The result was a badly deteriorating balance of trade position.

At the same time that the balance of trade was showing an increasing deficit, the capital account position began to worsen. High interest rates, stimulated by the large borrowing needs of the American government, attracted foreign investment and reduced American investment abroad. The net result was a change from a net surplus in the capital account to a net deficit. In other words, the United States went from being a creditor nation to being a net-debtor nation. In fact, to feed the rising domestic debt—both government and private—the United States had turned to foreign lending sources to the extent that the United States became the greatest debtor nation in the world owing more than foreign borrowers like Mexico and Argentina.

Interest rates also help explain the decline in the value of the dollar. Since the early 1980s, interest rates in the United States have declined, reducing the attractiveness of dollar-denominated deposits and thus the value of the dollar. At the same time, though, the economic growth rate of

ECONOMICS T⬤DAY 20.2

A Closer Look at the Balance of Payments

Just like an individual or a corporation, a country produces a deficit when it spends more than it takes in. And the nation (or individual or corporation) unavoidably must run down its wealth or borrow to finance that deficit. When a deficit occurs between countries, resulting from their trade and capital flows with one another, it is called a balance-of-payments deficit. In the balance-of-payments terminology, wealth is called international reserves. It is composed of gold, strong currencies that other nations are willing to accept (traditionally the dollar), and special drawing rights (SDRs) at the IMF. The table below lists the main types of transactions involved in a nation's balance-of-payments accounting.

Economists distinguish between the balance of trade and the balance of payments, and they use several different, but related, measures of both of these concepts (see the table below). The official settlements balance is the payment which is required when there is a balance of payments deficit. It measures changes in official reserve balances and short-term capital among governments.

Source: Table from "The Balance of Payments" from *Federal Reserve Bank of Minneapolis Quarterly Review*, Summer 1983. Reprinted by permission.

A Nation's RECEIPTS	less Its PAYMENTS	equals The Nation's BALANCE OF PAYMENTS[1]
EXPORTS of Merchandise	IMPORTS of Merchandise	
Services	Services	Balance of Trade
Private and government aid	Private and government aid	Balance of Goods and Services
CAPITAL INFLOWS From	CAPITAL OUTFLOWS From	Balance on Current Account
Investment	Investment	
Government borrowing	Government lending	
Long-term private borrowing	Long-term private lending	
Short-term private borrowing	Short-term private lending	Basic Balance[2]
Liquid	Liquid	
Nonliquid	Nonliquid	
SALES of Reserves	PURCHASES of Reserves	Official Settlements Balance

[1] Each balance in this table is a cumulative measure of all the items above it.

[2] The basic balance is also known as the balance on current and long-term capital account.

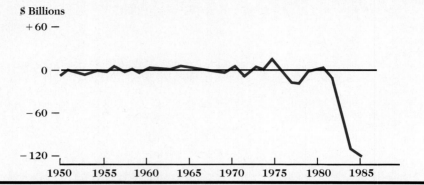

FIGURE 20.7 *American Balance in Current Account* This figure shows the deteriorating American international account. Using the balance on current account, in billions of dollars seasonally adjusted, the account showed a surplus during most of the post–World War II period. Since 1980, the account has dropped into a severe deficit position.

the United States has slowed. In the early stages of the recovery from the recession for 1981–82, the growth of the American economy was outstripping the growth of other Western democracies. The economic vitality of the American economy made it an attractive investment. As recovery has slowed, investors have found alternative investment possibilities. This has reduced the demand for dollar-denominated deposits and lowered the American exchange rate.

During the rapid rise in the value of the dollar, central banks also entered into exchange markets to try to provide greater stability. Translated in an American perspective, central banks tried to moderate the rising dollar exchange rate to help balance the American trade account.

The American dollar exchange rate did decline beginning in 1985. In fact, it fell rather precipitously. Concern shifted from an overvalued dollar and its implications for American trade, to the impact of loss of confidence in the dollar. This loss of confidence seems to reflect skepticism about the vitality of the American economy, especially the large federal government deficit.

The fluctuations in exchange rates that have occurred during the 1980s have caused observers to question the international financial system with its flexible exchange rate regime. Many economists and policy makers in the United States and abroad have called for reform of the system, perhaps even a return to a fixed-rate system. To understand the lessons behind a call for financial system reform we need to look at the structure of the financial system which allows relationships between nations. We also need to examine

ECONOMICS TODAY 20.3

Why Doesn't a Declining Dollar Reduce the Deficit?

Historically, the United States trade account balance and the value of the dollar have moved in opposite directions (as the dollar declines in value, the trade account improves). In September, 1985, the Group of Five (United States, Japan, West Germany, Great Britain, and France) agreed on the need for a weaker dollar, in large part to stem the tide of protectionist sentiment in the United States Congress, and set forth policies to achieve this goal. After a slow decline which began to appear in March, 1985, the dollar began a plunge in late 1985 which continued throughout 1986. Using the textbook theory and historical precedent, one would have predicted that the American trade account would improve with this decline in the value of the dollar.

The traditional scenario makes sense. As the American dollar declines, it takes more dollars to purchase imported goods. For example, since the September 1985 agreement, the dollar's value in terms of the Japanese yen has declined from 240 to the July 1986 value of 156 (a 35-percent decline). That should result in a Japanese product price increase such that something costing $10 in mid-1985 would have sold for well over $13 in mid-1986. By the same token, American products would prove more attractive to foreign buyers so our exports would have increased. The net result, one would expect, would be a decline in the trade deficit. But, it didn't happen.

The American trade deficit was about $123 billion in 1984, over $148 billion in 1985, and was projected at $170 billion for 1986. Surely this isn't the trade deficit reduction we would expect given the decline in the value of the dollar. Why didn't the deficit improve?

One explanation is that manufacturers in the nations with which we conduct most of our trade (Europe and Japan) have simply absorbed the currency swing by reducing their profit margins. Rather than lose their market share of American sales, producers lowered prices and cut their profits by lowering their production costs at home or by moving production facilities to lower labor cost regions. Another explanation is that the dollar's decline against the yen and most European currencies has not been matched by declines relative to the currencies of Canada and the newly industrialized countries of Asia. As a result, the imports from these countries still have a price advantage over American products and American exports face a price disadvantage. Finally, some argue that it takes 18 to 24 months for a currency decline to result in a trade account adjustment. If this is the case, the trade balance should begin to improve in 1987.

---

alternative financial arrangements between countries as they have existed over time. This perspective will allow us to consider the international financial system reform proposals.

International Financial System

The discussion in the first part of this chapter assumed a flexible exchange-rate regime for international financial arrangements. Under a flexible exchange-rate system, demand and supply factors in the exchange market determine rates of exchange. Central banks are one type of actor in exchange markets. Another important force is entrance of central banks into the exchange market; that force is not dictated by any formula or set agreement. Such a flexible exchange-rate system is relatively new in the history of the international financial system. An alternative, a fixed-rate regime, dominated throughout the nineteenth century and the first half of the twentieth century. An examination of the gold-based fixed exchange system and the evolution of the flexible exchange-rate system will provide a basis for evaluating suggestions for reform of the present international financial system.

Gold Standard, 1821 to 1914

Chapter 1 included a discussion on the gold standard. A domestic gold standard specifies that circulating currency is redeemable upon demand for gold. An international gold standard specifies that all countries' central banks and other financial institutions are required to redeem their monetary liabilities at a price established in terms of gold.

Pegging currencies to gold and using these *fixed parity rates*, established prices for currencies, as a basis for international exchange transactions, stems from the early part of the nineteenth century. The British Parliament set the value of the pound in terms of gold in 1816; other countries followed, such that international transactions among countries based on gold formed the foundation for the international financial transactions as early as 1821.

In adopting the gold standard, a country set the price of an ounce of gold. By equating the established price of gold of different currencies, countries established the rates of exchange for their currencies. We can illustrate the arrangement by looking at the United States and Great Britain after the United States returned to gold in 1879. (The United States had suspended specie payments during the Civil War and did not begin to redeem currency in specie—gold—until 1879.) Britain had set the price of gold at 77 shillings and 10½ pence per ounce. The United States set the price at $10.67 per ounce. After adjusting for slight differences in the purity of British and American gold coins, the exchange ratio was established at £1 = $4.865. This set the exchange rate for British/American international transactions.

Adopting gold-based exchange relationships required the countries involved to maintain the fixed exchange rate between their currencies. Although no firm treaty bound countries to this arrangement, functioning as a gold standard country carried with it a responsibility to adhere to unwritten rules.

Adhering to these rules meant that countries' money supplies, tied to their gold reserves, automatically adjusted in response to international trade and capital flows. Consider this illustration. Country X begins to experience rising rates of inflation, perhaps as a result of rapid economic growth causing demand stimulus. As its price level rises, its level of exports declines; they are relatively more expensive. Its imports increase; they are relatively less expensive. Under a flexible exchange rate regime described in our discussion of the law of one price, exchange rates would adjust. But under the gold-based, fixed-rate system, the rates are all immutable. The imbalance in the trade account, assuming no offsetting change in the capital account, will create a balance of payments deficit. Country X has agreed to redeem its monetary liabilities in gold. In so doing its gold reserves decline and, according to the domestic gold standard, the supply of money must adjust downward. This money supply reduction will stem the rising price level as it slows down the rapid economic growth. Automatically, price stability is restored. The international gold standard helps control price inflation. Figure 20.8 shows that during periods when the gold standard was in place, inflation was held in check. Of course, the domestic economy was tied to international economic events.

The gold standard remained in place until World War I disrupted the international financial system. After the war, and the inflation it brought, most countries attempted to return to the gold standard at the prewar parity

Source: From "The Classical Gold Standard: Some Lessons for Today" by Michael D. Bordo, Federal Reserve Bank of St. Louis *Review*, May 1981, p. 9. Reprinted by permission.

FIGURE 20.8 *Price Movements Before and After Gold Standard* Proponents of some form of a gold-based international exchange regime point to the behavior of prices during and since the gold standard was in effect. The wholesale price index trend line was steady (actually slightly downward) during the gold standard era compared to the noticeable upward trend since the abandonment of gold.

rates. This meant restoring the purchasing power of their currencies which was not an easy task. In reestablishing the domestic gold standard, countries were also seeking to restore gold as the basis for international transactions. They did so but in a slightly modified form.

Gold Exchange Standard, 1925 to 1933

After World War I, with an unanticipated shortage of gold relative to the expanding international economy and the increase in the number of nations needing gold reserves as a result of the fragmentation of the old Austro-Hungarian Empire, countries established a variant of the gold standard. The *gold exchange standard* concentrated gold holdings with central banks, minimizing its use as a circulating medium, and allowed some central banks to hold reserves in the form of foreign exchange (for example, government securities) denominated in the currency of one of the major gold reserve nations (the United States or Britain).

In economizing on gold reserves, thus eliminating the need to revise parity prices for the major world currencies, the goal of this system was to restore the fixed exchange rate system for international exchange which was in place before the war.[1] Worldwide, people wanted to "return to normalcy" and the gold-based exchange-rate system was part of this desire.

The gold exchange standard did not remain in effect for very long. Countries discovered that the disruptions to their domestic economies were too great. Most European countries were running huge trade deficits because they needed to import goods as they recovered from the war. Because of these trade deficits, the fixed exchange rate system forced continuing belt tightening. The effects on unemployment forced most European countries to abandon the gold exchange standard/fixed exchange rate system and let their countries "float" in exchange markets. The world wide economic depression drove the remaining countries off the gold standard. Not until after the depression and World War II was a new international financial system devised.

Up to the post–World War II restructuring of the international monetary system, gold or gold exchange had formed the foundation for international exchange transactions. After the war, countries attempted to create a new system, a *treaty-based international monetary regime*; that is, a "set of rules or conventions governing monetary and financial relations between coun-

---

[1] The rules of the game were not exactly the same as before. The gold reserve nations, the United States and Britain, were not tied to the automatic adjustment mechanism as before the war.

tries. . . . A monetary regime specifies which instruments of policy may be used and which targets of policy are regarded as legitimate. . . ."[2]

As victors in the war, the United States and Britain were dominant forces in restructuring the system. Their goal was to create a monetary system which insured the autonomy of national economic policies rather than subjecting domestic policies to the corrective pressures of the gold standard regime. With this goal in mind, the Western economic powers convened to establish new financial arrangements for the postwar world.

Bretton Woods, 1946 to 1971

The United Nations Monetary and Financial Conference met in Bretton Woods, N.H., during the final stages of World War II. The major allied powers constructed an entirely new international financial system. The Bretton Woods Agreement had three distinct parts, all of which are important in the international financial sphere. One of these established a new international financial system.

The International Bank for Reconstruction and Development (*The World Bank*) was funded by member nations for the purpose of postwar reconstruction in Europe. As that task was completed, the World Bank has provided financial assistance to developing countries.

Plans for an International Trade Organization were drawn up. Although this organization was never formed, the planning process did lead to adoption of the General Agreement on Tariffs and Trade (*GATT*) which has been instrumental in reducing tariffs.

The International Monetary Fund (*IMF*) is a multifaceted organization. Seen now primarily as an agency to lend funds to member nations for offsetting their balance of payments deficits, the provisions of the IMF treaty really established a new international financial system.

Unlike under the previous financial systems, countries now signed a formal treaty specifying operating procedures for international exchange. In joining the IMF, a country agreed to declare the value of its currency in terms of either gold or the dominant currency, the American dollar. Further, a country agreed to make its currency *convertible*, meaning it was freely exchangeable for other currencies, thus eliminating all exchange restrictions. Finally, the treaty required a country to maintain its currency's exchange value by not letting it deviate more than 10 percent either way from its parity value.

---

[2] Richard Cooper, "Prolegomena to the Choice of an International Monetary System," *International Organization* 29 (1975): 64–65.

The American dollar became the key international currency. The United States set its value at $35/ounce of gold. Many countries *pegged* their currencies to the dollar, meaning they would maintain their values with the dollar. As such the dollar served as the medium for payment for international transactions. Many central banks accumulated dollars as a store of value.

Throughout the 1960s, signals indicated that the Bretton Woods arrangement was flawed. As long as the American economy performed well, countries were not concerned. But, as Germany and Japan recovered from the war-time devastation, and their economies began to compete with the American economy, countries realized that the established parity rate ($35/ounce of gold) had overvalued the dollar. Its actual purchasing power was considerably less. Especially when the American economy faltered or its trade deficit widened, this overvaluing meant a loss of confidence in the dollar which resulted in redemption of dollar holdings for gold. For example, the American gold stock declined by $2,275 million in 1958 and continued to decline through the decade except for 1969, averaging nearly $800 million per year.

The idea of devaluing the dollar was repugnant to American political leaders. The dollar's strength was representative of overall United States military and economic dominance. While the official position opposed not only devaluation, but any movement from fixed exchange rates, an increasing number of economists were proposing some form of adjustment to par values or a flexible exchange rate system.[3]

One explanation for the pressure on the dollar was that an international liquidity shortage existed. Evolving out of this position was the call for a new form of international money. By the mid-1960s, the United States supported the idea for an IMF reserve arrangement to expand liquidity. In the late 1960s, the IMF created SDRs. *Special Drawing Rights (SDRs)* is essentially an international reserve asset. The IMF issued this new form of international money. Member countries could draw upon this new reserve asset to help settle international payment accounts. The value of SDRs was originally tied to gold and later to a weighted basket of sixteen currencies. As these currencies changed in value, the value of the SDRs changed.

The Bretton Woods System, with its relatively fixed exchange rates, held together fairly well. The system was very dependent on the stability of the American dollar and the American economy. When the Vietnam War inflation began to disrupt the American economy and create trade deficits in the American international account, the Bretton Woods exchange rate sys-

---

[3] See *International Monetary Arrangements: The Problem of Choice*, Fritz Machlup and Burton G. Malkiel, eds. (Princeton, N.J.: International Financial Section, Department of Economics, Princeton University, 1964).

tem began to show serious strains. The worsening trade deficit in the United States, the rising price level, and the continuing outflow of gold caused the United States to take dramatic action.

In August, 1971, President Nixon announced his "New Economic Policy." The country was stunned when Nixon announced a wage and price freeze. The president went on to acknowledge the worsening international monetary crisis and then declared that the United States was suspending gold convertibility and would halt measures to support the dollar in exchange markets; essentially, he was recognizing that the dollar was overvalued. These announcements shook the Bretton Woods regime and forced reconsideration of the international financial arrangement.

Smithsonian Agreement, 1971 to 1973

After the United States "closed the gold window" a group of ten Western trading nations met at the Smithsonian Institution to work out a compromise agreement for currency realignment. The agreement included a depreciation of the dollar by approximately 9 percent and the associated adjustment in European and Japanese currencies. This recognized what exchange markets had signaled for years, namely that the American dollar was worth less than it had been.

With the restructured currency values came a new exchange rate regime. By devaluing the dollar it was hoped that the American balance of payments deficit would decline. Nations agreed to maintain the new exchange rates by entering exchange markets and by adjusting domestic policies. The uncertainty and instability of the international economy meant that to maintain the fixed exchange rates, countries would have to accept domestic turmoil. Countries were unwilling to do so, and the Smithsonian Agreement crumbled within two years. The alternative was a floating or flexible exchange rate system.

Floating Exchange Rates, 1973 to Present

Floating exchange rates were not really chosen; they were accepted by default. The changes in the international economy, including the worldwide inflation, precipitated by oil price increases and the deteriorating position of the United States, forced countries to resort to the uncertainty of a flexible exchange rate system rather than subjecting their domestic economies to turmoil.

This period is described as one of floating exchange rates because the major currencies float against one another. Many countries, particularly smaller and developing countries, still peg their currencies to one of the major world currencies and use their central banks to maintain exchange rates in line with that pegging.

The largest trading nations do allow their currencies to float. Estimates place the level of world trade conducted at floating rates at between two-thirds and four-fifths of the world's total. Interest rates, the vitality of the economy, and government policies influence exchange rates under a floating rate system.

Evaluating the Current Regime

Four criteria are useful for assessing the effectiveness of the floating exchange rate system:

- Ability to achieve the macroeconomic goals of price stability, high employment and economic growth
- Efficient adjustments in external payments
- Enhanced volume of world trade
- Ability to adjust to changing global economic conditions[4]

Whether looking at these criteria from the perspective of one country or many, the conclusion seems to be the same; the floating exchange rate system is not facilitating global economic goals. The past fifteen years have seen continuing monetary disturbances, high rates of inflation, recession throughout the world, a Third World debt crisis, and highly volatile international mobility of capital. The international economy has been far from stable. Beyond this, the imbalances between countries, especially the United States and Japan, are threatening free trade. A rising tide of protectionist sentiment, calling for tariffs on foreign-produced goods, could force retaliation by other countries and an overall reduction in the level of world trade.

As a result of the problems with the existing exchange rate system, many are calling for reform of the international monetary system. When this happened at Bretton Woods, the postwar economic dominance of the United States helped force a new system. Creating a new system now will prove more difficult.

---

[4] For a more complete discussion see Morris Goldstein, "Whither the Exchange Rate System?" *Finance and Development*, International Monetary Fund (June 1984): 2–6.

A New International Financial System?

In the years since the abandonment of the Bretton Woods Agreement, numerous economists and policy makers have suggested even more reform packages. While many economists favor a return to some form of fixed exchange rates, policy makers are usually more reluctant to return to such a structure. The major concern with a fixed exchange rate system is that it makes domestic macroeconomic policies subservient to international market stability. Few countries seem willing to accept such regimentation. During its first four years, the Reagan administration consistently argued that the free market should determine exchange rates.

The wide fluctuations in the value of the dollar and the increasingly large American balance of payments deficit have created a greater sensitivity to reform discussions. While the United States is no longer in as dominant a financial position as it was during the Bretton Woods regime, American views still carry considerable weight among Western financial leaders.

As recently as June, 1985, at the Tokyo Summit, the finance ministers and central bank governors of the ten major Western nations concluded that the existing system needed no major institutional change. But in the spring of 1986, President Reagan called for a study to determine whether the time was right for an international conference to revise the world's monetary system.

Proposals for international monetary reform range from the reestablishment of a modified gold standard with fixed exchange rates to a floating exchange rate regime with fixed international money growth rates. Many of these proposals were outlined at the Congressional Summit on Exchange Rates and the Dollar, organized by Senator Bill Bradley and Congressman Jack Kemp in November, 1985. The Congressional Summit was an indication of growing American interest in reform.

Milton Friedman has suggested an international monetary rule that would require central banks to expand their money supplies at steady, moderate rates. Political activist and Reagan advisor Lewis Lehrman calls for a return to the gold standard and reestablishment of fixed exchange rates. Ronald McKinnon, from Stanford University, has outlined a program for harmonizing the monetary policies of the industrialized economies to bring their collective money supply under control and to reduce fluctuations in foreign exchange rates.[5]

---

[5] These proposals are discussed in Tamir Agmon, *et al.* ed., *The Future of the International Monetary System* (Lexington, Mass.: Lexington Books, 1984).

ECONOMICS TODAY 20.4

Gold and Platinum Signal More Than Recording Industry Success

Record producers watch sales to see if their recording artists' hits will bring gold and platinum records. As such, gold and platinum are signals to market observers. The primacy of these metals as highly valued commodities is evidenced in commodity markets as well as in the record industry and there, too, gold and platinum are signals, in this instance of investor confidence or concern with market conditions.

Gold and platinum contracts are traded much like contracts on other basic commodities. Gold contracts trade on the Commodity Exchange and platinum on the Mercantile Exchange in New York (as well as on regional exchanges around the country). Their prices are expressed in terms of American dollars.

These metals are important industrial commodities and since they are in relatively short supply there is speculation as to their availability. Political turmoil in South Africa (which provides 60 percent of the Western world's

gold and 80 percent of the platinum) and the possibility that the South African government will cut off shipments in retaliation for economic sanctions being placed on it have caused the price of these commodities to skyrocket. In the summer of 1986, gold prices were nearing the $400/ounce mark (after months of hovering around $350) and the price of platinum had surpassed $500/ounce. Both price levels represent psychologically important milestones (much like the 2000 Dow Jones stock market level).

There's more to the price fluctuations of gold and platinum than speculation about their availability to meet industrial demand. Both metals are used as hedges against inflation. When world price levels rise, or even when there are indications that they may rise (such as when OPEC announces a reduction in the supply of oil), investors turn to stable

commodities because they maintain their purchasing power. Concern about the exchange value of the dollar also sends investors to gold or platinum rather than holding dollar-denominated deposits.

As such, rising prices for gold and platinum may indicate that investors are concerned about the reappearance of inflation or the disruptive effects of political events. During the run-away inflation of the 1970s, gold prices soared well above the $400/ounce level and when there was an attempt on President Reagan's life, there was a flurry of activity which actually caused the suspension of gold trading. Many analysts watch gold and platinum price trends to get a handle on investor expectations. Gold and platinum prices can therefore be thought of as signals for financial markets.

McKinnon's plan has some of the same features as the one outlined by Yale University Professor Emeritus Robert Triffen.[6] His plan would create stable but adjustable exchange rates and a symmetrical process for both surplus and deficit countries to adjust their imbalances.

The IMF would be strengthened and serve as the vehicle for cooperation and consultation by central bankers. Finally, the SDR would become the principal reserve asset. Triffen's plan also calls for a greater flow of resources from developed to developing countries. Concern about the Third World debt crisis is driving much of the discussion about reforming the financial system.

---

[6] Triffen explains his plan in "Correcting the World Monetary Scandal," *Challenge* (January/February 1986): 4–20.

Most discussions about reform incorporate the need for greater cooperation between central banks with the goal of greater macroeconomic policy coordination. Despite the continual presence of national concerns, there is some evidence of central bank cooperation. In March, 1986, the Federal Reserve, the West German Bundesbank, and the Bank of Japan acted together to reduce interest rates. The rapid decline in the exchange value of the dollar is putting pressure on foreign central banks to agree on at least a general level for exchange rates and then to cooperate to stabilize exchange markets. The call for cooperation in exchange markets requires a coordination of domestic monetary policies. The latter may well present a barrier to international reform.

The drive for reform of the international financial system is occurring at the same time that a financial revolution is sweeping the globe. The same kinds of market deregulation that the United States has experienced are taking place throughout the world. For example, the London Stock Exchange was deregulated in late 1986 with far-reaching implications; the possibility of an offshore banking facility in Tokyo is becoming real. At the same time, financial innovation is creating new financial instruments, many of which link domestic markets to the international exchange market. These changes will influence the scope of international financial reform. These changes in the international nature of financial institutions and operations are the focus of the next part of this chapter.

Financial Institutions and the International Sector

Financial institutions operate in the international exchange market. For the most part, the institutions that perform financial services domestically do the same internationally. The changes that are occurring internationally, therefore, have implications for the domestic financial system. The internationalization of banking is one such change. But to understand fully the linkage between the international and domestic sectors, you also need to explore the markets in which these international banks operate. Finally, the chapter explores some of the international issues which are challenging the structure and stability of the American financial system.

Internationalization of Banking

The rapid changes in the domestic American financial system are parallel with international developments. Two surges in the expansion of international banking are important. The first was just after World War I, resulting in about 2000 international banking operations. The second was during the 1960s and early 1970s; the latter surge brought the number of foreign banking branches and subsidiaries to over 4500.[7]

The internationalization of banking involves a rather small proportion of banks; only about 200 American banks have foreign branches or subsidiaries. Nonetheless, this movement has far-reaching implications. The internationalization of banking is prompted by two major factors. First, deregulation of domestic markets and associated technological innovations are encouraging major financial institutions to expand the scope of their operations to take advantage of new markets in the face of increasing domestic competition. Second, the unprecedented magnitude of international capital flows in the 1980s has generated new financial instruments for moving funds across national borders. Commercial banks are facilitating the development of these instruments to take advantage of new business opportunities.

For years, the structure of international banking was mostly unchanged. Select major banks in the world money centers handled international investment transactions and facilitated international trade. While the number of commercial banks actively engaged in international banking is still not large, the overall trend is significant.

The first major expansion of American banks into foreign countries began in the 1970s; in 1950, only seven American banks had foreign operations. American banks expanded into the international market for a number of reasons. First, banks followed their domestic business customers as they expanded into foreign countries. Second, banks wanted to take advantage of the expanding quantity of international currency transactions. Third, they expanded to avoid restrictions on growth in this country caused by Regulation Q interest-rate ceilings and Regulation D reserve-requirement costs. Foreign markets offered the potential for high returns and attractive opportunities for growth.

Foreign banks in this country began to appear in increasing numbers during the 1970s. In large part, foreign banks opened American operations to take advantage of the growth in trade with the United States and to facilitate the rising tide of foreign investment in this country. Beyond these motivations, the unique role of the dollar as an international currency prompted large foreign banks to establish a large dollar deposit base which could be done more cheaply by opening American branches than by acquiring dollars

---

[7] The expansion eased somewhat during the 1970s as oil price hikes disrupted international lending. The accumulating debt of many developing countries which contributed to the collapse of Continental Illinois made many banks skeptical about expanding too rapidly.

in the international exchange market. In 1983, 226 foreign banks from 52 countries operated 558 offices in the United States. By 1985, the number of foreign banks had risen to 260.

The involvement of an American bank in a foreign country or a foreign bank in this country usually moves through a four-stage developmental process. Initially a bank may help finance the trading activities of local import or export firms. Next, the bank may make loans to foreign banks for their operations. As the firm becomes more sophisticated in international finance, it will extend loans to nonfinancial foreign firms or individuals. Finally, a bank may establish a foreign branch or an Edge Act office—an office outside its state of charter for the facilitation of international trade.[8]

The rise of international banking has prompted changes in the structure of American banking. Initially, American branches of foreign banks had a real competitive advantage over domestic banks. Foreign branches were not subject to reserve requirements or interest-rate ceilings. The 1978 International Banking Act brought foreign bank branches under American regulatory provisions. This helped eliminate their competitive advantage.

United States restrictions still prevented American banks from competing effectively in the international arena. So-called off shore banks began to proliferate. An *off shore bank* is a bank operation which does not deal in the currency of the country in which it is located. In most instances, this allows the bank to escape regulation. Without reserve requirements and other regulatory restrictions, these banks can extend loans at lower interest rates and offer higher interest rates to depositors. The development of *swap arrangements*, the conversion of a loan extended in the international market into the currency denomination and maturity desired by the borrower, made off shore banks attractive to American borrowers. Large numbers of off-shore banks were opened in England, Luxembourg, the Bahamas (where much American business was diverted) and Singapore.

To allow American banks to compete, a 1981 Federal Reserve ruling authorized American banks to establish International Banking Facilities. *IBFs* are limited-service banking offices established to handle off shore loan and deposit activities for foreign customers. IBFs are essentially free-trade zones; they are exempt from reserve requirement restrictions. They have allowed American banks to compete in the international market without having to move operations from this country. Much of the off shore banking business returned to American money centers, especially New York. In

---

[8] For a full discussion of the process see Donald Baer and David Garlow, "International Banking in the Sixth District," Federal Reserve Bank of Atlanta *Economic Review* (November/ December 1977): 127–34.

1981, IBF assets were $60 billion; by 1985, they had risen to over $200 billion.

The internationalization of banking has facilitated the extension of loans across national boundaries. In this country, we have heard a great deal about the extent of foreign-held domestic debt. The greatest publicity surrounding this phenomenon probably occurred during the large OPEC price hikes which resulted in huge revenue flows to oil producing countries. Much of that money came back into the United States in the form of investment. Foreign funds continue to finance the massive debt accumulation in the United States.

The purchase of American debt issues, both corporate bonds and government securities, has risen slowly but steadily during the 1980s. Estimates place the portion of publicly held U.S. Treasury securities owned by foreigners at about 15 percent, approximately $230 billion. Although declining American interest rates may result in less foreign ownership of American debt, some economists express concern that foreign ownership may make American interest rates more volatile. Foreign ownership of American debt is an issue of continuing controversy in the area of internationalization of banking and capital markets.[9]

In a similar vein, some observers have criticized the American international banking expansion for hastening the flight of capital from developing countries. In many cases, domestic American banks or international lending agencies, such as The World Bank, lend funds to developing countries to aid in economic expansion only to find that the funds return to the United States through foreign branches of American banks. Morgan Guaranty Trust estimated in May, 1986, that $198 billion has fled the turmoil of developing countries, mostly in Latin America, for the stability and relatively high returns of U.S. banks.[10]

Major international banking institutions conduct most of the business in the international financial market. An American bank, Citicorp, is among the largest banks worldwide and is the most active American bank in terms of foreign deposits. Other major American banks, for example, Bank America and Morgan Guaranty Trust, are also active. Smaller American banks establish correspondent bank relationships with these larger banks so that international transactions can take place in even small communities.

International banks perform the same functions as domestic banks—they gather deposits from surplus spending units which they make available

---

[9] The issue of foreign investment in the United States is discussed in a February 24, 1986 *The Wall Street Journal* article entitled, "Analysts Fret Over Holdings of Debt Issues by Foreigners."

[10] See "Foreign Money Finds Haven in U.S.," *The Wall Street Journal* (May 27, 1986).

to deficit spending units. Deposits collected in one country may be lent in another. This international activity is conducted through international money markets.

International Money Markets

The growth of the external, or international, currency market facilitates international monetary activities. Due to its initial prominence in Europe, this market is often called the Eurocurrency market. Because of its widespread acceptance the dollar has served as the basis for the Eurocurrency market. *Eurodollars* are deposit liabilities denominated in American dollars, of banks located outside the United States.

The Eurodollar market is quite distinct from the international exchange market. In the latter, one currency is traded for another; in the former, international banking activities occur with the transactions denominated in American dollars. This is a mechanism for transferring funds without working through the exchange market. Money in the Eurocurrency market is held in time deposits or Eurodollar certificates of deposit. A *Eurodollar CD* is a negotiable receipt for a dollar deposit at a bank located outside the United States. These deposited funds become the pool of resources allowing the extension of loans.

A multinational bank may generate funds in one foreign currency and extend loans in another country with another currency. For example, a bank might collect deposits in Saudi Arabia and extend a loan against these deposits in Italy. The deposit and loan are denominated in dollars; the transactions take place through the Eurocurrency market.

The Eurocurrency market is attractive because it is unregulated. Reserve requirements against deposits do not apply nor do any domestic interest-rate restrictions. There are no barriers on entry into the market, so competition is intense. Interest rates are attractive for both depositors and borrowers. The Eurocurrency market links countries and their currencies into a massive global financial marketplace.

The Eurocurrency market has been a major source of credit for the international economy. *Eurobonds*, simply debt securities that are sold outside a borrower's country in any one of a number of currencies, amounted to $135.5 billion in 1985. That is a 70 percent increase over 1984. American firms, as well as European and Japanese companies, raise funds by issuing Eurobonds because the cost of borrowing is less than in domestic markets. Rates are lower for a number of reasons, including tax law revisions designed to encourage American borrowers to attract foreign investors.

The expansion of the Eurocurrency market is represented by the development of *Euronotes*, one, three- or six-month short-term negotiable money market notes that are similar to American commercial paper. Estimates place the quantity of Euronotes outstanding at more than $45 billion. The Eurocurrency market has developed the same kinds of financial instruments found in domestic markets.

The deterioration in the value of the dollar along with its erratic behavior in the exchange markets during 1984 to 1986 combined with the increasing value of the yen has given greater prominence to the Japanese currency. Most currencies in East Asia are pegged to the dollar and the predominate quantity of Eurobond issues are in dollars, but debt denominated in currencies other than dollars has increased. The volume of Eurobond issues denominated in yen increased by 600 percent from 1984 to 1985 while dollar-denominated Eurobond issues increased by 50 percent. European bond issues amounted to only $374 million in 1982; in 1985 that had jumped to $6.5 billion.

Whether denominated in yen or dollars, the Eurocurrency market transactions have grown tremendously. This market facilitates international banking and blurs the national boundaries for financial transactions. The internationalization of banking and the growth of the Eurocurrency market are among the issues in a changing financial marketplace which present challenges to the American financial system.

Challenges to the American Financial System

Just as is the case with the domestic financial system, bad debts and competition in the international sector are challenging the American financial system. The *international debt crisis* has already had some dramatic effects on the United States. The problems of Continental Illinois National Bank owed much to bad international loans. In June, 1984, Continental Illinois had nonperforming loans, most of them international, that amounted to 132 percent of its common equity. The free-lending policies that characterized American commercial bank behavior toward developing countries in the 1970s changed abruptly when oil prices declined and recession disrupted international trade.

American banks participated actively in international lending. The International Monetary Fund reported in 1985 that American banks had loans of $90 billion outstanding to developing countries. And while large banks are primarily involved, some major banks created syndicates involving smaller banks in order to generate sufficient funds to extend sizeable loans to foreign countries. Therefore, while the bulk of foreign debt, about 62 percent, is held by the nation's nine largest banks, smaller American banks hold over 16 percent of the debt of developing nations, according to IMF reports.

The international debt crisis is a worldwide problem. American banks' exposure in many developing nations makes a resolution of the crisis particularly important in this country. But the magnitude of developing countries' debts its somewhat overwhelming. Table 20.1 illustrates the externally held debt of the major debtor countries.

The magnitude of foreign debts is already haunting American banks. Citicorp, the United States' largest bank holding company, had net loan losses on international loans of $186 million in 1983, up from only $18 million in 1980. To head off further losses, American bankers can only work to *restructure* these foreign debts, that is, stretch out the repayment over a longer period at lower interest rates to make current period payments more manageable. In Brazil, for example, a consortium of New York banks agreed in February 1986 to cut their spread (that is, their margin over the variable interest rate) by one percentage point (from 2.125 to 1.125) on one-third of Brazil's debt. This will save Brazil, and cost the banks, about $320 million in interest payments for 1986. At the same time, the repayment deadline for $15.5 billion of short-term debt was "rolled over" for another year.

While it may seem that the banks are adhering too strictly to the old adage, "a rolling loan gathers no loss," they really have little choice. They are buying time, hoping to avoid losses, while finance ministers try to work out plans to save the debtor countries from defaulting. United States Treasury Secretary James Baker in October, 1985, proposed a far-reaching plan which requires reform of state-managed economies of the fifteen major debtor nations in the hope of stimulating economic recovery. In return, the plan provides for additional aid from the World Bank. Unless the restructuring plans or Baker's recovery program begin to move bank loans from the nonperforming to the performing category, more banks will have to write off the loans and absorb losses.

Thus, while American banks continue their expansion into international financial markets, they are trying to extract themselves from some

Country	Debt ($billions)
Brazil	102
Mexico	97
Venezuela	28
Chile	18
Peru	14
Colombia	13

Source: **United Nations Economic Committee for Latin America and the Caribbean, as reported in** *The Economist* **(April 12, 1986). Reprinted by permission.**

TABLE 20.1 *Developing Countries' External Debt, Spring 1986*

questionable loans and they are exercising greater caution in the extension of new loans to avoid a replay of the current crisis.

Competition, although not a crisis like the foreign debt problem, is challenging major American banks; Japanese banks are currently presenting the greatest challenge. European banks continue to press for a greater market share in both international markets and within the United States.

Table 20.2 lists the top ten banks outside the United States. Japanese banks dominate in *Fortune*'s list of the largest 100 non-U.S. banks, holding the top five positions and placing 30 banks among the 100 largest. Japan has more banks in the 100 largest than France, Britain, and West Germany combined. If American banks are included, the top ten changes somewhat; Citicorp is number one (with assets of over $175 billion) and Bank America is ranked seventh (assets of approximately $123 billion). In an overall ranking of commercial banks, Japan leads with 25 in the top 100, to 19 for the United States, 10 for West Germany, and 8 for France and Italy.

The smaller number of commercial banks in foreign countries means that Japanese and European banks have tremendous resources available for worldwide expansion. The bank consolidations occurring in the United States will only begin to move the United States toward the European model. These large banks are well positioned to expand further their international financial operations.

Beyond the competition in global markets, competition is increasing in domestic markets. A relatively small number of banks can be considered "global consumer banks." Citicorp, Bank America, and Chase Manhattan in the United States, Barclays, Lloyds, and Standard Carter in Britain, Credit

	Assets ($ billions)
1. Dai-ichi Kangyo Bank	165.7
2. Fuji Bank	147.8
3. Sumitomo Bank	140.5
4. Mitsubishi Bank	135.2
5. Sanwa Bank	129.5
6. Banque Nationale de Paris	124.0
7. Caisse Nationale de Credit Agricole	123.8
8. Credit Lyonnais	112.3
9. National Westminster Bank	104.7
10. Industrial Bank of Japan	98.5

Source: From "The Largest Banks Outside the U.S.," *Fortune*, August 4, 1986, pp. 206–207. Copyright © 1986 Time Inc. All rights reserved. Reprinted by permission.

TABLE 20.2 *Largest Commercial Banks Outside United States, 1985*

Lyonnais in France, Mitsui, Sanwa, and Mitsubishi in Japan are all establishing a presence in retail markets around the world. These giants will compete for retail banking space in the population centers of Asia, Europe, and the United States. Not only will large American banks compete with foreign banks, but so too will regional banks find an increasing pressure in American markets by foreign banks.

Chapter Conclusion

The international financial system is among the more interesting aspects of money and financial institutions. At the same time, many people perceive it as the most confusing part of the world of finance. The international financial system is an extension of the domestic system. The primary difference is that multiple currencies are involved.

Exchange relations result from different national currencies; they influence trade and investment. Relations between nations, the arrangements they use to facilitate trade and investment, present a major problem for a smoothly functioning international system. Policy makers who ultimately conclude arrangements for international financial relations, must consider the domestic implications of international trade and investment flows. If these flows begin to work against one country, for whatever reason, the domestic economy may suffer. This has been the American experience during the 1980s. As a result, people are demanding relief from imports (through tariffs) and calling for reform of the system. But arrangements that have operated for the last fifteen years are slow to change.

One aspect of the international financial system that is not slow to change is the internationalization of banking and financial markets. Technological advances allow bankers to link domestic markets into a global market. With this linkage come global banking operations. The internationalization of banking presents challenges for the American financial system but it also brings countries closer together. As this happens, cooperation in foreign exchange markets and the coordination of domestic macroeconomic policies may well follow.

Consider these Questions

1. How did the foreign exchange market evolve? Must a currency trade in the market to allow international trade? Consider that the Russian ruble does not trade in the international exchange market. Yet in the summer of 1986, the United States sold thousands of tons of grain to the Soviets. How was this possible? Does it mean the exchange market is unnecessary?

2. Use the purchasing power parity theory to explain the movement of the dollar relative to the yen over the last few years. What economic conditions in the United States and Japan contributed to this movement?

3. Can the forward market rates signal trends in exchange rate movements? What other factors might intervene to influence the difference between spot and forward market rates?

4. What accounts for the deteriorating American balance of payments position? How has the trade portion of the account changed? What about the capital account?

5. Why, despite the declining value of the dollar, did the American trade position continue to worsen during 1985 and 1986?

6. What's the difference between fixed and flexible exchange rates? How is government policy affected by each type of exchange rate system?

7. The gold-based exchange rate system is often described as a *laissez faire* system which functions automatically. Explain why this claim is made.

8. How did the gold exchange standard meet the increasing liquidity needs of the post–World War I world? Why didn't the world's money supply increase dramatically under this arrangement?

9. The Bretton Woods Agreement provided for the American dollar as the international currency. Why? Would this system have continued to work if the United States had not experienced inflation?

10. How are SDRs similar to the arrangements of the gold exchange standard?

11. The European Economic Community, the so-called Common Market countries, have established a trading currency called the European Currency Unit (ECU). Do you think a uniform international currency is at all likely. Who would control such a currency?

12. When there is intervention into the exchange market during a period of floating rates, the arrangement is sometimes referred to as a "dirty float." Why would countries enter the exchange market when rates are floating? Has there been any recent evidence of coordinated central bank entrance into the exchange market? What was the effect?

13. How would you evaluate the flexible exchange rate system?

14. Why would an American bank consider expansion abroad?

15. What advantages do off shore banks offer to customers? How can banks in a "land-locked" financial center like Chicago participate in off shore banking?

16. Explain what is meant by the flight of capital from developing countries. Should international lending agencies try to prevent the flight of capital?

17. How can there be a Eurodollar and a Euroyen in the same market?

18. Treasury Secretary Baker's plan for restructuring international debt calls for developing countries to conform to certain conditions before additional aid is provided. Is this a good idea? How do you think developing countries will react?

19. What's the likelihood of a dozen or so global banks dominating both international and domestic financial markets? Explain your response.

Suggestions for Further Reading

Aliber, Robert Z. "International Banking: A Survey." In *Journal of Money, Credit, and Banking* 16, 4 (November 1984, part 2): 661–684.
A thorough review of the literature relating to international banking. Mostly nontechnical. Excellent bibliography.

Bordo, Michael D. and Anna J. Schwartz, eds. *A Retrospective on the Classical Gold Standard 1821–1931*. Chicago: University of Chicago Press for the National Bureau of Economic Research, 1984.
A collection of articles on the functioning of the gold standard.

Baughn, William H. and Donald R. Mandich, eds. *International Banking Handbook*. Homewood, IL: Dow Jones-Irwin, 1983.
This handy book has all the information you need to know about international banking.

Boyd, John H., David S. Dahl and Carolyn P. Line. "A Primer on the International Monetary Fund." In Federal Reserve Bank of Minneapolis *Review* 7, 3 (Summer 1983): 6–15.
Short, simple explanation of the IMF.

Chrystal, K. Alec. "A Guide to Foreign Exchange Markets." In Federal Reserve Bank of St. Louis *Review* 66, 3 (March 1984): 5–18.
Another short, clear explanation. This provides an analysis of the structure of exchange market and how participants interact in the market.

Kubarych, Roger M. *Foreign Exchange Markets in the United States*. Federal Reserve Bank of New York, 1983.
Good description of the structure and functioning of the exchange market with attention to exchange rate determination.

Makin, John H. *The Global Debt Crisis*. New York: Basic Book, Inc., 1984.
Excellent survey of origins, magnitude and implications of the international debt crisis.

O'Dell, John S. *U. S. International Monetary Policy*. Princeton, N.J.: Princeton University Press, 1982.

Very readable survey of the role of the United States in the changing international financial system. Looks closely at transition from Bretton Woods to flexible exchange rate regime.

Prochnow, Herbert V., ed. *The Eurodollar*. Chicago: Rand McNally and Company, 1970.

Collection of articles on the Eurodollar. Although some of the articles are outdated those on the emergence of the market, definitions and mechanics, and principles involved in its operation are essentially timeless.

Solomon, Robert. *The International Monetary System, 1945–1976: An Insider's View*. New York: Harper and Row, 1977.

For many years, Solomon was the Federal Reserve's top international economist. He reflects on his experiences and in the process provides a fascinating account of international monetary development.

———. "International Banking Survey." In *The Economist* (March 22, 1986).

A comprehensive review of the internationalization of banking with the focus on consumer banking activities of the global banking firms.

Glossary

Number in parentheses refers to chapter or chapters in which each term is discussed.

A

Accord of 1951 (16)   agreement between the Fed and Treasury which freed the Fed from responsibility of pegging interest rates on government securities.

Adaptive expectations (12)   expectations that are average of observations of past changes.

Aggregate demand curve (9)   curve representing combinations of output and price level at which the commodity and money markets are simultaneously in equilibrium.

Aggregate supply curve (9)   curve representing short-run relationship between aggregate output and the price level.

Anticipated income theory (5)   commercial banking theory which prescribes utilization of a loan portfolio that will provide a regular and continuous flow of funds.

Asset allocation theory (5)   theory of commercial banking which suggests matching maturity structure of assets to that of liabilities.

B

Balance of payments (20)   accounting record of a country's trade and investment activities with other nations.

Balance of trade (20)   accounting mechanism which indicates one nation's net flow of goods and services vis-a-vis another nation.

Bank charter (6)   government agency's granting of permission to operate a commercial bank; may be granted by either state or federal government.

Bank failure (6)   supervisory agency places bank in receivership because it cannot meet its obligations to its depositors; the bank "goes out of business."

Bank holding company (6)   a corporation established to hold the stock of one or more commercial banks.

Bank holiday (4)   euphemism for temporary closing of banks or other depository institutions to allow for provision of liquidity and solvency.

Bank merger (6)   combining two or more commercial banks into a single operating unit.

Bank of the United States (4)   early American attempts at central banking. Private banks, chartered by the federal government; the 1st BUS operated from 1791 to 1811 and the 2nd BUS from 1816 until 1836.

Bankers' acceptances (2)   promissory notes issued by individuals or firms that are guaranteed by a depository institution.

Barter (1)   system of exchange where goods and services are traded directly without benefit of medium of exchange; necessitates double coincidence of wants.

Board of Governors of the Federal Reserve (16) twelve-person board appointed by the president for fourteen-year terms and charged with responsibility of governing the functioning of the Federal Reserve System.

Bond (3)   a fixed interest security or promissory note with specified repayment schedule.

Branch banking (4)   allows commercial banks to operate multiple offices.

Bretton Woods System (20)   1946 multinational conference constructed a new international financial system with fixed exchange rates based on the American dollar; the system lasted until 1971.

Business cycle (8, 11)   Fluctuations in economic activity following regular patterns of expansion and contraction.

C

Capital account (20)   net of capital flows between two countries.

Capital market (2)   portion of financial marketplace dealing with securities with maturities over one year, for example, corporate stock, commercial mortgages, etc.

Central bank (4, 16)   public institution serving as government's bank and responsible for monetary policy.

Certificate of deposit (2) an account with a financial firm in which the firm agrees to repay a specified sum on a designated date; the CD may be negotiable or nonnegotiable.

Classical economics (1, 8) school of thought prominent during eighteenth and nineteenth centuries which described economic activity in terms of freely functioning markets and competition.

Commercial Loan Theory (5) traditional theory of banking specifying extension of short-term, self-liquidating loans; sometimes referred to as real bills loans.

Commercial paper (2) short-term, unsecured promissory note in denominations of $1000 that are issued by well-established business and financial firms.

Commodity money (1) goods, or commodities, which are used as medium of exchange.

Comptroller of Currency (6) U.S. Treasury official who charters, regulates, and examines national banks.

Conduct (13) behavior of firms in the marketplace including the strategies they employ in production, pricing, and product promotion.

Consumer Price Index (2) index number, sometimes referred to as Cost of Living Index, which measures changes in the prices of a specified set of consumer goods purchased by the average household.

Contestable markets hypothesis (13) challenges structure-performance hypothesis by arguing that market structure is determined by industry characteristics and does not in and of itself serve as a deterrent to competition.

Contractual saving institution (4) financial institution that accepts funds under contractual arrangement with savers and dictates payment and repayment arrangements; includes insurance companies and pension funds.

Correspondent bank (6) a bank which acts as agent for another bank, mainly for check clearance, in return for compensation.

Crowding-out effect (9) reduction in private consumption or investment expenditures as a result of a rise in government expenditures.

Current account (20) value of flow of goods, services, and other current receipts and payments between two nations.

Cyclical unemployment (11) unemployment associated with insufficient job opportunities during certain phases of the business cycle.

D

Debasement of currency (1) practice of reducing the metal content of coins without reducing nominal value.

Default risk (3) risk arising from possibility that a loan and/or its interest payment will not be paid to lender.

Defensive open-market operation (17) Federal Reserve purchase or sale of securities designed to offset factors which might destabilize economic conditions.

Deficit spending unit (2) any economic unit with liabilities in excess of assets and therefore needing to borrow funds.

Depository institution (4) financial institution that accepts deposits and issues transactions accounts; includes commercial banks, savings and loans, credit unions, and mutual savings banks.

Depository Institution Deregulation and Monetary Control Act (14) sweeping financial reform legislation passed in 1980 which, among other things, made all depository institutions subject to Federal Reserve requirements and gave all institutions access to Federal discount window; first step toward deregulation of financial industry.

Differential efficiency argument (13) suggests that the link between market concentration and above normal profits is more the result of operating efficiency by the large firms than from anticompetitive behavior.

Direct finance (2) direct transfer of funds from SU to DU; sometimes referred to as disintermediation because no financial intermediary is involved.

Discount rate (17) rate of interest the Federal Reserve charges depository institutions for borrowing through the discount window.

Discount window (16) Federal Reserve banks lend funds to all depository institutions through this "window," so called because borrowing institutions used to present corporate bonds at these windows for discounting.

Disinflation (11) decline in rate of inflation, not to be confused with deflation.

Double coincidence of wants (1) arrangement whereby someone who wants something finds someone else who has that item and is willing to trade it for something the first individual wants to exchange.

Dual banking system (6) chartering of commercial banks by both the federal government and state governments.

Dynamic Open-Market Operations (17) Proactive Fed actions to change reserves moving economy toward new level of economic activity.

E

Econometric model (10) a formally specified mathematical model of part or all of the economy where the parameters of the model are estimated using econometric techniques.

Economies of scale (4) reduction in average cost of operation resulting from increasing level of output.

Economies of scope (2) savings acquired through simultaneous production of many different products.

Edge Act corporation (20) the subsidiary of an American bank that is engaged primarily in international banking.

Endogenous variable (8) a variable whose value is determined within the framework of an economic model.

Equation of Exchange (10) updated version of quantity theory of money specifying that $MV = PT$.

Eurodollars (20) deposit liabilities denominated in American dollars which are located in banks outside the United States.

Exchange market (20) interaction of buyers and sellers of world currencies that establishes the price of one currency in terms of another; market is linked across political boundaries by telephone and telex hookups.

Exchange rate (20) price of a foreign currency in terms of the domestic currency.

Exogenous variable (8) one whose value is determined outside an economic model but which may influence endogenous variables.

Expectation theory (13) explains shape of yield curve in terms of investors' expectations about future interest-rate movements.

F

Federal debt (17) total amount owed by the federal government; represents accumulated annual deficits.

Federal deficit (17) annual shortfall of federal revenues for a given level of expenditures.

Fed watching (17) professionals who observe Fed actions and public policy pronouncements to anticipate effects of Fed actions in financial markets.

Federal Depository Insurance Corporation (FDIC) (6) government agency established in 1934 to insure small deposits (up to $100,000) at commercial banks and to supervise commercial bank operations.

Federal funds (2, 5) excess reserves on deposit with Federal Reserve bonds which are lent to depository institutions in large denominations for one or two days.

Federal funds rate (5) interest rate on overnight loans between banks of funds in deposit at Fed.

Federal Open-Market Committee (FOMC) (16) seven members of Board of Governors and five Federal Reserve district bank presidents comprise this committee which establishes specific money policy targets and undertakes open-market operations to advise those targets.

Federal Savings and Loan Insurance Corporation (FSLIC) (15) federal government insurance fund for personal deposits at savings and loans.

Fiat money (1) paper currency declared legal tender by government.

Finance company (4) financial institution that generates liabilities through issuance of its own commercial paper or by securing bank loans and then uses these funds to specialize in consumer and business loans.

Financial futures (2) contractual arrangements providing for the right or option to buy or sell a financial instrument at a predetermined price before some specified time in the future.

Financial intermediary (4) any individual or institution (usually a financial institution) which brings together surplus units and the funds users' deficit units.

Financial market (2) market which facilitates transfer of funds from surplus spending units to deficit spending units.

Fixed exchange rates (20) international financial system in which countries agree to peg currencies according to a fixed schedule.

Fixed Growth Rule (19) proposed reform in Federal Reserve policy that would require money supply expansion according to a prescribed growth rate.

Float (16) credit extended by Fed in check clearing process. Depository institutions receive credit for checks when depositing even though it takes time for Fed to process transfer of funds; difference between Fed balance sheet item cash in process of collection and deferred availability cash items.

Floating exchange rates (20) international financial system in which market forces are allowed to change the exchange rates between currencies.

Forward market (20) market for exchange rate transactions involving bank deposits of various currencies for some designated future date.

Fractional reserve system (7) practice by depository institutions of maintaining only a fraction of deposit liabilities as reserves to meet withdrawals and deposit transfers.

Frictional unemployment (11) unemployment associated with movement between jobs.

Full employment (11) level of employment resulting when economy is totally utilizing its existing resources. Economists think this results in about 5 percent of work force being unemployed.

Functioning four (1) Functional properties of money—medium of exchange, unit of account, standard of deferred payment, and store of value.

G

Garn-St Germain Act (14) 1982 legislation to complement DIDMCA primarily by providing expanded operating freedom to thrift institutions, thus increasing the degree of competition in the industry.

GNP Price Deflator (2) Price index used to adjust gross national product for price level changes.

Gresham's Law (1) prediction that when given two currencies, where the intrinsic value of one currency departs from its legally declared value, the currency with the higher intrinsic value will be withdrawn from circulation and held.

H

Herfindahl Index (13) measure of concentration in a particular market; it is the sum of the squared market shares for every firm in the market; maximum H-index, representing total concentration is 10,000; the smaller the H-index, the less the market concentration.

High-powered money (16) Federal notes in circulation and depository institution reserves; same as monetary base.

Hunt Commission (14) 1971 Presidential Commission that first made recommendation for sweeping changes in the financial industry.

Hyperinflation (11) excessively large increases in the general price level.

I

Income (11) a flow of earnings for some specified period of time.

Indirect finance (2) transfer of funds from SU to DU through financial intermediary.

Industrial Organization Model (13) model of industrial behavior in market economy which focuses on the market structure, firm conduct, and performance.

Inside lags (19) lags in monetary policy's effect resulting from the time it takes to recognize, diagnose, prescribe, and decide on instrumentation.

Instrumental targets (18) variables which respond to monetary policy actions within a few weeks.

Interest rate (2, 3) price of money; commonly thought of as annual rate of return for borrowing or lending money.

Intermediate targets (18) variables that respond to monetary actions only after 3 to 6 months.

International Monetary Fund (20) created by Bretton Woods agreement to assist in world trade primarily by making loans to countries that need assistance.

Interstate banking (15) bank operations that extend beyond the traditional state boundaries.

Investment (8) flow of expenditures devoted to increasing and maintaining the stock of capital (plant and equipment) in the economy.

Investment company (4) financial institutions that generate funds by selling stock, then pool acquired funds for investment in a diversified portfolio of assets.

IS Curve (9) curve representing locus of points of equilibrium between interest rates and income levels for the money market.

J

Junk Bonds (17) bonds issued by companies whose ratings are below those normally accepted by the credit market.

K

Keynesian Economics (8) school of economics originating from the work of John Maynard Keynes and his disciples which accentuates the income-generating effect of total expenditures.

L

Law of One Price (20) specifies when two countries produce an identical good, the price of that good, transportation costs excluded, will be the same throughout the world.

Legal tender (1) property of a currency established by law that makes it fully acceptable for payment of all debt.

Liquidity (1) a quality of an asset which allows it to be immediately sold or redeemed for money without risk of loss of capital value; money, by definition, is completely liquid.

Liquidity management (5) theory of contemporary banking which stresses attention to management of liabilities as well as assets to maximize profitability while maintaining liquidity.

Liquidity preference theory (3) identifies the overall demand for money and system's supply of money as factors determining the interest rate.

Liquidity premium theory (3) specifies that the rate of return on long-term securities be equal to the average of current short-term rates and expected short-term rates plus a premium to compensate investors for loss of liquidity on long-term securities.

LM Curve (9) curve representing locus of points of equilibrium between interest rates and income levels in the goods market.

Loanable funds (2) funds available for lending in financial marketplace.

Loanable funds theory (3) identifies the demand for credit or loanable funds and the supply of credit as the factors determining the interest rate.

Lucas Critique (12) Robert Lucas argued that econometric models based on adaptive expectations will provide erroneous results.

M

M1 (2) narrow empirical definition of money which includes components of money supply most often used in exchange transactions, namely coin, currency held by the public, non-bank travelers' checks and checkable deposits at financial institutions.

M2 (2) broader money supply measure including M1 plus savings and small denominations time deposits (under $100,000) at depository institutions, money market deposit accounts and overnight repurchase agreements and Eurodollar balances.

M3 (2) broadest money supply measure including M2 plus large denomination time deposits (over $100,000) and long-term repurchase agreements.

Marginal efficiency of investment (8)   the demand curve for investment relating the level of investment spending to the interest rate.

Market risk (4)   loss on an investment resulting from decline in the value of an asset.

Market segmentation theory (3)   differentiates between short- and long-term securities indicating that supply and demand in these various markets determine the overall yield curve.

Medium of exchange (1)   object that serves the intermediary function for exchange transactions; one of the functions of money.

Mercantilism (1)   economic philosophy prominent during the sixteenth and seventeenth centuries that saw precious metals as the key to the economic power of a country.

Monetarism (1)   school of thought often associated with Milton Friedman that views the money supply as the dominant factor determining nominal income and as the principal cause of instability in the economy.

Monetary base (7)   monetary measure that includes Fed's liabilities (currency in circulation plus reserves) and U.S. Treasury liabilities (coins in circulation); sometimes called high-powered money.

Monetary transmission mechanism (18)   process whereby monetary policy actions, usually open-market operations, are translated into changes in real economic variables.

Money (1)   any uniform object which is accepted as a means of payment for goods or services not because it has intrinsic value but because it can be used again for the same purpose.

Money market (2)   portion of financial marketplace dealing with highly liquid financial instruments such as Treasury Bills and commercial paper.

Money market deposit account (2)   deposit accounts authorized by Garn-St Germain Act that require minimum balance ($500), pay unregulated interests, and have restrictions on withdrawals.

Money market mutual fund (15)   essentially an open-ended investment company where funds held are used in acquisition of various credit instruments.

Money multiplier (7)   technically, ratio of the money supply to the monetary base; more commonly, the ratio of change in deposit liabilities, generated by extension of loans, to the initiating change in reserves.

Multiplier effect (8)   ratio of change in income to the initial change in expenditure (*C*, *I* or *G*) which demonstrates that the initial expenditure produces a multiple increase in income.

N

National Banking Act (4)   1864 legislation designed to strengthen financial systems by encouraging unified currency through issuance of national bank notes and imposing consistent operating regulations on national banks.

Natural rate of unemployment (11)   rate of unemployment implied by the basic structure of the economy which cannot be permanently affected by demand management policies.

Near money (1)   assets that can be quickly and easily converted into money.

Nominal variable (2)   an economic measure that is not adjusted for price level changes.

O

Offshore banks (20)   banks that do not deal in the currency of the country where they are located.

Okun's Law (11)   identifies statistical association between loss in aggregate output and rise in unemployment rate. Specifically, the law states that there is a 3 percent decline in real output (called GNP gap) for every 1 percent increase in unemployment.

Open-Market Operations (17)   Federal Reserve purchase and sale of securities in the secondary market.

Operating targets (18)   variables affected almost immediately by monetary policy actions.

Outside lags (19)   time it takes for implementation and initial evaluation of monetary policy action to begin to have any effects.

P

Performance (13) measurable result of firm behavior in the marketplace, such as profitability, technical efficiency, or economies of scale.

Permanent income hypothesis (10) notion developed by Milton Friedman which identifies permanent income as the weighted average of expected future receipts.

Phillips Curve (11) curve depicting trade-off between rate of change in money wage rates (more commonly now inflation) and the unemployment rate.

Policy ineffectiveness proposal (12) strictest version of rational expectations school which argues that macro policies will be ineffective due to public expectations and actions.

Present discounted value (3) translation of some future payment or stream of payments into its value now, given a particular interest rate.

Privatization of money issue (19) proposed structural reform calling for elimination of legal tender monopoly of federal government and allowance of all financial institutions to issue money subject only to market forces.

Purchasing power parity theory (20) exchange rates between countries will adjust to reflect changes in the nations' price levels or relative purchasing power of the countrys' currencies.

Q

Quantity theory of money (10) theory of demand for money that gained prominence before writings of Keynes and which has been revived in more sophisticated forms; expressed in its simple form as the equation of exchange, $MV = PT$, it shows impact of changes in quantity of money on prices given constant velocity of money and short-term limitations on total output.

R

Rational expectations (8) theory explaining that individuals using all available information form expectations about the future which are, on average, correct. When applied to macro policy, the theory argues that any attempt to stabilize the level of output and employment is ineffectual and possibly counterproductive.

Real variable (2) an economic measure adjusted for price level changes.

Reciprocity agreements (15) agreements between states, usually in close proximity, allowing the expansion of financial institutions across state lines.

Regional interstate banking (15) bank operations that extend across state lines within a specific geographic region usually as a result of reciprocal agreements between the states involved.

Regulation Q (14) Fed regulation phased out by DIDMCA which placed ceilings on interest rates payable on deposits.

Repurchase agreements (2) essentially a short-term loan whereby parties agree to sale/purchase of security with repurchase/resale on a specific date.

Reserve ratio (or reserve requirement) (7, 17) portion or percentage of deposit liabilities that depository institutions are required to hold as cash or as deposits at the Fed.

Reserves (7) depository institutions' portion of deposits which are held as vault cash or maintained on account with the Fed.

Return on assets (6) a bank's net income as a percentage of the average of beginning and end of year assets.

Return on equity (6) a bank's net income as a percentage of average annual equity capital.

Risk (4) probability that an investment will result in a loss rather than generating a return; the greater the probability of loss combines with the size of potential loss to determine degree of risk.

S

Say's Law (8) specifies that the production of goods results in income for workers which, in turn, fuels demand for the goods produced.

Secondary market (17) financial markets for trading of securities previously issued.

Securitization (5) contemporary technique of pooling or packaging loans into securities for sale in the secondary market.

Shiftability thesis (5) theory of commercial banking stressing extension of loans based on their shiftability or saleability.

Solvency (5) possessing, or having access to, sufficient assets to cover liabilities; having a positive net worth.

Special Drawing Rights (SDRs) (20) an international reserve asset for international payments created by the International Monetary Fund.

Spot market (20) exchange rate transaction involving immediate exchange of bank deposits denominated in different currencies.

Structural reforms (19) proposed changes which would affect the entire financial system, for example, returning to a metallic-based currency system.

Structural unemployment (11) unemployment resulting from mismatch between workers' skills and those necessary to fill existing job vacancies.

Structure (13) significant features of a market which affect behavior of prices and firms within the market, for example, barriers to entry or product differentiation.

Structure-performance hypothesis (13) hypothesis in industrial organization which ties performance of firms to structure of an industry; specifies that the more concentrated an industry, the less competition in that industry.

Supply-side economics (8) school of thought that emphasizes the role of productivity and saving in level of overall economic activity.

Surplus spending unit (SU) (2) any economic unit with assets greater than liabilities and thus with funds available for lending.

Swap agreements (17, 20) reciprocal currency exchanges between central banks whereby there is a simultaneous purchase and sale of a currency with different maturity dates; this essentially allows one central bank to swap its own currency for a foreign currency with the promise to repay, or swap again, at some future time.

T

Tactical reform (19) refers to changes in the way the Fed conducts its monetary policy, for example, institution of the fixed growth rule.

Target cone (18) range of growth rate for money supply specified by the Federal Reserve; range expands over time to provide cone.

Term structure of interest rates (3) the relationship or structure between interest rates on securities with various maturities but similar risk.

Transaction deposit or account (2, 5) funds in an account at a depository institution which are available immediately for transfer through the checking system; such deposits include demand deposits, share draft accounts, NOW accounts, and ATS accounts.

Treasury Bill (2) short-term (one year or less) promissory note issued by the federal government through the Federal Reserve banks; traded in an active secondary market.

U

Unit Banking (4) restricting chartered commercial banks to a single facility (preventing branching).

V

Velocity of Money (10) the number of times the money supply "turns over" in a given period of time.

W

Wealth (11) stock of accumulated income.

Y

Yield Curve (3) graphical representation of yields on a particular type of bond for various terms to maturity.

Index